GILLES KEPEL

JIHAD

THE TRAIL
OF POLITICAL
ISLAM

Translated by Anthony F. Roberts

I.B. TAURIS

LONDON · NEW YORK

In memory of Michel d'Hermies

master

friend

New edition published in the UK in 2006 by I.B. Tauris & Co Ltd
6 Salem Road, London W2 4BU

First published in the UK in 2002 by I.B. Tauris & Co Ltd

Copyright © I.B. Tauris & Co Ltd 2002, 2003, 2004, 2006

Originally published as *Jihad: Expansion et Déclin de l'Islamisme* © Éditions Gallimard, 2000

The right of Gilles Kepel to be identified as the author of this work has been asserted by the authors in accordance with the Copyright, Design and Patents Act, 1988.

ISBN 1 84511 257 1
EAN 978 1 84511 257 8

A full CIP record for this book is available from the British Library

New edition typeset by Rowland Phototypesetting Ltd, Bury St Edmunds, Suffolk
Printed and bound in India by Replika Press Pvt. Ltd.

Acknowledgments

This book is the result of more than five years' research, the greater part of which was made possible by a grant from the Fondation Singer-Polignac. I wish to extend my deepest gratitude to those who conferred this grant, as well as to Mr. Jean-Pierre Machelon, the former assistant director of the Département des Sciences de L'Homme et de la Société at the CNRS, for his trust in me and for his invaluable advice. In the course of my travels, which led me from Indonesia to the continent of America, I enjoyed the hospitality of many different institutions, notably that of the French research centers in Tehran (IFRI), Tashkent (IFEAC), Amman (CERMOC), and Cairo (CEDEJ); these I would like to thank, as well as the cultural sections of the French embassies in Algeria, Indonesia, Malaysia, Morocco, Pakistan, Senegal, and Sudan, who, by inviting me to hold conferences in their countries, also made it possible for me to pursue my studies *in situ*. Likewise, the Abdulaziz Foundation in Casablanca, the Bouabid Foundation in Rabat, the Codesria in Dakar, the Inesg and the Ena in Algiers all furnished me with forums in which to discuss the different themes of my work.

Those themes first emerged during my tenure as visiting professor at New York University and Columbia University, and I am deeply grateful to Richard Bulliet, Robert Paxton, and Martin Schain and for their invitation to fill this post. Likewise, Leonard Binder at the University of California (UCLA) encouraged me to give form to my ideas, and his rigorous and stimulating critique was of immense value to me.

I am grateful to him for having published an article that would become
the basis for the present work, and to Abdou Filali Ansari and Hassan
Aourid, who brought out an Arabic version of it. I also owe an incalculable debt to the Fondation Nationale des Sciences Politiques for the
use of its excellent library and for the kindness and patient assistance
of its staff, and above all to the students of the Programme Doctoral
sur le Monde Musuman, who in the course of their seminars had to
endure the various phases of my project's development and who
responded by enriching it with suggestions and critiques drawn from
their own experience.

Other colleagues and friends who reviewed my work and so gener-
ously sacrificed their time and energy to help me understand situations
that I myself had difficulty mastering are too numerous to mention in-
dividually. Nevertheless, I would like to acknowledge my great debt to
them all, especially Mahmoud Azab, Xavier Bougarel, David Camroux,
Andrée Feillard, Nilüfer Göle, Ibrahim Gharaibeh, Ruth Grosrichard,
Mohammed Hikam, Enes Karić, Jean-Francois Legrain, Rémy Leveau,
Aboul Manaich, Naoufel Brahimi El Mili, Ahmed Rashid, Yann
Richard, Olivier Roy, Ghassan Salamé, Mariam Abou Zahab, and
Malika Zeghal. I also wish to thank all those at the rue de Chevreuse
who gave me their unfailing support over the last five years. This
English-language edition was revised and updated as of December
2001; for their contributions to its publication I am grateful to my
translator, Anthony F. Roberts, and to my editors at Harvard University Press, Joyce Seltzer and Susan Wallace Boehmer.

And finally, I would like to make special mention of my children,
Charlotte and Nicolas, who bore my various protracted absences with
such patience. I want them to know that their presence and their love
have helped me more than words can say, and that without them I
could never have done my work at all.

Contents

Publisher's Foreword

When we first published Gilles Kepel's *Jihad* in the aftermath of the attacks on the World Trade Center (but well before the Anglo-American invasion of Iraq and its fallout), the book's thesis was a novel one: radical Islamism had seen its heyday and had in fact declined. If the 1970s and 1980s promised to unleash extremist Islam as a social and political force across the breadth of the Middle East, the 1990s saw that movement's demise.

What place is there today for Kepel's book, which has received such critical acclaim? In fact, recent events in Bali and in Madrid, in London and in Iraq have only proved his thesis: the political attention and aggression of extremist Islam has shifted away from the domestic, and onto the international scene. Osama bin Laden's focus of toppling what he saw as the corrupt, anti-Islamic Saudi regime has been extended to attacking the abstract evil of Western cultural and political global hegemony. In the period after September 11th, Kepel commented:

It seems clear that Al Qaeda's aim was to engineer a very spectacular attack, which would prove that the enemy was weak and not worthy of being feared. The masses they wanted to reach out to, it was hoped, would join in the jihad against the West to liberate themselves. But the problem is that such a closely-knit conspiratorial movement is both the basis of their success and, at the same time, the reason for their ultimate failure. They have no way to reach out to the masses. They have no charities. They do not spread the word. They have no way to deal with grass roots politics. So, they cannot mobilize. They can only use the exemplarity of symbols, and the media, to convey a message to the masses. Bin Laden became a mastermind in using the media—particularly after he singled out the new Arab media, such as the Al-Jazeera channel, as the main medium of his political message.[1]

Across the Middle East, the domestic politics of Arab Islamists have tempered. The fervor of religious forces inside the Middle East, clamoring for arch-reactionary sharia-driven government, has near disappeared, with the peculiar exception of Saudi Arabia. Iran's radical Islamic Revolution of 1979 has become what one might go so far as to call 'post-Islamist'. The 'Islamist' government of Turkey under Tayyep Erdogan has more in common with early twentieth-century Christian socialism than it does with the politics of such fiery ideologues as Sayyid Qutb or Mawdudi. Algerian Islamists, in such close proximity to the doors of power in Algiers, have moderated their message. And in Egypt, the Islamist terrorist attacks of the 1980s and early 90s are a thing of the past. In the face of Hosni Mubarak's fierce campaign against their members, and the middle classes' rejection of their militarization, such groups as the Muslim Brotherhood and Gamaat Islamiya have toned their politics down. Political Islam has tried to become respectable: Lebanon's Hezbollah dedicates most of its efforts to providing welfare for the poor in the south; it has several seats in the Lebanese parliament. Even the Palestinian group Hamas stood for local government elections for the first time in 2005. Only Saudi Arabia, caught between its Westernization programme and Islamic radicalism continues to suffer from the threat of Islamist revolution.

But if extremist Islamist politics have for the most part fled the domestic, social arena in the Middle East, they have, by no stretch of the imagination, disappeared. Jihad has gone global. To understand that change, we must examine not the recent history of Middle Eastern countries, but the history of Jihad's new enemy: Western policy in the region.

The invasion and occupation of Iraq in the spring of 2003, aimed ostensibly to disarm and topple the government of Saddam Hussein. But its first and longer term objective was to close the Pandora's box that the US opened back in the 1970s, when it armed, abetted and

---

[1] 'The Trail of Political Islam', published on 'Open Democracy.net', 3rd July 2002.

financed dangerous local allies who were, in the end, to turn against them: Saddam Hussein (whom the US backed against the fundamentalist Khomeini revolutionaries in Iran), and the jihadists, precursors of the Taliban, of Afghanistan whom the US backed against the Soviets.

In the short-term, this was a policy that worked: Saddam Hussein and Ayatollah Khomeini fought themselves to a murderous, eight year standstill that paralyzed their countries; and the US policy of arming Islamist mujahedeen against the Soviets is believed, in some Washington circles, to be the root cause of the Soviet Union's demise. But it was a policy with blow-back—and its consequences were only felt later. The US, ruefully aware of its Vietnam debacle, fought their wars by proxy. Those proxy warriors, trained to battle, have now turned against them. Post-invasion Iraq has now surpassed Palestine as a rallying point for global jihadism.

The Palestine issue itself remains as intractable as ever. The continued agony of the conflict and the US' unwavering support for uncompromising Israeli policies in the territories has shattered the image Washington would have of itself as the 'honest broker', the 'peace-maker', the progressive 'democracy-building' benevolent world power. The much-vaunted Israeli withdrawal from Gaza in 2005 looks set to have little impact on the conflict. Palestine, seat of the third holiest place in Islam, the Dome of the Rock, remains on the lips of jihadists the world over.

Jihadism remains as complex a phenomenon as any movement spread across countries, continents and cultures. Today, for the reasons outlined above, it must be seen as a primordially political, rather than religious, movement. Gilles Kepel's book and its primary theses have become even more important and relevant today.

London, January 2006

Preface

Since the attacks of September 11th 2001, the term "jihad" has gained currency in a number of European languages. In the eyes of much of the press and the public (and even amongst certain political leaders), it has become synonymous with "terrorism", and hence come to represent the ultimate target of the "war on terror" launched by George W. Bush. In the Muslim world, a significant proportion of public and media opinion sees this "war on terror" as a "crusade" directed against Islam—following the American president's use of the term in the wake of the bloodbaths in Washington and New York.

The semantic development of these terms, however, extends beyond these narrow usages. Although English is not my native tongue, I have had to explain to a number of acquaintances in the Arab world, during the year following 9/11, that in English the term "crusade" has acquired a metaphorical character. It refers, in the mind of the speaker, more generally to "mobilization" without necessarily carrying the connotations of a war between the Cross and the Crescent, or indeed of Richard the Lion Heart, Saint Louis or Saladdin. Similarly, "jihad"—now a relatively common first-name in the Arab world, even amongst Palestinian and Lebanese Christians—does not exclusively imply armed attack against non-Muslims. In Islamic Iran, the campaign to reconstruct the country after the ravages of the Iran-Iraq war, was directed by an organization called *"jahad-e sazandegui"* translated into English as the "reconstruction crusade". How then can one fully understand the terms employed when they have been adopted by organizations, each more belligerent than the next, on whom—to exaggerate only slightly—the future of the planet depends?

The usage and employment of the word "jihad" depends on the identity, as well as the political and social agenda, of those who hold a monopoly on the term's meaning at any one time. Today, the militants are controlling the meaning. By designating, in the Muslim context, all efforts to propagate Islam as "jihad", in their eyes the word comes to signify a holy war against all "infidels" who they stigmatize as such. (Even today, many "bad Muslims" continue to pay for this incrimination with their lives.) Above all, in the language of those movements that have rallied around the figure of Osama bin Laden and waged terrorist warfare since the mid-90s, "jihad" represents the ultimate justification of otherwise unacceptable violence. Obviously, a suitable socio-political and cultural climate is necessary for the propagators of this belief to win over their public and gain support for the translation of their bellicose and supposedly God-sanctioned doctrine into actual —and inevitably bloody—acts. This book seeks to review the circumstances that made such developments possible, and attempts to ascertain what conditions determined the political successes and failures of those Islamic groups that have emerged since the 1970s.

How has the Muslim world evolved in the period following the attacks of September 11? Has the appeal of those factions preaching anti-Western jihad increased, or has its allure expired? What indeed is the future of relations between the US, Europe and the Islamic world? The consequences are actually far more contradictory than those imagined by the perpetrators of the attacks or by the apostles of "the Clash of Civilizations". The Muslim world did not unite behind Osama bin Laden and his associates. Other than an initial outburst of enthusiasm amongst certain youths in the Middle East and South-West Asia, and occasionally in the West amongst the children of immigrants from these areas, very few Muslims attempted to capitalize on these acts. The bloody provocation of September 11 (preceded a few days earlier by the assassination of Northern Alliance commander Ahmed Shah Massoud in northern Afghanistan) had the dual objective of exposing the American superpower's vulnerability and luring it into a conflict in Afghanistan. It was hoped in Kabul that America could be provoked to engage in a war that would result in Afghanistan becoming a cemetery for US troops just as it had been for Soviet forces in the 1980s.

That objective was not reached. The Taliban regime was overthrown, and the succeeding government headed by Hamid Karzai has successfully eliminated the majority of Al Qaeda's bases throughout the country. Many Al Qaeda fighters and suspected militants have been arrested and transferred to the prisoners' camp at Guantanamo Bay. Legal or not, their interrogation may have facilitated the large number of subsequent arrests of suspected operatives in the US, Europe, Africa and Asia. It has also given investigators an insight into the size, capacity and complexity of the network whose leaders—notably bin Laden and his Egyptian adjutant, Ayman al-Zawahiri—have shown no sign of life since December 2001.

In Pakistan—the principal hub for militants moving between their Afghan sanctuary and the rest of the world—successive governments have tacitly permitted armed groups of Sunni extremists to operate with the support of considerable material and human resources. With strong backing from the US, General Pervez Musharraf has attempted to break with the policies of his predecessors and crush the authority of these movements. It is likely to be a long, hard haul. As the killings of American journalist Daniel Pearl and ten French engineers working in Karachi have demonstrated, General Musharraf is far from having reached his objectives; and his situation is not helped by Pakistan's fragile regional position and effective cold war with India over Kashmir. Long after September 11, however, Southwest Asia—the principal operations zone for networks linked to bin Laden—has neither exploded, nor risen up in arms at the instigation of the jihadists.

This represents an important failure for those who had hoped that the Muslims of the world would unite against the "impious" Western armies setting foot in Afghanistan, the "land of Islam"—as had been the case when the Red Army entered Afghanistan in December 1979. Hardly had the Muslim troops of the Northern Alliance appeared on the front lines to fight the Taliban, than some of Islam's most influential Islamic preachers withdrew their support for the Kabul regime. One notable example of this was the Egyptian Sheikh Qaradawi, who denounced the government in Kabul on the religious program that he hosts on the pan-Arab channel, Al-Jazeera. This and other denunciations essentially refuted the connection between the Taliban's plight and jihad, thus robbing it of the all-significant transnational Islamic support.

These same clerics also took immediate pains to distance themselves from the September 11 attacks by denying those who had committed them the status of martyrdom, referring to them rather as suicide victims who would burn in hell. Indeed, for the clerics, the radical escalation provoked by bin Laden threatened to drag the Islamic world into an immediate and suicidal confrontation with the West, particularly given the disproportion of forces. They had to disassociate themselves from Al Qaeda, from the attacks on the US and from the Taliban, while at the same time finding an outlet for the anger of an increasingly radical Muslim youth.

They did this by transferring the aspirations of the jihad movement to the Palestinian intifada, and to the suicide bombings perpetrated by Hamas and Islamic Jihad against Israeli civilians. The pretext used was that all Jewish citizens of Israel, including women, served in the national army. In the eyes of these *imams*, Israel represented a legitimate target for any form of jihad because of its usurpation of an Islamic land. Thus the notion of a just war against Israel was strategically used to compensate for the bad press received by the jihad movement for supporting the Taliban and bin Laden.

In this manner, one of the consequences of September 11 was to shift the epicenter of tensions in the Muslim world from South-West Asia back to the Middle East, in one of a series of pendulum swings between the two zones that has been recurrent since the 1980s. The Middle East had been ripe for this particular sway since the initiation of the second intifada in September 2000 by Yasir Arafat. Arafat considered the Oslo peace accords to have been little else than a placebo, particularly given that Israeli colonization had continued, and that the Palestinian Authority had been deprived of its revenues. Criticized for his authoritarianism, and for the corruption and incompetence of his entourage, the Palestinian president hoped that a controlled uprising would help him to recover his lost prestige by forcing concessions from Israel.

On the Israeli side, Ariel Sharon immediately perceived that casting himself as the protector of the imperilled Jewish state would facilitate his quest for power. Aided by the cynical and provocative visit he paid to the Al-Aqsa mosque on Jerusalem's Temple Mount, Sharon triumphed over Benjamin Netanyahu as leader of the Likud, and then succeeded Ehud Barak as prime minister. September 11 transferred the principal focus of jihad to a political landscape full of scheming and torment, in which demonstrations of force were favoured over genuine attempts to build a lasting peace.

Given Sharon's insistence that Arafat and bin Laden must be treated as equals, each suicide attack has reinforced Washington's support of Tel Aviv, and increasingly united the two capitals in their common "war on terror". That, in turn, has assured Sharon of the benign neglect of George W. Bush while Tsahal (the Israeli Defense Forces) reoccupies Palestinian territory, destroys its infrastructure and plunges its population into misery. For the Palestinians, confusing a national struggle and the kind of terrorism embodied by suicide attackers has proved to be a political disaster in both the eyes of the world, and of the intellectuals and civilians in the West Bank, Gaza and Jerusalem who have called for their immediate halt. In taking the intifada hostage, Islamic radicals waging jihad have won only a momentary and illusory victory, one for which the Palestinian population crushed by repression has paid an exorbitant price. How can this impasse be overcome and the spectre of jihad be eliminated while simultaneously allowing the people of the region to live in security and dignity? Many in Washington believe that only an offensive against Baghdad and the replacement of Saddam Hussein with a pro-Western government stands as an adequate response to the September 11 attacks, and makes positive headway in resolving the Israeli-Palestinian conflict. Is the only option military intervention, or are its perverse effects in fact more damaging than the conflict it is seeking to quell?

This is the dilemma confronting President Bush. As the master of a military might unrivalled on the planet, the United States is free to do as it pleases. In doing so, however, it must determine whether its Middle East policies will drown the last fires of jihad, or fan the coals that risk engulfing the entire Middle East in flames.

Introduction

On September 11, 2001, within the space of twenty minutes, two American airliners struck the twin towers of the World Trade Center in Manhattan. The towers subsequently collapsed, with the loss of almost three thousand lives. At the same time, another hijacked jet crashed into the Pentagon, while a fourth, probably aimed at the White House, failed to reach its target and plummeted into a field in Pennsylvania.

Never in its history had the mainland United States been the target of so massive an attack. The surprise bombing of Pearl Harbor by Japan was the only precedent in living memory—and this had been an assault against a military base on a distant Pacific island. The carnage of September 11 was deliberately aimed at civilians and struck at the principal symbols of American hegemony: commercial and financial power, military supremacy, and—missing its target in this third case only—political power. This was a seismic event with incalculable consequences. It exposed the fragility of the United States' empire, exploded the myth of its invincibility, and called into question all the certainties and beliefs that had ensured the triumph of American civilization in the twentieth century. Many feared that it was only the first in a series of planned atrocities.

Quite apart from the infamy of the massacre, the agony of the victims and their families, the grief of America, the precipitous drop in the nation's stock markets, the threat of bankruptcy among several airlines, and a more general upheaval in the world's economy, the cataclysm of September 11 was visually shattering. The sight of the jetliners flying headlong into the skyscrapers, followed by the buildings' awesome collapse, will remain deeply engraved on the collective memory of humankind for generations. The images, broadcast all over the planet by television, instantly sent shock waves rolling outward, magnifying the original impact.

The exactness of the terrorists' synchronization had two powerful and immediate effects. The first, clearly, was to terrorize and appall by the sheer numbers of innocent victims, with whom everyone could identify. The second was to mobilize the support of Muslims whom the authors of the attack wished to win over to their cause—to arouse emotional sympathy and enthusiasm and to galvanize with an example of victory won by violence. The purpose of this book is to shed light on this second effect of September 11, by placing these recent events within a historical perspective that covers the unfolding of the Islamist movement over the last twenty-five years of the twentieth century.

After a few days of hesitation, the leaders of the United States laid the blame for the massacre squarely on the shoulders of former Saudi billionaire Osama bin Laden and on the Taliban regime in Afghanistan that had given him sanctuary. On October 7 bin Laden responded with a televised message in which he exulted that "Allah had blessed a vanguard group of Muslims, the spearhead of Islam, to destroy America." Though he stopped short of personally claiming credit for the attack in that broadcast, the cumulative evidence seemed conclusive enough to provoke a massive retaliation. By the end of September, American and British forces were deployed around Afghanistan, and the Taliban was ordered to surrender bin Laden or face destruction. From his base in Kandahar, Mullah Mohammad Omar, the Commander of the Faithful of the Islamic Emirate of Afghanistan, responded by calling the world's Muslims to join him in a *jihad*, or holy war, against the United States and its allies, should they attack his country.

The United States also sought to build alliances and isolate the other side before the opening of hostilities in Afghanistan. The United Arab Emirates was persuaded to break off diplomatic and commercial relations with the Kabul regime—which was vitally important, given that the Taliban's economic and financial access to the outside world was mainly directed through this channel. American troops were prepositioned in the former Soviet republic of Uzbekistan, an unprecedented event for which the *quid pro quo* would be giving the Kremlin a free hand in dealing with the Chechen uprising.

The president of Pakistan, where the Taliban's strongest contingent of supporters reside, also gave his support to the United States. Taliban members were mostly drawn from Palistani *madrassas* affiliated with the Deoband School of India—a movement theoretically capable of mobilizing hundreds of thousands of students who, in blind obedience to their teachers, would pass on Mullah Omar's call to jihad. World television relayed the images of orchestrated demonstrations in Pakistan, in which bearded, turbaned men burned American flags and brandished portraits of bin Laden; these are Deobandis, as are the paramilitary groups who specialize in butchering Pakistani Shiites and waging guerrilla warfare against the Indian army in eastern Kashmir. However, the Deobandis' capacity for mass mobilization was very much open to question in a country of 160 million people exhausted by internal struggles, whose very cohesion would be imperiled by a fresh plunge into religious radicalism. For many years, U.S. support has been vital to the survival of Pakistan, a nation barely fifty years old with a history of persistent unrest. This was the reasoning behind its president's decision to throw in his lot with the Americans. Besides, Pakistani *realpolitik* needed the "strategic depth" of a friendly Afghanistan in a region where India, Shiite Iran, Russia, and the former Soviet Republics of Central Asia are all viewed with mistrust by Islamabad.

By late October, American planes had carpet-bombed military targets in Kabul and other strongholds of the adversary. Like chess players, the terrorists behind the September 11 attacks seem to have anticipated well in advance that the United States would seek military revenge against Afghanistan. Three days before the passenger jets struck New York and Washington, Commander Ahmed Shah Massoud, the leader of the Afghan opposition to the Taliban regime, was assassinated in his fief in the Panshir Valley by two North Africans carrying Belgian passports. The men were purportedly there to interview him and were carrying journalists' cards issued by a radical Islamist news organization based in London.[1] The two killers died with Massoud when their booby-trapped camera exploded. Massoud was far and away the most credible figure around whom the United States might have united opposition to the Taliban regime, when they launched their offensive after September 11. The assassination of Massoud was clearly a prelude to the attack on American soil. It was meant to preclude the unification of Afghan opposition to the Taliban. The murder slowed this unification somewhat, but soon Northern Alliance forces, many of them true to Massoud's legacy, if trained and equipped by the United States, would spearhead the ground offensive against the Taliban regime.

The terrorism of September 11 was above all a provocation—albeit a provocation of gigantic proportions. Its purpose was to provoke a similarly gigantic repression of the Afghan civilian population and to build universal solidarity among Muslims in reaction to the victimization and suffering of their Afghan brothers. In this second act of the terrorists' drama, the roles are reversed: the attacker becomes passive, and he himself is attacked, while the original victim of terrorism becomes the prime mover. Should the United States and its allies succeed in identifying their target with precision and thereby limiting the ravages of war among the civilian population, which the terrorists would undoubtedly use as a human shield, then there would be no third act. On the other hand, had the repression gotten out of control and caused huge numbers of civilian casualties—what military spokesmen bloodlessly describe as "collateral damage"—the trap would have closed and the third act, that of solidarity, would have begun. The terrorist actor would then have attempted to become the catalyst of a mass movement of outrage, driven by the language of jihad against the "impious" invaders of Islamic land who massacre innocent Muslims.

Thus, for the anti-terrorist coalition, the objective was to isolate and wipe out bin Laden's organization, Al Qaeda, and its Afghan protectors while minimizing civilian losses. For bin Laden and the Taliban, the goal was to rouse the Muslim world in solidarity against the American offensive and sweep Islamists to power in Muslim countries throughout the world.

For all its political successes in the 1970s and 1980s, by the end of the twentieth century the Islamist movement had signally failed to retain political power in the Muslim world, in spite of the hopes of supporters and the forebodings of enemies. The waning of the movement's capacity for political mobilization explains why such spectacular and devastating new forms of terrorism have now been visited on the American homeland. As we will see in the chapters that follow, Sep-

tember 11 was an attempt to reverse a process in decline, with a paroxysm of destructive violence.

The last twenty-five years have witnessed both the waxing and waning
of the militant Islamist movement—a phenomenon whose emergence
was as spectacular as it was unforeseen. In the 1970s, at a time when
the decay of religion in the private sphere appeared to be an irrevers-
ible trend of modern life, the sudden expansion of political groups
proclaiming the Islamic state, swearing by the Koran alone, calling for
jihad, and drawing their activists from the world's great cities was an
event that cast into doubt a host of previous certainties.[2] Worldwide,
the initial reaction was dismay: in the eyes of leftist intellectuals, both
among Muslims and in the West, Islamist groups represented a religious variant of fascism, while for middle-of-the-road liberals their
members were no more than born-again medieval fanatics.

But gradually, as Islamist numbers increased, critics of the movement began to pay closer attention. The left discovered that Islamism
had a popular base; consequently, Marxist thinkers of every stripe,
casting about for the mass support so critical to their ideology, began to credit Islamist activists with socialist virtues. Some sought to
open a political dialogue; others even converted to the creed. Meanwhile, it began to dawn on people further to the right that Islamists
were preaching moral order, obedience to God, and hostility to the
"impious" materialists—meaning communists and socialists. This was
reason enough to generate approval among conservatives, and ample
funds when necessary. Even though the popular attitude remained generally hostile, more and more people began to view Islamism as the authentic creed of modern Muslims—and to see in it perhaps the outline
of an Islamic civilization within the multicultural world of the coming
twenty-first century.

Thus, barely a generation after many Muslim nations won their independence, the Islamic world entered a religious era that largely canceled out the nationalist period which preceded it. The theoretical basis
for the Islamist movement was devised in the late 1960s by the ideologists Mawdudi in Pakistan, Qutb in Egypt, and Khomeini in Iran. But it
did not emerge as a potent political force until after the Israeli-Arab
war of 1973. The overall winners of that conflict were Saudi Arabia and

the other oil-exporting nations, who saw the price of oil soar beyond all expectation, making the Persian Gulf states unconscionably rich. The first phase of Islamism—upheaval—was sealed by the 1979 Islamist Revolution in Iran. Khomeini's radical regime galvanized the masses and mobilized the deprived against injustice. The Saudi royal family, by contrast, as Custodians of the Holy Places of Mecca and Medina, threw their fabulous wealth behind a more conservative approach. The Saudis exalted moral rigor above all else and were ready to fund the growth of any group or party that preached their creed, anywhere in the world.

So from the outset the Islamist movement was two-pronged. First, it embraced the younger generation in the cities, a class created by the postwar demographic explosion in the Third World and the resultant mass exodus from the countryside. Though poverty-stricken, these young urbanites had access to literacy and some education. Second, it included the traditional God-fearing bourgeoisie, the descendants of mercantile families from the bazaars and souks who had been thrust aside during the process of decolonization. In addition to this devout middle class, there were also doctors, engineers, and businessmen who had gone away to work in the conservative oil-exporting nations and had rapidly become wealthy while being kept outside the traditional circles of political power. All these social groups, with their different ambitions and worldviews, for the space of a generation found in the political ideals of Islamism an echo of their frustrations and a reflection of their hopes and dreams. Not surprisingly, the most enthusiastic propagandists were young intellectuals, freshly graduated from technical and science departments, who had themselves been inspired by the ideologues of the 1960s.

The equivocal nature of Islamism's message, within which the devout Muslim capitalist could make common cause with the slum-dweller, allowed the movement to spread rapidly in the early 1980s. Its religious cast, which effectively made militants accountable to God alone, provided a grace period before they were required to show concrete political results in the real world. By promising to re-establish social justice on the model of the first state of Islam set up by the Prophet Mohammed in Medina, the Islamists held out a vision of utopia. They also gave expression to the populace's visceral hostility toward regimes gnawed by corruption, bankruptcy (both economic and moral), and authoritarianism—for, broadly speaking, such was the order of things throughout the Muslim world at that time.

But contradictions at Islamism's core sharpened as well during this second phase. The question of who would control this potent new religious and political force was a matter of growing concern to the various powers in the region. Some tried to stifle it, others to encourage it; all interfered with it in one way or another. The Iranian revolution had given other established regimes much food for thought; it was only too clear that by alienating the mullahs, the shah had isolated himself, losing support within Iranian society. By contrast, Khomeini triumphed because he was able to unite, in a single irresistible dynamic, the merchants, the poor, and even the secular middle classes, who believed that, in the aftermath, they could easily outflank this charismatic but impotent old man—or so they thought.

The entire decade of the 1980s was overshadowed by a power struggle between the Saudi monarchy and Khomeini's Iran. Tehran sought to export its revolution, just as the Russians had once exported theirs. Riyadh set out to contain this ploy, just as the Americans had contained the Soviets during the Cold War. Countries between these two poles, such as Egypt, Pakistan, and Malaysia, encouraged their homegrown Islamist militants, whom they perceived as allies against the enduring threat of socialism. But they were not always able to control the genies of social change once released, as was proven in 1981 when the Al-Jihad group assassinated Egyptian President Anwar Sadat.

With the exception of Iran, all the regimes in power in Muslim countries during the 1980s concentrated their efforts on strategically dividing the various components of the Islamist movement. The guarantees they gave to the devout middle class were designed to detach them from the poor. Political leaders feared that the constant but ineffectual rioting of the Muslim masses would eventually grow into full-blown revolution and sweep more radical elements into power. By making concession after concession in the moral and cultural domains, governments gradually created a reactionary climate of "re-Islamization." They sacrificed secularist intellectuals, writers, and other "Westernized elites" to the tender mercies of bigoted clerics, in the hope that the latter, in return, would endorse their own stranglehold on the organs of state. Saudi Arabia in particular distributed largesse, fostered allegiances, and cultivated the loyalty of the devout middle class by giving it access to the financial benefits offered by a new Islamic banking system.

In 1980, with the blessing of the Gulf oil-producing states and the West, Iraq's Saddam Hussein declared war on revolutionary Iran. Though himself once the head of a secularist party, the Baath, he now mobilized the forces of religion in his own country in order to keep them out of Khomeini's control. Tehran retaliated with terrorism, taking Western hostages through the Hezballah in Lebanon and disrupting the pilgrimage to Mecca to tip the balance of power in its favor.

But in the end, the decisive battlefield proved to be Afghanistan, where a successful jihad was financed by the oil monarchies of the Gulf and the Central Intelligence Agency of the United States.

As far as the United States was concerned, this holy war in Afghanistan had one explicit goal: to set a Vietnam-like deathtrap for the Soviet forces that had invaded Kabul in December 1979 and thus to precipitate the collapse of the Soviet empire. As far as the Gulf oil states were concerned, Afghanistan's function was to divert the attention of the world's radical militants away from the Saudis' lucrative partnership with the American "Great Satan" by focusing their loathing on the Soviet invader.

The Afghan jihad against the Soviets became the great cause with which Islamists worldwide identified, moderates and radicals alike. In the minds of many Arabs, jihad supplanted the Palestinian cause and symbolized the shift from nationalism to Islamism. In addition to the local *mujahedeen,* or holy warriors, the international brigades in Afghanistan hailed from all over the Muslim world—Egypt, Algeria, the Arabian peninsula, and Southeast Asia. They lived in closed communities, where they received intensive training in guerrilla warfare techniques and built up a variant of Islamist ideology based on armed struggle and extreme religious rigor.

Up to 1989, the intelligence agencies of Saudi Arabia, Pakistan, and the United States were convinced that the bearded freedom fighters who had come to do battle with the Soviet Evil Empire on the hilly Afghan terrain were firmly under control and were demonstrating a pro-West Islamist alternative to the road taken by the Iranian revolution. In that year, Islamism reached its peak of intensity as a political force. During the Palestinian *intifada,* or uprising, the hegemony of the Palestine Liberation Organization came under threat from the Islamist Resistance Movement (Hamas). In Algeria, the Front Islamique du Salut won decisively in the first free elections since independence. And in the Sudan, a military coup d'état catapulted the Islamist ideologue Hassan al-Turabi to power. When the Soviet Army finally evacuated Afghanistan in 1989, the triumph of jihad and its Saudi sponsors was sealed.

In 1989, Khomeini, whose losses had forced him to sign an armistice with Iraq, more than made up for his failure to export revolution by issuing his famous *fatwa* (or legal opinion—in this case, a death sentence) against Salman Rushdie, author of *Satanic Verses.* With this gesture, the Iranian ayatollah symbolically expanded the *Umma,* the world, ruled by the laws of Islam straight into Europe and the West. He claimed the right to condemn to death a citizen of the United Kingdom in the UK—and the West took him seriously. In the same year, the wearing of the veil by Muslim schoolgirls in France sparked a nationwide debate that demonstrated the extent to which the Islamist movement had penetrated second-generation immigrants. And while all this was going on, the sudden collapse of the Berlin wall, signaling a more general implosion of the Communist system, opened the way for the Umma to extend its political reach beyond the Iron Curtain and gradually to embrace the new Muslim states of Central Asia, the Caucasus, and finally Bosnia, in the heart of Europe. The evaporation of militant socialism created a vacuum that Islamism seemed ideally qualified to fill.

But the movement's veneer of invincibility was misleading. For one thing, Islamism's popular base was far from secure. The fragile alliance between the young urban poor and the devout middle class, which was held together by intellectuals preaching the doctrines of Islamism, was ill-prepared for any kind of protracted confrontation with entrenched state authorities. With increasing success, governments figured out ways to pit the two camps against one another, exposing the underlying conflict between their true social agendas and their shared but vague desire to set up an Islamic state and implement the *sharia—* the code of law based on the Koran.

Contrary to the expectations of some and the fears of others, the final decade of the century did not fulfill the promise of the 1980s. Wildly extremist groups like the Armed Islamist Group in Algeria, the

Taliban in Afghanistan, and Al Qaeda led by bin Laden took center stage. From Paris to New York, spectacular terrorist attacks were carried out by militants claiming to belong to the Islamist movement. As an amalgam of different social groups held together by a shared religious belief, the movement began to unravel, and the violence hastened its decline. Indeed, the decade was noteworthy mainly for terrorism and disintegration within the ranks of the Islamist movement.

The detonator for this collapse was the invasion of Kuwait by Saddam Hussein's army in August 1990. Iraq had already been devastated by eight years of fruitless conflict with Iran. Saddam calculated that his attempt to seize Kuwait, whose rulers epitomized the egotism and selfish luxury of the oil states, would receive the broad support of most Arabs and Muslims, especially the poor. By threatening Saudi Arabia and forcing the kingdom to summon the assistance of an international coalition led by the United States, Saddam called into question the Saudi dynasty's religious legitimacy. The Saudis were forced to rely on the protection of "infidel" soldiers, whose presence "sullied" the sacred birthplace of the Muslim faith; and consequently, Saddam declared invalid the Saudi claim to the custodianship of the Holy Places of Islam.

The Iraqi attack on Kuwait demolished the Islamic consensus that the Saudis had laboriously built and kept intact throughout the maelstrom of the Iranian revolution. The radical fringe of the Islamist movement, as well as the young urban poor who identified with it, turned against the kingdom and against the international networks it controlled—networks with which the devout middle classes of the various Muslim nations were closely allied. In addition to dissidence in the name of Allah that began emerging within Saudi territory in 1991, a much wider disintegration of the Islamic consensus was exposed when Afghanistan jihad fighters based in Peshawar, Pakistan, began to turn on their Arab and American paymasters. Exultant at the success of their holy war and persuaded that they alone had brought the Soviet empire to its knees, these groups now felt themselves fully capable of bringing down other infidels in power, beginning with "impious" regimes in the Muslim world, especially the one in Saudi Arabia.

After the fall of Kabul to the local mujahedeen in April 1992, these holy warriors dispersed to other countries, in particular Bosnia, Algeria, and Egypt. There, they attempted to transform domestic conflict into a jihad that they themselves could direct. In Bosnia they were unable to inject Islamism into the civil war, and their failure to do so was sealed by the signing of the Dayton Accords in 1995. In Algeria, their technical experience of guerrilla warfare was initially useful to the local Islamists, but the extreme ideology and violence they endorsed cut them off from social milieus that had formerly been most friendly to them. In Egypt, too, though the ruthless assassination of Sadat had been absorbed, the militants managed to alienate a population that could not identify with the modes of action and doctrines worked out in the mountain camps around Peshawar.

In all three cases, the signs of failure began to show by 1995. Around that time, the terrorists carried out a series of attacks whose very technical success did irreparable damage to the political goals of the people behind them. The effect of camp training among the Afghans was felt even in France, where all the best-trained terrorists arrested following the attacks of 1994 and 1995 were found to have spent time in Peshawar. A gulf had opened between the aims of the 1990s jihad extremists and the social, political, and cultural aspirations of Muslims during the 1980s, and it brought the Islamist movement to a standstill.

Then in September 1996 the Taliban ascended to power in Kabul, accompanied by coercive measures against women and summary executions of "sinners." The country had slipped into bloody anarchy after 1992, with each of the regional powers supporting a different faction of the ruling coalition. The arrival of the Taliban, armed and funded by the Pakistani secret service (ISI), brought a semblance of order by concentrating power in the hands of a single party. After four years of devastation, murder, rape, and pillage at the hands of the mujahedeen faction commanders, the appearance of the "religious students" in Kabul in 1996 was a temporary relief to the population of the capital.

The United States and Pakistan both supported the rise of the Taliban. For Washington and Islamabad, it scarcely mattered that a retrograde version of Islam in its most literal and ossified form daily trampled the rights of men and women into the dust. At least order reigned—and that order guaranteed a friendly state on Pakistan's northwest flank, which relieved the pressure on the frontier.

What was more, a huge pipeline project was afoot to extract oil from

Turkmenistan, to the north of Afghanistan and Iran. The shortest route to a tanker port led across Iranian territory to the Persian Gulf, but the United States opposed this kind of involvement with its enemy, the Islamic Republic. Instead, the Americans pushed for a pipeline running through Afghanistan to Pakistan, as proposed by the three interested oil companies—two American and one Argentine. The Taliban guaranteed order, and the oil companies showed their customary willingness to cut a deal with the most reactionary regimes, so long as oil flowed unimpeded. The project never came to fruition, however. A drop in the price of crude made the operation financially unattractive, and American feminists threatened to withhold their votes from the Democratic Party if President Bill Clinton did not distance himself from a regime that so blatantly deprived women of their human rights.

Nevertheless, the Taliban remained firmly in place, living off the proceeds of contraband and opium, as Afghanistan quickly became the world's largest poppy grower.[3] Having neither interest nor competence in health care and other social matters, the Taliban turned over to humanitarian organizations in Kabul the management of these services.[4] For a long time the Taliban reaped the benefits of American indulgence, while Saudi Arabia, which had spent a fortune dislodging the Soviets from Afghanistan, found itself in close ideological agreement with the rulers of Kabul.

Osama bin Laden, who had waged jihad in Afghanistan against the Soviets with American and Saudi blessings, by the early 1990s had become an embarrassment for the Riyadh regime. He likened the stationing of U.S. troops on Saudi soil to the Red Army's invasion of Aghanistan—and wished to extend to the former the jihad he had fought against the latter. A refugee in Islamist Sudan, he was strongly suspected of having played a role in the failure of Operation Restore Hope in Somalia in 1992 and in the attempt to assassinate Egyptian President Hosni Mubarak in Addis Abbaba in June 1995. By early 1996 the Sudanese Islamist regime, seeking to break out of its international straitjacket and having already handed over the terrorist Carlos to the French authorities, offered to hand over the exiled bin Laden to the United States. The Americans doubted—or feared—the outcome of a trial in which the prosecution would have very little evidence to convict and suggested instead that bin Laden be extradited to Saudi Arabia. But King Fahd— unwilling to cut off the head of an outlaw who still had many powerful friends in the kingdom—declined the poisoned gift.

Bin Laden eventually left the Sudan for Afghanistan on May 18, 1996, after the various states involved agreed by default that he should be allowed to do so.[5] Bin Laden was not yet viewed as public enemy number one by the United States; burying him in Afghanistan, a desperately poor country without modern communications, was seen as a way of cutting off access to his financial empire. This proved to be wishful thinking. A few weeks later, on August 23, 1996, bin Laden published his first "declaration of jihad on the American occupiers of the Holy Places," demonstrating his intent to forge an effective partnership with the Taliban and his determination to defend the Saudi "great merchant" class—the group into which he himself was born—who were oppressed by the monarchy.[6]

That year is an important marker in the decline of the Islamist movement: it had become clear that none of the three principal fronts of the jihad—Bosnia, Algeria, and Egypt—which had been opened after Afghanistan by the salafist-jihadist militants trained in the military camps of Peshawar, had fulfilled their earlier promise. As a consequence, in the years that followed, many Islamist leaders, ideologists, and intellectuals would advocate a clean break with armed struggle and seek ways of integrating the Muslim cultural heritage with democratic values, in opposition to the authoritarian behavior of the regimes in place.

From the spring of 1997 onward, several participants in the Islamist coalition were looking for ways to escape the cul-de-sac into which they had been led by the extremists. The election of President Mohammed Khatami in Iran—against the will of the clerical establishment of the Islamic Republic but with the overwhelming support of the urban middle classes and young people born after the revolution—was the most striking symbol of a yearning for change and moderation. Similar signs were coming from other countries, where Islamists had been powerful and where their faltering ideology was giving way to a search for a new social compact with the formerly despised secular middle classes. This compact was formulated around respect for human rights and an aspiration for a Muslim version of democracy—until recently a Western concept that was taboo in Islamist circles. In Indonesia, a lay Muslim president was elected after the fall of Suharto, who had flirted seriously with the Islamist intelligentsia. In Algeria, the new government formed by President Abdelaziz Bouteflika included militant secularist figures as well as moderate Islamist leaders. In Pakistan, Prime Minister Nawaz Sharif, a protector of the Islamist movement, was overthrown by an army general claiming the mantle of Ataturk, Pervez Musharraf. In Turkey, the Islamist Prime Minister Necmettin Erbakan, in the space of a single year, had to leave power, dealing a death blow to the alliance between the Turkish devout middle class and the young urban poor. In the Sudan, another military leader thrust aside Hassan al-Turabi, the Islamist *éminence grise* of the regime. All these events indicated that the ideology of the Islamist movement and the alliance of classes it had created were beginning to go their separate ways by the end of the twentieth century.

The extremist wing of the movement found itself facing a political impasse. It rejected the democratic references invoked by the moderates; and as a result, raw terrorism in its most spectacular and destructive form became its main option for reviving armed struggle in the new millennium.

The attack of September 11 offers certain similarities but also a number of very striking differences when compared with the terrorism of the 1990s. If we juxtapose the declarations of bin Laden and his lieutenants on October 7, 2001, with those broadcast by him in 1996 and 1998, we see that the basic ideological justifications for terrorism followed the same lines. According to bin Laden, the United States' invasion of the land of Islam by "occupying the territory of the Two Holy Places" (in the form of American military bases in Saudi Arabia) justified a defensive jihad, like the one against the Soviet Union after the Red Army entered Kabul in 1979. The difference lay in two additional references in the October 2001 broadcast: "As we speak, a million children are dying, killed in Iraq . . . Today, Israeli tanks are ransacking Palestine." The mere mention of these conflicts, the blame for which bin Laden laid squarely on America, was a ploy that reached out to sympathizers beyond the Islamist movement and presented bin Laden as the champion of all those who condemned American policies in the Middle East.

As far as one can judge from newspaper editorials, debates on the Al-Jazeera pan-Arab satellite TV station, and a crescendo of street demonstrations, the attacks on the United States took place at a moment when anti-American resentment in the Arab world had grown virulent. Despite ten years of embargoes against Iraq, with intermittent bombing campaigns, Saddam seemed firmly entrenched in his position of absolute power, while the Iraqi people, caught between the hammer and the anvil, were suffering far worse that ever before. Furthermore, in September 2000, bitterness surrounding the stalemate of the Israeli-Palestinian talks came raging to the surface in the form of a new uprising called the Al-Aqsa intifada, after the Grand Mosque in Jerusalem. Whatever the responsibility imputed to each camp in this resumption of violence, it created unprecedented tension in the region and radicalized the positions of the two adversaries. An outlet was now available for expressing countless political, economic, and social frustrations. Support in the Muslim world for the Palestinian revolt, galvanized by the televised shooting death of a Gaza child, Muhammad al Durra, was fed by images of suicide attacks, which were broadly endorsed even when they killed Israeli civilians—and even though they were specifically condemned by the PLO leader, Yasir Arafat.

The Israeli army retaliated with "ripostes" and "preventive attacks" using guided missiles so electronically complex that no Arab army could expect to match them. This feeling among Muslims of having the odds stacked against them very soon turned against the United States, which was adjudged guilty of guaranteeing total military superiority to Israel. The Palestinians accused the new Bush administration of benignly neglecting Ariel Sharon's militarist policies and of abandoning the impartiality expected of the world's only superpower, without which there could be no resolution of the conflict.

This was the background against which the images of September 11 appeared on the televisions of the Muslim world—a *kamikaze* operation that pushed the usual scenario of suicide attacks on civilians to a hideous extreme with the massacre of thousands.[7] It is possible that the people behind the attack timed the operation to coincide with a period when passions in the Muslim world were running sufficiently high to give political engagement the edge over universal morality. They may have calculated that these passions would overwhelm any sense of indignation or outrage over the murder of civilians among those whose sympathy they hoped to win, while rallying them to the cause that had dealt so terrible a blow to the American enemy.

Thus far, Muslim populations have shown no signs of actively approving the long-term objectives of the terrorists or of mobilizing en masse to support them in reaction to the American onslaught in Afghanistan. To begin with, no one has formally claimed responsibility for September 11 or articulated its purpose. While this initially complicated the American response, it also inhibited support for the cause of the attackers because, apart from a desire to inflict damage on the United States, the goals of that cause remain vague. The greatest strengths of terrorism—its suddenness, its use of surprise, and its anonymity—are also its greatest weaknesses when the time comes to reap real political dividends.

The assumption that bin Laden and his network are behind the plot rests on an impressive array of evidence, including the infamous November 9 tape in which bin Laden seems to incriminate himself. Nevertheless, by refusing to acknowledge responsibility directly, the former Saudi billionaire deprives himself of any capacity to structure and unite behind him a mass movement capable of winning power in the Muslim world. He remains merely a symbol, an icon, whose only real contacts are with the activists belonging to his secret organization. Al Qaeda is cut off from the world by its strictly clandestine nature and is thus deprived of the means to win over large numbers of new recruits or to mobilize and control whole populations. To communicate with the outside world, bin Laden's organization relies on uncertain channels within the mass media, which carry news and images all over the planet but at best are capable of provoking only an immediate emotional reaction of solidarity, a fleeting enthusiasm.[8] This reaction is instant but short-lived, because its prompters have none of the social relay points of a well-entrenched movement that might be capable of translating such emotion into civil disobedience—unlike the vanguard Leninist party in 1917, or the Iranian clergy in 1978.

As icon or symbol, bin Laden and his companions have been at pains to construct an image of themselves modeled on the Prophet Mohammed and his followers. Mohammed was forced to flee idolatrous Mecca in 622 and settle in Medina, where for eight years he carried out daring raids on his enemies before returning in triumph to

Mecca in 630. Like the Prophet, bin Laden fled "hypocritical" Saudi Arabia in a kind of latter-day *Hegira,* coming eventually to the arid mountains of Afghanistan, from which he carried on his holy war under the guidance of Allah. (In his October message, instead of taking credit for the attack, bin Laden presented it as a miracle, the will of God: "America has been struck in one of its vital organs by Allah the All-Powerful.")

The desire to identify his group of comrades with the earliest Muslims, with the companions of the Prophet and their successors—whose example is very much alive in the heart of anyone brought up in an Islamic culture—was further strengthened by the disproportionate, "heroic" dimension of the war, waged by a small group of fighters against the two greatest empires in the world. Just as the early Muslim horsemen annihilated the Sassanid empire, so the jihadists, as they saw it, had brought down the Soviet empire by defeating the Red Army in Afghanistan. Likewise, just as the first caliphs hurled back the Byzantine empire, conquering all its southern and eastern provinces from Syria to North Africa, so today's activists have set off an earthquake that they expect will rock the foundations of the empire of America.

But alongside their seventh-century religious symbolism, the terrorists responsible for the September 11 attack demonstrated a technical sophistication that is very much a product of our own time. For sheer mastery of spectacle and symbol, their awesome feat far surpassed Israel's military technology or the U.S. Army's performance during the Gulf War. The suicidal leaders of the group had trained as pilots in the United States. They came from well-off backgrounds, were university-educated, spoke the languages and understood the cultural codes of the Western societies within which they moved. At least fifteen of the nineteen hijackers were from the Arabian peninsula, but all of them carefully masked any outward signs of belonging to the Islamist movement.[9] Appearing thoroughly bland in their Western clothes, they entered bars and drank alcohol, used cell phones, computers, and automated banking machines, shaved their faces, and consorted with women. They seemed cut off from the mosque network, the usual venue where sympathizers were recruited and converted. By contrast, the terrorists of the 1990s—including the activists arrested in France after the 1995 campaign and those responsible for the 1993 attack on the World Trade Center—nearly all were from a lower social stratum.

They were small tradesmen, convicts, unemployed men, and petty delinquents from disinherited urban groups whose poverty and youth
made them ripe for revolt. Their bombs were homemade and amateur-
ish, and the means and funds behind them were minimal. These limi-
tations kept their violence at a level that states were more or less able to
contain.

Perhaps the most troubling characteristic of this new brand of terrorist is this paradoxical ability to conceal his true nature and to preserve his extreme convictions intact while exposing himself to Western
culture down to its most intimate detail. Part of the explanation for
this extraordinary level of self-discipline may be found in the ideological axis around which the Islamist movement revolved in the final
quarter of the twentieth century: the Afghan jihad. The camps around
Peshawar—through which many thousands of militants passed in the
1980s and 1990s—offered training that combined ultra-religious ideological brain-washing and fascination with violence. The experience
of the terrorists in these camps may provide some of the keys to the
mystery.

Is this terrorist vanguard capable of mobilizing the masses, of permanently altering the present world order, of crushing the regimes
in power in the Muslim world, and replacing them with an Islamic
state—more than ever the dream of the militants after the apocalypse
of September 11? Such a strategy would not be unique to contemporary radical Islamism. Two decades back, when the communist system
was fading fast and the working classes it claimed to represent were
turning away from it in disgust, a number of armed groups (the most
extreme being the Red Brigades in Italy, the German Red Army Faction, and the Carlos network) also seized terrorism as the ideal way to
inflict spectacular damage on the enemy. It was their vain hope that the
revolutionary consciousness of the masses could be revived and mobilized, through a cycle of provocation, repression, and solidarity.

The Islamism of today and the communism of yesterday are different in both nature and scale, and it remains to be seen whether the terrorist strategy of bin Laden's Islamist militants will come to the same
end. But we should remember—in a context where the unleashing
of murderous violence is still provoking powerful emotions and pas-

sionate reactions—that terrorism does not necessarily express the true strength of the movement to which it claims to belong. Despite the devastation it can cause—even such shocking devastation as the entire world witnessed on September 11—desperate terrorist acts do not translate easily into political victory and legitimate power.

And as it happened, bin Laden and Mullah Omar's hopes to ignite in their fellow believers the fire of a worldwide jihad against the West failed miserably, as the Northern Alliance fighters, backed up by U.S. air attacks, launched a sweeping ground offensive that met with little resistance. Kabul fell on November 13, two months and two days after the September 11 attack on America. Among demonstrations of joy and liberation, residents of Kabul rushed to barber shops for a clean shave and waited in long lines to reclaim old TV sets, as Kabul television programming was soon to be back on the air. Only the Taliban strongholds of Kunduz and Kandahar resisted for a few more days, due to the presence there of Arab jihadists who fought to the death, convinced they had no hope of pardon or mercy. Images of Arab prisoners traded to U.S. troops by Afghans, and of Pakistani and foreign Islamists spat upon, molested, or killed by locals, went around the Community of the Faithful. Gone were the proclamations of endless solidarity from Muslims worldwide that the radicals had tried to buttress in the wake of the U.S. bombings on Afghan soil.

The Taliban regime crumbled as fast as it had surged (though, at the time of this writing, the fate and whereabouts of Mullah Omar and Osama bin Laden are unknown). It had been puffed by Pakistani will—with American blessing—in 1994; and it was wiped away by American might—with Pakistani sighs of relief—on December 6, 2001, when the last combatants surrendered in Kandahar. The last Islamist movement in control of a state in the Sunni Muslim world had vanished.

In the meanwhile, U.S.-led forces and Northern Alliance Afghan fighters were tracking the last Al Qaeda Arabs hiding in the Tora Bora mountain range, though no trace of bin Laden had been found by mid-December. Very little remained of the sound and fury that had been heard in radical Islamist circles after September 11. The gigantic provocation against America and the West had backfired, and the Muslim masses that the militants hoped would answer Mullah Omar's call to jihad now witnessed the infamous catastrophe that befell bin Laden's bloody utopia. In that autumn of fury that will mark forever the first year of the new millennium, the world witnessed, in a snapshot, the rise and fall of the most extreme version of Islamism. The battle the militants lost was but the cumulative result of the Islamist movement's long expansion and decline during the last quarter of the twentieth century—a process that this book will now attempt to unfold.

PART I

EXPANSION

CHAPTER

1

A Cultural Revolution

On August 29, 1966, Sayyid Qutb, one of the original theorists of modern Islamism, was hanged in Egypt. The event was recorded on the inside pages of the international press and soon forgotten. Some sympathizers protested, as did former members of the Muslim Brothers, an organization dissolved in Egypt twelve years earlier and already consigned to the past by the world's newspaper editors and diplomatic corps. Nevertheless, the hanging symbolized the rift that had occurred between the then-dominant Arab nationalists, as personified by President Gamal Abdel Nasser, and contemporary radical Islamists.[1]

By the end of the next decade, the balance of power between these two competing ideologies had shifted, and the Islamist movement had become a potent mobilizing force in Egypt and elsewhere. Many people, whether they were enthusiasts or passive observers, sincerely felt that Islamism carried within it the seeds of the future for the Muslim world. Qutb's contribution had been vital, along with that of two other major figures, Mawlana Mawdudi (1903–1979) of Pakistan and Ruhollah Khomeini (1902–1989) of Iran. Mawdudi and Qutb thought along similar lines and exercised influence among the Sunni Muslims. Khomeini operated within the framework of the Shiites. But all three men shared a vision of Islam as a political movement, and they all called for the establishment of an Islamic state. While opposing the secular nationalism that had dominated the 1960s, they also rejected the view within traditional Islam that relegated political combat to a secondary concern.

But in other ways these men represented three very different approaches. Qutb advocated a clean break with the established order, a strategy that attracted a cross-section of Muslim youth from both educated and deprived backgrounds but alienated most clerics and the middle class. Mawdudi, by contrast, viewed the establishment of an Islamic republic as a task to be undertaken slowly, step by step. While his more moderate approach found favor with the Pakistani middle classes, it did not achieve support among the masses. Only Khomeini was able to create a workable coalition of all the interested parties: the disinherited, the middle classes, radical intellectuals, and clerics. Consequently, the Islamic revolution succeeded in Iran, whereas it failed in other countries.

Modern Islamist ideology did not materialize in a vacuum. It emerged within a tradition from which it borrowed and exaggerated certain elements while downplaying others. Together, the three ideologists of contemporary Islamism whom we will examine were responsible for the intellectual gestation of this movement in the 1960s. We will see how these three men and their followers tackled the then-dominant nationalists and how they related to the popular religion of the brotherhoods and the more learned theology of the clerics, or *ulemas*.

The first Islamist onslaught was against nationalism, and its aim was to substitute one vision of world community for another. Prior to the 1970s, nationalist ideology predominated in most Islamic countries. It was shaped by home-grown elites who had fought to break the stranglehold of European colonization and who led their countries to independence in the aftermath of World War II.

Nationalist sentiments among Arabs, Turks, Iranians, Pakistanis, Malaysians, Indonesians, and others had fragmented the historic "land of Islam" *(dar el-Islam)* into communities with clearly different priorities. The nationalists took control of the tools of modern communication—newspapers, books, radio, and television—and placed them at the service of ideals, such as freedom and equality, translated and adapted from the European Enlightenment. This project of emancipation—which was propounded in the vernacular language of the people—allowed nationalists to thrust aside the religious establishment in their pursuit of secular goals. Above all it sidelined the ulemas, who had traditionally exercised sole control over the written language and had used it as a vector for the expression of religious values.

The nationalist intellectuals had been educated mostly in European-style schools within the Muslim world but nevertheless had been refused access to mid-level and higher employment by colonial administrations. Because the colonials had governed using the official language of their homeland, a key objective of the nationalist struggle for political independence was to establish the local idiom as the official language of the nation's citizens. Having brought the written word into the secular sphere, these newly empowered elites began using it to express the values of nation, state, and modernity as they understood them. But with the passing of time, their strict censorship of books and the media transformed the written word from an instrument of independence and freedom into a propaganda tool for tightening the new rulers' authoritarian grip on society.

It was at this juncture that Qutb and Mawdudi entered the fray. Their writings rejected the values of the nationalists and reactivated Islam as the sole cultural, social, and political standard for behavior among Muslims. The first battle they chose to wage in this cultural war was over interpretation of the past. Having established independent states, the nationalists wished to propound a version of history that would feature them as agents of a radical and decisive break with everything that had gone before. Turkey would no longer be the Ottoman empire; the Arab states would no longer be colonies of Europe; Pakistan would no longer be attached to India. A new era had begun.

But for Qutb and his followers, the post-independence history of the Muslim states had no inherent value.[2] Qutb stigmatized it with an Arab word from the Koran, *jahiliyya*, which describes the state of ignorance or barbarism in which the Arabs are supposed to have lived before the revelation of Islam to the Prophet Mohammed, at the beginning of the seventh century AD. The Muslims of the nationalist period were ignorant of Islam, according to Qutb; just like the pagan Arabs of the original jahiliyya who worshipped stone idols, Qutb's contemporaries worshipped symbolic idols such as the nation, the party, socialism, and the rest. By denying the nationalists' pretension to have founded history and by consigning them metaphorically to the pre-Revelation abyss, Qutb staked out a radical position that sparked a cultural revolution. His principal works, *In the Shadow of the Koran* and *Signposts on the*

Road, written in the 1960s, eventually became bestsellers all over the Islamic world. In them, he called for a "new Koranic generation" to build on the ruins of nationalism a contemporary Islamic community, just as the Prophet and his generation had built a Community of the Faithful (Umma) on the ruins of Arab paganism, which they had destroyed.

By placing his hopes for the future in a single generation, Qutb set his ideas within a clear historical time frame. He spoke to the young, born after independence, who had come along too late to benefit from the vast redistribution of spoils that followed the departure of the colonial occupiers. To win the allegiance of this young cohort, he had to address them in the language in which they had been educated, but he also had to subvert it. Thus, Qutb devised a new way of writing about Islam that was simple and straightforward, very different from the complex rhetoric of the ulemas, which was laden with traditional references and pedantic commentary. Qutb spoke directly to his readers, using the modern idiom to get simple points across.

In order to belittle nationalism as an ideal, he resorted to two concepts that Mawdudi in Pakistan had invented: sovereignty *(hakimiyya)* and adoration *(ouboudiyya)*.[3] These he made the criteria of difference between Islam and non-Islam, Good and Evil, Just and Unjust. Within Islam, Allah alone has sovereignty, being uniquely worthy of adoration by man. The only just ruler is one who governs according to the revelations of Allah. When sovereignty is vested in an "idol," whether a nation, party, army, or people, and when this idol becomes an object of mass adoration, as happens so often under the orchestration of authoritarian nationalist regimes, then evil, iniquity, and falsehood reign. The result is anti-Islam, jahiliyya.

The force of Qutb's rhetoric and his extraordinary attraction for younger people during the 1970s derived from his radical and imaginative break with the present. At a stroke, he demolished the utopian thinking that underpinned authoritarian nationalism, just as the Prophet himself had broken the idols of the pagans and replaced them with the Islamic ideal. There was no need to define this ideal or to lay out a new program—his listeners already had internalized the original experience of the Prophet and his companions and could draw inspiration from this knowledge.

The weakness in Qutb's theory lay in the latitude he allowed for the interpretation of exactly what the Prophet's experience had been and how it should be reproduced in the context of the twentieth century. Qutb died before he could clarify his views on this important point, and those who claimed his mantle—ranging from sectarian cranks who wrote off the whole of society as "impious" to militants who reserved this adjective exclusively for regimes in power—found themselves in a state of ideological confusion that in the long term did great damage to the Islamist movement.

The Muslim Brotherhood

In the early 1960s, when Qutb was writing the works that, after his death, would make him the greatest ideological influence on the contemporary Islamist movement, he was in prison, locked up by Nasser for belonging to the Society of Muslim Brothers.[4] Created in 1928 in colonial times, then broken apart in 1954 by Nasser's new state, the Brothers over the years developed a model for twentieth-century Islamist thought and action based on the work of the society's founder, Hassan al-Banna (1906–1949). Qutb's early inspiration had come from the Brothers—but at the end of his life, he was able to draw conclusions from their failures as well as their successes, and to confront the new situation created by the disappearance of colonialism and the rise of an independent state that was hostile to Islamist ideals.

In the 1920s, when the Society of Brothers was founded, the Muslim world was in disarray. Ataturk abolished the Ottoman caliphate in Istanbul in 1924, which for so long had symbolized the unity of the faithful, and replaced it with a secular Turkish nationalist republic. The land of Islam was divided up by the Christian powers at the same time that it was being eaten away from the inside. The Muslim Brothers formed their society in Egypt in order to reclaim Islam's political dimension, which had formerly resided in the person of the now-fallen caliph. Confronted by the Egyptian nationalists of the time—who demanded independence, the departure of the British, and a democratic constitution—the Brothers responded with a slogan that is still current in the Islamist movement: "The Koran is our constitution." Islam, for the Brothers, was a complete and total system, and there was no need to go looking for European values as a basis for social order. Everything was made clear in the Koran, whose moral principles, the Brothers claimed, were universal. This doctrine was shared by the entire Islamist movement, whatever their other views. All agreed that the solution to the political problems facing Muslims lay in the setting up of an Islamic state that would implement the law of the sacred texts of Islam—the sharia—as the caliph had done in the past.

Within a few years the Muslim Brothers had evolved into a mass movement that touched in particular those urban lower-middle classes who had only recently become literate and were fired by a religious vision of the world. Banna and his disciples managed to politicize this religious zeal by shifting its focus away from the traditional realms of piety and religious ceremony and onto urban colonial society. The Islam of the Brothers raised the standard of "Islamic modernity" as an alternative to the modernity of Europe. The exact meaning of Islamic modernity has never really been settled, and this ambiguity has allowed a wide variety of social groups to assemble under its umbrella. If we describe European modernity as the dividing of society, politics, religion, and culture into separate fields or discourses, then the Brothers were opposed to it during the 1930s, just as their heirs are today. Their Islamic version of modernity entailed a "complete and total" blend of society, state, culture, and religion, a blend with which everything began and ended. The social order they envisioned contained no internal contradictions. Political parties were scorned because their quarrels disturbed the unity of the Community of the Faithful, thus weakening it in its struggle with the enemies of Islam. Espousing this philosophy, the Brothers could thrive among the politically marginalized and discontented among the lower middle classes in cities and simultaneously be on cordial terms with the entourage of King Farouk, who saw the Brothers as a useful counterweight to the secular nationalists. In each case, the Brothers preached the unity of the faithful, placing special emphasis on personal morality.

The ambivalence inherent in the Brothers' message has not gone unnoticed, and it has been interpreted in a variety of contradictory ways over the passing years. Left-leaning Arab intellectuals have traditionally regarded the Brothers as a populist movement whose aim was to enlist the masses and dilute their class awareness with a vague religious sentiment—a tactic that, ironically, played into the hands of the established order. This analysis pointed out similarities to the workings of European fascism during the same period, the 1930s. But in the 1980s, a new interpretation of the brotherhood's ideology appeared among progressives, who saw the Islamist movement of their own time as a continuation of what the Brothers had begun. By offering a way for disenfranchised groups who had not come to terms with the culture of Europeanized elites to enter modern society, the Brothers assisted the process of democratization. Thanks to them, according to this view, the people could gain political power through, rather than in spite of, their Islamic culture. This debate over the merits of the Brothers' Islamic ideology is still under way today.[5] But both analyses tend to reduce Islamism to the expression of the bottom-line interest of a single social group: either the reactionaries who manipulate populist movements or the "people" whose cultural authenticity is idealized.

The history of the Muslim Brothers in the period between the world wars illustrates the socially ambiguous nature of the twentieth century's first Islamist movement. Exactly this same ambiguity was still apparent when Islamism reached its high point in the 1980s. It was powerful when it succeeded in uniting, through its cultural reference to Islam and its evocation of a fully reconciled Islamic society, various layers of society—urban and rural working classes, students, royal courts, and so on. But when the interests of its different components clashed, this shared culture and religion were not sufficient to maintain a unified front.

In 1949, during the political violence that marked the last years of the Egyptian monarchy, Banna, the founder of the Muslim Brothers, was assassinated. The Brothers played their part in the mayhem of this period, just as other parties did. The Secret Apparatus, which was the paramilitary arm of the Brothers, went so far as to practice systematic terrorism. The proponents of a fascist interpretation of the Brothers' ideology saw in this violence a corroboration of their analysis, while those who viewed the Brothers as progressives imputed the violence to an extreme wing of the movement.

When Nasser and his comrades took control of the Egyptian state in July 1952, the Brothers at first welcomed the seizure of power by "sons of the Egyptian people," who were very similar socially to the majority of the members. They also approved of the dissolution of the political parties that had menaced the unity of the faithful, and they saw in Nasser's Egypt an opportunity to build a society without divisions, guaranteed by the implementation of the Islamic order, as they themselves had recommended. But Nasser's nationalist agenda quickly collided with the Islamism of the Brothers, and the two camps found themselves vying for the same grassroots support among the cities' lower middle classes.

The conflict led to bloodshed, when an attempt on Nasser's life in 1954 was blamed on the Brothers. Their organization was dissolved, their members were jailed or exiled, and several of their leaders were hanged. At the time, it was felt that the Brothers had been politically annihilated and that they were in any case no more than a holdover from colonial times. They no longer had a place in a society that was aggressively modernizing under the banner of authoritarian nationalism, while moving decisively toward socialism and alliance with the Soviet Union. The decapitated movement now began a sojourn in the desert that was to last two decades in Egypt but that ultimately allowed it to spread to foreign countries and renew itself, notably by confronting the reasons for its failure against Nasserism. This reassessment by followers like Qutb, and the contrasting perspectives that came out of it, formed a blueprint for the Islamist movement of today, from its most radical to its most moderate elements.

But the Brothers' failure in their social struggle with Nasser had little to do with these political maneuvers. The fact was that Nasserism could rely on the support of low-ranking city workers, students, and rural people because it held out the hope of social advancement and integration as soon as political power had been secured. In the final analysis, any ideology's attractions, and the limits of those attractions, depend on how it adapts to the perceived needs of a society. The successes and failures of the Islamist movement in the twentieth century, from the time of the Muslim Brothers to the present, show this trend very clearly. This conclusion is far removed from a teleological view of history which holds that Islamism, for better or worse, is a necessary outcome for the Muslim world.

Sayyid Qutb's Squabbling Heirs

The success of the Society of Muslim Brothers derived from its capacity to muster widely different groups in support of its program, while recruiting members through charitable activities such as dispensaries, workshops, and schools near mosques. As their numbers rapidly increased, the Brothers perceived themselves to be an organization of the

Egyptian people, and the development of an ideal Islamist society was their most cherished dream. While reviling colonialism, they carefully fostered relations with King Farouk's entourage, and the sovereign granted Banna himself an audience.

Nasser's repression changed the situation completely. The Islamist movement that rose from the ashes of the Brothers found itself not only persecuted by a state to which it was implacably opposed but also alienated from the general population. This alienation was both physical (since the Islamist leaders were either in exile or in prison) and spiritual, for despite Nasser's propaganda and coercive methods, the Egyptian people were firmly behind him. He was the nemesis of the Brothers: and it was during Nasser's repression that Qutb defined the times as jahiliyya. This modern barbarism must be struck down, he wrote, just as the Prophet struck down the original jahiliyya and built his Islamic state upon its ruins.

This path diverged radically from the original way of the Brothers. It meant that the members of society as a whole were no longer viewed as Muslims. In Islamic doctrine, this is a very serious accusation, called *takfir*. The term derives from the word *kufr* (impiety), and it means that one who is, or claims to be, a Muslim is declared to be impure: by takfir he is excommunicated in the eyes of the Community of the Faithful. For those who interpret Islamic law literally and rigorously, one who is impious to this extent can no longer benefit from the protection of law. According to the consecrated expression, "his blood is forfeit," and he is condemned to death.

Takfir is a sentence of last resort. The ulemas, who are in principle the only people authorized to pronounce takfir after taking all the prescribed legal precautions, have always been reluctant to use it. Used wrongly and unrestrainedly, this sanction would quickly lead to discord and sedition in the ranks of the faithful. Muslims might resort to mutually excommunicating one another and thus propel the Umma to complete disaster. Qutb, who died before he could fully explain his theories, left unclear his use of the term *jahiliyya* and its dire consequence, *takfir*.

Three different readings were offered by those who took Qutb as their reference and debated his ideas in prison camps and elsewhere. The most extreme considered that impiety was endemic all over the world, except of course within their own corps of authentic believers.

They pronounced a general takfir on everyone else, even their fellow prisoners. The second reading confined the excommunication to the rulers of the state, whom they condemned as impious because they did not govern according to the injunctions contained in the holy texts. All other believers they spared. The third reading suggested an allegorical interpretation of the most controversial passages in Qutb's work: rupture with society (jahiliyya) should be understood in a spiritual sense, not a material sense. Most of the adherents of this view were Muslim Brothers who were out of jail or living outside Egypt. They recognized Hassan al-Hudaybi, Banna's successor, as the Supreme Guide of their organization, and they saw themselves as preachers, not judges. Thus, to show society how to make itself more Islamic, they needed to preach, not condemn.

At the end of the 1960s, these three interpretations were confined to a mostly clandestine movement. Intellectual battle lines were drawn between the younger faction and the remnants of the Brothers. The young radicals wished to break off all contact with the state and punish society for its passive acceptance of an impious government, while the Brothers, who were by now well-established in Saudi Arabia and Jordan, were horrified by radicalism, preferring political compromise wherever possible to direct confrontation with the state. The 1954 repression in Egypt had left deep scars.

Nevertheless, the Brothers patiently awaited their hour, which came in June 1967 with the Six Day War. Israel's catastrophic defeat of the Arab armies dealt a crippling blow to the Arab nation-states; Nasser himself offered to resign, though he later dramatically reversed himself. Still, the consensus around nationalist values was beginning to crumble. The modern Islamist movement, rebuilt around the ideas of Qutb, was at last able to command a hearing. Furthermore, by the beginning of the 1970s, the movement was no longer circumscribed by the Arab context, for by then the contribution of Mawlana Mawdudi, on the Indian subcontinent, was being felt.

Mawdudi, an Islamist Politician

Because Arabia was the site of the Islamic Revelation and Arabic is the language of the Koran, there has been a tendency in the West to reduce the Muslim world to the Arab world and scarcely admit the existence of a "peripheral Islam," which is viewed as subordinate. Yet at the close of the twentieth century, Arabs represent less than a fifth of the world's one billion Muslims, whose demographic centers lie in the Indian sub-continent and Southeast Asia. The same oversimplification often appears when the contemporary Islamist movement is at issue. Islamism is not confined to Saudi Arabia or even the Middle East; it has deep roots in India and Pakistan as well. Through Mawdudi's followers and other lesser-known networks, such as the Deoband schools in which the Taliban were trained, Islamist texts in Urdu—the written language of northern India—were broadly translated into Arabic and English and thereafter exercised a major influence on the global development of the Islamist movement throughout the twentieth century.

By contrast with Egypt, where Nasser crushed the Muslim Brothers in 1954 and created a hiatus between the colonial era and our own, the Islamist movement on the Indian subcontinent has developed steadily from the 1930s right up to the present. During the decades of Islamist persecution in Cairo, Mawdudi worked away in Pakistan to fine-tune the theories and concepts that would allow Islamic ideology to adapt to the new political conditions created by the rise of "irreligious" independent states.[6] At a very early stage, Mawdudi laid the cultural foundations for a future Islamic republic, defined in opposition to the Muslim nationalism that led to the birth of Pakistan in 1947.

To a much greater extent than the Arab Islamist theorists, Mawdudi acted squarely within the general framework of his culture. He was a prolific author and journalist in Urdu, a written language that uses Arabic characters and descends from Sanskrit, though it blends in many words deriving from Arabic, Turkish, and Persian derive.[7] The composite idiom of the Muslim conquerors of the Indian subcontinent, Urdu was adopted as the national language of Pakistan at that nation's creation in 1947; indeed, it symbolized the political identity of Pakistani nationalism in its opposition to India, which chose Hindi as its official language. Pakistani nationalists had an ambiguous relationship with Islam: they wanted to make Pakistan a "Muslim state" on the Indian subcontinent, but not an "Islamic state." (Analogously, Israel, which came into being the following year, was qualified by secular Zionism as the "state of the Jews"—Herzl's *Judenstaat*—but not the "Jewish state.") The nationalists wished to unite in a given territory all Muslims of the subcontinent, regardless of the intensity of their religious zeal. Their goal was to make them citizens of a modern nation whose institutions would be modeled largely on those of Great Britain.

Inventing this new nation required major population shifts, which were accompanied by resistance and shocking massacres. The country consisted of two distinct zones 2,000 kilometers apart: present-day Pakistan (then called West Pakistan) and the future Bangladesh (formerly called East Pakistan). Bangladesh's secession from Pakistan in 1971 exposed the fragility of the original edifice, which had counted on religion alone to unify the nation. While Urdu was the spoken language of Muslims near Delhi, it was not spoken at all by the people living in the territories of the new state. Yet it was adopted as the written language of the nation and thus became the principal vehicle for communicating the nationalist ideas of the ruling elites.

Mawdudi's first book, *Jihad in Islam*, was published in Urdu in the late 1920s, roughly coinciding with Banna's creation of the Society of Muslim Brothers in Egypt. From the start Mawdudi was against the project for a circumscribed "Muslim state," which would give power to the nationalists. Instead, he agitated for an Islamic state covering the whole of India. For him, all nationalism was impiety, more especially as its conception of the state was European-inspired. Apart from this, he had nothing but contempt for the ulemas, whom he accused of having collaborated with the British occupiers since the fall of Muslim-held Delhi in 1857. Mawdudi favored what he called "Islamization from above," through a state in which sovereignty would be exercised in the name of Allah and the sharia would be implemented. He declared that politics was "an integral, inseparable part of the Islamic faith, and that the Islamic state that Muslim political action seeks to build is a panacea for all their [Muslims'] problems."[8] For him, the five traditional Pillars of Islam (profession of the faith, prayer, the fast of Ramadan, pilgrimage, and almsgiving) were merely phases of training and preparation for jihad, the struggle against those of Allah's creatures who had usurped His sovereignty.[9] By the pen of Mawdudi, religion was turned into an ideology of political struggle. To carry out his jihad, he founded, in 1941, the Jamaat-e-Islami, which he saw as the vanguard of the Islamic Revolution, on a Leninist model. Mawdudi made explicit references to the "vanguard" of the earliest Muslims, who gathered around the Prophet in 622 during the *Hegira* (flight), broke with the idolatrous people of Mecca, and departed to found the Islamic state of Medina. His own party was intended to follow a similar course.

Mawdudi was the first twentieth-century Muslim thinker to build a political theory around the original break that led to the founding of Islam. In transforming this break into a strategy for action, he was inspired by the avant-garde European political parties of the 1930s. Qutb and his successors did the same; but instead of building up clandestine organizations and transforming the rupture with ungodly society into violent confrontation, Mawdudi's party existed in complete legality for most of its history. It continues to do so today, even though its founder and many of its leaders have been imprisoned from time to time. Mawdudi's holy war to build an Islamic state found expression through full participation in the political system of Pakistan, rather than radical opposition to it.

In contrast to the Egyptian Muslim brotherhood of 1930–1950, but also in contrast to Islamic parties of the late twentieth century such as the Turkish Prosperity (Refah) party or the Algerian Front Islamique du Salut (FIS), the Jamaat-e-Islami did not attract a mass following and its impact on elections remained consistently weak. Its social base was confined to the educated middle class, and it never seems to have penetrated to the poorer levels of society, where the Urdu language was not understood. Significantly, Mawdudi and his acolytes used Urdu for their speeches and sermons. Above all, the social agenda of the party remained highly ambiguous. It proclaimed its absolute hostility to capitalism, but socialism was the real target of its wrath. In the gestation of the contemporary Islamist movement, Mawdudi's contribution was largely that of a pioneer; he was the first person to give expression to the theory of cultural rupture with nationalists and ulemas alike. Moreover, he maintained the continuity of his Pakistani party at a time when many Arab Islamists were demoralized by repression. And in general his intellectual influence played a part in reorganizing Islamism to confront the then-triumphant forces of nationalism.

Toward the end of the 1960s, the bisecting influences of Qutb and Mawdudi prepared the ground within the Sunni Muslim world for the emergence of the Islamist movement over the next ten years. One influence came from the Middle East, where Islam had dominated for fourteen centuries and where European colonization had been unable to challenge its primacy. The other came from the Indian subcontinent, where most of the population was still Hindu despite ten centuries of Islamic political domination. When the British empire broke that domination in 1857, Muslims felt besieged and threatened. According to

Mawdudi, an Islamic state was the only possible safeguard for endangered Muslims; nevertheless, his call for a cultural break with the past was not an incitement to social revolution so much as a call to take part in the political institutions of Pakistan. The divide between the Islamist avant-garde and society did not translate into guerrilla warfare, uprisings, or resistance.

Meanwhile Qutb, in adopting Mawdudi's notion of an Islamic state, established a much more radical program of action. For him, the vanguard's role was to destroy the ungodly state, to break with it immediately, and to refuse to be compromised by association with a political system from which it could expect nothing. Qutb promoted revolution as a way to seize power—a concept that was absent from Mawdudi's thought—and in the process he found many followers and imitators among the radical youth of Islam. But neither Mawdudi nor Qutb gave any explicit social content to their theorizing. Qutb may have depicted Islam as the instrument of social justice, but in no way did he present himself as the mouthpiece of the disinherited, as did the Shiite revolutionaries in Iran. He identified the main fault line within society as being between Islam and jahiliyya, but nothing in his discourse infers that there might be a contradiction between "oppressed" and "oppressors"—or between the Iranian revolution's "disinherited ones" and "men of arrogance."

Khomeini, the Revolutionary Cleric

In 1971 Muhammad Reza Pahlavi, shah of Iran, organized at Persepolis a series of grandiose festivities, to which he invited elites from around the world. At the height of his power, the shah was celebrating the 2500th anniversary of the Iranian monarchy, whose heir he claimed to be—despite the fact that he was merely the son of an army officer who had seized power in a coup d'état in 1921 and then crowned himself king in 1925. By invoking the spirit of Cyrus the Great, the shah sought to create an eternal Iranian identity that would legitimize his monarchy and, at the same time, reduce his country's Islamization to the status of a historical accident. No doubt the guests at Persepolis would have laughed had someone suggested the notion that within eight years an elderly cleric in a turban would shock the entire planet by sweeping the shah from power in an Islamic revolution. Yet at that very moment, from his exile in the Shiite holy city of Najaf in Iraq, Ayatollah Khomeini was publishing a book entitled *Islamic Government*.[10] This volume contained transcripts of a series of lectures that included every one of the most important dispositions made by the Islamic Republic after it came to power in 1979.

Khomeini's book, which was barely noticed at the time, eventually precipitated a Shiite intellectual revolution that was without precedent among Sunni Muslims. For the first time a leading Shiite cleric had thrown his full weight as a doctor of the law behind the ideas of modern Islamist intellectuals. Mawdudi and Qutb, neither of whom had received any clerical training, had seen their ideas attacked by the ulemas, whom they had criticized very harshly. Although militant Sunni Islamism became a social movement after the mid-1970s, it remained handicapped by this conflict with the ulemas. But in Iran, from the beginning of the decade, a revered cleric was preaching the destruction of the established order. Khomeini was able to mobilize networks of supporters and disciples much more effectively than were intellectuals educated along modern lines; and this was one reason why the Islamic Revolution had no counterpart in the Sunni Arab world.

During the 1960s, while Qutb was being persecuted in Egypt, Iranian Islamism was taking shape around two poles. Young militants had begun to reinterpret Shiite doctrine within a revolutionary context, inspired by Marxism and the concerns of the Third World. At the same time a section of the clergy, symbolized by Khomeini, began to confront the shah by adopting virulently anti-modernist positions. The ayatollah's political genius lay in appropriating the aspirations of the young militants. Their endorsement allowed Khomeini to include in his audience the educated urban middle class who otherwise would have remained aloof from a personality perceived as preposterously traditional and reactionary.

The most influential intellectual figure for the young militants—apart from Khomeini—was Ali Shariati (1933–1977), who belonged to a strictly religious family and had studied in Paris, where he had been influenced by exiled Algerian independence fighters. The ideals he learned from leftist intellectuals and Third World revolutionaries such as Jean-Paul Sartre, Che Guevara, and Frantz Fanon were passed on to the Shiite militants. In the process, he reread religious doctrine, whose interpretation he disputed with the "reactionary" clergy.

One of the central doctrines of Shiite Muslims is the martyrdom of Imam Hussein, son of Ali, the fourth caliph of Islam and the grandson of the Prophet.[11] The imam was defeated and put to death in 680 at Karbala, in the south of present-day Iraq, by the armies of the Sunni caliph of Damascus, whom the Shiite supporters of Ali's family viewed as a usurper. Traditionally, the ceremony of commemoration involved what was called "Shiite lamentation," in which the faithful ritually flagellated themselves, weeping copiously for the martyr Hussein and his family and reproaching themselves for failing to come to his aid. Throughout Shiite history, the clergy have made this rite the symbol of a retreat from the world, and from politics and power in particular. Shiites also believe that the twelfth imam, Ali's descendant Muhammad al-Mahdi, who disappeared in 874, will return to the world at the end of time. During his "occultation," the world will be filled with shadows and iniquity; light and justice will return only with the coming of the Messiah. Politically, the consequence of this doctrine was a quietist attitude toward politics: the Shiite faithful viewed political power as evil and debased, yet rendered it lip service (taqiyya), without rebelling against it. They were devoted to their clerics, whose hierarchy was organized under the aegis of the greatest interpreters of the sacred texts, the "grand ayatollahs"; clerical independence was guaranteed by almsgiving (zakat) on the part of the faithful.

This state of political-religious equilibrium, punctuated by periods of mourning and celebration of the martyrdom of the imams, was attacked by Ali Shariati for its compromise with "iniquitous" earthly powers in the expectation of a heavenly reward and the return of the Mahdi. But where his Marxist friends would have rejected the entire system as another opiate of the people, Shariati attacked only the reactionary clergy. He claimed that the true interpretation of Shiite doctrine lay not in flagellation, quietism, and awaiting the Messiah but in continuing the fight against state injustice begun by Ali and Hussein. It was futile to bewail the martyrs' fate; instead, their example should be followed by taking up arms against the shah, the iniquitous monarch of the day, just as they did in their time against the usurper Sunni caliphs. In this doctrine, Shariati was in line with the thinking of Qutb, who called on his disciples to destroy the impious state as the Prophet Mohammed himself had destroyed idolatrous Mecca. Both preached a return to the fundamental message of religion, the blotting out of the compromises of recent history, and a clean break with the established political order.

In contrast to Qutb, who mostly expressed himself in the language of Islamic doctrine, Shariati allowed some of the tenets of Marxism to penetrate his writings and statements—most notably the idea of class struggle. He did not hesitate to replace the traditional formula that opens all pious Muslim discourse, "In the name of Allah the compassionate, the merciful," with "In the name of the God of the disinherited," which in traditional circles amounted to blasphemy.[12] When he translated Frantz Fanon's *The Wretched of the Earth* into Persian, Shariati rendered the difference between "oppressors" and "oppressed" with the Koranic terms *mostakbirine* (the arrogant) and *mostadafine* (the weakened or disinherited), thus transposing the theory of class struggle into the terminology of Islam and giving it a central importance that it did not have in traditional doctrine.

Shariati acted out of conviction—his own faith was profound and completely sincere—but also out of a sense of opportunity. According to him, the failure of the generally atheist progressive movements such as Marxism to mobilize the masses and seize power in the Muslim world between 1960 and 1970 could be imputed to their cultural distance from the populace, who perceived the universe through the prism of religion. Nonetheless, Shariati's own Islamic formulations yielded a curious hybrid mixture that also failed to convince the masses he sought to mobilize. His influence, direct or indirect, was most clearly felt by the Islamic-Marxist Iranian movements, notably the People's Mujahedeen, who found most of their recruits among the student population. These students were engaged in armed struggle against the shah's regime, but despite their spectacular terrorist actions, they too were failing to strike deep roots among the people.[13] And even though Shariati's lectures were highly successful, he himself remained an isolated figure. His death in London in 1977, shortly before the start of the Iranian revolution, passed almost unnoticed. Shariati's subsequent fame, which was confirmed after the revolution by the massive reprintings of his works, was due to the fact that Ayatollah Khomeini appropriated most of his ideas and wove them into the traditional tapestry of religious scholarship, of which he was an acknowledged master.

Born in 1902, a year before Mawdudi and four years before Qutb,

Khomeini assumed leadership of a minority faction of the high Shiite clergy in 1962. This faction opposed the quiescent attitude of the majority of clerics and openly rejected the Pahlavi dynasty. Khomeini himself had been a teacher in Qum, one of the holy cities of the Shiites; he had always held aloof from the political fray, preferring to write conservative doctrinal tracts. Now he took a stand against the shah's "White Revolution," whose program not only threatened the clergy's considerable landholdings but also proposed the emancipation of women, the swearing-in of elected officials on a holy book that need not necessarily be the Koran, and a referendum to endorse these measures. Khomeini's scandalized objections to all this galvanized the opposition, and the commemoration of Hussein's martyrdom in June 1963 was transformed into a demonstration against the regime.

The following year, Khomeini issued a violent denunciation of the legal immunity given by the shah to U.S. military advisers in Iran, accusing the monarch of selling out the nation for a few American dollars. For this he was immediately deported to the Holy City of Najaf in Iraq until October 1978, at which time he moved to Neauphle-le-Château near Paris prior to his triumphant return to Tehran on February 1, 1979.[14]

Before 1970, Khomeini's opposition to the shah was mostly expressed in moral and religious terms; he did not call for the revolutionary overthrow of the regime in the name of Islam.[15] But that year, a series of lectures, the minutes of which would later be published under the title *Velayat-e Faqih: Hokumat-e Islami* ("Islamic Government: Under the Guardianship of a Doctor of the Law," abridged to "Islamic Government"), represented a radical break with the Shiite stance of political passivity, and specifically with the previous attitudes of Khomeini himself. He now called for the overthrow of the monarchy and the establishment on its ruins of an Islamic government, of which a doctor of Shiite law would be the supreme guide. With this message, he exploded the entire intellectual edifice that endorsed submitting to the clergy and compromise with a bad prince while awaiting the Messiah. Instead, Khomeini preached the outright takeover of power by that very clergy.

This major alteration of course within the dominant Shiite tradition was lifted directly and without acknowledgment from Islamist revolutionary thinkers, particularly Shariati. The objective was to seize power after driving out the iniquitous sovereign. But while Shariati denounced reactionary clerics and saw "enlightened" intellectuals *(rawshanfekran)* like himself as the future guides of the revolution, Khomeini attributed this role to the religious cleric, the *faqih.* This of course meant Khomeini himself, as the history of the Islamic Republic was later to demonstrate.

This hijacking of activist intellectual ideas was further confirmed by the systematic use of terms like *mostadafine* and *mostakbirine* in Khomeini's post-1970 speeches—terms that had been almost completely absent from his earlier pronouncements.[16] In making himself the unofficial representative of the disinherited (a vague concept that was eventually expanded to include the bazaar merchants opposed to the shah), the ayatollah of Najaf succeeded in doing something that no one in Sunni Islam ever had accomplished before. He attracted the support of the traditional rural and urban base that had always followed the lead of a cleric of acknowledged stature, as well as the backing of the more modern social elements of the cities—students, the salaried middle class, and other progressive-minded workers. These people were receptive to a line of thinking that empowered them as harbingers of the future, in opposition to the "arrogant" oppressors clustered around the shah and his court.

But in the early 1970s, these ideas still had a long way to go. Their impact on Sunni and Shiite Muslims was limited to militant circles. They were largely unknown to the intellectuals of the cities, for whom nationalism was still the primary political reference point of the time and whose eventual opposition to established authority hinged on the various adaptations of Marxism then in vogue. Nor were they taken seriously by governments, which were more concerned with the spread of subversive ideas in the universities following the European and American student movements of 1968. Finally, they struggled to gain ground within Islam itself, which was controlled by socially conservative clerics who saw themselves as voices of conscience and reproof with respect to a government they never dreamed of overthrowing or replacing, as well as by mystical and pietist groups without explicit political objectives.

In the late 1970s Islamism gained a solid foothold within society by eventually winning control of the direction of Islam. It accomplished this by imposing its own values and marginalizing or dismissing other interpretations of the Muslim religion. It also forged alliances with some of the clerics and a few of the pietist movements, with whom its relations were complex and changeable. To comprehend these developments, we need to understand the general context of the Muslim religion at the dawn of modern Islamism, when its militants were struggling to be heard.

CHAPTER

2

Islam in the Late 1960s

From Morocco to Indonesia and from Turkey to Nigeria, the countries of the Muslim world in the late 1960s were not politically united behind their common adherence to Islam. Rather, the elites in power belonged to communities built around local or regional nationalisms (such as Arabism) or to one of the blocs created at Yalta at the end of World War II. Nonetheless, Islamic institutions, educational establishments, brotherhoods, and an architecture of mosques and places of prayer preserved the unique characteristics of the Muslim world. Among the various Muslim countries, a constant interchange of men, ideas, and funds created links and biases in favor of one religious interpretation or another. No state could afford to be indifferent to these networks, because if they got out of control they might do harm at home and even comfort a rival state.

It happened that several religious movements, which at the time had very little political visibility, were maintaining or developing a presence in various countries and regions throughout the Islamic world. All these movements were later caught up by the great upheaval of Islamism, and often their reaction to the movement's growing strength was an important factor in the success or failure of Islamist militants in establishing themselves within society at large.

We have seen that one of the greatest traumas to affect Islam in the early twentieth century was Ataturk's abolition of the caliphate in 1924. The caliphate was already a spent political force at the time, but it represented the ideal of spiritual unity within the Muslim world.[1] During World War I, when the Ottoman empire was the ally of Prussia and Austria-Hungary, the sultan in Istanbul, in his capacity as Commander of the Faithful, had called upon all Muslim subjects of the British, French, and Russian empires to wage jihad against their colonial masters. This call to arms had little practical effect, but nevertheless the Allied High Command was concerned enough to actively support those Muslims among the colonial soldiers sent to fight and die in the trenches. In France, official acknowledgment of Francophile Islam eventually led to the building of the Grand Mosque in Paris in 1926.[2] The idea behind this structure was to stop Muslims within the French empire from falling under the influence of transnational religious movements militating against colonialism, while keeping a close eye on the traditional Islam of the brotherhoods and the ordinary populace.

In 1927, a year before the creation of the Society of Muslim Brothers in Egypt and two years before Mawdudi published his first book, a movement began developing in India which by the end of the twentieth century was to become the most important single element of re-Islamization worldwide. This was the Tablighi Jamaat (shortened to Tabligh), or Society for the Propagation of the Muslim faith.[3] The Tabligh claimed to be outside politics. The aim of its founder, Muhammad Ilyas, was to use intensive religious discipline to bring back those errant Indian Muslims who had succumbed to the lure of Hindu culture or otherwise allowed their devotion to Islam to falter. Ilyas preached the exact and literal imitation of the Prophet as the personification of Islamic virtue, in the belief that if the faithful practiced this in their daily lives, they would be able to break all habits and other "impious" behavior that contravened the strict rules of Islam. For example, a Muslim about to make a journey would pray just as the Prophet did under similar circumstances. He would sleep, if possible, just as tradition has it that Mohammed slept, lying on his right side on the ground, facing Mecca with his hand cupped beneath his cheek. And whenever he could, he would dress in a white *jellaba*. This movement sought to break the bonds between its disciples and their corrupt environment and to bind them to a community of strict obedience.

In places where Islam was a minority religion, the approach was initially successful. Later, as the Tabligh's influence spread, it gained ground wherever Muslims found themselves living outside their traditional milieus—having moved from the countryside to the town, for example, or away from their countries of origin to places where their religious customs were destabilized by more secular lifestyles. Its effect was to reassert certain immutable standards within a familiar religious framework.

The Tabligh was opposed to the traditional Islam of the brotherhoods and mystics and condemned as idolatry the widespread practice of venerating tombs. But it strongly objected as well to the politicizing of Islam by Mawdudi, Qutb, Khomeini, and their successors. For the founders of the Tabligh, a man should not sit back and expect the state to implement Islam within society; he should do it himself, through his efforts to convert others. The extraordinary expansion of the movement, which today can be found around the world wherever there are Muslims, was also due to one of its articles of faith, which urges adherents to travel widely and function as, in Ilyas's words, "a mobile school, an itinerant monastery and a beacon of truth and example, all in one." Because the Tablighis, following the example of the Prophet, moved about exclusively on foot, over the course of seven decades they gradually built up a remarkably dense network across the globe, from which new waves of militants spread out in their turn.

During the 1960s, the Tabligh moved its operational center from Delhi in India to Raiwind, close to Lahore in Pakistan. Even at that stage the movement was already spreading in all directions from the small mosques where its wandering adepts spent their nights among groups of believers. To these they preached a rigorous, unifying vision of Islam, rooted in the Indian subcontinent instead of the Arab Middle East. By the 1970s, the Tabligh had become an advance guard for the political Islamists, some of whom used its network of contacts and former adherents for their own specific objectives. Nevertheless, they attracted little attention because of the discreet way they operated at the grassroots level, studiously avoiding publicity and politics.

The Tabligh was a striking example of a fluid, transnational, informal Islamic movement, and by the late 1960s it was more influential than any other. But it shared the field with a multitude of similar groups, most of which pursued cultural and social objectives instead of political aims. As soon as they gained access to significant numbers of Muslims, they became de facto mediators between the secular authorities and the mass of ordinary people. Consequently, the state was obliged to bring them to heel—co-opting them when they proved open to collaboration, and containing and repressing them when they were hostile or indifferent.

With the noteworthy exception of the Soviet Muslim countries, which had to wait another twenty years, by the late 1960s the majority of Muslim nations had won their independence from their colonial occupiers. The regimes that assumed power in the new Islamic nations could be divided ideologically along lines roughly corresponding to the two major power blocs: the Communists and the West. On one side were progressive socialist countries closely aligned with Moscow; these included Nasser's Egypt, Baathist Syria and Iraq, Muammar el-Qaddafi's Libya, Algeria under Ahmed Ben Bella and Houari Boumedienne, Southern Yemen, and Sukarno's Indonesia. Leaders of these nations viewed traditional Islamic institutions as thoroughly reactionary, placed restrictions on their independent social functions, and submitted them to rigorous controls with a view to using them as conduits for their own socialist ideology. On the other side were Islamic nations allied with the West. The stances of these governments ranged from a pronounced secular bias (as in Turkey and, to a lesser extent, Tunisia under Habib Bourguiba) to an exclusive reliance on Islam as the basis of the regime's legitimacy (as occurred in Saudi Arabia).

In monarchies where the traditionally dominant classes—the tribal aristocracies, landowners, and bazaar merchants—had maintained their own positions of political strength following independence, religious dignitaries remained in the forefront of society. But wherever the more modern urban groups had succeeded in driving out the pashas and sheiks, the dignitaries of Islam were sidelined. These states seized religious endowments (*waqfs* or *habous*), which consisted of considerable lands and buildings "bequeathed to God" by the faithful, along with funds that allowed Muslim clerics to manage and maintain them.[4] In compensation, the ulemas were granted salaries as state employees, but this new arrangement severely curtailed their independence.

Under Turkish secularism, which was unique in the Muslim world, the state did not remain neutral in religious matters, as it does in Western democracies, or aloof from religious activities. On the contrary, Turkey placed strict limits on these activities and exercised very careful control. Muslim brotherhoods and all parties that might call into question the legitimacy of the state's secular constitution were pro-scribed, while education was closely monitored by state officials who promoted an "acceptable" version of Muslim doctrine and practice. The secular character of the republic founded by Ataturk was the leg-acy of Comtean positivism, but it also owed a lot to the institutionaliz-ing of Islam by the Ottoman empire. One of the duties of the sheik of Islam, chosen by the sultan-caliph, had been to make sure that the state's authority was not undermined by overzealous clerics.[5]

Likewise, in the socialist Arab countries, the religious legitimacy of regimes was carefully fostered, but religious issues were kept out of the public eye, which was supposed to be trained instead on the battle against imperialism and Zionism. Thus, Egyptian, Syrian, and Iraqi schoolbooks of the 1960s went out of their way to impress upon chil-dren that socialism was simply Islam properly understood. Pamphlets demonstrating the inherently socialist nature of Islam were to be found all over the Muslim world.[6] Yet even this socialist version of Islam was kept under close surveillance.

Theoreticians of "developmentalism" have tended to equate mod-ernization with secularization. But nowhere in the Muslim world of the late 1960s did religion vanish from popular culture, social life, or day-to-day politics. Islam was merely handled in different ways by different regimes, and was combined with nationalism in ways that varied ac-cording to the social class of those who had seized power at the mo-ment of independence.

Broadly speaking, Islam during this period ranged between two ex-tremes. Popular Islam emphasized devotion; the relationship of indi-viduals with God was generally orchestrated by spiritual guides, living or dead, including founders of mystical brotherhoods such as the Sufis. Islamic scholarship, on the other hand, tended to emphasize an intel-lectual rapport with the divine, based on reading and interpretation of sacred texts by the ulemas. This term designates those who are officially acknowledged as scholars of the Koran (the sacred text of Islam, re-vealed to the Prophet by God), of the Hadith (a collection of the tradi-tions of the Prophet, including his sayings and deeds), and of the full body of jurisprudence developed by their ulema predecessors after spe-cial training in the religious schools or universities and the award of a diploma. This distinction between popular and learned Islam, which has existed throughout the history of the religion, is neither absolute nor exclusive. Some of the greatest mystics of Islam were scholars, just as they were in the Jewish and Christian traditions, while many scholarly Muslim clerics circulated among the mystical brotherhoods. Nevertheless, the distinction allows us to see the various ways one can practice Islam, and to comprehend the religion's pluralism. The emergence of Islamism in the 1970s, by contrast, tended to reduce Muslim practice to a single, political dimension.

The Resilience of the Mystical Brotherhoods

In the late 1960s, the popular Islam of the mystical brotherhoods still supplied a major social bond for both city-dwellers and the rural populace. Prior to the demographic upheavals of the 1970s, the majority of the population in Muslim countries consisted of illiterate farmers. The mystical brotherhoods mediated between the traditional beliefs, some of them pre-Islamic, of the uneducated masses and the bookish culture of Islam. For instance, a brotherhood of Upper Egypt might have rituals that included funerary barges similar to those that carried the dead across the Nile in pharaonic times; in the Indian subcontinent or the Indonesian archipelago, the brotherhood might ornament the tombs of Muslim saints with Hindu trappings (monumental staircases, lakes containing sacred crocodiles, garlands of carnations like those used to decorate statues of Shiva).[7] In black Africa, the Muslim *marabouts* (spiritual guides) were the inheritors of fetishism.

Popular religion organized around familiar and accessible saints who could serve as intercessors with the Prophet and who dispensed their *baraka* (blessings) among the faithful was important in several ways. In addition to soliciting and collecting donations and supervising their expenditure, religious leaders also managed large tracts of agricultural land and organized trade networks that made use of the wide dispersion of adepts around the world.[8] They provided the populace with a means of social integration, found work for people, shared subsidies, and arranged marriages. Equally important, these brotherhoods afforded governing regimes political stability by maintaining social peace in exchange for the state's recognition of the organization's central role and its guarantee of the inviolability of its property, tax exemptions, and so on.

The European colonialists understood the function of the brotherhoods as intermediaries. They fought them for a while, then came to terms with them. Photographs of marabouts from French North and West Africa with the rosette of the Legion of Honor pinned to their *burnouses* or *boubous* are among the clichés of colonialism. With independence, however, the political destiny of this brand of organized popular Islam was determined by the answers to a number of questions. How deeply were the brotherhood leaders compromised by association with the colonial power? Had they participated fully in the struggle for national independence? How great was their influence among the masses? How ready were they to cooperate with the new regime? What was the state's ideological attitude toward them? All these factors counted. In Algeria, the persistence of pro-French sentiment among leaders of the Muslim brotherhoods (who were consequently known as the *Beni oui-oui*, the "Yes-men" tribe) and their general lack of participation in the war of independence waged by the Front de Libération Nationale (FLN) between 1954 and 1962 made it impossible for them to co-opt the incoming regime, with its military supremacy, its armed resistance, and its leaders' lack of sympathy for the "superstitions" and "idolatries" of "religious reactionaries." Indeed, the state viewed the marabouts as obstacles to independent Algeria's march toward socialism. The Algerian brotherhoods were dispersed, and their properties were confiscated to further a program of agrarian reform. In the intermediate period, this created an institutional vacuum in Algeria's religious life that posed very little danger for the regime up to the end of the 1960s. But as we shall see, between 1985 and 1990 this vacuum was filled by the rapid growth of the Algerian Islamist movement.

In republican Turkey, the brotherhoods were methodically repressed from 1925 onward but nevertheless experienced a spectacular rebirth following World War II, mainly in rural areas. The sheiks sold their disciples' votes dearly to the newly created political parties, in exchange for whatever advantages they could get.

Following independence, most regimes in Muslim countries tended to seek a *modus vivendi* with popular Islam, on the assumption that the social unrest caused by their disappearance would do more harm than good. The spiritual guide of a brotherhood—a sheik, marabout, or pir, depending on the region—normally commanded total obedience among rank-and-file members. The brotherhoods were generally too far removed from the inner circles of politics to sustain regular criticism of the state's initiatives. This contrasted sharply with the scholarly ulemas, who monitored the regime religiously and made sure that whatever the state did was in strict conformity with the injunctions of the holy texts.

Thus, in Egypt, Nasser looked to the traditional Egyptian brotherhoods for support against the more radical Muslim Brothers and the Islamists. But these older groups were ill-adapted to attract the mass of educated youth who grew up in the cities, and eventually their influence waned. By contrast, in Senegal, called "the paradise of the brotherhoods," the traditional groups were able to retain the upper hand in both town and country. The *mourid* and *tidjan* "khalif-generals," of whom most Senegalese saw themselves as disciples, controlled agricultural and commercial revenues. With the departure of the French, they also found themselves holding most of the keys to political influence as well. When Islamism began to appear in Senegal in the late 1970s among students who were inspired by the Iranian revolution or educated in Arab universities in the Middle East, it immediately collided with the power of the marabouts. Radical Islamism was allowed a hearing only so long as it did no harm to the marabouts' interests; as soon as the movement showed signs of doing so, the religious leaders smashed it.

While most Muslim governments in the 1960s were tolerant of popular Islam, the one state that proscribed the brotherhoods even more strictly than secular Turkey or Algeria (where the prohibition was eventually lifted) was Saudi Arabia. Here, the scholarly Islam of the ulemas claimed a monopoly on religious matters and dictated the only acceptable discourse on the central values of society and political order. Mystics and secularist intellectuals were held in particular opprobrium.

The Saudi monarchy originated with an alliance in 1745 between the amir Muhammad ibn Saud and a puritan reformer, Muhammad ibn Abd al-Wahhab (1703–1792), who was a virulent campaigner against the "superstitions" that had adulterated Islam's original purity. The Wahhabi sect that sprang from this alliance is crucially important to an understanding of contemporary Sunni Islamism drawn from the thinking of Qutb and Mawdudi. The two currents share certain major points of doctrine—notably the imperative of returning to Islam's "fundamentals" and the strict implementation of all its injunctions and prohibitions in the legal, moral, and private spheres. But whereas

Islamism tolerates revolutionary social groups as well as conservatives, Wahhabism entails an exclusive conservatism within society.

The similarity of the two movements had a decisive effect on the fortunes of Sunni Islamism, for it was in Saudi Arabia that many of the Egyptian Muslim Brothers driven out by Nasser found refuge after the mid-1950s. At that time, the Saudis were beginning to profit substantially from their oil revenues, and the Brothers from abroad arrived just in time to supply a class of organizers and intellectuals who were better educated than their Saudi counterparts. They played an influential role at the University of Medina, completed in 1961, where the doctrine of the Brothers was taught to students from all over the Muslim world. Many of the refugee Brothers built up personal fortunes which they partly reinvested in Egypt after Nasser's death in 1970, contributing to the creation of an Islamic banking sector that would eventually finance the militant Islamist movement. Well before the full emergence of Islamism in the 1970s, a growing constituency nicknamed "petro-Islam" included Wahhabi ulemas and Islamist intellectuals and promoted strict implementation of the sharia in the political, moral, and cultural spheres; this proto-movement had few social concerns and even fewer revolutionary ones. Indeed, the contrast between the *tharwa* (wealthy) Islamists and the *thawra* (revolutionary) ones was a standing pun in Arabia. Qutb's advocacy of revolution and his denunciation of existing regimes, including those of the Arabian peninsula, as anti-Islamic or jahiliyya were generally viewed by those in power as exaggerations, brought on by the tortures endured by the Brothers in Nasser's jails. Nevertheless, Sayyid Qutb's writings, which were edited and published by his brother Muhammad Qutb in Saudi Arabia, were held in high esteem by his growing contingent of followers there.

So from the late 1960s onward, Saudi Arabia, a conservative country, held a somewhat aloof but far from unsympathetic attitude toward radical Islamist thought, whose harshness it sought to temper rather than confront. During the Cold War, this Wahhabite-Islamist trend prospered under the protection of the Saudi monarchy, whose worst enemies were Nasser and the socialist alliance and whose closest ally was the United States. Hence, in the early 1970s Islamism was kindly looked upon by the Western bloc, and Muslim regimes contending with leftist oppositions broadly encouraged their bearded Islamist students. They had no way of knowing that by the end of the decade many of these same students would build up a virulent opposition to the established order.

For the time being the Saudi monarchy seemed quite capable of containing Islamism and making it serve the kingdom's own international purposes. In 1962, the Muslim World League, a non-government organization funded by the Saudis, had been founded in Mecca; this was the first coherent and systematic institution whose avowed intent was to "Wahhabize" Islam worldwide and thereby negate the influence of Nasser's Egypt.[9] It operated by sending out religious missionaries, distributing the works of its main ideologists (Ibn Taymiyya and Ibn al-Wahhab notably), and above all by raising funds for building mosques and subsidizing Islamic associations.[10] The league identified worthy beneficiaries, invited them to Saudi Arabia, and gave them the recommendation *(tazkiya)* that would later provide them with largesse from a generous private donor, a member of the royal family, a prince, or an ordinary businessman. The league was managed by members of the Saudi religious establishment, working with other Arabs who either belonged to the Muslim Brothers or were close to them, along with ulemas from the Indian subcontinent connected to the Deoband Schools or to the party founded by Mawdudi.

The Ulemas at the Crossroads

Thus, by the end of the 1960s, Saudi Arabia was the only country in the Muslim world in which the ulemas had not lost control of the public debate over the central values of society. Everywhere else, they had also lost much of their traditional independence from state control. Indeed, they became tantamount to state officials, helping governments by issuing *fatwas* (religious rulings) and publicly endorsing state policies. These routine endorsements were occasionally mitigated by resistance to particular initiatives that were judged non-Islamic, but in the main the ulemas were weakened by having to share their role as arbiters with secular intellectuals.[11]

Secular intellectuals in the Muslim world judged society according to criteria that stemmed from the European Enlightenment, transmuted into local languages. Their reference was not to transcendental truth but to norms based on human rights and reason such as democracy, liberty, progress, and socialism. This contrasted with the views of the ulemas, for whom society's organization must conform with the prescriptions set out in the sacred texts of Islam. Because of their training, the clerics saw themselves as holding a monopoly on knowledge in this area, and they disparaged any nonclerics who ventured to comment on the holy texts. The unfortunate secular intellectual who ventured any kind of allegorical interpretation of the Koran, or even worse, the former cleric who betrayed his peers by suggesting a sacrilegious reading or by questioning the conventional meaning of a point of dogma was anathema. In extreme cases, intellectuals who had been censured by the ulemas were later assassinated by fanatics or driven into exile by the threat of death. Consequently, by the late 1960s, most secular intellectuals in the Muslim world tended to avoid religious questions, which no longer appeared to play a central role in the organization of society; nor did they bother to challenge the ulemas' position as Guardians of Islam, because it seemed largely irrelevant to them.

At Egypt's Al Azhar, the prestigious thousand-year-old institution to which ulemas come from all over the world for instruction, Nasser's government undertook a major reform in 1961.[12] The university was effectively placed under direct state control with a view to bringing its teachers and pupils into line and illustrating the compatibility between Islam and Nasserist socialism. The Azharis were given military uniforms and found themselves marching in step under the orders of army officers. Some of the students and teachers submitted to these changes; other ulemas, since they could not resist openly, merely dragged their heels. However, the religious reform was taken seriously by Nasser's opponents abroad, so seriously that in the following year the Saudis founded their own Muslim World League, as we have seen.

By linking the reformed Azhar institution too directly to the state, Nasser's regime deprived it of credibility. The ulemas found themselves no longer effective in their traditional role as intermediaries between the state and the people, preaching obedience to the regime while remaining free to criticize it and make it promote justice. The religious hierarchy now appeared too dependent on political leaders. A vacuum had been created, to be filled by anyone ready to question the state and criticize governments in the name of Islam, whether that person had received clerical training or not.

The two other Arab countries with ancient training institutions for

Muslim clerics were Tunisia, whose Zitouna mosque and university were founded in Tunis in 734, and Morocco, where the Qarawiyyin in Fez dates from 859. Bourguiba in Tunisia, who had received a secular education under the French during the Third Republic and depended for his support on the urban middle class, had struggled hard and long against French colonialism, and this record gave him political legitimacy. With strong support behind him, he rejected the clerics out of hand and emptied the Zitouna of its substance by directly abolishing the ulemas as an organized body. In a succession of striking symbolic acts—drinking a glass of lemonade on television during the fast of Ramadan and forbidding the slaughter of sheep for the feast of Eid al-Kebir (or Id al-Adha, the ritual commemorating Abraham's sacrifice)—he drove home the secularization of Tunisian society.

Nevertheless, Bourguiba took care to justify his acts in religious terms: economic development became a jihad, a holy war that dispensed with certain ritual obligations that might compromise its success. In contrast to Egypt, where the reform of Al Azhar was intended to controll and co-opt the ulemas, Tunisia under Bourguiba simply swept them from the scene, leaving the Supreme Combatant with a free hand to make use of Islam as he chose and only when he felt the need to do so. The total absence of the ulemas in Tunisia produced a backlash in the 1970s, when the Mouvement de la Tendance Islamique (MTI) rapidly annexed the religious field, unopposed by the weakened clerics, and forced the state into a campaign of fierce and ruthless repression.

When the French protectorate in Morocco came to an end in 1957, the ulemas, who were loyal supporters of Mohammed V, conferred full Islamic legitimacy on the king. This support proved a great asset when he met with opposition from the urban middle class. Nevertheless, while he showered the ulemas with prerogatives and honors, Mohammed V was careful to deprive them of any possibility of independent and potentially critical expression.[13] His son, Hassan II, who came to the throne in 1961, arrogated to himself all authority to speak for Islam, claiming direct descent from the Prophet (hence his title of Sherif) and adopting the title of Commander of the Faithful (amir al mouminine), by which he made his very person sacred. As such, he received the act of allegiance (baya) of the ulemas, of the descendants of the Prophet, and of the other members of the dynasty; but this allegiance had no contractual dimension.

The Moroccan ulemas played an institutional role, but it was limited to endorsing the dispositions of the Commander of the Faithful, who remained the ultimate reference where Islam was concerned. In the late 1960s, religion in Morocco was broadly based, legitimate, and under tight control. When the Islamist movement began to emerge at the start of the following decade, its followers, who spoke the language of religion, settled into society without attracting official attention or causing trouble. But it encountered much more difficulty in contriving a political rupture with the state without calling into question the monarch's sacredness, a taboo to which the mass of the populace was resolutely opposed.

In Algeria, where there was no national institution for training ulemas (traditionally, they went to the Zitouna or the Qarawiyyin), the Association of Algerian Ulemas was founded at Constantine by Abdel Hamid Ben Badis in 1931.[14] Doctrinally, they had much in common with the Egyptian Muslim Brothers founded three years earlier, but their impact was limited to groups of literate people in the cities—unlike Hassan al-Banna's movement, which appealed also to the broader populace. In 1954, at the outset of the war of independence, the association held aloof from the militant freedom fighters of the FLN, whose piety they suspected. They did not join the insurrection till 1956, two years later, at which time they supplied an Islamic justification for a war of independence whose fighters were called mujahedeen (combatants of the jihad) and whose dead were described as chouhada (martyrs of the faith).[15]

When independence came in 1962, President Ben Bella, then a militant socialist, viewed the association of ulemas and all other religious manifestations—including brotherhoods and marabouts—as hopelessly reactionary. In 1966 an association called Al Qiyam (The Values), which dared to protest the hanging of Qutb in Egypt, was dissolved. During that decade and the next, a conservative Islamic movement grew up within the FLN, humorously dubbed "Barbéfélène" (FLN with beards). But still there were no ulemas in Algeria of any special note, so when Algerian Islamism began to gather real momentum in the early 1980s (ten years later than in most other countries), the Algerian regime was obliged to import Egyptian ulemas to direct the Islamic university at Constantine. The religious field was quickly taken over by intellectuals of the Front Islamique du Salut (FIS), who encountered few doctors of the law or other scholars of religion capable of defending a vision of Islam that differed from their own.

This late 1960s weakening of the ulemas everywhere in the Arab countries except Saudi Arabia was also perceptible in the wider Muslim world. Nevertheless, the ulemas managed to hang on to their institutional positions, the importance of which varied from country to country. In Turkey, the *madrassas*—traditional religious schools that had trained the ulemas under the Ottoman empire—had been abolished by Ataturk after his proclamation of the republic. The 1950s and 1960s saw the creation by the state of schools for *imams* (spiritual leaders) and preachers (*imam hatip lisesi*), which expanded steadily right up to the end of the century.[16] Confronted by the persistence of a rural Islam that the state viewed as archaic and anti-republican, the government had opted to train a generation of "modern" clerics to believe that Turkish secularism and Islam, when properly understood, were perfectly compatible; they were given a part-religious, part-secular curriculum. This initiative, like the reform of Al Azhar by Nasser's state in 1961, was intended to produce a number of politically trustworthy ulemas, and its scope was to remain limited. But neither of those objectives was fully achieved. The schools for preachers were a great success, abruptly offering instruction to an entire class of young men from rural areas who had been bypassed by the secular school system. They were afforded social mobility without secular indoctrination. Those who were educated in this way continued to favor their original cultural values over the objectives of the state, and from the 1970s they supplied a base for the various Islamist political parties successively launched by Necmettin Erbakan, who in 1996 became the first nonsecular Turkish prime minister in 75 years.

At the other extreme of the Muslim world was Indonesia, which won its independence in 1945. At that time a divide ran between the ulemas of the Nahdatul Ulema, founded in 1926 and allied with various other militant Islamic groups, and the secular nationalists, whose leader, Sukarno, was an open admirer of Ataturk.[17] Eventually the state was founded not on Islam but on a set of five principles *(panca sila),* one of which was nationalism and another, faith in a single God. This compromise, which mollified the non-Muslim minorities (Chinese, Christian, and Hindu together formed about 10 percent of the population), also took account of the fluid nature of Islam in Indonesia, which was characterized by its assimilation of local practices and beliefs, especially in Java, the most populous island.[18]

Nevertheless, in 1949 the most fanatical partisans of a fully Islamic state began a thirteen-year guerrilla war against the army, whose younger officers were thus trained to fight a religious insurrection.[19] The ulemas and other militant Islamic groups were organized into political parties who actively participated in the bloody repression of the Indonesian Communist party in 1965. They welcomed the "new order" of General Suharto in 1967. But by delegating control of the nation to the army, Suharto marginalized the religious institutions whose influence appeared to threaten his regime's stability. Thus, by the early 1970s the Indonesian ulemas, along with all the other groups working to install Islam as the basis for the nation's government, had become greatly enfeebled politically, even though they had the support of many millions in a nation of 150 million people. Despite harassment from the regime, they succeeded in preserving their networks of education and solidarity in the form of Koranic schools and mosques. These networks were to become a central political asset at the end of the decade, when militant Islam made its reappearance among Indonesia's youth.

The Pakistani Exception

When Pakistan was founded in 1947 on the basis of "Muslim nationalism," a bitter conflict immediately ensued about how the notion of Muslim nationalism should be defined. This pitted the modernizing elites trained by the British against the various Islamic movements; the result was that the ulemas managed to play a more important role in Pakistan than in most other countries. Well-organized as they were, they relied on networks of traditional madrassas, whose pupils and former pupils provided them with a powerful religious base.

Present-day Pakistani Islam is the heir to a series of movements created in reaction to the British empire's dethronement of the last Muslim sovereign in Delhi in 1857. Like their co-religionists in the rest of the world, the Muslims of India yielded political power to the colonialists; but unlike the others, they found themselves in a minority of one to three to the Hindus, whom they had dominated for ten centuries. The most significant movement of Islamic reaffirmation, called the Deobandi movement, was founded in 1867 in the town of Deoband north of Delhi.[20] Its goal was to train a corps of ulemas capable of issuing fatwas on all aspects of daily life, and of examining society's conformity with the prescriptions of Islam, rigorously and conservatively interpreted. In fact, the Deobandi approach in India was similar to that of the Wahhabites in Saudi Arabia. Provided they adhered to a corpus of precise rules, the Deobandis reasoned that Muslims as a minority community could continue living in a non-Islamic society without coming to serious harm.

The Deobandi madrassas were well-entrenched throughout northwest India at the time, notably in the territories that would later become Pakistan—and in little more than a century thereafter produced fatwas estimated in the hundreds of thousands. In our own time each madrassa of any size includes a "fatwa center" *(darul ifta)* where the ulemas sit on the ground with their Islamic texts in easy reach, writing out fatwas all day. This they do in response to questions as to the validity of actions about which they may have been asked verbally, by letter, or by telephone.[21] By systematizing this practice, the Deobandis have built up a self-sufficient system that has allowed them to live "Islamically," whatever their political or social environment. But in contrast to adepts of the Tabligh, who steer well clear of politics, the Deobandis habitually pressure the state to allow their concepts of Islam to spread throughout society and into national legislation.

From the outset the ulemas of Pakistan were in a strong position to negotiate with the government, structured as they were around a network of religious schools, the bulk of whose pupils came from traditional urban and rural backgrounds and were either too poor to send their children to state schools or else unwilling to do so. The ulemas demanded more funds to finance their schools (which, as boarding establishments offering free instruction, remained very popular with the masses) and above all insisted that the state should guarantee jobs to their alumni, whose only skill lay in their mastery of classical religious knowledge. To this end they militated for the Islamization of the law, the government, and the banking system, among other things, which would create uses for the special aptitudes of their pupils and assure them jobs and positions of influence.

During Pakistan's infancy, a variety of religious factions campaigned hard for full Islamization of the new nation, including Mawdudi's Jamaat-e-Islami, created in 1941. In addition, there were several ulema political parties—unusual in the Muslim world—which gave expression to the special interests of their own professional groups and networks of pupils without seeking effective power for themselves. The two main ulema groups were the Jamiat-e-Ulema-e-Islam (JUI, the Association of Ulemas of Islam), a Deoband offshoot, and the Jamiat-e-Ulema-e-Pakistan (JUP, the Association of Pakistani Ulemas), run by ulemas who were tolerant of mysticism. In particular they were prepared to live with the Barelwi cult, whose veneration of saints was abhorred by the Deobandis.[22]

The army officers and Westernized elites who held power in Pakistan during the 1960s adopted a political approach that was broadly designed to reduce the influence of the various religious movements. Their success in this was partial and temporary, in contrast (for example) to that of Nasser in Egypt. Where Nasser had a number of options and could rely on the sheer strength of the Egyptian national identity to control the Islamic pretensions of the Muslim Brothers and the ulemas of Al Azhar, the less fortunate Pakistani leaders collided head-on with the Muslim nationalism on which their country was founded. Without Islam, Pakistan would not exist. Islam was the only element that united the population and justified the state's separatism from India. Other than Islam, very little else was held in common by the Pashtuns, Sindhis, Punjabis, Baluchis, and Muhajir refugees from India who made up the Pakistani population—not to mention the distant Bengalis, who would secede in 1971. When national identity is directly dependent on Islamic identity, those who can define the latter most cogently will be best qualified to maintain the nation's cohesion. For this reason the ulemas, alongside Mawdudi and his party, were able to withstand the onslaughts against them in 1960s Pakistan, whereas the Muslim Brothers of Egypt were crushed by repression.

By the end of the decade, Islam exhibited many more contrasts than conventional wisdom has allowed. Traditional Islam, though challenged by the emergence of intellectuals who had freed themselves from its customs and teachings and who based their worldview on knowledge acquired in the West, had otherwise come through unscathed. It maintained its appeal among the urban and rural poor, whose lives were barely affected by the changes. The real beneficiaries of independence had been the middle and lower-middle classes of the cities, who identified with the nationalist rulers. In contrast, prior to 1970, the poorer elements of Muslim society seldom appeared on the political scene and were remarkably quiet and weak by comparison with the decade that followed. At the same time, they were undergoing a phenomenal demographic explosion whose effects remained hidden until the 1970s, when an impatient new generation came of age whose outlook had been shaped only superficially by the traditional religious environment of the ulemas and mystical brotherhoods. This generation was wide open to ideas that transformed the familiar language of Islam, as the region tried to grapple with population explosion, rural exodus, and unprecedented wealth from oil exports. These ideas came from the Islamist ideologists and formed initially around the catalytic thinking of Qutb, Mawdudi, or Khomeini. But they took shape in different ways in different milieus, according to the political, social, and religious structure of each country.

3

Building Petro-Islam on the Ruins of Arab Nationalism

The 1970s were marked by the sudden emergence of militant Islamist movements in most of the world's Muslim nations. This growing unrest reached its peak with the triumph of the Iranian revolution in February 1979. A new Islamic Republic was built on the ruins of the shah's "impious" fallen government, and the precepts established by Ayatollah Khomeini at the beginning of the decade were now the law of Iran. These events overturned all preconceptions and all the common wisdom about Islam. What had previously been viewed as a conservative, somewhat retrograde religion, whose social and political relevance was declining in the face of progress and modernization, suddenly became the focus of intense interest, hope, and dread. The radical Islamist movement itself, whose very existence had been unknown to all but a very few, was now associated with a revolution whose contours were vague but whose essential nature appeared to be as radical as it was virulently anti-Western.

The politicizing of Islam during this decade was not confined to the Iranian revolution, even though that uprising was its most spectacular manifestation. Five years earlier, the financial clout of Saudi Arabia had been amply demonstrated during the oil embargo against the United States, following the Arab-Israeli war of 1973. This show of international power, along with the nation's astronomical increase in wealth, allowed Saudi Arabia's puritanical, conservative Wahhabite faction to attain a preeminent position of strength in the global expression of Islam. Saudi Arabia's impact on Muslims throughout the world was less visible than that of Khomeini's Iran, but the effect was deeper and more enduring. The kingdom seized the initiative from progressive nationalism, which had dominated the 1960s, it reorganized the religious landscape by promoting those associations and ulemas who followed its lead, and then, by injecting substantial amounts of money into Islamic interests of all sorts, it won over many more converts. Above all, the Saudis raised a new standard—the virtuous Islamic civilization—as a foil for the corrupting influence of the West, while still managing to remain a staunch ally of the United States and the West against the Soviet bloc (unlike the Iranians).

The year that began in Tehran with the victory of the Islamic Revolution to the battle cry of "Down with America!" ended with the Soviet invasion of Afghanistan. This called forth a massive commitment by the CIA and Saudi Arabia to the cause of Afghan jihad. American and Saudi aid to the mujahedeen was largely funneled through Pakistan under General Mohammed Zia ul-Haq, a fervent admirer of Mawdudi; indeed, several of Mawdudi's close associates were ministers in Zia's Islamabad government.

The Islamist upsurge of the 1970s was not merely a revolutionary, anti-imperialist movement that roused the impoverished masses by the skillful use of religious slogans, as in Iran. Nor was it simply an anti-communist alliance forged by the Americans and the Saudis. To measure its full impact we need to identify its many dimensions and investigate the different periods of gestation, the networks, the lines of communication, the tendencies and ideas that composed it, within the context of the demographic, cultural, economic, and social realities of the decade. Which groups took part in the Islamist movement? How did they succeed or fail in forming alliances to win power or gain the support of large segments of the population, and who exactly fought against them? Why were some movements crushed by the regimes in place, while others were torn apart by governments that co-opted their more moderate elements, and still others were eventually successful at engineering a revolution?

The Crisis of Arab Nationalism

Arab nationalism sought to bring together heterogeneous social classes by dissolving them into a sublimated Arab unity. But over time, the nationalists split into two fiercely opposed camps: progressives, led by Nasser's Egypt, Baathist Syria, and Iraq, versus the conservatives, led by the monarchies of Jordan and the Arabian peninsula. In this Arab cold war, the antagonists agreed about only one thing—confrontation with Israel—and even this consensus was dealt a potentially crippling blow by the Arabs' defeat in the Six Day War of June 1967. It was the progressives, and above all Nasser, who had started the war and been most seriously humiliated militarily. Nasser's spectacular resignation immediately after the defeat—even though he retracted this later and used the situation to eliminate his domestic rivals—marked a major symbolic rupture. In effect, the nationalists' pledge that the Zionist state would be annihilated was itself destroyed by the 1967 rout.

The trauma experienced at the time by Arab intellectuals resulted in much soul-searching, of which the most relentless example was *Self-Criticism after the Defeat* by the Syrian philosopher Sadeq Jalal al-Azm.[1] Later on, conservative Saudis would call 1967 a form of divine punishment for forgetting religion. They would contrast that war, in which Egyptian soldiers went into battle shouting "Land! Sea! Air!" with the struggle of 1973, in which the same soldiers cried "Allah Akhbar!" and were consequently more successful. However it was interpreted, the 1967 defeat seriously undermined the ideological edifice of nationalism and created a vacuum to be filled a few years later by Qutb's Islamist philosophy, which until then had been confined to small circles of Muslim Brothers, prisoners, and convicts sentenced to hard labor in camps.

Egyptian students would eventually play a key role in the ideological expansion of Islamism, but not before taking a detour to the left. As the avant-garde of revolt against Nasser's regime, they were led at first by socialists who pushed for renewed hostilities against Israel and imputed the defeat to treacherous generals and profiteers within the military. February 1968 saw the first student insurrection, which was backed by workers from the industrial city of Helouan on the outskirts of Cairo. In the fall, another wave of agitation in the Nile delta and Alexandria saw demonstrations by students linked to the Muslim Brothers—who were still a tiny minority.[2]

For Nasser, the creation of a leftist ideological caucus was a major threat because it challenged his legitimacy as a progressive. At the same time, the Palestinian cause, which Egypt and the other Arab states had used to spur nationalist sentiment, was passing out of those states' con-

trol, with the arrival in 1969 of Yasir Arafat as the head of the autonomous Palestine Liberation Organization. By gaining control of their
own destiny and embodying Arab resistance to Israel after the military
debacle of 1967, the Palestinians filled the space in the student psyche
that Nasser's nationalism had vacated.

Meanwhile, in 1970, tensions between King Hussein of Jordan and
the Palestinian organizations installed in the Jordanian refugee camps
resulted in the bloodbath of Black September, during which the Palestinians suffered the heaviest losses in their recent history.[3] Here it was
not the Jewish state but a government run by fellow Arabs that attacked
the new champions of Arab nationalism. It was a massive blow to the
nationalist cause, at the very moment when the death of Nasser (also in
September) eliminated its most charismatic leader.

The crisis of Arab nationalism seemed to be a boon to the leftist students, occasionally supported by workers, who championed Palestinian
resistance. This period was short-lived, however. The Arab states, including those that described themselves as progressive, quickly mobilized their resources against this leftist threat, which they saw as being patterned after the Western student uprisings of 1968. Meanwhile,
the attractions of the left did not extend beyond student groups, the intellectual circles of the cities, and scattered nuclei of committed workers. Its radical proposals—expressed in European Marxist language—
frightened the middle classes and were incomprehensible to the uneducated masses. Thus, paradoxically, Islamism's key to success lay in exploiting both the fears among government elites and the disappoint-
ments among leftist intellectuals. Conservative governments, on the
Saudi model, encouraged Islamism as a counterweight to the Marxists
on university campuses, whom they feared. And some of the young
leftist intellectuals, as they took stock of their failure to impress the
masses, began to convert to Islamism because it seemed a more genuine discourse.

The events of Black September 1970 in Amman demonstrated the
explosive nature of popular discontent, when mobilized by forces of
the left against authoritarian governments that recently had been defeated on the battlefield. Nevertheless, the Jordanian Muslim Brothers
had supported King Hussein during the showdown with the Palestinians, and this lesson was not lost on other Arab leaders. Anwar Sadat,
Nasser's successor, having first consolidated his power in Egypt by ar-

resting the pro-Soviet Nasser supporters during his "corrective revolution" of May 15, 1971, gradually began to release all the Muslim Brothers and their associates from prison. The freed Brothers quickly gravitated toward the fertile political ground of the universities, where the beginning of the 1972–73 school year was marked by incessant agitation for a new war against Israel. The student question had become central to domestic politics, and an Islamist organization, the first of its kind, was founded at the polytechnic faculty of Cairo University. For the moment its impact was minimal compared with that of the Marxists, but it at least made its program known and in doing so was aided by the secret services, even though some militants were uncomfortable with this.

By encouraging the Islamists, Sadat gave up the Egyptian state's monopoly on ideology, as well as the strategy of containing religion on which his predecessor had relied. Where Nasser's state had mobilized nationalist crowds and suppressed all dissent, Sadat compensated for the ideological weakness of his regime by allowing autonomous religious figures to express themselves and neutralize the left. This relative liberalization of religion occurred while the political arena remained under tight control. There was no press freedom worthy of the name, and no free exchange of ideas except in the mosques, where the Islamists were able to use the religious framework to their advantage. This Egyptian phenomenon had its equivalents in other Muslim countries, notably Tunisia, Algeria, and Morocco, where the mostly francophone leftist students found themselves confronting Islamists who no longer took their cue from books published in Paris's Latin Quarter but drew on Arabic sources published in Saudi Arabia.

The Emergence of Militant Islamism

During the 1970s, the first generation to be born in the era of independence came of age in most of the Muslim world. These young people had no first-hand recollection of the anti-colonial tide of liberation that had legitimized the nationalist regimes under which they lived, and thus they were out of step with elites in government. Unlike their elders and parents, they had been born too late to benefit from the jobs and social advancement created by independence and from the sharing out of property abandoned by the departing settlers and colonists.

Between 1955 and 1970, population growth in the Muslim world approached 50 percent—a demographic change of spectacular proportions. By 1975, with urbanization and literacy advancing apace, the cohort under 24 years old represented over 60 percent of the total population.[4] The world of Islam, which had always been predominantly rural and governed by a small urban elite with exclusive access to reading and writing, now underwent a radical transformation with the arrival of this mass of literate young city dwellers. The newcomers were confronted with challenges of every kind, for which the traditional knowledge passed on to them by their uneducated parents was largely useless. Their situation was in stark contrast with that of their parents and ancestors, who had had no choice but to remain in the roles to which they had been born, having known only the narrow confines of their village. The social and cultural chasm between the two generations was wide and deep, and there had been nothing like it since the dawn of Islam.

The young urbanites of the 1970s were far from prosperous, however. They crowded together under precarious conditions on the edges of cities—in the *bidonvilles* of the Maghreb, the *achwaiyyat* of the Middle East, and the *gecekondu* of Turkey.[5] But secondary schooling and, to a lesser extent, higher education in the cities had given this new generation not only access to newspapers and books but also great expectations of upward mobility. Young people were now able to select and compare information sources, to express themselves formally in public, and to confidently oppose the ruling national elites, by drawing on their own intellectual resources. This was a cultural leap forward, but it was not matched by the expected social progress. The result was frustration that quickly turned to resentment of the elites, who were accused of monopolizing state power and depriving the young of the influence and wealth that was their due.

Social and political discontent was most commonly expressed in the cultural sphere, through a rejection of the nationalist ideologies of the ruling cliques in favor of Islamist ideology. This process began on the once left-leaning university campuses which were now, in the early 1970s, controlled by Islamist movements. The Islamist intellectuals propagated the ideas of Qutb, Mawdudi, and Khomeini, who had not achieved a mass following because their advocates had been neither numerous enough nor angry enough to embrace theories of total revolution—even though they had been sufficiently versed in their own modern, written languages to understand the discourse and identify with the principles involved.

By the early 1970s the Islamist intelligentsia taking shape on the campuses of Egypt, Malaysia, and Pakistan began to spread throughout the Muslim world, courtesy of the networks and financial clout of the Saudi Wahhabites following the 1973 war. At first the goals and tactics of the intellectuals were diffuse; it was only after parting company with the nationalists that they began to focus on Islamism as their weapon in a new battle for political domination, and to find recruits in various milieus whose class interests were more diverse.

Among the new recruits, two social groups were particularly susceptible to Islamist persuasion. One was the huge mass of young urban poor from deprived backgrounds, whose parents had come in from the country. The other was the devout bourgeoisie, a class excluded from political power and economically hemmed in by military and monarchical regimes.[6] These two groups were both committed to the sharia and to the idea of an Islamic state, but they did not view that state in quite the same way. The former imbued it with a social-revolutionary content, while the latter saw it as a vehicle for wresting power for themselves from the incumbent elites, without fundamentally disturbing the existing social hierarchies.

This divergence of interests lies at the very heart of contemporary Islamism. The Islamist intelligentsia's role was to gloss over this clash of social agendas and reconcile the two groups to the shared pursuit of power. The intellectuals did this by concentrating on the moral and cultural dimensions of religion. They won the broadest base of support—and in Iran it was broad enough to carry them to power—when they mobilized both the young urban poor and the devout bourgeoisie with an ideology that offered a vague social agenda but a sharp focus on morality. Everyone in the movement could understand and interpret this ideology as they chose, given the opaqueness of the religious language in which it was couched. On the other hand, wherever the coalition between the young urban poor and the devout bourgeoisie dissolved, the more radical and more moderate elements canceled one another out and the Islamist movement failed to seize power. In Algeria, for example, the Islamist intelligentsia's ideology was too weak to unify the two groups, and as a result a civil war raged from 1992 to 1998 between the radical Groupe Islamique Armé (GIA) and the moderate

Armée Islamique du Salut (AIS). The extortion and blackmail practiced by Algerian radical groups on Islamist notables beginning in
1994–95 are just two examples of the terrorist tactics that some radicals
used to shock the pious bourgeoisie. The ruling elites—taking advantage of the fears of the middle class that they would be the first victims
of the young revolutionaries if state repression ceased—succeeded at
dividing the two groups.

Similarly, in Egypt, terrorism directed against tourists was disastrous
for the incomes of the local middle classes and others who lived off the
tourist industry. This helped the state to discredit the entire Islamist
movement, most recently after the massacre at Luxor in the fall of
1997. Several other Muslim states contrived to use these divisions to
entice segments of the Islamist intelligentisa and the devout bourgeoisie into the ruling camp, by making an ostentatious display of token
Islamization while keeping the old social hierarchies intact. This was
notably the case in Pakistan and Malaysia at the close of the 1970s.

The essential contradiction between the radical goals of the young
urban poor and the conservative goals of the bourgeoisie that lurked
behind the apparently united front of Islamism explains how the
movement could be outflanked by forces and interest groups from
both right and left in a given country or at the international level. The
massive financial clout of Saudi Arabia—a reactionary monarchy if
ever there was one—and the American policy in the 1970s of encouraging the expansion of the Islamist movement were never intended to
empower the young urban poor, for whom implementation of the
sharia and social revolution were one and the same thing. Rather, Riyadh and Washington were eager to shore up the devout bourgeoisie,
whom they felt were best equipped to neutralize these dangerous new
classes; and they were willing to pay in the coin of religious words and
symbols whenever necessary. The nationalists, whose principal weapons were coercion and repression, were too discredited by 1970s to do
this.[7]

In the Communist world, on the other hand, the target group was
just the opposite: by drawing on the strength of the masses, Islamism, it
was hoped, might turn into an anti-imperialist and anti-capitalist force
to overthrow the bourgeoisie.[8] The support of the Iranian Communist
party (the Tudeh) and the USSR for the revolution in Iran, the rallying
to the Islamist banner of many former Marxists from all over the Mus-

lim world, and even the enthusiasm of French Communist municipal authorities for young Islamist organizations in France's deprived immigrant areas were all prompted by the fact that the venerated masses were joining the Islamist movement.

The Victory of Petro-Islam and the Wahhabite Expansion

The war of October 1973 was started by Egypt and Syria with the aim of avenging the humiliation of 1967 and restoring the lost legitimacy of the two states' authoritarian regimes. The Arab armies successfully broke through the Israeli front lines on the Suez Canal and the Golan Heights, only to be threatened by an all-out counteroffensive. This retaliation was halted when the Arab oil-exporting nations declared an embargo on oil destined for Israel's Western allies. An armistice was eventually signed on the Cairo-Suez road, 101 kilometers from the Egyptian capital, at the point of the Israeli forces' farthest advance.

The Arab states emerged with a symbolic victory that allowed Sadat and Syrian President Assad ("lion" in Arabic) to present themselves respectively as the Hero of the Crossing (of the Suez Canal) and the Lion of October. However, the real victors in this war were the oil-exporting countries, above all Saudi Arabia. In addition to the embargo's political success, it had reduced the world supply of oil and sent the price per barrel soaring. In the aftermath of the war, the oil states abruptly found themselves with revenues gigantic enough to assure them a clear position of dominance within the Muslim world.[9]

Saudi Arabia—the home of the holy sites of Mecca and Medina—now had unlimited means with which to further its ancient ambition of hegemony over the Community of the Faithful. During the 1960s the nationalist dynamic had diluted the political importance of religion; the war of 1973 again reversed the situation. The Wahhabite doctrine's only audience outside the Arabian peninsula was in religiously conservative milieus belonging to disparate international groups, including Muslim Brothers associated with Indian and Pakistani networks as well as Black African and Asian Muslims. All of these had passed through Mecca and returned to their own countries to preach in the Arab style and purge Islam of "superstition."

Prior to 1973, Islam was everywhere dominated by national or local traditions rooted in the piety of the common people, with clerics from the different schools of Sunni religious law established in all major regions of the Muslim world (Hanafite in the Turkish zones of South Asia, Malakite in Africa, Shafeite in Southeast Asia), along with their Shiite counterparts.[10] This motley establishment held Saudi-inspired puritanism in great suspicion on account of its sectarian character. But after 1973, the oil-rich Wahhabites found themselves in a different economic position, being able to mount a wide-ranging campaign of proselytizing among the Sunnis. (The Shiites, whom the Sunnis considered to be heretics, remained outside the movement.) The objective was to bring Islam to the forefront of the international scene, to substitute it for the various discredited nationalist movements, and to refine the multitude of voices within the religion down to the single creed of the masters of Mecca. The Saudis' zeal now embraced the entire world, extending beyond the traditional frontiers of Islam to the heart of the West, where immigrant Muslim populations were their special target.[11]

The propagation of the faith was not the only issue for the leaders in Riyadh. Religious obedience on the part of the Saudi population became the key to winning government subsidies, the kingdom's justification for its financial pre-eminence, and the best way to allay envy among impoverished co-religionists in Africa and Asia. By becoming the managers of a huge empire of charity and good works, the Saudi government sought to legitimize a prosperity it claimed was manna from heaven, blessing the peninsula where the Prophet Mohammed had received his Revelation. Thus, an otherwise fragile Saudi monarchy buttressed its power by projecting its obedient and charitable dimension internationally. This religious policy also helped people forget that American military might was the ultimate guarantor of the kingdom and that the Saudi regime whose ulemas vilified the West for its impiety actually depended very heavily on the United States and its allies for survival. It was a ploy that protected the House of Saud throughout the years of abundant oil revenues, until the 1990–91 Gulf War finally exposed its essential weakness.

Through its network of proselytism, its subsidies, and the flow of immigrant labor that it attracted, the transnational Saudi system insinuated itself into the relationship between state and society in the majority of Muslim countries, by attracting immigrants to the oil-rich states. Around 1975, young men with college degrees, along with experienced professors, artisans, and country people, began to move en masse from the Sudan, Pakistan, India, Southeast Asia, Egypt, Palestine, Lebanon, and Syria to the Gulf states. These states harbored 1.2 million immigrants in 1975, of whom 60.5 percent were Arabs; this increased to 5.15 million by 1985, with 30.1 percent being Arabs and 43 percent (mostly Muslims) coming from the Indian subcontinent.

The social and economic impact of these migrations to the Gulf states was enormous. In Pakistan in the single year 1983, the money sent home by Gulf emigrants amounted to $3 billion, compared with a total of $735 million given to the nation in foreign aid.[12] Elites in the home countries viewed these oil revenues as a windfall, offering temporary relief for regimes threatened by fast-growing populations. Moreover, immigration lightened the burden of unemployment back home, notably among high school and college graduates, at a crucial moment when the first generation after independence—the offspring of the baby boom, the rural exodus, and mass literacy—were entering the job market, a generation that was otherwise prone to social discontent. By injecting cash into national economies through remittances to their families at home, immigration created new flows of wealth, goods, and services that evaded state control. Finally, immigration ensured rapid upward social mobility for most migrants, who returned home much richer than when they left. The underpaid petty functionary of yore could now drive back to his hometown at the wheel of a foreign car, build himself a house in a residential suburb, and settle down to invest his savings or engage in trade. Moreover, he owed nothing to his home state, where he could never have earned enough to afford such luxuries.

For many of those returning from the El Dorado of oil, social ascent went hand in hand with an intensification of religious practice. In contrast to the bourgeois ladies of the preceding generation, who liked to hear their servants address them as Madame, in the French style, a respectable spouse would now wear a fashionable *hijab* (veil) and her maid would call her *hajja* (the title given to those who perform the pilgrimage to Mecca).[13] Many who had lived in the oil-rich monarchies of the peninsula had grown rich in this Wahhabite milieu—and not surprisingly it was to this milieu that they attributed the spiritual source of their material prosperity.

In the last years of the 1970s and during the next decades, former migrants who followed the religious example of the Saudis became more and more prominent. Some lived in new residential areas around mosques, which were built in what was called the Pakistani "international style," gleaming with marble and green neon lighting. This break with the local Islamic architectural traditions illustrates how Wahhabite doctrine achieved an international dimension in Muslim cities. A civic culture focused on reproducing ways of life that prevailed in the Gulf also surfaced in the form of shopping centers for veiled women, which imitated the malls of Saudi Arabia, where American-style consumerism co-existed with mandatory segregation of the sexes.[14]

Alongside these social changes, inexhaustible funds were now available to promote the *dawa*, or call to Islam, through Wahhabite preaching. The Muslim World League, founded in 1962 as a counterweight to Nasser's propaganda, opened new offices in every area of the world where Muslims lived. The league played a pioneering role in supporting Islamic associations, mosques, and investment plans for the future. In addition, the Saudi ministry for religious affairs printed and distributed millions of Korans free of charge, along with Wahhabite doctrinal texts, among the world's mosques, from the African plains to the rice paddies of Indonesia and the Muslim immigrant high-rise housing projects of European cities. For the first time in fourteen centuries, the same books (as well as cassettes) could be found from one end of the Umma to the other; all came from the same Saudi distribution circuits, as part of an identical corpus. Its very limited number of titles hewed to the same doctrinal line and excluded other currents of thought that had formerly been part of a more pluralistic Islam.

This mass distribution by the conservative Riyadh regime did not always prevent more radical elements from using the texts of the faith to further their own objectives. The author most respected by the Wahhabites, Ibn Taymiyya (1268–1323)—a primary reference for the Sunni Islamist movement—would be abundantly quoted to justify the assassination of Sadat in 1981, for example, and even to condemn the Saudi leadership and call for its overthrow in the mid-1990s.

The Saudis' push for doctrinal uniformity was accompanied by their liberal distribution of money for building mosques. More than 1,500 were built around the world in the last half century, paid for by Saudi public funds.[15] Their proliferation from the mid-1970s onward was one of the most visible changes in the landscape of the rapidly urbanizing Muslim world. Donations from the Gulf states played a leading role in this at the beginning, but other interested parties soon invested considerable sums of money when it became clear that controlling the crowds assembled in these places of worship, as well as the sermons they heard, was an issue that no power—least of all a state—could afford to ignore.

Tapping the financial circuits of the Gulf to finance a mosque usually began with private initiative. An ad hoc association would prepare a dossier to justify a given investment, usually citing the need felt by locals for a spiritual center. They would then seek a "recommendation" *(tazkiya)* from the local office of the Muslim World League to a generous donor within the kingdom or one of the emirates. This procedure was much criticized over the years, given that in some cases the donated sums were diverted from their original objective.[16] The Saudi leadership's hope was that these new mosques would produce new sympathizers for the Wahhabite persuasion.

As it turned out, their policy was reasonably effective in limiting the devastating effects of the 1979 Iranian revolution on Saudi hegemony over Islam. But it proved powerless a decade later to contain the enthusiasm unleashed in the Muslim world by Saddam Hussein when he denounced the alliance between the Saudi monarchy and the West during the Gulf War. The limits of the kingdom's policy of religious propagation had been reached: its immense financial generosity had won it a following that was more venal than sincere, and the Wahhabization it wished to implement had tended to fluctuate with the price of a barrel of oil. Yet once Saudi Arabia had opted for the propagation of Islam as a tool for gaining influence abroad, it had no choice but to finance all those who claimed to belong to Sunni Islam, and to run the risk of underwriting revolutionary groups that were actively hostile to Riyadh.

In addition to increased migration and the spread of Wahhabite propaganda, a third consequence of the 1973 war was a shift in the balance of power among Muslim states toward the oil-producing countries. Under Saudi influence, the notion of a worldwide "Islamic domain of shared meaning" transcending the nationalist divisions among Arabs, Turks, Africans, and Asians was created.[17] All Muslims were offered a new identity that emphasized their religious commonality while downplaying differences of language, ethnicity, and nationality. This proposition did not necessarily correspond to any kind of demand on the part of the people to whom it was presented. It often stimulated such a demand, however, when it appeared to promise some kind of upward social mobility, political progress, or economic advantage; and at the very least it supplied a set of stable guidelines for behavior during a decade when Islam was buffeted by the combined effects of population expansion, rural exodus, international migration, mass education, and rapid urbanization.

The beginnings of the "Islamic domain of shared meaning" go back to a time when Arab nationalism was in deep crisis. In September 1969 an Islamic summit was held at Rabat after an extremist from Australia had tried to burn down the Al-Aqsa Mosque on the Temple Mount in Jerusalem, which Israel had occupied for two years. This incident in the ongoing Israeli-Arab conflict was taken as an attack on Islam in general and hence a pretext to mobilize all Muslim states, not merely Arab ones. The creation of the Organization of the Islamic Conference (OIC) quickly followed. From a full complement of 29 at its founding, the OIC's membership increased to 55 by the time of its eighth summit in Tehran in November 1997.[18] The installation of an OIC general secretariat in Jeddah, Saudi Arabia, demonstrated the strong Saudi commitment to an organization whose charter explicitly stated among its purposes promoting Islamic solidarity between member states, consolidating their cooperation in all areas, and, most notably, "co-ordinating all efforts to protect the Holy Places, supporting the struggle of the Palestinian people to recover their rights and liberate their land, and . . . strengthening the combat of all the Muslim peoples, so as to safeguard their dignity, their independence and their national rights."

The impact of the OIC on world history has remained slight, largely because of political divisions among its members and nonpayment of dues except by the oil states and Malaysia. Nevertheless, it has served as a forum for identifying causes, such as that of the Palestinians, and giving them an Islamic rather than nationalist slant. In 1974 the PLO was admitted as a member state of the OIC; in 1979 Egypt was excluded for making peace with Israel; and in 1980 Afghanistan suffered the same fate for passing under Soviet control. In each of these cases (and in the critical positions adopted toward Iran during the 1980s), the OIC gave an institutional gloss of consensus to the views of Saudi Arabia. In December 1973, when oil prices were at their peak, the OIC made the decision to create the Islamic Development Bank, with headquarters in Jeddah. The bank became operational in 1975 and proceeded to finance development projects in the poorest Muslim countries, mostly using funds from the Gulf nations within the framework of the Islamic banking system (see below).[19]

In addition to the formal framework of the OIC, one of the principal vectors of Saudi influence was control of the pilgrimage to Mecca, a rite symbolic of the unity of the Community of the Faithful throughout the world. The *hajj*, or pilgrimage, offered the promise of salvation to all devout Muslims; yet prior to the advent of modern air travel, it had remained a difficult undertaking that was rarely accomplished by the vast majority of the faithful. In former times, the hajj conferred incomparable prestige on the fortunate few. Ordinary folk had to be content with lesser pilgrimages to the tombs of saints scattered around the Muslim world.

In 1924–25, after expelling the Hashemite dynasty, King Abd al-Aziz ibn Saud finally took control of the holy cities Mecca and Medina. Immediately, the Wahhabites smashed the tombs of the imams—especially of Fatima, the daughter of the Prophet, whose veneration by the Shiites they condemned as idolatry—and then reorganized the hajj according to their own lights. King Saud's first act was to make the pilgrimage more attractive to pilgrims—as they supplied his kingdom with the bulk of its revenue before oil money changed everything. In 1926, 90,000 pilgrims visited Mecca; by 1979 the figure had reached 2 million, and since that time it has stabilized between 1.5 million and 2 million per year.[20] Vast numbers of Muslims from all over the world now realize their dream of the hajj.

In 1986 the king took the title of Custodian of the Two Holy Places, the better to emphasize Wahhabite control of the greatest and most sacred annual assembly of Muslims on earth. This control operated as an essential instrument of hegemony over Islam. It had been and still was violently opposed, first by Saudi dissidents who attacked the Grand Mosque at Mecca in November 1979, at the dawn of the fifteenth century of the Hegira, and second by Khomeinist Iran, which contrived to turn several pilgrimages into violent demonstrations.[21] Finally, it was strongly contested by Saddam Hussein and all the other radical opponents of the Saudi regime, following the Gulf War of 1990–91.

The Role of Banking and Finance

As a dynastic and tribal regime, within which birth and lineage were a precondition of access to oil wealth and power after 1973, the Saudi system was wide open to attack from social groups who did not happen to be "well born." Among Islamists who were out of favor with the rulers in Riyadh, the Saudi princes were painted as lazy, incompetent hypocrites, wallowing in luxury, debauchery, alcohol, pornography, and all manner of immoral behavior abhorred by religion. This classic bourgeois reproach to the high-living aristocrat is common to every society—with the difference that the ultimate moral reference here was the Koran.

The Islamic financial system constituted an important link between the tribal aristocracy of the Arabian peninsula, which controlled Allah's "gift" of oil revenues, and the devout middle class of the Muslim world. It allowed the two to associate in an economic partnership, while paying mutual lip service to piety. This buttressed both the Saudis' leadership of the Community of the Faithful and the political position of the devout bourgeoisie in each individual Muslim state, while binding them to the Wahhabite monarchy. With emphasis on charity and social work through collection and distribution of zakat (alms) and its financing of small businesses, farmers, and shopkeepers who otherwise would have no access to conventional banking systems, the Islamic banking and finance system deliberately set out to promote social cohesion and integration.[22]

Doctrinally, Islamic finance had one basic principle, the prohibition of fixed interest rates, which was condemned by the Koran as usury (riba). The ulemas were unanimous in condemning usury as a crime more terrible than fornication with one's own mother, but they reached no hard-and-fast consensus on the similarity between usurious practice and lending at fixed interest rates.[23] Several fatwas issued by eminent religious dignitaries made a distinction between the two terms, making it all right for good Muslims to engage in conventional banking operations under certain conditions, since the prohibition of interest rates was actually founded on other philosophical considerations. For example, by agreeing on a predetermined rate of interest, lender and borrower could protect themselves against future uncertainties, thereby giving themselves a hedge against the supremacy of the divine will, as expressed in the Arabic saying "insha Allah," God willing. A similar regulation in the insurance business prohibited insuring against the future risk of an accident or disaster that God might choose to visit upon us.[24]

Since modern economies function on the basis of interest rates and insurance as preconditions for productive investment, many Islamic jurists racked their brains to find ways of resorting to them without appearing to bend the rules laid down by the Koran.[25] The problem loomed ever larger as more and more Muslim states entered the world economy in the 1960s. They clamored for fatwas that would allow them to attract the savings of the faithful, who lived in terror that the acceptance of profits derived from fixed-rate investments would send them straight to hell.[26] This loose approach prevailed throughout the Muslim world until the 1970s, at which time the total ban on lending with interest was reactivated, in tandem with a general re-Islamization in the cultural and political domains. Technically, this "strict" Islamic financial system rested on a single basic principle: fixed rates of interest being prohibited, the profit or loss incurred by an investment had to be a function of the risks run.[27] The enforcement of this prohibition was ensured, in an age of international banking systems, by a watchdog committee of ulemas (the sharia board). This committee verified the legality of operations, canceled those that were tainted with usury, and applied their funds to pious endeavors such as those of the Islamist humanitarian organizations.

The leading theorist of Islamist finance was the Iraqi Shiite Ayatollah Baqir as-Sadr (who was killed in April 1980 by Saddam Hussein's regime).[28] His book *Our Economy (Iqtissaduna)*, published in 1961, advocated an economic system exclusively based on the principles of Islam. At that time the Muslim countries were either integrated into world capitalism or else were participants in the Soviet-sponsored socialist system without subscribing to any particular economic theory. According to as-Sadr, the Islamic economy was part and parcel of the kind of Islamic state he advocated, in the political footsteps of Sayyid Qutb and Khomeini: in other words, he saw it as a clean break with the economics of the non-Muslim world. But just as in politics, the implementation of this economic idea had to be put off until objective conditions were favorable—and this did not happen until 1973, when the tidal wave of petro-dollars changed the entire waterfront.

Another economist, the Egyptian Ahmad al-Naggar, tried a non-ideological experiment aimed at finding a way of mobilizing the cash savings of people who had no confidence in state-run banks. In 1963 he created a rural savings bank at Mit Ghamr in the Nile delta, which applied Islamic economic principles without specifically advertising

the fact, for fear of Nasser. Instead, Naggar emphasized the social character of his enterprise: by circumventing rates of interest, he appealed
to a broad spectrum of small savers who had hitherto remained outside
the official nationalized banking system, successfully attracting their
money and financing projects which allowed some of them to climb
the ladder of society. The poorest investors were given interest-free
loans (qard hassan) based on their own non-interest-bearing deposits
in current accounts. More substantial depositors looking to invest were
allowed to share in the profits or losses of the businesses financed by
the savings bank.[29] Finally, the bank established a zakat fund that accounted for 2.5 percent of its capital and was used as alms for the
needy.[30] This experiment was closed down by Egypt in 1968, in spite of
the large sums it had collected, on the pretext of management problems. It is still referred to today by Islamic bankers when they want to
advertise their social and proletarian credentials.

Contemporary Islamic finance really took off after the war of October 1973, with the recycling through the banking system of the petro-
dollar windfall.[31] In succeeding years, the expatriates who came to work
in the oil-exporting countries found themselves with an abundance of
cash. This new, transnational Muslim middle class, which had been
drawn to the faith at the same time that they were growing wealthy in
the monarchies of the Gulf, now sought a model investment for their
savings that would shelter them from confiscations, nationalizations,
and other machinations they had reason to believe were practiced by
the official banks of their own countries—especially when those banks
were controlled by the government. Many also wished to make substantial profits from their investments and even to take risks, once their
private needs were taken care of. In fact, they were more than ready to
support a private banking system that transcended borders and corre-
sponded to their own social identity, now expanded to include both
their native countries and the countries in which they had earned their
newfound wealth. Islamic banks responded well to this unprecedented
demand, and they ultimately played an important role in consolidating
the new social group constituted by their depositors, while creating a
devout middle class that was loyal to Saudi interests because it was dependent on them.

The Islamic financial system had two spheres that were perfectly
distinct from one another, even though they shared the same basic

logic. The first sphere supplied a mechanism for the partial redistribution of oil revenues among the member states of the OIC by way of the Islamic Development Bank, which opened for business in 1975. This strengthened Islamic cohesion—and increased dependence—between the poorer member nations of Africa and Asia and the wealthy oil-exporting countries.[32] The second sphere was the exclusive domain of private investors and depositors. After a few experiments in Egypt, this resulted in the creation of Islamic commercial banks, which began to appear in July 1975. Another threshold was reached with the creation of transnational holding companies: DMI (Dar al-Mal al-Islami: the House of Islamic Finance), whose foundation was announced in June 1981 by Prince Mohammed al-Faisal al-Saud, son of the assassinated King Faisal, and the Al Baraka (Divine Blessing) group, established in 1982 by a Saudi billionaire, Sheik Salih Abdallah Kamil. In addition to their banking activities, these companies specialized in investment funds; and the 1980s, which saw a major expansion in the Islamic financial system, also witnessed a huge diversification of its investment instruments.

In Pakistan, Malaysia, and Jordan, and even in states as secular as Turkey and Tunisia, Islamic banks, often accompanied by highly favorable fiscal incentives, began springing up everywhere in the 1980s.[33] In three countries, Pakistan, Iran, and Sudan, the banks were summarily "Islamized" by the state, and in Iran they have remained nationalized ever since. Elsewhere, the initiatives mostly came from the private sector. By 1995, there were 144 Islamic financial institutions worldwide, including 33 government-run banks, 40 private banks, and 71 investment companies.[34]

The stakes in this process were both national and international in significance. For Saudi Arabia and the political-financial markets of the Gulf oil monarchies, the banks provided an opportunity to tighten their links with the local devout middle class in all these countries. For other states, the interest lay in attracting those same classes and keeping them out of radical Islamist movements. As for the radical Islamists, they saw a golden opportunity to establish a war chest outside the control of the established regimes and use it to finance their overthrow. The interaction between finance and militant religion played an especially important role in Egypt and the Sudan, as we will see. Thus, banks became one of the most important factors in the Islamist expansion of the 1980s, because the political attitude of the devout middle class hinged on what became of them.

The middle class tended to adopt different attitudes according to the circumstances prevailing in each country, but in general it used the emergence of the banking system to promote its interest as a new social and cultural entity with a voice of its own. All this led to heightened visibility and respectability for the Islamist cause, which became significantly more middle class in aspect as the 1980s went on. It remained to be seen whether the new bourgeoisie would sacrifice its financial interests to militant zeal, if forced to choose between the two.

Islamism in Egypt, Malaysia, and Pakistan

While Saudi Arabia was consolidating its grip on the Umma after 1973, Islamist movements were beginning to gather strength in most other Muslim countries. The three most powerful Sunni groups were to be found in Egypt, Malaysia, and Pakistan, but their effects were strikingly different. They were at their most militant in the Nile Valley, where Sadat himself died at their hands. Nevertheless, the militants ultimately failed to seize power and set up an Islamic state in Egypt or in the other two nations.[1]

During the summer preceding the October war of 1973, the Gamaat Islamiya (Islamic Associations) suddenly came to life in student circles, on the occasion of the first summer camps organized for their members. Militants and sympathizers attending these camps were initiated into the "pure Islamic life"—which involved regular daily prayers, ideological training, an apprenticeship in the skills of the preacher and the tactics of proselytism, socializing within the group, and more. A skeleton network of cadres was planned that would eventually make the associations the dominant Islamic voice in the universities of the Arab world. In 1977, the associations won a majority in the Egyptian Students' Union, whose procedures had been democratized by Sadat in 1974 at a time when he was convinced that a leftist threat no longer existed.

The success of the associations was due mainly to their offer of an "Islamic solution" to the social crisis that was affecting Egyptian universities at the time. In the 1970s, the numbers of Egyptian stu-

dents more than doubled to half a million, while university infrastructures remained unchanged. As a result, learning conditions degenerated alarmingly and a chasm opened between the cultural aspirations
of the students—many of whom were the first in their families to attend university—and their ability to find jobs. Modern, secular values
of instruction were called into question: the Gamaat denounced them
as lies, incapable of reflecting social reality. Instead, the radicals offered
their own vision of Islam as a system that was "complete and total,"
that could not only interpret the larger world but also transform it.

On the level where students actually lived, the associations were
masters at combining practical services with the inculcation of moral
standards. For example, when the students were confronted with hid-
eously overcrowded transportation systems, the Islamists used generous donations to purchase minibuses for women students. When this
service became overwhelmingly popular, they restricted it to those
women who wore the veil. Thus, the privatization of transport became a way of responding "Islamically" to a social problem. Similarly,
to reduce the discomfort and harassment that overcrowding in class-
rooms caused to female students, Islamists responded by segregating
the sexes—which in the beginning was something of a relief to the
girls. But they went on to make sexual segregation a norm of behavior
on campus. The same approach was applied to dress. "Islamic gar-
ments" (veil, long, billowing cloak, and gloves) were offered to students
for next to no cost, as a response to a social problem, namely, the high
cost of fashionable clothes. But this uniform, worn by hundreds of students, had the added effect of demonstrating visually the Islamists' cultural control over the universities.

Issam al-Aryan, a young doctor who was one of the main theorists
of the Gamaat, published an article in 1980 claiming that "when the
numbers of female students wearing the veil are high, we may take it as
a sign of resistance to Western civilization and the advent of *iltizam,*
the strict observance of Islamic laws." In addition to wearing the veil,
Aryan identified sporting beards and white jellabas by male students
and mass attendance at the two great celebrations of Eid al-Fitr and Eid
al-Kebir as indications of a powerful Islamist movement. The feast days
provided the associations with an opportunity to show their growing
strength by inducing thousands of the faithful to gather for prayers in
every one of the great cities of Egypt.

Until 1977, when Sadat flew to Jerusalem to initiate peace talks with the Israelis, the Egyptian government and the Gamaat Islamiyya were close allies. The press, which was controlled by the regime, was effusively complimentary. The "Believing President," who sought to establish the reign of "knowledge and faith," saw the Islamist student intelligentsia both as a tool for containing a younger generation that was quick to protest and as a source of cultural and moral values. Moreover, Sadat had allowed the Muslim Brothers to return from their Nasser-imposed exile in Saudi Arabia, where some had grown rich, and to share in *infitah,* or economic opening. Sadat set this process in motion in 1975 to restore initiative to the private sector and dismantle the state-run economy that Nasser, on the advice of the Soviets, had imposed. The success of the Brothers was the model that most of the emigrés who went to the Gulf states after 1973 sought to imitate. The money and contacts in oil-producing countries brought home by these devout members of the middle class made them highly interesting to the Egyptian government, which did its best to win their support. They fit neatly into the moderate wing of the Muslim Brothers, which only occasionally referred to the "overly radical" works of Sayyid Qutb. This wing was led by Omar Telmesani, who had been imprisoned by Nasser and was released by Sadat in 1971. Telmesani began publishing the monthly *Al Dawa* (Call to Islam) in 1976 and was permitted some editorial freedom at a time when the rest of the Egyptian press was tightly muzzled.

Sadat's gamble—imitated by many other Muslim leaders in the years that followed—was to encourage the emergence of an Islamist movement which he perceived as socially conservative. In exchange for political support, he allowed the Islamist intelligentsia considerable cultural and ideological autonomy and gave the devout bourgeoisie easier access to certain sectors of the newly privatized economy. It was up to these favored Islamists to hold the line against more radical groups whose goal was to subvert society.

This gentleman's agreement fell apart in 1977. The year began with riots against the policy of economic opening, the social consequences of which were causing much alarm. Then a radical Islamist group, the Society of Muslims (known to the police as Al Takfir wa-l Hijra, "Excommunication and Hegira"), defied the government by kidnapping and murdering a cleric. Finally, in November, a month after the group's trial, Sadat went to Jerusalem to make peace with Israel. At a stroke, this action laid waste the good relations he had built up with the Islamist intelligentsia and the devout bourgeoisie, for whom peace with the Jewish state was anathema.

The appearance on the political scene of Al Takfir wa-l Hijra showed that the Islamists were not confined to moderates cosseted by the regime but included a growing radical fringe which turned to terrorism in the years that followed. This group sent shock waves through the Muslim world far beyond Egypt, and the term *takfiri* (one who excommunicates other Muslims) passed into colloquial Arabic as a description of the more sectarian elements of the movement, which had been hatched in Nasser's penal colonies by students arrested during the 1965 police raids.

In 1977 the leadership of this movement had devolved on a young agricultural engineer named Shukri Mustafa. Shukri pushed Qutb's incomplete theories to their limits. According to Shukri, the world was jahiliyya (barbarity without Islam) because nobody in it was a true Muslim except his own disciples. Based on a visionary interpretation of the sacred texts, he pronounced takfir on all the Muslim world, with the exception of his disciples, for being kafir (impious, non-Muslim). According to Islamic doctrine, one who is kafir can be put to death. Later, Shukri severed his followers from the rest of the world by interpreting Qutb's jahiliyya as a clean break rather than a mere spiritual abstraction (Qutb himself was never clear on that point). Striving to imitate the Prophet, who fled idolatrous Mecca, where his life was at risk, to seek refuge in Medina, Shukri installed his followers in caves in Upper Egypt or in communal apartments. While in this self-imposed domestic exile, Shukri planned to build up the strength of his group until it was sufficiently numerous to conquer Egypt, cast down the jahiliyya, and establish true Islam—in the same way that the Prophet came forth to conquer Mecca, returning there in triumph eight years after his flight into exile.

The sect found its recruits in modest social milieus that had remained untouched by Sadat's economic liberalism. It offered a community life that broke all ties with Egyptian culture, particularly the ties of matrimony. Shukri reshuffled marriages as he saw fit, and families whose daughters, sisters, and wives were "enticed away" attempted to sue him in court. But the state refused to intervene against what it saw as a marginal movement that posed no political threat in the short term. Shukri's followers were forbidden by him to work as government clerks and so eked out a living as small traders. Some were sent away to work in the Gulf states, from which they sent money back home by post. In short, the sect cobbled together followers from the lowest echelons of society, by offering a set of answers to the tensions they faced in the loosening economic climate of post-Nasser Egypt.

The religious authorities soon denounced Shukri's ideas, which a cleric of Al Azhar, Sheik Dhahabi, compared to Kharijism. This doctrine dated back to the earliest years of Islam, whereby takfir was pronounced against any Muslim accused of sin. Subsequently, rivalries between the Society of Muslims and another radical Islamist group that had enticed away some of Shukri's people degenerated into armed clashes. When the Egyptian police arrested some of the combatants for disturbing public order, Shukri retaliated by kidnapping Sheik Dhahabi and holding him hostage. When the authorities refused to negotiate, Sheik Dhahabi was murdered. Shukri's own arrest, trial, and execution shortly followed.

The trial of Shukri and Al Takfir wa-l Hijra demonstrated the failure of the state's strategy of co-opting the student intelligentsia and the devout bourgeoisie as bulwarks against unrest among the young urban poor. Through Shukri, the military prosecutor incriminated the entire Islamist movement, as well as the religious institution of Al Azhar, despite the fact that one of its own clerics had been murdered in the case. The prosecutor denounced Al Azhar for its inability to teach "true Islam" to young people, who as a consequence had fallen into the clutches of the "charlatan" Shukri Mustafa. This affair was the prelude to a total break between Islamism and the Egyptian regime, which occurred one month later when Sadat made his historic voyage to Jerusalem. The president could not allow his peace initiative to be called into question, and when Islamists began denouncing "the shameful peace with the Jews," Sadat dissolved the Egyptian Students' Union, confiscated the property of the associations, closed their summer camps, and even severely censored the monthly magazine of the Muslim Brothers.

As tension rose steadily during this time, the Islamists were unable to present a united front against the government. Telmesani and his friends adopted the stance of a respectful opposition. The columns of their monthly paper *Al Dawa* were filled with advertisements for corporations belonging to Muslim Brothers who had made their fortunes during their exile in the Gulf; but they also included advertisements for state-funded companies. Neither the accommodations between the devout bourgeoisie and the government nor their complementary nature was affected by political vicissitudes. The moderate middle classes were unlikely ever to pose a violent threat to the regime's stability, and for lack of an uncompromising opposition platform they lost touch with the radical militants among the students and the young urban poor, who consequently took up the battle against Sadat entirely on their own.

After 1977, the old strategy of preaching openly to students on campuses now devolved into clandestine actions around the poverty-stricken edges of Egypt's great cities (Cairo, Alexandria, and the major conurbations of Upper Egypt, Asyut, and Minia). Most of the suspects arrested after Sadat's assassination and the insurrection of Asyut in October 1981 would come from one or the other of these places. The more politically inclined militants gathered under the aegis of a shadowy group called Jihad, whose chief theorist was a young electrical engineer, Abdessalam Faraj. Faraj's pamphlet, *Al Farida al Ghaiba* (The Hidden Imperative or The Missing Obligation) refers to the ulema's obligation to declare jihad against any ruler failing to implement the precepts of Islam, even if he calls himself a Muslim. In Faraj's view, the religious clerics of Egypt had betrayed their trust—and this lapse authorized him, with his electrician's degree and his knowledge of the works of Ibn Taymiyya (which he quoted at length from a volume distributed widely by the Saudis), to take their place. He declared jihad against Sadat, calling him an "apostate of Islam fed at the tables of imperialism and Zionism." The writing of this text, which was directly in line with the theories of Qutb, was followed almost instantaneously by the assassination of Sadat himself. It exactly expressed the split that had taken place in the ranks of the Islamist intelligentsia, a split that eventually proved an insurmountable handicap to the Egyptian movement.

In addition to Faraj's denunciation of Sadat's regime, his call for violent action to overthrow it, and his condemnation of the ulemas' betrayal, Faraj launched a savage attack on moderate elements among the Islamists. According to him, the Muslim Brothers who had opted for legal opposition to the system were guilty of underestimating its fundamentally impious character. By taking part in the political process, they merely strengthened that which they sought to weaken. To set up an Islamist state, Faraj and his co-conspirators carried out a coup de force—the assassination of Sadat himself, during a military parade to commemorate the crossing of the Suez Canal on October 6, 1981. They hoped that this action would cause a "mass uprising," the prelude to a "people's revolution."

During the interrogations that followed their arrest, the culprits turned to exactly these expressions used in reference to Iran, where the revolution had recently triumphed. The difference was that the Iranian Islamists had been able to mobilize not just the mass of Iran's impoverished urban youth but also the bazaar merchants and even the secular middle class around the banner of a cleric, Ayatollah Khomeini. By contrast, Faraj and his friends had cut themselves off completely from the devout bourgeoisie of Egypt, while heaping abuse on the clerics whose "missing obligation" had been their first target. They were thus unable either to transform Sadat's assassination into a general rebellion in the name of Islam or to unite the opposition against the regime. They failed to seize power, even though at the moment of his death Sadat's unpopularity had reached new depths. He had filled Egypt's prisons to bursting with people of every political stripe, including the most moderate, and Sadat himself had lapsed into an isolation bordering on paranoia.

Sadat was succeeded by Hosni Mubarak, the vice president. An uprising instigated in Asyut by the Jihad organization was crushed by army paratroopers, and radical militants were hunted down in the working-class areas of the city. Thereafter, the Al Azhar hierarchy devoted considerable time and effort to proving that the ideas of Faraj and his companions were "deviant" and did not represent the thinking of Ibn Taymiyya. The ulemas pushed their claim that they alone were competent to interpret the great texts of Islamic tradition, which were beyond the grasp of ordinary "ignorant" people led by graduates in electrical engineering. Yet it had been the Saudis' massive distribution of these radical texts, so beloved of Wahhabite clerics, that had made them accessible to young people with education. These youth had duly absorbed the moral and conservative message the Saudis intended them to absorb; the trouble was, they had also paid close attention to its destabilizing subtext.

The predicament of Egypt at the end of the 1970s was the first instance of the political failure encountered by Islamists when their three components were disunited. But it also shows the bankruptcy of a regime which, in the hope of maintaining social order, sought to co-opt both the devout bourgeoisie and the moderate Islamist intelligentsia, by giving the former greater access to a privatized economy and giving the latter control of morality and culture. After Sadat's visit to Jerusalem and the signing of peace with Israel, the foreign policy of the Egyptian government came head to head with the fundamental tenet of Islamists, including those of its moderate wing: namely, hostility to Jews in general and to the Jewish state in particular. The positions taken by the Islamist intelligentsia, which were perfectly welcome as long as they attacked the Marxists on the left, became a destabilizing factor when they opposed the government's own policy of peace with Israel. The bourgeois component of the movement, even though it avoided direct confrontation, was overwhelmed by the groups of young urban militants and students, who fervently supported the idea of jihad.

The Egyptian Islamists, despite their initial setback, played a pioneering role in the later development of a wider movement. Their example was studied closely by militants all over the Muslim world, from sub-Saharan Africa to Central Asia—not least because of the sheer prestige of the country that had produced not only the Muslim Brothers but also Sayyid Qutb himself.

Business, Ethnic Tensions, and Islamism in Malaysia

In the early 1970s, Malaysia suddenly burst into the front of the Islamic stage. Now, to their amazement, travelers saw large numbers of young Malaysian women favoring the Islamic dress made fashionable on Egyptian campuses over the traditional brightly colored sarongs of Southeast Asia.[2] Mosques, installed with loudspeakers, blared the message of Friday preachers through the streets of Kuala Lumpur, exhorting the faithful to be better Muslims and quoting from the works of Mawdudi. A powerful Islamist movement was clearly under way.

Known by the name of Dakwah (from the Arabic dawa, the call to Islam), this movement emerged in earnest after traumatic riots on May 13, 1969. As in Egypt, where the end of the 1960s saw exhausted nationalists grudgingly surrender to Islamist demands, the 1969 confrontation in Malaysia exposed the fragility of the nationalist blueprint. Moreover, it made possible a political expression of religion—which in this region was mixed up with ethnic conflicts and the unequal distribution of wealth between indigenous Malays and the descendants of Chinese immigrants.

Strategically positioned on the straits separating the Indian and Pacific Oceans, Malaysia won its independence from Great Britain in 1957. Previously, the British colonialists had imported Indians to work the country's rubber plantations and had allowed the Chinese to engage in trade, starting from Singapore, which was part of colonial Malaya. By the time of independence, ethnic Chinese made up about a third of the population and controlled practically all of Malaysia's wealth; the majority of the Chinese were non-Muslim. The native Malays, or Bumiputra, were all faithful to Islam, which had been carried to the straits on the ships of Omani and Indian merchants during the fourteenth century. Most Malays lived in rural communities, or *kampungs,* where they had remained largely aloof from modernization. They numbered slightly more than half of the population of the newly independent nation, while Indians, some of whom were Muslims, made up the remaining 15 percent.

Malaysia's first problem as an independent country was how to maintain this delicate ethnic balance, for the Bumiputra, being the majority, immediately demanded the lion's share of the country's wealth. The established regime was made up of elites from all three communities, sharing power according to a system devised at the end of the colonial era. It soon found itself under pressure from a new generation of native Malays who had passed straight from a traditional, illiterate life of rural subsistence farming to the outward-looking, Chinese-oriented towns, with their rich network of overseas contacts and written culture. This conflict came to a head with the 1969 riots, which degenerated into an anti-Chinese rampage and severely tested the Malaysian state's ability to manage a multiethnic society.

The young Bumiputra attending school in the towns found themselves culturally disadvantaged by the supremacy of the English language—a holdover from colonialism. Thus, they determined to impose Malay, which most Chinese had difficulty mastering, as the national language.[3] In the aftermath of the riots, the regime backed down on this point, opening the way for systematic "positive discrimination." At the expense of the Chinese, Malays were given priority in the distribution of places in the state university, along with public employment and influential jobs within the administration. A closed elite supervised the granting of state authorizations and permits. The new balance that emerged in the 1970s saw the transfer of part of the wealth and influence of the Chinese to the Bumiputra. The Chinese were encouraged to go out and increase their wealth even further, so that the Malay elite could continue to benefit.

Still, during the 1970s the mass of young Malays had little or no access to such politically generated revenues. Faced with rural exodus, population explosion, new access to literacy, they felt the need to assert their own identity against the Chinese and to pursue their ambitions of national domination. The folklore of the kampung was of little help to them in the sophisticated, Chinese-oriented cities. Instead, it was Islam, in its most militant form, which came to their rescue. As in Egypt and elsewhere, Islamism offered a way to make sense of the structural upheavals that had characterized the last decade. Moreover, it offered hope to the faithful, by suggesting that they seize the levers of power and master the process of change instead of meekly submitting to it. To this was added, in the case of Malaysia, the problem of ethnicity: by raising their Islamic cultural profile, the young Bumiputra who had come from the countryside placed themselves on an equal social footing with other ethnic groups who had been in the cities longer. Those who embraced Malay Islamism found it an excellent showcase for their ethnic singularity. This explains the sheer breadth of Islamism's success, which became more spectacularly apparent at a much earlier stage in Malaysia than in the Middle East.

The most important Malaysian group, ABIM (Muslim Youth Movement of Malaysia), became active in 1971. Its goal was to make "better Muslims" of the young, to incite them to purge their faith of rustic "superstitions" rooted in the original Hinduism of the peninsula, and generally to "civilize" them. ABIM's Islamist intellectuals were part of the student milieu and offered their recruits a citified religion founded on written texts (notably Malay translations of Mawdudi). They advocated a clean cultural break; their idealized Islamist society emerged as a vague conceptual umbrella capable of sheltering a variety of different social groups. Likewise, their disciples favored different levels of political engagement, ranging from bringing down the established order to consolidating it.

The decade was one of profound discontent. The Malay farming community felt increasingly left behind, as its less-educated sons went unhappily to work in the new factories. There, they produced Japanese, Taiwanese, and Korean goods for Chinese-Malaysian subcontractors who took advantage of the low prevailing wage in the region. In 1974, violent demonstrations by young factory workers erupted at Baling, a town in the north; and around the same time students made common cause with squatters in the slums that ringed Malaysia's cities. ABIM supported the protesters, and the organization's leader, Anwar Ibrahim—then a 27-year-old fresh from the university—paid for his audacity with a two-year jail sentence. The regime had drawn a bright line that Islamist intellectuals crossed at their peril. They were entitled to preach, open schools, establish charitable organizations, and generally ease the passage of impoverished rural youths to the capitalist way of life in the cities. But under no circumstances were they to help overthrow the established order by giving popular discontent some kind of religious expression.

Apart from ABIM, Malaysia's government had to reckon with the full spectrum of the Islamist movement—from the local equivalent of the Muslim Brothers to fanatical sects and groups of armed extremists. The Malaysian Islamic Party (PAS) was represented in Parliament and occasionally joined governing coalitions: its stronghold was the rural state of Kelantan, where its president was frequently elected chief minister. In short, the PAS was part of the system, playing a strictly defined role as the institutional opposition. Founded in 1951, it was a relatively old party whose basic tactic was to keep pushing for a greater degree of Islamization, which the government could not refuse for fear of appearing impious. This political ritual of *kafir-mengafir* ("each calling the other kafir") resulted in the apportionment of more and more public funds to Islamization and a proliferation of decrees: to regulate the work of Muslim civil servants so that the hours of prayer and the month of Ramadan could be observed, to codify the wearing of the veil, and to oblige restaurants to serve halal (the Islamic equivalent of kosher) products. Nevertheless, in the 1970s, at a time when the Dakwah student movement was in full flower, the PAS was not a force to be reckoned with among the urban young.

At the other extreme was a sect which emerged in 1968, the Darul Arqam.[4] Founded by an inspired preacher, Ashaari Muhammad, this ambiguous group had developed its own notions of what constituted

Islamic purity. Its adepts wore long green or white Arab-style jellabas, with an ample black turban tied low over their foreheads. Tables, chairs, and televisions were anathema to the sect. In Malaysia and other countries of the region, Darul Arqam managed to establish no fewer than 40 communities living its version of the Islamic life, as well as over 200 schools, charitable associations, and dispensaries specializing in the "Islamic" rehabilitation of young drug addicts. They also ran a variety of processing units for halal food products. While not as radical as Al Takfir wa-l Hijra in Egypt, the group preached rejection of the impious environment and socialized its followers in a closed milieu represented as a prototype of the true Islamic state. Finally, under the combined pressure of the Iranian revolution, tension in the Middle East, and militants returning from abroad, more radical figures emerged within the movement to preach jihad, martyrdom, and the destruction of Hindu temples as symbols of impiety. The most spectacular of these militants was Ibrahim Libya, a young firebrand belonging to the PAS whose opinions had been formed by a period of study in Libya; he was killed by police in 1985.

During the decade following the 1969 riots, a ruling coalition of the three ethnic groups dominated by the native Malay party, UMNO (United Malay National Organization), set out to promote Islamization. The idea was to give symbolic retribution to Malaysian Muslims and make them proud of their religion, without alienating the other 40 percent of the population, which included the industrious Chinese. The state was careful to reaffirm its secular nature at regular intervals; the Islamic laws it promulgated did not concern non-Muslim citizens, who were protected by the state from persecution by radical preachers. The framing of Islamization was one of the most delicate and crucial tasks facing the Malaysian state.

In the second half of the 1970s, the PAS joined the governing coalition, agreeing to keep its adherents in line in return for promises of a more sustained process of Islamization within the native Malay community. However, its exclusively rural base offered no access to the main trouble spots, which were in the urban shantytowns and on campuses. Because it was unable to act as a mediator for the regime, the PAS was ejected from the government in 1978. As in Egypt, the regime went looking for a moderate partner among the Islamist groups through which it could promote morality while maintaining the status quo.

The state found an Islamist interlocutor in the shape of Anwar Ibrahim of Abim. Anwar had been freed from a two-year stint in prison in 1975, and under his direction the Islamist movement became extraordinarily popular among the new generation of city dwellers and students. Anwar's personal charisma inspired many conversions to Islam. In 1982, to everyone's surprise, and at the request of Prime Minister Mahathir Mohamad, he joined the UMNO governing party.[5] Mahathir, who had already served as a minister during the 1970s, had played a central role in the state's Islamization policy, where his chief concern had been to prevent uncontrolled Dakwah groups from monopolizing Islamic affairs. To that end, he himself had presided over the building of grandiose mosques and had liberally subsidized competitions in Koranic recitation. In addition, he had personally overseen the annual pilgrimage to Mecca and was responsible for a number of new faculties of Islamic sciences for the study of the sharia.

With the arrival of Anwar in the government, the state's commitment to Islamization accelerated. Courses on Islam became compulsory for all Muslim schoolchildren and students, thus creating jobs for graduates of the sharia faculties, and in 1983 the International Islamic University was inaugurated at Kuala Lumpur. With Anwar as its president and a Saudi professor of Egyptian origin as its director, the university's first allegiance was to the Wahhabite sect of Islamism.[6] Teaching in both English and Arabic, the university educated an international Islamist elite in the concept of the "Islamization of Knowledge"—according to which the goal of all science, whether exact or social, was to glorify the divine revelation incarnate in Islam. Graduates of the university, many of whom had scholarships funded by the Gulf states, were trained to reproduce the conservative Islamist establishment on the international stage.

When Anwar became minister of finance, he created Bank Islam in 1983. Prime Minister Mahathir ceremonially inaugurated the Islamic banking system in Malaysia by opening the bank's first account. The government's intention was to attract the savings of the newly urbanized Bumiputra middle classes and wage-earners, who had been touched by the ideology of the Dakwah. These people had profited from the new economic policies that, in the wake of the 1969 riots, shifted significant wealth from the Chinese to native Malays. The Malays demonstrated their loyalty and gratitude to the regime through their use of halal funds managed by young Muslim bankers—the pick of the devout middle class involved in the world of finance. The banking system even provided jobs for graduates in religious studies: they were given places on the sharia boards which made sure that transactions and investments were untainted by charging interest.

In this way Anwar Ibrahim brought forward the elite of Malaysia's Islamist students, to whom he gave positions of power and influence. They moved straight into jobs in the Islamic banking system or in the bureaucracies of the Organization of Islamic Conferences, Islamic non-governmental organizations, and the like. Beneficiaries of his largesse were turned away from the path of revolution, which might otherwise have led them to challenge the status quo.

Nevertheless, a number of hostile militant groups had not yielded to the government's blandishments. Darul Arqam was one of these; and it was a further source of worry to Mahathir's intelligence services that many high government officials belonged to the group, which was suspected of having the long-term goal of infiltrating the government and then seizing power, even though its main source of recruitment lay among the impoverished younger generation in the cities. By the mid-1990s Darul Arqam had around 10,000 members and as many as 200,000 sympathizers. Its assets, derived from its commercial activities, were estimated at $120 million. Its leader had been living in exile since 1988 but kept up a steady barrage of attacks on the regime's corruption, all in the name of Islam.

From the government's point of view, Darul Arqam's assaults on its religious legitimacy were unacceptable. But the destruction of the movement might be a long-term undertaking, given the extreme sensitivity surrounding anything involving Islam. In 1986 a book by the group's founder, Ashaari Muhammad, was singled out for condemnation: its author claimed to have met the Prophet in person and now exhorted his disciples to prepare for the coming of the Mahdi, or Messiah, with whom some had identified Ashaari himself. In the summer of 1994, a judgment of the National Council of Fatwas of Malaysia finally declared the sect to be "deviant" and its activities illegal. Having been extradited from his refuge in Thailand, the founder apologized on television and the police set about dismantling the group's educational, charitable, and commercial institutions and closing down its communes.

When Islamists set themselves up as an alternative to the regime, threatening its existence and claiming equal religious legitimacy, they crossed the line. What happened to Darul Arqam in 1994 was merely a prelude to what would happen four years later to Anwar Ibrahim. But so long as the Islamist organizations preached upright moral conduct and helped contain sections of the population that might otherwise have been restive, the Malaysian government, as in Egypt, afforded the Islamist movements a wide berth. These arrangements were designed to consolidate and give structure to the new devout middle class, whose members were educated in town but originated in the country. Their success right up to the late 1990s was due to Malaysia's participation in the expanding arena of Asian capitalism, for which the country's Chinese entrepreneurs were largely responsible. The Chinese business community had more or less gracefully accepted the discriminatory policies against them, while remaining the principal architects and beneficiaries of Malaysia's new economic openness toward other nations. The financing of Islamization did not seem too great a price to pay for this opportunity. As for the young Chinese who found themselves barred from Malaysian universities, they mostly went to Australia or the West to complete their studies, making full use of their community's international contacts. In the process, they acquired much better diplomas than their Muslim compatriots who were educated locally.

Mahathir, carried aloft by the "Asian miracle" of the 1990s, seized the chance to present his country as the fruit of a happy union between strict Islam and modern capitalism. The twin minarets of the national oil company's Kuala Lumpur headquarters, inaugurated in 1997 as the world's tallest buildings, were emblematic of the new Malaysia. Mahathir now aspired to hegemony over a wider Islam. Malaysia's influence, he believed, would one day supplant that of the Arab Gulf states, whose prosperity was entirely dependent on oil revenues. A tireless champion of Muslim and Third World causes, the prime minister (for whom "Western values were merely Western, while Islamic values were universal") founded the Institute for Islamic Understanding (IKIM) in 1992, with the stated aim of projecting the Malaysian model of Islamization around the world. IKIM emphasized its "modernity" as well as its compatibility with markets and inter-ethnic relations; it organized a steady flow of seminars and lectures, notably in Western countries.

When the 1998 economic tide turned the Asian miracle into an Asian crisis, Malaysia—with its extreme dependence on foreign markets—was hit hard. The most prominent casualty of this disaster was Anwar Ibrahim himself—Islamist intellectual, heir apparent to Mahathir, and darling of the newly Islamicized younger generation. Under suspicion of plotting the prime minister's downfall, Anwar was stripped of his office, jailed, beaten by his guards, and publicly vilified as a sodomite by the government-controlled Malaysian press.[7] By attacking him on a point of private morality, the regime cut straight to the heart of Islamist ideology, which holds that all relationships within society, including private relationships, must conform to moral norms. Anwar and his many defenders among Malaysia's younger generation had no alternative but to plead slander, because by their lights all deviant behavior was criminal. Here they fell into a trap of their own making by denying themselves any recourse to a defense based on a right to privacy.

The conviction of Anwar revealed the true relationship between the Islamist intelligentsia and the state. The prime minister had few qualms about ridding himself of the former head of ABIM, given that he now believed Islamization and its moral influence had done its work in weaving Malaysia's urban youth into the fabric of society. From his point of view, the important thing was that part of the Islamist movement had identified with a government that had improved its members' social condition. The political impotence of Anwar and his friends, despite a broad campaign of support, showed that cooperation with the government had deprived Islamist intellectuals of any ability to mobilize an opposition front. They were caught in a contradiction by an authoritarian regime to which they themselves had given strength and sustenance.

The government continued along its course of Islamization without Anwar, tightening its totalitarian moral hold as the recession deepened. In January 1999, the prime minister's office announced that Muslim couples would henceforth be issued electronic cards to prove their married status, so that the Islamic police could determine on the spot, with a bar-code scanner, whether two people of different sex found together were married or whether they should be arrested for *khalwa*, consorting illegally.[8] The regime soon discovered the political advantage of an intrusive morality that produced a series of spectacular scandals, just in time for the tightly controlled elections of November.[9]

Inevitably, within the ranks of the Islamists who had formerly been courted in exchange for condoning the state's policies, there was a bitter reaction. Munawar Anees, a friend of Anwar who was freed from prison and expelled from Malaysia after massive international pressure was brought to bear on his behalf, voiced a change of heart on his arrival in the United States. An intellectual of Pakistani origin and a frequent castigator of the West in the columns of the newspaper he had founded, Anees described his own career and its culmination in Mahathir's nightmare dungeons:

> Like so many others in the Muslim world, all my adult life I saw Western conspiracies everywhere I looked. I thought the West's sole objective was to keep our heads firmly under the water. After this revealing experience, I find that my Western friends were the ones who succeeded in saving me, whilst Mahathir, a Muslim, has done everything in his power to destroy me . . . He has shown that even though he calls himself a Muslim, his heart is blind to all compassion. Tyranny is the consequence, the demonstration that his concept of "Asian values" is entirely bankrupt. My own tragedy, and Anwar's, should make our Muslim co-religionists think harder when they consider the West and its role in the world. At a time when we are preparing to build our collective destiny in the 21st century, which values will be the most beneficial to us—those of Mahathir, or those of Jefferson? Mahathir himself has made the choice on my behalf.[10]

This change of heart among certain Islamist intellectuals, who turned to democracy as an alternative to the Faustian bargain of serving an authoritarian regime, occurred in other Muslim countries as the twentieth century came to a close. In post-1970 Malaysia, it was a result of the slow annexation by the state of the language of militant Islam. This co-optation allowed Mahathir to neutralize the urban generation of young Malays and to integrate them ideologically into a system which transformed religious zeal into a social identity. As a result, neither discontent nor dissidence could ever be expressed in Islamic terms. Darul Arqam was crushed for attempting to do so.

Anwar Ibrahim, the champion of Malaysia's newly Islamized younger generation, shared power with the establishment but was incapable of installing an Islamist state or applying the sharia of social justice to which his supporters so keenly aspired. Anwar and the Islamic cadres he brought into the administration, the banks, the press, and the educational system of Malaysia contrived to fill the ranks with devout bourgeoisie, but they never approached being a threat to the establishment's social hierarchy. And just when Anwar thought his moment had come, when he appeared to have the backing of the international financial establishment as well as that of Western leaders, the autocratic Mahathir Mohamad struck him down.[11] Because they had failed to hold themselves aloof from the government, in their hour of need the Islamist intellectuals of Malaysia found that their capacity to mobilize support among the disinherited young had been lost. It remains to be seen if they will prove able to build a new set of Malaysian values in the future, and if so what the place of Islam will be within it.[12]

Legitimizing Dictatorship in General Zia's Pakistan

The Malaysian experience showed how an authoritarian regime, by co-opting Islamist intellectuals, could check unrest despite ethnic difficulties, while at the same time projecting local capitalism into the global economy and maintaining the social status quo. The Pakistani situation was similar in many ways, except that the Islamization policies of General Mohammed Zia ul-Haq led to more violence, lasting well beyond his years in power.

After deposing Prime Minister Ali Bhutto with a coup d'état in July 1977, Zia made the implementation of the sharia the ideological cornerstone of his eleven-year dictatorship. While the world's attention was riveted by Iran's loudly anti-Western revolution, neighboring Pakistan followed its own quieter course. In 1979, the year of Khomeini's return to Tehran, Zia decreed a broad series of measures to Islamize the Pakistani state and society in such a way as to avoid revolutionary excesses and strengthen the established order, while retaining the overall support of America and the Gulf states. In light of the Iranian revolution and the 1979 invasion of Afghanistan by the Red Army, Zia's Pakistan became not only the main bastion of American policy in this region but also the main point of distribution for American aid—the deciding factor in the jihad against the Soviets in Afghanistan.

Zia and Khomeini each acted in the name of Islamization, but the two men differed widely in the meaning they gave the term.[13] Zia contrasted Pakistan's evolution toward an Islamic state with the revolution preferred by Iran. In Iran, the destruction of the shah's governing elite and its replacement by men of the devout bourgeoisie was conditional on the mobilization of impoverished young people in the cities. Iranian Islamic intellectuals were obliged to identify with the "disinherited." But in Pakistan, Islamization served to associate devout bourgeoisie and Islamic intellectuals with a system that allowed the governing elites to remain, in the form of a military hierarchy. More significantly, it prevented the masses from rebelling in the name of Allah.[14]

Although Pakistan lies in the geographic and demographic center of the Muslim world, its position within that world was distinctly marginal prior to the 1970s. A continuing rivalry with India froze Pakistan within the local political environment of the subcontinent. But farther afield a number of factors were to unite during the decade to give it a more prominent role on the Islamic stage. The secession of Bangladesh in 1971 reoriented the remainder of the country (originally West Pakistan) toward the Middle East, notably the Gulf oil states, from which millions of Pakistani migrant workers had begun to send home remittances after 1973.[15] At the same time, the rapid growth of Pakistan's population, from 65 to 121 million between 1970 and 1990, made it a demographic heavyweight—the second most populous nation in the Muslim world after Indonesia, which had 183 million people in 1990, and over twice the size of Egypt, the largest Arab country with 56 million people, or Iran with 59 million. So the policy of Islamization carried out by the state under General Zia strongly reinforced the nation's presence in the counsels of international Islam. One of the most powerful symbols of this was Zia's creation of the International Islamic University (identical to the one in Kuala Lumpur) in 1980 in Islamabad, where the leading Wahhabites and the Muslim Brothers gathered.[16]

Pakistani nationalism went through an acute crisis at the beginning of the 1970s, similar to the one in Malaysia and the Arab world. This was provoked by the secession of Bangladesh from the state that had been created in 1947. The Indian military offensive which neutralized the Pakistani army and precipitated the splitting of Pakistan was a disaster on a scale with the Arab defeat by Israel in the 1967 war, and the nationalists likewise had to take all the blame. Thereafter, a phase of re-newed support for socialism, presided over by Ali Bhutto (from 1970 to 1977), provoked an even more powerful Islamist reaction, which carried the movement to the forefront of politics.[17] Although he him-self belonged to a wealthy landowning family, most of Butto's sup-port came from ordinary working people in the cities and rural areas. Bhutto had won the leadership of the Pakistan People's Party (PPP), whose motto was "Socialism, Islam, and Democracy."

The Bhutto years began with a confident program of nationalization and agrarian reforms. But poor results coupled with high-handedness and corruption soon provoked vigorous opposition in the form of the Pakistani National Alliance (PNA), which was spearheaded by the party founded by Mawdudi, the Jamaat-e-Islami (JI). At the instigation of the JI and the Jamiat-e-Ulema-e-Pakistan (JUP, an ulema party), the PNA adopted as its slogan the Nizam-e-Mustafa (Social Order of the Prophet), in other words the installation of an Islamic state and the im-plementation of the sharia. To head off the danger, Bhutto gave his own program a much more pronounced Islamic slant, substituting the "Egalitarianism of the Prophet" for socialism and making Friday the official day of rest instead of Sunday. Finally, he manipulated the elec-tions of 1977 and emerged as the entirely unconvincing victor. While the debate degenerated into sporadic violence between supporters of the PPP and the PNA, Bhutto pressed ahead with measures forbid-ding alcohol, horse-racing, and nightclubs, announcing that the sharia would be fully applied in Pakistan within six months.[18] Indeed, it was: but by General Zia, the army chief of staff, who overthrew Bhutto in July 1977 and had him hanged in April 1979.

To stabilize what was to be the longest-lived of the three military dictatorships Pakistan had known since independence, the general—a great admirer of Mawdudi—promoted Islamism to the status of of-ficial state ideology. Using the PNA's own political slogan, he proposed to turn the Social Order of the Prophet into the Islamist justification and religious guarantor of a state run by martial law. For this he needed the support of the Islamist intelligentsia. The Jamaat-e-Islami applied itself with zeal to this role as the regime's ideological arm. It was rewarded with ministerial responsibilities, with numerous oppor-tunities to infiltrate the state system and the upper echelons of the administration, and with a share of the American and Saudi aid to the Afghan mujahedeen, some of which it brokered.[19]

For General Zia, the promotion of Mawdudi (though not for long; he died in September 1979) and his disciples was a way to block the restoration of democracy and justify martial law by presenting it as a vehicle for setting up a true Islamic state. The years of dictatorship proved fruitful for the devout middle class, who saw its ambitions reflected in the Islamist party. The funds brought home by the Gulf emigrés (who returned as wealthy as they were pious), the flow of American and Saudi aid to the Afghan jihad, and the highly profitable trade between Pakistan and Afghanistan opened up lucrative new possibilities for this social group.[20] As for the Islamist-inclined cadres and wage-earners of Pakistan, the presence of the JI in government helped them to reach the highest levels of public service. For this reason, the devout middle class was not tempted to ally itself with the disinherited younger generation to overthrow the ruling elites. A place, quite simply, had been made for them. General Zia had contrived to break up the PPP, thus rolling back the danger of socialism, he had satisfied the middle class, and he had seduced the Islamist intelligentsia, which identified with Mawdudi. Indeed, the latter now accepted its subordination to the ruling group from which the military hierarchy was drawn.

Zia's intentions were made clear by the Islamization measures enacted in 1979.[21] These included an examination of all existing laws to verify their conformity with sharia; the introduction of an Islamic penal code including corporal punishment or hudud (severing thieves' limbs, stoning adulterous women, whipping drinkers of alcohol, and so on); and the Islamization of education and of every aspect of the economy. In each one of these domains, the regime took particular care to prevent Islamic judicial decisions from escaping the control of the military hierarchy and contravening established social hierarchies. From 1980 onward, proliferating requests for verification of Islamic conformity in the laws were submitted to a federal sharia court, which filtered them carefully to avoid any suggestion of excess. As to the Islamic penal code, in Pakistan as elsewhere it served to apply one or two exemplary penalties that gave the government the moral high ground, at the expense of civil liberties—especially women's civil liberties.

The Islamization of education and the levying of Islamic taxes had a yet more important long-term effect, well beyond the calculations of the government, which saw this process as an opportunity to exercise tighter control of the religious field while manifesting its sympathy with the poor through the zakat. This "legalized" giving of alms to the needy, one of the five pillars of Islam, was treated as a private matter in most contemporary Muslim states. Zia's state broke with tradition by levying it on bank accounts each year during Ramadan, to the tune of 2.5 percent of net deposits. As a tax, it was more pedantic than efficient: its real function was to showcase the piety of the military regime and project an image of social justice, by taxing the urban middle and upper classes (the only people who had bank accounts) and redistributing the proceeds to the poor. The real lives and conditions of tens of millions of Pakistanis were entirely unaffected by the zakat.[22] The only clear consequence was the transformation of the religious landscape of the nation.

From the years of Zia's dictatorship right up to the present day, the alms tax has steadily contributed to polarization and rising violence. From the outset, the Shiite minority, who made up 15 to 20 percent of the population, argued that they were already paying the zakat voluntarily to their ayatollahs, and in any event they objected to the idea of the state's meddling in religion. The regime was forced to give way and exempt all Shiites from paying the tax. Naturallly, this caused outrage among the more conservative Sunni ulemas, who were deeply hostile to Shiism and feared that large numbers of Pakistanis would declare themselves Shiites to avoid the levy. This was only one of many issues that would lead to bloody confrontations between militants of the two communities in the 1990s.

The funds raised by the zakat served to finance the traditional religious schools, the madrassas.[23] These were controlled by the ulemas, the majority of whom were linked to the Deobandi movement. The control of this educational network represented a major advantage, since the zakat donations provided education, board, and lodging to large numbers of Pakistan's poor youth. Conditions in the schools were regularly condemned by human rights agencies as crowded and undisciplined, and the Pakistani madrassas taught religion to their pupils within a highly rigorous and traditional perspective, giving them a deeply retrograde worldview.[24] The policy of financing the madrassas by distributing the proceeds of the zakat to their more needy pupils afforded the state some control over a potentially dangerous social group.

At the same time, bridges were built between the systems of religious and state education. By making courses in Islam obligatory for all pupils and students, the government ensured a steady supply of teaching jobs for graduates of the madrassas, whose diplomas were rated equal to the national ones provided their programs were modernized. By giving opportunities for state employment to the protégés of the ulemas, these measures raised the prestige of their schools.

The effect of all this, when coupled with funds from the zakat and the population explosion then in full force, was a mushrooming in the numbers of madrassas during the 1980s.[25] This naturally gave the ulemas—especially the strict Deobandi ones—far greater power over the poorer Pakistani young, not to mention a sizable contingent of young Afghans, given that they also took care of large numbers of refugee children. In the fullness of time this generation produced the Taliban, whose name means "madrassa pupils."

When the state began to meddle with them as a *quid pro quo* for supplying zakat funds, the heads of many of the largest madrassas opted to fall back on their own resources. These resources were sufficient to keep them out of Zia's debt and so to preserve their independence, however great the general's apparent zeal for Islamization. By adopting this tactic, the Deobandi ulemas kept their political power intact; they were able to stand aloof from the regime because they held the key to social peace, given that they were able to mobilize at will both the urban and the rural youth in their schools. Moreover, as they later demonstrated in Afghanistan, they were perfectly capable of transforming their pupils into jihad militants, ready to kill and be killed for the cause. In the final analysis, Zia needed the ulemas more than they needed him; they controlled the more unstable groups within society, over which the regime had no hold at all.

Unlike the ulemas, the middle-class disciples of Mawdudi had great difficulty resisting the dictator's compromising advances. Substantial numbers from the devout middle class went over to the regime and prospered as a result. The Jamaat-e-Islami was now redundant as a representative of their interests. From the mid-1980s, tensions began to appear within the movement between those who were worried by the party's loss of autonomy and those who favored a continuing collaboration with Zia.[26] The JI now had to compete with the parties linked to the ulemas, who lost no time in taking advantage of their prestige among the young people graduating from the rapidly expanding madrassas.

Caught in this dilemma, the most restive factions of the Islamic intelligentsia—the Mawdudite students belonging to the Islami Jamiat-e-Talaba (Association of Islamic Students, IJT)—became increasingly radical. After a two-year honeymoon with Zia—during which they eliminated the left from the universities by force, as their Egyptian counterparts had done on Sadat's behalf—they began to clamor for the movement to distance itself from the regime. By the time this finally came about, in 1985, it was too late to build a credible rationale for opposing a government whose ideological accomplice the JI had unquestionably been. At the elections following Zia's death in August 1988, the party paid heavily for its past when Benazir Bhutto's Movement for the Restoration of Democracy swept to power. Mawdudi and his disciples had given their unconditional approval to the hanging of her father, Ali Bhutto, in 1979.

During Zia's years in government, the collaboration of the Jamaat-e-Islami supplied a ringing religious endorsement for his tenure of power. Furthermore, it enabled him to broaden his base to include the devout middle class, which calculated that its best interest lay in supporting the movement. This group rallied to the regime, receiving economic advantages in return for keeping Zia in power for what turned out to be an unusually long period by Pakistani standards. The general was less successful with the students, but despite their occasional outbursts of violence they never became a serious political threat. The bulk of the impoverished younger generation, many of whom were under the influence of the ulemas in the madrassas, benefited from the redistribution of the zakat and from new job opportunities. Finally, without managing to bring the ulemas themselves on board as he had done with Mawdudi and his followers, Zia was able to keep them neutral. He took advantage of the suspicion between traditional clerics and modern Islamists to play them off against one another, thus dividing the religious establishment, the better to rule it.

Thus, the state policy of Islamization was an overall success for the Pakistani dictatorship, which used it to win the support of the different social groups with which it had to cope. After the execution of their leader Ali Bhutto, the secular, urban middle class and the ordinary working people who had voted for the PPP were too weak to oppose Zia, who interpreted any challenge to his authority as an attack on Islam and repressed it mercilessly. Nevertheless, the dictator's excesses allowed Benazir Bhutto's opposition party to gather momentum, and in 1988 Zia himself was assassinated.[27] The dictator's death brought about a change of regime, but the effects of his Islamization policy endured. Those effects continued to reverberate in the violence that afflicted the Pakistani religious landscape during the decade that followed, in the aftermath of the Afghan jihad.

CHAPTER

5

Khomeini's Revolution and Its Legacy

The year 1979 will be remembered in history for the victory of the Iranian revolution and the proclamation of the Islamic Republic. Of all events in the contemporary Muslim world, this one has been the most scrutinized and analyzed by those who would unearth the causes of a tidal wave that nobody predicted, not even the protagonists themselves.[1] The developments of the 1970s had affected only a limited number of people; after 1979 there was nobody within the Muslim world or outside it who was unaware of militant Islamism. It became the subject of innumerable conferences, books, and research projects funded by major international foundations, and it benefited (or suffered) from heavy press coverage that stressed its most spectacularly violent and paradoxical dimensions.

Iran had enjoyed great prosperity in the years prior to the revolution, largely due to the high price of oil, of which it was the world's second largest exporter after Saudi Arabia. The shah prided himself on possessing one of the world's most powerful armies and having access to highly sophisticated American military equipment, which he used to police the Gulf and block Soviet expansion to the Indian Ocean. But the maintenance and handling of this military hardware required large numbers of American personnel, whose presence on Iranian soil provoked the fury of Ayatollah Khomeini. In 1964 he openly accused the shah of abdicating national sovereignty. The result was a fifteen-year exile, during which the ayatollah developed his political theology for the future Islamic Republic of Iran and from which he returned victorious in February 1979, carried aloft by the triumphant revolution.

What accounts for this dramatic turnabout? A primary factor was political unrest within Iran's student radicals, middle classes, and urban poor. Beneath the brilliant surface of modernization that the shah had projected and promoted, Iranian society was developing serious flaws. The monarchy and Savak (secret police) had muzzled debate on the regime's policies; the imperial system that had encouraged the growth of an educated urban middle class, through a system of schools substantially superior to those of Iran's neighbors, denied that class any semblance of political voice.[2] At best, its members could become functionaries and managers in the imperial administration. The absence of free speech and a free press inhibited the development of a democratic culture in Iran. Liberal and socialist intellectuals preserved the legacy of the National Front led by Mohammed Mossadegh, the prime minister whose nationalist government was toppled by a CIA-backed coup that brought the shah to power, but in the early 1970s this clique had little or no influence in Iran, despite the aura of its leaders.

The vacuum created by the absence of democratic institutions provided a space for radical sentiment to grow. It began among Iran's students, who by 1977 numbered close to 175,000. Of these, 67,000 were studying abroad, mostly in the United States. Student radicalism in Iran drew on two main ideological sources: Marxism in its various forms, and a movement within Islam that came to be called socialist Shiism. Young Marxists were at the forefront of Iranian emigration, having been savagely repressed by the Savak at home, and they eventually came to represent all shades of the international communist movement, from Maoism and Trotskyism to the pro-Soviet orthodoxy of Iran's Tudeh party ("the masses" in Farsi). In Iran, as in other parts of the Muslim world, the early 1970s saw a blossoming of Marxist groups in intellectual circles with access to European culture. But the ideas of these student activists did not filter down to ordinary people, to whom this radical discourse remained foreign. Because the intellectuals were much more in step with the bookish culture of proletarian internationalism than with grassroots Persian society, an attempted uprising in the early 1970s provoked by the Marxist-Leninist People's Fedayeen, which sought to graft the ideology of Mao and Che Guevara onto Iran, ended in bloody failure.

Aware of this intellectual gap, a few young Marxists began projecting all the messianic expectations of communists and Third World peoples onto revolutionary Shiism. Ali Shariati was the most outspoken representative of this movement; his fame and influence among Shiites had no equivalent in the Sunni Muslim world. Socialist Shiites viewed the seventh-century death of Imam Hussein (the original "oppressed" one—*mazloum*) at the hands of the Sunni Umayyad Caliph as the analog of the Iranian people's modern oppression by the shah. The movement found its most militant expression in the guerrilla tactics of the People's Mujahedeen, whose acts of violence were comparable to those of the fedayeen.[3] The mujahedeen's activities won the sympathy of the regime's opponents, but the group failed to enlist recruits beyond its core constituency of students. The educated, secular middle class as yet saw no reason to involve itself in so violent and radical a struggle. In purely practical terms the movement presented no immediate danger to the empire, which brutally repressed it nevertheless.

Rapid modernization, fueled by petro-dollars, destabilized two other important Iranian social groups: the traditional devout middle class associated with the bazaar, and the masses of young immigrants from the countryside, who had been drawn to town by the promise of prosperity, only to end up in the packed slums of Tehran.[4] These two groups benefited only partially from Iran's economic expansion under the shah. Although the bazaar prospered as the volume of goods and merchandise rose, its share of the market shrank in comparison with that of the new commercial elite, whose success was linked to the imperial court and depended on exclusive access to Iran's two most profitable businesses, oil and military hardware. Like the devout merchants in the bazaar, the immigrants from the countryside and the ordinary working people of the cities were also doing better than before, but economic uncertainty and dreadful living conditions contributed to unrest among this population.[5]

Culturally, both the devout middle class and the urban working class were alienated from the secular, modernist ideology favored by the regime. They viewed the world and their place in it through the filter of Shiism as preached by their clergy. In the bazaars, traditional life was spatially structured around the mosques and *imamzadehs*—tombs of saints much venerated by Shiites in their devotions. In the anarchic, jerrybuilt slums on the outskirts of the city, the primary source of order was Shiite places of worship, where citizens gathered to listen to their turbaned clerics teach the Koran and the deeds of the great imams.[6] Here, religious leaders not only indoctrinated the masses but also functioned as agents of social stabilization and containment. They blessed the profits of the bazaaris, redistributed their alms, and educated the children while fathers and elder brothers went into the city center, seeking work and wages.

Yet the relationship between the imperial power and these religious networks was strained. The mullahs, ridiculed as "black" reactionaries because of their dark robes, saw the numbers of their traditional madrassas cut by the state, which sought to replace them with modern, government-controlled schools—a policy that drew fury from the exiled Khomeini. The Shiite clergy was hierarchical and organized under the authority of ayatollahs, the most respected of whom were "sources of imitation" (marja-e taqlid). As recipients of the zakat (alms), they were independent, both financially and politically, from the state authorities, to which they paid only lip service (ketman). Their situation contrasted sharply with that of Sunni ulemas in other countries, with whom the state usually maintained close relations—rewarding them with political offices, paying their salaries, and in return receiving their blessing. During the reign of Muhammad Reza Pahlavi, the Iranian clergy added to the Shiites' traditional distaste for the regime a much more specific hostility provoked by the shah's open mistrust of the mullahs. Thus, in the mid-1970s, Iran's bazaars and slums contained a readily identifiable devout middle class and an impoverished younger generation, both of whom were culturally estranged from the ideology of a state that essentially ignored their existence. At the same time, they were strongly structured by the Shiite clergy, in whose hierarchy the state had no reliable representation. Quite the opposite was the case in most Sunni-dominated countries.

In addition to their hostility to the shah, the clergy were suspicious of the revolutionary ideas of Khomeini, who wanted to bring down the Pahlavi empire and replace it with a theocracy (velayat-e faqih) in which the supreme power would be held by a faqih, or cleric, specializing in Islamic law. This, of course, meant Khomeini himself, and most clerics joined the grand ayatollah Shariat-Madari in opposing it. They were content to stay with their policy of quietly procuring as much autonomy from state interference as possible for their schools, their charitable work, and their financial resources. They had little desire to win for themselves a political power that in theological terms they believed to be impure. They preferred to await the return of the hidden imam, the Messiah who would replace the shadows and iniquities of the world with light and justice.

Despite Iran's growing social discontent and the political frustration it engendered, the imperial system functioned without serious difficulty until 1975, when a 12.2 percent drop in oil prices created major economic and social stresses. The regime reacted by launching a large-scale anti-speculation campaign that hit the bazaar very hard; its best-known merchants were thrown into prison and publicly humiliated. From that moment on, the merchants bitterly opposed the shah, and their guilds *(asnaf)* became conduits for the mobilization of men and means to bring him down. At the same time, the new measures against speculation upset the modern bourgeoisie by obliging companies to sell a part of their capital to their employees, without winning much credit from the workers themselves.

As the shah's isolation grew, the support of his principal ally, the United States, was weakened by the election of Jimmy Carter to the White House in November 1976. The brutal tactics of the Savak became a target of the new American president's human rights policy, and Carter himself applied pressure on the shah to liberalize Iranian civil society. Naturally enough, the secular middle class took this criticism as a signal that the United States had withdrawn its unconditional support for the Pahlavis. The year 1977 saw a spate of meetings and demonstrations by the liberal opposition, which for the first time in many years was not repressed by the regime. The clergy took very little part in this short-lived "Tehran spring."[7] Though the secular middle class was the first group to shake off political apathy, it proved incapable of taking the lead in a general resistance to the shah. It lacked the charisma necessary to rally the bazaaris and the urban poor around its cause, and it did not have an organized party base capable of mobilizing these social groups with slogans they could understand. Meanwhile, the student-led Marxist movements were too weak for mobilization, having been decimated by repression or distanced by exile. The way was open for a clerical splinter group led by Khomeini.

The "moment of enthusiasm" that transformed agitation against the shah into an Islamist revolution was triggered by a purely fortuitous event. This was the publication by a Tehran newspaper of an insulting attack on Khomeini in January 1978. The ayatollah was in exile at the time, living at Najaf in Iraq; but the entire opposition, including the secular middle class and those pious Muslims who opposed the doctrine of velayat-e faqih, rose up in his defense. Khomeini then unleashed his own partisans: on his instruction, the bazaar closed down completely, and a number of people were killed during a series of demonstrations in the holy city of Qum. A celebration on the fortieth day after these deaths led to another wave of bloody demonstrations in Tabriz, the metropolis of Iranian Azerbaijan.[8] Thus began a spiral of provocation, repression, and polarization that rose steadily until the shah was forced to depart. Through their religious rhetoric, Khomeini and his disciples orchestrated these demonstrations, bringing into the streets, shoulder to shoulder, students from the madrassas and impoverished urban youths to be shot down as martyrs by the police, while the bazaar guilds raised funds for the victims' families.

As the movement became more radical, Khomeini was able to mobilize the entire network of mosques in Iran, where the majority of mullahs who had hitherto withheld endorsement of his doctrines now fell into line behind him.[9] This clerical network was supported by over 20,000 properties and buildings throughout Iran, where people gathered to talk and receive orders. The system had no equivalent among the secular opposition or among the Shiite socialists, who had done their best to rid themselves of clerical influence. Now they found themselves having to obey the ayatollahs, who controlled the lion's share of the resources available to support the revolution.

In the meantime, Khomeini adjusted his political rhetoric in order to appeal to an audience beyond his immediate circle of followers. In 1978 he made no mention of the doctrine of theocracy, which was bitterly contested among the clergy and would have scared away the secular-minded middle class had it known of it and understood its possible consequences. On the other hand, he made abundant reference to the "disinherited" (mustadafeen), so vague a term in Khomeini's parlance that it encompassed just about everyone in Iran except the shah and the imperial court. He borrowed the word from Shariati and had never used it before the 1970s.[10] After Shariati's death in exile in June 1977, the term had become a rallying cry of the Shiite socialist students, who maintained a strong distrust of the clergy. In making use of this vocabulary, Khomeini (who had always refused to condemn Shariati while he was alive, despite the demands of other clerics) won the approval of substantial numbers of younger Islamist intellectuals.[11] Bearded young engineers, doctors, technicians, and lawyers, whose counterparts in Egypt had clashed head-on with the ulemas of Al Azhar in the last months of Sadat's regime, now fell into line behind Khomeini. Thus, when he left Iraq in October 1978 for his final period of exile at Neauphle-le-Château on the outskirts of Paris, Khomeini was able to carry with him several figures from this group, notably the future short-lived president of the Islamic Republic, Bani Sadr.

In November 1978 Karim Sanjabi, one of the leaders of the liberal National Front, made a pilgrimage to Neauphle to join Khomeini, while the head of the Tudeh Communist party officially recognized the ayatollah as his guide. At this time Khomeini announced that the goal of the revolution was to establish "an Islamic Republic which would protect the independence and democracy of Iran." Here he employed a term—democracy—that he would denounce as "alien to Islam" only a few months later, during the debate over what the new republic should be called. The general submission to Islamist cultural hegemony reached its climax during the most spectacular demonstrations against the shah, on December 10 and 11, 1978, corresponding to the ninth and tenth days of the Muslim month of Muharram, when Shiites commemorate the martyrdom of Imam Hussein. On these days Khomeini ordered hundreds of thousands of people to defy the shah's curfew by shouting "Allah Akhbar" from every terrace and rooftop in Tehran. It was a powerful demonstration of the Islamist cultural grip on the revolution. One month and five days later, the shah was driven out of Iran forever.

This Islamist victory was made possible by Khomeini's extraordinary ability to unify the various components, religious and secular, of a movement whose single point of departure was hatred of the shah and his government. Khomeini allowed each group to invest the movement with its own particular political dreams, which were not dispelled until the purges began in the aftermath of victory. The fusion of the revolutionary clerics with the young Islamist intellectuals mobilized the bazaaris and ordinary working people to unite in the common expectation of an Islamic Republic and the implementation of the sharia—

without calling attention to the very different aspirations projected upon this nation by their respective class interests. This alliance also caught the imagination of the secular urban middle class. Incapable of asserting a cultural identity of their own, they felt obliged to go along with the dominant Islamist philosophy so that any benefits of revolution would not pass them by.

Upon his return to Tehran on February 1, 1979, Khomeini had to take account of the contradictory expectations of the immense host that had come together to welcome him home. His response was to set about eliminating all of his secular allies and establishing a theocracy. He first named a provisional government under Mehdi Bazargan, a devout Muslim engineer trained in France. This administration combined clerics with representatives of the National Front middle class, which alone was capable of making the state function. But the real power resided in the secret Islamic Revolutionary Council, which included a majority of ulemas loyal to Khomeini and from which the National Front was entirely excluded. Institutionalized as the Party of the Islamic Revolution in February 1979, this organization represented the Islamist intellectuals who, under clerical control, eventually produced a new official ideology for the nation.

The ordinary working people of Iran had played an important part in the revolution.[12] They made up the bulk of the 1978 demonstrators, even though they had no autonomy of expression whatsoever.[13] They had physically taken possession of places from which they had formerly been excluded, such as the main avenues of central Tehran and the university campus. In return, they expected the shah's overthrow to be followed by the satisfaction of their immediate demands—improved living standards, higher salaries, occupation of the property of the "corrupt ones," proper development of the temporary housing in which many of them lived, recognition of so-called illegal settlements, free public services, and much more. The Khomeinist clerics who controlled them through their *komitehs* (equivalents of the French Revolution's Comités de Salut Public, committees of public salvation), operating from mosques and tekiyehs all over the country, made sure that these demands were expressed in Islamist terms. Very rapidly, the komitehs became the backbone of a second power within the state, along with the militia, the army, the revolutionary tribunals, and the Islamic foundations, which inherited the financial empire of the Pahlavi

Foundation, as well as the property of the *taghuts*, or devils, and the sundry other "corrupt ones" who had been hanged, shot, or driven into exile. Bazargan's provisional government had no control at all over the komitehs, and since he had made it his goal to re-establish order, meaning a social order condemned as iniquitous by the young urban poor, he quickly became the target of their attacks. The leftist movements, who viewed the komitehs favorably as nascent soviets, immediately joined the hue and cry against him.

Khomeini's defeat of the secular middle class and liberals was accomplished both judicially and politically within a few months. Following the referendum approving the Islamic Republic in March—enshrining Islamism in the nation's very name—an Assembly of Experts was elected in August. This assembly, which was dominated by the ulemas and the PIR (Party of the Islamic Revolution) now devised a new constitution. This contained articles establishing the velayat-e faqih and gave absolute power to the Guide, in the person of Khomeini. Objections to this theocracy were raised by the liberals, the Kurdish (Sunni) minority, one of the leftist parties, and a few clerics, who called it a restoration of dictatorship. Confronted by this coalition of his opponents, and on the pretext of protesting the shah's admission to the United States for treatment of the cancer that would kill him shortly afterward, 500 "students in the line of the imam" (Khomeini), led by a PIR official, stormed the American Embassy on November 4, 1979.

The U.S. diplomats inside were taken hostage and held until January 1981, following Ronald Reagan's defeat of Jimmy Carter for the presidency. Having no authority whatsoever to free the hostages, Bazargan resigned, setting a political seal on the crushing defeat that the secular middle class had already suffered in the streets. Shortly afterward, Ayatollah Shariat-Madari, the leader of those ulemas who had opposed Khomeini's theocracy, was placed under house arrest. He remained incarcerated until his death in 1986.

By the end of 1979, the only surviving players on the Iranian political stage were the Islamist intellectuals, the young urban poor, and the devout bourgeoisie. The revolution accelerated following the hostage crisis, as bands of working-class youths went into action, led by fanatical clerics and left-wing Islamist militants who had been galvanized by the takeover of the American "nest of spies." Publication of the embassy's secret files brought to light U.S. contacts with a number of middle-class liberals. These revelations were promptly used as a pretext for new trials, executions, and confiscations of property. A sequence of events had begun to unfold that might lead to a total overthrow of the social hierarchy, going well beyond a mere change of regime. If this process was allowed to go too far, and if the young urban poor were permitted to win their autonomy and perhaps even free themselves from Islamist ideology (as they were encouraged to do by the Marxist groups and People's Mujahedeen that had infiltrated the komitehs), then intolerable pressure would be brought to bear on the clerics. It would also adversely affect the interests of the devout bourgeoisie in the bazaar, who were regaining the economic position they had lost in the years of the shah, by recovering the market share formerly held by capitalist "devils" who had been exiled, jailed, or shot.

Thus, the Islamist left, and the Shiite socialists who depended on poor urban youth for their support, now posed the primary threat to Khomeini's power. The strategy he used to eliminate them was the same one that had crushed Bazargan and the liberals. Khomeini first exposed them to power, then sapped it away through the komitehs, *pasdarans* (Guardians of the Islamic Revolution), and other organs controlled by his networks. Thus Bani-Sadr, representing the Islamist left, was elected President of the Republic with Khomeini's support in January 1980. In April of that year, the leftist groups and mujahedeens who had taken control of the campuses were driven out by the pasdarans. The University of Tehran was closed down until such time as it could be thoroughly purged. In May, the new Parliament—in which the PIR held the majority—became the true focus of power in Iran and imposed its own prime minister. President Bani-Sadr was now subjected to a war of attrition, and he finally left the country in June 1981 with the aid of the People's Mujahedeen. A general Mujahedeen uprising followed, which was put down in spite of the spectacular assassination of Bani-Sadr's successor and other PIR leaders in 1982, the bloodiest year of the revolution. In early 1983 the leaders of the Tudeh party, who were the last to be arrested in Khomeini's campaign to annihilate the Iranian left, confessed Soviet-style on television to the charge of spying for Moscow, before acknowledging Islam's superiority over communism.

The obliteration of the Islamist left led to a blanket prohibition of all dissent from the line taken by the Islamic intellectuals, in accordance with Khomeini's theory of *vahdet-e kalimeh* (oneness of discourse). Iran's urban youth and working poor were left without a spokesman to express their interests in social rather than religious terms. Nevertheless, they remained mobilized in the expectation that their basic demands would be met. Their demonstrations had brought down the shah; they had helped to eliminate the liberals and their allies; and they had always supported Khomeini. When Saddam Hussein's army invaded Iran on September 22, 1980, it handed Khomeini a perfect opportunity to mobilize this remaining sector of the population one last time, in such a way as to exhaust it politically and expend its energy in a paroxysm of martyrdom. At the front, the regiments of ill-trained young Iranian volunteers *(bassidjis)* were cannon fodder for the Iraqis. Hundreds of thousands of the most active and motivated militants gave their lives to defend their fatherland and its revolution, while millions more of their countrymen were pinned down for years in the trenches. Thus the soldiers of Year II of the Islamic Republic entirely vanished from the domestic political scene, and with them went any possibility that the impoverished urban working class might find some way of advancing its specific interests.

The killing of so many young men brought about the symbolic death of their class as a collective political protagonist in Iran. From that point on, the political significance of Shiism changed completely. Earlier, under the influence of Shariati and then during the revolution, the commemoration of Imam Hussein's martyrdom at Karbala had become a pretext for the struggle against the modern incarnation of the oppressor-caliph of old, namely the shah. Religious energy was externalized, and its goal was to change the world. This contrasted sharply with the dominant Shiite tradition, which had always foregone activism in favor of grief and lamentation, culminating with the self-flagellation of the *ashura* ritual. The appalling butchery of the eight-year war against Iraq gave the younger generation of poor Iranians an incentive to return to the former tradition of martyrdom, pushing the ritual of self-flagellation to the point of self-immolation—the ultimate sacrifice. No longer at issue was the transformation of the world, for the revolution had clearly failed to satisfy that expectation; rather, the young men developed a new desire—a longing for death—as a response to the failure of Iran's revolutionary utopia and the pressures of war with Iraq. The Shiite death wish took on massive dimensions with the sacrifice of the bassidjis at the front. The volunteers wrote letters and last testaments to their families, asserting their longing for death in the crudest, most detailed vocabulary of Shiite martyrology. What these tragic documents describe in religious terms is no less than the political suicide of the young urban poor of Iran in the 1980s.

Khomeini's regime celebrated the martyrdom of the nation's young by cloaking itself in the legitimacy their sacrifice conferred. To this day, hyper-realist murals can still be seen in Iranian cities, displaying portraits of war martyrs whose names drip with blood. These murals evoke the fountain of blood that decorated the principal war cemetery in Tehran. The Islamic Republic made it very clear that it governed in the name of the fallen disinherited, the worthy emulators of Imam Hussein. But despite the slaughter at the front, the numbers of those who stayed behind continued to grow at an unprecedented rate; and with time the regime was obliged to take initiatives that would win the support of these tens of millions of young men. What it did was to combine both moral and economic considerations.

First, the wearing of the veil and full Islamic dress was made compulsory in April 1983, just after the last leftist movements had been crushed. The komiteh members, finding themselves with no atheist leftists to harass, turned to policing their neighbors' morals, hunting down and prosecuting ill-veiled women *(bad hejabi)* according to strict criteria of garment lengths, shapes, and colors that still remain in force and are posted in all public places in Iran. The women most likely to be ill-veiled belonged to the secularized cultured middle class, whereas the komitehs found their recruits mostly among ordinary working people. These recruits began to see themselves as guardians of the values of the Islamic Republic whose duty it was to persecute the remaining members of the middle class who had somehow managed to hang on to their social status and cultural capital. The poor were able to exercise moral retribution in the name of God, and this seems to have compensated them for their own exclusion from the political arena.

Second, the Islamic Republic set in motion various mechanisms for allocating material and symbolic resources to reward the families of the young urban poor who had first made the revolution and then sacrificed their lives on the Iraqi front. The families of martyrs were entitled to send their remaining children to the university without having to pass the entrance exam. In addition, they were given grants, lodgings, and subsidized food by foundations run by the clergy. The beneficiaries of this largesse had every interest in perpetuating Khomeini's regime. They were ready to fight to keep power in the hands of the clergy and the Islamist intellectuals claiming loyalty to the ayatollah. The regime thus came to represent the interests of the devout bourgeoisie of the bazaar, which by the middle of the 1980s had wrested control of the entire economy.

The Ripple Effect of the Iranian Revolution

At first, the Islamic Revolution in Iran was able to draw on deep reserves of sympathy among opponents of authoritarian regimes throughout the Muslim world. Before purges, executions, and atrocities tarnished its image, the revolution demonstrated that a movement springing from a broad spectrum of society could bring down a powerful government, even one closely connected to the United States. This victory was enough to make world leaders who had hitherto paid little heed to Islam begin to take its revolutionary potential much more seriously. Through Khomeini, the example of the Iranian revolution convinced many observers that Islam had supplanted nationalism as the principal factor in the political, social, and cultural identity of certain countries.

Regimes in Muslim countries viewed the shah's fate as an object lesson, and many of them became ostentatiously religious, in the hope of avoiding what had befallen the Persian monarch, who had never bothered to hide his contempt for the "men in black." Governments sought to head off social movements that, by annexing the vocabulary of Islam, threatened to unite everyone with an ax to grind and bring down the established power. The ulemas, having been steadily harassed during the nationalist period, now found themselves fawned upon by princes eager for the Islamic legitimacy their blessing could confer. In return, the clerics demanded greater control over culture and morals, avenging themselves on their secularist intellectual rivals—whose influence they diminished through the intimidation and censorship governments were suddenly willing to brandish on their behalf. Through the ulemas, Muslim elites sought accommodation with the devout bourgeoisie, whose approval or neutrality sanctioned the repression of the more radical Islamist intellectuals at work among the young urban poor. The partnership was an uneasy one, with each side looking for advantage and seeking to impose its own conditions. In general, the ulemas came out on top, as representatives of proper standards and values within society and within the Islamic movement itself. The losers were the bearded engineers, computer scientists, and physicians who had spearheaded the Sunni radical groups throughout the 1970s and had held the sheiks in low esteem.

The Muslim world as such had been under Saudi religious domination since the creation of the Islamic conference in 1969 and the triumph of petro-Islam in the war of October 1973. But after 1979 the new masters in Iran considered themselves the true standard-bearers of Islam, despite their minority status as Shiites. As far as they were concerned, the leaders in Riyadh were usurpers who sold oil to the West in exchange for military protection—a retrograde, conservative monarchy with a facade of ostentatious piety. In the winter of 1978–79 a Khomeini follower in Paris predicted to an Arab journalist: "Be patient . . . we shall see what happens to the Saudis six months after our return to Iran."[14] Nine months later, at dawn on November 20, 1979—the first day of the Muslim fifteenth century—the Great Mosque at Mecca was stormed by several hundred Saudi dissidents, who were dislodged only after a ferocious two-week siege.[15] Nothing suggests that the attackers, who belonged to an extreme Saudi Wahhabite sect, had been in contact with Tehran, though Iran probably had something to do with the less serious Shiite uprising that took place in Hasa, Saudi Arabia's oil-rich eastern province, while the Mecca siege was under way.[16] Still, for the Saudi leaders, the balance they had so carefully constructed over the last decade was under serious threat. Their Islamic legitimacy had been spectacularly called into question in their own territory, and their ability to maintain order in Islam's holiest places had been found wanting.

The Iranian revolution's propaganda was aimed directly at the "Islam of the people"; it incited them to rise up against the impiety of their leaders, despite their claim to be following the dictates of the Koran and the sharia. The Saudi policy, on the other hand, had been to finance the expansion of Islamism around the world, the better to control it—through the Muslim World League and the Organization of the Islamic Conference—and to prevent groups bent on changing the status quo from appropriating Islam to themselves. The combination of the words "Islamic" and "Revolution" was, for the Saudis, an exceedingly dangerous proposition. Moreover, this revolution had flowered in an area of the Muslim world in which Sunni Wahhabite proselytism had no representation; the Shiites were viewed as out-and-out heretics in most Saudi religious circles.

Thus, after 1979 two conflicting strategies for dominating the Muslim world were in play. Iran's strategy sought to replace the supremacy of the Saudis throughout the Community of the Faithful with that of Khomeini. It took care to play down Shiism, since more than 80 percent of all Muslims were Sunni. Its target constituency was younger Islamist intellectuals belonging to the radical fringes of society. Saudi Arabia's strategy sought to mobilize its decade-old system for the propagation of Islam worldwide in order to counter the Khomeinist threat. The Saudis took care, first, to emphasize the Shiite nature of the revolution, thereby making it less easy for Sunni Muslims to swallow, and, second, to denounce the revolution as a vehicle for Persian nationalism.

The threat of Persian nationalism served as an excuse for Saddam Hussein's attack against the Islamic Republic in September 1980. But he had other motivations as well. Saddam meant to take advantage of the revolutionary chaos within his neighbor's borders to snatch an easy political victory and in the process to broaden Iraq's narrow access to the sea by regaining full control of the entire Shatt al-Arab estuary, which the two countries had shared uneasily since the Algiers agreement in 1975. At the same time, by militarizing his own society, he hoped to consolidate his recently won power while preventing Iraq's narrow majority of Shiites from mobilizing against his regime, as the Iranian Shiites had done against the shah.[17] In April 1980, Saddam executed Iraq's main Shiite personality, Ayatollah Baqir as-Sadr, a supporter of Khomeini; and as soon as war broke out five months later Saddam directed a campaign of savage repression against all potential Shiite militants.[18]

Saddam was encouraged to act by those who feared that events in Iran would spill over into other countries. The rich Arab monarchies of the peninsula felt especially threatened and were eager to supply financial and moral backing for a war that would mobilize modern Arab nationalism against non-Arab Iran. With the exception of Syria, Iraq's traditional rival, the Arab states staunchly supported Baghdad against Tehran. Saddam was also backed by the West, which was horrified by the Iranian revolution. Ironically, in the decade to follow he would be identified as the primary enemy of the United States and the Gulf nations.

Throughout the war, both the Arab states and Iran laid claim to Islamic credentials, the better to rebut the other's use of them. Control of the rhetoric of Islam and appropriation of its vocabulary had become a central tactic in the quest for power and legitimacy. The supporters of Saddam claimed the original Islam of Arabia, which had triumphed over Sassanid Persia at the battle of Qadissiya in 636; the Iraqis even named their military offensives after this event. Tehran was quick to react, branding Saddam Hussein as "impious" because he was a leader of the secular Baathist party and hence an apostate. Consequently, the Iranian military offensives were named after the battles won by the first Caliph, Abu Bakr, against the Arab tribes that had apostasized Islam (hurub al-ridda).[19] Claiming Islam would henceforth be a symbol of political power; and the ongoing battle of reference and anachronism would project the real physical war into the realms of ideology and doctrine.

In the Arab Middle East, the revolutionary enthusiasm of the Khomeinists found its principal expression in the gradual Islamization of the conflicts in Palestine and Lebanon. Each in its own way had embodied the cause of Arab nationalism, and neither had been particularly affected by religious ideology prior to the revolution. In Palestine, the PLO had adopted a political line that included both Christians and Muslims.[20] But the beginning of the 1980s ushered in a difficult period for the organization. Cut off from Egypt since Sadat's 1977 visit to Jerusalem and his signing of the Israeli-Egyptian peace treaty in 1979, inactive in Jordan since the Black September crackdown in 1970, and ruthlessly suppressed within the Israeli-occupied territories, Arafat's militants had focused their energies in Lebanon. Since 1975 they had been heavily engaged in the civil war between the mainly Maronite Christian right and the "Islamo-progressives" with whom the PLO identified. The latter had little to do with Islamist ideology, which at the time was hardly a factor in Lebanese politics.[21] Instead, it merely described the creed of most of those opposed to the Maronite elites (who had dominated politics since the time of the French mandate,

1920–1946) and who also identified with all the other Arab causes, notably that of the Palestinians.[22]

For as long as the PLO was caught up in the Lebanese conflict, in which cruelty, banditry, and shifting alliances quickly overshadowed principle, it was unable to pay much attention to the struggle against Israel, its main reason for existence. The PLO's predicament became even more dire when an Israeli attack on southern Lebanon in 1982 destroyed Palestinian infrastructures and forced the PLO to move its headquarters from Beirut to Tunis. This disaster was followed by a Syrian offensive that drove Yasir Arafat and his supporters out of Tripoli in December 1983.[23] In exile, far from its theater of operations, the PLO leadership now seemed to be directing a seriously weakened cause whose power to mobilize its supporters was about to be extinguished. In the eyes of the younger Arab generation of the 1980s, it was not the Palestinian cause but the Afghan jihad that was truly attempting to substitute Islamic ideals for a discredited nationalism.

In Palestine itself, the Muslim Brothers, which had been in existence for much longer than the PLO, were tolerated by the Israelis because the Brothers' concerns were mainly charitable and pious. The Jewish state saw them as a nonpolitical outlet for the frustrations of the occupied Palestinian people and an inoffensive substitute for the militant nationalism of the PLO. The Brothers, who were well-represented in Gaza, were mostly engrossed with the re-Islamization of the populace, as opposed to the secular nationalism preached by the PLO. They preferred to tip the balance of power within Palestinian society toward themselves before tackling Zionism—a move which they felt to be premature, given the overwhelming military might of the state of Israel.[24]

Among Palestinian students at the University of Zagazig in Lower Egypt, a group of militants who were equally tired of the Brothers' "quiescence" and the PLO's "impiety" were particularly enthusiastic about the Iranian model. Their leader, a medical doctor named Fathi Shqaqi, had published a slim volume entitled *Khomeini: The Islamic Alternative (Al Khumaini: al hall al Islami wa-l badil)*, which after 1979 could be found on every street corner in Cairo. Dedicated to "the two great men of this century," the "martyr Hassan al-Banna, founder of the Muslim Brothers," and "the Revolutionary Imam Ruhollah Khomeini," this work provided the most explicit apology for the Islamic Revolution to come from within the Brothers' network.[25] Shqaqi and his friends made reference to Iran in criticizing the nationalism of the PLO, which had gained nothing for the Palestinians on the ground. Equally, they condemned the "discretion" of the Muslim Brothers of Palestine, who had forsaken the political struggle against Israel for the relative comfort of preaching and good works.

As far as Shqaqi was concerned, the victory of the Islamic Revolution "demonstrated that even against an enemy as powerful as the Shah, a jihad of determined militants could overcome all obstacles." Therein lay the path to liberation of Palestine: armed struggle and combat for Islamization, combined in a single great jihad. This strategy found expression in the creation of the Islamic Jihad organization, which was conceived as an activist, militant vanguard capable of striking heavy blows at Israel and opening the way for the establishment of an Islamic state in Palestine.[26] Islamic Jihad would make possible an escape from the double impasse into which the social works of the Brothers and the diplomatic initiatives of the weakened PLO had led. Around the concept of jihad would emerge a single movement toward Palestinian liberation—or so it was hoped.[27]

From 1983 onward, a succession of violent, high-profile attacks showed the determination of these activists. In one incident in October 1986, militants threw grenades at a party of elite Israeli conscripts on their way to take their oath at the Wailing Wall. Acts like this were supposed to shatter the aura of invincibility that the Jewish state had previously enjoyed and strike fear into the heart of the "enemy." Nevertheless, Islamic Jihad proved unable to give leadership to the movement. The Israelis targeted it for ruthless repression, and (as we will see) the intifada which it eventually sparked was quickly taken over by the PLO and the Muslim Brothers, both much more powerful organizations. Still, in the first years of the 1980s when the Palestinian movement was seemingly in decline, Islamic Jihad's leaders were inspired by the Iranian example and as a consequence played a vital role in relaunching and Islamizing the Palestinian cause. They brought a strongly Islamist dimension to the purely Arab nationalist movement that it had previously embodied.

A Legacy in Lebanon

The Iranian revolution's heaviest impact in the Middle East was felt not in Palestine, where it was merely a source of inspiration for jihad, but in neighboring Lebanon. To all appearances, the country seemed to be fertile ground for revolution. A period of civil war since 1975 had crushed the authority of the state, which was now incapable of fulfilling its constitutional role as guarantor and arbiter of the balance between Christians and Muslims. Syria's occupation of part of Lebanon's territory in June 1976, on the pretext of keeping the peace, was gradually leading to a de facto Syrian protectorate. Meanwhile, the 1982 Israeli invasion had established a security zone along the frontier between the two countries that was patrolled by the Army of South Lebanon, a militia paid by Israel. Its existence completed the shift in the balance of power by eliminating the Palestinian military presence in the area. There was a clear political vacuum, and the pro-Khomeini Shiite Hezbollah movement moved in to fill it.

Before 1982, the Shiite community was viewed as the poor relation in the Lebanese family of religions. Traditionally concentrated in the infertile zones of the Jebel Amil in the south and the Bekaa valley, the Shiites had obtained a barely adequate share of political positions in the government at the time of the 1943 National Pact—which gave the Maronite Christians the permanent presidency of the Republic and the Sunni Muslims the presidency of the Council of Ministers. The Shiites had to be content with the presidency of the Chamber of Deputies, a largely ceremonial post that was appropriated as a personal fiefdom by the members of a few prominent Lebanese Shiite families. The Shiites were mainly based in the countryside and had not shared to any great extent in the drive toward modernization and education that had created a class of elites within the other religious communities and had turned Beirut into the intellectual capital of the Arab world. In Shiite society, it was the religious dignitaries who maintained the strongest grip. The village traditions and poverty of the Shiites led to much higher birthrates than in other communities, so that by the 1970s their numbers had increased sufficiently to upset the demographic balance on which Lebanese politics was based, with no redress forthcoming. Worse, a sizable portion of the younger Shiite generation, who could no longer make a living on the land, began to migrate to the southern outskirts of the capital, where they constituted a poor, highly discontented, and very numerous bloc of urbanites who had little respect or time for the Lebanese state.[28] This unrest was markedly worse among the Shiites than among the other communities. It incorporated, in an extreme form, the principal elements that led to the emergence of

Islamist movements in the 1970s, namely, demographic explosion, rural exodus, projection to the margins of cities, and growing literacy.

It was within this milieu that a cleric arriving from Iran in 1974, Imam Musa Sadr, created the Movement of the Disinherited (Harakat al-Mahrumin), better known by the name of its militia, Amal (Hope).[29] Its objective was the social advancement of the underprivileged youth of the community. Without taking the path of religious radicalization that would characterize the Khomeinist version of Shiism, this movement achieved a transformation of attitudes comparable to the one Shariati had achieved in Iran. Sadr replaced the traditional Shiite passivity, wailing, and gnashing of teeth over the martyrdom of Imam Hussein in 680 with a movement of real protest that completely redirected the thrust of Shiite symbolism. He turned Hussein's martyrdom into the doctrinal template for a general mobilization against social injustice, which for the first time raised the despised Shiites of Lebanon to the level of a real political force by giving them a sense of personal dignity. When the civil war broke out in the following year, Amal joined the "Islamo-progressive" camp, even though Sadr himself made no secret of his hostility to socialism and communism.[30] Many young Shiites were killed fighting in the vanguard of the Muslim forces against the Christian rightists.

In August 1978, Imam Sadr himself mysteriously vanished while on a visit to Libya. Many thought he had been eliminated on the orders of Colonel Muammar el-Qaddafi, for reasons that are unclear; his most fervent supporters were convinced that, like the hidden Imam of the Shiite tradition, the Mahdi (Messiah), he would return at the end of time.[31] In any event, he was replaced as head of Amal by a secular politician, Nabih Berri, who lacked Sadr's charisma. In March of the same year, the Israelis mounted their Litani operation, a prolonged incursion into southern Lebanon designed to weaken the PLO's base. The immediate consequence was a mass exodus of Shiites to the suburbs of Beirut, swelling the ranks of impoverished young people around the capital.

Despite the social discontent of the young Lebanese Shiites and the enthusiasm with which they greeted Khomeini's victory in February 1979, both Amal and the dignitaries of the Shiite community repeatedly asserted their complete independence from events in Iran. The Lebanese clergy had produced no emblematic figure to replace the lost

Imam Sadr, and the most resolute supporters of Khomeini were to be found among the little-known younger clerics returning from their years of study in the seminaries of Najaf in Iraq. There they had learned the ideology of the velayat-e faqih and looked on while their former classmates seized power in Tehran; now they dreamed of an Islamic republic of their own. Alas, this dream seemed beyond reach in the context of Lebanon's religious diversity, while the Shiite community itself, circumscribed by the networks of Amal, appeared to be more concerned by the state of affairs in Lebanese society than with ideological experiments borrowed from Iran.

Thus, the influence of the younger clerics remained minimal until 1982. In July of that year, Israel launched its Peace in Galilee operation to drive all Palestinian military groups out of southern Lebanon and put an end to the PLO's rocket attacks on Jewish towns in northern Galilee. The Israeli army penetrated to the outskirts of Beirut, driving the PLO before it; at the beginning it received qualified sympathy from those Shiites who had bitterly resented the fedayeen's presence in the southern areas of Lebanon. For a while the Shiites seemed relieved by the expulsion of the Palestinians. But the Israeli occupation persisted, and over time this again upset the regional balance of power. Most importantly, it made possible the establishment of a pro-Western regime in Beirut, so that leaders of the Maronite community, freed of the PLO and enjoying Israeli military might as a counterweight to the power of Syria, were emboldened to sign a peace treaty with the Israelis.

The Syrian government in Damascus, which lacked the means to fight a conventional war with the Israeli armed forces in Lebanon, reacted to the Israeli presence there by encouraging the most uncompromising elements in the Shiite community to spearhead a counteroffensive against the new status quo. Syria authorized the deployment of several hundred Iranian pasdarans, or revolutionary guards, in the Bekaa valley which it controlled, thereby enabling the Islamic Republic to participate directly in Lebanese politics and giving it what was to be its only real opportunity to export its revolution with any measure of success. During the same period, a split had occurred in the ranks of Amal when the organization's official spokesman, Hassan al-Mousawi, created Islamic Amal, hewing to Khomeini's line. In the second half of 1982, Ayatollah Mohtashemi, the Islamic Republic's ambassador to Damascus, brought together various Shiite groups and clerics who shared the same views in the Bekaa, the south, and the Beirut outskirts, under the single banner of an organization that was named, after the manner of the Iranian Khomeinist party, Hezbollah (Party of Allah).[32] In December, at Baalbek, the Islamic Republic of Lebanon was proclaimed. This initiative was more symbolic than real, even though the Islamic Republic did issue its own postage stamps. It had nothing to legitimize it but the control of a portion of Lebanese territory by its religious militia, just as the Maronite and the Druze militias controlled their mountain strongholds, and the Syrian and Israeli armies controlled the east and south of the country. However, it did express Khomeini's determination to project his Islamic Revolution beyond the frontiers of Iran, and this signaled danger for Iran's enemies in the region.

For the remaining years of the 1980s, the Lebanese Hezbollah operated as an agent for the growing radicalization of the Shiite community and as a tool for Iranian policy. Within the community, a major charitable program was set in motion, with the generous logistical and financial support of Tehran.[33] Aid was distributed to the young urban poor through a network of religious clerics affiliated with the party. Thus, Hezbollah successfully brought together two of the principal components of modern Islamic movements: the disinherited young, whose ideological allegiance it contested with the more community-minded Amal, and the intellectual extremists grouped around the younger clerics. The latter quickly produced the kinds of militant views and ideology that would serve (they hoped) to galvanize the masses and project them into an Islamic utopia completely divorced from Lebanon's reality. But Hezbollah failed significantly in its attempt to attract the devout Shiite middle class, because the community's traditional leaders were attentive to the real balance of Lebanese society, to which Nabih Berri's Amal movement seemed better attuned. They preferred to keep their distance from Iran.

During the first years of Hezbollah, no devout bourgeois element existed in its leadership that proved capable of steering it toward social moderation. Since its funds came from abroad—mostly from Iran—the movement was under no domestic pressure to be politically realistic, and in consequence its radicalism knew no bounds. It blended the social violence of the disinherited, the aspirations to martyrdom of Khomeinist preachers, and the political interests of Syria and Iran, which used its acts of terrorism to further their own objectives. Syria's principal goal was to annihilate the influence of Israel and the West in Lebanon. Iran was determined to exert pressure on the West by holding its citizens hostage and creating a counterweight to the support given to Iraq by Europe and the United States during the eight years of Saddam's war, beginning in September 1980. Hezbollah took the methods of popular mobilization introduced earlier by Amal and redirected them along Khomeinist lines. For example, instead of using the celebrations of Hussein's martyrdom as a vehicle for heightened community awareness, the movement transformed them into violent demonstrations against the "enemies of Islam." Land and buildings were occupied and redistributed in the zones controlled by the party, where the government's authority could no longer protect the rights of owners. This of course made Hezbollah extremely popular among impoverished Shiite youth, from whom it was able to recruit militants prepared to embrace martyrdom for the cause, as the Iranian *bassidjis* had done on the Iraqi front. These militants in turn gave the movement a singular capability to strike wherever it wished. Other less fanatical militias had no such capability.

In 1983 Hezbollah carried out two operations that assured it instant geopolitical star status. Following the Israeli invasion, Christian militiamen had massacred Palestinian refugees in the camps of Sabra and Shatila near Beirut on the 15th and 16th of September 1982—in full view of Israeli armed forces, who did not intervene. This atrocity caused an international scandal; and a multinational force of American, Italian, and French troops was dispatched to Lebanon to prevent a repeat of it. Damascus, Tehran, and their local allies perceived this force as a reinforcement of the Western presence in Lebanon. On October 23, 1983, Hezbollah launched massive suicide attacks against the French and American contingents, followed on November 4 by bombing the Israeli army headquarters in Tyre.[34] The carnage convinced the three countries to withdraw their troops, which effectively ended the pro-Western realignment of the Lebanese state and delivered lasting hegemony in the area to Syria. The Hezbollah, a popular movement supported by Iran and encouraged by Syria, had shown itself capable of inflicting decisive military defeats on three powerful Western nations, as well as on Israel—and of following them up with a political triumph. This lent the movement an aura that was perceived well beyond the ranks of the Shiites, among all those who opposed the presence of Israel and the West in Lebanon.

In the summer of 1982, to further the interests of the Islamic Republic, Hezbollah embarked on a hostage-taking campaign, using small groups to snap up the citizens of countries on which Tehran wished to exert pressure. This campaign reached a crescendo between 1984 and 1988; a few of the kidnappings were money-driven or linked to local concerns, but most obeyed a logic whereby Hezbollah itself was no more than a subcontractor for Iranian initiatives. This perhaps explains why it never claimed responsibility for acts perpetrated by the variously named groups that signed the communiqués demanding ransoms and threatening or announcing the "executions" of their victims.[35] Instead, it presented itself as an intermediary seeking to find solutions; it even received ransom money on behalf of orphans and the disinherited, which was channeled to its social works.

Hostage-taking was the bitterest aspect of the confrontation between the Islamic Republic and its enemies in the mid-1980s. It was the means whereby Tehran loosened the stranglehold imposed by the war with Iraq and the hostility of the Arab and Western states; and it served as a dire warning that any initiative taken against Iran would be followed by terrorist retaliation. The goal of many kidnappings was to obtain freedom or amnesty for Shiite militants jailed in various countries on charges of bombings or assassinations. For example, a group of Khomeinist activists, including some Lebanese citizens, were arrested and condemned to death in Kuwait for (among other things) their part in the bombings of the U.S. and French embassies in December 1983.[36] In France, a Lebanese Shiite revolutionary, Anis Naccache, who was closely associated with the Iranian establishment, was imprisoned following an assassination attempt on Shahpur Bakhtiar, the shah's last prime minister and a determined opponent of the Islamic Republic who was living in Paris. France had lent Saddam its most advanced fighter-bomber, while refusing to repay a debt to Iran contracted in the days of the shah and linked to the European nuclear power program.[37]

By playing on public opinion in the countries concerned, Tehran's hostage-taking seriously affected domestic politics. In the case of France, major elections in 1986 and 1988 were turned to advantage by the terrorists and those controlling them. In the United States, hostage-taking sealed the fate of Jimmy Carter, who was severely defeated at the polls by Ronald Reagan after failing to find a solution to the first and most spectacular kidnapping, that of the American diplomats in Tehran, who were held for 441 days. Ironically, it also adversely affected the presidency of Carter's successor. Since the days of the shah, the United States had controlled the supply of spare parts to the Islamic Republic's army, whose materiel was almost exclusively American-made. After the storming of its Tehran embassy in 1979, the United States had retaliated by freezing all Iranian assets and arms supplies. As a result, American hostages were seized in Lebanon, so as to pressure the U.S. government into mitigating its policies. Secret negotiations were conducted in 1985 with a view to giving Iran the spare parts its armed forces so badly needed in exchange for the liberation of these hostages in Lebanon. The talks broke off when they were exposed by a faction within Iran that opposed them, thereby igniting the "Irangate" arms-for-hostages scandal that would dog Ronald Reagan throughout his tenure as president.[38]

As it turned out, Hezbollah was the only real success story in Iran's effort to export its revolution. Minor Lebanese clerics had mobilized impoverished young Shiites using themes, slogans, and actions similar to those that had been effective in Iran; the movement had then gone on to blackmail hostile states with terrorism. But these gains were circumscribed in both time and space. And nothing comparable to the Lebanese Hezbollah, which was directly inspired by Khomeini, emerged anywhere else in the Muslim world. The collapse of the Lebanese state, the fragmentation of the country into enclaves controlled by rival militias, and the various foreign contingents there all favored it. By contrast, the militant political culture of Sunni Islam was too resistant to Shiite symbolism for any significant headway to be made by the small groups of activists attempting to bridge the doctrinal gulf between the two sects. The Pakistani, Indian, and Gulf Arab Shiite communities lacked the social and demographic makeup of their brothers in Lebanon, where the recently urbanized and educated Shiite poor were far more numerous—and more genuinely disinherited—than the poor of other faiths.

Exporting the Revolution to the Muslim World

In Africa, some younger black intellectuals with a modern education saw Tehran's example as an opportunity to shake up the traditional Islam of the brotherhoods, whose rituals they found suffocating. At the same time they were eager to distance themselves from the modern European example, which they associated with colonialism and imperialism. In the early 1980s, a surge of Islamist enthusiasm in Senegal was directly attributable to the return from Iran of such a group of young intellectuals. The most prominent of these belonged to a family of *marabouts*, the Niassenes, who were members of the Tijaniyya Brotherhood. One of them founded a French-language militant paper in 1984, whose name in the Wolof language, *Wal Fadjri* (The Dawn, from the Arabic *fajr*), represented "the proclamation of a radiant sunrise after the long night that has beset the world since the death of the Prophet Muhammad . . . in the last four years, the situation has changed radically! Glory to Allah! The face of the world is transformed, and mankind's very foundations have been shaken since the project of an Islamic society has emerged as a practical and viable alternative to all others."[39] Among other things, *Wal Fadjri* published long extracts from Khomeini's writings, a defense of Iran's position against Iraq in the war, declarations on the unity of Shiite and Sunni Islam, and a series of bitter attacks on Saudi Arabia and the Organization of Islamic Conferences. One of its headlines ran: "The OIC admits Egypt to membership: the trash goes into the garbage can."[40] The founder's brother, who lived in the town of Kaolak, southeast of Dakar, earned himself the nickname the Ayatollah of Kaolak; he was much given to burning the French flag in public and issuing passionate denunciations of French imperialism and its "accomplice," traditional Islam.[41]

All this quickly aroused the hostility of the state and the pro-Saudi networks, and at the same time clashed with the vested interests of the marabouts.[42] Worse, no alternative was offered to the forms of social integration or access to resources and property procured by the Brotherhoods for their *talibes* (disciples), in exchange for their compliance. Radical movements of this type, notwithstanding the financial aid provided to some of them by the Iranians, eventually proved incapable of holding the allegiance of those young people whose enthusiasm they had at first aroused. As time passed, a few of their leaders and intellectuals were absorbed by the Brotherhoods and joined the local Islamic establishments they had formerly condemned: others transformed their militant political enterprises into successful commercial ones. *Wal Fadjri*, which began as a radical Islamist publication, has been a respectable liberal newspaper since 1994, coupled with a radio station, on-line services, and a projected privately owned TV channel.[43]

At the beginning of the 1980s the impact of the Iranian revolution was broadly similar in most other Muslim countries. Young militants from Southeast Asia, as well as from certain communist countries and Western Europe, began to make the pilgrimage to Tehran, and a few of them converted to the Shiite faith and wholeheartedly embraced the Khomeinist cause. But because there was no Shiite tradition in their home countries, most of them chose to work within already consti-tuted Sunni Islamist groups such as the ABIM in Malaysia, whose leader Anwar Ibrahim had visited Khomeini.[44] Confronted by govern-ments anxious to contain the spread of Islamist ideas, the Iranian revo-lution's inspirational message was diluted within the more general Islamist movement, within which the twin influences of Saudi Arabia and the Muslim Brothers were also very strong.[45]

Like the French and Bolshevik revolutions before it, the Iranian rev-olution held out great hopes for those in other countries who sympa-thized with its goals, and Europeans especially viewed the upsurge of militant Islamism among their immigrant Muslim populations with mounting concern. In France, for example, the mostly Iranian "stu-dents in the line of the Imam" tried in vain to mobilize immigrant workers from North Africa and convert the social conflicts of the early 1980s, notably within the automobile industry, into a Khomeini-in-spired jihad against the "satanic" West. A few tracts were distributed at the gates of striking factories, but this initiative quickly fell apart for lack of a common culture and a real presence among the grassroots working class. Most of the ringleaders in France were deported in De-cember 1983, as the atmosphere within the exiled Iranian community turned violent and the different factions began fighting among them-selves in the streets and metro stations of Paris. The French govern-ment, unsettled by a phenomenon it had failed to analyze in any depth, delegated the management and surveillance of Islam among France's two million North African residents to the Algerian authorities, which promptly took control of the Grand Mosque in Paris.[46]

In the United Kingdom, a group of pro-Iranian intellectuals formed around a journalist, Kalim Siddiqui, the founder of the Muslim Insti-tute. Siddiqui set in motion a series of radical initiatives that attracted wide press coverage; the most notable one came in the wake of the

Salman Rushdie affair in 1989 (see Chapter 8), when he created a British "Muslim Parliament" designed to ape the one at Westminster. But here again the tenuous presence of a few radical intellectuals who were held in deep suspicion by the madrassa-educated British Muslim leaders prevented the Iranian Islamic Revolution from making any significant converts once its novelty had worn off.[47]

Thus, the direct impact of these avant-garde revolutionaries remained slight, though that was not apparent at the time. In the early 1980s, people involved in politics the world over were still reeling from the unexpected Islamic Revolution in Iran and so were unable to assess its strengths and weaknesses with detachment. In the minds of some Western leaders, Islam in general became associated with the successes and excesses of the Khomeinists. But as leaders in Tehran were aware from a very early stage, the revolution was far more vulnerable than it appeared to outsiders. The international conferences and congresses the Khomeinists organized attracted only marginal Islamist intellectuals and young ulemas, few of whom carried any weight in the religious councils of their home countries. The Iranian propaganda apparatus and the polyglot publications it distributed could not begin to compete with the heavy artillery of the Saudis.

For this reason, Iran, following its own line of Islamic populism, chose to concentrate on what was at once Saudi Arabia's weakest point and its principal token of legitimacy—namely, the organization of the annual pilgrimage to Mecca. The leadership in Tehran felt quite competent to galvanize crowds of militant pilgrims within a gathering of at least two million, after having successfully orchestrated the mass demonstrations that led to the triumph of the Islamic Revolution. Mecca is deeply venerated within the Shiite tradition, even though the faithful also journey in great numbers to the holy places of their own saints—the tombs of Imams and members of the family of the Prophet at Najaf and Karbala in Iraq, Machad and Qum in Iran, and the Damascus mausoleum of Sayeda Zeinab in Syria. The symbolic importance of the largest gathering of Muslims on earth had already been noted by revolutionary Shiite thinkers, and Ali Shariati himself had written a book detailing the uses that might be made of it by the disinherited in their struggle against the enemies of Islam. The first hajj after the revolution, in September 1979, offered a golden opportunity for Iranian pilgrims to make their opinions known without directly locking horns with the

Saudi authorities, against whom they had two major complaints. In the first place, the Wahhabite conception of the pilgrimage was seen as hostile to Shiite sensibilities, given that the Saudi Custodians of the Holy Places had demolished the tombs of the imams in Medina, leaving no trace of them beyond nameless ruins within a high-walled cemetery.[48] Second, the care taken by the Saudi monarchy to prevent any kind of trouble was in direct contrast to the revolutionary spirit with which the Iranian leadership viewed the event.

The first serious incidents took place during the 1981 hajj. Despite the warnings of the authorities in Mecca and a succession of prior negotiations with Tehran, a section of the 65,000-strong Iranian contingent defied the Saudi monarchy by brandishing portraits of Khomeini and chanting anti-American slogans at the wellspring of Saudi Arabia's authority and pre-eminence in the Islamic world. For Iran, whose territory had been invaded a year earlier by the Iraqi army with the implicit support of the Arab states, the pilgrimage had provided an opportunity for a confrontation in which it had no reason to show the slightest restraint. In 1982, the Saudi authorities, fearing new incidents that might further tarnish their legitimacy, were obliged again to negotiate with Khomeini's representative on the pilgrimage, the hojjat-ul-Islam Khoeiniha, a singularly virulent cleric who had recently inspired the students of Tehran to overrun the American Embassy. To no avail: demonstrations took place nonetheless, leading to pitched battles with the police, scores of injuries, and hundreds of arrests. Khoeiniha himself was one of those detained.

From 1983 to 1986, the two adversaries reached a compromise that clearly exposed the weakness of the Saudis' position and their need at all costs to avoid conflicts that would be disastrous for their image. In exchange for an Iranian pledge of moderation, they had to accept an enlargement of the Iranian pilgrim contingent to 150,000 people and allow them to hold gatherings not only to exalt their revolution but also to verbally abuse its enemies both within Islam and outside it.[49] Thus, the Riyadh monarchy managed to save face only by making concessions in an area where it had formally exercised absolute sovereignty.[50] Meanwhile, the war with Iraq had turned to Iran's advantage, and Saudi prudence appeared eminently advisable.

The 1987 pilgrimage took a far more dramatic turn. On July 31, following an authorized demonstration at Mecca, the Iranians were suspected by the Saudi police of an intent to surround and take over the Grand Mosque. They were prevented from approaching it. The fighting that followed left over four hundred dead and horrified the entire Muslim world. The exact circumstances were unclear, with each party blaming the other: what was certain was that four years of relative truce had come to an abrupt end. In November, Iran called a conference with the stated aim of liberating Mecca from the "clutches of the Saud family," but the international participants were confined to the usual fellow travelers of the Islamic Revolution. No other major political force in the Muslim world would back Iran. The month before, an extraordinary session of the Muslim World League had been fully attended by partisans of the Saudi version of events, and now it was clear that the political advantage had swung back in the direction of Saudi Arabia, which regained full control of the hajj by achieving an Islamic consensus in favor of re-establishing order.

In the year that followed, Saudi Arabia won agreement at a session of the Organization of the Islamic Conference for its project to attribute to each Muslim country the quota of one pilgrim for every thousand inhabitants. Iran, finding its contingent reduced by two thirds and all demonstrations explicitly banned, had no choice but to boycott the pilgrimage altogether and break diplomatic relations with the kingdom.[51] About the same time, Iraq's armed forces went back on the offensive, and on July 18, 1988, Iran had to accept a cease-fire, bringing the eight-year war to an end. To safeguard the revolution, Ayatollah Khomeini had been forced to "drink the poisoned chalice" and renounce his vow to "punish the aggressor" Saddam Hussein. The Saudi regime immediately took advantage of Tehran's weakened state to regain full control of the pilgrimage to Mecca. Iran continued to boycott the hajj in 1989, showing clearly that it had lost the initiative on this front.

But in the meantime it had regained it elsewhere, with the death sentence on Salman Rushdie issued by Khomeini's fatwa on February 14. Once again, the revolution had devised a spectacular initiative to escape the clutches of its enemies.

6

Jihad in Afghanistan and Intifada in Palestine

For the leaders of the United States and their conservative Arab allies, particularly Saudi Arabia, the Islamic Revolution in Iran was a source of growing concern. In its first months, the ferocity of its anti-Western and revolutionary slogans had caused alarm, but America had remained in touch with the government of Mehdi Bazargan nevertheless. The events of late 1979, however, dramatically changed the way the United States and its allies viewed the revolution. The takeover of the American Embassy in Tehran and the internment of its staff on November 4 were followed immediately by the Soviet Army's invasion of Afghanistan at the end of December. In the Cold War world, in which anything that was bad for Washington was good for Moscow and vice versa, the dramatic confluence of these two events brought the region into the geopolitical spotlight as never before. The Islamic Revolution had disturbed the West and its Muslim allies because of its unpredictable nature and its violent religious language. At the same time, by destabilizing one of the United States' principal military allies in the world's richest oil-producing region, the revolution made it easier for the Soviet Union to fill the political void. In rushing to the aid of a beleaguered communist government in Afghanistan, the Soviets appeared suddenly to be very close and threatening. Thus, the Islamist question became part and parcel of the wider American-Soviet struggle, whose end—paradoxically—it would eventually hasten. In December 1979, the Soviet Union appeared to have everything going its way: the Red Army was in Kabul and the Americans were humiliated in Tehran. Yet within ten years the Soviet system had collapsed, and the Afghanistan debacle had been a key contributor to its demise.

The American strategy of containment, designed to "trap the Russian bear," turned on massive aid to the Afghan resistance, a large proportion of whose members belonged to the Islamist movement: indeed, all of the mujahedeen claimed to be Muslims of one kind or another.[1] Saudi Arabia and the wealthy conservative monarchies of the Gulf also contributed freely to the Afghan jihad. All were glad to join the United States in an effort to keep the Soviet Union out of their backyard, while providing an outlet as radical as that of the Iranian revolution, though distinct from it, for all the Sunni Islamist militants who dreamed of striking a blow at the impious, as Khomeini had done. By making the Afghan jihad the central militant cause of the 1980s, the Saudi government shielded their American ally—which supported the holy war—against the wrath of Sunni activists, making sure that the Soviet Union would replace America as their principal scapegoat.

Thus, Saudi Arabia and the Gulf monarchies were able to burnish their prestige and religious legitimacy, despite the continuing verbal broadsides from Tehran. But their allies were far from predictable—especially the Afghan mujahedeen (of whom only a very few factions adhered to the Wahhabite line) and the partisans of Armed Jihad, the most extreme wing of the worldwide Islamist movement. In the camps and training centers around Peshawar—the capital of the Pakistani Northwest Frontier province where three million Afghan refugees were living—there was a great gathering of international Islamists.[2] Arabs mixed with Afghans and other Muslims from every corner of the world and exchanged ideas based on their different traditions. Arab funds, abundant American weaponry, and trade in heroin were the mainstays of camp life, which was heavily infiltrated by the Pakistani Inter-Service Intelligence agency (ISI) and the American CIA, as well as by the leading organizations of Pakistani Islamism, notably Mawdudi's Jamaat-e-Islami and the Deobandi madrassas.[3] For once these organizations were prepared to go beyond their local bases into the arena of international Islam; and as they did so, many unexpected ideological cross-fertilizations and grafts emerged. In general, that network answered the purposes of the states that had underwritten it (the United States, Saudi Arabia, the Gulf states, and Pakistan) by playing a key role in the discomfiture of the Soviets and creating a focus of attention for the jihadists of the world, as well as an alternative to the Iranian revolution. At the same time, however, the network developed its own logic, which before long began to work against its original patrons.[4]

When the Red Army intervened in Afghanistan in December 1979, the Soviet Union's objective was to come to the aid of an ally in difficulty, as it had done after the "Prague spring" in Czechoslovakia in 1968. The Afghan communists had seized power on April 27, 1978, with a coup d'état by officers committed to socialism. This group was divided into two factions, the People's Party (Khalq) and the Party of the Flag (Parcham). Like their inveterate enemies the militant Islamists, the coup officers were drawn mostly from the first Afghan generation to be educated in towns at modern, Western-style schools.[5] At the insistence of the Soviet leadership, which feared a rapprochement between the Afghan regime and the two allies of America—Iran under the shah and Pakistan under General Zia ul-Haq—in December 1978 the Afghan leaders signed a treaty of friendship that bound their country to the Soviet Union. They went on to implement a policy of radical agrarian reform, compulsory literacy, and the imposition of socialism, through thousands of arrests and summary executions. Not surprisingly, this alienated the bulk of the population. The khalq faction, the most extreme, then wiped out the parcham in a purge that reached into the leadership of the khalq itself: the parcham leaders who survived went into exile in Moscow.[6] In April 1979 there was a general uprising, and by December of that year the party had lost control of all but the cities and was facing a rising tide of resistance accompanied by the wholesale emigration of trained officials fleeing the purges. The Soviet intervention of December 27 was designed to halt the regime's suicidal policies, which threatened the very foundations of the "socialist edifice." The head of the khalq was executed and replaced by his parcham rival, Babrak Karmal, who had arrived with the Soviet troops.

In the West, the Russian advance on Kabul was viewed with horror. It was understood as a fresh twist on the "great game" played between the British and the Russians in the nineteenth century, in which the czar's ultimate objective was to win access to the Indian Ocean and Britain's was to block him. In the post-1945 context, the invasion of Afghanistan was construed as an explicit violation of the world balance of power agreed upon at Yalta, and as a threat to Western security that was all the greater for Afghanistan's proximity to the Persian Gulf oil fields. For their part, the leaders of the Muslim world were divided over this new development and uncertain how they should react to it. In 1979 the USSR still had a number of clients in the Arab world—Syria, South Yemen, the PLO, and Algeria were all dependent on Soviet support—and none of these wished to embarrass Moscow. The summit of the Organization of the Islamic Conference at Taif, Saudi Arabia, in January 1981, which had reached a consensus on the idea of launching a jihad for the liberation of Jerusalem and Palestine, refused to do the same for Afghanistan.[7] Instead, it confined itself to calling on all Islamic states to cooperate with the UN secretary general in bringing an end to a situation that was "prejudicial to the Afghan people."[8]

The call for a jihad in Afghanistan and its day-to-day implementation were not initiated by Muslim states as such but by transnational Islamic religious networks. They were assembled around ulemas and institutions that were already in place, such as the Muslim World League, or created ad hoc by the conservative salafists, whose ideology fell somewhere between Saudi Wahhabism and the Muslim Brothers. The Afghan jihad saw itself as an offshoot of ordinary Muslim society, and it rode a wave of popular approval not unlike the one Khomeini enjoyed, with his exaltation of the "Islam of the people." At the outset, ulemas with recognized credentials issued fatwas interpreting the Soviet intervention as an invasion of the territory of Islam (dar el-Islam) by the impious. This made it possible to proclaim a "defensive" jihad, which, according to the sharia, obliged every individual Muslim to participate (fard ayn).[9] The operation was delicate, however, because transnational fatwas called on the allegiance of believers to a cause to which their own government might be opposed (for instance, if the government were allied to the Soviet Union), and as such were an intrinsic threat to social order. Furthermore, the fluidity of the Islamic religion and the absence of a hierarchy of authority within it (in contrast with Catholicism, for example) made it very easy to manipulate. The more intransigent ulemas might use such a fatwa as an excuse for the declaration of a jihad elsewhere, thus creating an uncontrollable spiral of disorder and violence, as actually occurred in the late 1980s.

It was vital, then, that the appeal to all Muslims to join in the jihad in Afghanistan should be both widely broadcast, like its Iranian alternative, and meticulously controlled, so that it would not one day turn upon its instigators. The Saudi promoters of the operation had to walk a tightrope. Until the mid-1980s, international Islamic solidarity was expressed largely in financial terms. It complemented America's military support of the Afghan mujahedeen and was channeled by Pakistani institutions and associations, who redistributed aid to those closer to them. But from 1985 onward, it took the form of growing numbers of foreign jihadists, most of them Arabs, who gathered at Peshawar and then moved on to Afghanistan itself.

The Afghan mujahedeen belonged to a heterogeneous group of movements under the umbrella of Islam, through which they expressed their outraged rejection of the communism that had been imposed from above by the April 1978 coup. They ranged from adherents of traditional Sufi mystical groups to the Muslim Brothers and sundry devotees of the Wahhabite doctrine. In social, ethnic, political, and military terms, the various movements of the mujahedeen included several distinct components. There was an obvious fault line between the predominantly urban and student make-up of the Islamist associations and the more traditional religious groups from rural and tribal backgrounds. The former were inspired by the Egyptian Muslim Brothers, with whom the founding generation of Afghan Islamists had studied at Al Azhar in Cairo. After its first appearance in 1958 in the theology faculty in Kabul, this movement had continued to develop gradually throughout the 1960s, when the works of Qutb and Mawdudi were being translated. In 1968, the Organization of Muslim Youth was founded in Afghanistan and went on to win the 1970 student elections.[10] As in other countries, the applied science departments (engineering and so on) provided a significant platform for recruitment.

In contrast with the Islamist intellectuals of Egypt and Iran, who were seeking in the mid-1970s to mobilize impoverished urban youth, their Afghan brothers lived in a country where, at that time, more than 85 percent of the population still dwelled in the countryside. There had been no full-scale migration to the cities, and most young people in Afghanistan were controlled by rural networks of brotherhoods and tribal structures. Like the communists, who emerged from the same student-based, urban milieus and methodically infiltrated the Afghan army until they were ready for the putsch of April 1978, the Islamist militants tried to compensate for their relative lack of influence among the ordinary populace by seizing power in a coup d'état. An uprising launched in the summer of 1975 was swiftly crushed, however, and the surviving activists fled to Peshawar, where their movement experienced its first major schism.[11]

This schism had an ethnic as well as a political dimension. The Jamiat-e-Islami (Islamic Association), led by Burhanuddin Rabbani, a graduate of Al Azhar, specifically set out to recruit Persian speakers; at the same time, it sought common ground with tribal leaders and the non-Islamist and anti-communist intelligentsia.[12] As a result, it evolved toward a moderate version of Islamism, which made it popular with the Western friends of the Afghan resistance but narrowed its possibilities of access to the Saudi system. Conversely, the Hezb-e-Islami (Islamic party) led by Gulbuddin Hekmatyar, a former activist from the Kabul University engineering faculty, preferred to enroll members of the Pashtun tribe and was implacably hostile to any form of political compromise. This gave the Islamic party great credit with the Muslim Brothers, Mawdudi's Pakistani Jamaat-e-Islami, and the Saudi networks.

At the time of the communist coup in April 1978, the Afghan Islamist intellectuals were isolated: their ideas had not taken root among the general population, and they themselves were forced into exile. But the policies of the new masters of Kabul, which amounted to a forced march toward socialism, provoked a massive uprising in the name of religion, which was at first perceived as a resistance for safeguarding Afghan identity in the face of a determined communist attempt to destroy the culture.[13] This allowed the Islamists to secure a respect in Afghan society that they had formerly lacked. However, in the year before the Soviet intervention, most of the revolts going on in Afghanistan were still organized by the tribes or by the traditional religious factions; and among the Islamists it was the jamiat of Rabbani that seized control of the movement, largely because of the battlefield successes of Commandant Ahmed Shah Massoud.

The Red Army's invasion suddenly thrust the majority of Afghans into the resistance. They signed up spontaneously or else were obliged to do so because Soviet bombings and the destruction of crops and herds had driven them from the land and turned them into mujahedeen operating from bases close to the frontier. At the same time, massive foreign aid was provided to them: they were perceived by the West as freedom fighters and by the Saudis as the vanguard of the Umma and the jihad. The "Afghan cause" received disproportionate means with which to wage war, and this would quickly change its scope and meaning. In Peshawar, the resistance was made up of a coalition of seven parties that the Pakistani authorities recognized and to whom it distributed arms, ammunition, and funds from foreign governments. All this was orchestrated by the government of General Zia ul-Haq, who had implemented the sharia in Pakistan in 1979 and who was backed by the Jamaat-e-Islami founded by Mawdudi. This party was the main channel of Arab financial aid to the resistance, and it naturally favored the group that was closest to it, Hekmatyar's Hezb party.[14] Access to Saudi largesse was also the main reason for the creation in 1980 of an Islamist party that was virtually nonexistent in the field but whose leader, Abdul Rasul Sayyaf, an eloquent speaker of Arabic and a man of impeccable Wahhabite credentials, was henceforth to receive ample subsidies.[15] Groups closest to the Wahhabites and the Muslim Brothers got the lion's share of funds.[16] Thus the seven parties—three traditional and four Islamist—saw their funds allocated according to ideological criteria that placed Hekmatyar and Sayyaf in a position of clear advantage, while Rabbani's less-favored jamiat owed its share to the military successes of Massoud against the Soviets, which were hailed as victories of the jihad as a whole.[17]

The transplanting of the parties onto Pakistani soil, in the midst of three million refugees, also favored the spread of Islamist militant ideas over those of traditional Islam, with its emphasis on symbolic sites, the land, and the hierarchies of rural and tribal society. The first generation of literate, urbanized Afghans were educated in the camps of Peshawar, through the networks controlled by the Hezb party. The Hezb used its massive Arab subsidies to build a recruiting base within the now "detribalized" younger generation, which had been transformed by the circumstances of their exile into an impoverished urban youth that was highly receptive to Islamist ideology.[18] This educational effort was also extended by the Deobandi madrassa network over all the rest of Pakistan. The children of the Afghan refugees were taken in by the madrassas as boarders, cut off from their families and traditional environments, and made to mix with young Pakistanis of different ethnic origins—Pashtuns like themselves, but also Punjabis, Sindhis, and Baluchis.[19] Classes were conducted in Arabic and Urdu, and they contributed toward the building of a "universal Islamic personality" structured around Deobandi ideology. This was perfectly adapted to a population of young refugees with no state of their own that they could trust to apply the laws of Islam. Crucially, they were educated to put Deobandi doctrines into action through obedience to the fatwas produced in the madrassas in a spirit of conservatism and religious rigor.

This host of young Afghans, trained in the spirit of jihad at schools to which nobody had paid much attention previously, gave birth to a hybrid movement. In the decade that followed, when these Afghans came of age, they formed the mainstay of the Taliban in Afghanistan and of the Sunni extremist militants of the Sipah-e-sahaba in Pakistan, the Army of the Companions of the Prophet, who massacred Shiites and carried the jihad to Kashmir. Unlike the Hezb Islamists of Hekmatyar, whose goal was to "Islamize modernity," meaning to domesticate Western techniques and knowledge and put them to work on behalf of the Islamic state, "fundamentalists" of the Deobandi persuasion rejected such things out of hand. From the creation of Pakistan in 1947 until they became enthused by the spirit of jihad in the 1980s, their project for society had avoided all political violence.[20] Their sudden adoption of violent methods was one of the more unexpected effects of the Islamist ferment in southwest Asia during that decade.

For General Zia ul-Haq, who had been mistrusted by the West ever since his execution of Ali Bhutto in March 1979, the Afghan imbroglio arrived at the right moment to strengthen his regime. In a region shaken to its foundations by the ongoing chaos in Iran, Pakistan became the strategic hub of American policy and the beneficiary of the fourth largest foreign aid package voted annually by Congress.[21] Zia was the intermediary in everything that affected the Afghan resistance. By 1982 the jihad was receiving $600 million in U.S. aid per year, with a matching amount coming from the Gulf states.[22] This steady flow of money spurred the nation's economic growth and stabilized the regime. The downside was the wholesale theft of aid money, to which all parties turned a blind eye as long as the Russians remained in Afghanistan but whose devastating consequences opened the way to far worse things as the decade drew to a close. Huge consignments of light weaponry were delivered by the CIA and unloaded at the port of Karachi; much of it was promptly sold on the local market before the residue could be trucked overland to its official recipients, and as a result Karachi became one of the most violent cities in the world. For the return journey, the trucks were loaded with heroin extracted from poppies grown in Afghanistan and in tribal zones along the Pakistani frontier and exported via Karachi.[23] The greed and profits resulting from the criminal side effects of American and Arab aid to the resistance swiftly became a major headache for the United States. Later, following the Soviet withdrawal from Afghanistan, the Arab states inherited the problem when heavily armed, uncontrolled groups backed by access to such funds began propagating jihad wherever they chose.

Arab aid, which was unfettered by the kinds of legal constraints prevailing in the United States, came from a variety of public and private sources. Beyond their avowed intent to check the growing power of Khomeini's Iran on the Islamic world scene, these funds produced a whole range of delicate coordination and attribution problems. Three arms of the Saudi administration (the intelligence services directed by Prince Turki Al-Faisal, the ad hoc support committee chaired by Prince Salman, the governor of Riyadh, and the Muslim World League) formed the main channels of transmission.[24] But in order for aid to reach those for whom it was intended and serve the interests of its donors, in a region where it was open to all manner of abuse, and given the huge sums at stake, trustworthy agents were needed on the spot. Thus, Arab volunteers were recruited to make the journey to the Pakistani-Afghan arena—an area of the world which until that time had been largely unknown to them. Initially, they served as correspondents of the Saudi Red Crescent and the other Islamic humanitarian agencies. But from about the middle of the decade onward, they came as combatants in the jihad, at least to receive training in the handling of weapons, if not to use them against Soviet troops.

Throughout the 1980s, the key figure among these Afghan Arabs, as they came to be known, was a Palestinian university professor named Abdallah Azzam. A Muslim Brother, Azzam acted as the connection between these Arabs and Wahhabite interests in Saudi Arabia and presided over the doctrinal back-and-forth between the Afghan and Palestinian causes. Intellectually, he helped place the Palestinian cause firmly within an Islamic perspective, as the December 1987 intifada got under way in the occupied territories, as we will see. And finally, he was the leading contemporary mouthpiece of the jihad, popularizing the concept of armed Islamic struggle that would be developed further in the 1990s by much more radical activists, notably the Algerian GIA.

Azzam was born near Jenin in northern Palestine in 1941.[25] He studied the sharia in Damascus between 1959 and 1966, where he joined the Muslim Brothers at the age of eighteen, becoming their representative at the Syrian university level in 1960. After taking part in the Arab-Israeli war of 1967, he was one of the few Islamists to become involved in armed struggle against Israel at a time when the Palestinian Muslim Brothers were favoring charitable and social work over political activism. In 1970, the year of the PLO's Black September in Jordan, Azzam broke with the Palestinian leadership, whom he accused of committing their forces to the overthrow of King Hussein instead of the struggle against the Jewish state. After completing his studies at Al Azhar in Cairo and receiving his doctorate in 1973, he became a professor of the sharia at the University of Jordan, while supervising the university's youth sector for the Muslim Brothers. Upon being evicted from his university post a few years later, he moved to Jeddah in Saudi Arabia, where he taught at Abd al-Aziz University. One of his students there was the young Osama bin Laden.

Around this time he rejoined the Muslim World League and was placed in charge of its education sector. According to his hagiography, which was published after his assassination, he met a group of Afghan pilgrims in Mecca in 1980; moved by what they told him, "he concluded that the cause he had sought for so long was the cause of the Afghan people"—a formula that was all the more remarkable in that, as a Palestinian, Azzam embodied that which was held to be the Arab cause par excellence. But by the 1980s the Palestinian struggle had lost its luster for Islamist militants; indeed, Azzam's engagement in the Afghan cause via a pious jihad made it possible for him to place the predicament of his own people in a new perspective. According to other sources, he was sent to Islamabad by the Muslim World League to teach at the International Islamic University that opened there in 1980—an institution funded in part by the league and supervised by the Muslim Brothers.[26]

In 1984 Azzam moved to Peshawar and in 1985 took part in the creation of the Council of Islamic Coordination, which included a score of Arab "humanitarian Islamic organizations" in support of the Afghan resistance, under the aegis of the Red Crescent of Kuwait and Saudi Arabia, the two main contributors of the 600 million Arab dollars given annually to the Afghan resistance.[27] He proved to be a trustworthy partner for the Saudi establishment, and with his religious erudition was able to exercise a strong influence on the unpredictable jihadists who had begun to pour into Pakistan from the Middle East. In 1984 Azzam founded the Bureau of Services to the Mujahedeen to receive, supervise, and organize all these people.

In December of that year, the first issue of his magazine *Al Jihad*—priced in dollars and Saudi rials—was published in Arabic.[28] *Al Jihad* galvanized fresh support for the Afghan cause. In addition to news from the front, it contained doctrinal texts and editorials written by Azzam that were immediately republished as tracts throughout the Arabic-speaking world, before being translated into local languages and English. Eventually they would furnish the material for an Internet site that popularized the ideas of their author within the international Islamist movement.[29]

Azzam's priority was to demonstrate that the jihad in Afghanistan was an obligation for all good Muslims. This was the theme of his best-known booklet, *Defending the Land of the Muslims Is Each Man's Most Important Duty*.[30] For this, he invoked the authority of eight ulemas who had issued fatwas on the subject, notably Sheik Ben Baz, the future mufti of Saudi Arabia, and other Wahhabites and Muslim Brothers such as the Syrian Said Hawwa and the Egyptian Salah Abu Ismail. Every Muslim, he proclaimed, had an obligation to participate morally *(bi-l-nafs)* and financially *(bi-l-mal)* in jihad.[31] In effect, "If the enemy has entered Muslim lands, the jihad becomes an individual obligation according to all doctors of the law, all commentators of the Sacred Texts, and all the scholars of tradition (those who assembled the words and deeds of the Prophet)."[32] In this, Azzam rose up against any man who would call the jihad "a collective obligation" *(fard kifaya)* to be left to the politicians, who would advise Muslims against going to Afghanistan, and who would take the view that "it was better at this time to acquire learning than to join the jihad."[33]

The burden of his argument was that the faithful committed a capital sin if they did not participate morally and financially in the Afghan holy war.[34] Moreover, any Muslim who considered himself capable of doing so had the right to take up arms without the authorization of any other individual, "not even the authorization of the Commander of the Faithful, if such a one exists."[35] It followed that the "impious" leaders of certain Muslim countries had no right to intervene. Afghanistan was merely the first example of an Islamic land usurped by infidels, whose reconquest by jihad was absolutely required. "This duty shall not lapse with victory in Afghanistan, and the jihad will remain an individual obligation until all other lands which formerly were Muslim come back to us and Islam reigns within them once again. Before us lie Palestine, Bukhara, Lebanon, Chad, Eritrea, Somalia, the Philippines, Burma, South Yemen, Tashkent, Andalusia . . . Our presence in Afghanistan today, which is the accomplishment of the imperative of jihad and of our devotion to the struggle, does not mean that we have forgotten Palestine. Palestine is our beating heart, it comes even before Afghanistan in our minds, our hearts, our feelings and our faith."[36]

These writings of Azzam belong to a great tradition of jihad doctrine within Islam that has existed since medieval times. His predecessors were the authors of the Hanbali school, especially Ibn Taymiyya, whom he quotes freely. The novelty of Azzam's work lies not so much in its content as in its context. Other contemporary Islamist writers called for a jihad before he did, but their effect was purely rhetorical, because there were no organized masses to make them a reality. The jihad for the liberation of Jerusalem, for example, was scarcely more than a religious gloss on the state of war with Israel, directed on the battlefield by the Arab states and to a lesser extent by the PLO. These entities operated in accordance with their own political or national imperatives, and until the intifada of December 1987 those imperatives were very far from condoning a popular uprising. But Azzam's exhortations were delivered under entirely different circumstances, because what he called for actually came about. He spoke directly to would-be activists from all over the Muslim world, most from Arab countries (between 8,000 and 25,000 according to some estimates), who had come of their own accord and who had full access to weapons and training camps.[37] Azzam himself attracted an important retinue, and he was frequently seen in the company of Egyptian Sheik Omar Abdel Rahman, who visited Peshawar regularly after 1985 to stir up the Arab combatants and generally preach jihad with the blessing of the CIA and Saudi diplomats.

Strictly speaking, the Arabs seem to have played only a minor part in fighting the Red Army.[38] Their feats of arms were largely perpetrated after the Soviet withdrawal in February 1989 and were highly controversial. In March of that year, during the siege of Jalalabad, an Arab contingent won notoriety by chopping "atheist" Afghan prisoners into small pieces and packing them in boxes. This caused consternation in the ranks of the Afghan mujahedeen.[39] For the international jihadists, the journey to Peshawar was above all an initiation, a socialization of the Islamist networks; thereafter, for some of them, it turned into a radicalization process, as they came into contact with militants who were much more extreme than their Saudi sponsors. In the mid-1980s, "jihad tours" were arranged for rich young Saudis, who attended summer camps lasting several weeks. The experience included a foray across the border and photographs taken on location. From time to time they encountered representatives of European humanitarian organizations, to whom they showed the strongest antipathy. Later, young militants from the poorer classes—East Asians, North Africans, and even a few "Beurs" from the outskirts of French cities—were sent to spend some weeks taking part in the jihad. The ostensible purpose was to strengthen their devotion to the cause and to give them a taste of war that would help them carry the fight to their own impious leaders back home.

Eventually, the most experienced activists, some of whom had already served prison sentences in their own countries (such as a good many of the Egyptian Islamists arrested after Sadat's assassination in October 1981), began to assemble around Peshawar. Their presence was facilitated by the sympathy of private Arab benefactors, while the states that had jailed them were relieved to see them vanish into the mountains of Afghanistan. These were educated men, many of whom were fluent in English and competent with computers; indeed, some of them were valued informers for the Pakistani and American intelligence services. Osama bin Laden, scion of a family of construction magnates in Saudi Arabia and the Gulf, was an emblematic jihadist figure; because he belonged to the Saudi inner circle, his religious zeal was deemed harmless both to the monarchy, with which his family's business was closely linked, and to the American agencies, for whom this well-born young man was an ally in the struggle against communism.

After the Soviets withdrew from Afghanistan in February 1989, the Americans reduced their aid to the resistance, which now showed itself incapable of bringing down the Kabul regime. Since November 1987 the Afghan government had been led by Muhammad Najibullah, former head of the KHAD, the Afghan equivalent of the KGB. The debacle of the communists, whose empire in Eastern Europe collapsed the same year, led to the dissolution of the Soviet Union in December 1991 and the consequent withdrawal of the Afghan question from America's list of strategic priorities. For Saudi Arabia, the struggle with Iran for precedence in the Islamic world no longer presented the threat of ten years earlier; in July 1988 Ayatollah Khomeini himself had been forced to make peace with Iraq. His country was exhausted and his pilgrims had been unable to make the hajj to Mecca because of his refusal to submit to pilgrim quotas. From Washington's standpoint, there seemed to be no bona fide freedom fighters left in Peshawar.

Moreover, members of the U.S. Congress had begun to express alarm at the burgeoning heroin trade and the involvement in it of mujahedeen leaders. Hekmatyar and Sayyaf were branded as extremists who were no better than Najibullah; their supplies of American arms were abruptly cut off. At the same time, the Arab states began to express concern at the prospect of Kabul falling into the hands of Islamist extremists in alliance with militants made more effective by exile in the land of the jihad. It was within this context of increasing international skepticism and bitter internal rivalries within the resistance itself that Abdallah Azzam was killed on November 24 by anonymous assassins. Thus, the herald of the jihad—who now wanted to redirect it toward Palestine—was eliminated at the precise moment when some of those who had supported him in the Muslim world were letting it be known that as soon as the Russians were gone, the fight would be over.

Nevertheless, Saudi Arabia and the Pakistani intelligence services pressed on with their aid to Hekmatyar. Benazir Bhutto, who had come to power in Pakistan after Zia's death in August 1988, was unable to do anything about this, despite her hostility to the Afghan ally of her sworn enemy, the Jamaat-e-Islami. But the disunity of the mujahedeen, the solid positions in northeastern Afghanistan held by Commandant Massoud, Hekmatyar's main rival, and the continuing resistance of Najibullah's regime all combined to prevent the Hezb leader from taking Kabul and setting up the hoped-for Islamic state, friendly to Saudi Arabia and a docile client of Pakistan. Afghanistan itself was divided into many zones, each controlled by warlords who were more or less affiliated with one another but fundamentally attached to their ethnic and tribal bases. Many of these survived only by trading in arms and opium. By 1990, the spirit of jihad was rapidly yielding to dissension (fitna) in the Community of the Faithful.

As Central Asia was drifting into disarray, Saddam Hussein invaded Kuwait on August 2, initiating events that would lead to the Gulf War—and posing a much greater threat to Saudi Arabia's supremacy in the Islamic world than Iran ever had. Hekmatyar and his followers in Afghanistan, along with a substantial majority of Arab jihadists, took sides against Riyadh, effectively turning against their principal sponsor. This in the long run was to sound the death knell of the "modern" Islamists in Afghanistan and open the way for the Taliban to seize power there. It also began the scattering of Arab jihadists to every remote corner of the earth.

The Islamization of the Palestinian Cause

During the 1980s, the Islamic world to some extent marginalized the Middle East by focusing so hard on the rivalry between Saudia Arabia and Iran. The lines of force moved eastward—to the Iran-Iraq battlefront during the war between those two countries, and then on to Afghanistan and Pakistan during the years of the jihad. The Palestinian cause, which formerly embodied the Arab identity and gave it its clearest direction, had lost much of its militant capacity and attraction. Weakened by Israeli repression in the occupied territories, the PLO had compromised its original message with its inglorious foray into Lebanon's complex civil war, before being expelled militarily from Lebanon after the 1982 Israeli invasion. Finally, in December 1983, Arafat and his loyalists were forced to evacuate Tripoli in Northern Lebanon, following a Syrian offensive in support of the Palestinian groups opposing the PLO; the strength and boldness of this opposition had increased as the PLO faltered.

With the intifada, which began in late 1987, the Palestinian cause regained the aura it had lost. This movement won worldwide attention and local popularity through its street tactics, whereby young Palestinians armed with nothing but stones confronted the Israeli army of occupation. This uprising caused such severe damage to the international image of the Jewish state and its moral identity that Israeli leaders were forced to consider an official recognition of the PLO. The process began to take shape after the 1990–91 Gulf War and eventually resulted in an Israeli-Palestinian "declaration of principle" in September 1993, along with the July 1994 installation of an autonomous Palestinian authority in Gaza led by Yasir Arafat.[40]

In recovering its prestige through the intifada, the Palestinian cause also partly altered its image. Previously, it had embodied Arab nationalism and a set of ideals that, on the international stage, fitted naturally into the socialist, Third World camp. It had remained outside the emerging "zone of Islamic influence." The jihad in Afghanistan had supplanted Palestine as a pole of identity and even as a battlefield for many young Arabs, though Abdallah Azzam unflaggingly reminded his readers that Palestine and Afghanistan were part of the same struggle among all Muslims whose lands had been "usurped by the enemy." The 1970s Palestinian camps in Lebanon had been replaced in the imaginations of the young by the jihadist camps of Peshawar. The financial priorities of the Gulf oil states had altered accordingly, a fact lamented by a PLO leader of the time, who said he would have been happy if his organization could receive "only 10% of the aid sent to the mujahedeen in Afghanistan."[41] The intifada altered all these perceptions, allowing the Islamists to raise their profile dramatically in the occupied territories, especially Gaza. The PLO was visibly losing its monopoly on the symbolic representation of the Palestinians, and it would have to fight hard henceforth to keep overall control.

By this point, the Islamic Jihad group, which drew its inspiration from Khomeini's example, had burst onto the scene by spectacularly murdering a number of Israeli soldiers. It managed to reconcile the struggle against Israel with Islamist demands, in contrast to the nonreligious but militarily engaged PLO and the devout but politically quiescent Muslim Brothers. However, Islamic Jihad was unable to build a mass following or even a network of support within the population. The emergence of a powerful Islamist movement initiated by the intifada was principally due to a change of heart among the Muslim Brothers, who abandoned their traditional quiescent stance and embarked on a jihad against the Israeli occupant by creating the Hamas movement a few days after the start of the uprising.

The intifada officially commenced on December 8, 1987, when an Israeli truck smashed into two Palestinian taxis, killing four people. The day before, an Israeli had been stabbed in Gaza, and the collision was interpreted by young Palestinian refugees in the camps as a deliberate act of revenge rather than an accident. There were angry protests, and large crowds gathered.[42] But to the surprise of the PLO leaders abroad and the Muslim Brothers, these demonstrations turned into a durable uprising instead of dispersing quickly, as they had always done before. The intifada took place within a political and social context similar to the one that prevailed during the 1970s Islamist emergence in Egypt, if its specifically Palestinian characteristics are discounted; the Egyptian movements began to develop seriously some twenty years after Nasser's seizure of power in 1952, when a new generation came of age and demanded its due from the only government it had ever known. In exactly the same way, the intifada broke out twenty years after Israel's occupation of the Palestinian territories in June 1967. The young of 1987 had never known anything other than occupation and a PLO-managed resistance movement. The PLO preserved its special access to grassroots Palestinians by redistributing funds it received from the Palestinian diaspora and the oil-producing Gulf monarchies; but at the same time the PLO appeared militarily and politically strangled by Israel and was thus perceived to be incapable of satisfying the aspirations of a younger, deeply displaced generation of Palestinians.

In demographic terms, the birth rate of the occupied territories was among the world's highest.[43] Half the population was under fifteen years of age, and 70 percent of it was under thirty. Education was available to most, and in 1984–85 there were more than 30,000 adult Palestinian students inside and outside Palestine. But only 20 percent of those with secondary school diplomas or higher education were able to find work when they completed their studies. The Islamic University of Gaza (founded in 1978 and run by the Muslim Brothers) had a permanent complement of 5,000 students, to which were added those of the other Islamic institutes in Hebron and Jerusalem.[44] As the first educated generation from Palestinian families of generally modest means, most of these graduates left school to face unemployment or, at best, journeyman work inside Israel. For a while, social upheaval was avoided through infusions of international aid, emigration to the oil-producing states, and private remittances from Palestinians abroad. But the collapse of oil prices in 1986 considerably restricted the flow of funds and jobs, while at the same time new tensions were raised by Jewish colonization in the territories. This was spurred by floods of new Jewish immigrants from Russia and a growing number of obstacles raised by Israel to bringing in any kind of economic development and investment that might contribute to the affirmation of an independent Palestinian entity.[45]

This tense situation inevitably favored the emergence of the younger generation as an independent political force. Indeed, youth was the principal characteristic of the intifada—a form of protest that no Palestinian leader of any party had foreseen. From the start, the most violent demonstrations took place in the refugee camps of Gaza, where the poorest people were found.[46] The other social groups that eventually joined the uprising were villagers (many of whom were day laborers in Israel) and shopkeepers: but these held back until early 1988, when it became clear that the movement would continue and that their political and economic interests would be damaged more seriously by abstention than by participation.[47] Nevertheless, throughout the four or five years of the intifada the *shebab,* or young people, played a central role in it, in the conviction that they had nothing to lose by any confrontation, however violent.[48]

The PLO and Hamas were soon competing for control of the intifada. Each party attempted to mobilize and organize the shebab, whose allegiance might alter the direction of the struggle while preventing them from joining forces with its rival. Hamas, with its Islamist emphasis, had a significant advantage: the acute social and demographic tensions in the occupied territories in 1987 were very similar to those that had fostered the emergence of Islamism elsewhere. But the PLO, unlike the discredited nationalist regimes of other Arab countries, was not running a tangible state against which the young could vent their wrath. In spite of its weaknesses and shortcomings during the 1980s, the organization still embodied the resistance and the promise of independence, and Yasir Arafat himself still possessed a political legitimacy among young Arabs far greater than that of any other Arab chief of state in the region. So although the uprising was aimed exclusively at the Israeli occupants, Islamist competition caused massive problems for the Palestinian nationalist movement all the same.[49]

The Muslim Brothers met on December 9, 1987, around their leader, Sheik Ahmad Yassin, and published a communiqué six days later that called for the intensification of the uprising. It was signed by representatives of the Islamic Resistance Movement.[50] But the Brothers did not

acknowledge the paternity of this movement until February of the following year: its initials in Arabic (HMS for Harakat al-Muqawama al-
Islamiyya) were later compressed into the simple name Hamas ("zeal")
under which Palestinian Islamism was to become world-renowned.
During the first hesitant months, the Brothers were racked by fear that
if they declared their support, Israeli repression would crush both the
intifada and their organization along with it. But their worst nightmare
was that the deprived younger generation would slip away from them
and join other groups like Islamic Jihad or the PLO. For this reason,
they represented Hamas to Palestinians as an operational entity that
enjoyed some kind of autonomy from the Brothers. But their uncertainties also reflected the discomfort of a movement run by respectable
religious clerics, doctors, chemists, engineers, and teachers—that is, by
intellectuals from the devout middle class—when confronted with a violent, spontaneous revolt by young men from the impoverished underclass. The Brothers decided to acknowledge their responsibility for
Hamas in February 1988, when the shopkeepers finally entered the political arena. After the shebab had forced their hand, the bazaari confronted the Israeli police by closing their stalls in obedience to calls
for a general strike. The shopkeepers were traditionally close to the
Brothers, and from the moment when the devout middle class and
the souk traders swung their support behind the uprising, a powerful
Islamist dynamic was under way.

The impoverished young were no longer viewed as an unpredictable
political entity by the Brothers but as ideal recruits to their cause—
even more so in March 1988 when the Israelis annihilated the cells of
Islamic Jihad, thus clearing the political and religious field of Hamas's
most radical rival. Thereafter, Hamas set about channeling the random
fury and resentment of the young into pious zeal for the promotion of
its own social agenda. This operated on three levels: private, social, and
political. Through the strong moral content of its message, Hamas
turned the deprived young into a tool of Islamic authenticity with a
duty to punish the vices of the secular bourgeoisie, whose Western
morals and ways were denounced as an effect of "Jewish depravity."
This in turn called into question the ethical legitimacy of their elite status. Attacking un-Islamic cultural activities such as the trade in alco-
holic beverages and even throwing acid into the faces of middle-class
women who spurned the veil were part of the same logic, which sought

to make the re-Islamized lower class the standard-bearers of social values against the secular elites. A similar phenomenon had occurred in 1978 when the clergy took control of the popular movement during the Iranian revolution; also, a little later, in Algeria, with the appearance of armed Islamist groups in that country. This moral reference served to galvanize the poor as an incarnation of the pure and true "people of the Umma," in their struggle with the "corrupted ones," and it drove them straight into the arms of the devout middle class.

The PLO, which was also caught short by the unfolding of the intifada, immediately detected a challenge to its political primacy. PLO leaders viewed the uprising as a spontaneous movement of the shebab tending to sideline older and more established politicians. Beginning in January 1988, a complex balance was established between the young nationalist cadres of Gaza, the West Bank, and Jerusalem (Fatah, PFLP, DFLP, and the communists) and the exiled PLO leadership in Tunis, which was struggling to regain some kind of initiative. The Unified National Leadership of Uprising (UNLU) was the point of equilibrium between Arafat's headquarters abroad and the new generation fighting within Palestine, whose origins were humbler and who for the first time found themselves in positions of responsibility.[51] The challenges facing the UNLU leaders were many and various: they had to contend simultaneously with Israeli repression, the growing power of Hamas, and the threat of absorption by the PLO leadership in Tunis. The answer to their problems lay in their capacity to mobilize the shebab, direct their actions toward political goals that were clearly identified and anti-Israeli, and generally to offer their young recruits an alternative to the Islamist identity proposed by their rivals.

From the summer of 1988 onward, Hamas and the UNLU vied openly for the allegiance of the prime movers of the intifada, each publishing its own calendars of "compulsory" strike action and work days. Violent clashes followed, from which the Islamists emerged the victors, forcing the UNLU to allow them their own schedules. This was the first time in the history of the Palestinian movement that the Islamists had succeeded in imposing their will on the nationalists. Their growing power in the field was reflected ideologically by the publication of a Hamas charter on August 18, laying out Hamas's difference from the PLO, whose own constitution had hitherto been the only reference. It made clear that the jihad to liberate Palestine, a Muslim land usurped by infidels, was each individual's religious obligation. This echoed the proclamations made by Abdallah Azzam on Afghanistan and Palestine, from his base in Peshawar: "There will be no solution to the Palestinian problem except through jihad. All these international initiatives, proposals and conferences are perfectly futile and a waste of time."[52] Above all, an opportunity had arisen to take a stand against the process of negotiation that the Palestine National Council, the PLO's "parliament," had begun after its meeting in Algiers on November 15, when it proclaimed an Independent State of Palestine while simultaneously accepting the existence of Israel.

Islamists and nationalists now scrambled for advantage. Hamas appealed to those opposed to the PLO's diplomatic initiative, calling the organization a hostage to "Israeli duplicity." Any escalation of the struggle with Israel favored Hamas's strategy. As for the PLO, the continuation of the intifada helped to increase pressure on the Israelis to make concessions to the Palestinian cause. In the competition between the two, the main objective was to win the support of the "popular committees." These had sprung up all around the towns, camps, and villages of Palestine, and they now orchestrated resistance on a daily basis, organized regular patrols, repaired the steel shutters of shops and padlocks broken by the Israeli army, and generally promoted survival tactics in a climate of constant boycotts and strikes. The committees also forced the wholesale resignations of Palestinian functionaries and policemen, leading to private penury, a chronic shortage of public funds, and slow economic asphyxiation.[53]

In 1989, growing material difficulties combined with political deadlock, when Israel refused the PLO's offer to negotiate after the Algiers congress. Deadlock naturally favored the radicalization of the people and the influence of the Islamists. What was more, Hamas benefited from its effective access to the Muslim Brothers' network of mosques and charitable organizations, which had profited from Israeli indulgence in the past. In September the Jewish state, now thoroughly alarmed by the success of the Islamists, changed its strategy and began to take repressive measures against them, arresting and imprisoning Sheik Ahmad Yassin and over 200 other leading activists. Like Sadat in Egypt, who had encouraged the Gamaat Islamiya against the leftists in the university before cutting them down, Israel sought to smash a movement which, although it was a thorn in the side of the UNLU, had

now become a formidable enemy of Israel, too, by reason of the growing numbers of young men who were enlisting in its rank and file.

But repression only served to increase the legitimacy of the Islamists
in the eyes of those living in the occupied territories. Their jailed leaders were replaced by younger men, who were less experienced politically and whose excessive zeal soon led to random, unfocused acts of
violence. Much the same happened in the ranks of the nationalists,
whose elites had been repressed more comprehensively and for much
longer by Israel. In 1990, the third year of the intifada, Hamas's influence in several Palestinian trade unions that had formerly been controlled by PLO partisans increased. And for the first time, the Islamists
won elections within the professional unions, reflecting their penetration of the salaried middle class.[54] Simultaneously, they succeeded in
netting a major share of Arab aid from the Gulf states: in 1990, Kuwait
contributed $60 million to Hamas and only $27 million to the PLO.[55]
The Palestinian Islamist movement had managed to mobilize the devout bourgeoisie as well as the impoverished young—especially those
in the camps, who were losing patience with Arafat's failure to produce
results from his peace offer to Israel.

In response to this challenge, the PLO suggested that Hamas join the
Palestinian National Council in April 1990. The PLO's hope was that
Hamas could be transformed into a minority opposition that would
submit to the will of the majority and be more easily controlled, like
the PFLP, the DFLP, and the Communist party. But Hamas demanded
almost half of the seats in the council, the resurrection of the pledge to
eliminate Israel, and the proclamation of jihad as the only means of
liberating Palestine.[56] If these conditions had been accepted, Hamas
would have become the dominant force in the PNC, and all the PLO's
diplomatic efforts made since the Algiers resolutions of December
1988 would be negated. The PLO rejected the demands out of hand,
and skirmishes between militants of the two factions began to occur on
an almost daily basis in the field. Hamas felt itself to be in a position of
strength: it had built up a dynamic that appeared to be all the more irresistible after the Gulf War of 1990–91 struck a crippling blow at the
PLO, whose leaders had declared for Iraq against Kuwait and Saudi
Arabia. A proliferation of uncontrolled acts of violence, the killing of
hundreds of real or suspected "collaborators with Israel," and a general
lack of response to the UNLU's calls for strike action all clearly demon-

strated that the PLO had lost control of the uprising. The conditions appeared to be in place for Islamists to oust nationalists in Palestine, just as they had elsewhere. The jihad in the occupied territories now replaced the holy war in Afghanistan, which was gradually winding down, as the major focus and symbol of Islamist militancy.

At the moment of the Gulf crisis in 1990, Palestinian Islamism was able to take advantage of the intifada to mobilize the devout middle class side by side with the young urban poor and thereby challenge the PLO's dominance. The last Arab nationalist cause looked ready to enter the Islamist zone of influence, in the wake of Afghanistan but ahead of Algeria and Bosnia. But because of Yasir Arafat's uncanny ability to rebound and seize control of events, even after two decades of adversity and trial, things would fall out differently.

7

Islamization in Algeria and the Sudan

Less than a year after the outbreak of the intifada, Algeria—another country that had once embodied Arabism, Third Worldism, and anti-imperialism—slipped into the sphere of political Islam. In October 1988, Algeria experienced its most serious riots since independence in 1962. The young urban poor, who had been marginalized by the military hierarchy ruling through the apparatus of the Front de Libération Nationale (FLN), took decisive control of the streets and showed that they were now a major independent force. As in Egypt and Palestine, this event involved the first generation to reach maturity without having known any regime other than the one against which they were protesting. Again, a population explosion had thrust the children of the *fellahs* (farmers) into the cities and their outskirts, where conditions were precarious; and again, this mass of young people had had access to education for the first time in the country's history. Education had raised great hopes among these youth—hopes that were mostly drowned in a welter of frustration when hard-won degrees turned out to be worthless on the job market. In 1989, 40 percent of Algeria's population of 24 million were under 15 years of age; the urban population was in excess of 50 percent of the total population; the birthrate was 3.1 percent per year; and 61 percent of adolescents were attending secondary school. The official unemployment rate was 18.1 percent of the working population, though in reality joblessness was much higher; in 1995 it rose—again officially—to 28 percent.[1]

The young urban poor of Algeria were mocked as *hittistes*—from the

Arab word *hit*, "wall." This jibe derived from the image of jobless young men with nothing to do all day but lean against a wall. The joke was that, in a socialist country where in theory everyone was supposed to have a job, the profession of a hittiste consisted in propping up walls that would otherwise collapse. The hittistes were assumed to be passive—unlike the Iranian disinherited ones, who were glorified by religious movements and hailed as the messengers of history and the Revelation.

At the time of the October 1988 riots, oil and gas represented 95 percent of the nation's exports and supplied more than 60 percent of the government's yearly budget. Under Presidents Ahmed Ben Bella (1962–1965) and Houari Boumedienne (1965–1978), the Algerian state was a kind of popular democracy cum oil. The state used its oil revenues to buy social pacification by subsidizing imported consumer goods. Taking the Soviet Union as its model, the regime banned all opposition to the FLN, whose legitimacy was rooted in its successful war of independence against France (1954–1962). In reality, under the veneer of socialism and the unity of the revolutionary family around the FLN, most of the actual holders of power (the military top brass and the party *nomenklatura*) came from the Arabic-speaking east side of the country. Excluded were the people of central and western Algeria, as well as Kabylia, despite the fact that they too had paid dearly in blood during the war of independence.

This balance of power, maintained by subsidies, socialism, repression, and official ideology, was ultimately dependent on the fragile economic equilibrium created by the high price of oil. In 1986, when oil prices collapsed, half of Algeria's budget was wiped out and the whole structure fell down in ruins. Worse, the population explosion had created a demand for food, urban infrastructure, housing, and employment that continued to increase. The malfunctioning of the planned economy was accompanied by corruption on a grand scale; and the expansion of an informal commercial sector, the *trabendo*, in which prices were wildly speculative, just added to the hardships.[2] The construction industry in particular had failed spectacularly to keep pace with the housing demand; the result was the kind of slums and overcrowded urban conditions that invariably lead to social eruption.

It was in this deteriorating climate, punctuated by continual strikes, that riots broke out on October 4, 1988. Mobs of impoverished Algerian youths attacked such symbols of the state as buses, road signs, and Air Algeria agencies, along with any automobile that looked expensive. The focus of the rioting was the Riad al Fath (Victory Gardens) shopping mall on the heights overlooking the capital, a symbol of untrammeled consumerism and the meeting-place of the *tchi-tchi*, Algeria's "golden youth." The police, taunted as Jews by the young demonstrators, who had seen nightly TV reports of the Israeli armed forces repressing the intifada, counterattacked ruthlessly, and hundreds of demonstrators were killed. The Algerian regime could hardly have foreseen that its ritual anti-Zionist rhetoric would be turned against it in this way. The October uprising was mostly spontaneous, rich in signs of social fury and derision of the ideology in power. Near Riadh el-Fath, the Algerian national flag was torn down and an empty couscous sack was hoisted in its place. But these days were much more than a "couscous riot" or a "student rampage that turned ugly," as commentators and government representatives described them. They marked the emergence of the young urban poor as a force to be reckoned with. The once ridiculed hittistes had shown that they could seize and hold power in the streets, shaking to its foundations a regime that had excluded them and whose legitimacy they scorned.

Nevertheless, the revolt was never transformed into a structured political movement. Left to themselves, the urban poor proved incapable of pressing home their demands. The vocabulary of socialism had been largely discredited by the Algerian government's use of it, so the left was no more capable of giving direction to the uprising than any other political faction. The Islamist movement instantly understood that this impasse represented a golden opportunity.

The salafist faction had preserved its grassroots support in Algeria for many years. The Association of Muslim Ulemas, founded at Constantine, Algeria, in 1931 by Abdel Hamid Ben Badis, three years after the founding of the Muslim Brothers in Egypt, shared the same strict attitude that made religion the absolute focus of private life and society. But it had never pushed the idea of an Islamic state and even less the theory of nationalist struggle. Like the Deobandis of British India or the Palestinian Muslim Brothers under the pre-intifada Israeli occupation, Ben Badis and his companions thought it both dangerous and futile to confront the overwhelmingly powerful colonial occupant: just a year before the founding of their association, the French had celebrated the centenary of the conquest of Algeria amid scenes of great pomp and circumstance. On the other hand, Ben Badis fought resolutely against any attempt to assimilate Algerians and French, a move that would blur Islamic identity, of which he and his friends were the guarantors and defenders. They considered their principal enemies to be secularization and the "superstitions" propounded by the marabouts. They were also deeply suspicious of the nationalists, who were influenced by socialism and European ideas, with the result that when the FLN started its insurrection in 1954, they held back for two years before deciding to join it.

The FLN, like most of the other nationalist parties in the Muslim world, was split over what attitude it should adopt toward Islam. Led by Western-educated elites, the FLN viewed religion as a means of uniting a population that had little understanding of modern trends— especially in the countryside—and of clearly demarcating their difference from the Christian colonists. Thus, the November 1954 uprising was proclaimed "in the name of Allah," without making the FLN a religious movement. When independence finally came eight years later, Islam was sidelined by Ben Bella's regime, which at the time was more engrossed with Moscow and Havana than with Mecca. The marabouts and their brotherhoods (the *zaouias*), who owned large tracts of land, had to surrender their property to the nation as part of agrarian reform and in reprisal for their complaisant attitude toward the colonists. The ulemas were treated slightly more leniently, on account of their (late) participation in the war; but any attempt at independent expression brought an immediate clampdown from the Marxists in power. In 1964 the ulemas were stigmatized by one newspaper as "les ulemas du mal" (ulemas of evil). In 1963, a group of religious intellectuals and party members founded the Al-Qiyam al-islamiya (Islamic Values) association, to fight against Westernization and champion the idea of an Islamic state as the necessary outcome of the war of independence. In this they were close to the ideas of Sayyid Qutb; indeed they sent a letter to Nasser in August 1996 asking for Qutb's pardon, just a few days before he was executed. The association was later dissolved, but its influence persisted even within the otherwise sealed circle of power.

The eviction of Ben Bella by Boumedienne in June 1965 was followed by a campaign of Arabization and Islamization that allowed its advocates to exercise wide control over Algerian education and culture.

Among the Egyptians who were recruited at this time to Arabize and de-Frenchify the school system was a substantial contingent of Muslim Brothers on the run from Nasser's repression. The Egyptian contingent trained a whole generation of strictly Arabophone teachers who agreed with their ideas and later formed the basis for the broadly Islamist intelligentsia who made up the Front Islamique du Salut (FIS), of which Ali Benhadj, also a teacher and the "number 2 of the FIS," would one day become the symbol.

Officially proscribed as a political party, Algerian Islamism remained one of the components of government power, although its influence was confined to the cultural domain, with no direct bearing on political decisions. It was only in 1982, a decade after the emergence of Islamism in the Middle East, that Algerian Islamists began to express genuine opposition to the regime.[3] Right away, two major factions became apparent: an extremist group that opted for armed struggle and soon went underground, and a reformist group that sought to influence the regime's decisions without upsetting the status quo of society. The radicals were led by Mustafa Bouyali, a veteran of the war of independence who was born in 1940. Bouyali broke violently with the regime, which he declared impious.[4] A gifted, inflammatory preacher, he called for the application of the sharia and the setting up of an Islamic state by jihad. In the mid-1970s he gathered around him a small cadre of determined partisans, all of whom were avid readers of Qutb and behaved very much like his Egyptian disciples at the time. Bouyali was relentlessly harassed by the Security Services and was eventually forced to go into hiding in April 1982 before founding the Mouvement Islamique Armé (MIA), a loose association of tiny groups of which he was proclaimed the amir. Among his followers, most of whom joined the FIS and the armed Islamist movement after 1992, was Ali Benhadj himself.

By carrying out a series of bold attacks, the MIA established itself as the first serious challenger to the power of the FLN. It conducted an underground resistance for five years, until Bouyali himself was killed in February 1987. The MIA was a melting pot for a number of experiments, fusing several components of the international Islamist imagination of the time as well as that of modern Algeria. When it launched its jihad in the Mitidja (the plains surrounding Algiers), the Saudi-sponsored Afghan mujahedeen had already been fighting the

Red Army for two years and had become the heroes of the Islamic world. Because the Soviet Union was a close ally of the Algerian regime and supplied most of its military equipment, for the radical Algerian Islamists the struggle against the former was a prelude for the struggle against the latter. Several hundred of them made the pilgrimage to the camps of Peshawar, and one, Abdallah Anas, became the son-in-law of the Islamist theorist Abdallah Azzam and then his successor, after the older man was murdered in November 1989.

By fighting out of the same areas held by the FLN during the war of independence, the MIA laid claim to its legacy, symbolically perpetuating the original conflict and demonstrating that in the eyes of its militants those currently holding power in Algeria were no better than the departed French colonialists. At the time, this attitude seemed barely relevant: but with the hindsight of the civil war of the 1990s, when the much more significant resistance forces of the Armée Islamique du Salut and the Groupe Islamique Armé entered the field, the actions of Bouyali and his followers may be seen for what they were: a link between the two Algerian wars, illustrating a clear continuity of method, along with an ideological shift from nationalism to Islamism.

The year in which Bouyali took the resistance underground also saw the appearance of militants seeking to put pressure on the regime to increase the pace of Islamization without recourse to armed struggle. In November 1982, incidents between francophone Marxist students and arabophone Islamists at the University of Algiers led to the death of a Marxist. The fighting began with a strike staged by the Arab-speaking clique to protest their slim prospects of entering any professional career, despite the regime's propaganda and authoritarian measures of Arabization. This they contrasted with the rich openings available to their French-speaking fellow students, who monopolized all the best-paid jobs because they were conditional on a knowledge of French. At the end of a prayer meeting involving several thousand people, Abassi Madani, a teacher at the faculty and a former member of the FLN who had broken with the party, presented a fourteen-point list of complaints. Specifically, he demanded "respect for the sharia in government legislation and a purging of elements hostile to our religion," along with a separation of the sexes in the educational system. This was the first organized public demonstration by the nonviolent Islamist opposition to break out of the framework authorized by the single-party regime. It was instantly repressed: Madani served two years in prison, and most of the known figures in a movement that was still confined to a few university professors and preachers were arrested.[5] These men formed a kernel of the intelligentsia around which the young urban poor and the devout middle class gathered after 1988.

To eradicate this religion-based challenge, the Algerian regime set about constructing an Islamic legitimacy of its own. In 1984, the National Assembly of the People (the "parliament" controlled by the FLN) voted in favor of a family code inspired by the strictest Islamic ideals, by which women's rights were heavily curtailed. A policy of state-financed mosque construction was inaugurated, and the preachers appointed to them were controlled by the Ministry of Religious Affairs; these were meant to counter the proliferation of small, unofficial prayer rooms in the poor areas of the cities, in which unlicensed preachers held sway. Finally, in 1985, the Amir Abd el-Kader Islamic University was inaugurated at Constantine, with its own cathedral-mosque, the plan being to provide Algeria with a training center for distinguished imams.[6] In the absence of local ulemas of any repute who could give their blessing to the regime, the Algerian government (headed since 1979 by Boumedienne's successor, Chadli Benjedid) imported from Egypt two of the most revered sheiks in the Muslim world, Muhammad al-Ghazali and Yusuf al-Qaradawi. Both were fellow-travelers of the Muslim Brothers and very much in favor with the oil monarchies of the Arabian peninsula.[7] Although their recruitment was an implicit admission of the moribund scene among Algerian ulemas, the importation of two imams belonging to this school of thought showed the regime's desire to strengthen the religious dimension of the FLN's nationalist ideology, which was making no headway with either the younger generation or anyone else whose interests were not served by the status quo. The two imported preachers gave only lip service to the government while encouraging the "Islamic awakening" at work in society.

Thus, at the moment when the riots broke out in October 1988, there existed in Algeria an Islamist intelligentsia made up of teachers and students who were actively preaching in working-class areas and against whom the state was unable to bring forward any credible ulemas to express its own side of the argument. The contrast with Egypt was all too obvious: after all, President Mubarak had managed to enlist all the principal dignitaries of Al Azhar against the assassins of Sadat, thereby heading off the expansion of radical Islamism. He was able to do this because ordinary people revered the doctors of the law who represented this thousand-year-old institution and held their opinions in high esteem.

As a result, by the end of the 1980s the Algerian Islamist militants had swept all their religious rivals off the beach. The bigoted faction within the single party (called Barbéfèlène, the bearded FLN, by local wags) had much in common with the Islamists, and many of them rallied to the FIS or sympathized strongly with it from 1989 onward. The world of the brotherhoods had been dismantled at independence, and now there were no ulemas worthy of the name for the state to use against the Islamist activists. As soon as the riots began, the militants set about building bridges to the young urban poor, and within a few months the small circles of believers that had formerly gathered round a few scattered preachers had been transformed into a movement with the force of an earthquake.

Exactly how the "days of October" started remains a mystery. Rumors circulated in Algiers that power struggles within the government apparatus were to blame, along with provocateurs sent to destabilize President Chadli, whose political and economic decisions in the face of Algeria's crisis were hotly contested.[8] Whatever the initial spark may have been, the blaze roared through the gangs of hittistes and other young people with extraordinary speed. Confronted with widespread looting in the capital, the Islamist preachers called a crisis meeting. Sheik Mohamed Sahnoun, an 81-year-old cleric, a former member of the Ulemas' Association, and a figure renowned for his intransigence toward the regime, made an appeal for calm on the evening of October 6. This had no effect other than to position the Islamist intelligentsia as the obligatory intermediary between the government and a society up in arms against it. On October 10, following a demonstration orchestrated by Ali Benhadj from the Kabul Mosque (built by veterans of the Afghanistan jihad in the Belcourt quarter of Algiers), a gunshot caused panic in the huge crowd, and several dozen people were trampled to death. Benhadj immediately issued an appeal in which he framed the people's demands in the terminology of political Islamism, effectively setting up the Islamist intellectuals as spokesmen for Algeria's impoverished urban youth. This alliance was sealed with the creation of the FIS in March 1989.[9]

On the evening of October 10, President Chadli announced a series of reforms and met with Sahnoun, Benhadj, and Mahfoud Nahnah, the Algerian representative of the Muslim Brothers, thereby legitimizing them as interlocutors.[10] The uprising petered out. After sacking a few subordinates, Chadli was re-elected as head of state in December, and in February 1989 he imposed a constitution that ended the era of the single party in Algeria. He hoped to avail himself of a much stronger presidential institution that would allow him to put together coalitions of the various parties as he saw fit (nationalists, Islamists, Marxists, and Berberists) while preserving the main characteristics of the system that had been in place since 1962. In short, he underestimated the strength of the dynamic that the Islamists had set in motion in October, a mis-calculation which soon pushed his regime into crisis and the country into full-scale civil war.

On March 10, 1989, the birth of the FIS was proclaimed at the Ben Badis Mosque in Algiers. Its fifteen founders represented a number of different approaches, ranging from advocates of armed struggle and followers of Bouyali (such as Ali Benhadj) to FLN veterans (such as Abassi Madani) whose aim was to Islamize the regime without alter-ing society's basic fabric. The movement was not fully represented: personal animosities and rivalries over precedence ruled out figures like the Muslim Brother Nahnah, the Constantine Islamist Abdallah Jaballah, the elderly Sheik Sahnoun, and Muhammad Said, the head of the *djazarists*.[11] The government was later able to use some of these men to obstruct the FIS, but in the first year of its existence it made spectacular progress in binding together the disparate social groups of Algeria, in a way that bore a close similarity to the events of 1978 in Teheran.

As in Iran, a steady proliferation of demonstrations launched by the Islamists enabled them to maintain a climate of permanent mobiliza-tion. For the first time the unemployed young were able to express their resentment against the regime and their support for a revolution-ary blueprint for society, which, after twenty-five years of inertia, now seemed within their grasp. From 1989 onward this project took the form of the *doula islamiya* (Islamic state), for which the intellectuals of the FIS clamored in their harangues. The new multiparty system made possible the emergence of about fifty different political formations, but of these only the FIS had a coherent network of preachers already in place. This network allowed it to give structure to a mass movement that lambasted the state and the FLN. Indeed, the former single party was able to survive only because of its massive apparatus and the vested interest of its cadres, though it went through a period of acute moral crisis. As to the democratic parties that advocated a non-religious approach to politics while also rejecting the FLN, these were confined to ethnic and regional bases (such as Kabylia for Hocine Ait-Ahmed's Front des Forces Socialistes) or to a restricted sector of the francophone middle class (such as Said Saadi's Rassemblement pour la Culture et la Democratie, RCD).

The power of the FIS was demonstrated by its victories in the first free elections since Algerian independence, in June 1990 and December 1991. These successes were due to the party's Khomeini-like ability to unite the poor urban youth and devout middle class through the intermediary of a dynamic Islamist intelligentsia. The intellectuals knew how to produce an ideology of mobilization in which everyone had something to gain: they even managed to annex a part of the nationalist discourse and detach it from the FLN. This strength—as long as the movement was still being carried forward by its initial spirit and the government was still being found wanting (that is, until the "insurrection strike" of June 1991)—was well served by the two heads of the party.

The first head, Ali Benhadj, the lowly schoolteacher and former companion of Bouyali, now the prophet of jihad, was only 33 years old in 1989. He rode a lightweight motorcycle, and he was an incomparable speaker in the mosques, using classical Arabic or Algerian dialect to enthrall the tens of thousands of hittistes who hung on his words, making them laugh or weep at will, one moment whipping them into a frenzy of fanaticism and the next reining them in.[12] The other head was Abassi Madani, a 58-year-old war veteran, university professor, and academic, who went about in a luxurious Mercedes (supposedly given to him by an Arab monarch) and knew how to talk to the shopkeepers and traders, as well as to the "military suppliers."[13] All these he weaned away from the regime by arguing that investment in the FIS would deliver a guarantee for the future of their businesses.

The inroads made by Benhadj and Madani were reversed as soon as the regime began repressing the party after the failure of the June 1991 strike. First, the traders and entrepreneurs who had earlier been attracted by the FIS's promised reforms began to have second thoughts about the movement's real intentions and about the balance of power within it. They were also frightened by the growing radicalism of Benhadj's associates and the threat of a savage hittiste backlash against them. At this juncture the dual nature of the FIS leadership became a weakness. In Iran, Khomeini had remained to the end the sole and unique figure who could exalt the disinherited on the one hand while reassuring the bazaar on the other. The Algerian Islamist movement, with its two leaders, was incapable of sustaining unity between the poor urban youth and the devout middle class as Khomeini had done. During the civil war, Algerian Islamism split completely into two opposing factions: the Groupe Islamique Armé (urban poor) and the Armée Islamique du Salut (middle class).

In the first months of its legal existence (which commenced in September 1989), the FIS showed its power again and again. The first edition of its weekly publication, *Al Munqidh* (The Savior), 200,000 copies of which were distributed in October, demanded the liberation of those members of Bouyali's group still in detention by order of the regime. At the end of the month, an earthquake laid waste the Tipasa region of Algeria, and the government's callous attitude to the catastrophe contrasted starkly with the devotion and effectiveness of the FIS-inspired doctors, nurses, and rescue teams who arrived in ambulances bearing the party's insignia. One month after the FIS's creation, it was already demonstrating its readiness to take the reins of power from a corrupt and faltering regime and had showed a degree of mercifulness that won favor well beyond the movement's circle of immediate supporters. In the first six months of 1990, the party organized marches and gatherings and applied steady pressure on the state, from which it was finally able to extract the promise of early legislative elections. On June 12, the FIS triumphed on the municipal and regional ballot, winning control of a majority of the country's communes.

The young urban poor had turned out in record numbers to elect the first generation of FIS officials. These mayors and municipal councilors were of course the Islamist intellectuals who supplied the party with its cadres; many were teachers, but given the large numbers of seats to be filled, there was also a high proportion of representatives from the devout middle class. This was the first time that shopkeepers and small businessmen with local reputations had achieved any kind of access to political responsibilities, which, apart from defectors from the ex-FLN, had hitherto been confined to lackeys of the regime co-opted by the single-party apparatus.

The victory of the FIS in the 1990 municipal elections modernized the Algerian political system and sealed the alliance between the three components of the Islamist movement. It brought better services to the deprived, thanks to the budget of the Islamic municipalities (*baladiya islamiya*), which allowed the FIS to give the urban poor a foretaste of the coming Islamic state by deploying charitable activities on a large scale. In the euphoric climate that prevailed among the movement's sympathizers, there were abundant testimonies to the justice, equity, order, and general civic virtue of the elected FIS officials, in contrast to the corruption, waste, arbitrariness, and inefficiency that had formerly prevailed.[14] These virtues were attributed to religious rectitude founded on a strict respect for the injunctions of the sharia, as demonstrated to the world by the application of "Islamic morality."

In the following weeks and months, female municipal employees were forced to wear the veil; liquor stores, video shops, and other immoral establishments were "persuaded" to close their doors; women of easy morals (or those thought to be) were persecuted; and the coastal municipalities busied themselves organizing separate bathing for the sexes, banning indecent clothing on beaches, and so on. As in other countries where the Islamist movements made inroads, the first effect of this avalanche of moral prohibitions was to point the finger at the Europeanized secular middle class whose members were more or less emancipated from traditional taboos, to deprive them of all legitimacy as proponents of the values of modernity, and to hand over their elite positions to the devout bourgeoisie. At the same time, it allowed impoverished young men, humiliated and forced into abstinence or sexual misery by the crowded family conditions in which they lived, to become heroes of chastity who sternly condemned the pleasures of which they had been so wretchedly deprived.

In the context of Algeria, this translation of social and political conflicts into the moral sphere was accompanied by a linguistic dimension that was specific to the Maghreb. The struggle to eliminate the French language attained jihad proportions: in the most trivial Islamist propaganda, French was perceived as the vector of the West's most pernicious aspects, especially nationalism and secularism. Thus, Ali Benhadj declared his intention "to ban France from Algeria intellectually and ideologically, and be done, once and for all, with those whom France has nursed with her poisoned milk."[15] Notions like this, voiced after the victory of the FIS in the municipal elections, were music to the ears of the hittistes and the Arab-speaking graduates of the secondary and higher-education establishments, who were sick of being beaten in the job market by their French-speaking contemporaries. On the other hand, these sentiments were alarming to the urban middle class, whose members had supported the FIS in the elections of June 1990 out of disgust with the FLN but were still eager to watch the 8 o'clock news on French television, which they received through what the Islamist militants called "paradiabolic" dishes. At first the Islamists tried to destroy all satellite dishes in Algeria, but when this proved impractical they reverted to training them on the Arabsat satellite, which broadcast various Saudi programs.

In Iran the secularized petite bourgeoisie had backed Khomeini because he professed openness and the inclusion of every element of society in his revolutionary project. Also, during the early days of the revolution he concentrated his attacks on a single enemy, the shah. In Algeria, by constrast, as soon as the FIS was in control of local power following its success in the municipal elections, the preachers who harangued the young urban poor took issue not only with the regime but with a whole sector of society for its "francization." This imprecise notion, with which the FIS exposed a substantial sector of the urban middle class to the wrath of the hittistes, was—not unreasonably—construed as a threat.

As it turned out, in electoral terms the high point of Islamist influence was reached at the June 1990 municipal elections. In the first round of the December 1991 legislative ballot a year later, the party lost nearly a million votes (though it still won comfortably) because the possibility that it might win power had begun to frighten a substantial segment of Algerian society. Khomeini, faced with the same dilemma, had taken great care not to scare any social group unduly before the shah was deposed and he himself was well established in Teheran. Moreover, the ayatollah had focused his attacks on the monarchy, from which he offered a radical break, and this exacerbated the shah's isolation. In Algeria, the heads of the FIS did not make such a clean break with FLN ideology. Instead, they claimed to be partisans of the FLN's "true" line and denounced the perversion of FLN ideals by the "sons of

France" who had diverted the movement from its original course.[16] In its publications, the Islamist party presented itself as the legitimate heir of the 1954 War of Independence, which it described (retrospectively) as a jihad to install the Islamic state but which had been betrayed by the "French-speaking communists" who usurped power in 1962.[17]

A similar view of history allowed more socially conservative leaders like Madani to maintain close links with the bigoted, Arab-speaking faction of the former single party, just as it allowed President Chadli to stay in touch with the leaders of the FIS, whom he still hoped one day to include in a government coalition. Thus, in contrast to the Iranian situation whereby the Islamist movement had seized power because of its ability to unite society and isolate the regime, after mid-1990 the Algerian FIS began yielding to pressure from its most radical fringe, and in doing so alienated a significant proportion of the urban middle class. Its leaders, represented by Madani, were further hamstrung by their attempt to find a compromise with the FLN, whose politics they wished to correct and whose legitimacy they craved for themselves. This desire to effect a hasty purge coupled with an inability to make a clean break with the old regime was largely responsible for the FIS's ultimate political failure.

In the year that followed the June 1990 victory in the municipal elections, the Algerian government gave the impression of gradually losing control of events and of merely reacting to the Islamist party's initiatives. The FIS monopolized attention with its marches, rallies, and barrage of new projects in the communes it controlled. The state of dual power that seems to characterize all revolutionary periods had arrived in Algeria. The outbreak of the Gulf War in January 1991, with the offensive against Iraq by an international coalition led by the United States and supported by Saudi Arabia, was the pretext for giant demonstrations in support of Baghdad. These in turn supplied an opportunity for the FIS to take to the streets and outflank the regime.

At the end of one of these demonstrations, which had been headed by a detachment of Afghan-garbed jihadists fresh from Peshawar, a uniformed Ali Benhadj delivered a harangue in front of the Ministry of Defense in which he demanded the formation of a corps of volunteers to join the forces of Saddam Hussein. The symbolism of this demand was twofold. For one thing, such an intrusion onto the army's turf was a direct affront to the military hierarchy and a danger signal for the cohesion of the armed forces, whose chiefs concluded that the Islamist mobilization had to be stopped forthwith. For another, the Iraqi affair exposed the hidden fault lines within the FIS itself. Madani, who owed a debt of gratitude to the oil monarchies for their earlier financial support, adopted a pro-Saudi stance. But he had to defer to Benhadj, who supported Iraq and rode the popular enthusiasm for Saddam. The young urban poor were in a position to impose their views and passions on the party, and the party's leaders were unable to channel those views and passions. For the middle classes living in dread of hittiste vengeance, this moment was a turning point.

The tension between the regime and the FIS, and the contradictions within the FIS itself, began to peak in late May, when a project surfaced for the realignment of electoral districts in the election at the end of the next month. The effect would have been to reduce the party's majority by judicious gerrymandering. Madani, concluding that he had been betrayed, called for a general strike. The ensuing demonstrations quickly degenerated into violence, with the young urban poor heavily engaged. The government was obliged to surrender one of the largest squares in Algiers to the FIS, which proceeded to hold mass sit-ins there for a full week. At this point the army intervened to put an end to the situation, which could at any moment turn into a general uprising.

On the evening of June 3 a state of emergency was declared, the demonstrators were dispersed by tanks, and the army nominated a new prime minister, Sid Ahmed Ghozali, who promptly postponed elections until December. The army then turned its attention toward the local FIS bosses, removing the "Islamic municipality" signs on the town halls won by the movement in the previous year. Benhadj called for a general uprising, and Madani threatened to unleash jihad if the soldiers did not return to their barracks. It was too late: the army was already deployed, and popular support for the FIS had been sapped by its hesitations during the month of June. In short, the FIS had lost the initiative to the generals, who now took over the day-to-day running of Algeria. On June 30, Benhadj and Madani were arrested for sedition and thrown into prison, where they remained for the duration of the upcoming civil war.

This unexpected debacle widened divisions within the Islamist movement. The working partnership of Benhadj and Madani was supplanted by a gaggle of lesser characters who fought each other for pri-

macy. Those in favor of armed struggle coalesced around the residue of
Bouyali's followers and the Afghanistan veterans. These now began to
go into hiding; they were prepared for direct military action, scorning
the electoral process, which they viewed as a fraud. Their first spectacular operation was a bloody assault on a frontier post, in the course of
which a group of "Afghan" veterans cut off the heads of some wretched
army conscripts at Guemmar on November 28, 1991. The date was
carefully chosen to celebrate within four days the second anniversary of
the martyrdom of Abdallah Azzam in Peshawar. It marked the beginning of a jihad on Algerian soil. The Afghan experience—and reference—furnished a complete vocabulary to go with methods and traditions resurrected from the War of Independence, itself made topical by
the popular legend of Mustafa Bouyali.

The party, which had little control over this crowd of armed bandits,
began to see defections among its most radical founding members,
who criticized Madani's "politician's" approach. At the same time, the
party won new adherents among djazarist technocrats who saw in this
new weakness an opportunity to take control of its structure. A conference called at Batna on July 25–26, 1991, allowed a young engineer,
Abdelkader Hachani, who followed Madani's line, to seize control of
the party apparatus and strike a compromise between the different factions, giving the djazarists the lion's share of influence. Although the
leaders arrested in June were still in jail, and in spite of the pressure exerted by the army, which, having won the political initiative, first imprisoned then released Hachani and his companions, Hachani decided
to participate in the legislative elections, the first round of which took
place on December 26. The FIS opposed two other Islamist parties then
in contact with the regime, Abdallah Jaballah's Nahda and above all
Mahfoud Nahnah's Hamas party. These siphoned off a number of electors from the devout middle class, which was now seriously worried
about the direction in which Algeria seemed to be going. And a large
number of younger radicals who no longer believed in the electoral option did not vote at all. The net result was that the FIS lost over a million votes (25 percent of its support) by comparison with the municipal elections of June 1990.[18] Nevertheless, it still won handily, with 118
deputies elected in the first round against 16 for the FLN and over 47
percent of the popular vote.

This victory completely killed off President Chadli's project to entice a part of the Islamist elite into a manageable coalition, while the forecasts for the second round of elections suggested that the FIS would win an absolute majority in the Parliament. The army promptly "resigned" Chadli on January 11, 1992, called off the elections scheduled for January 13, and dissolved the FIS itself on March 4. The entire FIS apparatus was dismantled, thousands of militants and locally elected FIS officials were interned in camps in the Sahara, and Algeria's mosques were placed under tight surveillance.

A civil war ensued that would drag on for the rest of the decade. The net result was that the Front Islamique du Salut was annihilated as a mass party: its organization was smashed by the coup d'état of January, to which it was unable to devise any riposte. The alliance it had managed to forge between the young urban poor and the devout middle class, at the instigation of the Islamist intelligentsia, had proved incapable of taking power. Again, the contrast with Iran is telling. There, a single charismatic figure, Khomeini, enabled the Islamist movement to overcome the social divisions of its base and attract the whole of society, in a process that completely isolated the shah's regime. Even though the FIS was by far the strongest electoral force in the country at the moment of its dissolution, it had already passed its peak—which, in hindsight, was the triumph in the June 1990 municipal elections. Electoral success merely caused it to strengthen its grip on its natural support within society, while alienating the secular middle classes. This class, whom the FIS had branded "sons of France," was convinced thereafter that it would be the first victim of the hittistes.

In Iran, the middle classes and even the Communist party rallied wholeheartedly around Khomeini, and a strike organized by the oil industry workers—not otherwise known for their interest in religious ideology—dealt the final blow to the imperial regime. In Algeria, the government succeeded in retaining the backing of minority social groups, whose resistance to the FIS eventually proved crucial. It also kept control of the army, whose top brass had everything to fear from an Islamist movement whose leaders had given them no guarantee of survival. Nor did the armed forces' rank-and-file go over to the FIS, as the Iranian soldiery went over to Khomeini, despite Benhadj's appeal for a general mutiny in 1991. The Algerian regime also held its traditional support within the "revolutionary family" (the veterans of the War of Independence who had taken over the property of the colonial

French in 1962) and who, having used violence as a means to enrich themselves, were afraid that similar violence would deprive them of the spoils they had seized. The Iran of the shah did not possess any social group whose privileges were directly linked to the perpetuation of the monarchy. Finally, and above all, members of the secularized urban middle class in Algeria, who had received few benefits from the system, who had suffered from its corruption and nepotism, and whose condition was dismal to say the least, nevertheless grew apprehensive that they too would be targeted on account of the clothes they wore, the food they ate, or the lives they led. The consequence was that all of these groups, who were in a minority but who nonetheless held positions of responsibility within the social and administrative framework of Algeria, threw their support behind the coup d'état. In Iran, of course, their counterparts had gone the other way, into the arms of Khomeini.

Confronted by a coalition united in its fear of them, the Islamists were suffering on account of the very thing that had made them so successful in the first place: the fact that their young preachers had met with no effective opposition in the religious field. In Egypt, their counterparts had collided head-on with the ulemas of Al Azhar after Sadat's assassination, while in Iran the Shiite clerics had been rewarded for embracing the ideas of Shariati. In Algeria, by contrast, the Islamists entirely controlled the direction of Islam between 1988 and 1992 and set the tone for all FIS propaganda. Nevertheless, their youth, their ardor, their virulence, and their political immaturity prevented them from winning secular middle-class support to go along with that of the hittistes and the devout bourgeoisie. The civil war would accentuate this flaw in the Islamist alliance, when the devout notables of the ex-FIS would themselves become the prey of gangs of young proletarianized jihad partisans.

The Military Coup of the Sudanese Islamists

In 1989, a crucial year for the worldwide expansion of the Islamist movement, a durable regime built on Islamist foundations failed to materialize in Algeria despite the FIS's initial triumph. Paradoxically, the most significant victory occurred not in Algeria but in the Sudan, under the aegis of Hassan al-Turabi. Turabi's success resulted from a military coup d'état and had no popular dynamic whatsoever. Instead, it was the consequence of a long process of infiltration by the Islamist intelligentsia of the Sudan's state apparatus, army, and financial system, with the cooperation of an emerging devout bourgeoisie.

In the Sudan, the Muslim Brothers appeared on the scene in 1944, fifteen years or more after the creation of the organization in Egypt by Hassan al-Banna.[19] Banna's group was quick to gain a foothold among the Egyptian middle classes, but his Sudanese followers were confined to educated and intellectual circles until the mid-1960s. As in other countries of Black Africa, in the Sudan the Muslim religion was tightly controlled by mystical brotherhoods, which gave short shrift to the rigorous, city-oriented approach of Banna's disciples and their plans to Islamize a state and social structure from which they felt excluded.[20] The Sudanese brotherhoods were basically divided into two branches, represented by two separate political parties. The Ansars claimed the inheritance of the Mahdi or Messiah, who led the jihad of 1881 against the British; after independence in 1956, they became the Umma party.[21] Their rivals, the Khatmiya, were traditionally closer to Egypt and were represented politically by the Democratic Unionist party.

Both favored a traditional approach to politics: the allegiance of their militants to individual leaders was similar to the devotion of Sufi disciples to their master, who in return distributed his baraka to them and gave them his protection. The Ansars were led by the al-Mahdi family, and their strength was in the rural areas, with overall control over the country's agricultural economy. The Khatmiya, under the aegis of the al-Mirghani family, were especially influential in the souk and in Sudanese commercial networks. Among educated urban people, who were very sparse during the 1960s, the Islamist movement had to compete with the largest Communist party in the Arab world. The Communists were strongly entrenched in the university and had great influence among railway workers, in a country that depended on an extensive railway system bequeathed by the British. Arab nationalism also had its proponents, as it did elsewhere in the region. But the Sudan was only partly Arab in its makeup.[22] The south, which was mostly animist and Christian and scarcely Arabized at all, was firmly opposed to any national project associated with Arabism—meaning, with an Islamic ulterior motive—because it feared that its Black African identity would be swiftly annihilated by any such development.

In this highly circumscribed context, a charismatic leader emerged who was eventually to lead the Sudanese Islamists to victory in the putsch of 1989. Hassan al-Turabi was born in 1932 into a family of religious dignitaries claiming to descend from a minor mahdi and who also had the gift of baraka. He received a traditional Koranic education before studying law at the University of Khartoum, from which he emerged with a law degree. He then went to London, where he earned a master's degree in 1957, followed by a doctorate in Paris in 1964. In the same year, on his return to Khartoum, he became the head of the capital's law faculty. In October of that year the military dictatorship that had run the country since 1958 was overturned and replaced by a civil government with strongly socialist leanings.

At the age of 32, Turabi was a polyglot intellectual with a double claim to legitimacy, both traditional and modern. He played his role with gusto, utilizing his Western training to build an original Islamist political movement named the Islamic Charter Front (ICF) from the matrix provided by the Muslim Brothers. He copied his organization from that of its main rival, the Sudanese Communist Party, while at the same time breaking with the logic of the Muslim Brothers, who confined themselves to preaching pure religion. At the legislative elections of April 1965, the ICF won only seven seats (two of which were in constituencies reserved for candidates with diplomas, the left taking the remaining eleven seats).[23] At the student elections in the same year, the ICF reaped the fruits of its careful proselytism at the university, taking 40 percent of the votes and coming in a close second to the left, which won 45 percent.[24] In the assembly, the domination of the Umma party, with sixty-six seats, demonstrated the pre-eminence of politicians from the milieus of the brotherhood, in a country that was still over 80 percent rural.

Its leader, Sadiq al-Mahdi, was named prime minister. Turabi, who became Sadiq's brother-in-law, allied the ICF with the Umma; in this way his movement obtained access to the constitutional committee, which went on to propose that Islam become the state religion, with the sharia as its source of law. This was a golden opportunity for a minority party of intellectuals to graft itself onto the leading brotherhood, whose principal characteristic was its reference to the mahdi, and to bring it up to date by demanding the contemporary implementation of the sharia just as it had been applied by the late nineteenth-century Mahdist state. This tactic made it possible for the Islamist movement to install its supporters at the heart of the Sudanese political establishment. But by giving the sharia a central position in the Sudanese identity, it alienated non-Muslims, who constituted 30 percent of the population, mostly in the south. This led to extreme tension and eventually to civil warfare in the south. Against this background, General Djafar Nimayri seized power with the support of the Communists, Nasser's Egypt, and the Khatmiya brotherhood. The ICF was promptly dissolved, and Turabi spent seven years in prison.

With no real hold on the bulk of the population, whose allegiance was shared between the two main brotherhoods and their political arms, the Sudanese Islamists fell back on a patient strategy of winning over students—who constituted the intellectual breeding ground for a new generation of the devout middle class. From prison, Turabi wrote a book entitled *The Place of Women in Islam*, which, although it insisted on the wearing of the veil, also encouraged women to take part in public life. This angered traditionalists but allowed Turabi's movement to recruit large numbers of female students; previously, the leftist parties (secular and communist) had been the only ones offering a vision of the future that took account of women's dreams of emancipation. At the same time, the Communist party—on which Nimayri had depended heavily at the time of his coup—fell out of favor with the dictator and was dismantled. This was a blow from which it never recovered, and one which greatly facilitated the Islamist penetration of the academic elite, whom the Communists had dominated.

By 1977, the regime's support had eroded dangerously on account of its economic failures and the army's lack of progress in its southern offensive. Nimayri's solution was to launch an initiative of "national reconciliation," freeing opposition leaders from jail and allowing political exiles to return home. Turabi and his people now began to play a major role, infiltrating the top echelons of the government where their education, frequently acquired in the West, made them indispensable in putting the state back on track. This pragmatic approach was described by Turabi himself as the "jurisprudence of necessity." It consisted in placing Islamist supporters in every available position of power, and it was a direct consequence of the restricted, elitist nature of the organization. Unlike the Egyptian Muslim Brothers or the Algerian, Palestinian, and Iranian Islamists who began by preaching to the masses, Turabi and his friends were adept at Islamizing society from the top down, in the mold of Mawdudi and the Jamaat-e-Islami of Pakistan, or Anwar Ibrahim's ABIM in Malaysia. In other words, the conquest of the state by an "enlightened elite" eventually made it possible for Turabi to bring his Islamist project to fruition.

The Islamists were able to serve as intermediaries between the Sudan and its Red Sea neighbor Saudi Arabia, which, by reason of its new-found financial muscle following the war of October 1973, was eager for a rapprochement with a country capable of exporting large num-bers of immigrant workers.[25] At the same time, the Saudis were concerned to prevent the Sudan from drifting into the Communist camp, while the Sudanese themselves, like any other poor Muslim country in Africa, were eager to attract Arab funds from the Gulf. In the fall of 1977, the Faisal Islamic Bank opened a branch in the Sudan. For Nimayri's government, this offered an opportunity to attract Saudi Funds, which comprised some 60 percent of the bank's startup capital.[26] So popular was this novelty that by the mid-1980s the Faisal Bank was the second richest concern in the country, in terms of the money it held on deposit. The bank was run by Islamists, some of whom had been received by Prince Faisal in Saudi Arabia during Nimayri's perse-cution in the early 1970s; one of its directors was later to become an important figure in Turabi's regime.[27] Like the Al Baraka Bank founded shortly afterward, it not only provided jobs for young militant gradu-ates, allowing them to raise their social status through its network, but also attracted deposits from bazaar merchants and Sudanese citizens based abroad.

These banks were considered to be among the strongholds of the lo-cal Islamist movement, which, unlike its Egyptian and Algerian coun-terparts, had little or no popular base but recruited most of its people from the younger, educated elites. They would play a key role in struc-turing a devout lower middle class that would ally itself with the Islamist intellectuals and army officers to seize power in 1989 by a coup d'état. Turabi's associates naturally monopolized most of the jobs made available by the banks, reaping employment and wealth as a reward for their activism as students—a development comparable to that which occurred in the Malaysian banking sector. In addition, the banks pro-vided low-interest loans to investors and businessmen linked to the movement, and this in turn encouraged the emergence of a devout middle class directly dependent for its economic success on political contacts and ideological inspiration. Finally, the banks were successful in finding new depositors, notably among local traders deprived of access to conventional institutions that were entirely focused on foreign business—and these became commercial as well as political clients.

Thanks to the Saudis' support for their Sudanese fellow-Islamists, the latter were able to transcend their original bases in intellectual and university circles. They now became the spokesmen for an emerging, newly educated devout middle class that had escaped the influence of the non-religious parties (nationalist or communist) as well as the traditional brotherhoods. The Saudi-Sudanese connection, with Turabi's National Islamic Front (NIF) as its intermediary, was also expressed through the African Islamic Center, which was richly endowed by the Gulf states and headed by a party member from 1979 onward. The center's function was to train preachers and young elites from French- and English-speaking African countries, to imbue them with the salafist view of Islam, to provide them with the means to compete effectively with Christian missionaries, and in general to usurp the role formerly played by the brotherhoods.[28]

The final eight years of Nimayri's regime were marked by a growth in the influence of Turabi's adherents, who were given a free hand to set up cells within the state apparatus on condition that they did not challenge the dictator himself. Nimayri saw their enthusiasm for Islamizing the law as an opportunity to tighten his own control over a population that had grown tired of the regime's corruption and inertia, and in doing so to shift the emphasis of social conflict to the religious plane. With this prospect in mind, in September 1983 Nimayri issued a decree to make the sharia the law of the country. Thieves' hands were cut off, adulterous couples were stoned, alcohol was banned, and the Islamization of the banking system was officially inaugurated. In January 1985, Mahmud Muhammad Taha, an intellectual who wanted to revise certain items of Islamic dogma, was publicly hanged.[29] In March, Nimayri suddenly became alarmed by the extent of the influence wielded by Turabi and his entourage, whom he called the "Satanic Brothers." It was too late. Turabi had to wait only a month in prison before Nimayri's regime collapsed entirely.

During the four-year democratic interlude between the fall of Nimayri and the coup d'état of June 1989, the Sudanese Islamic movement consolidated its positions, creating in 1985 the National Islamic

Front. The NIF won 51 seats out of 264 at the parliamentary elections of April 1986, and 21 out of the 28 seats reserved for graduates with diplomas. By comparison with the elections of 1965, it had obtained a clear mandate from electors of the educated middle class, even though the results as a whole showed that it had failed to impress the masses (unlike its Algerian counterpart). On the other hand, these years were used to infiltrate the military hierarchy, which the Algerian Islamists had never managed to do. Crucially, the NIF gave an ideological justification for the war being waged against the animists and Christians in the south, which they depicted as a jihad. The reverses sustained in this war had forced the government to negotiate with the southern rebels, and on June 30, 1989, it suspended the Islamic laws as a preliminary to a campaign for national reconciliation.[30]

A successful coup d'état was mounted on the same day by General Omar Hassan al-Bashir, supported by Islamist officers, and this put an end to the reconciliation project. It quickly became clear that Turabi, although he was placed under house arrest for a while along with other political leaders, was the real power behind the new regime. As in Pakistan in 1977 when General Zia ul-Haq brought down Ali Bhutto prior to proclaiming the birth of an Islamic state based on the ideas of Mawdudi, the Islamic intellectuals and the devout bourgeoisie influenced by them won power in the Sudan without having to mobilize the people on their behalf. In both cases, a section of the military hierarchy had embraced Islamist ideology.[31] There was no need to appeal for the help of the young urban poor, whose social demands might have uncontrollable consequences for the establishment. In both cases, Islamist ideology found more receptive ears among army officers because the Jamaat-e-Islami in Pakistan, like the NIF in the Sudan, was able to supply a full religious justification for unsuccessful wars like Pakistan's Bangladesh debacle of 1971 or Nimayri's campaign against the southern Sudanese animists and Christians.

Finally, setting up an Islamist military dictatorship involved several years of savage repression against the secular middle class, a repression symbolized in Pakistan by the hanging of Ali Bhutto in 1979. In the Sudan, where political customs were traditionally much less harsh and where marriages and tribal alliances between the ruling elites had always given physical protection to politicians who might find themselves temporarily disgraced, the 1989 regime provided a rude awakening. Purges and executions were immediately carried out in the upper ranks of the army, while civil and military officials were subjected to "reeducation" to make them adopt the Islamist view of the world. People were routinely interrogated and tortured in "ghost houses"—anonymous villas used by the security services. This was denounced by international organizations, but Turabi dismissed the abuses as minimal, attributing them to the "extreme sensitivity" of his compatriots.[32] Nevertheless, associations, political parties, and independent newspapers were all banned, and their leading figures were imprisoned.

The brutality of the first years of the NIF's regime enabled it to consolidate its control of the state by filling government positions with its own men, whose origins were in the Islamist intelligentsia or the devout middle class. The long-term objective was to destroy the power of the traditionally dominant political parties, which had close ties to the brotherhoods, and to replace them with a new, modern elite.[33] At the same time, the NIF came down even harder on intellectuals or members of the non-Islamist middle class, forcing many of them into exile to prevent them from constructing any kind of alternative. Finally, the NIF compensated for its lack of mass support by heavily favoring the Fallata, a hitherto marginal group of tribesmen from West Africa whose loyalty and willingness to do the government's dirty work were all the more fervent because they risked forfeiting everything should the NIF lose its grip on power.[34]

This policy enabled Turabi and his friends to remain firmly in control for a decade. Turabi was greatly admired by most other comparable movements in the Arab world, particularly by the leaders of the Tunisian Mouvement de la Tendance Islamique (MTI) and the Palestinian Hamas, which held the Sudan up as a worthy example.[35] The Sudan also won the sympathy of nationalists and leftist militants in the region, who applauded the anti-imperialism of Turabi's speeches and turned a blind eye to the repression of their comrades in Khartoum. In contrast to General Zia's pro-Islamist government in Pakistan, which also took power through a military coup but which then received massive American support in its battle against the Soviets in Afghanistan, the regime in the Sudan had attracted, then cultivated, the displeasure of the United States. Among other things, the exactions of the army and militia during the unending war in the south had aroused the opposition of many Protestant and Catholic organizations, which had clout in both Washington and the capitals of Europe. This closed off any access the Sudanese leaders might have had to the various forums of Islamic-Christian dialogue, through which the Islamist movements in many other countries had managed to establish contacts with those in power in the West.

In this sense, the NIF, although it had come into being through a coup and was led by elites trained in Great Britain and the United States, was as unpopular with the Americans as Khomeini's regime before it, being classed as a rogue state that actively supported terrorism. Like the Iranians, the Sudanese contrived to parlay Western sanctions and hostility into a kind of legitimacy, seizing on them to blame America for the economic disasters of the preceding decade and to call for a sacred union.[36] Turabi himself—who had supported Saddam Hussein during the Gulf War of 1990–1991, temporarily cutting his country off from Saudi aid—used the situation to rally international support beyond the Islamist movement, portraying his country, one of the poorest nations on the planet, as a symbol of resistance to imperialism.

In April 1991, an Arab and Islamic conference in Khartoum brought together all the leading Islamists from the Arab Middle East, Iran, Afghanistan, and Pakistan, as well as Yasir Arafat and the Egyptian Nasserists. All reiterated their solidarity with Iraq and proclaimed themselves an alternative to the Saudi-dominated Organization of the Islamic Conference, though they had nothing like its financial means. This gathering was followed by a second conference with the same objective, in December 1993, and then a third, in March–April 1995.[37] These gave Turabi a forum with which to establish his own presence on the international scene through the media, which he handled with consummate skill, and to strengthen his hold on his own country.[38] In this way his regime was able to mask its own narrow origins and its lack of mass support among the people, while projecting the image of a revolutionary state willing and able to represent the progressive Muslim masses of the world. It could do this because, after 1989, the NIF was not only the sole Sunni Islamist movement to have taken control of a legitimate state but also the only one ready to fill the vacuum left by Khomeini's death, which took place in the same month as the Khartoum coup d'état.

8

The Fatwa and the Veil in Europe

Khomeini died on June 3, 1989, less than four months after enjoining the world's Muslims to execute Salman Rushdie, the author of *The Satanic Verses*. This stunning fatwa was the true political legacy of the ayatollah, and it brought to a close the decade-long ascendancy of Islamic movements which began with the mullahs' seizure of power in Tehran in 1979.

Iran had been forced to abandon its long war against Iraq, which had been dragging on since 1980, and to relinquish its hope of bringing down Saddam Hussein. Meanwhile, Saudi Arabia still maintained its grip on the direction of Islam worldwide, despite Tehran's attempts to destabilize the Saudi regime. The fatwa was above all a move to regain the initiative. With it, Khomeini gave expression to the deep outrage of many Muslims over a book that they viewed as an affront to their honor, religion, and culture. His bold action contrasted strongly with the powerless of Riyadh and its international networks to prevent the book's publication. A further effect of the fatwa of February 14 was to shift the focus of Islamic opposition away from southwest Asia and into the heart of Western Europe—which was outside the traditional borders of the faith—where Salman Rushdie lived as a British subject. At a stroke, dar el-Islam was made universal, and its politics was expanded to include Muslim immigrants to the West, who became first the hostages and then the actors in a worldwide struggle for control of Islam. In the decade that followed, the West was to become a new battlefield for these contending forces.

February 15, 1989—the day after Khomeini issued his fatwa—
marked the triumph of the jihad sponsored by the United States and
Saudi Arabia in Afghanistan. On the orders of Mikhail Gorbachev,
Soviet forces completed their withdrawal from Afghan territory. It
was expected that in the aftermath a coalition government would be
formed in Kabul to include the various mujahedeen groups based in
Peshawar and sponsored by the Pakistani and Saudi governments. Although another three years of fighting would occur before the Afghan
capital fell into the hands of the mujahedeen, at the time it appeared
that Sunni-dominated Saudi Arabia had scored another significant
point in the affirmation of its leadership of Islam, particularly since the
Shiite faction within Afghanistan did not belong to the victorious coalition.

But the Soviet withdrawal went almost unnoticed in the world's media, riveted as they were by Khomeini's announcement of the day before. This publicity coup thrust Iran back into contention for political
primacy within Islam. The broadcasting of the ayatollah's brief text
"condemning to death" the author and publishers of The Satanic Verses
and calling upon all zealous Muslims "to execute them immediately
wherever they might be" was accompanied by images of Islamists sacking the American Cultural Center in Islamabad, Pakistan, on February
12. Five people were killed and dozens were injured in this riot, among
them the head of the Deobandi ulemas, Maulana Fazlur Rahman. The
dramatic images demonstrated that even America's substantial support
for the Afghan jihad, all of which was funneled through Pakistan, could
not avert the destruction of one of its institutions by a mob protesting
Rushdie's book, despite the fact that the author was in no way connected to the United States. For good measure, television coverage of
the fatwa included scenes filmed a month earlier in Bradford, England,
where a large population of Muslim immigrants publicly burned copies of The Satanic Verses at the instigation of the town's Council of
Mosques.

These outbreaks of violence against a work of fiction surprised and
outraged the West. Comparisons were made with the fanaticism of the
Spanish Inquisition and the book-burnings of Nazi Germany. The
Bradford militants argued that a novel in which characters identifiable
as the wives of the Prophet Mohammed were depicted as prostitutes
was an insult to the honor of Islam and a mockery of its beliefs. It did

not matter to them that Rushdie's intention had been to write a work of fiction about the upheavals in the lives of those large numbers of Muslim immigrants who settled in Europe in the last quarter of the twentieth century. In their eyes, the case against the author was compounded by his own Muslim origins, which qualified him as a blasphemer and—if he did not repent—an apostate, a criminal for whom the prescribed sentence of the sharia was death.

The first months of the Rushdie affair, between the publication of the novel in September 1988 and the Bradford book-burning on January 14, 1989, were orchestrated from India and Pakistan by the disciples of Mawdudi. Thereafter, the campaign was directed by their representative in Britain, the UK Islamic Mission.[1] The group began by activating the various Saudi networks, which vainly exerted pressure on the British government to ban Rushdie's novel. The Deobandi and Barelwi associations next took the initiative, working at the grassroots to organize street protests in Britain and Pakistan against the novel and its author. This approach was in stark contrast to Saudi Arabia's customary cautious diplomatic efforts and its distrust of popular movements. The third and final phase, initiated by Khomeini with his fatwa on February 14, was a blend of grassroots mobilization and international action seasoned by the threat of terrorism.

Added to the two rivals of the 1980s—the Wahhabite Saudis, the Jamaat-e-Islami, and the Muslim Brotherhood on one side and the Iranians on the other—was a third competitor, the Pakistani ulemas. The ulemas were dominated by the Deobandi faction, whose influence on international Islam was to grow steadily throughout the 1990s and to eventually spawn the Taliban. On October 3, 1988, the Leicester Islamic Foundation, which was controlled by the spiritual followers of Mawdudi, circulated extracts from *The Satanic Verses* around the Muslim associations and mosques in Britain. Barely a week had passed since the novel's publication; the Leicester Foundation now asked Muslims to join a campaign of petition-signing to have it banned and withdrawn from sale, with a public apology from the author. This idea was instigated by the Jamaat-e-Islami of Madras, India, which had already forced moves by Muslim politicians in India to stop the book from entering Rushdie's own country of origin. The Indian prime minister, Rajiv Gandhi, who was facing a close election in which he badly needed the votes of India's 150 million Muslims, agreed to suppress the novel on October 5. Rushdie himself roundly denounced this decision, whereupon an ad hoc Muslim Action Committee, meeting at the house of a Saudi diplomat in London the following week, broadened the campaign against him by calling for British blasphemy laws—originally designed to protect the Church of England—to be extended to other religions. The United Kingdom's legal safeguards for freedom of expression precluded this; nevertheless, the majority of Muslim states fell into line and forbade importation of the book, which was officially condemned by the Saudi-dominated OIC on November 5.

The first phase of the mobilization against Rushdie's novel was low-key. The disciples of Mawdudi in the UK, a well-organized group of intellectuals, for the time being had little leverage over a largely working-class immigrant majority badly affected by unemployment; Deobandi and Barelwi's influence was prevalent among them. However, the goal of Mawdudi's disciples was to win the support of their co-religionists and to gain moral and political ascendancy over them by defending the honor of Islam, and the anti-Rushdie campaign offered an opportunity to broaden their base among younger, less affluent urban Pakistanis in Britain. Unlike their parents, this second generation of immigrants was both literate and fluent in English, having been educated in the UK; they were able to understand the issues raised by Rushdie's book.

At the same time, the Mawdudist elite was eager to preserve its relationships with British institutions. The latter saw them as valid representatives of Islam; and the Mawdudi disciples preferred the tactic of diplomatic pressure backed by Saudi financial muscle, which (they hoped) would prove effective. They remembered, for example, how Riyadh had provoked an outcry at the beginning of the decade by discouraging the broadcast by the BBC of a documentary entitled "Death of a Princess," about the resolution of a case of adultery within the Saudi royal family. But *The Satanic Verses* was not yet seen as an issue important enough to warrant the intervention of Saudi diplomacy, or even the threat of commercial reprisals against the United Kingdom.

At the end of December, the attorney-general in Westminster ruled that British law offered no grounds for a civil suit to withdraw *The Satanic Verses* from circulation. This failure of the first phase of the campaign opened the way to street demonstrations by Barelwi and Deobandi militants. These people were not greatly concerned about a book written in English, whose themes were well outside their customary sphere of interest; nor were they guided by geopolitical considerations. Theirs was merely a gut reaction to something they perceived as an affront to Islam, or rather to the strict rules of behavior prescribed to the faithful by the madrassas. For the leaders of these groups, whose authority hinged on absolute acceptance of immutable, untouchable Muslim dogma, any text that might instill doubt—especially in the young, who were more susceptible to the blandishments of Western culture—constituted a grave threat. This danger was especially acute in the United Kingdom, because the mullahs' position and power as the main intermediaries between the British authorities and the Muslim community depended on maintaining a cultural barrier between their own people and British society as a whole. The "blasphemy" perpetrated by *The Satanic Verses,* if not nipped in the bud, might embolden young Muslim Indians and Pakistanis to imitate Rushdie's heroes; that is, they might break with traditional patterns of thought and even cease to obey their religious instructors. Thus, the campaign of the mullahs was conducted in defense of their own vital interests—hence, the Bradford book-burnings and the rioting at the American Cultural Center in Islamabad. Even so, the real or symbolic violence of these demonstrations of large crowds of ordinary people had no direct political sequel. Nor did it affect the judgments of those who wielded real power in the Muslim world. This contrasted with the campaign of the Mawdudists, which was quickly taken up by powerful Saudi interests but found no echo in the streets.

By issuing his fatwa immediately after the Islamabad riots, Khomeini gave the cause a political dimension it had previously lacked and made it an instant worldwide phenomenon. Until that moment, the campaign had focused on banning the novel, and in that strategy the Saudi network had failed. Now, Khomeini's campaign called for the execution of the author himself—a British subject with no connection to Iran. The Guide of Tehran became the unchallenged champion of all those Muslims disgusted by what they perceived as Riyadh's spinelessness. Furthermore, the symbolic dividends the Saudi kingdom had expected from its Afghan jihad, whose success was confirmed by the Soviet withdrawal on February 15, vanished. Finally and above all, Khomeini appeared to have transcended the traditional frontiers of Islam. According to Islamic law, no fatwa could be valid outside those areas governed by a Muslim prince and in which the laws of the sharia were applied. Now, at a stroke, the ayatollah had placed the entire world under his jurisdiction. Not only did he symbolically impose his will upon both Sunnis and Shiites outside Iran, he also contrived to rally the immigrant Muslim peoples of Europe to the banner of Islam. This double upheaval was to have dramatic effects on the balance of forces existing within the Muslim world, on the way that world perceived the West, and on the way Islam itself was perceived by Westerners.

The coup restored Khomeini's position at home. He had been confronted by a "pragmatic" trend led by the president of the Parliament, Hashemi Rafsanjani, whose aim was to re-establish links with the West following the inglorious end of the war with Iraq. Khomeini's fatwa had the effect of once again electrifying the political atmosphere in Iran. He appealed to the disappointed and deprived multitudes of the faith, offering a new moral and religious "crusade" to distract them from the social discontent of a nation in which the deepening poverty of the masses contrasted with the substantial enrichment of a pious commercial bourgeoisie with links to the mullahs. Abroad, he sowed confusion among the Saudis and their allies, dividing and weakening them. Saddam Hussein interpreted this political disarray as a military opportunity, and the result was his invasion of Kuwait and the subsequent Gulf War of 1990. Finally, a number of militants who had taken part in the Afghan jihad and were considered by Riyadh to be well out of the extremist anti-American, Iranian orbit now gave their support to Khomeini—among them the Egyptian Sheik Omar Abdel Rahman, who would later become famous in connection with the 1993 bombing of the World Trade Center in New York.

At the end of the OIC conference of foreign ministers on March 16, 1984, Saudi Arabia and its fellow "moderate" states were obliged to accept a communiqué declaring the author of The Satanic Verses an apostate. This supplied a doctrinal justification for the fatwa—by judging Rushdie's blasphemy according to the categories of Islamic law— while avoiding handing down an explicit death sentence to a British subject residing in England.[2] In his final great political act before dying, Khomeini had succeeded in confounding his adversaries. As his future successor Ayatollah Ali Khamenei expressed it: "He is the Guide of all the Muslim communities, not only of the Iranian nation. Muslims throughout the world are linked in their hearts. As Guide of the Islamic Umma, he is pledged to defend their rights."[3]

The "communities" over which Khomeini wished to further extend his authority were made up of people who had emigrated to Western Europe. This migration in some cases dated back to the first decades of the twentieth century and had its roots in a quest for work.[4] European industries needed cheap basic manpower, and the immigrants needed income that they could send back to their home countries. Nothing about this exchange was specifically Islamic; the migration was not linked to the faith or to its expansion. In fact, many Christians from southern Europe were also traveling northward to find work at that time. When most of the Muslim nations won their independence at the end of World War II, the movement broadened considerably because of Europe's huge need for workers to carry out reconstruction under the Marshall Plan and because of a population explosion in the Third World.

Prior to the mid-1970s, most people designated as immigrant workers were male, and they migrated to countries where unemployment was low. No real settling process took place: the workers, like the European authorities, saw themselves as itinerants rather than immigrants, who would go back home once their contracts ran out and would be replaced by others, according to the regular ebb and flow of migration. France and Great Britain received citizens from their former colonial empires, in North and West Africa and the Indian subcontinent, while most Muslim immigrants to Germany came from Turkey.

Prior to the war between Israel and the Arab countries in October 1973, Islam was an issue of minor political importance in the Third World, where the various forms of nationalist ideology predominated. Immigrants referred to themselves first and foremost in terms of their nationality, especially if independence was the recent reward of a long struggle, as in Algeria. As for those who saw the world in terms of religious categories, they tended to perceive Western Europe as *dar el-kufr* (the domain of impiety)—that part of the universe governed by non-Muslims, where the sharia was not applicable—in contrast to dar el-Islam. In real terms, this meant that Muslim religious life in France and Germany had almost no visibility whatever: mosques and places of prayer were few and far between. Nevertheless, there was a minimal respect for certain prohibitions, such as the consumption of pork and alcohol (the latter not so strictly observed) and for the carrying out of daily prayers and the fast of Ramadan. But these rituals were practiced on an individual basis and were rarely identified locally as collective religious endeavors.

The Indian and Pakistani Muslims of Great Britain were an exception. For a hundred years past they had been accustomed to keeping to their own creed within the context of the Deobandi and Barelwi movements, in a subcontinent where they formed only one fifth of the population (unlike North Africans, Africans, and Turks, who came almost exclusively from Muslim countries). They had applied the sharia to themselves without provoking the intervention of the state: and on arrival in the United Kingdom after World War II, many of them transposed to the British context the patterns they had developed in the environment of Hinduism, strictly observing the prohibitions and turning inward as a community in order to preserve their way of life. For example, in order to eat ritually slaughtered (halal) meat, which was not available in the shops at that time, they had to band together and buy a sheep. The community also prayed together and looked out for one another's interests. Gradually, a fabric of Muslim associations built up in Great Britain, with a network of mosques that organized the people as a proper religious community—much stricter than was the case among the Turks in Germany or the North Africans in France at that time.

The 1973 October war, which played a crucial role in the rise of conservative Islamism on the Saudi model, had an unexpected and no less considerable effect on the future of the Muslim populations in Western Europe. The rise in oil prices was reflected in double-digit inflation and a sudden, massive increase in unemployment, which immediately affected workers without qualifications, that is to say, immigrants. European governments took measures to restrict immigration in the hopes of reducing unemployment; they also counted on the probability that those who found themselves out of work would go home. But the immigration strictures had exactly the opposite effect: immigrants realized that they would be better off being unemployed in Europe than unemployed at home. Consequently, most of them chose to settle down. Within a few years, wives were brought over, and children came along, either arriving as very young immigrants or being born in the host country after 1973. By the end of the 1980s, these children had grown up as the first significant generation of young Muslim adults born or educated in a European country—speaking its language, engaging with its local popular culture, and either enjoying full citizenship or desiring to do so.

Between 1973 and 1989, Islam in Europe was dominated by political issues linked to immigrants' countries of origin. It also reflected the social constraints prevailing in host countries, where immigrants found life difficult. Omnipresent unemployment hindered their integration into society and upward mobility. Newly arrived women often stayed home like recluses because they were unable to speak the local language. Their children, educated in English, German, French, and Dutch, became their indispensable intermediaries with the world outside the home; yet these modern young people often spurned the generational hierarchy and disparaged the folk culture of their parents.

In this unstable context, where traditional points of reference seemed obsolete and the host society seemed impenetrably hostile, a new Islamic identity began to develop. People who had gambled on the unknown were now trying to get their bearings, especially the fragile, ill-educated, unemployed segment of the immigrant population. From the outset this group attracted the attention of the more pietist Islamic movements, which were accustomed to providing order and structure in the daily lives of the faithful through strictly codified practices. The renewed success of the Deobandis and Barelwis in Great Britain was paralleled by that of the Tabligh, a movement originating in India that regulated the lives of its adepts with strict discipline (its original purpose had been to help them break with the Hindu environment). The Tabligh had particular success in the French North African milieu, where they had never before won a foothold. For many West Africans, the strong support systems of the Mouride and Tijan brotherhoods had insulated their talibes (disciples) from the destabilizing effects of migration—at the price of a ghetto-style home life. In the Turkish diaspora of Germany, the brotherhoods banned by Ataturk's state (Nurcus, Nakshbandis, and Suleymancis in particular) performed an identical role.

Before the Islamic Revolution in Iran, European authorities were largely indifferent to Islam, though they appreciated it as a conservative religion hostile to revolutionary ideologies and communism and as a stabilizing resource for people who, they still hoped, would one day return to their countries of origin. During the major strikes among immigrant workers in France between 1975 and 1978, the administration had discreetly encouraged the opening of prayer rooms, which were quickly taken up by Tabligh preachers; these they saw as bulwarks against leftism and the key to social peace. But Khomeini's return to Tehran, his harangues in favor of exporting the Islamic Revolution, and the violent actions attributed to Iranian "students in the line of the Imam" attending European universities completely transformed the image of Islam. Henceforth, it was associated by the TV news with the machine-gun-wielding mullahs of Tehran. At the same time, the Saudi-inclined Muslim World League had begun opening offices in Europe, with a view to financing the building of mosques through local associations whose economic dependence they hoped would evolve into ideological support for Wahhabism.

Thus, the emerging field of European Islam was, from the start of the 1980s, an arena of intense competition for the various currents then struggling for primacy in the wider Muslim world. But Paris, Bonn, and Brussels, whose main worry was the greatly overestimated Iranian threat, were caught short by the growth of a religious movement that their police services had no idea how to handle. Their response was to assign the management of Islam to foreign states or institutions over which they had some kind of hold, thus passing on the job of keeping order and eradicating the "epidemic" imported from Tehran. The Algerian government, which ran the Grand Mosque in Paris from 1982 onward with the consent of the French authorities, took care that French Algerians (who formed the majority of Muslims in France) did not offer a breeding ground for Islamist ideas inspired by the movements then gathering around Bouyali in the Algerian maquis or around Abassi Madani at the University of Algiers. The department of religious affairs attached to the Turkish premier rushed its own preachers and teachers to Germany to rebut the ones inspired by the brotherhoods and by Necmettin Erbakan's Islamist movement, which were taking advantage of German freedom of speech to escape the restrictions imposed by Ataturk's strict secularism.

At that time, the Islamist intelligentsia in Europe was represented by students who had grown up inside the Muslim world until high school. A number of these were committed to the work of preaching and proselytizing, but it was hard for them to connect with the immigrant workers and the unemployed, since they had no appreciation of their experience. This first Muslim generation—marked by the trials and difficulties of immigration, threatened by the dwindling number of blue-collar jobs after 1977, and worried by the education of numerous children who were acquiring a culture over which their parents had almost no control—were more attracted (if they thought about religion at all) to Islam's more reassuring pietist forms. They had little time for militants who preached the virtues of an Islamic state, denounced the "impious" nationalist governments of their home countries, and seemed generally bent on stirring up trouble.

But by 1989 an entire generation of children of immigrants had come of age in Europe. Though they were acculturated to Europe, they faced major difficulties because of the uncertain job market, compounded often by poor school records. For the first time, a class of young urban poor who were much more receptive than the older generation to radical Islamist militants appeared on the European scene. The militants were young people as well; in the main they were students from North Africa, the Middle East, Turkey, or Pakistan, with a high intellectual capacity and full mastery of the languages of their home countries. The immigrants' children often had little or no knowledge of these languages but were nevertheless strongly attracted to Muslim culture, in which they discerned reassuring roots.

The success of Islamist ideology among this new generation also benefited from disappointed hopes in the great causes of the 1980s. In France, the SOS-Racisme movement had sought to bring all young people together, regardless of creed or color, in a great groundswell of protest against racism. It had been used by President François Mitterrand to lambast the National Front and divide the right, but in the end had petered out, leaving memories of spectacular initiatives that had had no real effect on society. The Beur movement (after the French slang word reubeu, "Arab"), which tried to build up a distinct identity for young Frenchmen of North African descent by drawing on the cultural cross-currents of both nationalities, quickly arrived at the boundary of its possibilities and lapsed into the promotion of a "beurgeoisie" confined to the educated elite. Many who had initially joined these movements felt bitterness and disenchantment about the way they had allowed French cultural values to marginalize the Islamic influence.

All this was fertile ground for the Islamist dawa, Muslim Brothers off-shoots, the Pakistani Jamaat-e-Islami, and the Turkish Refah party, all of which started to vigorously exhibit their presence in Europe. They adapted their various messages to suit a milieu of young urban poor who seemed to them ripe for conversion. There was a sudden blossoming of Islamist preachers in French, English, German, and so on, with sermons and lessons in the mosques and translations of the works of Sayyid Qutb and Mawdudi—in contrast to the previous decade, during which the languages of immigrants' countries of origin were the only vehicles for spreading the message.

Furthermore, prior to 1989 European territories had been "sanctuarized" by the Islamist movements that had taken root in them: they were places where militants and sympathizers could be recruited, who would then go home to their native countries to carry on the only fight that was worth the candle, against the regimes of the ungodly. Everything had been done to avoid conflicts with European authorities— and the expulsions of the Khomeinist militants who had tried to stir up trouble among immigrant workers in Europe in the early 1980s served as a reminder that the balance of forces was weighted against them. Within European Islam, the social and political dimensions of preaching had been detached from one another. Charitable work, help for the needy, and maintenance of the moral framework of everyday life were all taken care of by pietist groups and apolitical brotherhoods backed up by the consulates and their official imams, who also organized courses of religious education for children. As for the Islamist movements, they trained their own recruits for the ideological struggle against the established governments of Algeria, Morocco, Tunisia, or Turkey, and against the Indian presence in Kashmir, while exerting no pressure on host states.

The new generation of young European adults of Muslim origin turned this situation around completely. Unlike their parents, who were unfamiliar with the laws and cultural codes of their host countries and whose worldview had been formed during the era of colonial domination, the children were fully aware of their rights and quick to voice their complaints and tackle the institutions of the countries whose languages they spoke and whose citizenship they either possessed already or were about to claim. The forces of law and order in France, Britain, and Germany, as well as the education and justice systems, were held responsible for immigrants' failures in the schools, for their problems in finding work, for the high incidence of police harassment they experienced. These problems had already been raised by the antiracist movements of the 1980s; they now returned with double force, because by the end of the decade antiracist groups had lost their prestige and the new generation was growing apace. The Islamist intellectuals rushed into this perceived breach; abandoning the sanctuarization strategy, they decided to intervene in European politics by making themselves the spokesmen of the young urban poor, whom they characterized for the occasion as an "Islamic community."

This change of course was matched by a theoretical shift: now that Muslims were full citizens of European states, they could no longer belong to the territory of dar el-ahd, or the domain of contractual peace. In Islamic doctrine, this term designates the portion of the dar el-kufr (domain of impiety) in which the faithful can live in peace. In the old days, the dar el-ahd covered those territories whose sovereigns had signed a peace treaty with the Commander of the Faithful: here, Muslim merchants, seamen, and travelers, for example, could go about their business peacefully. This was in contrast to the dar el-harb (domain of war), where Muslims were obliged to wage jihad. During the 1980s, only the militants of the Lebanese Hezbollah, who carried out the Paris bombings of 1985 and 1986, had acted as though Europe was part of the dar el-harb. The vast majority of Muslims in Europe up to the end of that decade thought of it as belonging to the dar el-ahd.

In the "domain of contractual peace" it was out of the question to demand the implementation of the sharia, since the sovereign was kafir (impious). It was thus impossible for Islamist organizations claiming to speak for their "community" to operate within this context. For this reason, from 1988 onward Islamist organizations began to characterize Europe as dar el-Islam. The large number of Muslims who had become citizens of European countries should now organize themselves into an Islamic community, apply the sharia, and intervene as such in local politics.

In Germany, Great Britain, and the Netherlands, this doctrinal evolution did not translate into tangible changes. Each of these states was already encouraging its so-called minority populations to organize themselves on a community basis. In Germany, where naturalization laws made access to citizenship for a Turk very difficult, even if he had been born and educated in the country, support of minority communities was the compensation offered for the denial of civic integration through naturalization. The immigrant population was therefore all the more inclined to live in closed groups, to speak its own language, to buy provisions in ethnic shops, to have picnics together in public parks, and to veil its women—given that its members had no particular opportunity to assimilate as Germans. By multiplying the outward signs of difference in this way, the immigrants strengthened the case of those who advocated German blood as a restrictive definition of *Heimat.*

In the United Kingdom, where British citizenship was easy to obtain without having to speak English or show any other signs of acculturation or political allegiance, the state emphasized community identification over individual integration. Thus it prolonged the communalist tradition of the British Indian Empire, whereby the religious identity of Hindus, Muslims, and Sikhs conditioned their political representation and made the notables of each community the public representatives of their co-religionists. In Bradford, Birmingham, and elsewhere, the Council of Mosques was delegated a number of mediating functions by the municipalities, vis-à-vis their flocks. These included the management of unemployment, charitable work, and so on. In return, the imams urged their congregations to vote for whichever Labor or Conservative candidate for Parliament promised to support, for instance, the creation of all-girls' schools, so young Muslims would not be exposed to coeducation, which was perceived as licentious. They also expected their prospective MPs to guarantee halal food in school lunchrooms and to provide all kinds of other goods and services that favored a closed community and therefore strengthened the authority of the religious hierarchy.

In France, where the two traditions of secularism and Jacobinism were opposed to the introduction of religion into public life and indeed of any community that set itself up as a screen between the citizen and the state, the new direction sought by Islamic intellectuals quickly degenerated into conflict centered on the wearing of the veil in educational establishments. The logic of republican integration required that all pupils should be equal, beyond the diversity of their social, ethnic, or religious origins, when it came to acquiring knowledge and fulfilling the duties of citizenship. They should not parade their religious denomination, which would tend to confirm their difference instead of making common ground with their fellows. Now that France counted as dar el-Islam, militants felt that Muslim schoolchildren should be authorized to respect the prescriptions of the sharia, as interpreted by the disciples of Qutb and Mawdudi, and that women and girls should wear the veil. The movements in France that took up this cause had identified, with great discernment, a directive that allowed them to commence a process of controlled rupture with the state. For potential adepts and sympathizers, the law of God should take precedence over the regulations of French schools. This devaluing of schools relative to religion would reverse the cultural balance between the "disinherited" young urban poor, with their immigrant background, and the "arrogant" institutions of the state. By forcing the French government to modify its definition of secularism, the Islamist militants would raise their prestige as representatives of their community and would win the support of the young, for whom they had already organized holiday camps and training courses. These camps and courses, which replaced the activities of the declining Communist Party, were modeled on those of the Gamaa Islamiya in Egypt, where the norms of the "pure Islamic life" were conscientiously absorbed.

The first "affair of the veil" took place in the fall of 1989 and was followed by a succession of others into the mid-1990s. The Union des organisations islamiques de France (UOIF) played a leading role in this protest. Though close to the Muslim Brothers, they were also favored by influential figures in Saudi Arabia. They owned a chateau in France, which they used to train imams specializing in young European Muslims, under the high patronage of the Egyptian-Qatari Sheik Yusuf al-Qaradawi. Every year, at the end of December, the union organized a major gathering that brought it high visibility: prominent Islamist personalities from all over the world were invited, as well as French university academics and ecclesiastics. These speakers addressed thousands of young people bussed in from the outskirts of France's principal cities.

By involving itself in the dispute over the veil, the union's strategy was to secure its role as the Islamic community's intermediary with the authorities. In exchange for concessions from the government, it would exert itself to keep control of the potentially unstable youth element and fight against delinquency, drug addiction, and violence. This "community logic," which went in tandem with the classification of

France as part of the dar el-Islam, was aimed at making control of Islam an issue in French domestic politics; until then, it had been linked only to foreign policy matters, whether in North Africa or the Middle East. No longer a part of the domain of impiety, France should in theory have had a solid guarantee that no jihad would be unleashed on its territory—a doctrine that would be called into question by the terrorist attacks in the Paris metro carried out in 1995 at the instigation of the Algerian GIA (as we shall see in Chapter 13).

Thus, by 1989 the Islamist organizations active in France were seeking a foothold among the young urban poor who dwelled in the projects (banlieues), with a long-term strategy that excluded violence. Instead, they looked for support among the democratic sectors of French society, to whom the controversy over the veil was presented in the guise of freedom of expression and belief. In the media, the Islamist intellectuals gave the leading role to young Muslim girls, who insisted on their wish to gain access to modern education while protecting the intangible values of their religion from impurity by wearing the veil. For these girls, as for their brothers whose beards demonstrated their religious fervor in imitation of the Prophet, the republican model had failed to keep its promise to "integrate the individual." Though completely acculturated and even assimilated into French society by their progress through the schools, some young people of Muslim origin found themselves pushed to its edges, crushed by unemployment and even forced into criminal ways. Community solidarity, reinforced by a religious identity along Islamist lines that praised the disinherited ones and disparaged those in power, seemed to some children of immigrants to be a viable alternative—so much so that it actually sparked a movement to convert non-Muslim British, French, and German citizens living in the projects.

It was against this backdrop that Ayatollah Khomeini issued his sensational fatwa condemning Rushdie to death. The call came at a moment when European Islam was in a state of uncertainty, without being in any way the cause of that uncertainty. Like the Iranian revolution ten years earlier, which had coincided with the appearance of France's first mosques, the fatwa's main effect was to create antagonisms and to reinforce the clichés whereby Muslims in general were associated with fanaticism and violence. But it also undermined those Islamist associations on both sides of the English Channel whose patient work at the community level had aimed to reassure the European authorities that the Islamists could keep the peace among a potentially turbulent younger generation.

In the United Kingdom, those of Mawdudi's followers who had been behind the first campaign against *The Satanic Verses,* as well as the Barelwis and Deobandis who had instigated the book-burning in Bradford, would have nothing to do with the fatwa. They had called for the censuring of a novel, they said, not for the assassination of its author. But a certain number of young Pakistanis, exasperated by unemployment and unable to see any prospect of relief in the existing community-assistance networks, seized the opportunity to vent their fury and defy the authorities in bitter demonstrations calling for Rushdie's head. A pro-Iranian activist, Kalim Siddiqui, pushed the logic of rupture to its extreme expression by creating a Muslim parliament parallel to the one at the Palace of Westminster, whose "elected" members claimed to legislate in the name of all Muslim believers in the United Kingdom. This deliberately provocative minority initiative had little effect in the long term, other than to serve as a reminder that, historically, the exacerbation of communalist identities had often resulted in the breakup of societies. In other European countries, the Rushdie affair had little impact: while many believers rejected his book as an insult to their faith, most were completely indifferent. The issue seemed mainly to concern Iran and the Indian subcontinent; Arabs and Turks were unmoved by a controversy that one Saudi minister described as "marginal" and "imaginary," whose principal result was "to make Islam look like easy prey to whoever felt like attacking or harming it."[5]

Still, the year 1989 marked the high point of Islamist expansion, twenty years after the ideas of Qutb, Mawdudi, and Khomeini first began to circulate among students and young intellectuals and found an echo among the new generation of disinherited urban poor and the devout middle class. The decade that began with the Iranian revolution and was dominated by the figure of Khomeini ended in a spectacular publicity coup; the storm raised throughout the world by his fatwa had demonstrated that an Islamist movement predicated on threats of violence could still mobilize the masses. In that same year, which was marked by Khomeini's death, an Islamist regime seized power in the Sudan, and the FIS in Algeria seemed poised to take over that country's government. In Palestine, the last Arab nationalist cause had been obliged, since the outbreak of the intifada, to reckon with the vigorous Islamist element of Hamas. Everywhere in the Muslim world, governments were having to make concessions to opponents who clamored for the sharia and to seek religious legitimacy from ulemas who gave them support in exchange for control over the field of ideas and values, from which secularist intellectuals were in full retreat. Finally, beyond the societies of the traditional dar el-Islam, the movement was making inroads in Europe through the first generation of young adults born of immigrant parents. It even called into question France's deep-rooted secularism; the year when all parties were supposed to celebrate the 200th anniversary of the French Revolution in a spirit of consensus will instead be remembered in France as the year of the Islamic veil controversy.

Of course 1989 was also the year when communism finally collapsed, as symbolized by the fall of the Berlin wall in November. This followed on the heels of the final Soviet withdrawal from Afghanistan on February 15, which had sealed the Red Army's defeat by the jihad. In the eyes of its militants (who forgot the help of U.S. funds), Islamism not only had brought down the whole edifice of communism but also could look forward to new territories added to dar el-Islam from among the nations of the now-dismantled Soviet empire. From Bosnia to Chechnya to Central Asia, a whole new section of the world seemed ready to join the Community of Believers and become prey to the activists. But it was not to be. The last decade of the twentieth century did not fulfill this abundant promise, despite the ardent hopes of Islamist militants around the globe.

PART II

DECLINE

9

From the Gulf War to the Taliban Jihad

On the morning of August 2, 1990, the foreign ministers of the Organization of the Islamic Conference, assembled in Cairo, learned that Saddam Hussein had just invaded Kuwait.[1] A Muslim state, which had hosted the preceding OIC summit and had supplied the OIC's current president, had just been wiped off the map by a fellow member of the organization. The Iraqi army, having seized control of the emirate almost without firing a shot, advanced to the Saudi frontier and threatened to make incursions toward the province of Hasa, where the kingdom's richest oil wells were located. In just three days Saddam might conquer the whole of Saudi Arabia.

On August 7, King Fahd, the Custodian of the Two Holy Places (Mecca and Medina), appealed to the United States for military assistance. In Operation Desert Shield, several hundred thousand non-Muslim soldiers, all of them part of an international coalition with a mandate from the United Nations, landed in Saudi Arabia. They saved the monarchy, but in the process they ruined the entire edifice the Al-Saud family had so patiently erected since the 1960s to dominate the Islamic world.

The Saudi system had survived the repeated attacks of Ayatollah Khomeini during the preceding decade, and by financing the Afghan jihad it had preserved its credibility with even the most radical Sunni militants. Thanks to the Islamic financial and banking network, Saudi Arabia had maintained contact with the devout middle class of the wider Muslim world, and through the OIC its diplomacy had achieved a degree of consensus among the Muslim states. The Muslim World League and other transnational organizations working along the same lines spread the Wahhabite message to the beneficiaries of Saudi largesse: few opponents other than Shiites were prepared to act on the anathemas hurled at Riyadh by Tehran. Though there had been ups and downs, in general the Sunni Islamist movements had managed to bridge the gulf between the young, poor urban extremists and the devout bourgeoisie moderates. Medical students and engineers predicted to all who would listen the coming reign of the sharia, which would be built upon the ashes of socialism and of a Western world completely devoid of moral standards.

The person responsible for destroying the social consensus the Saudi state had built around these Islamist values was a figure who was anything but a shining example of piety. In 1980 Saddam Hussein had sent to the gallows, among thousands of others, Baqir as-Sadr, one of the foremost Islamist thinkers of the late twentieth century. In contrast to Khomeini, the Iraqi president had no claim to religious legitimacy: the Baathist party that had brought him to power was doctrinally secular and had been consigned to hell in many a mosque. During the war against Iran (1980–1988) it had begun using religious formulas to counter the charges of apostasy leveled at it by Tehran, but lying just beneath the party's fiery Islamic vocabulary was an ever-present Arabism. Iraq's war was being waged against Persians in the name of Islam, because Arabs had been the first to recognize the Prophet's revelations.

After the invasion of Kuwait, Saddam Hussein appropriated to himself all the grievances against the Saudis formerly trumpeted by his Iranian enemies. He called the kingdom an American protectorate unworthy of governing the Holy Places, and the presence of over 500,000 American soldiers on Saudi territory during the conflict seemed to bear out this argument. Saddam's condemnation was all the more telling in that it did not come from a Shiite Persian but from a Sunni Arab—from the very heart of the Islamic zone that Riyadh had marked out with such painstaking effort and expense. By giving a populist dimension to his calls for jihad (thus compensating for the weakness of his doctrinal justification), Saddam Hussein wrecked the inner equilibrium of the Islamist movement, to the lasting detriment of the bourgeoisie and the conservatives. The cumulative effect of the 1980s had been to force the Islamists to bring together their various components and mask their divergences behind a shared ideology; this process began to reverse in the early 1990s, when mere doctrine could no longer hide the social rifts within the movement. The radically different trajectories of the middle classes and the disinherited young became more and more painfully obvious—and as a result the former became vulnerable to attempts by established governments to win them over, while the latter drifted in the direction of violence and terrorism. The consensus built around a conservative Wahhabism, which had attracted allegiances in every quarter thanks to its religious rigor and financial generosity, and which had added an international dimension to the alliance between the devout bourgeoisie and the young urban poor, would never be the same again after the Gulf War.

The record of the last ten years of the twentieth century might at first glance give the appearance that the power of political Islam was growing in all areas, from secular Turkey, where the head of the Refah Islamist party became prime minister in 1996, to post-communist Bosnia, where power fell to the Islamist Alija Izetbegovic, who had to compromise with a highly secularized society. Among radicals, the Algerian civil war echoed the terrorism in the Nile Valley, which temporarily wrecked the Egyptian tourist industry; the Taliban took power in Kabul in 1996, two years after their first appearance on the scene; Islamist guerrillas in Chechnya had been defying the might of Moscow since 1995; in the same year a series of violent attacks had been launched in France; in August 1998 there were simultaneous bombings of American embassies in Kenya and Tanzania; and finally, on September 11, 2001, the bloody attack on the World Trade Center and the Pentagon shocked the world. But despite this appearance of growing influence worldwide, the deeper reality was that the two opposing camps within the Islamist movement were no longer able to provoke social upheaval on a scale that could lead to a lasting success like that of the Iranian revolution. The recurrent violence of the decade was above all a reflection of the movement's structural weakness, not its growing strength. No ideologist worthy of the name had come forward to take the place of Mawdudi, Qutb, and Khomeini, and their imitators were unable to offer an overall vision that transcended social antagonisms.

The extremist groups published their own manifestos, in which the struggle against "deviant" fellow Muslims took up as much space as attacks on the "ungodly." As for intellectuals linked to the devout middle class, they were obliged to take a stance in favor of democracy, the rights of man (and woman, too), and freedom of expression, themes on which the founding fathers of Islamism had been ambiguous, not to say downright hostile. This stance allowed them to forge alliances with their secular counterparts against authoritarian regimes, but it also forced them into revisions of doctrine that tarnished their Islamist credentials and made them vulnerable to dogmatic zealots. This crisis within the movement, which continued throughout the 1990s, was revealed for all the world to see in the yawning chasm opened up by the Gulf War and by Saddam Hussein's ideological offensive against Saudi hegemony.

The Aftershocks of the Gulf War

The war had lasting effects on two levels. Internationally, it shattered the aura of religious legitimacy that had been so painstakingly acquired by Saudi Arabia, and the Saudis were to feel the effects of this loss for years after Iraq had been crushed on the battlefield. In every other Muslim country, the war backed Islamists into a corner, focusing attention on their squabbles, forcing them to choose sides between the two Muslim antagonists, and eventually provoking the emergence of an alternative Islamism within Saudi territory, which was directed against the Saudi royal family.

During the war that Iraq had initiated against Iran, a Popular Islamic Conference had convened in Baghdad in 1983 with a view to hammering out a religious argument to counter Tehran's fulminations against Saddam's regime of Baathist apostasy. The participants were Islamic personalities of the Saudi persuasion. Following the invasion of Kuwait on August 2, 1990, the Iraqi government, having lost the support of the Popular Islamic Conference (PIC), set about detaching from Riyadh the Sunni Islamist movements originating with the Muslim Brothers and their affiliates. To this end, Saddam Hussein—whose flags had suddenly been struck with the words "Allah Akbar" and who had taken care that footage of himself praying on the shore of conquered Kuwait City was broadcast on international TV—sought to make of the rape of Kuwait a kind of moral and social jihad. He claimed that the royal family of the emirate, the Al Sabahs, reigned over an artificial state created by the British; they were no more than pawns of the West, using their oil revenues to enrich themselves rather than their people. By annexing Kuwait, the argument ran, Iraq was recovering a "natural" province stolen from it in the nineteenth century and broadening its access to the sea. Saddam maintained that he was working for the unity of Arabs and Muslims, and he swore to place at the disposal of the "disinherited" the revenues that the emirs would otherwise have squandered on palaces and casinos. He stripped Islamic dogma of its subtleties, appealed directly to the yearning for justice that has always inspired Islam (in common with most other religions), and blended it with Third World ideology and Arab nationalism. Thanks to Kuwait's black gold, Iraq would, according to Saddam, become a great Arab power and the shining defender of the poor nations of earth against the new American world order.

To justify the annexation of the emirate, the Iraqi propaganda machine pieced together a composite discourse. The idea was to concentrate the anti-Western sentiment that was simmering all over the Muslim world quite independently of the ideological conflicts between nationalists and Islamists and to use it to strengthen a single populist cause. At the same time, however, the war divided the Islamists, setting them at one another's throat because of the attacks against Saudi Arabia, which Baghdad intended to strip of its religious legitimacy. For Riyadh, which had succeeded in containing a similar onslaught from Iran for a period of ten years by playing on Shiite marginality and the Persian-ness of Khomeini and by financing a diversionary jihad in Afghanistan, this new challenge was much more serious. It came from the Sunni Arab world, and from a neighboring state whose troops were massed on its frontiers—at the same time that Saudi Arabia itself was hosting more than half a million "infidel" soldiers. Accompanied by their Christian chaplains and Jewish rabbis, this foreign army had been called to the assistance of a country that the Wahhabites prided themselves on having made sacred to Islam, and within whose borders the open practice of any other religion was forbidden.

All the international organizations on the Saudi payroll that had struggled in the past to defeat Nasserism and contain Iran were now mobilized against Saddam Hussein. Nonetheless, a certain number of habitual Saudi clients did not answer the call, or did so reluctantly, making clear their discomfort in combating a populist cause that held certain attractions for ordinary Muslims everywhere. For the first time since the war of October 1973, petro-dollars were not sufficient to secure allegiances, because the reputations of the ulemas and Islamist intellectuals might now be tarnished by fulsome praise of Saudi Arabia. The Saudi government had to go begging for the support of institutions like Al Azhar in Cairo, which for two decades Riyadh had believed it could browbeat with its financial clout but whose prestige had remained unphased. Al Azhar's official opinions seemed less questionable than the fatwas of Sheik Abdelaziz bin Baz, the principal Wahhabite ideologist.

The OIC, which was in session at the moment of the invasion of Kuwait, voted to express its solidarity with the emirate and to condemn the Iraqi annexation. But five of its members, in addition to Iraq, did not approve the resolution—among them were the PLO, Jordan, and the Sudan—while two others, one of which was Libya, abstained.[2] In September, the Muslim World League convened a conference in Mecca, chaired by the leader of the Afghan Jamiat party. Over two hundred participants, many of whom had benefited handsomely from Saudi largesse, condemned the invasion and justified in the name of Islam the appeal for help from non-Muslim armies. But most of the more important Islamist movements refused to compromise themselves, seeking instead a middle ground between their base support, which favored Iraq, and the always-welcome financial aid provided by the Gulf monarchies. Immediately after the Mecca conference, their leaders reassembled in Amman at the invitation of the Jordanian Muslim Brothers. They sent a delegation to the capitals concerned by the conflict, and to Tehran. Their final communiqué appeased both parties by acknowledging their grievances, but mostly criticized the American and Western military presence around the Holy Places of Islam. This was a direct reproof to Saudi Arabia.

As the clock ran down on the January 15 United Nations ultimatum to Iraq and the launching of Operation Desert Storm became imminent, the two adversaries scheduled for that date two separate meetings of the Popular Islamic Conference. The conference that took place in Baghdad called for a jihad against the West, whose soldiers were accused of sacrilege against Mecca and Medina. The participants reflected the popular support that Saddam Hussein had managed to rally to his cause: in addition to the Islamists, these included a number of ulemas who were sensitive to the enthusiasms of their constituencies (such as the heads of the Grand Mosque in Marseille and Paris) and a sprinkling of Arab nationalists. The rival conference, which was held at Mecca, was attended by the sheik of Al Azhar and Mohammed al-Ghazali, one of the most respected figures among Islamic conservatives, along with the Saudis' most loyal clients. These participants denounced the "wayward" ulemas who supported Saddam Hussein—demonstrating in the process that Saddam had succeeded in dividing Islam to his advantage, whereas Riyadh had formerly held it together under its umbrella of religiosity and generosity.

After the cessation of hostilities and the defeat of Iraq, the "war of the conferences" continued in other venues. On April 25 it was Cairo's and Khartoum's turn to receive, simultaneously, the representatives of the two camps determined to dominate the political expression of Islam. In Cairo, the home of Al Azhar, whose sheik had supported his colleagues in Mecca when they were in trouble, the lords of Arabia showed their gratitude. Various Islamic institutions in Egypt suddenly found that their projects had been deemed worthy of funding. The crushing of Iraq by the American, European, and Arab allies had left a feeling of bitterness at the grassroots, and the ulemas who had given the war the stamp of legitimacy had suffered deep ideological wounds. It was a matter of urgency that the Saudi aid which had been siphoned off by the war should be reactivated and the flow of social goods restored.

In Khartoum, at the invitation of Hassan al-Turabi (the *éminence grise* of a regime that had supported Iraq), an Arab and Islamic People's Conference brought together Muslim Brothers and similar movements from all over the world, along with Yasir Arafat and other Arab nationalists who had come out in favor of Baghdad. By borrowing the name of the Iraqi People's Islamic Conference, which had broken up in January, it aimed to capitalize on the groundswell of sympathy for Saddam Hussein in the Muslim world, and to add to that what remained of Arab nationalism—notably among intellectuals, who in general had more finesse and discretion in handling people than their Islamic militant colleagues. The goal, of course, was to blend all these ingredients into an international Islamism with a much more radical program—colored by populism and Third World ideology—than the one offered by the Wahhabites. It saw itself as a durable alternative to such puppets of Saudi control and influence as the OIC and the Muslim World League, and it called other meetings in 1993 and 1995.[3] But in the long term, Khartoum was unable to compete with these well-oiled, liberally financed organizations. Nevertheless, Turabi's initiatives testified to a continuing split within the Islamic world, which in itself reflected the social and ideological divisions operating within the movement in each Muslim nation.

Saudi Arabia Entraps Itself

The split within the Arab Islamist movement initiated by the Gulf War extended well into Saudi Arabia itself, where dissent began to run rife. Without question, the dynasty held an overwhelming advantage over a new opposition movement that was claiming to act in the name of Allah and of Wahhabism. All the same, this opposition was to contribute significantly to the shattering of the government's religious legitimacy, exposing at home the fragility of the balance on which Saudi Arabia's primacy in the Muslim world was based.

The massive presence of allied armies in the country between 1990 and 1991 aroused two kinds of reaction to the monarchy. The first gave voice to the expectations of the liberal middle class, which hoped to nudge the regime toward greater political openness. The second, which viewed demands like these as highly dangerous and subversive, denounced the Westernization of the kingdom that had come as a direct consequence of its complete dependence on American military support and called for a return to the founding puritanical spirit that the corrupt princes of the royal family had betrayed. There was nothing new in these charges: first Khomeini, then Saddam Hussein, had repeated them over and over. On the other hand, they were now being voiced for the first time by organized Saudi nationals, more than ten years after the foiled assault on the Great Mosque in Mecca by the ultra-Wahhabite Juhayman al-Utaybi in November 1979. As opposed to Juhayman's initiative, the new opposition had its own support and network within the religious establishment that had provided the government with its claim to Islamic legitimacy.

The liberal movement had two defining moments. One was on November 6, when seventy Saudi women drove their own cars into the center of Riyadh in protest against the law forbidding women to drive.

Although they were careful to proclaim their allegiance to Islam—pointing out that Aisha, the wife of the Prophet, had ridden her own camel—and announced that they were acting in the best interests of the monarchy whose legitimacy they did not question, the women nonetheless had broken a taboo. And in doing so, they had justified themselves with a precedent from Holy Writ, while Sheik bin Baz, the principal Wahhabite ideologist, had pronounced the exact opposite interpretation; thus, they were deemed to have contravened religious authority in addition to disturbing the peace.

Even though substantial numbers of princes, businessmen, and university professors supported the women's demands, the general furor against these "communist whores" engulfed all liberal expressions of solidarity. The women were shrilly denounced by reactionary elements of Saudi society, who seized on this pretext to vent their frustration over the evil influence of the foreign military presence within the kingdom. Consequently, the lady drivers were fired from their jobs and thoroughly repressed by the regime. The last thing the Saudi rulers wanted was a confrontation with the ulemas over the issue of women's rights, at a moment when it urgently needed fatwas approving its recourse to American forces during the war against Iraq.

In February 1991, while the coalition offensive was at its height, the Saudi liberals presented a fresh petition to King Fahd, calling for a constitution and the appointment of a consultative council. In the face of this pressure from liberals, the Islamists were quick to react with a petition and criticisms of their own.[4] Two preachers, whose sermons were distributed in cassette form, stood out as the most violent critics of the Western military presence in Saudi Arabia, whose soldiers they viewed as a new wave of crusaders. The first of the two, Salman al-Auda, was the imam of a mosque in the agricultural town of Burayda, near Riyadh in the province of Qasim, a region that had been more or less bypassed by the oil boom: he was 36 years old. The second, Safar al-Hawali, was five years older and a promising graduate of the Saudi religious establishment who had been trained first at the Muslim Brothers' Islamic University at Medina and then in Mecca. He belonged to a family that was among the dominant clans of the kingdom. In company with seven other preachers and Islamist university professors, the pair signed a letter of petition (khitab al-matalib) which was approved by Sheik bin Baz and presented to King Fahd in May 1991. It called for the appointment of a *majlis al-shura* (consultative council) that would be made up of ulemas, to temper arbitrary decisions by the monarchy; it would make sure that the kingdom remained true to Wahhabite norms, resisting the pernicious influence of Jews and Christians. In veiled terms, the signatories criticized both the Al Saud family's monopoly of power and the monarchy's loss of Islamic credibility after it was bailed out by impious foreign armies. Like the petition of the liberals, this letter demanded that the regime include in the decision-making process the educated middle class who did not belong to the royal family. With this demand, it called into question the dynasty's authority, while claiming the mantle of impeccable Wahhabite and Islamist rectitude.

King Fahd was obliged to take these demands into consideration in order to consolidate the religious base of his government, which had been severely shaken by the Gulf War. As a face-saving measure, he had the two young preachers taken to task by the Council of Ulemas for having made their epistle public, to the greater delight of Saudi Arabia's enemies, rather than keeping it discreet. The king took issue with its form, too, though not its content, which had, after all, been approved by Sheik bin Baz. Later, in November, he announced the nomination of a consultative council and the codification of the fundamental laws of the realm, which was completed in March 1992. The sixty members of the council were chosen by the king, who was not bound by any of their opinions; most of them belonged to the principal tribal families. The Nejd region around Riyadh, the homeland of the Al Saud, was much more heavily represented than other parts of the kingdom, while nearly 70 percent of the councilors had studied in the West, most of them at American universities. In fact, the composition of this assembly was much more satisfactory to the liberals than to the Islamists—with the result that the Islamists counterattacked the following September by making public a memorandum of admonition *(mudhakirat al-nasiha)*, as a basis for the demands of the religious opposition.

This latest detailed assault on the regime was immediately condemned by the Council of Ulemas and by Sheik bin Baz himself.[5] The memorandum set out a list of grievances against Saudi rule and suggested reforms to improve it by making it more Islamic—thus placing it squarely in the tradition of the *nasiha* (admonition) which the ulemas were traditionally permitted to offer princes to make them align what they did with the injunctions of the holy texts. The memorandum's principal demand was for real independence to be accorded to Muslim clerics in their dealings with the government, in recognition of their preeminence. Next, it called for the complete Islamization of laws and regulations (noting that Arabia, which had promoted interest-free banking in all other Muslim countries, had yet to practice it at home). Total Islamization was recommended as the only means of stamping out corruption, waste, violations of Muslims' rights, and other anomalies. A harsh assessment of the inadequacies of the Saudi armed forces during the Gulf War led to a recommendation that they be reconstituted along the same lines as the Israeli conscript army (!) and that all military alliances with non-Muslim powers should be terminated forthwith. In foreign politics, the criticism was focused on relations with the United States, on Saudi support for the Israeli-Arab peace process, and on Saudi friendship with states like Algeria whose governments were locked in combat with the Islamist movement.

All in all, the memorandum painted a picture of a kingdom ruled by an arbitrary regime, which only resorted to religion when it needed to cover up the turpitudes of its leaders. The document's clear aim was to wreck the Al Saud claim to any kind of moral leadership in the wider sphere of Islam. The authorities were much disconcerted, and they showed it, and this further encouraged the dissident factions. On May 3, 1993, six clerics (four of whom had signed the memorandum of admonition) created an organization to pass on the views of the Islamist opposition that was rapidly developing in the universities and mosques of the nation. Known in English as the Committee for the Defense of Legitimate Rights (CDLR), it claimed—in Arabic—the defense of the rules laid out in the sharia. Its shrewd use of the rhetoric of human rights won the approval of the Western press, while it followed a much stricter Islamist line in its dealings with its supporters in Saudi Arabia. The Saudi authorities reacted vigorously to this direct challenge when the official spokesman of the CDLR, Mohammed al-Masari, a physician trained in the United States, gave a spectacular interview, in English, to the BBC and obtained a rendezvous at the U.S. Embassy in Riyadh. The signatories and their sympathizers promptly lost their jobs and were thrown into jail, whereupon Amnesty International adopted Masari as a "prisoner of conscience." This forced the Saudi government to release him, and he left for London, where he revived the CDLR in April 1994.

For two years, Masari applied himself to superficially blackening the reputation of the regime through manipulation of the international media, without raising any groundswell of support within the kingdom itself. Unlike Sheiks Hawali and Auda, who belonged to powerful families, Masari was viewed in the upper echelons of society as a pariah and was not taken seriously.[6] Moreover, in doctrinal terms he was sadly lacking in ballast, as became evident when he was confronted by the barrage of fatwas issued by the regime's ulema supporters. In July 1993 Sheik bin Baz was promoted to the long-vacant position of Grand Mufti; meanwhile the government undertook a reorganization of its Ministry of Religious Affairs by an energetic cleric, Abdullah Turki. All the same, Masari was a gifted communicator; having been quickly propelled into the limelight by the Islamists in London, he supplied the newspapers with a steady stream of revelations (many of them hearsay) about the public and private vices of the Al Saud princes. He made feverish use of the fax machine to circumvent Saudi press censorship, just as Khomeini, fifteen years earlier, had short-circuited the shah's radio monopoly with his ubiquitous audiocassettes. Finally, Masari opened an Internet site, on which he published, in both English and Arabic, a steady stream of virtual communiqués and periodicals.

The media were delighted by this maverick who could make the Saudi monarchy tremble with nothing more than a fax machine and a modem; they cast him as a bearded postmodernist dissident inveighing against the Kingdom of Oil. Nevertheless, Masari's fame was based on a deep ambiguity. When he used the language of Shakespeare, Amnesty International, and Microsoft, he concentrated on human rights violations, corruption, and so on, endearing himself to the Western media. But when he spoke in the language of the Koran, he sought to give "definitive proofs of the Saudi state's contravention of sharia" (this was the title of a pamphlet he published in 1995). He even ventured to pronounce takfir (ex-communication) against all Muslims who obeyed the laws of Riyadh—an extremist posture that aligned him fairly closely with the Algerian GIA and its London representatives. In Saudi Arabia, this attitude destroyed much of his support among dissidents who wanted to win over the nation's leading ulemas, not to insult and vilify them.

Furthermore, the government had turned the screw of repression by arresting Hawali and Auda in September 1994, along with several hundred demonstrators assembled by them in Burayda. Other demonstrations organized the following year attracted only a small number of people, in a climate of repression rendered even more menacing by the public beheading of an Islamist militant who had assaulted a policeman. In November 1995 five Americans were killed in Riyadh. The fax and Internet had been supplanted by bombs, and dissidence had succumbed to violence. In February 1996 the CDLR was irrevocably split, and Masari gradually abandoned the front pages of the world's media to Osama bin Laden. Masari had proved unable to transform his virtual successes into solid backing on the ground or, in the last analysis, to unite the devout bourgeoisie of Saudi Arabia behind him and thus mount a serious threat to the power of the reigning dynasty.

The Proliferation of the Afghan Jihad

The Saudi monarchy, already weakened from within, was dealt another blow in the aftermath of the Gulf War. This time the perpetrators were the prodigals of the 1980s, the combatants of the Afghan jihad. Having been armed and funded by the kingdom, these *wunderkinder* of the Saudi Islamist movement now turned against it: and the most prominent among them was the billionaire Osama bin Laden, whose family held a position of hegemony over public works and construction in the peninsula, thanks to its close connections with the royal family.

After the Soviet withdrawal from Afghanistan on February 15, 1989, disagreements had begun to surface among the jihadists, who felt that their promised triumph had been thwarted. Mohammed Najibullah, the communist leader, was still in power in Kabul (where he was to remain until April 1992), and, with the withdrawal of the Red Army, the American ally had begun to pay attention to the voices that depicted some of the erstwhile Freedom Fighters as dangerous fanatics and heroin dealers. Hekmatyar and Sayyaf, the heads of the two most pro-Wahhabite factions in the resistance, were viewed by Washington as extremists as bad as Najibullah himself; all aid to them was quickly terminated. In Pakistan, Benazir Bhutto, who had been elected prime minister following General Zia's assassination in August 1988, had little sympathy with the Islamists who had been co-opted into power by the former dictator and executioner of her father, Ali Bhutto, in 1979. She set about weakening their stronghold, the Jamaat-e-Islami (the party founded by Mawdudi), which had thrown its weight behind Hekmatyar's Hezb-e-Islami in Afghanistan. In these circles the martyred Zia, the *chahid* as he was called, was greatly revered; even though the American ambassador had been killed along with him, his death was attributed to an American plot whose purpose was to bring the resistance into line following the Soviet defeat, in order to check the advance of the Islamist movement.

Anti-Americanism was on the rise within the Jamaat-e-Islami, even though one of the objectives of the jihad, from Saudi Arabia's point of view, had been to turn the ire of the militants against the Soviet Union and away from the American protector—despite Khomeini's excoriations against the "Great Satan." In this light, the November 1989 assassination of Abdallah Azzam—the Palestinian Muslim Brother who had founded the Bureau of Services for the Arab jihadists in Peshawar and had acted as the intermediary between the Saudi system and the most virulent activists—was a coup that favored the militants' emancipation from their patrons. Anti-Western sentiment, momentarily suspended while the CIA's weapons and dollars were flowing in, now returned with a vengeance. It was quickly translated into attacks on European and American humanitarian agencies in Peshawar, who were trying to help the Afghan refugees.

When Iraq invaded Kuwait on August 2, 1990, most of the Islamist movements of the region initially condemned the annexation of one Muslim country by another. Among the Afghans, Burhanuddin Rabbani, leader of the Jamiat party, and Hekmatyar, the Hezb chief, took part in the Mecca conference organized in September to oppose the invasion. In Pakistan, the Jamiat-e-Ulema-e-Islam (Association of Ulemas of Islam, or JUI) and the Jamiat-e-Ulema-e-Pakistan (Association of Ulemas of Pakistan, or JUP) called on Saddam Hussein to withdraw his troops, on the grounds that he was handing the West a pretext for a military intervention.[7] Before long this became the principal talking point of the conflict: from November onward, the entire Pakistani Islamist movement, seeing the war as an American-Israeli plot to dominate the Middle East, began to turn decisively against the Saudi monarchy. Particularly striking was the virulence of the head of the Jamaat-e-Islami, Qazi Hussein Ahmed, a Pashtun who owed his political rise to the Afghan jihad and to Hekmatyar; both organizations had been the main beneficiaries of Saudi and Kuwaiti financial aid for the entire decade of the 1980s. This about-face showed the degree of anger provoked in the region by Washington's abandonment of the jihad and, to a lesser extent, by Riyadh's betrayal. For the United States and Saudi Arabia, the Afghan and Pakistani causes had lost much of their strategic importance following the rout of the Soviets, the enfeeblement of Iran, and the death of Khomeini. Thereafter, all the Arab jihadists who were still on the spot adopted the same attitude as the local Islamist parties, freeing themselves from Saudi tutelage and then rising up against it.

The international brigade of jihad veterans, being outside the control of any state, was suddenly available to serve radical Islamist causes anywhere in the world. Since they were no longer bound by local political contingencies, they had no responsibilities to any social group either. They reflected neither the interests of the devout bourgeoisie nor those of the young urban poor, even though their militants were drawn from both classes. They became the free electrons of jihad, professional Islamists trained to fight and to train others to do likewise; they were based in Pakistani tribal zones, in smugglers' fiefdoms over which Islamabad exercised next to no authority, and in Afghan mujahedeen encampments. Around the most heavily involved militants gathered clouds of sympathizers, many of whom were in trouble in their own countries and unable to obtain visas to Western nations; they were stuck in Pakistan and obliged to survive in the direst circumstances. Young Islamists from all over the world came to join these men and learn the terrorist trade from them; some emerged later as the perpetrators of a series of attacks in France in 1995. Above and beyond the cause they claimed to serve, they constituted a pool of manpower that could be used by the secret services of a number of states who might find it opportune to manipulate unattached extremist militants.

This milieu was cut off from social reality; its inhabitants perceived the world in the light of religious doctrine and armed violence. It bred a new, hybrid Islamist ideology whose first doctrinal principle was to rationalize the existence and behavior of militants. This was jihadist-salafism.[8] In academic parlance, the term *salafism* denotes a school of thought which surfaced in the second half of the nineteenth century as a reaction to the spread of European ideas. It advocated a return to the traditions of the devout ancestors (*salaf* in Arabic). Exemplified by the

Persian Afghani, the Egyptian Abduh, and the Syrian Rida, it sought to expose the roots of modernity within Muslim civilization—and in the process resorted to a somewhat freewheeling interpretation of the sacred texts.[9] In the eyes of the militants, the definition of the term was quite different: salafists were those who understood the injunctions of the sacred texts in their most literal, traditional sense. Their most notable exponent was the great fourteenth-century ulema Ibn Taymiyya, whose work served as a primary reference for the Wahhabites. The salafists were the real fundamentalists of Islam; they were hostile to any and all innovation, which they condemned as mere human interpretation.

According to the militants, there were, however, two kinds of salafists, as they defined them. The "sheikists" had replaced the adoration of Allah with the idolatry of the oil sheiks of the Arabian peninsula, with the Al Saud family at their head. Their theorist was Abdelaziz bin Baz, Grand Mufti of Saudi Arabia since 1993 and the archetypal court ulema *(ulama al-balat)*. Their ostentatious salafism was no more than the badge of their hypocrisy, their submission to the non-Muslim United States, and their public and private vices, in the view of the militants. They had to be striven against and eliminated. Confronted by the "sheikist" traitors, the jihadist-salafists had a similarly supercilious respect for the sacred texts in their most literal form, but they combined it with an absolute commitment to jihad, whose number-one target had to be America, perceived as the greatest enemy of the faith. The dissident Saudi preachers Hawali and Auda were held in high esteem by this school, whose thinking was enlarged upon by a number of other theorists whose names and pseudonyms cropped up frequently in the London bulletins of the Algerian GIA. Among these were the Palestinian Abu Qatada and the (naturalized Spanish) Syrian Abu Musab, as well as the (naturalized British) Egyptian Mustapha Kamel, known as Abu Hamza. All three were veterans of the jihad in Afghanistan.

Hostile as they were to the "sheikists," the jihadist-salafists were even angrier with the Muslim Brothers, whose excessive moderation they denounced on the grounds that it led the Brothers to take liberties with the letter of the holy texts. Even Sayyid Qutb, the spiritual father of the radical element among the Brothers, was held in suspicion; in particular the jihadist-salafists condemned Qutb's reading of the Koran in his book *Fi-zilal al-Quran* (Under the Aegis of the Koran), which was seen as a collection of personal interpretations *(tawilat)* on the part of an author who had no training in theology, rather than a canonical commentary *(tafsir)* with real authority. As to the moderate Brothers who participated in the political games of the impious states, created parties, and stood at elections, they were branded as deceivers of the faithful because they gave bogus religious legitimacy to regimes that only deserved to be annihilated.[10]

These extreme views paralleled those prevailing in one of the early Egyptian groups of extremists, Al Takfir wa-l Hijra (Excommunication and Hegira), whose leader, the agronomist Shukri Mustafa, was hanged in 1978 (see Chapter 3). But Shukri, who declared impious (kafir) all Muslims who did not belong to his sect, was not so much a salafist as a visionary who interpreted the sacred texts as it suited him, without remotely adhering to the tradition defined by Ibn Taymiyya. Furthermore, he advocated withdrawal from godless society, at a time when the position of his adepts vis-à-vis the state was dire, to say the least; and he did not directly confront the Egyptian government until he was forced to do so, in circumstances that ultimately proved fatal to him. The jihadist-salafists, by contrast, took the view that the Muslim world was ready to go on the offensive and wage the great jihad that would ultimately lead to the proclamation of the Islamic state.

In this sense, they were the heirs of Abdallah Azzam and of the Egyptian group known as Tanzim al-Jihad (Organization of the Jihad), which had carried out the assassination of Sadat. Many of the militants who had gravitated toward the assassins after their arrest and trial in Egypt appeared in the Peshawar encampments in 1985–86, around the time that those who had received the lighter sentences began to be released from prison. One of the most prominent figures among these Afghan Arabs, the physician Ayman al-Zawahiri, was a case in point. There was an intellectual as well as a personal link: unlike Shukri, the murderers of Sadat had been careful to find grounds for their acts in Muslim tradition, citing Ibn Taymiyya to justify the execution of the "pharaoh." But they could not for all that be qualified as salafists. Their Islamic culture was rudimentary, made up of bits and pieces only, as illustrated in a short work authored by the group's chief theorist, an electrical engineer named Faraj. Later on, this intellectual weakness made them easy marks for the ulemas linked to the state, who scolded them in avuncular fashion and then brought them to heel like wayward youngsters.

The Tanzim al-Jihad had emerged from Egypt's impoverished underclass; it had no international dimension whatever. It was thanks only to the work of Abdullah Azzam that a local experience of this kind gave inspiration to a jihad that later spread all over the world. Azzam himself had remained a strict Muslim Brother, with close links to the Saudi establishment—for whose benefit he channeled the passion of the Islamist militants of the world. During the 1980s, when the struggle of the Afghan mujahedeen was at its height, his writings served to justify a clearly defined jihad, attracting to it a host of volunteers who might otherwise have chosen the way of revolutionary Iran. Later they re-emerged as a part of a far wider, indeed planetary, scheme for the future.

After 1989, the year of the Soviet withdrawal and Azzam's own assassination, this new dimension was unmistakable. In addition to Afghanistan, Azzam wrote, all other Muslim countries "usurped" by the ungodly had the duty to wage a holy war to recover their lost Islamic identity. At issue, first and foremost, were Azzam's native Palestine, Andalusia (which had been seized from the dar el-islam by the Reconquista—an old refrain of the Islamist movement), the Philippines of the Moro Liberation Front, the Muslim republics of the former Soviet Union bordering on Afghanistan, and finally South Yemen (which at the time was still communist and an abomination to Riyadh). Along with these came a series of states whose rulers either were not Muslims or were bad ones, a formula that made the list of potential victims virtually infinite. It was expanded in the early 1990s to countries on which Azzam was probably ill-informed, or where he had not foreseen that they might become fronts in the general global jihad that he envisaged. These were Bosnia, from 1992 onward; Chechnya, from 1995; Algeria (the homeland of his son-in-law), from the beginning of its civil war; and finally Kashmir, under Indian rule.[11] Azzam's disciples adopted on these nations' behalf the terms he had employed to rally foreign volunteers to the Afghan jihad.

Apart from a clear doctrinal affiliation, the jihadist-salafists had affinities with another movement that appeared at the same time, in the same region and Islamic context—the Taliban. They had in common an attachment to the literal aspect of the holy texts and the use of jihad to attain their objectives. But the Taliban, who belonged to the Hanafi Deobandi school, did not have the same doctrinal training as the Arab salafists; moreover, they came exclusively from the traditional madrassas, unlike the salafists. Their jihad was primarily directed against their own society, on which they sought to impose a rigorous moral code: they had no taste for the state or for international politics. The cross-fertilization between the two movements, their simultaneous emergence, the hospitality offered by the Taliban within Afghanistan to the principal jihadists, the fact that some of the latter spoke in their name—all these factors begged the question of whether the one had some kind of ascendancy over the other.

Both, then, were among the unexpected progeny of the Afghan jihad and the result of its hybridization with the Deobandi tradition, for which jihad had never been a priority since its birth in 1867. The Deobandi school had been created to permit the Muslims of India, who had yielded their power to the British in 1857 and immediately found themselves a minority within a population of Hindus, to survive as a community under difficult circumstances. The Deobandi ulemas had issued fatwa after fatwa whereby their disciples were enabled to follow the prescriptions of the sharia meticulously, within a state that would not apply them. They developed the guidelines for a *modus vivendi* within a non-Muslim society, in which neither jihad nor emigration to a Muslim nation was possible. At the creation of Pakistan, the Deobandi ulemas who were already resident in the territory of the new state or who chose to come there from India had created a political party, the Association of Ulemas of Islam (JUI), intended to protect their sacred way of life within the then highly secularized Muslim Pakistan and to negotiate for funds to support their madrassas.[12] Within the field of Islam proper, this allowed them to defend their specific identity against the Jamaat-e-Islami founded by Mawdudi—whose modernism and tendency to confuse religion and politics they roundly condemned—and against their rivals, the Barelwi ulemas, who had created the Association of Ulemas of Pakistan (JUP). By the sheer weight of the pressure group they formed, which included tens of thousands of pupils and graduates of their madrassas, they were now able to intervene directly in political life and to contest everything that appeared to compromise their view of the Islamic world order.

Their first victims were the Ahmadis, a sect whose disciples they denounced as apostates; several members occupied key government posts. Later, under Zia's 1977–1988 presidency, the dictator's determination to impose Sunni Hanafi Islam as the national norm, the levying of alms *(zakat)* directly on bank accounts, and the subsequent revolt of the 15–20 percent of Pakistanis who happened to be Shiites in July 1980 gave a new vocation to Deobandi militantism—the struggle against Shiism. This conflict was encouraged by the rivalry between Saudi Arabia and Iran.

In the context of the war between Iraq and Iran and the jihad in Afghanistan, Pakistan was bound to constitute a second front in the Sunni-Shiite conflict.[13] In 1980 a Shiite party had been set up to preserve the identity of the Shiite community against Sunni omnipotence, as a direct result of the intrinsic threat of the zakat. Entitled Tehrik-e Nifaz-e Fiqh-e Jafria (Movement for the Application of Jafarite [Shiite] Jurisprudence) and organized by a group of younger clerics, this party was much enthused by the Iranian revolution from 1984 onward. It received substantial aid from Tehran, which caused alarm among the various Sunni pressure groups. Saudi Arabia, which viewed this movement as the Achilles' heel of the jihad it was subsidizing within Afghanistan, immediately began giving substantial funds to organizations that were prepared to fight the Shiites. The Deobandis benefited on several counts. Funds to its madrassas were stepped up, allowing an increase in the number of children from poorer rural and urban backgrounds who could receive free board and instruction and be turned into potential anti-Shiite zealots.

In 1985 a Deobandi paramilitary youth movement was founded by a leader of the JUI in the Punjab, Haq Nawaz Jhangvi, who in 1990 would be assassinated at age 32. Entitled Sipah-e Sahaba-e Pakistan (Soldiers of the Companions of the Prophet in Pakistan), this movement's goal was to have all Shiites pronounced infidels (kafir), and it did not hesitate to resort to violence against them.[14] In the same spirit, two even more violent Deobandi movements surfaced in the mid-1990s: the Lashkar-e Jhangvi (Army of Jhangvi) in 1994, which specialized in assassinating Shiites, and the Harakat al-Ansar (Partisan Movement) in 1993, whose militants went off to wage jihad in Indian Kashmir, earning a grisly reputation for beheading captured Hindu soldiers as infidels.[15] This surge of fanaticism elicited a Shiite backlash, in the form of the Sipah-e Mohammed Pakistan (Soldiers of the Prophet

Mohammed in Pakistan, or SMP), which was created in 1994 and carried out a number of killings of Sunnis.[16]

This paroxysm of violence in the name of religion was not due simply to the regional and international context of the time, even though the military and financial manna that had fallen to the Afghan jihad had suddenly made funds and heavy weaponry available to extremist movements that effectively enabled them to exist outside the law. It was also the product of a deep social crisis specific to Pakistan and in particular to the southern Punjab, where the offspring of impoverished and ruined Sunni peasants, amid a continuing population explosion, found themselves confronted by mostly Shiite landowners and urban establishments dominated by the descendants of the refugees from India who had arrived in 1947 (the mohajirs).[17] Unlike the Jamaat-e-Islami founded by Mawdudi, which in general remained an elitist party of devout middle-class people with no grassroots support, the Deobandis embraced impoverished young people with no hope of climbing the social ladder, for whom violence was the main form of expression within a society that was profoundly non-egalitarian and obstructionist. The madrassas sheltered their pupils—their Taliban—from all these tensions for as long as their education lasted; they were also able to rationalize their charges' potential for violence by transforming it into a jihad against anyone designated kafir by the master—whether he was a Shiite neighbor, an "impious" Indian soldier, or anyone else—even a Sunni Muslim who was held to be a "miscreant." The Taliban became extremely devoted to their ulemas, after many years of education by them under conditions of intense intimacy. They had little or no contact with the outside world; much of their time was spent mumbling texts that they were taught to revere and apply even though they did not understand their meaning, and this experience left them with an esprit de corps that extinguished even the smallest expression of free thought or individual will. In the doctrinaire madrassas, it was a simple matter to turn pupils conditioned in this way into full-blown fanatics.

After the Gulf War, the radicalized Deobandi movement profited from two coincidences that allowed it to increase its influence and, when added to the violence in the Punjab and Kashmir, opened the way to the final victory of the Taliban in Afghanistan. Saudi Wahhabism had been badly damaged by the decision of the Pakistani

Jamaat-e-Islami and the Afghan Hezb-e-Islami to support Iraq, despite the fact that both had been heavily funded by the kingdom for a full decade. The Deobandi party (the JUI) had also demonstrated against the presence of impious soldiers in Arabia but had shown much less enmity to the Riyadh monarchy. Furthermore, the Deobandi ulemas were the sworn enemies of the *pirs,* or guides, of the Barelwi brotherhoods, who belonged to the other religious party, the JUP. The patron saint of these brotherhoods was buried close to Baghdad, and they were traditional recipients of aid from Iraq. During the war, their leader attended meetings of support for Iraq, at which he declared his "love" for Saddam; he also set up recruiting centers for volunteers to serve the Iraqi cause, which, according to him, enrolled upwards of 110,000 men.[18]

Riyadh, which had to maintain some kind of contact with religious developments in Pakistan, chose the lesser of two evils and switched its support from the now-mistrusted Jamaat-e-Islami to the JUI. In the JUI's favor were these facts: that it was not linked to the international networks of the Muslim Brothers; that it hated Shiites, Iraq, and the brotherhoods; and that its strict religious orthodoxy had many affinities with Wahhabite practice. Likewise, in Afghanistan, Gulbuddin Hekmatyar's Hezb, which had declared for Iraq, was steadily losing ground to Ahmed Shah Massoud and was unpopular in Riyadh. The way was now open for Saudi backing of the Afghan pupils of the Deobandi madrassas, the Taliban.

The other coincidence that helped the JUI and the Taliban, which came as more of a surprise to Western observers, was the advent of a second government headed by Benazir Bhutto—a Harvard-educated lady whose face had graced the covers of countless women's magazines in the West but who nevertheless encouraged a movement that was to imprison Afghan women behind their veils *(chadri).* Political maneuvering within Pakistan was behind this reactionary attitude, which could be traced to the efforts of Bhutto's Pakistani People's Party to break the coalition of the three religious parties (JI, JUI, and JUP). This coalition had thrown its weight behind her rival, Nawaz Sharif, the leader of the Muslim League and the spiritual heir of General Zia. In 1990 Benazir Bhutto was driven from power by the army, which supported Sharif's coalition, only to return in triumph in the 1993 elections. She had succeeded in detaching most of the Deobandis from her rival, and she now appointed the JUI faction that had backed her to positions of great power, with its leader, Maulana Fazlur Rahman, taking the post of chairman of the Parliamentary Foreign Affairs Committee.[19] At the same time, her government was preoccupied with the anarchy in Afghanistan, which had worsened since April 1992 when Kabul fell into the hands of a shaky coalition of mujahedeen commanders and former supporters of the communist regime. Bhutto had scant confidence in the policies of the army secret intelligence service (ISI), a bastion of Zia and Sharif supporters that favored the Hezb.

It was under these circumstances that her interior minister, General Babar, dispatched a convoy of trucks across southwestern Afghanistan to Turkmenistan in early November 1994. A mujahedeen commander, hoping to hold the trucks for ransom, intercepted them, but then several thousand heavily armed Afghan Taliban, who arrived in the nick of time from madrassas just across the Pakistani frontier, liberated the convoy. The next day, the Taliban seized control of Afghanistan's southern capital, Kandahar. Kabul fell into their hands in September 1996, and by the fall of 1998 they had forced their remaining adversary, Massoud, to withdraw to his own fief in the Panshir valley on the Tadjik frontier and had won control of 85 percent of Afghan territory.

The successes of the Taliban have been attributed to a combination of external and internal factors, but these take only partial account of the dynamic of this new brand of Islamist extremist, which appeared in the mid-1990s as a result of the breakup of the jihad in Afghanistan. The Taliban had several powerful protectors in their early years: for example, through Benazir Bhutto's alliance with the Deobandi leader Maulana Fazlur Rahman they were able to win the support of most of the Pakistani political establishment, even after Nawaz Sharif's return to power in November 1996. For Islamabad, an Afghanistan under Taliban control offered a number of initial advantages. Successive governments there, in their brief struggle to survive under highly volatile conditions, were unlikely to entertain long-term political solutions that might have negative effects. Pakistan's regional environment was fraught with dangers. Tense relations with India were kept at the boiling point by border clashes and by the "jihad of attrition" being waged by paramilitary Islamist groups in Kashmir, and this was made worse by the nuclear rivalry between Pakistan and India and by visceral hatred of the Iranian Shiites, who were linked with substantial minorities of their co-religionists in the subcontinent. As if these tensions were not enough, Moscow was deeply suspicious of Pakistan because it feared the destabilization of its own former Muslim republics (Uzbekistan, Tadjikistan, and Kirghistan) by Islamists from the south.

Rabbani, the head of the Afghan Jamiat party that controlled the coalitions of mujahedeen which ruled Kabul between 1992 and 1996, was able to find common ground along this Indo-Iranian-Russian axis, whereas Hekmatyar, Islamabad's protégé, was unable to do so. The collapse of the Soviet empire reopened the old trade routes between Central Asia and the Indian Ocean that had been blocked by the Russians since czarist times. Oil and gas from Turkmenistan, badly needed by overpopulated, energy-starved Pakistan, had to cross Afghanistan along the same road on which General Babar's provocative convoy had been liberated by the Taliban in November 1994.[20] If these roads were to be kept open, the country needed to be united under a single authority guaranteeing its security.

Since the start of the jihad, Afghanistan had been broken into dozens of fiefdoms ruled by mujahedeen commanders who held up travelers and merchandise for ransom whenever they chose. From 1994 onward, the Taliban slowly emerged in the eyes of the Pakistani political establishment as the only power capable of unifying Afghanistan and maintaining its vital links with Islamabad. In addition to their Deobandi theories, which made them the bitter foes of "ungodly" Shiite Iran, India, and Russia, most of the Taliban belonged to the Pashtun ethnic group, which was strong on the Pakistani northwest frontier around Peshawar and staffed the Pakistani officer corps and special services. This ethnic affinity allowed many to conjecture that an eventual Taliban state could be solidly aligned with Pakistan and would give Pakistan the strategic depth it needed to stand up to its three enemies in the region.

Outside help for the Taliban came in the form of logistical and military support. Internal factors also contributed to their success, especially the exhaustion of the Afghan people with their own chronic state of neglect, corruption, and insecurity. These reached unparalleled heights after Kabul fell into mujahedeen hands in 1992. Order completely broke down as the warring factions bombarded one another's quarters of the city. In the Pashtun areas, at least, the Taliban had been able to take control of district after district without firing a shot: their reputation for moral integrity had preceded them, and in the rural areas their ultra-strict attitudes toward women and society were perfectly acceptable to a population that adhered to the roughly similar tribal traditions of *pashtunwali*. On the other hand, they met stiff resistance when they reached Kabul and were foiled in their first attempt to seize the city, an objective they finally achieved in September 1996. The same happened in the predominantly Shiite regions of Western Afghanistan, where they devoutly massacred the "ungodly," notably at Mazar-e-Sharif in 1998. Yet it was religious ardor that impelled them to march forth on their jihad and give their lives for the cause in the conviction that as martyrs for God they would see the gates of heaven flung wide before them.

Once the Taliban had taken control of the capital, order was established and insecurity no longer stalked the ruins left by four years of internecine struggle among the mujahedeen. The new rulers immediately applied the Deobandi concepts taught to them in their madrassas not only to their own community of disciples but to the whole of Afghan society.[21] Pashtun-speaking, country-bred people as they were, the Taliban saw the *Dari*-speaking Kabulis, who had been accustomed to a modern urban lifestyle since the 1950s, as a corrupt mob who must be subjugated to the rules of sharia. Women were compelled to wear burqas in public and were forbidden to take jobs, with the result that many of those women who had lost their husbands, fathers, and brothers in the war were forced to beg in the streets surrounded by their starving children.[22]

In front of the government ministries, whose functionaries had been sent away to camps for religious re-education, the weeds grew unchecked. The Deobandi culture opposed ordinary public services, being traditionally focused on organizing the community in the meticulous respect for dogma without regard to the state, which it had firmly dismissed as "godless" ever since the conquest of India by the British. In Kabul, the Taliban did not so much take control of Afghan institutions as completely eviscerate them, erecting in their stead only three functions: morality, commerce, and war.

Morality, which is no more than the strict imposition of Deobandi norms on all citizens, was implemented by their "organization for the commanding of good and the hunting down of evil," shortened in English to the "vice/virtue police." Its operatives bore the same name as their counterparts in Saudi Arabia, the infamous *mutawia*, and like them were bearded young men from poor backgrounds who went around with truncheons enforcing the hours of prayer, the wearing of the veil, and Wahhabite rules of behavior in general.[23] Prior to September 2001, Afghanistan had extended the notion of hunting down all manner of evil to include whipping clean-shaven men, or even men with short beards. Televisions, video recorders, and music were also forbidden. The mental environment of a madrassa was re-created in the villages and cities of Afghanistan. Road blocks set up by the Taliban always included a pole around which were wrapped, like trophies, the tapes ripped from audiocassettes that had been seized from motorists. The only public spectacles that could be viewed were those the Taliban considered edifying: on Fridays, the enormous stadium built by the Soviet Union to celebrate the triumph of proletarian internationalism was enlivened by the flagellation of drinkers, the amputation of the limbs of thieves, and the execution of murderers by the families of their victims, who were lent machine guns for the purpose. The state took no responsibility for the punishment of miscreants, a fact that reflected its own virtual nonexistence; instead, it consigned the task to the moral community of the faithful, urged on by a populace that had been steadily migrating to the outskirts of the capital since 1996 and which was gradually "Pashtunizing" it at the expense of those wretched remnants of the middle class (educated in Persian) who had been unable to escape.

In addition to morality, the second function that survived in the Islamic Emirate of Afghanistan was commerce. The Taliban had initially reaped the benefits of Saudi financial aid at a time when the princes of the peninsula were all flying to Kandahar in their private planes to hunt wild game in the mountains. On their departure, they would leave behind their all-terrain four-wheel-drive vehicles as gifts for the locals.[24] After the Taliban took control of most of the country, commerce between Central Asia and Pakistan expanded considerably, as did trade in contraband goods brought from the free port of Dubai and traffic in heroin destined for American, Russian, and European markets. This commerce in turn allowed the Taliban to levy tolls on goods and vehicles in transit, which made them financially independent of their former paymasters abroad and thus able to stand up to them politically. In the medieval atmosphere of the Kabul bazaar, where bearded, traditionally garbed shopkeepers and customers met in silence, the stalls groaned with goods. Dealers and transporters clearly benefited from a regime in which the near absence of state power allowed them to prosper untrammeled by taxes and regulations.

The last of the three functions of the Islamic Emirate was war, and this was the only one that required a semblance of centralization. The ongoing struggle was waged from Kandahar, where the Commander of the Faithful, Mullah Omar Akhund, who has never been seen by any "infidel," resided. A former mujahedeen who lost an eye fighting the Soviets, he presided over his *choura* (council) at all times, deciding on offensives to be undertaken against the rebels, making known his responses to pressures from abroad, and, most notably, reiterating the conditions under which Osama bin Laden and the jihadist-salafists who surrounded him were allowed to remain in Afghanistan, despite the protests of the Saudis and the Americans.

The summary exercise of these three functions did not make the Islamic Emirate of Afghanistan anything like a modern state: in fact it was more a community organized according to Deobandi norms but merely "swollen" to the dimensions of a country subjected to moral coercion on the inside and jihad on the edges. It was entirely financed by tolls levied on the flow of the (largely illegal) commerce that transited across its territory. In this sense the Afghanistan of the Taliban was not comparable to the Islamic Republic of Iran or to Hassan al-Turabi's Sudan. Iran and the Sudan relied on efficient administrative machines, managed in a rational way the authoritarian Islamism of their societies, and became prominent participants in the wider sphere of Islam as well as in the international system. This was far from the case with the Taliban: their effect on the world was not made through a state, and they had no diplomatic relations with any country except their Pakistani sponsor and their principal commercial partner, the United Arab Emirates, since breaking with their former benefactor, Saudi Arabia. They were completely indifferent to politics, which for all the other Islamist movements affiliated with the Muslim Brothers, whether moderate or radical, was always a key aspect of their obsession with winning power. In Deobandi ideology there was no edifice of virtue; only the community itself, the sum of the faithful, duly constrained by a body of fatwas that allowed each to live in conformity with the sharia, could claim to be moral. The absence of state or political legitimacy negated any notion of citizenship and freedom, concepts that were entirely supplanted by belief and obedience.

The extension of the jihad beyond Afghanistan was also under way in Kashmir, being implemented by the paramilitary Deobandi movement Harakat al-Ansar, founded in 1993, and renamed Harakat ul-Mujahedeen in 1998, after its classification as a terrorist organization by the American State Department. Here again the Pakistani political and military establishment actively encouraged groups of this type, which found their recruits among the impoverished youth of the Punjab and effectively waged a proxy war against India. Such short-term logic, whereby the social tensions of an unstable province are projected onto a foreign "enemy," threatened to rebound upon the fundamental equilibrium of Pakistani society itself. What would happen to the mujahedeen who returned from Kashmir? Would they transform the jihad they have waged outside Pakistan into a domestic struggle which, after the anti-Shiite terrorism of Lashkar-e Jhangvi, might turn directly against the state, opening the way for a "Talibanization" of Pakistan? This was the outcome dreaded by many Pakistani intellectuals.

Nevertheless, the influence of the religious parties was in general not very great at election time, even though the JUI and the SSP benefited from a crossover of votes during their paradoxical alliance with Benazir Bhutto in 1993.[25] The activism of the most extreme groups, which recruited from the ranks of the "displaced" underclass, terrified the devout middle class. These found a champion in Nawaz Sharif, the leader of the Muslim League and prime minister in 1999. To gratify them, he initiated a project for the complete Islamization of the law, which was reactivated on a regular basis and just as regularly killed by a combination of practical difficulties in its application and the bitter hostility of the bulk of the legal profession. The young people from disinherited backgrounds who were the basic recruiting material for the madrassas and the activist movements linked to them were not for the moment likely to become autonomous political agents expressing precise social interests, who might successfully join forces with bourgeois Islamist groups aggrieved at the lack of any meaningful access to the system. The latter had been broadly integrated into government and did not appear to be motivated by revolutionary longings. In fact, with their connivance, the impoverished young were channeled through the madrassa network into religious parties and their paramilitary organizations, toward objectives that locked them into a culture of antagonism to Shiites, Christians, Ahmadis, and Indians. This effectively turned them in on themselves, absorbing their potential for social violence and unrest. And the state hierarchy remained unaffected, despite the sound and fury generated by the radical Islamists of Pakistan.

The downside was the terrible effect of all this endemic violence on the nation's image abroad. Pakistan began to be described as an out-and-out rogue state; and by the end of 1999 Nawaz Sharif was ousted by his chief-of-staff, General Pervez Musharraf, who boldly declared himself ready to follow the example of Ataturk. This was a sign that people in the higher echelons of the Pakistani government were beginning to have second thoughts about the policy of benign neglect toward the jihad.

Meanwhile, the collapse of the Soviet Union, hastened by the debacle of the Red Army in Afghanistan, opened new potential fronts to the radical Islamist movement, and in particular to the jihadist-salafists. In neighboring Tadjikistan, the newly independent state run by former communist cadres was challenged by armed opponents based in the south of the country, with Islamists playing a significant part.[26] In the autonomous Caucasian republic of Chechnya, on the margin of the Russian Federation but within its borders, an independent movement started by a former Soviet general was turned into something very like a jihad in 1995 by Shamil Bassayev, a young warlord. He was supported by a group of "professional Islamists" trained in the Peshawar camps and commanded by Ibn al-Khattab, a jihadist who had fought earlier in Tadjikistan and Afghanistan.[27] But these confrontations took place in areas that were little known to the rest of the world, and unlikely to rouse much enthusiasm. Their symbolic value was minimal, and above all no outside power was disposed to intervene because the shadow of Russia still lay heavy over these remote territories.

All the events that took place in the former Soviet republics were overshadowed anyway by the final year of the Taliban regime in Afghanistan, the effects of which were to be felt from Central Asia to the Caucasus. In early 2001, a number of related developments signaled an increased level of radicalization among the Taliban—a phenomenon that seemed difficult to understand if related to domestic politics only. The first bizarre sign was the destruction of two-centuries-old gigantic statues of Buddha that were carved off the cliffs at Bamyan, a predominantly Hazara—or Shiite—location in central Afghanistan. Enemies of paganism as they were, the Taliban had nevertheless been careful not to spoil their relations with the heterogeneous populations that lived under their yoke, so as to concentrate their military strength on the northern front in the hope of fighting a decisive battle against Commandant Massoud. The statues were part of the Shiite popular religious folklore, and their demolition was bound to raise very strong anti-Taliban feelings in a population where the embers of sedition and insurgency were never entirely extinguished.

On the international level, there was an outcry of fury worldwide. In Europe and America, the Buddhas were seen as works of art, and their destruction reinforced the feeling that the Taliban were a bunch of iconoclastic barbarians. But in Hindu and Buddhist Asia, the statues were perceived as religious symbols, and their destruction further alienated the Taliban regime. In the Muslim world, and in Islamist circles more precisely, there was great uneasiness. In Muslim-Brothers fashion, a delegation of ulema and conservative intellectuals headed by Sheik Yusuf al-Qaradawi—the most influential of Sunni preachers and the host of an Al-Jazeera Islamic talk-show—tried to persuade the Taliban to leave the statues in peace, giving as an example the way Muslim Egypt dealt with pharaonic temples. But to no avail; the statues were finally blasted.

Another bizarre occurrence during the final year of Taliban rule was the persecution of foreigners on Afghan soil. As we saw earlier, the Deobandi-trained "students of religion" had no interest in state machinery. Outside of war, commerce, and religion, they couldn't care less about what happened under their rule. In particular, they were uninterested in social works and unable to implement any social policy. But they needed a minimal flow of goods and services to stave off hunger riots and other demonstrations of unrest that might overthrow their pious rule. These social functions were left to foreign Islamist humanitarian organizations, which the Taliban welcomed. But these agencies could not deliver all that was needed. Hence, Western nongovernmental organizations were very much present in Kabul and provided the population with additional food, sanitary services, medical assistance, and so on.

Suddenly, in 2001, one of those NGOs came under fire: it was accused of Christian proselytism—a major crime under the sharia, since Muslims who convert to another faith are dubbed apostates and condemned to death. A number of Afghans, as well as foreign relief workers, were jailed, pending trial under "Islamic justice." That was of course a source of major concern abroad, and it annihilated the last sympathies the Taliban could mobilize within influential American circles which, up to that point, had protected them for sundry geopolitical reasons.

Why would the Taliban regime take such steps? Was this all merely fanaticism? Then why were such measures not taken earlier? Precise evidence is still lacking as of December 2001, though in retrospect it seems clear that the Buddha and NGO affairs were but a foretaste of the events that led to the cataclysmic attacks in autumn of that year: the Taliban regime had come increasingly under the influence of Osama bin Laden. The wealthy Arab jihadist networks surrounding him now had such clout that they were able to impose their own global ideological agenda on any attempt at local realpolitik the Taliban may have made.

Another sign reinforces this interpretation. In early 2001, British authorities had finally taken some steps to restrain "Londonistan" activists. As a result, the British capital was no longer the major hub for radical Islamist international activities that it had formerly been. Militants and their networks reverted to Kandahar, which was then perceived by many observers as an important "relocation" venue for Jihad, Inc.'s manifold business ventures. It looked as though Mullah Omar was becoming a puppet in bin Laden's theater—as though Afghanistan, on the international scene, was now no more than Al Qaeda's sanctuary and base of operations. The malevolent mission of those operations would become clear in the bright morning sunlight of September 11.

After the attack on America, the Taliban regime was doomed to head-on confrontation with the U.S. superpower; it could count on none of the benign neglect it had enjoyed in years past. On October 7, the U.S. Air Force began carpet-bombing selected sites in Afghanistan. In spite of bin Laden's declaration broadcast that same day on Al-Jazeera television to rouse the emotions and solidarity of the Muslims worldwide for Afghan brothers under threat, there was little hope left for the Taliban regime—that oxymoron of an Islamist state. On November 9, the forces of the anti-Taliban Northern Alliance, trained and equipped by the United States, took Mazar-e-Sharif, a major city close to the Uzbek border. A swift military offensive wiped away the Taliban regime in a few days. Kabul fell on November 13, among demonstrations of widespread joy by city dwellers, who turned on the music, flew kites from rooftops, played soccer, and rushed to barber shops for their first shave in five years. On November 25, the Taliban stronghold of Kunduz fell, while Arab, Pakistani, and other foreign fighters faced retaliation from a furious populace. And, finally, on December 6, Kandahar, the historic capital of the Taliban, surrendered. Though Mullah Omar was able to escape, on that day the bell tolled for this strange ultra-radical Islamist regime—once the beneficiary of American indulgence, now the victim of its wrath.

10

The Failure to Graft Jihad on Bosnia's Civil War

The breakup of the former communist state of Yugoslavia, due to the nationalist tensions between its various components, reminded the world of the existence of Muslim Slavs in the heart of Europe. These were the forgotten descendants of converts made by the Ottoman Empire at the time of its Balkan expansion in the fourteenth century.[1] In March 1992, Bosnia-Herzegovina, where most of the Muslims lived side by side with Serbs and Croatians, declared its independence, which was swiftly followed by an attack on Sarajevo, the capital of the new state, by Serb militias.[2] The war that ensued lasted for three years; 150,000 people were killed and "ethnic cleansing" forced two million to leave their homes and become refugees.[3]

In the Western press, this atrocity was repeatedly compared to those of the Second World War—especially when the first images emerged of skeleton-thin prisoners in concentration camps. Mass graves were also uncovered, showing evidence of a deliberate intent to carry out genocide.[4] In Islamic countries, which had hitherto been just as ignorant as the West about the existence of Bosnia, there was general enthusiasm about the creation of a new Muslim state in the heart of Europe. The Serbian aggression was viewed entirely in terms of Christian versus Muslim; it was perceived as a kind of crusade, a holocaust perpetrated for religious reasons. A wave of solidarity with their newfound Balkan co-religionists swept over the Muslim world. Having emerged deeply split from the Gulf War of 1991, the Umma had spread symbolically into Europe at the time of the fatwa against

Salman Rushdie in 1989; and now, suddenly, it found itself broadened westward into Central Europe through the Balkan conflict.⁵ The difference this time was that indigenous populations, not immigrants, were at issue.

But no sooner had this new Muslim land been recovered than it threatened to vanish in a welter of Serbian butchery, while the West, with its vaunted human rights, looked on silently. The defenders of Saddam Hussein were quick to denounce the double standards of those who had imposed embargos on Iraq, bombed its territory, and excoriated its leader and yet now were unwilling to punish Slobodan Milosevic's Serbia with anything more serious than a few feather-light sanctions. The blood of Muslims, so the saying went, was worth less than their oil. Among those Muslim states that had taken part in Operation Desert Storm, this widespread solidarity with Bosnia became a real headache. Islamist opposition activists used it as a pretext to accuse their regimes of inertia, of connivance with the West, and of a fresh betrayal of the Umma after the crime of assisting the international coalition to crush the armies of Baghdad.

Between 1992 and 1995, after the extinction of the Afghan jihad, the fall of Kabul in April 1992 (coincidentally, in the same month that Serb militias opened hostilities in Sarajevo), and the watering down of the intifada by the Israeli-Palestinian peace process, Bosnia became a major issue for the Islamic world. Unlike the Algerian civil war (which also began in 1992 but, being a struggle of Muslim against Muslim, had a far lower profile in the Community of the Faithful), the bloodshed in Bosnia brutally exposed the different strategies of each state and of each opposition movement striving for supremacy within Islam.⁶ As in the preceding decade, the same poles of influence were apparent: they were Iran, Saudi Arabia, and the many forms taken by the Islamist movement, from the Muslim Brothers to the jihadist-salafists. But the context was no longer the same as it had been in Afghanistan. Tehran had lost the revolutionary zeal whipped up by Ayatollah Khomeini in his time; the monarchy in Riyadh was still heavily in debt following the Gulf War, and under steady pressure from its domestic opposition. Jihad was a slogan to be used with the greatest care in Europe, where it was liable to provoke the kind of virulent response that was meat and drink to Serbian propaganda.

For all these reasons the Bosnian cause led to a low-intensity contest between the two capitals and their respective allies, mainly expressed through their support of Islamic humanitarian endeavor in a field that had hitherto been monopolized by Western charities. To these they opposed their own concept of charity, creating a polemic on the motives behind this activity. Jihadists from Peshawar, along with new recruits (a total of about 4,000 men), went away to fight in Bosnia; but they were unable to transform the war into a jihad in any meaningful way because the term struck no chord in the local Muslim population, as it had done among the Afghans. In general, Bosnian Muslims viewed their conflict with Serbians and Croatians in a very different light.

And yet the Bosnian Muslims had not been cut off from the great changes that had swept over the wider world of Islam since the late 1960s, despite the vitality of socialist ideology in Yugoslavia throughout the half century of Marshal Tito's dictatorship. In 1970, the year of Nasser's death and Khomeini's publication of *Towards an Islamic Government*, a text entitled *Islamic Declaration* was clandestinely distributed in Sarajevo. This text discussed a number of themes similar to those of Sayyid Qutb's 1965 manifesto. Its author, Alija Izetbegovic, had belonged to the pan-Islamic association Mladi Muslimani (Young Muslims), which was greatly influenced by the Egyptian Muslim Brothers. Founded in 1941, the Young Muslims were dismantled by Tito's government in 1949. Izetbegovic was first imprisoned for his ideas in 1946; in 1983 he was jailed again, following the trial of thirteen Muslims accused of Islamic fundamentalism in the aftermath of the Iranian revolution. Seven years later in March 1990, when Yugoslavia was beginning to fall apart, he created the Party for Democratic Action (Stranka Demokratske Akcije, SDA), whose original name, the Yugoslav Muslim Party, had not been approved by the authorities. In November the SDA swept the entire Muslim vote in the elections for the collegial presidency of the Yugoslav Republic of Bosnia-Herzegovina, while the nationalist Serbian and Croatian parties triumphed in their respective communities.[7] Izetbegovic, the former Young Muslim, was to become the first democratically elected president of a country whose population (like that of the Serbs and Croatians) was overwhelmingly secularized.[8] He had been able to attract votes by positioning his party at the very heart of a national identity defined by religious faith, within the context of rising nationalisms all over the crumbling federation of Yugoslavia.

Thus, there was an electoral coincidence between the message of a small but long-established pan-Islamic tradition and a population that was mostly uninterested in such ideology, being thoroughly disoriented by war and the breakup of Yugoslavia. This was hardly the moment for the leaders of the SDA to proclaim an Islamic state and apply the tenets of the sharia, despite the hopes of the jihad storm troopers who had come to Sarajevo dreaming of another Kabul. It was the United States, seconded by Western Europe, that brokered the Dayton Accords which ended the fighting. Bosnia thereafter was integrated into the European sphere, and the Islamic world forfeited any influence over its future with the forced departure of the Islamic "volunteers" from Peshawar, Cairo, and Tehran.

The failure to transplant jihad was an early indication of two entirely new phenomena that characterized political Islam in the 1990s. The first was the gradual opening of a gulf between the ideas of Islamist radicals and the needs of ordinary Muslims, in whose eyes utopian ideals were progressively losing their attraction. Second, there began to emerge among those same ordinary Muslims a blueprint for a Muslim democratic society that went beyond the Islamist model. It was suggested that traditional Islamic culture could find a way to allow Muslims to embrace the modern world without betraying themselves. This occurred at the conclusion of a war filled with atrocities that had been perpetrated in the name of a closed, exclusive interpretation of identity.

To understand these developments, we must see them within the context of the building of the Muslim identity of Bosnia-Herzegovina. This was first called in question by the military victories of Austria-Hungary and its subsequent takeover of the province from the Ottoman Empire, which was endorsed by the Congress of Berlin in 1878. Islamized Slavs had constituted a dominant minority of urban elites and landowners, who derived power and status from their links with Istanbul. The Austro-Hungarian occupation deprived them of this prestige and diluted their influence within the greater Yugoslav entity. Until the outbreak of World War I, the area was controlled by the Catholic Croatians favored by Vienna; after the war, the Orthodox Serbs dominated the independent kingdom of Yugoslavia from 1918 to 1941. This state of affairs was roughly similar to that of the Muslim Indians who, after the British victory over the last Mogul emperor of Delhi in

1857, suddenly found themselves a minority part of a state in which the sharia was no longer applicable and in which their own religious and political identity was called into question. Unlike India, where emigration *(hijra)* to an Islamic country was impossible for most Muslims, the Muslim elites of the Balkans who were most closely associated with the Sublime Porte (that is, the Ottoman caliphate) moved straight to Istanbul, where the Bosnian community was well represented at the sultan's court.

Moreover, there was in Bosnia no equivalent to the Deobandi movement, which erected a kind of community fence around the codification of religious practices in their strictest form. Instead, just as had happened in India, Bosnian society coagulated around communities defined by their religious belief, whose leaders represented them in their dealings with the Hapsburg state. When elections were organized by the occupying power (1910 in Bosnia, 1911 in India), they took place in a similar way, the electors being qualified according to religion and the property they held and voting for notables representing their own communities (Muslim, Serb, Croat, or Jewish in the one case, Hindu or Muslim in the other). Between 1918 and 1941, in a state that had begun by calling itself the Kingdom of the Serbs, Croats, and Slovenes, the identity of the Muslim population was seriously threatened. If this community wished to exist alongside the others, which inhabited regions where the population was more homogeneous, it had to transform itself into a nation.

Most of the Muslims lived between mainly Croatian zones in the west and Serbian zones in the east; thus they were caught in a vise between those who viewed them as Muslim Croats and those who viewed them as Muslim Serbs. As a result, Bosnia-Herzegovina lost its territorial autonomy and was divided into four departments *(banovinas)* in 1929. As religious affiliation became harder and harder to translate into political community, the Muslim party (Jugoslavenska Muslimanska Organizacija, Yugoslav Muslim Organisation, or JMO), which formed in 1919, found itself endangered at a time when the other vehicles of identity were moving forward rapidly. Apart from the Communist party, which also made inroads among the Serbs and Croats, a new pan-Islamic political faction came to the surface, which urged Muslims to militate for the re-establishment of a universal Community of Believers. Even more than their Arab colleagues, the Bosnian ulemas had been crushed by Ataturk's abolition of the Ottoman caliphate in 1924, because they had no other point of reference. The *reis üs ülema* (chief of the ulemas), who exercised supreme religious authority, was nominated with the approval of the Islamic powers in Istanbul. The younger religious generation turned to the Islamist movements that appeared in Cairo in the late 1920s, founding in 1936 the El Hidaje (Right Path) association and, in March 1941, the Young Muslims.[9] The latter, by recruiting among educated young people as the Egyptian Muslim Brothers had done, turned Islam in its purged, salafist form into a way of organizing society and opposing the rising tide of communism and fascism.

The Nazi invasion of the Balkans, which took place in the month following the forming of the Young Muslim party, resulted in some of their militants joining the Handjar (Dagger) SS battalion that was raised among the Bosnian Muslims by the Mufti of Jerusalem, Amin al-Husseini, an enthusiast of the Third Reich.[10] Afterward, the partisan movement led by Marshal Tito, the secretary general of the Communist Party, succeeded in enrolling a large number of recruits from the Muslim population. Tito offered a way out, in the face of the pro-Nazi Croatian Ustase and Serb Chetnik militias, each of which perpetrated appalling massacres in the zones it controlled. At the liberation, the Communist regime dismantled El Hidaje, which had collaborated with the Germans, and in 1949 the Young Muslims were also proscribed, four of their leaders being executed.

Paradoxically, Tito's Communist Yugoslavia seems to have laid the groundwork for a national Muslim identity in Bosnia on which the SDA was able to build. After fifteen years during which the official ideology favored political and cultural centralism with a view to melting all the components of the nation into a single Communist and Yugoslav entity, the 1960s brought a kind of détente. The decade emphasized the federal nature of the state and allowed a limited measure of free speech, which stood in stark contrast to the strict censorship prevailing in the Eastern Bloc. Unlike the other republics of the Yugoslav Federation (the "nation" of Serbs, Croats, Slovenes, Montenegrins, and Macedonians), Bosnia-Herzegovina did not include a Bosnian nation; it was more a grouping of Serbs, Croats, and others. But the 1961 census confirmed that there actually existed a distinct denomination of Muslims, in the ethnic sense of the word, and beginning in 1968 this denomination became a new "nationality." "Muslims" were now understood to be people who spoke Serbo-Croat and professed Islam as their religion, whatever their nationality (they might also be Kosovar Albanians, for example). This secular affirmation of a national identity founded on religious belief has its parallels with the definition of Muslims and Jews, respectively, at the creations of Pakistan in 1947 and Israel in 1948. It emerged at the juncture when the Muslims of Bosnia became the largest single group in that republic, when their elites were penetrating to the heart of the nation's political and economic apparatus. Specifically, Bosnian Muslims were in the forefront of Tito's campaign to promote Yugoslavia's international strategy at the head of the non-aligned movement, in which Egypt and Indonesia, among other Muslim countries, were active participants.

But the fact remained that Muslims were the only Yugoslav nation without a territory of their own. The process of secularization was continuing apace among them, as it was elsewhere; but, still, their only autonomous institutions were religious ones. The political, economic, and cultural structures existing within the framework of the Republic of Bosnia-Herzegovina were all pluri-national, including Serbs and Croats. The Islamic Community (Islamska Zajednica, or IZ), a structure run by ulemas that was the official religious intermediary with the government, assumed responsibility for the mosques and madrassas of Sarajevo, and it did its best to restore the most devout possible complexion to the Muslim nationality. This process was similar to the work of the ulema parties and the Jamaat-e-Islami in the first decade of Pakistan's existence, though on a far smaller scale. The IZ also favored the reaffirmation of the pan-Islamist faction repressed in the late 1940s; Alija Izetbegovic's 1970 *Islamic Declaration*, intended as a program for the Islamization of Muslims and Muslim nations, showed that its author was receptive to the new ideas that were appearing among Islamist thinkers all over the world.[11] They attracted students and pupils of the madrassas, many of whom were from rural backgrounds and did not belong to the elite Muslim families of Sarajevo who had benefited from the regime's modernizing initiatives.

Thus, a new generation of Islamist intellectuals surfaced in the 1970s. They had a lot in common with their equivalents elsewhere in the Umma at that time: they made the same references to thinkers among the Muslim Brothers and they came from the same social ori-

gins in newly urbanized milieus, at a time when the Muslim population of Bosnia was increasing very rapidly. But apart from this Islamist
intelligentsia, there were no other social groups liable to join it in creating a movement resembling the ones in Egypt, Pakistan, or Malaysia.
There was no devout middle class in the still-socialist Republic of
Bosnia, nor was there an impoverished urban youth with the potential
to unite for change. The Bosnian Islamists between 1970 and 1990 remained an intellectual minority, whose members were bound together
by past friendships and present trouble but did not in any way constitute a social movement.

The worst period they had to endure was the trial of thirteen of their
number in the spring of 1983, at a time when the ongoing Iranian revolution was causing considerable disquiet and Tito's death (in 1980)
had removed the keystone of the Yugoslav system. The competitive
nationalisms that eventually blew the federation apart were about to
ignite; and this political trial, which led to prison terms for Izetbegovic
and his main collaborators on a charge of fundamentalism, may have
weakened his initiative to project the Islamist message outside academic circles, but it gave him an undeniable legitimacy later when new
elites arose who were capable of embodying Muslim nationalism in the
coming times of uncertainty and war.

The creation of the SDA in March 1990 was the work of those who
had been jailed in 1983. In the interval they had gathered a following of
young imams, Islamist intellectuals educated in secular schools, and a
few personalities from the bazaars and the media. Yet this party, whose
base consisted of intellectuals who had little real contact with the wider
population, was able to impose itself in the institutional vacuum and
political disarray of a society in the process of very rapidly losing all the
basic touchstones so painstakingly constructed by Tito since 1945. It
presented itself as the best hope of Muslims who were deeply apprehensive that the confrontations between Serbs and Croats would cost
them dearly, given that both sides were set on proclaiming independent
states of their own and much tempted to include in those states the territory of Bosnia.

In the eight months between the founding of the SDA and the election of Izetbegovic to the presidency of the Bosnian Republic, the SDA
became a mass party, thanks to the support of notables linked to the
League of Communists. The most eminent of these was Fikret Abdic,

the head of the Agrokomerc combine, who had been implicated in a spectacular financial scandal in 1987 and had no previous affiliation with the Islamist movement. The SDA victory in the election of November 1990 was more marked in the rural areas and small towns of Bosnia than in Sarajevo, where the urban classes were more receptive to the programs of "citizens'" parties that were hostile to nationalism, whether they were Muslim, Serb, or Croat. But in general the three victorious nationalist parties (the SDA, the Serbian SDS, and the Croat HDZ) agreed to share power, as a coalition of circumstance and convenience from which the latter two were afterward gradually ejected; they landed in the arms of Serbia and Croatia proper.[12]

War broke out on Bosnian territory in April 1992, in the month following the proclamation of independence. This was rejected by the Serbian deputies of the SDS, though it was recognized by the European community—a fact that rendered the situation highly confusing, from the perspective of the Muslim world. The Muslims whose villages came under attack by the Serbs defined themselves in terms of nationality as much as religion, and they were far from devout practitioners of Islam. At the same time the party that represented them and for which most of them had voted, the SDA, had its roots deep in Islamism, with President Izetbegovic himself as its principal Bosnian advocate. Izetbegovic's thinking had evolved since his *Islamic Declaration* in 1970. A book published by him in 1988, entitled *Islam between East and West*, shows, like his later works, that he had moved away from the more radical ideas of his youth. His earlier aspiration to Islamic statehood had yielded to the principles of democracy, a subject much more likely to appeal to the secularized urban classes forming the bulk of the cadres and intellectuals of Sarajevo, who otherwise tended to hang back from a party whose origins seemed to them suspect.

As the war went on, the SDA found itself with a growing need for these people, with their technical, organizational, and military talents. They also proved to be excellent intermediaries with Western governments and intellectuals, whose good opinion was vital in promoting Sarajevo as a "capital of European culture" and in drawing a contrast between its openness and tolerance and the barbarity of the Serbian militias engaged in their campaign of ethnic cleansing. Thus in October 1993 the citizens' parties became participants in power, and Haris Silajdzic was named prime minister. After his departure from the government in January 1996, Silajdzic became a leading figure among the Muslim Democrats who criticized the SDA state.

The war severely tested the definition of Muslim identity in Bosnia, torn as it was between the Islamist vision of one section of the ruling elite and the secular values embraced by the majority of society. Those who were carrying out the atrocities of ethnic cleansing did not bother to inquire if their victims were devout or secularist. Yet the relentless campaign of persecution actually drove many people to a religious identification with militant Islamism—especially those who had lost everything and been driven from their homes. This was shown by the creation within the Bosnian army of a number of Islamic Brigades manned by refugees, in which the prohibitions and prescriptions of the sharia were strictly observed. The phenomenon remained a minor one, despite the encouragement given to it by leaders of the SDA, by the various Islamic charitable organizations from abroad, and by the jihadists trained in the camps surrounding Peshawar.

Islamic solidarity with Bosnia caused a sensation in the rest of the Muslim world and inspired numerous declarations of principle. But in real terms the Community of the Faithful was caught off guard by a situation in which the ways and means of intervening were awkward and subject to international constraints that were much more complex than those governing solidarity with Palestine or Afghanistan. With the exception of Iran, the states and organizations that wanted to help had very few contacts within Bosnian society, whose European character was new to their experience and highly disconcerting.

The Organization of the Islamic Conference (OIC), which was the natural conduit for this initiative, was dominated by Saudi Arabia but was pulled every which way by Iranian activism, the one-upmanship of opposition Islamist movements, and the uncontrollable initiatives of the jihadist-salafists, who persisted in treating Bosnia as the latest front in the never-ending holy war against infidels. Iran had for many years been in touch with the founders of the SDA: three of the accused in the 1983 trial had been arrested on their way home from one of the congresses for the unity of Sunnis and Shiites organized each year by Khomeini's regime for the greater discomfiture of Iraq and Saddam Hussein. And the Iranian revolution, modern and iconoclastic as it was, exercised more of an attraction for the European Islamist establishment of the SDA than did Wahhabite conservatism, with its musty medieval air, its dogmatism, and all its other "sclerotic" aspects that the *Islamic Declaration* had dismissed as long ago as 1970.

In 1992 Tehran was hyperactive in the course of two extraordinary conferences called by the OIC to discuss Bosnia: in Istanbul in June and in Jeddah in December. Alija Izetbegovic attended the Jeddah conference in hopes that he could pressure the U.N. Security Council into lifting its embargo on arms for Bosnia, given that the Serbs were using the weaponry of the former Yugoslav army.[13] Two resolutions came out of this, which on the one hand expressed the organization's solidarity with Sarajevo and on the other refused to overstep the mark laid down by the United Nations. The Bosnians were much more difficult to arm than the Afghans because they were under close airborne surveillance by NATO. Nevertheless, the embargo was circumvented by the Iranians in 1992, with weapons that transited via Turkey and the airport at Zagreb and were then delivered to the Bosnian zone after the Croatian forces had taken about a third of the total for themselves.[14] This supply channel benefited at first from the benign neglect of the American government, which saw the arrangement as a way of redressing the balance of power in the former Yugoslavia to the advantage of the Muslim-Croatian federation. Even though the trade-off was exposed when several tons of weapons were confiscated from an Iranian plane at Zagreb in April 1994, triggering a congressional inquiry in the United States, the channel continued to operate until the signing of the Dayton Accords in December 1995.[15] After that, American pressure eventually obtained the departure of the several hundred Guardians of the Revolution (pasdarans) sent to train the Bosnian military.

In addition to military aid of this kind, the Islamic Republic attempted to propagate its ideology in Bosnia through various SDA leaders, while implementing a number of charitable initiatives through the Iranian Red Crescent. Unlike the Wahhabite networks, the latter was able to project an image whereby the humanitarian mission came across as mattering just as much as Islamic solidarity. Indeed, according to a poll conducted at the end of the conflict, 86 percent of Bosnian Muslims had a "favorable opinion" of Iran, a resounding success that caused concern not only in the United States, which had done everything in its power to achieve the opposite result, but also among Tehran's opponents in the wider Islamic world.[16]

Confronted by the relative inertia of the OIC and the leaders of the

Sunni Muslim states, the Islamist opposition in each of these countries turned support of the Bosnians into a propaganda weapon with which to attack the religious legitimacy of governments whose passivity they condemned. Thus, in 1992 the Muslim Brothers in Egypt called for a jihad against the Serbs, with Afghanistan as its model. For the government and every other circle that saw the connection between the return home of the Afghan Arabs and the rising numbers of terrorist attacks in the Nile Valley, it was vital to avoid new disturbances, which were uncontrollable, whatever the question at issue. The state made it its business to take control of all initiatives of solidarity with Bosnia, strictly confining them to humanitarian and medical assistance. Any expressed desire to engage in armed jihad was firmly repressed.[17]

In Saudi Arabia, where the Islamic legitimacy of the dynasty had been under steady threat from within since the Gulf War and where Osama bin Laden's potential for mischief was as much a problem as the perennial rivalry with Iran, the government and those religious institutions within its orbit were all in favor of arming the Bosnians and even of an armed jihad in that country. At the same time they were afraid that a jihad would be taken over by groups hostile to Riyadh, as had happened in Afghanistan. So here again the emphasis was placed on humanitarian assistance, along with mostly ineffectual diplomatic initiatives and a jihad of the pen rather than the sword. This was implemented by a specialist branch of the Muslim World League and by a special fund administered by Prince Salman, the governor of Riyadh, who had supervised a similar effort in Afghanistan. Beginning in 1992, about 150 million dollars' worth of public and private aid from Saudi Arabia reached Bosnia.[18]

Apart from the Islamic humanitarian organizations based in the principal nations of the Arabian peninsula and Malaysia, the conflict attracted the attention of charitable groups collecting funds from Muslims all over Europe, especially the United Kingdom, where the cause was promoted by Muslim Aid, run by the charismatic Yusuf Islam (who, before his conversion to Islam, was the pop singer and songwriter Cat Stevens). In European Islamist circles, the cause of the Bosnian Muslims broke the monopoly on aid of Western organizations, both Christian and nonreligious, which had always been cast as missionary-inspired. It also provided an ideal opportunity to intervene in a moral domain that had become an important political element in international relations by the 1980s: namely, rallying the Muslims of Europe and promoting their coming together as full-fledged communities.

The Islamic specificity of this humanitarian cause prevented the dilution of funds by more nebulous, universal associations. The common European identity of the Bosnian Muslims and the descendants of Pakistanis, Moors, and Turks in England, France, and Germany, transcending the gulf between autochthonous people and immigrants, was a powerful motivating factor of which these associations made full use. Certain militants took the view that the atrocities visited on the native European, fair-haired, blue-eyed Bosnians who spoke the same language and belonged to the same race as their persecutors and who were generally secularized showed that it was futile for immigrant Muslims to try to assimilate into the dominant societies of Western Europe. The process had not helped the Bosnian Muslims one iota; the only real security, they preached, resided in a strengthening of the bonds of religion and community.

Some of the Islamic humanitarian organizations present in Bosnia, whose interests were managed by a Saudi-backed coordination committee (not unlike the Islamic Coordination Council created in Peshawar in 1985) sought to implement a brand of charity associated with the dawa, or propagation of the faith. This aroused its share of controversy, because the attribution of aid was sometimes linked to the performance of religious obligations of the strictest kind. There was even a rumor that women who went unveiled were disqualified from receiving aid and that people who did not regularly go to the mosque would be treated likewise. The confused war situation made it impossible to verify these facts, but such was the reputation of these associations.

A more radical form of propagation was promoted by the jihadist-salafists who arrived in Bosnia to wage holy war despite the opposition of their own governments. According to some estimates, there were as many as 4,000 of these, most of them from Saudi Arabia or the other countries of the Arabian peninsula, and they came to Bosnia after the mujahedeen took Kabul in April 1992. While the Egyptians and Algerians were beginning to return home to their respective countries— where many later took part in the military activities of the Gamaa Islamiya and the GIA—those who came to Bosnia had next to no idea of what a European Muslim country might be, viewing it as another zone of the Islamic Umma where they could behave as they had in Afghanistan.

One of the leaders of the Bosnian mujahedeen was the flamboyant figure of "Commandant" Abu Abdel Aziz, known as Barbaros (Barbarossa) on account of his carefully combed, two-foot-long beard, which he dyed with henna in imitation of the Prophet. A veteran of Afghanistan, where he first arrived in 1984 at the behest of Abdallah Azzam, Barbaros was looking for a new theater of jihad following the fall of Kabul and was torn between the Philippines and Kashmir. "There was only a fortnight's interval, and then the Bosnian crisis was upon us: it confirmed the saying of the Prophet, peace and blessings be upon him, 'Verily, the *jihad* will endure until the Day of Judgment.' A new *jihad* was beginning in Bosnia; we went there, and we joined the battle, according to God's will."[19]

Barbaros brought with him four former "Afghans," confirmed that the conflict was indeed a holy war, then petitioned for fatwas from three of the salafist ulemas who had already given their support to Abdallah Azzam for the war in Afghanistan.[20] Volunteers began to arrive in Bosnia, concentrating in the town of Zenica, which was easily accessible from Croatia. They fought either on their own initiative or as a detachment of the 7th Islamic Brigade of the Bosnian army, which was formed in September 1992. The ideological differences between them and the native Bosnian contingent eventually led to their enrollment in the El-Mudzahidun regiment, which was created especially for them in August 1993. Barbaros was in command of this structure. Thereafter, the experienced, heavily armed veteran jihadists fought a series of ferocious battles with the Serb militias, against whom they claimed in their propaganda to have struck several decisive blows that "saved Islam from extinction."[21] They were just as cruel as their opponents, and the photographs of grinning Arab warriors brandishing the freshly severed heads of "Christian Serbs" or crushing them with their boot-heels created such a furor that the Bosnian army had to regain control of them before their excessive zeal did any more harm to the Muslim image.[22]

Apart from their military activities, the "Afghans" used their free time to propagate their salafist ideas among the local Muslims. Specifically, they undertook the "purging" of Bosnian Islam, causing disturbances in the ceremonies of brotherhoods they deemed to be deviant, attempting to impose the veil on women and the beard on men, smashing up cafés, and generally transposing the Afghan experience to the Balkans, especially to the Zenica region. These practices, along with a number of sharia marriages to Bosnian girls that were not declared to the civil authorities, were anything but popular, and the press of the citizens' parties joined with intellectual democrats and even the pan-Islamist ideologues of the SDA in condemning them.[23]

The El-Mudzahidun brigade, to which President Izetbegovic rendered a public tribute on December 10, 1995, was disbanded after the Dayton Accords were signed in Paris. All foreign volunteers were invited to leave the territory of Bosnia-Herzegovina and allow themselves to be replaced by American peacekeeping forces.[24] For many of the jihadist-salafists this was a bitter experience, since the war they had sought to turn into a holy war had come to an end in an aura of Pax Americana. From their point of view the soldiers of the "ungodly" were moving in to occupy one of the territories of the Umma, a dire echo of the arrival *en masse* in Saudi Arabia of the coalition armies five years before. Bosnia had been snatched from Serbia's grasp, at the price of a shift into the Westernizing European sphere of influence. This was the reverse of what had happened in Afghanistan; and to make matters worse, their militant and inflexible version of Islam had taken root among only a few scattered groups of youthful extremists. Today, nothing is left of their presence except a few naturalized Arab subjects married to Bosnian women, who live in an Islamic village commune in a remote area of northern Bosnia. Their experience is not unlike that of Darul Arqam of Malaysia or of Shukri Mustafa in Egypt.

Yet neither the clumsiness of the humanitarian organizations, which identified charity and dawa too closely, nor the rigidity of the jihadist-salafists who confused Zenica and Jalalabad, nor even the Western schemes that they denounced were entirely responsible for the radical Islamist failure in Bosnia. The main cause was the emergence, in ordinary society, of a democratic attitude toward religion, which in many ways resembled the post-Islamist logic that has been gaining ground ever since the 1990s in other Muslim societies, including Iran, as we shall see.

At the postwar elections of September 1996, the SDA consolidated

its 1990 success and reaped the lion's share of the benefits accruing
from Alija Itzetbegovic's international stature and from a moral victory over Serbian aggression. The SDA's rival, the Party for Bosnia-
Herzegovina founded by former Prime Minister Silajdzic, did much
less well in spite of the indispensable role it had played in the restoration of the state since the autumn of 1993. Most of the criticisms of the
ruling party were focused on its monopoly of the government—since,
according to its adversaries, it strongly resembled Tito's Communist
party in its behavior. Indeed, a number of former Communist cadres
had joined the SDA, which earned them the Sarajevan nickname of
"watermelons": red inside, green outside. At the same time, the SDA
was accused of using Islam as a tool to forge its own legitimacy, and of
confounding muslims (small m, for national identity) with Muslims
(capital M, for religious creed). But this monopolizing of religion,
though it was fraught with the dangers of populism and one-party
government, also supplied a barrier against the radicalization of the
message or the actions of the party. The SDA could govern only if it
had the support of the secular urban middle class, the non-religious
former communist cadres, and rural Bosnia, home of the brotherhood-
based piety that had so shocked the Arab jihadists.

Every year, in the month of June, the highest officials of the SDA
presided over the celebration of the Ajvatovica, an ancient pilgrimage
Islamized by the brotherhoods, which—in complete disregard of Islamist or salafist orthodoxy—is the most important symbol of Muslim
Bosnia and the pluralism it has evolved for itself. Some of the party's
publications still contained references to the Islamization of society,
with special emphasis on Islam's strict moral order. These texts were
reminiscent of Izetbegovic's 1970 *Islamic Declaration.* Nevertheless the
president himself, without renouncing any of his former engagements,
continued to make public declarations that were tinged with political
realism. It appeared to be his belief that the installation of an Islamic
state, or any attempt to apply the sharia, would arouse the overwhelming opposition of Bosnian voters and seriously undermine the SDA administration.

Although the SDA's original founding fathers remained Islamist in
their outlook and kept firm control over the country's politics and ideology, the party had in recent times been transformed by society, which
had forged it in its own image rather than vice versa. As we shall

see later, a similar phenomenon occurred within the Turkish Islamist party, which in assuming power jettisoned some of its original doctrines and changed itself into an instrument for the political inclusion of the devout middle class. In Bosnia, the more dogmatic figures in the SDA aroused general hilarity by conducting a campaign against Father Christmas as being non-Islamic.

Enes Karič, a Muslim intellectual educated at the Sarajevo madrassa, a translator of the Koran, a collaborator of Silajdzic, and a one-time minister of culture, sums up the position in pluralist, democratic Muslim Bosnia today, in which nobody can use the sword of Islamic authenticity against other Muslims for political ends: "Bosnia is on the soil of Europe, and it is very important that Bosnian Muslims have for many years before now accepted the principle that they should practice Islam within the context of a civil society and a civil state." For him, religion should be able to function "without political interference as to what constitutes the 'real Islam,' which will never be the sole property of anyone, nor a tool in the hands of politicians who will use it for worldly or egotistical ends."[25]

Behind the idealism of these assertions, we may detect the failure of an Islamist campaign which in 1992 seemed to have international momentum but which three years later was rejected by Bosnia without ever bearing fruit. By 1995, the high season of jihad was drawing to a close in the countries where it had flourished. Its discomfiture in Bosnia was only a prelude to its fiascos in Algeria and Egypt a couple of years later.

11

The Logic of Massacre in the Second Algerian War

In the year the Bosnian conflict began, another civil war broke out in Algeria in which Islamism was to play a leading role. From 1992 to 1997, confrontations of unbelievable savagery and violence ripped the country apart, claiming over 100,000 dead. All this was the consequence of a coup d'état to cancel the result of a general election in January 1992, which the Front Islamique du Salut (FIS) was poised to win. The fighting that ensued between the Algerian army and Islamist militants in the bush and in the cities hastened the break-up of the coalition behind the FIS, bringing the devout middle class and the young urban poor of Algeria into more and more open conflict.

The devout middle class, whose members mostly identified with the leaders of the dissolved FIS, gave their sympathy to the Armée Islamique du Salut (AIS), the FIS's military arm, and then to the "moderate" Islamic parties, especially Hamas, founded by Mahfoud Nahnah. Meanwhile, the Algerian regime, gradually consolidating its military successes in the field, endeavored in 1995 to win back the approval of that pious bourgeoisie by undertaking a program of privatization and a switch to a market economy. The faction on the other side—the young Algerian poor in the cities—tended to identify very strongly with the swarms of armed groups that eventually came together under the banner of the Groupe Islamique Armé (GIA). Advocating total war against the government and rejecting all truces and compromises, the GIA's core consisted of former members of Mustafa Bouyali's Mouvement Islamique Armé (1982–1987), along with Algerian "Afghan Arabs." The result was a jihadist-salafist movement of extraordinary brutality, which overtook those groups still loyal to the FIS in 1994 and attracted, along with large numbers of hittistes, a sprinkling of intellectuals who had previously gone underground. The GIA was led by a succession of so-called amirs, all in their twenties, who rose to power and then were killed in combat one after the other; in the process it cut itself off from its grassroots Algerian support and exported terrorism to France in 1995.

The drift toward aimless violence culminated in wholesale massacres of civilians in the suburbs of Algiers in the fall of 1997, at a time when the AIS was declaring a "unilateral truce" with the government. Deprived of its popular component—radicalized Algerian youth and the jihadist-salafist intellectuals who had gone along with them—the Islamist movement as a whole was incapable of remobilizing as it had done between 1989 and 1991, when it provided the FIS with a critical mass of support that allowed it to control the streets and win elections. Consequently, the Islamist movement in Algiers was defeated. In the aftermath of the civil war, the Algerian government took care to maintain its grip on the political situation and was eager to absorb on its own terms parts of the devout bourgeoisie—who were, by this point, prepared to live with the regime.

The scale of the Algerian Islamists' shipwreck was not fully appreciated until 1996–97, when it became clear that the strategy of jihad had lost all popular support and that its proponents had lapsed into self-destructive terrorism. Prior to this, in 1994–95, violence and insecurity had reached such a pitch within Algeria that the state seemed no longer able to withstand them—to the point where some observers (notably in the United States) braced themselves for the advent of the "next fundamentalist state" in Algeria.[1] Many factors seemed to point to this outcome: the frustration of the majority of electors, who had voted for the FIS in December 1991, the conjunction of the two recent jihad traditions (Bouyali's native Algerian one and that of the returning "Afghans"), contrasting memories of the violence of the War of Independence—with its bush and the triumph of the colonels who hijacked power in 1962—and finally the fury of vast numbers of young people and their determination to have done with the "thieves" who ruled them.

Islamist leaders and opposition parties all over the Muslim world were riveted by the unfolding of the Algerian conflict, with each camp expecting a boost from the success of whichever faction it supported. In Egypt, where a wave of terrorism was sweeping through the Upper Nile Valley and where the radical group Gamaa Islamiya was exchanging messages of sympathy with the GIA, the Algerian conflict was followed intently. In France, where a very large Algerian population resided and links formed with Algeria over 132 years of colonization were still very strong, the civil war quickly acquired a domestic dimension. After a number of French citizens were killed in Algeria, the French police cracked down hard on militant Algerian Islamists within France's borders; and this impelled the GIA to expand the conflict to France. An Air France jet was hijacked in December 1994, followed by a series of terrorist attacks throughout the summer and fall of 1995.

Many questions remain unanswered as to who exactly was responsible for this campaign and for the tangle of manipulations by which the bloody history of the GIA was brought to a close. What is certain is that by losing the war on the ground, in an orgy of unspeakable atrocities, the GIA drastically weakened Islamism as a whole, not only in Algeria but in the rest of the Muslim world, where it was now obliged to expend much time and energy distancing itself from its more extremist elements. The Algerian disaster put the movement (except for the most radical groups) on the defensive, in notable contrast to the offensive optimism of the 1980s. Intellectuals linked to the devout middle class found themselves obliged to reformulate their theories to reassure society in general, and to do so some of them began to embrace the rhetoric of democracy. Although this set them apart from the extremists, it created serious dissensions within their own ranks. Indeed, the Algerian drama of the 1990s had major consequences far beyond Algeria itself.

When the electoral process was "interrupted" (to use the customary euphemism) in Algeria on January 13, 1992, several small radical groups that viewed elections and democracy as "ungodly" (kufr) were fully prepared for a jihad. They had inaugurated it in spectacular fashion with a bloody attack on the military outpost of Guemmar on November 28, 1991—two years, almost to the day, after the assassination of Abdallah Azzam in Peshawar. The head of the group responsible, the Afghanistan veteran Aissa Massudi (also known as Tayyeb al-Afghani) was later arrested, tried, and put to death. The attack, which the authorities blamed on the FIS so as to damage its electoral campaign (the party formally denied the charge), was the first indication of a jihadist-salafist contingent at the fringes of the Islamist party in Algeria. The jihadist-salafists had never believed that power could be won through the electoral process and thus had waited for the right moment to precipitate an armed struggle.

According to one of the Afghan veterans who founded the GIA, the idea of forming an armed group that would take power through jihad was hatched in late 1989, when jailed leaders of Bouyali's former Mouvement Islamique Armé were released. But the spectacular success of the FIS mobilization right up to the strike and uprising of June 1991 created a climate that appeared to favor a political victory for the Islamist movement and made the proclamation of a jihad seem unnecessary. It was only after the arrest of Madani and Benhadj at the end of the strike, which was taken as a sign that the regime was determined to use force to keep control of the situation, that the armed groups decided to go on the offensive at Guemmar. They judged that the conditions for a jihad were now in place, because there were more than enough militants sufficiently disenchanted with the electoral strategy of the party to go into action.[2]

This jihadist faction was actually made up of a number of different cells, nursing bitter rivalries of doctrine, personality, and experience. These differences later furnished a pretext for murderous infighting. There were two leading networks: former militants of Bouyali's MIA (among them Abdelkader Chebouti, Mansouri Meliani, and Ezzedine Baa) and veterans of Afghanistan such as Qari Said, Tayyeb al-Afghani, and Djafar al-Afghani—the latter was the amir of the GIA between August 1993 and February 1994.[3] To these were added a number of FIS dissidents, notably Said Mekhloufi, a former officer of the Algerian army, who later became the editor of the FIS's official newspaper, wrote a 1991 *Treatise on Civil Disobedience* advocating violence, and was excluded from the FIS's Batna Congress in July of the same year. Finally, there was a stream of young men with no experience in combat or activism, which increased steadily in volume from 1992 onward. All these members diverged widely in terms of culture and experience: the jihadist-salafists who had originally come together in Afghanistan had no trouble accepting the fairly similar but basic ideology of Bouyali's followers, and this group became a main source for the GIA's texts and proclamations. But other factions were also surfacing at about the same time. For example, the Qutbists (disciples of Sayyid Qutb) rejected salafism; the takfiris viewed society in general as impious and thus excommunicated it; and the djazarists (or Algerianists), an association of technocrats and intellectuals, turned to violence and joined forces with the GIA in May 1994.[4] The ideological fragmentation of the armed groups making up the GIA prevented them from joining forces militarily and later provided the pretext for purges and liquidations.

This disparate, tiny movement was thrust into the spotlight with the interruption of the January 1992 elections, which was followed by the arrest of most of the leaders of the FIS and the breakup of the party itself. Those who had previously gone underground now saw their strategy justified, and they were joined by considerable numbers of young men forced "into the hills" to escape the government's campaign of repression. In February, an armed group attacked the admiralty building in Algiers and policemen were assassinated. Armed confrontations began to take place regularly after Friday prayers, and scores of people were killed in every part of the country. In August, a spectacularly bloody attack on the airport in Algiers was blamed on the Islamists, whose sympathizers saw it as pure provocation.

But throughout 1992 things stayed relatively calm, by comparison with the frenzy of violence that would characterize the five years that followed. At this time the FIS's dismantled leadership showed itself incapable of holding its militants and electors in line and was unsure of what to do next. The mobilization seemed to be relaunched every week after Friday prayers. Its instigators expected a snowball effect comparable to the Iranian one masterminded by Khomeini in 1978, but the determination of the military hierarchy made that outcome untenable. The army commanders arrested more than 40,000 people and sent them to camps deep in the Sahara. For a while the military seemed to have the situation under control, but before long this massive relocation had an unforeseen consequence. The sympathizers and militants who had been removed and concentrated became much more radical while in custody, and by the time they were released (beginning in the summer of 1992) they were willing recruits for the armed insurgent groups.

The disarray of the FIS was demonstrated by the breakup of its decision-making structures. Commanded from within by a secret crisis cell that was rapidly taken over by Abderrazaq Redjem, a confederate of the djazarist leader Mohammed Said, it maintained two delegations abroad. These were the parliamentary delegation, run by the djazarist Anwar Haddam, and an organization controlled by Rabah Kebir, based in Germany, that was loyal to Abassi Madani. The two were not unified until September 1993, following the creation in Tirana, Albania, of the IEFE, or Instance Exécutive du FIS à l'Etranger (FIS Foreign Executive), which was supposed to speak with a single voice. In Iran in 1978, Khomeini had taken firm control by rallying the various elements of society, despite their differences, into a single revolutionary Islamist program. In Algeria in 1993, the FIS was broken by repression. The devout middle class it had attracted earlier was politically rudderless and marginalized, and the initiative gradually passed to more violent groups, in which the impoverished urban young had gained the upper hand by the time the civil war entered its most active phase in the spring of 1992.

While the FIS's leadership was falling apart (and giving the government the illusion that it had won an easy victory), the armed insurgent groups made a concerted effort at coordination. In March 1992, Chebouti and Baa, veterans of Bouyali's MIA, and Mekhloufi, a founder member of the FIS—all three of whom were salafists convinced at an early stage that jihad was necessary—created the Mouvement de l'Etat Islamique (MEI) in the bush, largely based in the area round Lakhdaria, south of Algiers. The MEI quickly attracted a number of militants from the FIS, which had been dissolved in the same month. At the same time, Meliani—another former aide of Bouyali—formed his own cell, attracting an assortment of "Afghan" veterans and younger urban militants. This group was blamed, among other things, for the attacks on the admiralty in February and on the airport in March. Arrested in July and executed in August 1993, Meliani was replaced by Mohammed Allal (nicknamed Moh Leveilley after the working-class area of Algiers that was his stronghold). Allal quickly made a name for himself as an urban guerrilla. On August 31 and September 1, 1992, a meeting was held at Tamesguida to unify all these people under the command of Chebouti. This was broken up by the Algerian military, which managed to kill Leveilley in the process. It was left to his successor, Abdelhaq Layada, an autobody mechanic from the Baraki district of Algiers who had discovered Islam during the October 1988 uprising, to make the decisive step—namely, the amalgamation of the three small groups into the unified GIA.

By the close of 1992, the armed movement consisted of two main branches. These were the MIA, led by "General" Chebouti, which was well-organized and structured and favored a long-term jihad based on a maquis like that of the War of Independence and of Bouyali. The MIA's struggle was mainly directed against the state and its representatives. In January 1993 a fatwa promulgated by Ali Benhadj from his prison cell gave the MIA the blessing of the number-two figure in the dissolved FIS. Layada, who represented the other branch, implemented the GIA's strategy of immediate action to destabilize the enemy, with repeated attacks designed to create an atmosphere of general insecurity. His verdict on the FIS was severe, and he declared impious those leaders of the party who had declined to take up arms on the pretext that they abhorred violence.

Initially, Layada, the first amir of the GIA, threatened journalists ("grandsons of France") and the families of Algerian soldiers. These threats were fulfilled a few months later, in the spring of 1993. In an interview published by the *Al-Shahada* (Profession of the Faith) bulletin in March 1993, Layada placed his movement within the context of contemporary history.[5] According to him, the greatest disaster ever to befall the Community of the Faithful was the fall of the caliphate in 1924. The Muslim Brothers and the Pakistani Jamaat-e-Islami had fought manfully during the struggle to establish an Islamic state against the ideas of jahiliyya (barbarity); this was all very well, but the overall results of the last seventy years were distinctly meager, according to Layada. The ungodly had everywhere succeeded in clinging to power, because the movements opposing them had hesitated to embrace jihad and to resort to armed struggle.

The one project of Islamic jihad that had achieved most of its objectives while yielding strategic experience that could be emulated on a global level was Afghanistan, according to Layada. In Algeria, where enemies of Islam trained by the French had seized power at the time of independence, a few preachers had continued to nurse the flame of resistance, until "the martyr Bouyali" arrived and became aware that the way to raise high the word of Allah was the way of jihad.[6] Yet he too remained isolated, according to Layada, "because the preachers lived in a world of dreams, mirages, and intellectual and operational naivety." Next had come the FIS, whose objectives were commendable but whose strategy was defeated by the forces of impiety and godlessness. Now the hour had come for jihad, for the launching of which "the GIA has assembled the necessary justifications according to Sharia." Layada went on to express his amazement that "those who issued fatwas to proclaim that the jihad was an obligation [fard ayn] for everyone in Afghanistan have not done likewise in Algeria and the other Muslim countries, whereas the basic principles that ought to guide them are exactly the same."

After a phase of preparation following the unification of the first jihadist cells in the GIA, Layada set about bringing together all other armed militants under his own command "according to a single intellectual principle: namely, the way of orthodox Sunni Islam as our pious ancestors understood it."[7] Referring to Oswald Spengler's theory of the decline of the West and Bertrand Russell's idea that the "white man has had his day," the amir went on to suggest that a new caliphate should be established by force of arms in Algeria. He divided the existing Islamist movements into two categories. On the one hand were those who gave their allegiance to the "godless government . . . and we shall be innocent of their blood, because Allah's judgment on them is made clear when he announces that 'he among you who pays allegiance to them, is one of their number.'[8] As to those who are not allied to the government, we say to them, 'why do you wait to join the caravan of the jihad?'"[9] Pleading for the combatants to unite, Layada sought to avoid the dissensions that, by the time his text appeared in March 1993, had transformed the victory of the Afghan mujahedeen over the Red Army into a fratricidal war.[10]

This interview—whether Layada was its real author or whether the editors of Al Chahada doctored it—places the GIA firmly in the line of the Afghan jihad and the saga of Bouyali. Layada suggests that the GIA is the natural outcome of the Algerian Islamist movement after the failure of the FIS. He sees his own vocation as rallying the disappointed FIS militants to turn the GIA into the single controlling organization for armed struggle. This double ambition took shape in 1993 during Layada's time as amir and came to fruition during the amirate of Cherif Gousmi in 1994. It was set in motion by a cycle of violence aimed not only at the Algerian government and its officials but also at all those men and women who were viewed as having links of any kind with that government.

Beginning in March 1993, a steady succession of university academics, intellectuals, writers, journalists, and medical doctors were assassinated. Not all of them were connected to the regime, but all—at least in the eyes of the young urban poor who had joined the jihad—were associated with the hated image of French-speaking intellectuals, with their inaccessible cultural assets. In military terms the regime was unscathed by this purge, but the myth of its easy triumph over the Islamist movement in 1992 was exploded. The visibility of the victims and their ties abroad meant that their murders greatly damaged the credibility of the state. More worrisome still, though less easily understood outside Algeria, was the regime's loss of control of mountain and rural districts as well as of the main roads and the working-class areas of the cities. These passed into the hands of the armed insurgents, revealing the fragility of the government and the tilt toward dissidence that was taking place across broad swathes of the population. Without actually enlisting with the still-embryonic GIA and MEI, many young men from humble backgrounds—who were more or less under the orders of local amirs—managed to expel the police from their neighborhoods and proclaim them "liberated Islamic zones."

This process, which was fairly well received at the time by a population who had voted overwhelmingly for the FIS and deplored the disappearance of the "fair" management of the municipality by the elected officials of the party, was reflected by a change in the social hierarchy within the Islamist movement itself.[11] During the period when the FIS controlled many municipal authorities (June 1990–April 1992), local power had remained in the hands of the devout middle class and the intellectuals of the party, who implemented a populist policy intended to satisfy the social demands of the impoverished urban young. This involved fighting corruption in public services, cracking down on crime, "improving" public morals, and so on. In 1993–94, when young militants seized local power by force, Islamist notables, entrepreneurs, and shopkeepers—united in their hostility to a government that had robbed them of their election victory in January 1992—initially funded the hittiste amirs, journeymen workers, and plumbers, whom they saw as tools for their political revenge. But as the months went by, their voluntary "Islamic tax" turned into a full-scale extortionist racket, operated by bands of armed men claiming to represent an ever more shadowy cause, while fighting one another for turf on which to continue their exactions. Meanwhile, the army, having withdrawn from these areas, surrounded them and turned them into ghettos.[12] The devout middle class found itself first pauperized, then victimized through extortion by gangs of deprived young men. Its members responded by deserting their districts, and this was a powerful contributing factor in destroying all semblance of social unity within the Islamist movement. In fact, in the long term it would lay the groundwork for a gradual return of the middle class to the government fold.

In political terms, this passage of influence from the devout bourgeoisie to the working class became clear when the GIA won supremacy over the FIS in 1993–94. Layada, who was arrested in Morocco in May 1993, was succeeded (after a period of indecision) by Mourad Si Ahmed, also known as Seif Allah Djafar (Djafar the sword of Allah) or Djafar al-Afghani (in recognition of the two years he spent in Afghanistan with Hekmatyar's Hezb-e-Islami). Aged thirty when he became amir in August 1993, this leader had not been educated beyond primary school and had made his living from trading in contraband goods *(trabendo)*.[13] Like his predecessors and successors, he was an underprivileged youth from the city. His amirate, which continued until his death in combat on February 26, 1994, was distinguished by an escalation of violence, as his alias would indicate. He began by expanding the GIA's base of support outside Algeria. From July 1993 onward, a weekly bulletin called *Al-Ansar* (The Partisans) was published in London by the international jihadist-salafist movement, under the supervision of two Afghan veterans, a naturalized Spanish Syrian named Abu Mousab and a Palestinian, Abu Qatada.[14] These two would supply doctrinal justifications for the GIA's actions until June 1996, keeping up a steady stream of pro-GIA publicity outside Algeria and maintaining contacts between the local and international jihad.

Within Algeria, Djafar al-Afghani managed to broaden the influence of his organization to include new groups, who used its name to claim responsibility for spectacular military actions and raise the struggle to a higher intensity.[15] On September 21, 1993, a group allied to the GIA killed two French surveyors at Sidi Bel Abbas in the west of the country. The communiqué claiming responsibility for this execution, signed by the new amir and published by *Al-Ansar*, indicated that godless foreigners as well as godless Algerians were legitimate targets for the jihad. This was the beginning of a deliberate campaign of murder against foreigners: twenty-six individuals were killed before the end of 1993.[16] Nor were those in the Islamist movement who opposed the war spared by "the sword of Allah": in November 1993 Sheik Mohamed Bouslimani, a popular figure who was prominent in Nahnah's devout middle class Hamas party, was kidnapped and executed after refusing to issue a fatwa endorsing the GIA's tactics.

The exacerbation of the violence forced the FIS-based groups to engage more actively in the fight so as to keep the GIA from outflanking them. In the summer of 1993, the djazarist Islamist intellectuals attached to Mohammed Said created the FIDA (Front Islamique du Djihad Armé, whose Arabic acronym means "sacrifice"), which specialized in assassinating secularist intellectuals, their bitterest adversaries. In March 1994, at the end of Ramadan, several hundred fighters of the MEI led by Abdelkader Chebouti attacked the Lambeze prison near Batna and freed all the Islamist inmates. Prior to this, in the middle of a month of fasting which saw a substantial increase in violence, Djafar al-Afghani had been killed in circumstances suggesting that the army had been given exact information on his whereabouts.

Yet al-Afghani's death in no way affected the growing strength of the GIA, whose new amir, Cherif Gousmi (also called Abu Abdallah Ahmed) was introduced by *Al-Ansar* on March 10. Before his death in combat on September 26, 1994, Gousmi achieved one of the chief objectives of the jihad—the unification of its troops—by absorbing some of the original adherents of the FIS. His amirate saw the high-water mark of GIA power, during which the use of violence was combined with precise political objectives. Gousmi, aged twenty-six when he took control, had been the imam and local representative of the FIS at Birkhadem before being sent to the Sahara camps in 1992. Thereafter, he joined the GIA as head of its religious committee, and within this context gave an interview to an Arab newspaper in Peshawar in January 1994.[17] The new amir appeared to have national and international militant credentials, along with experience in religious matters that made him a more influential personality than any of his predecessors or successors.

On May 13, 1994, Mohammed Said, Abderrazaq Redjem, and Said Mekhloufi met with Gousmi in a tent in the mountains, where the three leaders decided to give their allegiance *(baya)* to the amir and pool their resources within the GIA.[18] The "communiqué of unity, jihad and attachment to the Koran and the Sunna" that resulted was signed by Redjem on behalf of the FIS and by Mekhloufi on behalf of the MEI; it established a consultative council *(majlis al choura)* that included two jailed FIS leaders, Madani and Benhadj (who actually were not consulted).[19] But the real architect of unity was, without a doubt, Mohammed Said, whose charisma and culture set him head and shoulders above the rest. His influence would soon be felt on the GIA, which thereafter was the undisputed principal Islamist force in Algeria. Whatever the real intentions of the various signatories, the historic unification meeting acknowledged the ascendancy of a group that had emerged from the ranks of impoverished urban youth. One of the most prestigious Algerian Islamist intellectuals, the fifty-year-old Said, paid allegiance to an amir of only 26 years of age. This meeting showed quite clearly that the devout middle class had lost the initiative, and it confirmed the decline in its status within Algerian society.

The FIS's executive branch abroad, which was directed from Germany by Rabah Kebir, refused at first to give credence to the unity communiqué and organized a riposte favoring the creation of an Armée Islamique du Salut (AIS). The aim here was to furnish those of the middle class who favored the FIS with a mode of expression to match that of the jihad without obliging them to join the GIA, with its radical objectives. By excluding from its ranks the supporters of Mohammed Said and denying that Redjem had any right to sign anything on behalf of the FIS, the IEFE paved the way for the proclamation of the AIS on July 18, 1994.[20] This move united in loyalty to the FIS, and under the authority of its imprisoned leaders, a network of well-established resistance groups operating in Algeria's eastern and western regions. Their national amir, Madani Merzag, was the counterweight to the GIA amir, Gousmi, whose troops were present in central Algeria and the outskirts of Algiers. Very soon the two factions found themselves locked in bloody combat.

From the start, their political goals were different. For the FIS, the creation of a military branch in the form of the AIS was a tactic to facilitate negotiation with the government from a position of strength. In August, the month following the creation of the AIS, Abassi Madani wrote from prison to General Liamine Zeroual—who had assumed the presidency in the previous month—suggesting they work together toward a solution of the crisis on the basis of the original conditions set by the FIS. The regime did not respond, though Madani was transferred from jail to house arrest and three other FIS leaders were freed on September 13. On the same day, by contrast, Gousmi went public with a letter in which he violently criticized the strategy of the FIS, recalling that the GIA was not fighting a war in order to open a dialogue with "apostate" rulers, nor to establish the "democracy" of a "moderate Islamic regime favored by the West, but to purge the land of the ungodly" and establish through jihad an Islamic state. He reiterated the watchword inscribed on all the GIA's communiqués: "No agreement, no truce, no dialogue." On the ground, the GIA was gaining against the AIS, carrying out more and more executions of apostates and ungodly ones, as well as assassinations of foreigners (to which the AIS was opposed). But within two weeks of this declaration, on September 26, at the height of his power, Gousmi was killed.

The confused events that followed the amir's death and the installation of his successor, Djamel Zitouni, have been interpreted in various ways, and the absence of reliable sources precludes any firm judgment about what happened. While the FIS and AIS were weak, the GIA had in Mohammed Said a potential leader whose stature was far greater than that of any of the younger amirs. It was fully expected that he would consolidate his hold over the group and make it a tool to control the field and present a major threat against the government. He alone was capable of rebuilding the original movement, fragmented as it was by repression, radicalization, and terrorism, while at the same time appealing to those of the devout middle class who were not frightened by the djazarist faction to which he belonged. On October 6, *Al-Ansar* announced that the amirate had been conferred on Mahfoud Tajine, one of Gousmi's aides and a supporter of Mohammed Said. But the more intransigent salafists would not hear of a djazarist at the head of the GIA and staged an armed coup to replace him with Djamel Zitouni, who was formally presented as the new amir by *Al-Ansar* on October 27.[21]

Zitouni, the thirty-year-old son of a poultry merchant, had received a francophone secondary education. His mastery of written Arabic was as limited as his knowledge of the texts of Islam—unlike his predecessor, the imam Gousmi. After Zitouni's internment in the desert in 1992–1993, he joined the GIA and quickly attracted attention as a specialist in killing French citizens. The circumstances under which he came to power were so murky that he found his leadership quickly contested by many of the local phalange who made up the group: not only the djazarists, angry at his treatment of Tajine, but also a number of senior salafists of the Bouyali and Afghan generations. Where Gousmi had succeeded in unifying the armed movement, both Zitouni and his successor, Antar Zouabri, created dissensions within it that eventually proved fatal. From the first months of his amirate, rumors fueled by his AIS rivals—which many people took seriously—suggested that Zitouni was being manipulated by the Algerian special services. His shaky religious credentials, the odd manner of his assuming power, and the negative effects of the initiatives he took during his two-year amirate served only to heighten the speculation and mistrust surrounding him.[22]

It was this amir—probably the best French-speaker of any GIA leader—who unleashed a war of terrorism against France. In late December 1994, the GIA seized a French Airbus at the Algiers airport and flew it to Marseille, where the hijackers were neutralized by French police.[23] For a while it seemed that the organization had broken through to a new level and was now capable of carrying the war to France proper. Apart from the prestige the GIA acquired among the hittistes by striking this blow "at the former colonial power and bitterest enemy of Islam in the West," it expected to trigger a political dynamic whereby the French government, concluding that the price of terrorism within France was too high, would withdraw all support from the Algerian regime and hasten its collapse. But the dead and wounded in the bombings of summer and fall 1995 produced exactly the opposite effect, stiffening the resolve of the French authorities to combat an extremist Islamist movement that appeared to be imperiling civil order among young French Muslims whose families had recently emigrated from the Maghreb.

This new escalation of violence took place at just the moment when the FIS was preparing a "platform for a political and peaceful solution to the Algerian crisis," alongside several other opposition parties. This text was signed in Rome on January 13, 1995. The aim of the dissolved FIS was to demonstrate that it was still a central, unavoidable player on the political scene and that it might have ways of bringing an end to the armed struggle, if the regime would agree to negotiate, send the army back to its barracks, and give back the reins of power to the devout middle class. This initiative was a real challenge to the Algerian authorities, given that the Rome platform was receiving a favorable reception within certain influential circles in the United States. However, the project assumed that the FIS was still capable, in 1995, of controlling the young urban poor, the swollen battalions of the jihad, and the world of the devout entrepreneurs and shopkeepers—and this was no longer the case. The urban notables, exhausted by the predations of local warlords and their people, were more in favor of Hamas, the Islamist party run by Mahfoud Nahnah, which had agreed to collaborate with the government and defend their interests.

As to the GIA, in spite of Benhadj's support for the Rome platform, it conducted a virulent campaign against the agreement, "signed in the shadow of the Vatican," accusing the leaders of the FIS of being no more than "betrayers of the jihad, selling the blood of its fighters" to satisfy their own political ambitions.[24] In June, Madani and Benhadj were excluded from the consultative council of the GIA, to which they had been appointed (without their knowledge), after the unity meeting a year before. On May 4, Zitouni published a communiqué forbidding representatives of the FIS abroad from speaking in the name of the jihad and giving them a month to repent or die. Among the five leaders targeted was Sheik Abdelbaki Sahraoui, who was killed on July 11. This marked the beginning of a series of terrorist actions in France that continued unabated until the Algerian presidential election was held in November 1995.

The war against the French in metropolitan France was part of the complex struggle between the FIS, the government, and the GIA over the direction of the Algerian civil war. In organizing a broad-based terrorist campaign in France, the GIA's goal was to prove that the FIS was irrelevant to the armed struggle and to counter its preferred tactic of negotiating with the Algerian regime with the prospect of civil peace as its main bargaining chip. From this point of view, the government reaped a major advantage, because it now appeared in the eyes of Western leaders and Western public opinion-makers as the only force capable of stopping the terrorists who threatened them in their own back-yards. By this reasoning, the leaders of the FIS and a certain number of observers were strengthened in their conviction that Zitouni's GIA was playing into the hands of the Algerian government, and indeed that it had been thoroughly infiltrated by government agents.

In Algeria itself, dissension was growing within Zitouni's amirate. To affirm his hold on it, at the end of 1995 he published a 62-page tract entitled *The Way of God: Elucidation of Salafist Principles and the Obligations of Jihad Fighters*, in which he reiterated the line of the GIA and answered its detractors.[25] This text, which was unoriginal in its jihadist-salafist doctrine, attempted to lay to rest suspicions about Zitouni that had begun to surface within the ranks of the GIA itself, by furnishing a precise chronology of the various groups that had preceded it, from Bouyali's MIA to the series of amirs and their most significant achievements. Special care was taken to include Zitouni himself in their legitimate line. Again and again he incriminated the *Kharijites* (Islamist extremists) and other partisans of takfir, or excommunication of society as a whole, recalling that such people had been killed by the successors of the Prophet and that their contemporary heirs met with the same fate whenever they fell into the hands of the GIA. This was Zitouni's attempt to disassociate himself from the members of this faction: he had been accused of behaving like them in his February 1995 communiqué, when he gave the order that "for every pure Muslim woman arrested by the government, an apostate's wife would be executed." But if Zitouni spared society as a whole, in the hope that its members would join the ranks of the jihad fighters, he condemned out of hand the other devout Islamist factions as godless, particularly the Muslim Brothers and the djazarists. Their militants were enjoined to repent, adopt salafism, and adhere to the GIA, according to a precise procedure detailed in Zitouni's text.[26] As for those who betrayed their allegiance to the amir, they deserved instant death: a judgment that Zitouni went out of his way to justify with abundant quotations from the holy texts and salafist authors.

The year 1995 was marked by a series of major GIA purges. In June, Ezzedine Baa, the number-three figure in the Mouvement de l'Etat Islamique (which had merged with the GIA in May 1994) and a veteran of Bouyali's campaign, absconded back to the AIS: he was caught, judged, and executed.[27] In the following month, Abderrazaq Redjem announced that he too wished to rejoin the AIS and was mysteriously killed, along with Mohammed Said, in November. The GIA did not announce the two men's deaths in *Al-Ansar* until December 14, and then laid the blame on the security forces. In its issues of January 4 and 11, 1996, it changed tack and assumed responsibility for the killings, accusing the two men, as "members of the heretic djazarist sect," of plotting a coup d'état against Zitouni. These executions caused a sensation within the Algerian Islamist movement, given the prominence of the two victims. Indeed, they had the effect of isolating Zitouni, who found himself abruptly dropped by a number of regional GIA leaders, though for a few months longer he continued to benefit from the support of the principal jihadist-salafist theorist in London, the Palestinian Abu Qatada. Nevertheless the disquiet was such and the charges of manipulation so numerous, given that the deaths of the two men were perceived as placing in doubt the entire future of Algerian Islamism, that before long even *Al-Ansar* was demanding explanations from Zitouni. These were not forthcoming until the summer of 1996, when video cassettes were released showing two wretched friends of the victims (Abdel Haq Lamara, a djazarist university professor, and Mahfoud Tajine, who had been ousted by Zitouni after the death of Gousmi) "confessing" to the plot and humbly requesting summary execution for themselves, in a production as lurid as any Moscow show trial.[28]

This piece of "evidence" arrived too late to bolster Zitouni's image, however. As the spring wore on, militants began to desert in droves, accusing the amir of straying too far from the authentic jihadist-salafist line. On March 27, Zitouni kidnapped seven French Trappist monks from the monastery of Tibehirine, who were subsequently beheaded after the failure of negotiations with Paris.[29] The news of this latest massacre, on May 21, shocked even the most extreme fundamentalists, who pointed out that Islamic tradition had always enjoined respect for monks. Moreover, they feared that the killings would have disastrously negative effects, at a time when many Islamist representatives in the West had forged close links with Christian ecclesiastics.

However, the most decisive blow to the GIA was dealt by those in London who had previously given it legitimacy in the world's eyes through the publication of *Al-Ansar*. On May 31 1996, its editors suspended the bulletin. Then, on June 6, the two principal London ideologists of the jihadist-salafist persuasion, Abu Qatada and the Syrian Abu

Musab, joined with Zawahiri's Egyptian Gamaa Islamiya and a Libyan armed group to announce that they had withdrawn their support from Zitouni, who was guilty of "deviations" in the implementation of the jihad. He had, they claimed, "shed forbidden blood" by assassinating Said and Redjem along with several veterans of Afghanistan who had criticized the growing isolation of the GIA as a result of the amir's policies.[30] When other dissidents announced Zitouni's exclusion from the GIA and the return of the group to an authentic jihadist-salafist line, the amir found himself completely abandoned. Eventually, he was hunted down and shot on July 16 near Medea, probably by djazarists wishing to avenge the death of their leader in November 1995.

Zitouni's twenty-two months at the head of the GIA brought the Algerian jihad to its knees, and Antar Zouabri, his successor as amir, finished it off altogether. The GIA was especially split in Algiers, where the devout middle class, fed up with the endless violence and racketeering by gangs of young men in the name of jihad, participated en masse in the presidential elections of 1995 despite calls from the FIS to boycott them. More significant than the victory of Zeroual—a foregone conclusion—was the achievement of the man who finished second in the polls, the Hamas candidate Mahfoud Nahnah, who now emerged as a serious rival to the FIS among the religious petite bourgeoisie.

The terrorist campaign against France also emphasized the contradictions between the GIA and the FIS. The GIA exalted the enthusiasm of the disinherited in the cities every time the former colonial power was attacked, whereas the FIS leaders abroad had gone to great lengths to persuade the governments of Europe and the United States that their accession to power would guarantee social order and the expansion of the market economy within Algeria. Now, in 1996, the same governments were convinced that the FIS was no longer capable of controlling the armed struggle, that it had lost touch with the impoverished youth of Algeria, and that it now stood a far lesser chance of assuming the reins of power after the assassination of Said, a charismatic leader who alone had looked able to reconcile extremists and moderates, the poor and the middle classes, the jihadists and the djazarists. Finally, the growth of violence at every level of society and the indiscriminate killings—whether or not some were provocations or deliberately arranged by the security forces—were steadily eating away at the popularity the jihad had enjoyed in 1993–1994. The final break between a population that was growing more and more tired of the unending conflict and the armed Islamist groups was accomplished by the last amir, Zouabri.

A faction of the GIA that was considered questionable by the others nominated the 26-year-old Zouabri, amid general confusion. Born in a shack at "Houch" Gros next to a former colonial estate in the foothills of the Atlas near Boufarik, he had been an activist since adolescence; his brother Ali was also the leader of an armed formation. After returning from Iraq, where he was a member of the contingent sent by Ali Benhadj, Zouabri had taken part in various groups that later merged with the GIA. A close confidant of Zitouni, Zouabri continued where his predecessor had left off—with a strategy of ever-increasing violence and redoubled purges within the GIA. He killed anyone who questioned his authority and flatly rejected the criticisms of the international jihadist-salafists. With these methods he managed to re-establish a certain authority by early 1997, and he found in the Egyptian Abu Hamza—a veteran of Afghanistan and Bosnia who preached at the Grand Mosque in Finsbury Park, London—a new theorist abroad who was prepared to back up his jihad with the necessary fatwas.

In February, Hamza relaunched the publication *Al-Ansar,* having assured himself of Zouabri's salafist orthodoxy as laid out in a manifesto entitled *The Sharp Sword.*[31] Apart from justifying the various murders and liquidations that had taken place since Zitouni's time, this text presented Algerian society as being resistant to the jihad, whereas it should do battle against the impious as a Muslim community and join the struggle of the GIA. Yet only a small minority of Algerians were really supporting their religion by taking part in the holy war, according to Zouabri. Confronted by godless and apostate rulers, the majority of the people had "forsaken religion and renounced the battle against its enemies."[32] *The Sharp Sword* harbored no illusions about the jihad's unpopularity, in contrast to the triumphalist tone of the GIA's previous published texts. In practice, this attitude translated into a series of violent acts aimed at "punishing" a population that had betrayed the hopes placed in it.

The month of Ramadan (January–February) in 1997 was the bloodiest of the entire war, with horrific massacres of civilians, whose throats were cut with knives. It seems that the creation by the state of armed "patriot leagues" in villages where jihad militants were denied access contributed to the privatization and spread of the violence by adding the ingredients of vendetta and local dispute to the wider struggle between the GIA and the government. In the absence of reliable research or evidence, it is difficult to see who exactly was responsible for the wave of killings that characterized Zouabri's amirate and that culminated with the bloodbaths of August and September in Rais, Beni Messous, and Bentalha, where several hundred people lost their lives. The Algerian press laid the blame exclusively on the "GIA criminals" and gave special emphasis to the links between some of its founders and the FIS. By contrast, the exiled FIS party leaders refused to see the killings as anything other than provocations by the government security forces, whose aim was to alienate the population from the Islamist movement in general.

Whoever was responsible for the bloodletting, it led in September 1997 to two events that spelled the end of organized jihad in Algeria. These were the virtual disappearance of the GIA and the unilateral truce declared by the AIS. The GIA's final communiqué, signed by Zouabri, was issued at the end of September. It claimed responsibility for the massacres and justified them by declaring impious all those Algerians who had not joined its ranks. Thus, the GIA had finally chosen the option of takfir, the excommunication of society as a whole. Abu Hamza published this in the September 27 issue of *Al-Ansar,* along with a critical commentary, and two days later announced the closure of the bulletin and the termination of his support for Zouabri and the GIA, whom he accused of abandoning the line of jihadism-salafism by "condemning the Algerian people for impiety (kufr)."[33] After that date, the GIA, with no representation abroad, ceased to be able to publish its communiqués and lost its identity. This in no way brought an end to the violent actions of groups within Algeria, which continued to wage an erratic jihad led by independent commanders, with no cohesive structure nationwide. The last amir, Zouabri, has scarcely been heard of since that time.

The GIA vanished both as a structured entity and as the leading participant in the Algerian civil war, in a way that was even more confused and mysterious than the one whereby it came into existence in 1992. By pronouncing takfir against the whole of society in his final communiqué, Zouabri gave his blessing to a sectarian tendency within the group that gradually cut it off from any possible base within Algerian society, and even within the ranks of the young urban poor from whom its support had originally come. And indeed this class had emerged de-moralized and demobilized from five years of relentless violence, with little inclination to engage in an Islamist political project that would involve further sacrifices in the unequal struggle against the government.

On September 21, the same day that the GIA's final communiqué reached London, Madani Merzag, the AIS's national amir, called on all the fighters under his command to observe a unilateral ceasefire from October 1 onward. This again demonstrated the weakness of the armed wing of the FIS, which had already been exposed by the widespread massacres in September that had taken place while the AIS stood by powerless. As an "honorable" intermediate solution between defeat and surrender, the truce negotiated with the army high command allowed the AIS to keep its men together in the interval before they could be integrated into the security forces. In military terms, it reflected the conditions under which the government was prepared to give amnesty to the devout middle class who had supported the FIS—basically, its members would be granted clemency provided they gave their full allegiance to the regime.

Despite the disappearance of the GIA and the ceasefire with the AIS, massacres continued unabated throughout 1998. In the absence of any credible claim of responsibility, they were attributed to a continuing campaign of indiscriminate terrorism by armed groups that had formerly belonged to the GIA. Some of these had lapsed into pure banditry; others were settling scores among themselves or with the "patriots" who continued to harass them; and still others, according to a brand of logic akin to that which had prevailed at the end of the War of Independence, enlisted themselves in the service of landowners who needed to frighten illegal occupants away from property that would later become valuable with the advent of peace. Here again we have no reliable way of knowing exactly which groups were responsible, but after a year in which violence was not followed by any coherent political or ideological demands, it was clear that the social movement represented by the various categories of Islamism had more or less petered out. This made it possible for the regime to organize a series of elections aimed at institutionalizing the gradual return of peace in 1999. These culminated in May with the election to the presidency of

Abdelaziz Bouteflika, followed by a referendum of "national concord" in September, which attained a plebiscite.

After nearly a decade of civil war, the government had vanquished the Algerian Islamist movement. The young urban poor, who had rebelled in October 1988 and taken control of the streets on behalf of the FIS before supplying the GIA with its base of recruits, had been crushed as a political factor. The devout bourgeoisie, whose economic interests and cultural demands were now represented within the government by Hamas, was in the process of rallying behind the conditions set by a president who had expressed his respect for Abbasi Madani.[34] Madani had simultaneously expressed his desire to abandon politics. Ali Benhadj, the idol of the impoverished young, was still in prison; and Abdelkader Hachani, hated by the Islamist radicals but still the only political leader of the movement capable of negotiating on an equal basis with the government, was assassinated in mysterious circumstances on November 22, 1999.

Will the passage from socialism to a market economy, which had curiously enough been hastened by the civil war, now make it possible for the leaders of Algeria to absorb private entrepreneurs and businessmen into the system, who were formerly attracted by the FIS because they rejected the generals' "total control over the import-export economy"?[35] The reconstruction of Algeria, whose infrastructures have been neglected or destroyed over the last ten years of warfare, offer rich opportunities to these investors, provided that civil authorities manage to carry out the necessary political arbitration. But so far, endless bickering between the top brass and President Bouteflika has paralyzed any serious attempt at reform. While it seems unlikely that the social dynamic which allowed the emergence of the Islamist movement will begin all over again, after a war in which its ambition to seize control of the state has been literally drowned in blood, despair is the dominant feeling. And with violence resuming in the bush at the hands of unidentified "Islamist" radical gangs, the regime's military success over the militants is still short of the kind of political victory that would reconcile it with Algerian society as a whole.

CHAPTER

12

The Threat of Terrorism in Egypt

While civil war was ravaging Algeria, Egypt also was stricken by a wave of violence in which the state confronted groups of Islamist radicals. In 1992 the assassinations and bombings were just beginning in Algeria, the government was interning FIS militants in desert concentration camps, and the armed groups of the MEI and GIA were forming in the mountains. Meanwhile, in Egypt, the Gamaa Islamiya (Islamic Association) assassinated the secularist author Farag Foda and appeared to be operating openly in the Upper Nile region. Its militants, in addition to harassing and murdering members of the Coptic Christian minority, began in that year to kill tourists and police officers. In December, 14,000 soldiers and police surrounded and "cleaned out" the working-class quarter of Embaba on the edge of the capital, which the Gamaa had transformed into a liberated Islamic zone similar to the disinherited Eucalyptus and Baraki quarters of Algiers.

This simultaneous intensification of violence in the two countries occurred in the same year that Kabul fell into the hands of the mujahedeen. Several hundred Algerian and Egyptian "Afghans" had recently returned home. Trained to jihadism-salafism in Peshawar, these men now contributed to the radicalizing of the local jihad by applying their international experience. In both countries the regimes in place found themselves confronted by the success of "moderate" Islam among the middle classes. Hosni Mubarak had avoided an Islamist victory in Egypt's legislative elections, but the Egyptian Muslim Brothers had shown their strength in the sociopolitical areas that still remained open to them. In September, they won elections for control of the Egyptian bar, thereby consolidating their control of the professions; they already held a quorum among the doctors, engineers, dentists, and pharmacists, which were the preserve of the university-educated Egyptian middle classes. On October 12, following an earthquake that killed 500 people in Cairo and left another 50,000 homeless, the Brothers took the leading role in the emergency by supplanting cumbersome state organizations, just as the FIS had done during the Tipasa earthquake in October 1989.

The wave of violence in Egypt reached its height with the massacre of 60 people, most of them tourists, at Luxor on November 17, 1997. This took place shortly after the carnage at Rais, Beni Messous, and Bentalha in Algeria, and in both cases the killings were the last for which the organized armed Islamist movement took official responsibility. The radical limbs of the Gamaa Islamiya in Egypt and the Algerian GIA collapsed, pulverized by repression and loathed by the population. The historic leaders of the Gamaa had appealed in July for a general ceasefire. In Algeria, the AIS pronounced its unilateral truce at the end of September. Almost simultaneously, jihad was defeated in the two Arab countries where violence had been worst, opening the way for co-optation by the regime of an Islamist movement that had lost its popular support.

The parallels between events in Algeria and Egypt were due in part to the leadership of militants in both countries who had been trained in Afghanistan, but the events unfolded under very different political circumstances. The Algerian state was a recent invention, dating from 1962, the year of independence. From the start it bore the scars of war and was mistrusted by Algerians after the single-party government of the Front de Libération Nationale (FLN) lost its credibility during the 1980s. Government-sponsored religious institutions had remained embryonic; when the state created the Islamic University at Constantine, it was obliged to import ulemas from Egypt to give the institution some kind of legitimacy. This religious vacuum within the regime helped the FIS to mobilize the people in the name of Islam and thereafter to win elections between 1989 and 1991. It also facilitated the entry of a whole sector of the population into civil war.

In Egypt, by contrast, Mubarak's state was heir to a much older political structure, controlling an administration that was efficient despite
its top-heavy pharaonic bureaucracy. And in Al Azhar it possessed a religious institution that had managed to preserve its immense prestige
despite government meddling, the criticisms of Islamist militants, and
infiltration of its ulemas and teachers by the Muslim Brothers. Furthermore, unlike pre-1989 Algeria, where violent Islamist protest had been
confined to Mustafa Bouyali's bush, the Egyptian state, which had survived the assassination of its leader, Anwar Sadat, by the Al-Jihad group
in October 1981, had a long tradition of struggle against Islamism.
This went back to the founding of the Muslim Brothers on the Suez
Canal in 1928, the hanging of Sayyid Qutb by Gamal Abdel Nasser in
1966, and Sadat's ambiguous relationship with the Gamaat Islamiya
during the 1970s. Between 1992 and 1995, the spectacular shift toward violence in certain quarters of the Islamist movement did not
lead to a general civil war—even though pockets of territory temporarily passed out of the direct control of the army and police. In 1995, a
foreigner could live quite safely in Cairo; this was out of the question in
Algiers.

In military terms, the relative scale of the two confrontations as
gauged by the numbers of dead (about a thousand in Egypt, a hundred
thousand in Algeria) bears no comparison. But politically, the Egyptian
Islamist movement, which in 1992 appeared to be in full expansion at
every level of the population, emerged from five years of bitter and
fruitless struggle just as deeply split as its Algerian counterpart.

The June 1992 assassination of the author Foda by Gamaa Islamiya
militants is usually taken as the moment when a new phase in the
Egyptian conflict began, after a quiescent period of about seven years.
Following the death of Sadat in October 1981, a massive crackdown
had temporarily annihilated the extremist factions, dispersed their network of sympathizers, and forced the Muslim Brothers to distance
themselves from the militants of the Al-Jihad group. President
Mubarak then reintegrated into politics the opposition parties that
Sadat had driven out, going on to organize a legislative ballot in May
1984 whose result was a foregone conclusion. Nonetheless, the election
campaign was conducted under conditions of freedom that had not
been seen in Egypt for many years. The Brothers managed to elect a
few deputies, and the government felt confident enough to show clem-

ency to some of the radical militants who had been arrested in October 1981, most of whom eventually recovered their liberty.

Up until 1987, the militants kept a low profile. A few hundred, encouraged by the regime, joined the Afghan jihad by way of Saudi Arabia, while others set about gradually rebuilding the networks dismantled in 1981. Thus, the Islamist movement resumed its process of expansion, recovering the bastions it had held in Sadat's time and pushing into new areas. Beginning in 1984, the results of student elections again reflected Islamist dominance in most of Egypt's universities. By the mid-1980s, the majority of Egypt's twenty-two professional guilds had passed under the control of their younger Muslim Brothers members. Former activists who had been students in the previous decade, once they had earned their diplomas and begun working for a living, continued to practice dawa (preaching and activism) as they had done at the university.[1]

This penetration of the professions was reinforced by the enrichment of a devout middle class, whose prosperity went hand in hand with that of Islamic banks and investment funds, then in a period of strong growth. The Faisal Islamic Bank of Egypt, founded in 1977, was a typical case. Its managing director was a Saudi prince, Mohammed al-Faisal Al-Saud, a son of King Faisal; the very name was sufficient to inspire trust in devout investors and depositors. The bank initially required a minimum deposit of $200, which was several times the monthly salary of an Egyptian university professor. This signaled, first of all, that the Faisal Islamic Bank was looking for the business of cash holders wishing to see their savings increase according to the laws of the sharia. This, to all intents and purposes, meant expatriates. Forty-nine percent of the capital was held by leading Saudi families (such as the bin Ladens); the bank benefited from the cooperation of the Egyptian religious establishment (notably Sheik Mohamed Metwali el-Sharawi, the country's foremost television preacher, an ultraconservative) as well as of local businessmen and entrepreneurs with links to the government. It even won the approval of leaders of bourgeois Islamist groups.

All these made the bank's image irreproachably pious, earning it the trust of a whole class of potential depositors who were also mightily attracted by the possibility of gain. Even better, the Faisal Islamic Bank was able to offer returns much greater than the interest rates delivered by conventional banks, because it favored short-term operations in sectors where turnover was rapid. These returns served to finance consumption at a time when it was expanding strongly, thanks to the fallout from the new policies of economic openness and the increase in oil prices. The bank even speculated on the price of gold and other precious metals.

In 1980–1985, Islamic investments throughout the Muslim world underwent a spectacular expansion, leading to the creation of a hundred or so Islamic investment companies offering annual returns of around 25 percent. Many of these companies had shadowy origins in the black market, and consequently had plenty of experience in circumventing bureaucratic obstacles to make considerable profits. They attracted large deposits by blending the attraction of great gains with the religious guarantees supplied by the ulemas, whom they recruited to issue fatwas denouncing conventional banks and recommending their Islamic rivals. In Egypt, these institutions were at first encouraged by those in power, who saw in them an opportunity to win the backing of the devout middle class. They reasoned that if that class placed its money in Islamic banks and made substantial profits, it would be unlikely to join the radical opposition led by Islamist intellectuals who had spawned the assassins of Sadat and the extremist movements of the 1970s. Instead, members of the middle class would be economically integrated and would find it in their interest to perpetuate a political system that allowed them to enrich themselves.

But in 1988 the Egyptian state called a halt to this process, fearing that it would allow the Islamist movement to build up a war chest and hand the Brothers and their friends a financial independence that would lead to a hardening of their oppositional stance. Consequently, a campaign was launched against the banks in the press, in the same newspapers that had previously published page after page of advertisements on their behalf, as well as interviews with their managing directors and fatwas favorable to them issued by religious dignitaries. The link between some of the investment groups and militant extremists were exposed, and the companies themselves were denounced as fraudulent. Finally, they were ordered to modify their legal structure. The combination of all this adverse publicity created mounting panic among depositors, to a point where they attempted to withdraw their funds and drove some of the companies into bankruptcy, notably those whose investments carried the highest risk.

If the regime was ambivalent about the banking system, it cautiously encouraged the growth of the religious infrastructure, as an element that would give the government a certain legitimacy when bearded militants accused it of impiety or foot-dragging in religious matters. In 1985 the Egyptian state TV put out nearly 14,000 hours of Islamic broadcasts, ceding moral primacy on the airwaves to such preachers as Sheik Metwali el-Sharawi, known for his hostility to the Copts, and Sheik Mohammed al-Ghazali, who had close ties to the Muslim Brothers.[2] These ulemas saw themselves as the state's ideological rampart against "religious extremism," and they sought to gain advantages of status from this role.

Their first targets were secularist intellectuals, whose work they censured if, in their view, it "brought religion into disrepute." On this pretext, they condemned the complete version in Arabic of the *Thousand and One Nights* for its "obscenity." Meanwhile, the ban on serving alcohol aboard EgyptAir flights and the decrees promulgated by regional governors to make their states "dry" showed that the regime was beginning to give salafist conservative clerics a free hand in the domains of morality, culture, public manners, and daily life. In Parliament, Muslim Brothers applied steady pressure for the sharia to be applied to the letter—with the ultimate goal of scrapping all legislation they felt to be contrary to its prescriptions. When Rifaat al-Mahgoub, the president of the assembly, opposed the Brothers on that ground in 1985, he made the point that the judiciary, like the legislature, should remain independent of religious pressure, even from moderate Islamists. His initiative was followed by demonstrations organized by Sheik Hafiz Salama, a fiery preacher. The police quickly dispersed the protests, but they served as a warning that the Islamists once again felt strong enough to take to the streets.

Thus the Muslim Brothers, their allies in the religious establishment, and the regime conducted a kind of border war—the Brothers in order to extend their influence over the law, the economy, and the politics of the nation, the regime in order to confine the Brothers' influence to morality and culture. Meanwhile, the clandestine elements of the Islamist movement had divided into two main factions as a result of a dispute that had broken out among their jailed leaders following the assassination of Sadat.[3] The first faction was led by Lieutenant Abboud al-Zomor, one of the main conspirators who was serving a life sentence, and the physician Ayman al-Zawahiri, who had gone to Afghanistan in 1985.[4] For these two men, the jihad could succeed only if it destroyed the nerve centers of the impious regime by violence. What was needed was a small group of determined militants who would mount a coup and then set up an Islamic state, amid the grateful acclamations of a nation saved from tyranny. This was an Islamist version of the putsch scenario that Arab nationalist army officers had used all over the Middle East during preceding decades. It had no confidence in preaching (dawa), which the state had the means to control as long as the Islamist movement was weak—an idea that echoed the theories used by the electrician Abdessalam Faraj to justify the murder of Sadat. The Al-Jihad group (Tanzim al-Jihad), secretly reconstituted, was fully in favor of this option.

The second faction reused the name Gamaat Islamiya, which had became popular in the universities during the 1970s; it believed that jihad should be waged in tandem with a campaign of preaching and should reach into society itself.[5] There, "the compelling of good and the driving out of evil" would be the movement's goals. This faction envisaged open, widespread recruitment, the control of whole areas of territory seized from the state, and the imposition in those areas of the Islamic order. Militants understood this in moral terms (harrying individuals whose morality was suspect, forcing closures of video shops, hairdressers, liquor stores, cinemas, and so on). It also had a doctrinal-juridical aspect (Copts should be coerced into paying the protection tax prescribed by the sharia for non-Muslims living under Islamic domination) and a political-military one (state officials, policemen, and so on should be physically attacked at every opportunity). The spiritual guide of the Gamaa was the blind Sheik Omar Abdel Rahman, mufti of Sadat's assassins, who had become famous for his fatwas authorizing attacks on Coptic jewelers and goldsmiths (and their murder, if necessary) to finance the jihad.[6] Freed in 1984, the sheik had installed himself at the Fayyum Oasis, where he continued to fulminate against his pet hates. He was imprisoned briefly in 1986, released, and arrested again in April 1989, after which he spent several more months in jail following a violent confrontation between his supporters and the police. Having obtained a visa for the United States in the Sudan, he settled down to preach in Jersey City, where he remained until he was arrested in connection with the February 1993 bombing of the World Trade Center.

The erosion of security did not seriously worry observers until May 1987, when the former minister of the interior and a group of American diplomats narrowly escaped assassination. Meanwhile, attacks on Copts instigated by the Gamaa Islamiya grew more and more frequent in Upper Egypt. A rumor spread that Christians had surreptitiously sprayed the veils of Muslim women with a mysterious aerosol that made the veils display the sign of the cross after the first wash. That such nonsense could spark violent incidents showed how tense the atmosphere in the Nile Valley had become. The same year saw a decisive increase in the Muslim Brothers' representation in Parliament; in coalition with the Labor Party, which was led by a former Marxist turned Islamist, it obtained 17 percent of the votes and sixty seats. The government, which actually controlled the results, made clear that it now depended upon a strategy of dialogue with the devout middle class, on whom it relied for keeping social peace.

But the violence continued to grow, year after year, right up to the showdown of 1992. In the fall of 1988, at Heliopolis near Cairo, the security forces had to invade a quarter in which the Gamaa Islamiya had forcibly seized control. This signaled that the organization now had the capability to come out of its rural bastions in Upper Egypt and penetrate working-class areas of the capital.[7] In 1989 and 1990, continuing violence against the Copts in Upper Egypt and the growing strength of the Gamaa triggered a cycle of repression that included the siege of Sheik Abdel Rahman's mosque in Fayyum, wholesale arrests, and intermittent police brutality. This in turn ignited a vendetta against the security forces among the traditional sectors of society in Upper Egypt; this uprising came on top of the ideological confrontation between the state and the radical Islamists. For its part, the government maintained two simultaneous strategies up to 1993: heavy police pressure on the extremists, which was extensively covered by the media, and discreet dialogue with some of their number, mediated by religious dignitaries who had ties with the salafist faction or the Muslim Brothers. Government hesitation over which line to take was demonstrated by three changes of interior minister in three years; the militants construed this as a sign of weakness.[8] Despite thousands of arrests, the attacks became more and more brazen, culminating in the assassination of the former president of the Parliament, Rifaat al-Mahgoub, in the center of Cairo in October 1990.

At the beginning of 1992, which ushered in five years of "war," the Egyptian government found itself in a situation of relative fragility. However, the Islamist opposition was suffering—even more so than in Algeria—from divisions among the social groups that made it up, and notably from their differences in matters of doctrine and tactics. Muslim Brothers had won a solid foothold among the devout middle class; they had their own deputies in parliament as well as a funding network based on an Islamic banking system in which they were well represented. Furthermore, they controlled the professional unions and were able to extend their reach right down to ordinary working people through charities run by their members. The religious establishment on which the government had to rely after the assassination of Sadat, and which had full access to state television, was nonetheless vulnerable to the influence of the Brothers, given that such leading ulemas as Mohammed al-Ghazali and Yusuf al-Qaradawi were closely linked to them. But despite the mediating role they claimed for themselves, neither the Brothers nor the clerics had much control over the radical Islamist fringe. Nor could they influence the young urban poor to make common cause with the devout middle class against the government, as the FIS had done in Algeria between 1989 and 1991.

By 1992, Gamaa Islamiya and, to a lesser extent, Al-Jihad had succeeded in building an independent power base by patiently accumulating successes after the liberation of most of their activists in 1984. In the second half of the 1980s they established strongholds in the provinces of Asyut and Minia in Middle Egypt, where they benefited from social circumstances that favored their preaching campaign. The fall in the price of oil in 1985 stemmed the flow of emigrants to the Arabian peninsula, which had served as the main outlet for young rural graduates educated in the new, post-1970s universities of the Nile Valley. Many of these young graduates, who had frequented the Gamaa Islamiya in college, found themselves back in the villages and towns where they had started, living at the expense of relatives who had made sacrifices to give them an education. The Gamaa carefully weighted its rhetoric and ideology to transform the frustration of these unemployed graduates into an uprising against the established order, which it stigmatized as impious. This now-militant Islamist intelligentsia was able to mobilize the educated but impoverished Muslim youth of the valley to open revolt.

Upper Egypt had a traditional social fabric based on clan and family, among whom conflicts were frequently settled by violence and vendetta. Banditry organized around arms smuggling or the cultivation and sale of hashish was well entrenched and well favored by the local topography. The islands of the Nile, with their luxuriant vegetation and thick crops of sugar cane, as well as the cliff caves along the valley, offered plenty of cover for such nefarious activities. The state's presence was barely perceptible at the local level, where private interests controlled everything, and this in turn encouraged pockets of dissidence that had a long history in this environment. Finally, the rural area around Minia and Asyut, being so closed in on itself, had never entirely succumbed to Islam. In this province, Nilotic Christianity held out more successfully over the centuries than in any other part of Egypt, thanks to the monasteries. The proportion of Copts here was higher than anywhere else in the country—18 percent in the province of Minia and 19 percent in Asyut, whereas the national figure was closer to 6 percent.[9]

This situation offered fertile ground for the expansion of Gamaa Islamiya. It was able to organize and mobilize well away from the pressures normally brought to bear by the state. It established arms caches and training camps and put its theories into practice by tormenting the Copts in the vicinity. The relationship of coexistence between Muslims and Christians in the Nile Valley had been much tested over the centuries; long periods of calm had followed periodic flare-ups of tension, when some overzealous preacher stirred up his flock against the "arrogant" Christians. Strictly speaking, the holy texts enjoin the faithful to "humble and humiliate" Christians by forcing payment of a poll tax (jiziyya), which is imposed by the sharia in exchange for the status of protection (dhimma) they enjoy (or endure, depending on how you look at it). In 1911, a Coptic Congress held at Asyut raised the specter of a secession of Middle Egypt and the creation there of a Christian state. But the tensions and violence that began with the development of the Islamist movements in the 1970s and culminated twenty years later owed their gravity to a massive influx of desperately poor, mostly Muslim rural migrants, both workers and students, in cities like Asyut and Minia, where many prominent positions were held by Copts.

Alongside the old landowning notables, who had suffered much from Nasser's nationalizations, there had emerged a Coptic middle class who took full advantage of an advanced Christian educational system. To impoverished young Muslims aware of the ideology of the Gamaa Islamiya, this was frankly scandalous: the Copts, who should be humble and submissive, were visibly prosperous, while good Muslims suffered. This simplistic analysis ignored the fact that most of the Nile Valley Copts were, like their Muslim fellow citizens, very poor country people. Nevertheless it provided a clear and easily manipulated religious outlet for a massive social grievance—a grievance that was growing daily more explosive as emigration to the Arabian peninsula ground to a halt.

For this reason, anti-Christian agitation became the preferred means by which the extremists of the Nile Valley set about extending their influence among the region's disinherited youth. In their tracts and campaigns, Christians were always portrayed as perverse creatures who take advantage of their undeservedly superior position in society, or else as agents of foreigners and crusaders bent on converting Muslims to Christianity, and hence on corrupting them. Thus, a Copt from the region of Minia was accused of selling Muslim minors into prostitution and peddling videotapes of their activities.[10] Copt-owned pharmacies and jewelry shops were favorite targets for recurrent riots stirred up by radicals against the "arrogant'" Christians.

In 1992 the political situation in the valley was dominated by this kind of agitation, and the Gamaa Islamiya was quick to turn it to advantage. The state reacted savagely, with wholesale arrests and interrogations. This in turn provoked the clandestine Islamist movement, which by now was fairly secure in the strongholds it had built up in Middle Egypt, to raise the stakes and challenge the government head-on. This descent into total war, encouraged by the return in that year of the first groups of "Afghans" with their military training and fanatical jihadist-salafist indoctrination in Peshawar, took three forms: assassinations of prominent personalities, murders of tourists, and penetration of the most poverty-stricken areas of the capital—symbolized by the proclamation of the Islamic Republic of Embaba.

Militants of the Gamaa Islamiya assassinated Farag Foda on June 8, 1992. The purpose of this murder was twofold. The victim was, first, a symbol of secularist intellectualism, a longtime opponent of the application of the sharia, and a proponent of total war against the Islamists. Foda was also in favor of stiffening the anti-terrorist laws to combat fundamentalism and of normalizing relations with Israel. For all these reasons he was loathed by the religious establishment and the Muslim Brothers, who had repeatedly condemned his writings, and looked upon with suspicion by the nationalist left, for which the Zionist state was the perennial enemy. In killing him, the Gamaa selected a figure without much of a following in Egypt but who had a very high profile abroad; Foda's assassination was thus a direct challenge to the state, calculated to terrorize anybody who might be tempted to take similar public positions. Moreover, by targeting a radical secularist intellectual, the Gamaa transcended the brutality of the act itself and touched a deep chord among the same religious-minded people whom the state was trying to win over in order to provide itself with some kind of Islamic legitimacy. During the trial of the assassins, who would be sentenced to death in June 1993, Sheik Mohammed al-Ghazali was summoned as a witness by the defense. He announced that anyone born a Muslim who militated against the sharia (as Foda had done) was guilty of the crime of apostasy, for which the punishment was death. In the absence of an Islamic state to carry out this sentence, those who assumed that responsibility were not blameworthy. This reasoning sowed consternation in government circles and contributed to abandonment of the policy of mediation with the radical Islamists through the religious establishment and its contacts with the Muslim Brothers. It was behind a series of attacks by the Brothers on any attempt by secularist intellectuals to intervene in the debate on society's core values, by simply outlawing them.

Another victim was the university professor Nasr Abu Zeid, who was first pronounced an apostate on the basis of his writings, then summarily divorced from his wife by a tribunal on the pretext that an apostate could not remain married to a Muslim woman. Abu Zeid and his wife were eventually forced into exile in Europe, under threat of death.[11] Finally, in October 1994 Naguib Mahfouz, winner of the Nobel Prize for Literature in 1988, who had been regularly attacked by conservative clerics for the indecency of his novels, was stabbed by a Gamaa activist. These affairs showed, first, that the Islamist movement had allies in the Egyptian legal world, not only among the lawyers (whose bar association had been taken over by the Muslim Brothers in 1992) but also in the judiciary: it was Islamist judges, after all, who had imposed a divorce on Abu Zeid and his wife. These events also showed that the moderates and the extremists complemented one another's actions, with the latter executing victims singled out by the former, and the former pleading attenuating circumstances on behalf of the latter, should the need arise.

The targeting of non-religious intellectuals was meant to reunify the movement, even though in public the moderates deplored the fanaticism of militants who translated their words into deeds. Nevertheless, its consequences for Islamism's international image were disastrous, at a time when the Muslim Brothers and their allies were engaged in an intense charm offensive (vis-à-vis the United States in particular), with the aim of presenting themselves as the champions of civil society against totalitarian states and as the only power capable of neutralizing the radicals.

In tandem with the campaign of intimidation against intellectuals, Gamaa Islamiya launched an offensive against tourists during the summer of 1992. After exploding some homemade bombs in June, they went on to attack a cruise boat on the Nile and then a train. In October, an Englishwoman was killed, and in December several Germans were injured. The New York–based spiritual guide of the Gamaa, Sheik Omar Abdel Rahman, sent video cassettes to Egypt in which he described tourism as an enterprise of debauchery that promoted alcoholism and declared it *haram* (forbidden by religion). Part of the moderate wing of the Islamist movement backed the sheik, seeing the expansion of tourism—and especially Israeli tourism—as one of the consequences of the peace process so reviled in the Middle East. They deplored the deaths of innocent people but tended to blame them on police violence that had forced the young men of the Gamaa to defend themselves in any way they could.

In 1993, the wave of attacks spread to Cairo, where several foreign visitors were killed, and they continued sporadically for several years thereafter until the massacre at Luxor in November 1997. Like the attacks against secularist intellectuals, attacks against tourists led some moderate Islamists to see the state's impiety as an excuse for the rage of the radicals. In doing so they showed that they condoned the action and indicated that the Gamaa was providing a frame of reference for mobilization against the government, while obliging the other components of the movement to follow it, even if they did no more than pay lip service. Finally, the war against tourism was a no-risk gambit for those behind it: with a minimum of expense, they were able to strike a heavy blow at the Egyptian state, both financially and in terms of its image abroad.[12] The Western contacts of the moderate Islamists were able to point to the violence as evidence of the isolation and ineffectiveness of the state. They pleaded for accession to power of the devout bourgeoisie, which would be able to restore order while also being friendly to investors and businessmen. These arguments soon began to make an impression, notably in some American political circles.

However, the state was not the sole victim of the collapse of the Egyptian tourist industry. A major percentage of the Egyptian population—which was genuinely shocked by the deliberate and completely unprecedented slaughter of foreign visitors—depended on tourism for its livelihood. This included guides, hoteliers, restaurant owners, market vendors, members of the building trades, and chauffeurs, along with the families they supported. Whatever their political or religious preferences, they had to confront a sudden fall in their standard of living; this economic hardship eventually alienated them from those who had brought it about.

Still, the strategy of all-out radicalization chosen by the Gamaa Islamiya in 1992 was not without a certain logic, and its goal of pushing impoverished Egyptian youth into open revolt was making some headway in the "disinherited" areas around Cairo. Back in the fall of 1988, near Heliopolis, security forces had surrounded a quarter of the city that had been taken over by militants. The situation was far worse in the Embaba district, a shantytown not far from the campus of the University of Cairo, with a population of around one million (one twelfth of the total for the entire capital). Rural migrants from Upper Egypt were the main occupants of this deprived zone, which was desperately short of public services. It had become the symbol, even the caricature, for the implantation of radical Islamists in the capital.[13]

Some of Sadat's assassins had come from the area, though at that time Embaba and its slums had served more as a hideout than as a fertile ground for Islamist preachers. It was only after most of the militants were released in 1985 that Islamist penetration resumed there, with the objective of broadening the Gamaa Islamiya's recruiting base and building up the Islamist-dominated zone outside the state's control on the pattern of the dissident pockets in Upper Egypt.

The success of this operation was due to the coming together of Islamist intellectuals, activists from the 1970s, graduates and students from the university nearby, and the local *caids*. The latter were the traditional godfather types *(futuwwa)* who ran the district as they liked in the absence of any meaningful state authority. These gangsters, many of whom were adept at martial arts, were won over to radical Islamism at just the moment when the movement had adopted a strategy of violent confrontation with the government. Men who had a technical understanding of violence, of how to organize gangs and procure weapons and ammunition on the black market, were at a premium.[14] In short, the encounter between the Islamist intellectuals and the futuwwa created conditions for the enrollment of the impoverished urban young in the support of the Gamaa, which thereby became the unchallenged sociopolitical power in Embaba.

In 1984, Sheik Abdel Rahman toured the local mosques, the largest of which were taken over by his militants. Before long they were organizing everything: sporting activities, schools, militias that maintained Islamic order in the quarter and opposed any attempt by the police to assert control. The Embaba takeover, all the way down to the Islamization of its street names, was achieved by the substitution of the Gamaa for traditional institutions in settling disputes and mediating between families involved in long-standing vendettas. Finally, a network of charitable organizations was set up to take care of the needy, in association with the mosques.

The leading tribal families of the area were defeated by simple force of arms and obliged to sue for peace. Meanwhile, the Copts, who constituted an important minority grouped around twenty-one churches, suffered exactions very similar to the ones wrought on their fellow Christians in Asyut and Minia. Their shops were looted, their churches were torched, and they themselves were systematically beaten. All this was justified by the "hunting down of evil" preached by the extremists.

Such violent excursions naturally attracted young people with no political ax to grind, who took advantage of the occasion simply to steal what they could while the shopkeepers were being forced to pay their protection tax to the Gamaa.[15]

At Embaba, the younger people used the process of religious radicalization to assume the social roles that ought to have devolved on their elders—a phenomenon that recurred in the Algerian Civil War, when the hittistes from the poorest quarters took over from the FIS notables after 1991. As in Algeria, these young Egyptian men imagined that once they had established themselves, they would be able to prolong their offensive to a point where the state itself would be brought down. In Embaba, from around 1991 when the harassment of Copts began in earnest, the charitable dimension of the movement began to be obscured by a progressively looser interpretation of "hunting down evil," whereby common delinquents used the mantle of Islamism to cover straightforward racketeering. Just as they did later in the suburbs of Algiers with the GIA, a section of the population that had begun by sympathizing with the Gamaa Islamiya turned against them.

In late November 1992, in an act of bravado, Sheik Gaber, the military leader of the group, boasted to Reuters news agency that Embaba had become an Islamic Republic wherein the sharia was the prime law. The story shot around the world at lightspeed. Unlike the Algerian government, which had to opt for encirclement and "rotting away" of the liberated Islamic zones in the suburbs of Algiers, the Egyptian state met this blatant challenge with all-out force. In December 1992, 14,000 soldiers occupied Embaba for six weeks, arresting and removing some 5,000 people. This put an end to Sheik Gaber's short-lived Islamic Republic, without leading to the bloodbaths promised by his supporters, because the violence into which the movement had lapsed had alienated most of its local support.

Thereafter, huge sums of money poured into the area; police stations and social security facilities were built everywhere, while the mosques passed under the control of the Ministry of Religious Affairs (waqf), which appointed "trustworthy" clerics to run them. This reconquest of Embaba by the state was not accomplished by repression alone: the disappearance of the Gamaa's function as social intermediary, which it had achieved by force, allowed the emergence of a new elite of young political entrepreneurs, adherents of the ruling Democratic National

Party, who facilitated access to the sudden windfall of investment from the authorities.[16] Some of these had been, in their time, close to the radical Islamist movement; now they anticipated its gradual winding down in the coming years and changed allegiance.

The Authorities Strike Back at the Gamaa and the Brothers

By using force to break an alliance between the young urban poor and the radical Islamist intellectuals in a deprived quarter of Cairo, the Egyptian government warded off an immediate danger that might have led to a real revolution. But it still had to face another threat, this time from the Muslim Brothers, whose members and sympathizers had flexed their muscles several times in 1992. They had a solid foothold among the devout middle class; they threatened to take up where the extremists had left off, using their charitable activities to win over the impoverished masses; and they had clearly penetrated the religious establishment, to which the regime looked for support against the Islamist movement.

The success of the Brothers in the Egyptian bar elections in September was described as "the most important event to occur in Egypt since the assassination of Sadat," because it completed their takeover of the representative organs of the educated middle class.[17] Only the journalists remained outside their control. This meant that the legal domain—crucial to the political demands of the Islamists, which rested on the application of the sharia—was in the process of slipping away from the secularist jurists. The devout middle class believed that the Brothers would know how to steer the law in their chosen direction, from within.[18] They would use their position of strength to start proceedings against Nasr Abu Zeid and other nonconformist intellectuals, and to win the cases, thanks to judges who agreed with their ideas. It was a golden opportunity for the Brothers to cause maximum embarrassment to the government, by partially withdrawing the justice system from its sphere of control, and thereafter by imposing the sharia as soon as the opportunity presented itself.

The government's reaction was to recover its authority over all the professional unions, by demanding the presence of a quorum of voters in balloting: in the absence of such a quorum, judicial administrators were appointed.[19] This measure was naturally viewed as crass manipulation, and it led to protests at a time when the regime was still uncertain as to what position to take in regard to the devout middle class. Direct confrontation with the Muslim Brothers and their allies was decided upon early in 1993, after six months of vacillation that were used by the Brothers to press home their advantage. Following the Cairo earthquake in October 1992, the Brothers demonstrated that they could be far more effective in delivering social services than the official bureacracy, which was hobbled by red tape and ineptitude. Using the professional unions they controlled, as well as their network of charitable associations, the Brothers were able to contribute thousands of tents to the 50,000 people left homeless by the disaster. These tents had been assembled by the Brothers' aid committee for shipment to Bosnia and so were readily available; they bore the slogan "Al Islam huwa al hall" (Islam is the solution).[20] The work of the Brothers won them great popularity and visibility, in sharp contrast with the state's ineptitude, and it enabled them to collect substantial new funds, which the government promptly froze.

In reaction to police occupation of Embaba, Islamist militants killed three foreigners with a bomb set in a café in central Cairo in February 1993. And in the Nile Valley, fresh attacks against tourists fixed the spotlight on the government's evasive security strategy. The Brothers and their allies within the religious establishment saw this as an opportunity to offer to mediate between the police and the extremist "devout young people"; they claimed that they could restore order, whereas repressive measures had failed to do so. One mediation committee included the television preacher Mohamed Metwali el-Sharawi, the Muslim Brothers' ally Mohammed al-Ghazali, and Sheik Abd al-Hamid Kishk, a former star preacher of the 1970s, among other like-minded clerics and journalists.[21] With the approval of a number of government politicians, notably the interior minister, the mediation committee made contact with the jailed leaders of the Gamaa. On the basis of a document that acknowledged the justice of the radical militants' demands while rejecting violence, the committee suggested unifying the entire Islamist movement under its leadership, which meant closing the gap between the devout middle class adhering to the Brothers and the young urban poor whose allegiance belonged to the Gamaa Islamiya.[22]

Had this project come to fruition, the state's legitimacy would probably have been severely tested by the people it was attempting to woo, and the regime itself might have been seriously endangered.

After a final agony of indecision, the authorities opted for a strategy of head-on confrontation with the entire Islamist movement and rejection of those elements of the religious establishment that had coalesced around the Brothers. On April 18, Abdel Halim Moussa, the minister of the interior, was removed for encouraging the mediation committee. On April 20, Safwat Sharif, the minister of information, who had argued in favor of appeasement and was responsible for allotting disproportionate TV time to the Islamist preachers, was the victim of an attack imputed to Al-Jihad. And in June, Mohammed al-Ghazali himself appeared as a witness for the defense in the trial of Foda's assassins. Thus, the regime rationalized the hard line it had finally chosen, the purpose of which was to smash the Islamist groups' military arm and repress the Muslim Brothers politically and legally, while making no overtures to the devout middle class until the battle against extremism had been won on the ground.

From 1993 to 1997, the intensifying struggle led to hundreds of deaths. The government's response to a series of daring attacks—one of which nearly killed Mubarak himself in Addis Ababa in June 1995—was ruthless repression, and in the end the tide swung decisively in its favor. The Gamaa had failed to mobilize the urban masses after the setback in Embaba and was now obliged to fall back on sporadic sorties against tourists, Copts, and policemen from its bases in the Nile Valley.[23] Spectacular though they were, these acts never came close to tipping the balance in favor of the militants. By the beginning of 1996, the movement was beginning to show signs of exhaustion. Many of its most battle-hardened fighters, who had come back from Afghanistan in 1992, had been killed in combat, or arrested, condemned to death, and executed.[24] They could not be replaced by men of similar fighting skill, owing to the tight border controls introduced by the regime.

Abroad, Western sanctuaries were no longer available to known militants. Sheik Omar Abdel Rahman was jailed for life in the United States in January 1996, while the disappearance in Croatia of the Gamaa's European coordinator, Talat Fuad Qassem, in September 1995 had disrupted the international support networks that supplied the military and religious arms of the movement.[25] The result was that many new initiatives came to nothing. Several countries extradited militants back to Egypt; money transfers from supporters in the Arabian peninsula slowed to a trickle, forcing the Gamaa to resort to armed robbery of local citizens to keep itself in funds. The killings of collaborators and informants (such as country policemen) alienated otherwise neutral or sympathetic elements of the population from the radical militants and their works; a parallel development occurred in Algeria during the same period.

The state's strategy of confrontation began to cause internal divisions in the movement, and eventually the first call for a ceasefire came from the amir of Aswan in March 1996. This truce was far from unanimously approved; in the very next month, eighteen Greek tourists, fourteen of whom were women, were massacred in a Cairo hotel. The Gamaa, which had mistaken these people for Israelis, claimed responsibility for the attack in a communiqué entitled "There is no place for Jews in the Muslim land of Egypt," justifying it as "a just vengeance against the Jews, sons of monkeys and pigs, adorers of the demon *(taghut),* for the blood of the martyrs who died in Lebanon."[26] The movement had reverted to a strategy of struggle against the "distant enemy" (Israel), in the hope of broadening its base of support by attracting the sympathy of nationalists and people frustrated by the dead-end of the peace process. This further compromised the battle against the "enemy within" (the government), which was being waged under conditions of growing isolation.[27]

While the Egyptian government was scoring military successes against the Gamaa, political pressure was building on the Muslim Brothers in accordance with the strategy decided in the spring of 1993. The regime, and Mubarak himself, regularly accused the Brothers of being the "acceptable" face of violence and the matrix from which the terrorists came. Though there was little concrete and convincing proof for these assertions, this argument demonstrated to the devout middle class that the regime had no intention of negotiating with them from a position of weakness and that any attempt on their part to collude with radical groups and the young urban poor to put pressure on the government would be firmly resisted. It was also a signal to Western governments, some of whom had begun to listen to voices favoring the arrival in power of "moderate" Islamists in countries like Egypt and Algeria.

The very successes of the Brothers carried the seeds of division, which the Egyptian regime was able to exploit. The association was led by a gerontocracy of "historic" members from the pre-Nasser era, men who were staunchly against turning the organization into a political party. As the Supreme Guide Mustafa Mashur explained to the press in early 1996, the strategy of the organization consisted in maintaining a "presence" in areas outside institutional politics, whose rules and manner of functioning were controlled by the whim of the regime and were foreign to an Islamic state applying the sharia, to which they aspired. These areas included professional unions, charitable endeavors, mosques and their associations, the non-usurious financial and banking sectors, the universities, the press, the judiciary, and the Parliament. This presence would produce a "preaching" *(dawa)* that would ultimately persuade society to implement the "Islamic solution." But this strategy for winning power through social implantation was opposed by the younger generation, who had been influenced by university militancy in the 1970s and had been successful in professional elections in the mid-1980s.

In January 1995, one of the leading figures of that generation, Issam al-Aryan, vice president of the physicians' guild, demanded the legalization of the Brothers as a political party. He was immediately arrested, along with dozens of fellow doctors, engineers, and other middle-class figures. A military tribunal condemned them all to heavy prison sentences for forming an illegal organization, a charge that the Brothers and many observers dismissed as a fabrication designed to prevent them from taking part in the legislative elections of November–December 1995.[28] In January 1996, other members of the younger generation called for recognition of a party that was an offshoot of the Brothers but had no organizational ties to them. This party, called Al Wasat (The Center), included an Anglican Copt among its leaders.[29] It sought to occupy the center of the political spectrum and was specifically aimed at an educated middle-class electorate, which it planned to bring together around a religious core (as the Brothers had done during the professional elections). Al Wasat's program was based on civil liberties, human rights, national unity, and so on and thus departed from the ideology of the Brothers in subscribing, without ambiguity, to Western principles of democracy. In this it found itself in opposition not only to the Brothers, for whom an Islamic state applying the sharia was the only political system of any value, but also to the government, whose repressive practices were directly targeted by Al Wasat's insistence on civil liberties. The initiative was rejected out of hand by the movement's Supreme Guide, who viewed it as a threat to his authority; and it was disapproved by the government, which in early 1996 still had to consolidate its position and thus was unable to accept any project for rallying the middle classes that might compete with its own social vision and methods. In consequence, the leading advocates of the putative new party were arrested, and the project collapsed.

In 1996, the policy of Egyptian government leaders was zero tolerance for the Islamist movement; and the general decline of violence, despite a series of spectacular attacks, offered hope of success in the mid-term.[30] The government's hesitations of three years earlier belonged to the past, even at the price of abuses of democracy that drew protests from the West. And indeed the policy worked: by the following year the regime's crackdown had exhausted and scattered the Gamaa Islamiya. In July 1997, the Gamaa's imprisoned "historic" leaders called for a ceasefire, having drawn the inevitable conclusion from the failure of their war against the state that the excesses of their strategy had turned the people against them. This appeal was rejected by several exiled leaders but supported by Sheik Abdel Rahman from his New York jail cell. However, the militants in Egypt defied it with a campaign of assassination against policemen in the Nile Valley in September. This last offensive served only to highlight the deep divisions within the organization. The end came with the massacre of a group of tourists at the temple of Hatshepsut in Luxor on November 17, an act that was condemned by the Gamaa's European center but approved by the leaders who had remained in Afghanistan.[31] Since then, the Gamaa Islamiya has ceased to exist as a major perpetrator of political violence in Egypt.

Like the Algerian government, the Egyptian regime won the war declared on it by the radical Islamist movement in 1992. It began by destroying the Gamaa's base of popular support in Embaba, then caught the movement in the trap of its own drift into terrorism, which alienated more and more elements of the population the longer it went on. It also took care to block any move to reunify the Islamist movement, such as the one initiated by the mediation committee in 1993; later, it systematically thwarted the attempts by the Muslim Brothers to represent the devout bourgeoisie politically, by outlawing that organization. Nor did the regime leave any room for a Center Party, which, had it come to anything, would have competed with the government's own attempt to rally the middle classes.

Mubarak's state was able to do all this because the economic situation was favorable after the Gulf War. Part of Egypt's foreign debt had been written off as a reward for its participation in the alliance, and Egyptian émigrés, alarmed by the disappearance of Kuwait's bank for several months, began to put their savings in Egyptian banks instead. The policy of privatizing and modernizing the economy led to the emergence of a new class of entrepreneurs whose presence changed the Egyptian middle classes more radically in the space of ten years than anything else had in the thirty years since Nasser. The regime gambled that the growth of wealth would allow the social interest of the devout middle class to prevail over their ideological inclinations and that it would join the bandwagon of prosperity while at the same time deploying and funding a species of piety that would acknowledge political consensus, instead of encouraging the kind of confrontational Islamism embodied by the Brothers and the Gamaa. The retrieval of a whole series of symbols that had formerly been identity tags for militant Islamism, such as the hybridizing of Islamic emblems and their transformation into merchandise, all helped this process—thus, the chic hijab framing a carefully made-up woman's face, the beard cut in the latest Italian style, or the evening meals (maidat al rahman) served gratis during the month of Ramadan. Formerly offered under the Muslim Brothers' ubiquitous slogan "Islam Is the Solution," today these Ramadan dinners operate as a kind of charitable endeavor for companies and shops, which put out tables in front of their establishments.[32]

Once again, there is a parallel with Algeria. The Egyptian government seems to have gambled on the idea that market-economy Islamists would eventually absorb the energy of Islamic fundamentalism. But the market may do more than that: it may push those involved in it to express their preference for the kind of political pluralism and genuine democracy that Egypt and Algeria have yet to see.

13

Osama bin Laden and the War against the West

The jihad intensified in 1992 in Bosnia, Algeria, and Egypt, as soon as veterans of the Afghan war began arriving home from Peshawar. In Egypt as in Algeria, the combatants were native born; they had made the pilgrimage to the Afghan camps in the mid-1980s, discreetly encouraged to do so by their governments, which were only too happy to rid themselves of potential malcontents and troublemakers.[1] In Bosnia, the jihadists were all foreigners, Arabs for the most part, many of them Saudis. In Tajikistan—and in Chechnya after 1995—other Arab volunteers played an important role in the attempt to turn a local conflict into a full-blown jihad.

The dispersion all over the world, after 1992, of the jihadist-salafists formerly concentrated in Kabul and Peshawar, more than anything else, explains the sudden, lightning expansion of radical Islamism in Muslim countries and the West. These hardened veterans of the Afghan jihad excited the enthusiasm of zealots around the globe, who saw "heavy blows" being struck at the "godless" and the "apostates." In the last decade of the century, the bombing of the World Trade Center in February 1993 and the GIA's campaign against France in 1995 were the most striking examples of the new battlefronts opening up in the backyards of Islam's "enemies." Yet the savage violence of these operations, carried out by terrorist networks cut off from any social movement and manipulated by obscure forces, had an effect that was the exact reverse of the one their authors probably hoped for. By the turn of the century, the image not only of the extremist fringe but also of the

Islamist movement as a whole was badly tarnished. Worse, those voices in the West that had supported the idea of the Muslim Brothers entering government alongside other "moderates" from the devout bourgeoisie, as the only force capable of bringing an end to the cycle of violence, had fallen silent. The near impossibility of telling apart the various Islamist factions or of crediting one group with influence over another gradually led the West to distrust any interlocutor who claimed to represent Islamism; and this precipitated a series of crises and changes within the movement.

When Kabul fell into the hands of a coalition of Afghan mujahedeen parties in April 1992, the objective of the jihad was to all intents and purposes achieved. An Islamic state was installed on the wreckage of the communist government, even if the country was in a state of semi-chaos until the Taliban gradually took over. The Arab and international jihadists had no further reason to stick around, especially since the United States was pressing for the dispersal of all military forces in Afghanistan that could no longer be kept under control. Hundreds of fighters returned to their home countries; but many others found themselves physically prevented from doing so. Most Arab states viewed the veterans of Afghanistan as a real danger, and border controls were tightened against them. They constituted a kind of demobilized army of several thousand seasoned warriors, all without passports, in search of a place to fight or hide. As combatants they were ready to serve anyone willing to fund them and help them travel from one place to another around the globe.[2] Yet they were completely divorced from the social realities of the wider world around them, locked as they were into a sectarian religious logic.

The attempts of these extremists to export jihad were thwarted in Bosnia, Algeria, and Egypt, and in Western countries their plight was even worse. At first, Western nations, particularly France and the United States, which had served as sanctuaries and refuges for the "Afghans," became targets of violence and terrorism. During the 1980s the United States had played a pioneering role in financing the Afghan jihad, facilitating the movements and even the comings and goings on American territory of preachers and recruiters. In 1986, two years after his release from prison, the blind Sheik Omar Abdel Rahman obtained his first American visa through the CIA, which he used to attend conferences of Islamist students in the United States.[3] Next, he visited Pakistan, where he preached at Peshawar, lunched at the Saudi embassy in Islamabad, and was lionized at receptions heavily attended by Americans. The sheik was a leading figure in the campaign to recruit fighters who were ready to face martyrdom for the chance to enter paradise— and in the process bring about the fall of the Soviet system for the greater benefit of Washington, D.C.

Nevertheless, as an amir of the Gamaa Islamiya in his home country of Egypt, the sheik was in a delicate position regarding the regime of President Hosni Mubarak, whom he was wont to castigate at length in his sermons. On April 22, 1990, he was interviewed for an hour and a half by Interior Minister Abdel Halim Moussa, with a view to reaching a gentleman's agreement whereby Omar Abdel Rahman would call his supporters to order in exchange for an improvement in the detention conditions of the Islamist militants still in Egyptian jails.[4] Three days later the sheik left Egypt for the Sudan. On May 10 he was given an American visa in Khartoum, and he finally arrived in New York on July 18.[5] There he was taken in by Mustafa Shalabi, an Egyptian activist based in Brooklyn, who had set up a support center for the jihad in Afghanistan in 1986 with a view to raising funds and recruits in the States—and who was assassinated a few months after the sheik's arrival in New York.[6] In January 1991, Sheik Abdel Rahman applied for a permanent U.S. resident's visa, on the grounds that he was a minister of the El Salam mosque in Jersey City, commonly known as Little Egypt. With unusual rapidity, a green card was issued to him in April.[7] During this period, he traveled frequently to Europe and the Middle East, haranguing congregations on the need for jihad in Afghanistan. This continued until the fall of Kabul in April 1992.

Since the 1980s, all activities of this kind had been gratefully assisted and subsidized by the CIA. But from 1990–91 onward, other American interest groups had begun to question the perverse effects of this policy, and gradually these critics prevailed. The U.S. public and its leaders had a complete change of heart when the Islamist freedom fighters who had fought the Red Army and the "Evil Empire" were suddenly depicted as terrorists and fanatic criminals. Sheik Abdel Rahman was both the pivotal force and the instrument of this change.[8] In June 1991, while he was on a pilgrimage to Mecca, the American authorities noticed that he was an undeclared bigamist and had therefore lied on his administrative application.[9] They immediately began proceedings to remove his resident status. In June 1992, he filed for political asylum in order to forearm himself against an expulsion decision, and he began soliciting support from human rights jurists, without ceasing to preach jihad. In Jersey City, the sheik was surrounded by a circle of poor Arab immigrants, black converts, and Muslims from the Middle East and the Indian subcontinent who were enthralled by his sermons but cut off from the mass of American Muslims. It was in this small, precarious world, infiltrated by *agents provocateurs* and spies, that the first plan to destroy the World Trade Center was hatched.

The trials that followed the 1993 bombing of the WTC established the identity of those directly involved beyond any doubt. They were all close to Sheik Abdel Rahman and all had been swayed by his fiery sermons against America in particular and the West in general. On the other hand, the contention made by the American Justice Department that a wide "conspiracy" had been masterminded by the sheik himself was still open to doubt several years after the fact.[10] Quite apart from the practical impossibility of a blind man picking out targets he had never seen and could imagine only with great difficulty, it is hard to believe that his accomplices, who were anything but bright and had only the haziest idea of the nature of American society, could have imagined an attack of such spectacular proportions without outside help. At the trial, the defense stressed the role of an Egyptian informer infiltrated into the group by the FBI, whose recorded conversations with the accused showed that he openly incited them to carry out the attack.[11] Another theory has it that Saddam Hussein's Iraq, newly defeated in the Gulf War of 1991 and under heavy American military pressure, was the instigator; and this theory spotlighted the central role of a mysterious figure, Ramzi Yusef, in the logistical preparation of the bombing.[12]

In the absence of any certainty in this domain, we may at least take it for granted that the explosion which shook the famous twin towers—the emblems of triumphant American capitalism—on February 26, 1993, marked a symbolic twist in the special relationship between American authorities and those who had fought in Afghanistan.[13] These warriors became the object of unremitting repression. To an even greater extent than in Egypt and Algeria, the militants had engaged in terrorist violence (or had allowed themselves to be manipulated to that end) without being in step with any kind of broader social movement. They were crushed for a time. But they would come back with a vengeance on September 11, 2001.

While Sheik Abdel Rahman was waiting out his awkward exile in the United States, large numbers of other jihadist-salafists obliged to leave Afghanistan at the end of the jihad in 1992 were looking for asylum in European countries—where they hoped to build up new networks for funding, supplies, information, and communication. Scandinavia had a generous tradition of granting asylum, with equally generous financial provisions for its beneficiaries; also, the local authorities were for the most part ignorant of radical Islamism and those involved in it, and this allowed a number of militants to find a safe haven there. Copenhagen became the headquarters of the Egyptian Gamaa Islamiya in exile, while Stockholm provided the Algerian GIA with the wherewithal to publish and distribute its *Al-Ansar* bulletin. In these countries, the Muslim population was a tiny minority and possessed nowhere near the same explosive political potential as in France or Great Britain.

On the issue of asylum, London and Paris took positions diametrically opposite one another. London, still traumatized by the Salman Rushdie affair, freely gave safe haven to militants from all over the world. Paris, on the other hand, whose political landscape had for some time been disturbed by controversy over the wearing of the veil in state schools, kept its frontiers firmly closed to militants. Thus, in the final years of the twentieth century, Great Britain became the axis around which the small world that had coalesced at Peshawar in the 1980s revolved. In return for this hospitality, the militants declared Britain a sanctuary: no act of terrorism was committed there, and the refugee activists made no attempt to stir up the young Indo-Pakistanis who had demonstrated against the *Satanic Verses* in 1989. (Of course, most of the Afghan refugees in Britain were Arabs who were not directly in touch with Britain's Indian and Pakistani Muslims.) In France, by contrast, the government lived in dread of what might happen should the Arab jihadists penetrate and influence its three-million-strong North African population, many of whom originally came from Algeria, where the civil war was just heating up.

For these geopolitical reasons, the Egyptian leaders of the Al-Jihad group found themselves rubbing elbows with their counterparts of the

Gamaa Islamiya in London after 1992. They had the opportunity to re-structure or rebuild their Islamist movements and disseminate bulle-tins by fax or Internet. They also put pressure on the Egyptian govern-ment by denouncing torture and the arbitrary arrests and death sentences handed down by military courts.[14] London became a base for an ultra-radical faction of the Al-Jihad group, the Vanguard of Con-quest (Talai al-Fath), who were opposed to any suggestion of a ceasefire in Egypt.[15] Following the example of the Saudi Islamist Mohammed al-Masari— who sent out his bulletins by fax from London until the co-lossal bill he owed to British Telecom brought his activities to a halt— the partisans of Talai al-Fath inundated the newspapers with gran-diloquent proclamations that did not necessarily reflect their actual strength on the ground.

As had been the case in Peshawar, the concentration in "London-istan" of these groups led to a tempest of reciprocal excommunications and anathemas. On the other hand, London offered a space for free discussions and exchanges of views that could possibly lead to reconcil-iation between radicals and moderates.[16] The presence in one coun-try of the "international representative" of the Muslim Brothers, of the charismatic leader of the Tunisian Mouvement de la Tendance Islamique, Rashid al-Gannushi, and of the headquarters of the Islamic Foundation in Leicester run by members of the Pakistani Jamaat-e-Islami facilitated this free exchange of ideas.[17] The radical Syrian Omar Bakri, who managed to organize two mass meetings at Wembley Sta-dium in support of the jihad, made a number of contacts with these so-called moderate leaders before communication was cut off under pressure from the British.[18] All benefited from the presence in London of the daily newspapers *Al Hayat* and *Al-Quds al-Arabi* (Arab Jerusa-lem), which provided considerable media attention, ensuring that their discussions were followed all over the Arab world.

The centralizing function of the English capital reached its highest point of effectiveness during the Algerian Civil War. The GIA was able to build its image and establish its legitimacy thanks to the mediation of the jihadist-salafists publishing the bi-monthly *Al-Ansar*, "the voice of the jihad in Algeria and throughout the world," after they had relo-cated it from Stockholm. Run by two leading Afghanistan veterans, the Syrian Abu Musab and the Palestinian Abu Qatada, this publication kept open the lines of communication between the GIA in Algeria and the international salafist network, translating the GIA's activities into the latter's politico-religious language and categories. Everyone had something to gain by this communication. The Algerian activists, whose Islamic culture was rudimentary at best, found in the bulletin's support a religious endorsement of their violent acts, while the intellectual preachers in London found in it the social grounding that they lacked in England. Thus the GIA continued to operate in a curiously disjointed way, with the young urban poor doing the physical fighting at home while the Islamist intelligentsia abroad took care of propaganda.

Distance was a problem, however. Even with modern communication facilities, the link between London and the Islamist underground had to be indirect and was therefore vulnerable to all manner of interference and manipulation. Sometimes the actions of the GIA in Algeria seemed coherent only in light of the filtered, selective, largely unverifiable information and communiqués published in *Al-Ansar,* which were edited by non-Algerians with little real knowledge of the country, seeing it through a kind of "Afghan" prism. The two great crises of the GIA were thus quite naturally expressed at the interface between these two poles.

After the purges and the execution of Mohammed Said in the fall of 1995, the intellectuals in London gradually distanced themselves from Djamel Zitouni and eventually closed down *Al-Ansar* by June 1996. But in the following February, the bulletin was revived by the Anglo-Egyptian activist Abu Hamza, in support of Antar Zouabri's amirate, only to go out of circulation again following the massacres of civilians for which Zouabri claimed responsibility. After that, the GIA ceased to exist as such, though massacres carried out by its operatives continued as late as 1998. As soon as there was no more recognized Islamist intelligentsia speaking on its behalf, the GIA lost its composite identity and broke into a multitude of tiny groups that either fought one another to a standstill or fell back into simple brigandage.

In contrast to the British policy that turned London into the capital of world Islamism in the 1990s, Paris made access to French territory very difficult for Arab activists coming from abroad. A "Franco-French" network of FIS sympathizers had grown up alongside the

Fraternité Algérienne en France (FAF), whose weekly bulletin, *Le Critère*, published news of the jihad from the outset of Algeria's civil war. *Le Critère* was eventually banned by the authorities in a sharp demonstration of the limits to government tolerance.[19] On the other hand, Sheik Abdelbaki Sahraoui, a founder member of the FIS living in exile who supervised a mosque in the Barbès quarter of Paris, was viewed by Charles Pasqua, the French interior minister, as one of his most valuable intermediaries with Islamist circles.[20] The sheik discreetly used his strong moral authority to make quite sure that France remained a real sanctuary for all the party militants who had taken up residence there. He realized that rallying sympathizers, putting together funds for the armed struggle, and organizing clandestine deliveries of arms from the former Eastern Bloc were possible only if this business was kept strictly separate from French political concerns about Islamism within metropolitan France and from tensions in the *banlieues* about whether the veil should be worn by Muslim schoolgirls. The authorities were obsessed with the idea that the violence of Algeria's jihad might cross the Mediterranean and enter France, in the form of an activist-inspired intifada among second-generation immigrants in the poorest urban areas.

As we have seen, since 1989 the various Islamist movements based in France itself had pursued a very different course. The Union des Organisations Islamiques de France (UOIF) and groups resembling it had been in the forefront of the squabble over veils in French schools: they viewed the growing number of young French Muslims as a sign that France had become a part of the "land of Islam" (dar el-Islam). According to the UOIF, young Muslims ought to be able to apply the sharia to their personal lives without interference from the state. Guided by Islamist militants and at their behest, the UOIF saw its role as being a necessary intermediary between this new Muslim community in France and the French administration.[21] Once France was viewed as an Islamic land, radicalization or violence over foreign issues was unwelcome, and jihad on French territory was expressly forbidden. France, like Britain, was a sanctuary. At stake was the Islamist movement's credibility vis-à-vis the French authorities, whom they wished to convince of their crucial role as community mediators who could keep the social peace.

Prior to 1994, these "Franco-French" Islamist organizations did not mix or mingle with the support networks for the Algerian Jihad. The former avoided the Algerian question, and the latter stayed aloof from local Islamic affairs that it felt were properly the business of the French.[22] But in August of that year, following the GIA's assassination of five French officials in Algiers, French police rounded up a large number of people, including the leaders of the FAF and an Algerian imam, Larbi Kechat, the head of one of Paris's biggest mosques.[23] They were all interned at a military camp in Folembray, in the north of Paris, and some were later expelled to the Burkina. In the growing antagonism between the armed Islamist movement and the French state, the government had given unmistakable notice of its determination to maintain control. It would tolerate no repercussions of the Algerian conflict on French territory. During the crackdown on Algerian militants, the police did not disturb Sheik Sahraoui, however—he was providing France its sanctuary status.

The response from the Algerian jihadists was not long in coming and was preceded by worrying signs from Morocco. On August 24, a band of young terrorists murdered some Spanish tourists in a Marrakesh hotel, and their accomplices were arrested in Fez and Casablanca. All were found to be the sons of Algerian and Moroccan immigrants resident in France, in the Paris and Orléans regions. Reciprocal arrests made by the French police—and the trial that followed— revealed for the first time the existence of a transnational network based on young Muslims from the housing projects, trained to violence and the use of weapons.[24] Like the group centered on Sheik Abdel Rahman in the United States, this network included student idealists as well as young men on the dole who had records of delinquency and drug abuse—some of whom had committed robberies and hold-ups to finance the group. After discovering—or rediscovering—religion at the end of the 1980s, they were taken in hand by two figures whose previous careers had been shadowy, to say the least. One, a former leader of a radical Islamist movement in Morocco, had taken refuge in Algeria before moving on to France using an Algerian passport. As the group's principal activist and theorist, he had arranged for some of its members to spend time in the Afghan camps in 1992; thereafter, the group's activities had been directed toward destabilizing the Moroccan regime with spectacular terrorist attacks on Jews and tourists, after the fashion of the Egyptian Gamaa Islamiya. Like their New York counterparts, the conspirators in France were characterized by naiveté, rashness, fanaticism, and a rudimentary intellect. Most were sent to prison.

This sequence of events in the late summer of 1994 made clear that the sanctuary status of French territory was beginning to crumble under pressure from radical Islamist groups. For the first time, young French Arabs had been implicated in a well-organized armed operation with international ramifications, even though their shift to terrorist tactics had taken place abroad. This showed, at the very least, that some young people in French housing projects who came in contact with re-Islamization by way of extremist preachers in the mosques could be vulnerable to the call for jihad—despite the guarantees given by Islamist self-proclaimed community mediators. A year later, Islamist terrorism entered France itself.

Jihad against France

The holy war against France was launched by the Algerian amir Djamel Zitouni with the seizure of an Air France Airbus departing from Algiers on Christmas Eve, 1994. It reached its height with a series of attacks on French territory in the summer and fall of 1995 and continued with the massacre of the Trappist monks of Tibéhirine, who were found beheaded on May 21, 1996. To this day, this onslaught remains as hard to decipher as every other major Islamist terrorist operation against the West, including the World Trade Center attacks and other terrorist acts imputed to Osama bin Laden. Behind the people who carried out these operations were a number of obscure suspects, including Zitouni himself. The organizational structure of the GIA, with its leaders in Algeria, its outpost in London, and its terrorists in France, was diffuse and mysterious. But whatever the identities and calculations of those who planned and carried out the French jihad, it had a high profile and very important consequences for the future of the Islamist movement, both north and south of the Mediterranean.

When the Air France Airbus was stormed by gendarmes on the tarmac at Marseille-Marignane and its four hijackers killed, the best-informed observers pointed out that the war had reached a turning point and that henceforth it would be waged on French territory. But the expected onslaught did not begin in earnest until six months later, on July 11, 1995, when Sheik Sahraoui, the guarantor of French sanctuary, was assassinated in his mosque with one of his closest collaborators.[25] The murder weapon was later found in the backpack of Khaled Kelkal, who was shot by the police after a manhunt through the woods near Lyon on September 29. Eight attacks were carried out between July 25 and October 17, leaving 10 dead and more than 175 injured.

None of these operations was ever expressly claimed by the GIA as its work—if one discounts the litany of threats against France as the enemy of Islam and exhortations to President Chirac to embrace the Muslim faith. Nevertheless, the proven involvement in the attacks of people belonging to the GIA, the funds they received from one of the directors of *Al-Ansar* in London, and the declarations of one of the leading culprits during his trial in 1999 have convinced most analysts that Zitouni's GIA was behind them. By spreading terror in France, Zitouni had hoped, presumably, to force the French state to cut off its support for the Algerian government, thus hastening the regime's fall. But given the GIA's nebulous character and the fact that many FIS leaders in exile (as well as independent observers) suspected that it had been infiltrated and manipulated by the special services of the Algerian army, many analysts saw the war against France in 1995 as a plot from *within* the Algerian government itself to obtain exactly the opposite effect—a stiffening of Paris's support for Algiers and a ruthless repression of all the support networks in Algeria, France, and Europe available to the armed Islamists.[26] Whatever the merits of this theory, the fact remains that those who carried out these acts of terrorism, even though they may have had no clear understanding of the consequences of what they were doing, did claim to have the support of the GIA.[27]

After the arrests, the reports of the investigating magistrates and the declarations made in court built up a picture of young men of North African origin (as well as a few European converts), living in abject poverty and mostly out of work, who had turned to militant Islamism as a reaction to their wretched social conditions. Some were former drug dealers and petty criminals who had spent time in prison, where they had begun to embrace Islam. Both the preparation and execution of their attacks were unprofessional: they had very little money behind them, they survived on petty drug deals, they forged their papers amateurishly, and they had great difficulty making the simplest bombs out of gas containers. One of these bombs failed to explode and eventually yielded Kelkal's fingerprints. With the police on his heels, Kelkal disappeared to a makeshift camp in the woods, where he was provisioned by two friends driving an old red car. With the equivalent of only eighteen dollars in his pocket, he was finally caught and killed while waiting at a bus stop. Nothing about him or his confederates relates to the world of professional terrorism, with its sophisticated systems and its ability to exfiltrate suspects sought by the police.

The life of Khaled Kelkal, who had earlier—by chance—been a subject in a remarkable sociological study in 1992, illustrates the alienation experienced by a young man from the French *banlieue*, born in Algeria in 1971 and subsequently growing up in France.[28] Kelkal claimed to have been rejected by his schoolmates in a "highly thought of" *lycée* because he was the only Arab there; he felt "more comfortable" in the "outsider atmosphere, among thieves," especially since, in the public housing project where he lived, "70% of the young people stole." When he was sent to prison for robbery, he rediscovered religion through the "Muslim Brother" who shared his cell. His return to Islam gave him an opportunity to substitute another community for his gang of thieves, while representing a break with the "arrogant Westerners" whose "Christian religion . . . was a false religion."

In his narrative of the first part of his life, Kelkal mentions *The Auto-biography of Malcolm X*, which reached young Muslims of the French suburbs through Spike Lee's film and was distributed gratis on video-cassettes by Islamist associations. The film illustrates the same disappointment of a student who felt he deserved better, the same drift into delinquency, encounter with Islam in prison, and sense of redemption afterward that Kelkal described.[29] Abundant research into Islam in France during the 1990s now shows that this career, while hardly the norm, was by no means unusual. Social unrest, after the antiracist movements of the previous decades had run their course, led a certain number of young people to re-Islamization, which they perceived as a break with the past.[30] This sometimes took the form of verbal violence, as in "Islamic rap," or else was converted into political engagement by one or another of the Islamist organizations within France, such as Jeunesse Musulmane de France (JMF), which was linked to the UOIF, or Union des Jeunes Musulmans (UJM), which was firmly established in the Rhône-Alps region.[31] But this political engagement had never found an outlet in terrorism on French soil, because the Islamist social movement that emerged in the suburbs in the early 1990s had steadfastly refused to countenance violence.

Like the members of the Marrakesh network, Kelkal resorted to terrorism after being socialized by activists outside of France. At the end of his 1992 interview he declared: "I want to do something, I want to leave France altogether. *Forever.* And go where? Home, to Algeria. *There's no place for me here.*"[32]

And to Algeria he went, in 1993. The civil war was just beginning, and he returned to France a full-fledged "fanatic," according to testimony made at his trial by his then-girlfriend.[33] He organized showings at home of his GIA videos and was identified as a "reliable contact" by the Holland-based Ali Touchent, who had been appointed by the "Amir of the GIA" as the group's European representative. Thereafter, activist cells were established in Lyon, Paris, and Lille, where militants who had come expressly from Algeria met with young French recruits. These constituted the interface between the Algerian leadership and the Muslim youth of France's outer suburbs. According to the incomplete information available, it would seem that the terrorist attacks that followed were carried out by these cells, on the orders of Ali Touchent.

Thus the 1995 terrorist violence in France was an operation orchestrated from abroad but dependent on networks in which a few young Islamists from the suburbs had been enlisted. Although several dozen of them were involved, they were unconnected with the broader re-Islamization movement that was taking place at the same time, in the same milieu. Its organizations and leaders had kept well away from Algerian affairs. The terrorist operations were not intended to spark a youth uprising but to utilize some of their number to strike a blow at the French state, in the name of Algerian political issues and interests. The failure of the project, the dismantling of the networks, and the catastrophic image of militant Islam created by this latest wave of terrorism were later to hamper the movement's penetration of North African youth in France. The organizations claiming to represent that movement, which were seeking to promote a social dynamic within an Islamist perspective, found themselves confronted with pressures and dilemmas to which they could find no response.

For one thing, their credibility with the French authorities, to whom they had presented themselves as guarantors of public order because of their religious education of the young, was seriously impaired: they had signally failed, after all, to stop a few individuals from heading down the path of terrorism—individuals who had previously moved in circles where they were very much present. Their claim to exercise control at the community level had proven empty, at a moment when public order was under serious threat.

Moreover, among the more general Muslim population of France, the events of 1995 caused real outrage. They expressed indignation at the bombings and sympathy for the victims, and they absolutely rejected the exploitation of their Islamic faith as a pretext for terrorism. North African immigrants saw violence on this scale as a threat to relations with mainstream French society that they and their children had patiently constructed, at a moment when, despite the difficulties of the past, integration at last seemed possible.[34] Although the younger generation of North Africans initially expressed their admiration for Khaled Kelkal and their disgust at the way he was shot to death by the police, even those youth in the poorest suburbs saw no reason to go down the same dead-end street of violence.

Islamist organizations whose defense of the wearing of the veil in schools had previously attracted some sympathy now found themselves rejected as potential troublemakers. Worst of all, these organizations found themselves faced with a credibility problem in their own ranks, because after a decade of presence on the ground, they had nothing to show for it and no social platform whatever. Their success had been built in the late 1980s on the waning of the "beur" movement and SOS Racisme, which had promised much but delivered little. In those years they had been helped forward by the development of re-Islamization all over the world, which reached a climax in about 1989; they had also capitalized on their political successes over the wearing of the veil, the fight against drugs in the public-housing projects, and the creation of training institutions for imams (which had attracted generous funds from the Arabian peninsula). But despite these promising beginnings, they were confronted with the same obstacles as the secular antiracist movements they had supplanted: in the last analysis, they had nothing of significance to offer that might help with social integration and access to jobs. Their religious approach had proved of little help to people grappling with social conditions in France's low-income housing.

The Islamist line, which had been made so fashionable in the early

1990s by charismatic preachers (winning over the sympathy not only of journalists and academics but also of Christian ecclesiastics), had lost the attraction of novelty—and had never found a sound anchorage in society. This disaffection was made acutely clear when the UOIF, which for many years had held its annual meeting at Le Bourget on Christmas Day, attracting thousands of young people along with extensive press coverage, was obliged to cancel the event in 1997.[35] The reason given was that the public was no longer interested, and the cost of the operation was simply too high. The organization was taken over by leaders of Moroccan origin, whose moderation softened its image. The same thing happened with the Fédération Nationale des Musulmans de France, which was also headed by a team approved by Rabat.

Thus, the events in France in 1995 played a major role in the transformation of the Islamist movement, and the same was the case (though on a much larger scale) in Algeria and Egypt. The drift into terrorism cut off the most radical groups from the young urban poor whom they aspired to represent, and this also affected the alliance between poor youths and devout middle-class intellectuals. At the same time, the middle class, through the organizations they ran, had no choice but to adopt a more and more democratic and liberal stance in order to negotiate (from a position of weakness) their own participation in political life following the evaporation of their radical base. There was no more talk of breaking with the system, as there had been during the campaign over the wearing of the veil at the beginning of the decade.

Osama bin Laden, Apocalyptic Terrorist

The most complete and media-conscious drift into terrorism of any among the jihadist-salafist faction was that of Osama bin Laden. In 1996 the United States dubbed him worldwide public enemy number one because of a wide range of terrorist acts attributed to him, and as a result bin Laden had become, by the turn of the century, the new visage of the Evil Empire.[36] His name and face ensured the success of dozens of television programs, magazines, books, and Internet sites and justified a wide range of American policy decisions. Ironically, all of this exposure would make him a hero of anti-Americanism in the Muslim world.[37]

Born in 1957, Osama was one of the 54 sons and daughters fathered by Mohammed bin Laden. Mohammed, who belonged to a family of masons from the Hadramout region of South Yemen, emigrated to Saudi Arabia in 1930 and was recruited by the House of Saud. He delighted the Saudi monarchy with his flair for palace-building, and over the years this royal favor turned his family business into the largest construction company in Saudi Arabia and one of the largest in the Middle East. He obtained an exclusive concession for the extension and maintenance of the Grand Mosque in Mecca, the most sacred site of Islam, as well as that of all freeways leading to it from other major cities in the kingdom.[38] Mohammed's feats of engineering along the pilgrim road from Jeddah to Mecca, through the mountains of the Taif region, quickly established his reputation, and by the time of his accidental death in 1968, his personal fortune exceeded $11 billion. Today, the business's emblem is often the first thing passengers see plastered all over billboards when they land at a Middle Eastern airport.[39]

The bin Laden children were raised and educated from babyhood with Saudi princes, in spite of their father's modest Yemeni origins. Mohammed made up for his lowly birth by lavish expenditure on religious good works; he kept open house throughout the pilgrimage season, just like the royal family, entertaining ulemas and dignitaries from all over the Muslim world, as well as the leaders of Islamist movements in every part of the Umma. Thus, as a youth Osama was in regular contact with all those who were very much in favor with the Wahhabite circles of power. He studied engineering at Abd-al-Aziz University in Jeddah, where his course in Islamic studies (compulsory in Saudi Arabia) was taught by Muhammad Qutb, brother of the famous Sayyid Qutb. Abdallah Azzam, the future herald of the Afghan jihad, was another of Osama's teachers. Bin Laden reached adulthood as a young billionaire whose worldview was deeply colored by the ideas and doctrine of the Muslim Brothers and Saudi-style salafism.

After the Red Army entered Kabul in December 1979, Osama traveled to Peshawar with the blessing of the Jamaat-e-Islami, where he again encountered the leaders of the Afghan mujahedeen Islamist parties, whom he had last seen at the family table. Soon he was inquiring about the condition of the Afghan refugees and what kind of help he could provide for them. For the next few years he occupied himself in raising funds for the mujahedeen cause, becoming one of its most fer-

vent partisans in Saudi Arabia. In 1982 he moved his base of operations to Afghanistan, taking with him a substantial infrastructure, and
two years after that he established the first guest house for Arab jihadists in Peshawar, in collaboration with his former teacher, Abdallah
Azzam, who ran the Bureau of Services providing jihadists with the
help they needed. Between them, the two men did much to attract
and organize thousands of volunteers. These included many sons of
wealthy Saudi families for whom the jihad in Afghanistan was a kind of
summer camp; also present were revolutionary Islamist militants released that year from Egyptian jails, Algerian Bouyalists from the bush
on the run from their government, later a smattering of young men
from the French *banlieues* who would take part in the 1994–95 terrorist
campaign in France, and many others.

At that time, all volunteers were viewed favorably: in the eyes of the
Saudi establishment, to which bin Laden and Azzam were at this time
still close, the sacred cause of the Afghan jihad offered a chance to enroll potential troublemakers, divert them from the struggle against the
powers that be in the Muslim world and their American allies, and
above all keep them away from the subversive influence of Iran. In the
eyes of the United States, the goal of the Afghan jihad was more
straightforward still: the jihadists would do battle against the Soviet
Union, sparing American GIs, while the oil monarchies of the Gulf
would foot the bill, sparing American taxpayers. But at this very early
stage, Saudi intelligence services attempted to keep militant Egyptian
and Algerian radicals at arm's length from the well-born young men of
the Arabian peninsula. This did not, however, prevent them from making contacts that would come to fruition in the decade that followed.

In 1986 Osama established several camps of his own within Afghanistan. His wealth and generosity, the simplicity of his behavior, his personal charm, and his bravery in battle soon became legendary. In 1988
he established a database of all the jihadists and other volunteers who
had passed through his camps, and this gave birth to an organizational
structure built around a computer file whose Arabic title Al Qaeda
(The [Data]base) became famous only ten years later when it was portrayed by the American Justice Department as the key to an ultra-secret
terrorist network; this led to bin Laden's indictment for conspiracy. According to some sources, by 1988 Osama had broken with Azzam
for reasons that are still unclear; in the following year Azzam was mys-

teriously assassinated.[40] The Saudi regime had begun to have serious doubts about this loose cannon in Afghanistan, whose declared intent was the propagation of jihad all over the world; and in the same year that Azzam was murdered, the Saudis detained Osama during a visit to his homeland and stripped him of his passport.

In the months preceding Iraq's invasion of Kuwait in June 1990, the posturing of Saddam Hussein—who was still despised by the jihadist-salafist faction as an apostate—worried Osama sufficiently for him to offer the kingdom the services of his jihadist corps for the defense of the Saudi frontier.[41] But when King Fahd, the Custodian of the Two Holy Places, called in the troops of an international coalition led by the United States, bin Laden joined Sheiks Auda and Hawali and their circle in adamantly opposing the presence of infidel armies on Arabian soil. Thereafter Osama was harassed by the regime until, with the assistance of family contacts, he contrived to escape in April 1991. He first went to Pakistan and Afghanistan, and finally, at the end of the year, installed himself in Hassan al-Turabi's Sudan.

A major turning point had now been reached in the life of the man who was to become the most sought-after outlaw in recent history. Like many other Islamist militants coddled by the Saudi system during the 1980s, bin Laden broke radically with the monarchy and its American protectors over the Gulf War. In the Sudan, which shortly afterward found itself playing host to thousands of other jihadists from Afghanistan looking for sanctuary, he joined the motley coalition built by Turabi at the four Popular Islamic and Arab Conferences held from 1991 onward in Khartoum. It brought together the pan-Arabists, Muslim Brothers, radical Islamists, and—for a short period—PLO leaders, all of whom were united in their resentment of Operation Desert Storm and America's military triumph. Turabi's ambition was to create a focus of opposition to the conservative Saudi view of worldwide Islamism, thus taking advantage of the splits and realignments that followed the war. At the same time, bin Laden set about evacuating jihadists from Pakistan, where they were no longer welcome, facilitating their movements around the globe, and in many cases finding work for them in his building concerns throughout the Middle East. In addition to the Sudan, a number of these militants ended up in Yemen—the country of origin of Osama's family—which was well placed to provide a springboard on the peninsula for destabilizing its vast neighbor, Saudi Arabia. A powerful Islamist movement had long been present in Yemen, although by and large it remained aloof from bin Laden's objectives.[42]

Against this background, the first front against the United States was opened up on the Horn of Africa. In response to the civil war that was ravaging Somalia, a U.S.-led international force landed there in 1992 as part of the United Nations' Operation Restore Hope. The Islamists were quick to condemn it as an act of aggression aimed at threatening nearby Sudan and strengthening the West's grip on a region very close to the Middle East.[43] As a result, veteran jihadists from Afghanistan took part in military operations which ended in the massacre of 18 U.S. Marines in Mogadishu on October 3–4, 1993. The coalition forces departed from this fiasco ignominiously, taking with them the corpses of American fighting men in body bags. The retreat was celebrated as a triumph by America's enemies. The United States blamed bin Laden's organization for the loss of life, even though Osama himself, delighted as he was at the outcome, never claimed direct responsibility.[44]

In the wake of this event, bin Laden made major investments in Sudanese agriculture and the country's road network, turning himself into a pivotal figure in anti-Saudi Islamist circles—so much so that he was stripped of his Saudi citizenship in April 1994.[45] But when Khartoum came under heavy international pressure following the attempted assassination of Egyptian President Mubarak in Addis Ababa in June 1995, bin Laden changed from a welcome guest into a real liability. A year later, he was expelled from the Sudan.

In the summer of 1996, Osama returned to Afghanistan. In June, an attack on the American military camp at Khobar in Saudi Arabia that took 19 lives was imputed to him. Again, he did not claim responsibility, but on August 23 he released a *Declaration of Jihad against the Americans Occupying the Land of the Two Holy Places*. This eleven-page tract, best known by its subtitle *Expel the Polytheists from the Arabian Peninsula*, is crammed with quotations from the Koran, *hadiths* (sayings and stories) of the Prophet, and references to Ibn Taymiyya.[46] It is similar in form to the productions of the jihadist-salafist movement published in the GIA's *Al-Ansar* bulletin, notwithstanding the geopolitical vision it adopts. After recalling the sufferings visited by the "Zionist-Crusader" alliance upon Muslims in various countries around the world, it describes the "occupation of the Land of the Two Holy

Places" as "the greatest of all these aggressions." Thanks to the "awakening" of Islam, the aggression can be successfully repelled, "under the guidance of ulemas and preachers"—as were the crusaders and the Mongols in their time, when Muslims were guided by Ibn Taymiyya.

The five ulemas cited as references (Abdallah Azzam, Ahmad Yassin of the Palestinian Hamas, the Egyptian Omar Abdel Rahman, and the two Saudis Auda and Hawali) all stood at the intersection between the jihadist-salafist movement and the Muslim Brothers. For his own part, Osama positions himself squarely in their doctrinal camp and describes himself—since his flight to the mountains of the Hindu Kush in Afghanistan—as the point of departure for the reconquest. Bin Laden invites the reader to see a parallel with the Prophet's flight to Medina in Year One of the Hegira, prior to recovering Mecca and revealing Islam to the world.

Osama's declaration then goes on to stigmatize the deep injustice in Saudi Arabia. Above all he champions the claims of the higher social strata of the kingdom (his own class), referring to them as the "great merchants" to which the state is "indebted," who are suffering from the "devaluation of the *rial*," and so on.[47] Mainly he addresses himself to the devout midle class (and to some of the princes), in the hope of detaching them from the ruling dynasty. Then, in a reference to the "memorandum of admonition" of July 1992, he presents himself as the voluntary executor of all the demands and criticisms contained in the document.

Driving out the Americans, he claims, is the condition for reestablishing Islam in the peninsula. Invoking the words of his former teacher, Abdallah Azzam—for whom "jihad is every man's duty" (*fard ayn*) wherever Muslim lands are occupied by foreigners (as was Afghanistan by the Soviets)—bin Laden calls on all Muslims to join the jihad to expel the American occupant from the Land of the Two Holy Places. Making lengthy reference to Ibn Taymiyya, he invites the faithful to forgo their differences and unite against the Al-Saud family, who have "collaborated with the Zionist-Crusader alliance." His appeal is specifically addressed to the kingdom's armed forces, whom he exhorts to mutiny, and to Saudi consumers, whom he urges to boycott all American products.

The declaration of jihad goes on to praise the attack on the American barracks at Khobar in June 1996 and the October 1993 "victory" in

Somalia.[48] After invoking the "sons of Arabia" who fought in Afghanistan, Bosnia-Herzegovina, and Chechnya, it announces that the battle will continue until the Islamic state is established throughout the peninsula. A series of warlike poems and invocations to Allah conclude the document's blend of strident anathema and dubious strategy.

In this first manifesto, bin Laden appears to be venturing into the field of theory, whereas his early reputation was won as a master organizer, financier, and combatant. He brings together two powerful political currents: Saudi Islamist dissidence, whose proclamations were encompassed by the Wahhabite code of civility, and the call for jihad to liberate the land of Islam from foreign occupation, modeled on the preachings of Abdallah Azzam in Peshawar. He sets out to radicalize Saudi dissidence, by extending it to cover armed struggle; at the same time he seeks to turn those who are already jihadists against their former patrons, the United States and Saudi Arabia. In the 1990s, he claims, these two nations have assumed the roles of the Soviet Union and Communist Afghanistan in the 1980s—as godless invaders of the dar el-Islam and apostate collaborators.

But in this new struggle he mentions no strategic support comparable to that which the volunteers of the previous decade found in the United States and in several of the oil monarchies of the peninsula. The only two rogue states that had ever been able to offer him any semblance of support—Turabi's Sudan and the Taliban's Afghanistan—were impoverished and dependent. Within the worldwide Islamic fundamentalist movement at the end of the twentieth century, the enthusiasm of the young urban poor mobilized by the Pakistani religious parties and a few others around the figure of bin Laden himself seemed unlikely to turn into a powerful infrastructure. As for the contributions of his wealthy sympathizers, they had never obscured the general distaste of the devout bourgeoisie for a faction that attacks Riyadh and Washington head-on and threatens a wide range of vested interests.

In February 1998, bin Laden created the International Islamic Front against Jews and Crusaders, whose founding charter was co-signed by the leader of the Egyptian Al-Jihad Group, Ayman al-Zawahiri, one of his Gamaa Islamiya compatriots, and a few leaders of tiny Islamist cells in the Indian subcontinent. This short text, which contains abundant quotations from the Koran and the inevitable Ibn Taymiyya, repeats the customary tirades against the "Zionist-Crusader alliance" and raises the confrontational stakes to a new level by issuing a fatwa stipulating that "every Muslim who is capable of doing so has the personal duty to kill Americans and their allies, whether civilians or military personnel, in every country where this is possible."[49]

On August 7 of the same year, on the anniversary of the arrival of American troops in Saudi Arabia at the request of King Fahd, two huge explosions simultaneously destroyed the United States embassies in Nairobi (Kenya) and Dar-es-Salaam (Tanzania). The first left 213 dead (among them 13 Americans) and over 4,500 injured; the second left 11 dead and 85 injured (none of them American). The U.S. authorities immediately laid the blame on bin Laden. After American cruise missile attacks obliterated a chemical factory in Khartoum and leveled several training camps inside Afghanistan on August 20, Osama was indicted for conspiracy and a price of $5 million was placed on his head.[50] In a series of interviews given to the press from his Afghan hideout, bin Laden attempted to cast doubt on his direct implication in the African bombings, although he made clear his satisfaction that they had taken place.[51]

The killings in Nairobi and Dar-es-Salaam followed the same logic as those in Luxor in November 1997 and in Algeria at roughly the same time. Cut off from its roots within society, the extremist Islamist faction had resorted to a brand of terrorism that was more or less covered by religious justifications, and most of whose victims had nothing whatever to do with the designated enemy of the jihadists. Spectacular terrorism, because of the inevitable worldwide media attention it attracts, made it possible for extremists to pose as champions of the cause, and perhaps to regain popular favor by way of television, in the absence of any effective work at the grassroots level.

But resorting to spectacular terrorism was a high-risk gamble which, apart from emotional and momentary demonstrations of sympathy or solidarity, was bound to engender also a far greater, far deeper *angst* among the devout middle class, who feared that such explosions of violence might threaten its vital interests in the long run. But despite the bad odds, bin Laden seemed determined to follow that path. On October 12, 2000, a daring attack on *U.S.S. Cole*, which was refueling in Aden, Yemen, left 17 sailors dead.[52] Never had an American warship been inflicted such damage by a terrorist organization. Though many hints led to bin Laden, and a number of arrests were made, the criminal investigation proved frustrating—as if Al Qaeda had become a kind of brand name for anything anti-American in the area, as if a wide network of would-be accomplices took care to make proofs disappear and activists vanish. A number of questions remained unanswered: who was actually involved in that ring of attacks, from Khobar in June 1996 to Aden via the embassy bombings of August 1998, and also what was its purpose? If terrorism is a system of signs and signals sent to an adversary, what was the meaning embedded in that language? It could not be that the mere fact of U.S. world hegemony was at issue. Was it America's Middle East policy, and if so, what aspect of it? What did the terrorists, or the people behind them, want? What kind of trade-off, what kind of deal were they after, as they exercised such severe pressure on America? Maybe, at that point, the world should have taken bin Laden's words seriously. In his 1996 *Declaration,* he had voiced his hostility to the U.S. presence in Saudi Arabia and lambasted the Saudi royals, or at least some of them. He was adamant about the fact that, in his view, the kingdom had become an American protectorate. And it was known that, in some segments of the Saudi public, he had networks of friends who shared his vision. Was it thinkable that, whatever bin Laden's extremism, some wider groups willing to reshuffle the U.S.-Saudi relationship would discreetly push him forward, so as to send well-calculated advance warnings—warnings, perhaps, that oil money should go through different channels, that the great deal that had been brokered on board the *U.S.S. Quincy* in the aftermath of Yalta between Franklin D. Roosevelt and King Abd al-Aziz ibn Saud should be revised? And what had all this to do with the still largely mysterious bombing of the World Trade Center on February 26, 1993?

The gruesome attack that finally destroyed the World Trade Center on September 11, 2001, together with the crash of an airliner on the Pentagon the same day, was in line with this series of blows against American interests tracing back to 1993, though the unprecedented level of violence has changed its dimension altogether. As of early January 2002, we still do not know whether the apocalyptic destruction that resulted had been foreseen by the perpetrators of this crime against humankind, or whether they were taken aback by a cataclysm that exceeded even their expectations. That last hypothesis could be drawn, with all required caution, from the videotape that was seized by U.S. intelligence in Jalalabad after the flight of the Arab fighters in early December 2001 and subsequently aired worldwide. In a meeting with accomplices, bin Laden acknowledged that the toll of September 11 was much heavier than even he had hoped for.

Whatever the intent might have been, the attack on America meant that Al Qaeda and anyone suspected to be in touch with its network—which still remained fairly obscure—would be hunted down. Its infrastructure in Afghanistan, to the extent it was known, was destroyed within a few months. Whether these search-and-destroy tactics will prove sufficient in the long run against a rather fluid network, whose very name refers to a worldwide database of operatives, remains to be seen. Brick-and-mortar compounds and caches can be flattened by carpet-bombing, but websites and e-terrorism may prove far less difficult to delete.

14

Hamas, Israel, Arafat, and Jordan

The crushing of Iraq in the 1991 Gulf War had direct consequences for the Arab-Israeli conflict. It forced the political elites of Israel and the Palestinian Liberation Organization to engage in a peace process, which eventually broadened to include most of the Arab states. Thus, at the very moment when radical Islamist groups in Algeria and Egypt—stimulated by the homecoming of militants from Afghanistan in 1992—were resorting to jihad in order to establish Islamic regimes, the Palestinian Islamists were confronted with a major political challenge: the prospect of peace with Israel. If peace were achieved, the PLO would emerge at the head of a state recognized by the international community, after a half-century of nationalist struggle, and Islamist groups in Palestine, including Hamas and Islamic Jihad, would be severely handicapped.

The outbreak of the intifada in December 1987 had heralded a rapid growth in the influence of Hamas and, to a lesser extent, Islamic Jihad, both at the expense of the PLO, whose nationalist rhetoric had previously dominated the Palestinian discourse. The victory of the United States at the head of a coalition against Iraq in 1990–91 radically changed the complexion of the Arab-Israeli conflict. In a world where the Soviet Union no longer existed, the sole triumphant superpower found itself in a position to impose on the two adversaries a peace process that conformed to its interests. Israel, whose territory had been violated by a few Iraqi Scud missiles during the war, had left its military defense to Washington in order to avoid provoking Arab states by

launching a "Zionist" attack against the Iraqis. The Jewish state saw its
room for maneuver considerably reduced by an American government
led by Republicans, who were less sensitive to the concerns of the Jewish electorate than Democrats traditionally were. Moreover, President
George Bush had come to politics after a career in the oil business,
which made him amenable to the political reasoning of the Arab oil
monarchies of the Middle East, who were bent on recalibrating the
United States' regional policy in their own favor.

This momentary weakness of Israel was more than matched by
weakness on the part of the PLO, after Arafat's disastrous tactical mistake of throwing his support to Saddam Hussein. In retaliation for this
gesture, the states of the Arabian peninsula abruptly deprived the PLO
of the bulk of its funds—money that it counted on for redistribution
in the occupied territories. The severing of this lifeline obliged Arafat
to close numerous institutions whose existence depended on his largesse; many allegiances and contacts were damaged, but worst of all the
PLO lost much of its built-in advantage over Hamas, whose greater
prudence during the Gulf War was rewarded with petro-dollars.[1]

Thus, the conditions of a Middle East peace were worked out at a
time when Yasir Arafat's organization was politically and financially
weakened. Arafat's Palestinian Authority, which at the outset was to be
based in Gaza, gave the impression of being subjugated to the political whims of the ruling majority in Israel. There was a risk that the autonomous Palestinian territories would be transformed into so many
"Bantustans," as had happened to blacks in South Africa, and Arafat
into a Pétain-like figurehead.[2] This prospect opened up significant possibilities for the "Islamist alternative" offered by Hamas.

But the Islamist movement had a politically delicate hand to play. It
had significant social capital among the disinherited youth as well as
among the traders and middle class. It was up to the Islamist leaders to
make this capital bear some kind of political fruit, by exploiting the
disenchantment people felt with the foot-dragging of the peace process as well as with the authoritarianism and corruption of the Palestinian Authority's leaders. The Islamists had to maintain steady pressure without drifting into the outright terrorism of the radical Islamic
groups, which at the time were intoxicated by the idea of jihad.

The temptation to violence was very strong, given the level of Israeli
repression and the many frustrations and humiliations that had to be

borne. The young men who had come of age as participants in the intifada of 1987 refused to be content with fine words and a few crumbs of sovereignty combined with a wretchedly low standard of living. In this three-way political tug-of-war, Islamists could increase their own strength by using extremist tactics to provoke Israeli oppression and expose the PA's defenselessness. Hamas was able to maneuver with great skill in this climate between 1991 and 1994. It maintained coherence among its three elements of support: impoverished urban youth who were inclined toward violence, the devout middle class which saw its economic aspirations reflected in the movement, and the sophisticated Islamist intelligentsia—some based in the United States—who produced Hamas's political theories.

But like so many other Islamist movements gripped by the ideology of armed jihad, Hamas eventually fell into the trap of terrorism. Meanwhile, the PLO, despite a string of reverses, set about constructing a state apparatus and organizing general elections for January 1996. At this time Hamas was divided between its most radical and activist wing on the one hand and its more moderate sympathizers on the other, who wished to participate in the newly established political process, to found parties, and generally to turn their backs on self-destructive violence. In its drift toward terrorism, Hamas lost its ability to unite behind a single cause these different layers of society which, in the early years of the decade, had made it the most dangerous challenge to the system put in place by Arafat.

Under pressure from the United States, the Israeli government and the leaders of the PLO had no way to wriggle out of the peace process that took shape during the Madrid conference in December 1991. But at this stage the PLO was represented only indirectly, through individuals from the territories who were included in the Jordanian delegation, among them several who later demonstrated independent points of view. The PLO was adamant about changing the rules that disallowed its direct participation—rules which, in the view of its leaders, diminished its own stature and made it more vulnerable to the criticisms of Islamist and Marxist opponents who saw such compromises as surrender.

Hamas, on the other hand, despite being banned, succeeded in making electoral capital at the guilds' vocational election by rejecting a negotiated peace process in which the Palestinians seemed to be the losers.[3] In January 1992, the PLO had to enlist its secular opponents in the Popular Front for the Liberation of Palestine (PFLP) and the Democratic Front for the Liberation of Palestine (DFLP) to help prevent the Islamists from taking over the Gaza engineers' union.[4] In March, the Islamists won a decisive majority in the Chamber of Commerce at Ramallah, a secularized town with a sizable population of Christians. This demonstrated that Hamas had significant support among the middle class. In May, at the Nablus Chamber of Commerce elections, the PLO narrowly avoided defeat (48 percent against the Islamists' 45 percent) by repeated avowals of piety.[5]

While buoyed by this electoral demonstration of its strength among the devout bourgeoisie, Hamas was careful to maintain an escape valve for its radical, impoverished young. This it did by encouraging them to control the streets, in defiance of the PLO. In addition, the PLO "hawks" were taken to task by their Islamist opposite numbers, the Ezzedine Al-Qassam Brigades, who redoubled their harassment of Israelis.[6] The year 1992, though it saw a real decline in the intifada as a movement of mass disobedience and revolt, was nonetheless marked by an increase in the rate of assassinations of soldiers and civilians, mostly claimed by Hamas. On December 13, the fifth anniversary of the founding of the Islamist party, the Al-Qassam Brigades kidnapped an Israeli lieutenant at Lod (on Israeli territory) and demanded the liberation of the party's spiritual leader, Sheik Ahmad Yassin. Two days later, the hostage was found beside a road on the West Bank, bound hand and foot and stabbed to death.

This symbolic act of terror, which recalled the first killings of Israeli soldiers by Islamic Jihad, showed that Hamas was not afraid to provoke Israel, was not bound by a negotiating process that seemed bogged down, and was fully prepared to carry on an armed struggle. The murder had the added effect of strengthening support for Hamas among the most radical Palestinian activists and causing great international embarrassment to the PLO, which denounced it, thereby further alienating the extremists. Yitzhak Rabin's Labor government, which had come to power in June of that year, responded with an equally symbolic measure to assuage the outrage of the Israeli people; 418 leaders and activists of Hamas and Islamic Jihad were rounded up and deported to Marj al-Zohour, a mountain village in the south of Lebanon whose poetic name (flowering pastures) belies its harsh winter climate.

This move provoked angry riots in the occupied territories, where the departed Islamists became the heroes of the Palestinian youth. Meanwhile, the world's press trekked to the snowy hilltop where the outcasts were being held. There, the television cameras of the international news organizations found themselves filming not terrorist jailbirds but university students and teachers, doctors, engineers, and imams, many of whom articulately explained, in English, the political positions of Hamas, its hostility to Israel, and its defiance of the PLO. By targeting the Islamist intelligentsia, the Israeli government had intended to disorganize the movement, depriving it of its key theorists and organizers. Instead, the victims turned their exile into a successful public relations coup, in which they projected an aura of persecution and earned precious credentials as resisters of Israeli oppression. Israel's embarrassment was compounded when the U.N. Security Council voted the immediate and unconditional release of the prisoners.[7] While the peace negotiations dragged on and on, the deportees proceeded to organize seminars and conferences at Marj al-Zohour, calling the venue Ibn Taymiyya University in reference to the medieval thinker who was the main inspiration of their movement.

The net result of these events was that the PLO was forced to suspend participation of the Palestinian delegation in the peace negotiations. It had become the hostage of an operation over which it had no control, while the head-to-head confrontation between Israel and Hamas sapped its authority and diminished its status. Arafat urgently needed a significant advance in the peace process, if he was to overcome the misgivings of a Palestinian population that grew more susceptible to Islamist blandishments the more disenchanted it became with the PLO's leadership. Thus, in the very month that the deportees were taken to Lebanon, secret, direct contacts between Arafat's representatives and the Israeli government were initiated, which eventually resulted in the Oslo Declaration of Principles signed in Washington on September 13, 1993.

This declaration, which designated Gaza and Jericho as the first Palestinian territories to be placed under the PLO's direct authority, gave cause for satisfaction on both sides. Israel was able to divest itself of Gaza, where the cost of maintaining order had become prohibitive; and the Palestinian leadership was able to present its people with its first tangible results on the ground, a prelude to the creation of an independent state. The PLO expected this breakthrough to allow it to regain the political initiative it had lost with the recent successes of Hamas.

The signing of the Declaration of Principles did indeed restore the popularity of the PLO in the occupied territories, and in the short term it yielded the longed-for withdrawal of the Israeli army and the end of direct occupation in some areas. On the other hand, it facilitated the opening of an anti-Arafat front, where the various leftist opposition factions coalesced around Hamas. Five days after the signing, its militants gathered to heckle Arafat at a political meeting in Gaza. In November and December, student elections at the highly politicized Birzeit University resulted in a crushing defeat of PLO candidates by a coalition of their opponents.

With the new status quo of autonomy, Hamas found itself facing another political dilemma. It had to reconcile its maximalist position, calling for the liberation of all Palestine "from the River Jordan to the sea" and the installation of an "Islamic state," with the everyday aspirations of ordinary people, who wished to be rid of the Israeli occupiers as quickly as possible. They approved of the agreements that had brought autonomy about, even though they were unhappy with the heavy terms imposed by Israel. Hamas now found itself obliged to use violence to put pressure on Israel and the PLO—a strategy that had been successful in the past—but without entirely compromising the Israeli withdrawal from the occupied territories, for fear of exasperating ordinary Palestinians.

Hamas's dilemma also reflected the contradictory goals of the various components of its support, whose cohesion was sorely tested by the autonomy of Gaza and Jericho. The young urban poor, from among whom the largely independent Al-Qassam Brigades were recruited, mostly went along with Hamas's no-compromise stance and violent tactics, which were also endorsed by leaders in exile in Amman, who were regular visitors to Tehran. On the other hand, the devout middle class was eager to take part, even as an opposition party, in the installation of a new political power center that would control the economic resources on which their commercial activities depended (foreign aid being a major one).[8] Their expectations were reflected in various declarations made by Sheik Yassin and other leaders; none excluded the creation of a legal Islamist party or participation in elections.

On July 12, 1994, the PLO became the Palestinian National Authority. But the political situation was murky. On the previous February 25 an extreme right-wing Jewish colonist from neighboring Kiryat Arba had murdered over 30 Palestinian Muslims at prayer at the Tomb of the Patriarchs in Hebron. The riots that followed claimed the lives of scores of additional Palestinians. The PLO was reviled for negotiating with an adversary capable of producing such a mass murderer. Hamas, by contrast, received *carte blanche* to avenge the victims; and in April, a series of attacks inside Israel by Hamas suicide bombers left a dozen Israelis dead and many more wounded. Israel retaliated by closing its border with the territories and rounding up Islamists across the board. It was against this dire backdrop that the accords implementing the Israeli-Palestinian Declaration of Principles were signed in Cairo on May 4, 1994, regulating the transfer of sovereignty, the delineation of the territories evacuated, and the size of the security forces.

Beginning with the June installation of the PLO as the Palestinian Authority, Arafat's security forces took over responsibility from the Israeli army for the repression of Hamas—a tricky undertaking for the "men from Tunis," some of whom were setting foot on Palestinian soil for the first time in their lives.[9] The Islamists continued their campaign of terror through October, assassinating Israelis in Jerusalem, kidnapping and then killing an Israeli soldier when the hideout in which he was being held was taken by storm, and blowing up a bus in Tel Aviv with a suicide attack that left 20 dead. In early November, the revenge killing in Gaza of the military chief of Islamic Jihad (which Arafat blamed on Israeli security services) led to Arafat's being jeered by a Palestinian crowd at the chief's funeral, something that would have been unthinkable earlier.

On November 18, for the first time, the Palestinian Authority's newly installed police force opened fire directly on Hamas demonstrators outside the Grand Mosque in Gaza, killing 16 people. Arafat's moral position had now hit rock bottom and was scarcely improved by the various antiterrorist measures being undertaken by Israel. These included setting up numerous roadblocks and control points, along with bans on traveling in the West Bank or along the Gaza frontier. These restrictions made normal life impossible for the average Palestinian. Once the euphoria of the Israeli departure was past, it became only too clear that the autonomy agreements had yielded no improvement whatever in the conditions of daily life for the Palestinian people.

Again, Hamas appeared to be the main beneficiary of this dire situation.

The first months of 1995 passed in an atmosphere of continuing violence and suicide attacks within Israel. But violence was effective only insofar as it could improve the conditions for negotiation; and this it did by blocking the implementation of the peace accords in order to wring further concessions from the Israelis.[10] It was with this long-term hope in mind that the Palestinian population could tolerate violence, given the immediate price it had to pay in the form of Israeli retaliation and a dramatic fall in living standards. And thus it was that in 1995, the terrorism of Hamas, just like that of the GIA in Algeria and the Gamaa Islamiya in Egypt, turned counter-productive, because in that year the governments in Jerusalem, Algiers, and Cairo refused to yield.

Meanwhile, the suffering of the population continued to swell. And in Gaza, Arafat's government improved its capacity for repressing Hamas, by jailing several thousand Islamist leaders and militants. He dismantled their networks, interrupted their external sources of finance, and placed their mosques under surveillance. Finally, the Palestinian security forces—the area's principal local employer—began recruiting its troops from among the same impoverished urban youths who had been the driving force behind the intifada and who had served as the base of Hamas. The familiarity of these young men with their new prey made surveillance and policing easier.[11] All these shifting circumstances—to which we should add the crisis that struck Islamic Jihad when its leader was assassinated by Israel's Mossad—contributed to dissociating the radicals with poor backgrounds from those who came from the more moderate middle class.[12]

As was the case by the end of the intifada, the economically exhausted bourgeoisie earnestly hoped for some kind of resolution of the peace negotiations but was afraid that the domestic enfeeblement of Arafat would have negative consequences for all Palestinians.[13] Some "moderate" Hamas dignitaries then defected, and Hamas itself began negotiations with Arafat's government in the fall of 1995 to find a *modus vivendi* prior to the general elections of early 1996. Their failure to reach any agreement finally convinced the movement's exiled leaders that a boycott of the vote was their only option, thus leaving Arafat free to build the institutional framework of the Palestinian Authority to fit his own designs.

At this critical juncture, a Jewish terrorist from a right-wing religious faction assassinated Israeli Prime Minister Rabin on November 4. The Israeli campaign to elect a successor brought the Palestinian Islamists back to center stage. The assassination of the Hamas bombmaker Yahya Ayyache was followed by a series of spectacular suicide attacks by Palestinians that killed 63 Israelis and led directly to the election victory of Benjamin Netanyahu and his Likud party on May 29, 1996.[14] Netanyahu advocated a hard line, and in the eyes of Hamas his policy of obstructing the peace process could only play into the hands of the Islamists by making the task of the Palestinian Authority all the more difficult. But this strategy of provocation backfired: new attacks in March, July, and especially September 1997, which killed a total of 17 people in Jerusalem, achieved only a pitiless hardening of the Israeli attitude.[15]

The proven tactic of closing Israel's borders with the territories led, this time, to the economic strangulation of the Palestinians. Netanyahu's government also halted Israel's gradual withdrawal from the West Bank and relaunched Jewish colonization. The political advantages of terrorist acts against Israel thus began to seem more and more uncertain, possibly even negative, to a Palestinian population exhausted and demoralized by this never-ending struggle. It was also clear that the Palestinian autonomous government, despite criticisms of the authoritarianism, incompetence, and corruption of some of its leaders, had contrived in the absence of any credible alternative to impose its authority. The legislative council (meaning the Parliament elected in January 1996) saw the entry into politics of a number of local notables and members of the devout middle class, most of them linked to the PLO. They appeared interested more in pragmatic issues than in ideological proclamations and were inclined to get into step with "everyday Palestinians," who no longer expected the golden age promised by jihad.[16] Hamas itself, fearing a division in the ranks of Palestinians, believed that the Zionists had managed to avoid facing the movement and its program of jihad by hiding behind the Palestinian Authority. It was also aware, however, that if it confronted the PA militarily it would achieve one of the principal objectives of the Zionists.[17] The weakening of Hamas and the control by the Palestinian Authority security forces of the young urban poor had been two of the main objectives of successive Israeli governments.

The Palestinian Authority needed to be granted some political and economic dividends for implementing a policy that would achieve these goals—otherwise it would find itself in an awkward situation vis-à-vis Palestinian society. With Hamas ebbing by early 2000, the PA found itself alone in its relationship with Israel. There had been no major breakthrough toward the establishment of a viable Palestinian state, and, with unemployment high, the economic situation was gloomy. The two estranged Palestinian territories of Gaza on the one side and the West Bank on the other was beginning to look like a permanent rather than provisional arrangement—one that would leave Palestine a shattered entity. The Oslo peace process had reached a stalemate. Mounting frustration on both sides impeded any progress in the Israeli-Palestinian negotiations under the auspices of President Bill Clinton, then in the last months of his tenure.

Each camp contained factions that hoped to reap political benefits from renewed tension. The Israeli rightist Ariel Sharon saw an opportunity both to oust his rival, the former prime minister Benjamin Netanyahu, as leader of the Likud coalition and to shift the balance of forces toward the right whenever new elections took place. Tension with the Palestinians, he thought, would be perceived by voters as a threat against Israel's security, and they would cast their ballot accordingly. A highly publicized and heavily protected stroll Sharon took on the Mosque Esplanade in Jerusalem was interpreted by the Muslim populace as an intentional insult, and it ignited demonstrations of fury in retaliation. They developed into a full-blown uprising, encouraged by Arafat's Fatah organization (known as *Tanzim*, from its name in Arabic).

Arafat viewed this second intifada—called the "Al Aqsa intifada," after the mosque where Sharon took his stroll—as a means to mobilize Palestinian society anew behind his leadership and to pressure Israel into accepting the PA's demands for the creation of a viable Palestinian state. In his view, political tension should ultimately serve his cause: Israel could not bear it and would have to yield; meanwhile, he would appear on the domestic Palestinian scene as the champion of the nationalist cause, foiling any attempt by Hamas and the Islamist radicals of Islamic Jihad to outflank his own troops. Conversely, Sharon saw Palestinian turmoil as a means to win at the polls, and he succeeded. Confronting Israeli skepticism in the face of mounting insecurity and a radical breach of confidence in relations with the Palestinian Authority, Ehud Barak had called for general elections. Voters turned out *en masse* to elect a hawkish Knesset, with Sharon as prime minister.

From that point on, tension escalated to a level that had not been seen since the establishment of the Palestinian Authority. By mid-2001, Arafat was losing ground to the radicals, both Islamists and younger Fatah activists who believed that violence, not merely tension, was the only strategy capable of achieving the desired political outcome. Suicide bombers became the main symbols of this second intifada. They blew themselves to death in Israeli pizzerias and bus stations, killing as many Jews as they could, while Islamist religious authorities called for jihad. They claimed that Israeli civilians, including women, were legitimate targets because Israel was a military society where everybody, regardless of gender, performed military service. Lebanese Hezbollah had forced Israel to leave Lebanon by using suicide bombers; the same tactics would now be applied in the Al Aqsa intifada.

But this time, Israeli retaliation was severe. Sophisticated weaponry guided by intelligence reports targeted with precision many leaders of radical movements, while Arafat was pressured into taking extreme action against the terrorists. Gradually, Israeli military action destroyed, with a vengeance, the infrastructure supporting his political power. Images of this unnamed Arab-Israeli war of attrition shocked the Arab and Muslim world. The suicide bombers became heroes of the youth and of a wide segment of the populace—a development that put pressure on pro-West Arab governments. This demonstration of Israeli military might provoked rage and frustration, as it became only too obvious that no Arab army could match the Israeli Defense Forces and take up its challenge in the future.

One has to keep in mind this perception of the Middle East conflict when trying to understand the reaction of the "Arab street" to the events of September 11. The planes that crashed into the twin towers and the Pentagon were perceived both as a continuation of the terrorists' strategy of suicide bombing and as a fitting response to the Israeli (and Western) military challenge. For Arafat—who was filmed giving his blood for the New York victims—September 11 signaled that he was at risk of failing to keep the Al Aqsa intifada under control. For Sharon, whose propaganda machine equated the PA chairman with Osama bin Laden, September 11 provided an incentive to use force without restraint—since the West would now give *carte blanche* to any policies aimed at fighting terrorism, regardless of the methods or means. Palestinian Islamist radicals, following Al Qaeda's example, showed no more restraint than did Israel, and embarked on a fresh cycle of suicide bombings—a tactic that ultimately may harm Palestinian society as deeply as the sequels to September 11 may harm Arab societies as a whole.

The Muslim Brothers in Jordan

By the end of 1990, five months after Saddam Hussein's army invaded Kuwait, the international coalition forces stationed in Saudi Arabia, the Land of the Two Holy Places, were ready to launch Operation Desert Storm. King Hussein of Jordan, the West's principal interlocutor in the Levant, chose New Year's Day 1991 to nominate a new cabinet, 6 of whose 21 members belonged to the Islamist movement. Such heavy representation at the highest levels of power in Jordan reflected the influence the movement had won for itself in the parliamentary elections of 1989, when it captured 34 seats out of 80. In this small nation of 3.5 million inhabitants, more than half of whom were of Palestinian origin, the regime was in pressing need of help from the Muslim Brothers and their allies to contain public hostility to the coalition's war against Iraq. It was feared, with good reason, that the fury of the people might easily get out of hand and focus on Jordan's own fragile monarchy.

The Jordanian and Palestinian Muslim Brothers had a long, shared history. During the two decades when the West Bank belonged to the Hashemite kingdom (1948–1967), they had been part of the same organization. Since the Muslim Brothers' creation in 1946—the same year that Jordan itself became a nation—the organization had been a staunch defender of the throne.[18] It offered religious legitimacy to the monarchy in exchange for royal favor, at a time when the Brothers in other nationalist-dominated Arab countries were being hounded from pillar to post. By dint of prudent political maneuvering during the first decades of their existence, the Jordanian Brothers had won control of a network of mosques and charitable associations through which they exercised considerable influence over the devout population.[19] These religious venues offered the most effective field of action for local notables, while the central power remained in the hands of the Hashemite dynasty, which the Al-Saud family had expelled from Arabia in 1925.[20]

On the West Bank of the River Jordan, which Israel had annexed in the war of 1967, the Palestinian Muslim Brothers persisted in their strictly pietist attitude for twenty years longer, until the launching of the intifada and the creation of Hamas in December 1987. On the East Bank, in Jordan, they provided King Hussein, who had been threatened on several occasions by Arab nationalist conspiracies and by unrest among Palestinian refugees, with the priceless support of their networks in the cities. With the exception of Abdallah Azzam and a few dozen of his disciples, between 1967 and 1970 the Jordanian Brothers did not engage in the struggle against Israel, because they did not want to fight alongside the "secularists" from the PLO.[21] And in September 1970, when the monarchy itself became engaged in a bloody ten-day civil war with Palestinian guerrillas (including Al Fatah and the PLO), the Brothers loyally supported the monarchy. When the shooting ended, they received their reward. During the 1970s and 1980s, they took in and trained the Syrian Brothers, who were then engaged in a confrontation with Hafez al-Asad.[22] Certain individuals from among their militants and sympathizers were then given important posts in the royal administration, and they used these positions to recruit, in their turn, officials and administrators from within the brotherhood.

In 1984, for the first time since 1976, a partial election for Parliament was held. Three out of the eight available seats were won by the Brothers, with one more going to an "independent Islamist." This success at direct political involvement took place at a moment when the Islamist movement was expanding throughout the world. But locally, the electoral breakthrough occurred during a period of tension with the king, who had negotiated a rapprochement with Syria whereby the Syrian Brothers who had escaped to Jordan would be surrendered to Damascus and prominent, influential Jordanian Islamists would be removed from the administration.

In April 1989 riots broke out in Maan, in south Jordan, following an agreement with the International Monetary Fund that led to steep price increases for consumer goods. The rioters attacked symbols of state power, just as their Algerian counterparts had done; and just as happened in Algeria, the Islamists stepped forward and presented

themselves as intermediaries to help restore order and satisfy some of
the demands of the protesters. In both countries the movement was rewarded with the chance to take part in an open, relatively free vote. In
Algeria—a state governed by the army and ill-prepared for electoral
maneuvering—the FIS won a landslide victory in the municipal elections of June 1990. The Jordanian Brothers, in a country where the palace was very experienced in electoral politics, obtained 22 seats, to
which were added 12 independent Islamist members.[23] With more than
40 percent of the 80 seats available, the Islamists were now the largest single bloc in the assembly, but it still could not control the government.

The decision to take part in the elections was the consequence of an
internal debate between moderate Brothers (mostly drawn from the
devout middle class of the East Bank) and radical Brothers, whose
main source of support was among the Palestinian sector of the population, chiefly the more recently arrived refugees and young people
from the camps. The moderates were all in favor of political participation, and in the course of the 1990s they became more and more
committed to notions of democracy. The radicals, who were generally
hostile to democratic procedures, which they viewed as impious, nonetheless demanded their quota of candidates once the decision to take
part had been made by the majlis al-shura (consultative council) of the
brotherhood. Among the candidates were a number of preachers who
would later use the parliamentary forum as a pulpit.

The sociopolitical program of the radical Brothers did not include
any measures that threatened the status quo. It was mainly characterized by a wish to make the entire legislative apparatus conform to the
sharia and to strengthen religious education, which provided a source
of employment for many militants as well as a means to influence the
younger generation. As in other countries, Islamist ideology's chief
function was to mobilize social groups with different agendas into a
single force, by demanding the moral regeneration of an impious state.
But the long-term ideal was the installation of a true Islamic state. In
Jordan, this strategy's success hinged on maintaining an efficient pater-
nalist network of charitable associations linked to mosques, hospitals,
dispensaries, and schools, which offered help from the cradle to university for the country's neediest citizens. In a nation where health cover-

age was a mere token gesture and other public benefits were sorely lacking, the Brothers and their sympathizers were the leading providers of social services, along with various charitable associations sponsored by the queen.[24]

But the Brothers were also influential among the well-to-do middle class, to whom they offered social services for a fee. Because of these lucrative arrangements, they were able to build financial empires controlled by the various factions of their movement—among whom doctrinal and religious disputes were often merely a smokescreen for deeper struggles over market share.[25] For all these reasons, the mediation of the Brothers in the wake of the spring 1989 riots appeared indispensable to the Jordanian regime. They were admitted to Parliament—a concession they viewed as a chance to influence legislation and enshrine themselves in the nation's institutions.

This was the tense backdrop in Jordan against which Saddam Hussein's invasion of Kuwait on August 2, 1990, occurred. Here, as elsewhere, his action sidelined an Islamist movement that was torn between the Saudi sympathies of its devout middle class and the pro-Iraqi, anti-Western zeal of its impoverished urban base. Moreover, the sizable Palestinian contingent in Kuwait welcomed the Iraqi army, which they regarded as a pan-Arab liberating force—a view shared by their Palestinian compatriots in Jordan, among whom Saddam also enjoyed strong support. The final straw was the arrival of coalition troops in the Land of the Two Holy Places. This swung the religiously inclined sector of the public decisively against the Western camp, and the Brothers, including their moderate and pro-Saudi elements, all adopted this anti-Western line, taking their place at the head of what appeared to be a genuine popular movement.

For King Hussein, who for many years had maintained strong links with the United States, the overriding priority was to prevent his throne from being swept away by a tidal wave of unrest caused by the allied military intervention. His response was to name the first cabinet in Jordanian history to include seven Islamist ministers, one third of its total complement. The strategic ministries (defense, foreign affairs, interior, and information) remained under palace control, while the Brothers and their confederates received the ministries of education, health, religious affairs, and social development. This gave them control of the state budget and the distribution of government posts in the ministries they had won, and it completed their penetration of society through control of social services, governmental as well as charitable.[26]

However, the Brothers' political power was once again short-lived. On June 17—with the danger past, Iraq defeated, and its supporters in confusion—King Hussein abruptly named a new prime minister to bring Jordan into the Middle East peace process under the aegis of the United States. This eventually led to a treaty between Israel and Jordan, signed on October 26 at Wadi Araba, in a move that was anathema to most of the Brothers. They were not invited to join the new government, and thereafter the monarchy kept their opportunities for political expression to a minimum. An ad hoc modification of the Jordanian electoral law led to the loss of 6 of their seats in the Assembly in the 1993 elections (they were left with 16 out of their original 22). The Brothers went on to boycott the 1997 elections, expelling from their ranks all members who had taken a liking to power and had accepted government commissions or portfolios.

Participation in elections and in the government sorely tested the coherence of an Islamist movement that had nonetheless succeeded, unlike most of its counterparts in other countries, in preserving within a single organization—the Muslim Brothers—the overwhelming majority of its sympathizers. The Brothers in Jordan had never been seriously challenged by other Islamist groups—unlike Hamas in nearby Palestine, which had to cope with the rivalry of Islamic Jihad and then with the growing autonomy of the Al-Qassam Brigades; unlike the Egyptian Brothers, who yielded the initiative to the radical Gamaa Islamiya; and unlike the FIS in Algeria, which completely lost control of the GIA.[27] In 1990, a few dozen militants returned to Jordan from Afghanistan, where they had been galvanized by Abdallah Azzam, and created an Army of the Prophet Mohammed. In the early months of 1991, while Desert Storm was still raining bombs on Iraq, they used the combat techniques they had learned in the Peshawar camps against Jordanian shopkeepers, for selling alcohol, and against the nation's tiny Christian minority. These men were promptly arrested and jailed, before being pardoned in December by the king. Other small groups made up of former "Afghans" occasionally came to the surface prior to 1996, but without making much of an impression on a political-religious scene that the Brothers had cordoned off much more tightly than had their Egyptian counterparts.[28]

Apart from this extremist opposition, there was one other peculiarity in Jordan: the group of independent Islamists who emerged to take part in elections. These notables sought to capitalize on the Islamist movement without losing their individual freedom to maneuver by joining the Brothers' organization.

Just as they did everywhere else, the Brothers provided an umbrella for a host of different factions falling between the two poles of the young urban poor and the devout middle class. The former were mostly Palestinians from refugee camps and shantytowns, while the latter came mostly from traditional East Bank townships like Salt and Irbid. But the organization had no spokesman or Islamist intellectual of sufficient stature to mobilize the people—no one who could denounce the godless regime as the root of all evil and raise the street as well as the bazaar in fury against it, as Khomeini had done in Iran. The Hashemite monarchy had taken the utmost care to woo the most brilliant Islamist intellectuals into its privileged net. Thus Ishaq Farhan, an eminent university professor of Palestinian origin, was minister of education and later minister of religious affairs between 1970 and 1973. He suspended his previous activities in the hierarchy of the Brothers, though he recruited a number of their militants and fellow travelers into his government bureaucracy. Thus the Jordanian Islamist intelligentsia was reluctant to denounce their government, as the Brothers in other countries tended to do, so long as the monarchy depended on religious organizations and leaders to legitimize its own existence, and rewarded them, in turn, with influence and prestige. A Jordanian Islamist intellectual could easily find an occupation as an ideologist for the regime if he was prepared to make minor adjustments in his expressed opinions. This put a stop to more than a few budding radical vocations and in general disposed the Brothers much more to negotiation than to confrontation.

The doctrinal flexibility that prevailed in Jordan did not prevent the emergence of more vigorous views within the Islamist movement itself. By 1989 there were two clearly divergent schools of thought—the doves, who favored electoral participation and symbiosis with the political establishment, and the hawks, who were influenced in their radical rhetoric by the writings of Sayyid Qutb. For the Jordanian Brothers, the main difficulty was keeping within a single united organization all these conflicting layers of society, despite strong forces that pulled leaders of the devout middle class toward the system and pushed leaders of the young, urban poor away from it. To some extent, the coexistence of these opposing groups, each of which had the means to bring the organization's machinery to a grinding halt, produced a kind of reciprocal, balanced inertia. But on the other hand, a decisive split between them would have condemned the movement to the fate of its peers in the rest of the Arab world, who were fighting among themselves for control of the religious arena, to the delight of "impious" secular regimes.

A way out of this dilemma appeared in 1992 with the creation of a legally recognized Islamist party, under the name of the Islamic Action Front. Led by the former minister Ishaq Farhan (one of the more prominent doves and a future president of Zarqa University, a private institution), its purpose was to achieve full political participation, while the Brothers' paramount goal was preaching and social work. The party adopted the language of democracy, opening its ranks to women as well as men, while the Brotherhood remained hostile to unfamiliar democratic ideals and did not admit female members.[29] But Farhan's desire to play the institutional game had been dampened by the government's manipulation of the election in 1993 and also by the signing of the peace treaty with Israel in 1994. After that date, any participation in Jordan's institutions looked like a tacit endorsement of the "shameful peace with the Jews," which was despised by most Islamists. Pressure from the grassroots forced the party to boycott the 1997 elections, even though its head had officially announced that the IAF would participate. Thereafter, the Islamist movement, at a time when Jordan's ailing king was no longer directly controlling the nation's affairs, had to grapple with rising tension between its original, pragmatic, middle-class elite, who wished to join the political fray and had created the IAF with that objective, and a populist base that preferred to subordinate participation in the elections to ideological considerations.

After the death of King Hussein and the accession to the throne of his son, Abdullah II, in June 1999, the party gave guarantees of goodwill to the new sovereign, who had named an ex-Muslim Brother as his first prime minister. At the municipal elections in July, the IAF submitted its own list of candidates, most of whom were returned to office;

they were urban dignitaries who took over the city halls of the me-
dium-sized towns. However, in August the regime made an indirect
move against the Islamists by closing down the offices of Palestinian
Hamas, which were located on premises in Amman belonging to its
Jordanian fraternal organization and acted as a foreign headquarters.
On their return from a meeting in Tehran, the leaders of Hamas who
had Jordanian passports were jailed, and the others were expelled from
the country.[30] With this abrupt crackdown, the new Hashemite monarch showed that he could still influence events on the other side of the
River Jordan in order to satisfy Israeli, American, and PLO demands.

For Arafat, the foreign leadership of Hamas was an extremist cell
that he wished to eliminate, at a moment when he was looking for a
rapprochement with Islamists in the territories—notably with Sheik
Yassin, who now showed himself more open to negotiation. But the arrests by the Jordanian police also created a crisis of confidence between
the throne and the Palestinian component of the Jordanian Muslim
Brothers, which the hawks controlled. The repression of the exiled radical leaders of Hamas by the authorities in Amman was in line with
what most other Muslim countries were trying to achieve in the waning months of the twentieth century: namely, a rapid dismantling of
the Islamic movement by isolating and repressing the young urban
poor and their intransigent spokesmen and by embracing those of the
devout middle class who wished to participate in the political system.[31]
It remains to be seen if this tactic is a simple expedient for shifting the
balance of power decisively toward authoritarian regimes, by taking
advantage of the crisis situation currently affecting the Islamist movements, or whether the result will be a broadening of consensus through
democratic participation, following the example of King Hussein in the
early 1990s.

CHAPTER

15

The Forced Secularization of
Turkish Islamists

On June 28, 1996, in Ankara, Necmettin Erbakan, the leader of the Refah Islamist party, was named prime minister of the republic.[1] The event horrified the heirs of Kemal Ataturk, for whom the arrival in power of an Islamist politician represented a monstrous heresy against Kemalist dogma. Whatever their reaction, most observers saw the development as yet another episode in the triumphant advance of a worldwide movement that had already won control of the back country of Algeria, had threatened the Egyptian government, and had just unleashed a wave of attacks in France. In the months that followed, Osama bin Laden broadcast his declaration of jihad on the United States, and the Taliban seized Kabul. Islamism still seemed to be ascendant.

The Islamist government in Turkey lasted only a year, however, and its demise embodied the waning fortunes of political Islam around the world in the last years of the twentieth century. On June 18, 1997, the parliamentary coalition supporting Erbakan fell apart under pressure from the army high command, and the prime minister resigned. Six months later, on January 18, 1998, the Turkish Constitutional Committee dissolved the Refah party, without provoking the violence that some had feared. In the following year, the Fazilet (Virtue) party, which took Refah's place, was trounced in the general elections (parliamentary and local) of April 18, 1999, despite widespread expectations of a Fazilet victory. Whatever the role played by the military in the fate of Turkish Islamism, the movement had been compelled to function according to the rules of a pluralist, relatively democratic system, which for over twenty-five years had incorporated the Islamist movement as one of the main components of the nation's parliamentary life. For many Islamist militants and electors, pragmatic considerations were at least as important as their ideological and doctrinal beliefs.

To a great extent, Turkish Islamism anticipated the rise and decline that most of its fraternal organizations would undergo in other Muslim countries. It emerged in more or less the same period: Erbakan founded his first political party in 1970, the year Khomeini held his conferences on Islamic government. That was also the year of Nasser's death and the Palestinian Black September massacre in Amman; with these events, the Arab world began to see nationalist ideology giving ground to the doctrines of the Muslim Brothers. In the mid-70s, Erbakan was appointed deputy prime minister—one of the first Islamists in the world to exercise the responsibilities of government. During the 1980s he took advantage of the general expansion in Islamist influence, even though he had to share the dividends with the dominant political figure of the period, Prime Minister (later President) Turgut Ozal, who was also from a religious background.

Erbakan's new party, the judiciously named Refah (Prosperity) party, was designed to admit the devout middle class—many of whom had recently migrated to the big cities from the Anatolian plateau—into the capitalist economic expansion then under way in Turkey. Growing in tandem with the party was an original breed of Islamist intellectuals fully in touch with modern trends in Western thought. During the 1990s, Erbakan, who had built solid networks and contacts within the Turkish diaspora in the West, was able to broaden his audience significantly, winning more than one vote in five at the 1995 legislative elections. This made Refah the largest single bloc in the Turkish Parliament. The party had benefited from divisions among the secular right-wing parties, but above all it used its slogan "Adil Duzen" (Just Order) to unite its original constituency of the devout middle class and Islamist intellectuals with the young urban poor of the informal shantytowns "built overnight" (gecekondu).

When Refah came to power in the summer of 1996 at the head of a parliamentary coalition, it was the first Islamist party in the world forced to grapple with democratic constraints—constraints that the various elements of its electorate, under hostile pressure from the Turkish military, ultimately proved unable to withstand. In a "postmodern coup d'état," the army incited certain coalition deputies to renounce their support of Erbakan and bring down his cabinet in June 1997. This was followed by the dissolution of the Refah party for "antisecularist activities" a few months later. Contrary to the expectations of many observers, this did not lead to a revolt in the gecekondu or radical activity among the young urban poor. As it turned out, these urban youths had been neglected by the Refah-dominated government in favor of the devout middle class, and consequently the middle class was the only group to give their votes to Refah's successor, the Fazilet party, in April 1999. In losing the attraction it had formerly enjoyed for the various groups united in support of Islamist ideology, the party became a humdrum part of the Turkish political landscape and resigned itself to expressing the religious interests of a single segment of society, an expression it was forced to dispute with the extreme right nationalists, who were the principal gainers from Fazilet's 1999 electoral debacle.

Three Incarnations of Turkish Islamism

Erbakan, like many eminent Islamists, was trained as an engineer. When he founded the Party of National Order (Milli Nizam Partisi, or MNP) on January 26, 1970, he was already the head of the industrial branch of the Turkish Union of Chambers of Commerce.[2] Having crossed over from the Justice party—a right-wing array of militants with a religious background who had no tolerance for the official secularism installed by Ataturk— Erbakan was fresh from his election as an independent member of Parliament for the Konya constituency in central Anatolia, a conservative bastion and a traditional center for the religious brotherhoods banned by Ataturk in 1925. Erbakan himself was the disciple of a sheik of one of these brotherhoods.[3]

His political program had a double thrust, Islamist and technocratic. A keen advocate of industrialization, Erbakan was deeply hostile to the West and especially to the European Economic Community, which gave expression to the Islamist movement's trinity of demons: freemasons, Crusaders, and Zionists.[4] He declared himself in favor of the values of "order," among which he placed the moral conservatism of religion and the defense of social hierarchies—the special mission of the right. His targeted constituent at that time was the small Anatolian entrepreneur concerned with modernizing his business and gaining access to the technology and capital previously monopolized by the secular, cosmopolitan bourgeoisie of Izmir and Istanbul.

The MNP deliberately distinguished itself from the right-wing parties appealing to religious sentiment (like Suleyman Demirel's Justice party). Erbakan did not seek to annex religion as a support for yet another brand of conservative nationalism but instead saw belonging to Islam as the essence of Turkish identity. His was an Islam close in spirit to that of the Egyptian Muslim Brothers or the Pakistani Jamaat-e-Islami; but within the restrictive framework of the secular Turkish state, it could not express itself as such for fear of an immediate clampdown. The army carried out a coup d'état in March 1971, and on May 20 the Constitutional Council banned the MNP for jeopardizing the secular character of the republic in the first of three successive dissolutions of parties founded by Erbakan.

On October 11, 1972, the MNP was reborn under the name of the Party of National Salvation (Milli Selamet Partisi, or MSP).[5] A year later, during the legislative elections of October 1973, the MSP won nearly 12 percent of the vote, along with the balance of power between the two major parliamentary parties: Bulent Ecevit's social democratic People's Republican Party and Demirel's Justice Party. The MSP's deepest political inroads were made in Turkey's provincial towns, where the traditional guilds of craftsmen and shopkeepers were very powerful: as soon as the party entered the government, it championed the interests of these guilds.[6] As he controlled 49 members of Parliament and the key to any government coalition, Erbakan showed complete indifference to the political complexion of his partner in power—first Ecevit, then Demirel—but great interest in the major job-providing ministries assigned to the MSP (justice, interior, commerce, agriculture, and industry).[7] Control of these ministries allowed him to introduce his own reliable supporters into every level of the bureaucracy, and their influence would tell in the long term.

Erbakan also made sure that pupils at the "schools for imams and preachers" (imam hatip lisesi) could apply to universities on an equal footing with those who had attended secular schools, a measure that greatly contributed to the formation of an Islamist intellectual elite in the decades that followed.[8] With its overriding priorities of "heavy industry, morality, and spirituality," the MSP expressed the aspirations of this religious faction to take in hand the nation's modernization and give it an Islamic face. And indeed his MSP ministers fought openly against "Westernization," censoring films that they judged obscene, placing restrictions on the sale of beer, and opening prayer rooms in their office buildings.

The parliamentary instability of the last years of the 1970s, which resulted in a weak Turkish government and an average death rate from extremist violence of 20 people per day, eventually led to the third military coup d'état in modern Turkish history, on September 12, 1980. The Islamist movement had not been spared a certain radicalization during the time of domestic turbulence that followed the triumph of the Iranian revolution. Six days before the coup, at a meeting of the MSP in Konya to discuss the "liberation of Jerusalem," there had been calls for a return to the sharia. Delegates had also refused to rise during the playing of the national anthem and had brandished banners written in Arabic. These were serious affronts to Kemalist precepts, and the generals seized on them to justify their intervention. Like the other Turkish political parties, the MSP was dissolved, and its leaders, along with 723 of the most prominent political figures, were stripped of their civil rights. Erbakan himself was arrested and tried in April 1981, only to be released in July.

The third incarnation of Turkish Islamism, the Prosperity party (Refah Partisi), did not surface until July 19, 1983, and Erbakan was not officially acknowledged as its head until October 1987, when the ban on former political leaders of the 1970s was lifted by referendum. Nevertheless, it was during the first half of the 1980s, when the apparatus of the Islamist party was at its lowest ebb, that major changes took place which were to lead to the short-lived triumph of the Refah party. These changes also set Turkish Islamism apart from that of other countries and made the adoption of democratic ideals by many of its followers easier. Like its foreign counterparts, the movement benefited from the general Islamist expansion of those years, while sustaining the same contradictions; these it succeeded in overcoming by avoiding the drift toward violence that took a toll elsewhere in the final decades of the century. But it paid a heavy political price, in losing part of its doctrinal substance.

A radical faction did appear in Turkey at the turn of the 1980s, chiefly among militants fascinated by the Iranian revolution and by extremist Arab groups.[9] Buoyed by the attention paid to the "Islamist danger" by the generals who staged the coup, these militants mostly concentrated their efforts in the universities. A rich field of protest had been opened for them by a ruthless crackdown on students of both the right and left who had been the main activists behind the violence of the late 1970s. But this radical student Islamism never took hold in Turkish society, nor did it strike a chord with the impoverished youth of Turkey's cities, in contrast to the Egyptian and Algerian experience. In effect, when the Refah party was in its infancy, political Islam was dominated by figures from civil society, a fact that favored the emergence of autonomous Islamist intellectuals. This intelligentsia was much more concerned with finding a place in a pluralist system that was becoming progressively liberalized and with defining its role in a secular state than with promoting a dynamic of revolutionary alliance between social classes to bring down the "ungodly" government and build a new Islamic state on its ruins.

Furthermore, in the absence of an official, organized Islamist party, a sizable percentage of Islamist sympathizers joined the Motherland party (Anavatan Partisi, or ANAP), which was founded in May 1983 by Turgut Ozal and won a resounding victory in the ballot organized in November, the first one following the military coup.[10] This party was heir to the center-right party of Suleyman Demirel in the preceding decade, and accordingly it attracted the votes of the devout middle class in Anatolia, which was particularly impressed by Ozal's reputation for piety—his brother, Kerkut Ozal, was very closely associated with the religious brotherhoods.[11] Turgut Ozal had furnished the Kemalist generals with sufficient guarantees for them to authorize his party to take part in the elections, and his manifesto laid special emphasis on economic and political liberalism as the only solution for Turkey's current impasse. Employers and young educated professionals who were aware of trends abroad appreciated his policies favoring a market economy, rapprochement with Western Europe, and the restoration of civil liberties. Thus, the ANAP contrived to unite a number of differing sensibilities, opening to the devout middle class a possibility of access to circles of power and to modernity. This integrated this group into the dominant political system, making it all the harder for a broad-based, openly dissident Islamist movement to coalesce.

Meanwhile, the military command took measures of its own to

strengthen the state's control over Islam's forms of expression. In 1982, the ruling generals made religious education compulsory in state schools. As they saw it, this was a way of providing the young with a form of instruction that was free from "fanatical" or "extremist" influences.[12] General Kenan Evren, the head of the National Security Council, openly urged parents to send their children to these courses, rather than to the "illegal" Koranic classes whose promoters were prosecuted by the law.[13] This measure was similar to those taken during the same period by a number of leaders in other Muslim countries, with a view to controlling and forestalling the Islamist expansion of the 1980s. Its results in Turkey were just as ambiguous as they were everywhere else, for the religious personnel responsible for the "modern" teaching of Islam had in most cases been recruited to administrations headed by ministers of Erbakan's MSP in the second half of the 1970s.[14]

Another factor tending to bind the devout middle class to the government created by the September 1980 coup came from the Turkish-Islamic Synthesis (Turk Islam Sentesi, or TIS), a movement whose effect was to confuse the Islamist message. At its beginning, the TIS represented a group of conservative intellectuals who challenged the dominant position of leftist intellectuals in the university and the press during the 1970s.[15] It saw Islamic culture as a necessary moral complement to the values of law and order embodied in Turkish nationalism. Thus, the TIS became the *bête noire* for secularist militants, who gave it credit for the inroads made by political Islam during the previous quarter of a century and viewed its existence as a plot hatched by reactionary sectors of the government to hamper progress. It was true that the TIS had influenced the instigators of the coup, by supplying a doctrinal link between a few of them and Ozal's ANAP, which won the 1983 elections. The very existence of the TIS, and the attraction it held for intellectuals whose ideas were close to those of the Islamists, contributed to a certain toning-down of Islamists' views to suit the bourgeoisie.

As was happening simultaneously in Jordan, where the regime was deliberately courting theorists belonging to the Muslim Brothers (who subsequently lost all their radical drive and ceased to worry about stirring up the young urban poor), Turkey in the 1980s offered a number of job openings and other opportunities for social advancement, which operated as enticements to the counter-elites of the Islamist movement.

This progress was made easier by the rapid transition at that time from a controlled economy to a liberal one presided over by Ozal. The period was also one of remarkable freedom of expression in Turkey, by comparison with other countries of the Muslim world. An authentic marketplace of ideas, competitive and capitalist, had arisen, and the result was a burgeoning of written and audiovisual media in the private sector throughout the 1990s.[16] This market created jobs for large numbers of Islamist intellectuals in social organizations controlled by the movement. It also nudged their opinions closer to the mainstream, by obliging them to compete with others in media that depended financially on advertisers and shied away from any form of extremism that might alienate readers and spectators, thus reducing advertising revenue.

The Islamist counter-elites of the 1980s, embodied in the bearded engineer and the veiled female student, were proof of the arrival in force, within the educated urban world, of the children of the Anatolian migrants of the previous decade.[17] This generation brought Islamic culture and way of life—as transmitted by the brotherhoods and religious associations—back to center stage in the cities and universities of Turkey, which until that time had been regulated by the Western social codes imposed by Ataturk. A roughly similar phenomenon occurred in other Muslim countries, but the political and economic liberalism of Turkey at that time offered greater possibilities for social recognition, at the same time that it exposed people to the dominant culture of secularism.

Thereafter, tension between Islamists who favored a pragmatic approach and those who preferred a doctrinaire one continued to build. While politics was dominated by Ozal (who remained prime minister until 1989, then president of the republic until his death in April 1993), the pragmatic Islamists flourished. The doctrinaire faction came in on the coattails of Erbakan and his third political party, Refah, whose successes during the 1990s followed a decline in the popularity of ANAP after its founder's death. Indeed, the loss of Ozal was a mortal blow to ANAP and cleared the way for a full-scale expansion of the Refah Islamist party.

At the time of its creation in 1983, Refah was not authorized to present candidates at the parliamentary elections. Despite its steady gains at the polls, between 1984 and 1991 it never won more than 10 percent of the vote.[18] But in 1991 an alliance with the extreme right nationalists allowed Refah to cross this threshold—mandatory for any party looking to have seats in the Parliament—and bring it within sight of the best-ever returns of its predecessor, the MSP, in 1973 (11.3 percent). It was only after Ozal's death that Refah began making substantial gains, almost doubling its percentage in the March 1994 municipal elections and registering major symbolic victories by winning control of the city halls of Istanbul and Ankara along with those of 325 other cities and towns. On December 24, 1995, with more than 21 percent of the votes at the parliamentary elections, an Islamist party became Turkey's largest single party for the first time in the history of the modern republic. That Christmas Eve was a time of stunned consternation in the secular camp—even though the triumph of Refah was basically attributable to a split in the Turkish right, whose two parties each received slightly less than 20 percent of the vote.[19]

The doubling of the Refah vote in 1994–95 was a milestone (even though it was hardly comparable to the Algerian FIS's landslide victory in the municipal elections of June 1990 and in the first round of the December 1991 parliamentary elections).[20] It attracted a mass of new voters along with its traditional support among the devout middle class of Anatolia. It also reaped a windfall from ANAP's sudden decline. By the end of the 1990s the ultra-liberalism of this party had led to general corruption and an exponential inflation that had a significant effect on wages. Beginning in 1985, problems had arisen around the fact of Islamic expansion: the government had tolerated, or encouraged, the opening of new mosques and the institution of courses in the Koran, in the expectation that it would be able to control the growth and expression of religious sentiment. Instead, conflicts over religious practice had broken the consensus between the religious and the military camps of which Ozal was the guarantor and had promoted strategies of confrontation and rupture for which the Islamist party made itself the prime mover.

In 1986, the Higher Education Council—a state organization—refused to allow women wearing the veil to enter Turkish universities, a decision that led in January 1987 to demonstrations in Istanbul and Konya organized by Erbakan's confederates. The agitation over the veil created further problems for the government, which forced Ozal, who was in favor of the free wearing of the turban, to give way under pressure from the generals and then to expel the key Islamist-leaning members from ANAP in July. In 1989, the veil was forbidden at the universities by the Constitutional Council, which concluded its decision by noting that "the Republic and democracy are the antithesis of government by sharia."[21]

The government's willingness to tolerate a circumscribed form of Islam had collided head-on with the actions of militants seeking to press home their advantage by annexing symbolic positions of power. This pressure upset the secular norms established by Ataturk, whose ultimate guarantors were, in the eyes of the military commanders, themselves. As in France, where the first major confrontation over the veil in state schools also occurred in 1989, the Islamist argument had a twofold thrust. To Muslims, the wearing of the veil was presented as an obligation imposed by the Koran, to which the faithful must submit. To the rest of public opinion, it was portrayed as a fundamental issue of freedom of religion and individual expression, a "right of man" (or woman) that an authoritarian, secular government was denying to students, who should be free to follow the injunctions of the sharia should they choose to do so.[22]

Unlike the governments in most Muslim countries, which accepted or encouraged the wearing of the veil in schools and universities—conceding the social and religious domain to the Islamist movement while keeping politics under their own exclusive control—the Turkish state was determined to keep its grip on public morality as well as politics. This was the main symbolic issue over which battle lines were drawn between the secular establishment and the Islamists: and it led to a prolonged stalemate, with no decisive victory for either camp, since neither was prepared to lose face. However, real breakthroughs were made in the social and economic sectors, where Ataturk's state had known its most dramatic failures hitherto.

The move to a market economy, presided over by Ozal, coincided with the arrival in the major cities of entrepreneurs from small Anatolian towns seeking new contacts. At about the same time, the first generation of devout engineers from the same milieu, who had received their diplomas in the 1970s, reached an age when they could expect to take on major professional responsibilities. Privatization and liberalism suddenly offered them unheard-of business opportunities both inside and outside Turkey. The oil-rich Arabian peninsula, for example, was both an outlet for Turkish exports and a source of Saudi and Kuwaiti capital investment for the rapidly expanding Turkish domestic market, where Islamic banks and investment corporations had begun to spring up in the form of joint ventures.[23] For the regime in Riyadh, support for the emerging devout middle class in Turkey was part of a global political strategy to back this social stratum.

Moving to a market economy was also an economic windfall for religiously inclined entrepreneurs who had connections with Ozal's ANAP or with Erbakan's Prosperity party. A number of these devout Anatolian businessmen now had access to bank loans without interest, in obedience to Islamic law, from which the leading conventional banks had previously barred them. In 1990 they founded their own employers' association, the Musiad, in competition with the Turkish Employers' Federation, the Tusiad, which was run by the leading capitalists in Istanbul.[24] The Musiad was simultaneously a small business organization and an Islamist-leaning lobbying tool. Its members had set out to create a structure for mutual assistance in order to defend their specific interests against the secular bourgeoisie, in both the commercial and the cultural sphere. There was a clear ideological dimension to it— for example, the Musiad demanded a Muslim Common Market to rival the EEC's "Christian Club"—but it also maintained a steady pro-business attitude; its members hoped to use the organization to defend their market share and expand it to its limits. Combining Islamic morality with a frankly capitalist spirit, they aspired one day to gain entry to the Turkish economic establishment, from which their modest regional origins and comparatively backward way of life had hitherto precluded them. They also ardently desired to enrich themselves and to enjoy their wealth to the hilt, without overstepping the bounds imposed by religion.

The most prominent of these Islamic businessmen frequented a luxury seaside hotel, the Caprice, where they spent lawful holidays with their families and veiled womenfolk, bathed on separate beaches, wore Islamically acceptable swimsuits, and ate expensive meals at the halal three-star restaurant. They discussed business in the hotel gym. This situation had its parallels in the wealthy orthodox Jewish community in Israel, and it demonstrated the ambivalence of this class's commitment to strict religious observance. The question was a fundamental one: should one join the struggle for an Islamic state and the application of the sharia, enlisting the young urban poor, or should one opt for a comfortable ascent through the ranks of the established order, applying a judicious blend of pressure and compromise vis-à-vis the state?

Turkish Islamist intellectuals who had crossed over from the left or cut their teeth on the Third World ideology of the Iranian revolution mocked the Musiad and its "veiled high society," accusing it of a readiness to do anything for profit. One of the leaders of this faction, Ali Bulac, who foresaw a division of the faithful into poor Muslims and rich ones, admonished the latter as follows: "If you are to reconcile your pursuit of economic gain with your religion, you must read books other than the Koran. You need not go back fifteen centuries. If you look among the books written only a hundred years ago, you will discover that easily the most important one—unfortunately written by a Jew—is entitled *Das Kapital* and treats of exploitation and class struggle."

This devout bourgeoisie with its confused political goals at first divided its loyalty between Ozal's ANAP and Erbakan's Refah. Later, after Ozal's death in 1993, it moved decisively toward Erbakan, anticipating an Islamist triumph at the polls from which it could expect a return on its heavy investment. The Prosperity party appeared set to win the elections; it had made an effort to channel the dissatisfaction of ordinary working-class people in the cities who had missed out during the unbridled economic liberalism of the 1980s and showed itself capable of controlling them. It would receive their votes, which would make its victory all the easier, and would prevent their sense of grievance from spilling over into disorder. By the same token, Refah appeared more than likely to win the support of the "green capitalists." Its campaigns during the 1990s were amply funded. Its efficient organization depended on the various managers who had been recruited into government administrations since the time of the MSP ministers. It could also use the Anatolian municipalities that the party had controlled since 1989, and state facilities had been available for its use since the day it won 40 seats in Parliament in October 1991. And if that were not enough, it had hired an advertising agency to streamline its television image, in the awareness that too "Anatolian" and retrograde a look might put off potential voters who saw themselves as more urban and modern.[25]

Thus, Refah was able to make appealing its slogan of "Just Order," which came at exactly the right time to claim the votes of those who found extremely unjust the new division of wealth resulting from the triumph of capitalism during Ozal's years in power. Unlike the other parties, which found themselves critically short of militants, Refah was able to deploy an electoral activism that was already well established at the grassroots. Its workers went door-to-door, registering the preferences of each elector in a computer database, targeting waverers and following up by telephone until they pledged their votes, and generally canvassing every street of every constituency they hoped to win.[26] Unlike the MSP in the 1970s, Refah did not campaign during the municipal elections of 1994 or the legislative elections of 1995 on the heightening of Islamic identity. This would have lessened its impact. Instead, judging that its support among pious electors was secure (they accounted for 10 percent of the total votes), it focused its message on economic and social issues. This strategy enabled it to win an additional 10 percent of voters, who, although they had nothing against the Islamists, did not necessarily define themselves as belonging to their number and mostly belonged to a younger, poorer stratum of society.[27]

Thanks to its successes in these two elections, Erbakan's party looked as though it had brought together the three components required of any Islamist movement that expected to win political power—the devout middle class, the young urban poor, and the Islamist intelligentsia. It even attracted other groups, which liked the sound of its promises of change but did not subscribe to its religious ideology. As a result, Refah finished first in the legislative elections of December 1995. But it won little more than a fifth of the available votes, and its leader had to wait six months before he could take his place as prime minister of Turkey. Far from advancing triumphantly toward an Islamic state governed by the sharia, he had to submit to the political compromises and contortions of a parliamentary coalition, in a constant reminder that more than three quarters of Turkey's enfranchised population had not voted for him.[28]

The Implosion of Turkey's Islamist Government

The coalition of Refah and Tansu Ciller's center-right Right Path party was a trial by fire for the Islamists. Its ultimate failure was largely due to the pressures exerted on it by the military hierarchy and the political establishment. It was also a consequence of insurmountable contradictions between the Islamist political project and the practical reality of running a democratic state linked to the West and hampered by growing disenchantment at the ruling party's electoral base. Unlike the Algerian army, which in January 1992 brutally interrupted the elections that the FIS was on the point of winning, the Turkish army (which had mounted three coups before, in 1960, 1971, and 1980) did not need to use force in this case. The Islamist government trapped itself.

When the coalition government was formed in June 1996, the Refah party was itself allotted the post of prime minister and most of the secondary ministries that its MSP predecessor had held during the coalitions of the 1970s.[29] Some of these ministries allowed it to use state means to continue unhindered the mobilization and organization it had begun through its network of charitable associations and municipalities. But other ministries (justice and culture in particular) were flashpoints for conflict between the Islamist agenda and secular Turkish institutions. A project for constructing a Grand Mosque in the middle of Taksim Square in Istanbul, at the heart of a modern area that embodied the heritage of Ataturk, concentrated the opposition of the majority of the electorate more than it aroused the enthusiasm of the 21 percent who had voted for Refah. The same went for the proposed reconsecration to Islam of the Basilica of Saint Sophia, which had been transformed into a mosque by the Ottoman conquerors in 1453, then converted into a museum by the republic.

In the field of foreign policy, the Islamists loudly denounced Turkey's military alliance with Israel and promised to revoke it, but were quite unable to do so.[30] In fact, Erbakan, in his role as prime minister, found himself uncomfortably ratifying a series of trade agreements between the military industries of the two countries. This caused an outcry among other Muslim nations, to which he testily responded by quoting the Prophet himself: "Go out to look for knowledge . . . [military technology in this case] . . . where knowledge is to be found." In an attempt to recover the initiative against the Turkish military hierarchy by winning support abroad, Erbakan undertook two foreign tours with the express intention of creating a kind of Islamic Common Market. This was an idea originally floated by the pious middle-class businessmen of the Musiad, a sizable delegation of whom accompanied the prime minister to Iran, Indonesia, Nigeria, Egypt, and Libya. These trips had more than a hint of Ottoman nostalgia about them, aimed as they were at erecting Erbakan as the "paramount leader of the Islamic world." Instead, his global image was severely weakened by this misbegotten tour. In Tehran, the prime minister was asked to explain Turkey's close relations with Israel; in Egypt, he was bluntly put in his place by President Mubarak when he tried to plead the cause of the Egyptian Muslim Brothers; and in Libya he was harangued in a tent by Colonel Qaddafi, who delivered a speech in warm support of the Kurdish PKK (Kurdistan Workers' party), which was at war with Ankara, and demanded that the Kurds be given their independence forthwith.

The party congress of Refah, which was held the week after Erbakan's Libyan fiasco, demonstrated its ideological fragility for all to see. At a time when the prime minister should have been trumpeting his long-hoped-for triumph, proclaiming his Islamist beliefs, and lambasting secularism as he had been doing ever since the start of his career in the 1970s, the delegates found themselves gathered around a giant portrait of Ataturk, listening to their leader abjectly praising the founder of the republic and presenting the Refah party as Kemal's loyal heir. This speech was aimed at the secular establishment and the military hierarchy in hopes of winning over the 75 percent of the electorate that had not voted for Erbakan; instead, it enraged Refah's militants, who were accustomed to a completely different rhetorical tone.

Thus, on January 31, 1997, the Refah mayor of Sincan (an Ankara suburb bursting with Anatolian migrants) organized a celebration of Jerusalem Day at which groups of young men mounted a mock intifada and violent speeches were made against Israel, Arafat, and every national leader who had dared to sign agreements with the Jewish state. Slogans and banners were brandished demanding the application of the sharia, in the presence of the Iranian ambassador, who himself made a speech along the same lines. The following day, the army sent tanks into the streets of Sincan. The Iranian ambassador was expelled from Turkey, and the mayor was clamped in irons; when the Refah minister of justice came to visit him in prison, tensions reached the boiling point. On February 28, a meeting of the National Security Council was held, with representatives of the government and the army high command in attendance. A series of measures were taken against "reactionaries," which explicitly condemned many of the initiatives put forward by the elected Refah members of Parliament, including the prime minister.[31] Premier Erbakan was obliged to sign this document and then to face the criticism of his own militants.

The Refah party never managed to overcome the distrust of the secularist urban classes, however hard it tried. In the same month of February 1997, at nine o'clock every evening, vast numbers of Turks turned off their house lights and went into the streets carrying candles, promoting the theme of "A minute of darkness for a future filled with light." Hostile remarks made by the minister of justice were attacked by the protesters, who denounced his efforts to find inspiration in the sharia for a general reform of the justice system. Later, in March, Erbakan was jeered at the Prime Minister's Football Cup, with slogans in favor of secularism. It was an ominous sign when even the football crowds, who had been solidly behind the Islamist cause in other countries (notably Algeria), now rejected Refah.

In May 1997 Turkey's internal conflict was aggravated by the expulsion from the army of over 160 commissioned and noncommissioned officers suspected of Islamist sympathies, and by a controversy centered on the schools for imams and preachers that provided the bulk of the Refah party's workers. Among the measures taken by the National Security Council was one for prolonging obligatory public education from five to eight years, that is, from the end of primary level to the end of secondary school. Apart from raising the educational standard in general, this decision was aimed at the classes of the imam hatip lisesi, which were to be suppressed and reintegrated into the ordinary system. Islamic instruction per se would thus be reduced to three years from six, and strict limits would be imposed on the numbers of students, reducing them substantially. The Refah's militants demonstrated, chanting "Hands off religious schools." But there was very little response, because the campaign seemed to be directed against the raising of the compulsory school age and hence was perceived as retrograde.

Obliged to fall back on its base of pious voters, the Islamist party saw its authority challenged there as well. Fethullah Gulen, the head of a large Turkish Islamic association that controlled a broad network of private schools, a television channel, and numerous companies, called for Erbakan's resignation. Before long, pressure exerted by the military on various members of Parliament and ministers from Ciller's Right

Path party (Refah's coalition partner) forced them to withdraw their support. Next, a petition was laid before the Constitutional Court accusing Refah of violating the principles of secularism. On June 16, the prime minister resigned, in the hope that Ciller would take his place and maintain the coalition unchanged. But the president of the republic bypassed both leaders by calling on the head of ANAP, Mesut Yilmaz, to head an alliance united in its opposition to the Islamists and guaranteed by the army. This alliance would hold together until the elections of April 1999.

Thus, the failed Erbakan government represented a severe setback for the Islamist movement in Turkey. Refah failed to implement its Islamization program, and it came into conflict with the country's secular institutions, which it was unable to attack head-on without unleashing a revolutionary process that it did not have the means to control—and one in which the devout middle class and the small businessmen of the Musiad would never have participated in any case. Worse, the radical fringe rejected the compromises made by the prime minister and immediately lost interest in political participation. To the surprise of many, the dissolution of the party by the Constitutional Council in January 1998—a move that was criticized by many democrats, who saw nothing but political skullduggery in the legal arguments brought to bear—failed to provoke violent protest among the militants, as if Refah's failure in government warranted a fresh start.

In anticipation of this decision, a fourth reincarnation of the Islamist party surfaced in December 1997 under the name of the Fazilet (Virtue) party. Unlike its three predecessors, all of which had been firmly controlled by Erbakan, the new formation was distinguished by strong antipathies between the "old turbans" still loyal to him and a new "reformist" generation who held him accountable for earlier failures and eventually won control of Fazilet. The party's main concern was to maneuver its devout middle-class constituency into the Turkish mainstream; it abandoned all reference to what Islamist ideology might represent as a symbol of rupture with secularism and the West. The wearing of the veil was presented as a matter of personal choice and no longer as a religious imperative. Women who rejected the veil were appointed to Fazilet's central committee, and one of them did not hesitate to serve alcohol at a party reception or to sing in unison with Racai Kutan, the party leader.[32] Erbakan's many political parties had always held separate meetings for men and women and had never promoted women to positions of responsibility; Erbakan himself had always insisted that all versions of the national anthem played in his presence had to be sung by males only.

Nostalgia for the Ottoman caliphate was also out of fashion by late 1997. Unlike Refah, which had tried to put together an Islamic Common Market to rival the Judaeo-Christian European Economic Community, Fazilet supported Turkey's request to join the European Union. Like the Center party (Hizb al Wasat) that young reformist Muslim Brothers in Egypt had tried to create in 1995, or even the Jordanian Islamic Action Front, Fazilet made democracy its overriding political imperative. It sought access to power on behalf of the devout middle class it represented, discarding all doctrinal and dogmatic rigidity. Like its equivalents in Egypt and Jordan, it was obliged to take account of the aspirations of a social group that had altered considerably over the last quarter century: whose members were now much better educated; whose elites spoke English and were familiar with computers and the Internet; and who sought a place of their own in a liberal political and economic environment, where markets and democracy offered the best chance of making a profit or winning a share of power.

Today, the "constraints" of democracy chiefly concern the middle class that formerly took part in the Islamist movement but offer nothing of consequence to the young urban poor. Democratic principles emphasize a broadening of the foundations of power, rather than a radical questioning of social hierarchies. In Turkey, as in Jordan or Egypt, this devout middle class is now looking for an acceptable form of access to the system, a *modus vivendi* with the regimes in place and with the secular bourgeoisie. But their strategy deprives them of the solidarity and support of the young urban poor, who see nothing in a democratic project that can conceivably serve their interests. In losing this support, the devout middle class loses its strongest bargaining chip in its negotiations with the regime. Alone, the middle class has little capacity to cause trouble for established governments, and as a result governments see themselves as secure enough to impose their own conditions.

At the end of the twentieth century, democratization was under way all over the Muslim world. In the case of Turkey, it resulted in a severe setback for the Islamist cause at the April 1999 general elections. Fazilet surrendered the power won by Refah, being pushed into third position with less then 15 percent of the vote (compared with 21 percent in December 1995).[33] The party seems to have lost most of its support in the outskirts of the big cities and in rural zones but to have held the line in urban middle-class areas. Once again, a petition to dissolve the party for antisecular activities was laid before the Constitutional Council—a sign that the government wished to impose its own advance conditions on any future negotiations and take advantage of the weakened Islamist movement. By 2001, Fazilet was banned in its turn.

Symbolically, the separation between the Islamists and the rest of society was made very clear at the time of the appalling earthquakes in Turkey in August 1999. In the past, natural disasters like this were seized upon by local Islamist factions (the Algerian FIS in November 1989 and the Muslim Brothers in Cairo in 1992) as an opportunity to demonstrate the strength of their charitable networks and even to remedy the shortcomings of the state and offer themselves as a substitute for it. Nothing of the kind occurred after the Turkish Yalova earthquake. The Islamists were conspicuous by their absence, and the mobilization to help the victims was mainly carried out by secular associations, among which the Akut mountain-climbing group was especially prominent.

Conclusion

In December 1999, General Omar Hassan al-Bashir, Sudan's head of state, ousted the charismatic Islamist Hassan al-Turabi, *éminence grise* of the regime and perennial enemy of the United States and the conservative Arab governments.[1] A few days later, on December 29, the London-based Arabic daily newspaper *Al-Quds al-Arabi* (Arab Jerusalem) published an editorial by one of its most respected writers, Abdel Wahab al-Effendi. A native of the Sudan who was educated in England, where he now resides, and the author of a well-received if sympathetic book on Islamism in his native country, Effendi gave his article the following title: "The Sudanese Experiment and the Crisis of the Contemporary Islamist Movement: Lessons and Significance."[2] According to him, events in the Sudan are part of a long series of failures for the "Islamic renewal" movement of the late 1990s, which began with Afghanistan and continued with the ejection of Anwar Ibrahim, the Islamist deputy prime minister of Malaysia. Afghanistan was the movement's greatest triumph of modern times before it turned into its supreme catastrophe, notes the author. (As a good Sunni Muslim, he does not count the Shiite revolution in Iran among Islam's triumphs.) In Effendi's view, the Afghan and Sudanese disasters had one major characteristic in common, despite their different contexts: Islamists were solely responsible for both, with no interference by any foreign foe. In the end, the movement was better off when it was frankly repressed, as it was in Egypt or Algeria, for afterward it could bask in the glow of martyrdom.

In Afghanistan and the Sudan, the two countries where Islamists had seized and consolidated power, the movement had fallen at the first obstacle—that of resolving internal conflicts in a calm and democratic manner. The spectacle of triumphant militants on attack, massacring one another, was painfully eloquent: it crippled the moral authority to which they laid claim and "rendered meaningless the years and centuries of campaigns for the propagation of the faith." Worse, "their disagreements had nothing to do with religious matters but were concerned with glory and power! As sincere Muslims, they should have taken no account of these things, even had such attitudes not been sure to create divisions in the ranks of believers *(fitna)* . . . And what are we to say when they lead to the ruin of a country and the perdition of the faithful, turning people away from religion by disfiguring the image of Islam and of the men that profess it!"

Effendi deplores the fact that when Islamists achieved power, they ignored all democratic procedures "although Banna himself [the founder of the Muslim Brothers] acknowledged that parliamentary democracy was the system most closely approximating to Islam." And, he concludes, "if the Islamists do not succeed in resolving this problem, they will deal a mortal blow to our hopes of Islamic renewal, and bring down calamity upon Islam. And that calamity will be far worse than any visited upon it by communism or secularism—for Islamists can strike Islam in its most vital places, where its enemies have never yet managed to inflict a wound."

The anger and frustration of this disillusioned Islamist deserve special attention, given Effendi's international influence and the stature of the paper that published his article. *Al-Quds al-Arabi* is the flagship newspaper of anti-Zionism and the mouthpiece of radical Islamist and Arab nationalist causes.[3] If we discount the ideological language in which the message is couched, which is intended for in-house consumption by militants, the three factors pinpointed by Effendi are the same causes of Islamism's decline that we have examined in the preceding chapters: (1) the deflating of utopian dreams under the twin pressures of time and power, (2) the conflicts between the various components of the movement, and (3) the failure to implement democratic procedures. But where this sympathizer sees nothing more than clashes of personalities, I tend to see social antagonisms between the devout middle class and the young urban poor. And where Effendi makes democracy a touchstone of the Islamist movement from the time of Banna—an assertion that is worth discussing—I see in his references to democracy the yearning of the middle class and of a segment of the Islamist intelligentsia (Effendi among them) for an alliance with mainstream secular society whereby they can escape the trap of their own political logic.[4]

In Malaysia—Effendi's third example—the local Islamist prodigy Anwar Ibrahim was accused of homosexuality by Mahathir Mohamad, the dictator who had raised him to power. Anwar's supporters then found themselves facing a familiar dilemma. In the time of their prosperity, they had been the most fervent defenders of an authoritarian regime that co-opted, flattered, and enriched them.[5] They gave little thought to democracy, because they worshipped at the shrine of "Asian values," with Mahathir as high priest. But, says Effendi, Asian values were a fraud, based on the idea that, in Asia, community holds sway over the individual, thus making it possible to sneer at liberty as a shameful Western value. Later, when Anwar's men demonstrated against Mahathir, they found their staunchest allies among the democrats. Anwar's friend Munawar Anees, a well-known Islamist intellectual who habitually saw Western plots everywhere, suddenly found himself hounded by Mahathir's tame press and thrown in jail. On his release—which he owed to relentless pressure on the Muslim dictator applied by Western human rights advocates—he conscientiously re-examined his past anathemas against democracy, quoting abundantly from the works of Thomas Jefferson. Here again, it was to secular civil society that the "disillusioned Islamists" of the middle class and the intelligentsia turned. They wished to forge an alliance with civil society that would allow them to recycle themselves, with a minimum of loss, into the great market of globalization opening up at the dawn of the third millennium.

If the Afghan and Sudanese fiascos unsettled the microcosm of Sunni "Londonistan"—as it was nicknamed by the Islamist refugees, journalists, writers, activists, and "green financiers" who operated out of the British capital—the bankruptcy of the political program of the Islamic Republic of Iran supplied the first major setback to the general enthusiasm that had swept the movement along in the last decades of the twentieth century. The victories of the Sunni Islamists in Afghanistan and the Sudan, with weapons and money provided by Saudi Arabia and the CIA in the first case and with a military-religious coup d'état in the second, were in no way comparable to the authentic Islamic Revolution that had taken place in Iran. Quite apart from the Shiite particularity of that country, Khomeini's regime could be said to embody the Islamist utopia in its widest sense. Yet throughout the eight years of Iran's warfare with Iraq, a single social group, made up of bazaar merchants and business operators linked to the political-religious hierarchy, appropriated the Islamic Republic to themselves.[6] This seizure of power worked to the detriment of the shah's former elite, but above all to the detriment of the impoverished young people of Iran, who had been sent, first, to confront the bayonets of the imperial army and, if they survived, were then consigned to mass martyrdom in the Iraqi minefields once the revolution was secure.[7] The logic of Iranian officials echoed that of the French Revolution, whereby the *sans-culottes,* paid in the coin of morality and puritanism, were systematically eliminated from the nerve centers of the system. Those Iranian men who were fortunate enough to return from the front found themselves, once again, pushed to the bottom of the political ladder and stripped of all hope of social advancement, despite their sacrifices. As a consolation prize, the regime offered up the women of the Iranian middle class, who were forced to go about completely veiled or endure arrests and molestation at the hands of *pasdarans, bassidjis,* and other riffraff in battle dress. In 1989, Khomeini's macabre fatwa condemning Salman Rushdie to death was a further sop thrown in the direction of the radicals, to distract them from the fact that not only had the revolution failed to export itself in the face of Saudi containment but, worse, it had betrayed the expectations of its supporters, who henceforth would be fed a diet of symbols as a substitute for real gains in their standard of living.

Twenty years earlier, the population explosion in the Muslim world had served the Islamist cause very well, by corralling in the peripheral slums of its great cities a corps of young men who would later rise up on the movement's behalf. During the 1990s, however, the demographic trend reversed direction. A rapid and consistent falling-off in the birthrate followed the first population explosion among newcomers to the cities, where lodgings were hard to find and where women were obliged to plan their families to match the constraints of urban life. Ignoring the Islamists' ideological enthusiasm for a high birthrate (presumably because it supplied abundant souls ready to fight and die in the jihads of the future), young couples living in the metropolises of the Muslim world in the year 2000 made up their own minds about family size, consistent with their hopes for a better life. Their prospects for the future hinged on having two or three children instead of seven or more, which had been the norm twenty years before.[8]

Unlike their country-born parents who had lived through the trauma of rural exodus, urban young Muslims growing up in the 1990s knew nothing other than city life. They shared the same written culture as their fathers, but with an important difference: their fathers had belonged to the first generation taught *en masse* to read and write and had thus been separated from their own rural, illiterate progenitors by a cultural gulf that radical Islamist ideology could exploit. The children of these "bearded ones" were more likely to call into question the utopian dreams of this 1970s generation—and nowhere was this youthful rebellion more striking than in the Islamic Republic of Iran, two decades after Khomeini's triumph of 1979.

The twentieth anniversary of the revolution, in 1999, witnessed the coming of age of a generation who never knew the shah. However, it *did* know massive unemployment, moral repression, and a cataleptic social order that was completely dominated by the religious hierarchy, the "pious foundations" that control the economy in collusion with the bazaar merchants, and a whole crew of profiteers who preyed on the Islamic Republic. All of these elements opposed any reform that might conceivably reduce their power. In 1997, during the presidential elections, the younger generation of Iran had voted decisively against the candidate of the religious establishment, Ali Akbar Nategh-Nouri, and in favor of the candidate of "change," Mohammed Khatami. But the change offered by the new government has operated very gradually. The president himself is a turban-wearing product of the religious establishment, and his room for maneuver is severely limited by two other centers of power, the Parliament and the Supreme Guide of the Revolution, which remains in the hands of the conservative clan that controls the lion's share of Iran's repressive judicial apparatus.[9] The legislative elections of February 18, 2000, were won handsomely by reformist candidates, however—an unmistakable sign that Iranian society is turning its back on the social and moral order inherited from Khomeini.

The uncertainties about the way the transition from an Islamist to a post-Islamist era will be managed recall the arguments over post-communism in the former Soviet republics. In both cases, the unrest demonstrates the failure of a political blueprint that is now faded and unworkable. Muslims no longer view Islamism as the source of utopia, and this more pragmatic vision augurs well for the future.

The decline of Islamism goes well beyond the frontiers of Iran and Shiism. It affects the whole body of Islamist ideology, Sunnis included. Effendi's article deplores the incapacity of Sunni leaders who won power to implement the ideals to which they had subscribed when they were in the opposition; Effendi sees more authenticity in movements that are being actively repressed by state power. But the record of these groups is scarcely better: they have never managed to emerge the victors over their adversaries' strategies of confrontation or co-option. Confrontation was the path chosen by the Algerian and Egyptian governments; the violence against the state preached and put into practice by the most radical groups began auspiciously but eventually backfired. The militants never succeeded in enlisting the population in a general uprising, even when the Islamist cause was popular enough to win elections, as it did in Algeria. On the contrary, Algeria's paroxysms of violence—fanned by the jihadists from Afghanistan—caused ordinary people to shrink from an ideology that had turned into a blood-drenched nightmare. The moderate Islamist groups whose members belonged to the devout middle class found themselves incapable of controlling the spiral of violence of which they themselves were sometimes the victims. They were unable to sustain their role as intermediaries and guarantors of order *vis-à-vis* the state and foreign governments.

Between 1992 and 1995, the United States viewed a number of Islamist figures with favor. These men either lived on U.S. territory or were frequently invited there by semi-official American organizations, in the wake of the CIA's massive support of the Afghan jihad. The Central Intelligence Agency had established a wide network of operational contacts among militants, activists, and ideologists who might serve as valuable interlocutors for Washington should they ever seize power. Some American academics published books to the greater glory of the "moderate Islamists," in whom they saw the incarnation of civil society and the best hope for a market economy. Journalists with the same sympathies prepared their readers for the eventuality of Islamist triumphs in Algeria and Egypt, which in their eyes would offer nothing but advantages for the United States. But at the same time, other academics and pressure groups in the United States, many of whom were close to the pro-Israeli lobby and press, made it their business to claim that the so-called moderate contingent was only the smiling mask of terrorism and fanaticism.[10] The debate that ensued called upon the U.S. government to define the future direction of American policy toward the Islamists.

Among the elements that shifted U.S. foreign policy from benign neglect to a distinctly hard line was the extension (from around 1995 onward) of Islamist-inspired terrorism to the American homeland. The first attack on the World Trade Center in 1993, which still remains something of a mystery, was a terrifying demonstration of the Islamists' new jihad against the United States. More subtlely, the fate of Anwar Haddam was an example of this change. Haddam lived in the United States and acted as the official spokesman for the Front Islamique du Salut at the Rome Conference of Sant'Egidio in December 1994; there, he replaced Rabah Kebir, who had been conveniently prevented from leaving the German location where he was in exile. At the time of the conference, Washington was still in favor of defusing the Algerian crisis by allowing the Islamists to play a central role in the government. But by 1995 the terrorist spiral of the "war against France" and the daily carnage in Algeria, whatever the identity of those involved, made the Islamist option untenable, given the lack of interlocutors who could answer for its activities. Washington consigned that option to oblivion, and Anwar Haddam found himself jailed in the United States for an irregularity concerning his residence permit (the same tactic that had been used against the Egyptian Sheik Omar Abdel Rahman).

In the second half of the decade—prompted by figures like Effendi and Anees but also by the group of Muslim Brothers in their forties who were trying to create the Al Wasat party in Egypt in 1995 and by the "moderate" leaders of the Turkish Refah party who piloted the transition to the Fazilet party after 1997, as well as many others—the more clear-sighted Islamist intellectuals began to understand that the political ideology of their movement was leading to a dead-end. This was demonstrated in various ways: uncontrollable violence in Algeria and Egypt, ineffectual violence in Palestine, seizure of power followed by political and economic collapse in the Sudan and Afghanistan, religious civil war in Pakistan, co-option by a dictator and exhaustion of moral credit in Mahathir's Malaysia and Suharto's Indonesia, inability to live under the constraints of a government coalition in Turkey and Jordan. Last and most significant was the bankruptcy of the Iranian regime, on an inverse scale with the immense hopes that the revolution had inspired throughout the wider Muslim world.

We should bear all this in mind when we attempt to analyze the new directions taken by those militants and former militants who now, in the name of democracy and human rights, are looking for common ground with the secular middle class. They have put aside the radical ideology of Qutb, Mawdudi, and Khomeini; they consider the jihadist-salafist doctrines developed in the camps of Afghanistan a source of horror, and they celebrate the "democratic essence" of Islam. Islamists defending the rights of the individual stand shoulder to shoulder with secular democrats in confronting repressive and authoritarian governments. Choosing to wear the veil is no longer trumpeted as a sign of respect for an injunction of the sharia but is viewed as an exercise of the human right of individuals to freedom of expression.[11]

The *Islam 21* bulletin, which heads up a network of online websites, email, and discussion forums, is typical of these efforts.[12] Based in "Londonistan" and regularly broadcasting, in English and Arabic, the views of intellectuals like Effendi, the Tunisian Rashid al-Gannushi, and scores of others from every nation between the Maghreb and Southeast Asia, *Islam 21* proposed a "charter for the Islamists" in February 1999. This initiative would give priority to "questions of civil society, women's rights, the right to hold different opinions, and the need for an enlightened interpretation of religion." An editorial deplored the fact that "during the past decades, the Islamists, like all other political militants, had made it their principal business to win control of the state. This experience has been very costly and has proved feasible in only a very few cases. Furthermore, the mere seizure of power does not resolve problems and may even be a serious impediment to the wider Islamist project."[13] In the next issue of the bulletin, an article entitled "Islamism, Pluralism and Civil Society" further developed this theme, with Tocqueville freely quoted in support of it. Civil society, as a vehicle for opposition to despots, was presented as a panacea for the problems of the contemporary Muslim world, confronted as it is by "orientalists who continue to maintain that Islam and democracy are mutually incompatible . . . and ironically, that they are supported in this view by a small but vocal minority of Islamist militants who claim that democratic values have no place in Islam."[14]

Outside London, such developments are closely followed by large numbers of Islamist student organizations and by the preachers who have emerged from these groups in Europe and the United States. In the French-speaking world, a charismatic speaker named Tariq Ramadan, the grandson of Hassan al-Banna, founder of the Muslim Brothers, has become the champion of this line of thought. Refusing to go along with the logic of confrontation with the West, Ramadan sees European-style democracy as a mode of self-protection against the despotism that prevails in most Muslim states, and he urges his disciples to make the fullest use of the rights that citizenship confers. Himself a Swiss national, he yearns for intellectual status within the French academic and publishing worlds. As the author of a book printed by a Catholic publishing house and prefaced by an established Third World journalist with a communist background, Ramadan is determined to win acceptance for the active participation of Islamists in the democratic process.[15] His aim is to make Islamism legitimate by divesting it of all association with radical groups or individuals tainted by violence—such as those who waged Djamel Zitouni's GIA war on France in 1995.[16]

Some journalists, ecclesiastics, and teachers, intrigued by this speaker who appears to have broken with the ways and rhetoric of the past, see Ramadan as the new spokesman for a younger generation of Muslims in France and Europe and have given him broad access to the machinery of power. Others, more circumspect, are inclined to question his motives and the exact nature of the message he is transmitting to his youthful audience. Still others are prepared to gamble on the fact that, whatever the ideology underlying Ramadan's speeches, he at least urges his listeners and followers to better themselves within society and to integrate themselves as citizens. In the end, they feel, this will make young Muslims' identification with French society easier and will detach them permanently from radical Islamist ideology. In the same way, several decades ago, the children of proletarian and communist immigrants to France from southern and eastern Europe fell under the influence of the Communist party and the trade unions, while all the time engaged in a process of gradual integration and advancement within society. Today, these French citizens belong to the *petite bourgeoisie,* having lost all links with both Marxism-Leninism and their parents' native countries.

We have already witnessed a parallel situation among the devout small businessmen of Anatolia. Once these men had won access to the dominant economic circles of Istanbul and Ankara, during the Refah Islamist party's ascendancy, they were content to rest on their laurels. When Refah was forced out of power and dissolved under pressure from the Turkish military, these businessmen did not mobilize in the party's defense but opted instead to consolidate their social and economic position. This move worked to the detriment of an Islamist organization and ideology that could no longer be of use to them and which indeed had become an encumbrance to new alliances with their secular counterparts in the larger business world.

The same logic, pushed even further, was applied in Algeria after 1999, when a wealthy businessman with close ties to the "moderate Islamist" Hamas party that was part of the coalition government presented himself as a candidate to build a giant new brewery. The idea was to produce a European brand of beer locally and market it at a price low enough to attract those sectors of the population who—piety notwithstanding—wished to consume alcohol but could not afford imported liquor.

As the twenty-first century dawned, this dilution of Islamist ideology within a global market economy took place in an environment that was very different from that of the previous decades. During the 1980s, Islamism's growing strength was accompanied by the creation of a banking system that did not impose interest rates and of various investment funds that allowed people to speculate in conformity with the injunctions of religious law. At the beginning of the new century, these initiatives prospered only insofar as they had managed to capture a sector of the savings market based on purely economic considerations, and without much regard to the political idea that originally dictated their implementation during the years of Saudi hegemony. Likewise, attempts to legally substitute an "Islamic charter" of the Rights of Man for the Universal Declaration of the OIC made in Cairo in August

1990, when Iraq had just invaded Kuwait, was no longer a burning issue by the year 2000.

By then, the broader Islamist movement had lost its momentum to power and was neither capable nor desirous of substituting its specific language for the universal idiom it once dismissed as "occidental." Many Islamist parties and movements were bent on winning recognition as democrats and on denouncing repression by reference to the universal Western principles of human rights. They no longer sought to diminish that system by substituting their own ideas for it. Some people viewed this development as a cynical maneuver, like that of the modern communist parties, which used the parlance of democracy now and then, the better to dupe the "useful idiots" they needed to enlarge their base and their political networks, especially among the intelligentsia. When the Soviet Bloc was still relatively powerful, this strategy produced excellent results, attracting many sincere democrats who were seduced by the messianic aura of the workers' movement. On the other hand, with the coming of the crisis that was to sweep away the Eastern Bloc and its confederates, these currents of exchange began to favor the defection of communist militants, notably the managers and agents whose democratic contacts offered possibilities of re-conversion in various civil institutions and associations outside party circles.

This was one—but not the only one—of the possible outcomes of a dialogue between the Islamists (now less sure of themselves) and the secular democrats of the Muslim world. The latter, though they had been reviled for two decades for being the Westernized "sons of France" in North Africa and "brown sahibs" in Southwest Asia, still maintained networks of relationships, high educational levels, and the confidence of political and economic power circles worldwide. These circles held the key to vital investment decisions, in a time of general privatization and globalization.

When we consider the Muslim world as a whole, the opposition Islamist movements still face an unprecedented moral crisis. Their political project—which was always vague in its promises of a radiant Islamic state applying the sharia—now has a track record showing that it banks on the future but is mired in the past. The random violence of the 1990s, even though many suspected that it was stoked by the *agents provocateurs* of regimes that had an interest in doing so, was still fresh in people's memories. For this reason, the most moderate component of the movement was more and more vocal in its profession of democratic faith, seeking to distance itself from a militancy that clouded its political future. The devout middle class at Islamism's grassroots was probing for new alliances with its secular counterpart—and even with Christians, in states where both Muslims and Christians reside.

Thus, the Shiite Hezbollah party in Lebanon, which began as a terrorist cell doing the bidding of Khomeini, turned into a mass movement representing the disinherited and then became the embodiment of Lebanese national resistance to Israel.[17] In anticipation of a coalition, it is being courted by more than a few Maronite Christian leaders. The convergences between the cult of the Virgin Mary and the Shiite devotion to Fatima (the daughter of the Prophet, the wife of Ali, and the "mother of the Believers") are being quietly emphasized—perhaps as a prelude to a rapprochement between Christians and Shiites who, together, would form a broad majority of Lebanese opposed to a Syrian protectorate and to a predominantly Sunni Middle East.

The Muslim Brothers of Egypt—most in their forties—who formed the project for a centrist, democratic Al Wasat party in 1995, placed a Protestant Christian intellectual among their leaders, as testimony (as they saw it) to their open-mindedness. Elsewhere, from Indonesia to Morocco, Islamists participated in elected assemblies when they could and wherever they were permitted to do so; their representatives did not question the democratic principles undergirding such assemblies. Elected officials like these have set aside the sovereignty of God (*hakimiyyat Allah*) which Qutb and Mawdudi erected as the central criterion of an Islamic state. These original Islamic thinkers had viewed the sovereignty of the people (that is, democracy) as a form of idolatry—a pre-Islamic barbarism (jahiliyya) resurfacing in the twentieth century. The democratic system, which Ali Benhadj once scorned because 50+ percent of the electorate could make laws (such as allowing the consumption of wine) that violated the teachings of the Koran, were now widely venerated. In Turkey, Refah and Fazilet mayors were returned to office because of the efficiency with which they ran their municipalities; yet in the general election, where the issues at stake were far more explicitly political, the Fazilet party had difficulty holding the votes it had won in 1999. Paradoxically, the Islamist experience itself has produced some of the conditions that have led to its own obsolescence. In the ranks of veiled female militants demanding the application of the sharia, we see, in many cases, the first generation of women to speak in public outside their homes and beyond their domestic role. In doing this, they have collided with male militants bent on confining these women to a subordinate role in Muslim society. Some women, most notably in Turkey and Iran, have reacted by creating a form of "Islamist feminism" to counter the *machismo* that prevails in the movement. These protests may represent the first stirrings of tomorrow's Muslim democracy.

All this goes against the blinkered vision of those who make the doctrine of Islam itself an obstacle to the implantation of democracy in any of the countries where it is the dominant religion, and also to those who attribute to that doctrine a "democratic essence." Islam, like any other religion, is a way of life, one that is given its shape and form by Muslim men and women. These men and women belong to a world in which the annihilation of intellectual frontiers by modern telecommunications is threatening the fortresses of identity that Islamist ideology has sought to build. Quite apart from the internal causes of its decline, that ideology has been consistently incapable of reducing contemporary Muslims to an Islamist mass exclusively swayed by the imperatives of doctrine. The dissolution of that ideology is offering Muslims a new opportunity to take control of their future and free themselves from the straitjacket of dogma. This opportunity harks back to the great tradition of Muslim civilization throughout history, whose strength has always been an extreme sensitivity and receptiveness to change. This, in the time of its grandeur, allowed the Muslim world from Baghdad to Andalusia to absorb and draw sustenance from the contributions of Persian and Greco-Mediterranean civilizations.

Today, as Muslim societies emerge from the Islamist era, it is through openness to the world and to democracy that they will construct their future. There is no longer any real alternative. The young people of Iran, Algeria, and other Muslim countries all have relatives living abroad: they use the telephone, watch satellite TV programs, and see the bullet trains of modern civilization streaking across Europe and the United States. The regimes of the mullahs—the Front Islamique du Salut, the Sudanese Islamic Front, not to mention the Taliban—leave them cold. In Algerian hittiste parlance, these experiments are *perimés*—past their "sell-by" date.

But this march to democracy must face an obstacle that has nothing religious about it: the various sovereign states, as well as the elites that rule them, must also be prepared to make their modes of government democratic. In the late 1960s the hope of an Islamist utopia flourished in the repressive, authoritarian soil of almost every Muslim state as a consequence of the moral bankruptcy and economic failure of nationalism. Islamism, in its early decades, grounded itself securely in the rejection of impious (kufr) democracy, and this was all the easier because nationalist regimes that imprisoned, tortured, and executed their opponents, as well as driving them into exile, were apt to hide behind the slogans of liberty, socialism, and progress—ideals of which they were travesties. The Islamist way was attractive because God and the Holy Koran guaranteed its proper implementation on earth, unsullied by the perversions and manipulations of despotic generals, kings, or sultans.

The moral free hand enjoyed by an Islamist movement that wished to make a clean break with violent and corrupt political traditions did not survive the last thirty years of the twentieth century. People had time to observe its beatings of leftists in universities, its compulsory wearing of the veil, its "Islamic" investment swindles, its censorship of secular texts and terror campaigns against authors, and its bloodbaths of innocent civilians and tourists. To counter this, Islamist militants pointed to their successes—their charitable achievements, the new access to modern urban life that the veil afforded young girls from traditional backgrounds, the humanitarian organizations financed by the Islamic banking system, and so forth. Sociologists and economists will eventually work through these arguments and emerge with precise figures and data. But in the meantime, the political and moral record of three decades of militant Islamism was, to say the least, a far cry from what was hoped for at the outset.

At the dawn of the millennium, the initiative was with those regimes that had emerged victorious from confrontation with the Islamist movement, whether they did so by armed violence or by peaceful co-option. They now faced the task of absorbing and integrating the social groups that were left out at independence, and are still left out. They must assist at the birth of a Muslim form of democracy that would embrace culture, religion, and political and economic modernity as never before. The younger elites coming to power—from King Mohammed VI in Morocco to King Abdullah in Jordan, from the technocratic and military entourage of Algerian President Abdelaziz Bouteflika to that of the new president of Indonesia, Megawati Sukarnoputri—would have to be willing and able to share the fruits of democracy today, the better to preserve them for tomorrow. If these leaders neglected reform and drew immediate, selfish profit from Islamism's decline, then the Muslim world would very soon face a new crisis—expressed as either Islamist, ethnic, racial, religious, or populist. The choices these leaders made in the very near future would determine whether or not we would see again the flag of jihad as we did in the last quarter of a century or whether the Muslim peoples could take their own peaceful path to democracy.

For the pious middle class and the intellectuals closest to them, shifting from Islamism to the search for a common ground with secular groups and democratic ideologues was rather easy. But the failure of the Islamist utopia as an ideology has not had the same consequences for the young urban poor and the radicalized thinkers and activists, and the challenge has been much harsher. The young urban poor had nothing to gain from any kind of alliance between the devout and secular middle classes. They could not identify with them, and did not care for their language and political or economic agendas. On the road to prosperity, their former allies passed them by without so much as a backward glance. Within this disenchanted mass, volatile feelings could quickly catch fire if ignited by the right spark.

Among the jihadist-salafists, isolated as they were in the seclusion of their secret organizations and terrorist cells, from Londonistan to Afghanistan, any idea of a compromise with "Westernized" groups was loathsome. The mental world they inhabited was closed, though they were perfectly aware of the tremendous possibilities for action that new technologies provided, and many activists actually boasted training or a degree in applied sciences, such as engineering and information technology. The devout middle class considered these radicals the culprits responsible for the decline of Islamism, and rejected them as firebrands of violence who had finally scared everyone away from the movement and played into the hands of its enemies.

Such was the context in which the cataclysm of September 11 took place. In spite of what many hasty commentators contended in its immediate aftermath, the attack on the United States was a desperate symbol of the isolation, fragmentation, and decline of the Islamist movement, not a sign of its strength and irrepressible might. The jihadist-salafists who belonged to bin Laden's mysterious Al Qaeda network imagined themselves as the spark that would ignite the volatile frustration of the disenchanted ones in the Muslim world and stoke a firestorm. They had no patience for the slow building of a movement that would reach out to the masses, mobilize them, and guide them on the path to power. They put their faith in example and emotion, in immediacy and violence. They believed that once the great American Satan had been made to shake on its foundations, for all to see, then a sweeping tide of jihad could overtake the modern world. This delusion bore some similarity to that of the Jihad group of Egypt who assassinated Anwar Sadat in October 1981. Those militants, too, had thought that the sheer audacity and violence—both real and symbolic—of their action would spur the masses into a general upheaval, bringing down the regime and building on its ruins an Islamist state. But in both cases, those tactics suffered from a gross miscalculation, because the militants put too much faith in the emotional reaction of the Muslim masses, and no effort into organizing and mobilizing them. The ultra-radicals successfully implemented the first part of their plot—assassinating Sadat in 1981 and inflicting unprecedented damage, death, and destruction on the United States in 2001. But in neither case could the activists deliver on the second stage of their strategy. No Islamist state took shape in Egypt; Sadat's vice-president, Hosni Mubarak, who succeeded him, still holds power twenty years later. And America did not falter after September 11, despite weeks of mourning and disarray. Within a hundred days the U.S. army had wiped the Taliban regime from the face of the earth, and bin Laden was on the run, his secret cells dismantled or disbanded.

This does not mean that we shall not see other outbursts of terrorism that claim the mantle of jihad. The Israeli-Palestinian conflict in particular will be ripe for more violence, as long as the issues in the Middle East are dealt with as they were in the wake of September 11. But violence in itself, as we have seen throughout Part II, has proven to be a death trap for Islamists as a whole, precluding any capacity to hold and mobilize the range of constituencies they need to seize political power. Torn between those favoring rapprochement with democrats and those intoxicated by the mystique of jihad, the Islamist movement will have much difficulty reversing its trail of decline as it confronts twenty-first-century civilization.

**NOTES
GLOSSARY
MAPS
ABBREVIATIONS
INDEX**

Notes

Introduction

1. The Islamic Information Observatory, directed by Yassir al-Sirri. Al-Sirri asserts that he was tricked.
2. In 1992, Olivier Roy published *The Failure of Political Islam* (Cambridge: Harvard University Press, 1998), a book full of ideas that went against current opinion and forged the way for a new approach to the phenomenon of Islamism.
3. In 1999, the Afghan production of opium was estimated at 4,500 tons, about 75% percent of the world total. See Alain Labrousse, *Libération*, October 4, 2001.
4. The radicalization of the Taliban regime in 2001—which was demonstrated in the dynamiting of the monumental Buddha sculptures at Bamyan and the arrests of aid workers accused of Christian evangelism and followed by the departure of nearly all other aid workers in Afghanistan—weakened their support base among the local population. These developments may have been assisted by the growing ascendancy of foreign militants, most belonging to the Arab salafist-jihadist movement, who moved into the area around Kandahar and were linked to Osama bin Laden.
5. For an account of this episode, see Barton Gellman, "In '96, Sudan Offered to Arrest Bin Laden: Saudis Balked at Accepting U.S. Plan," *International Herald Tribune*, October 4, 2001.
6. Following the attacks on the United States, a number of analysts queried the nature and breadth of the ties, especially the financial ones, between Osama's networks and certain milieus on the Arabian peninsula—given the discontent in societies living on shared-out oil income, which today are experiencing a population explosion that is reducing each individual's share and building resentment against bloated royal families with privileged access to revenues.
7. For an overview of the various reactions among Egyptian intellectuals, see Amira

Howeidy, "Striking Hazardous Chords," *Al Ahram Weekly*, October 11–17, 2001, p. 7. Also my *Chronique d'une guerre d'Orient* (Paris: Gallimard, 2002).

8. During discussions with Egyptian students on October 16, 2001, I was struck by the confused feelings of both sexes, who sympathized with bin Laden as a champion of the resistance to the United states (especially after seeing his TV declaration on October 7) while deploring the civilian loss of life in New York and Washington and rejecting the Islamist cause as he exposed it.

9. The jihads in Bosnia and Chechnya—where the fighters were not locally-born, unlike in Algeria and Egypt—were already mobilizing people from wealthy Arabian backgrounds, as is shown by the "biographies of martyrs" on specialized Islamist Internet sites. On the itinerary of the secular middle-class Egyptian who piloted the first airliner into the World Trade Center, see "A Shy Child's Journey to Fiery Mass Murder," *International Herald Tribune*, October 11, 2001, p. 2.

1. A Cultural Revolution

1. Benedict Anderson, *Imagined Communities* (London and New York: Verso, 1991), esp. chs. 3, 5, 7.

2. Qutb's work has been the subject of numerous commentaries and analyses. To complete the brief presentation made here, see Gilles Kepel, *The Prophet and Pharaoh: Muslim Extremism in Egypt* (London: Al Saqi; Berkeley: University of California Press, 1985). For more detailed exegeses of Qutb's work, see Olivier Carré, *Mystique et politique* (Paris: Presses de la FNSP et Cerf, 1984), and Ibrahim M. Abu Rabi, *Intellectual Origins of Islamic Resurgence in the Muslim Arab World* (Albany: SUNY Press, 1996).

3. Mohamed Tozy, in *Monarchie et islam politique au Maroc* (Paris: Presses de Sciences Po, 1999), suggests as a translation of *ouboudiyya* "servitude" or "submission" (pp. 25–26). The Arabic root has both meanings.

4. The classic text on the Muslim Brothers is Richard P. Mitchell's *The Society of the Muslim Brothers* (London: Oxford University Press, 1969). In addition, Brynjar Lia's more recent *The Society of the Muslim Brothers in Egypt: The Rise of an Islamic Mass Movement, 1928–1982* (London: Ithaca Press, 1998), is key reading. In French, see Olivier Carré and Gerard Michaud, *Les Frères musulmans, 1928–1982* (Paris: Gallimard, 1983).

5. This debate is recalled in Lia, *The Society of the Muslim Brothers in Egypt*, pp. 6–7. Among the numerous books devoted to the question, Martin Kramer's *The Islamism Debate* (Tel Aviv: Dayan Center Papers, no. 120, 1997) provides a useful synthesis presenting the points of view of the protagonists of the American, British, French, and Israeli academic worlds.

6. Two books by S. V. R. Nasr are my principal sources for details of the works and political life of Mawdudi: *Mawdudi and the Making of Islamic Revivalism* (Oxford: Oxford University Press, 1996) and *The Vanguard of the Islamic Revolution: The Jamaat-i Islami of Pakistan* (London: I. B. Tauris, 1994).

7. The term comes from the Turkish word *ordu,* "army."

8. Nasr, *Vanguard of the Islamic Revolution*, p. 7.

9. See S. Abul ala Mawdudi, *Fundamentals of Islam* (Lahore: Islamic Publications; 1st Eng. ed. 1975), pp. 249–250.

10. The text is available in an annotated English-language edition in *Islam and Revolution: Writings and Declarations of Imam Khomeini,* trans. with commentary by Hamid Algar (Berkeley: Mizan Press, 1981).

11. For an examination of these questions, see Yann Richard, *Shiite Islam: Polity, Ideology, and Creed* (Oxford, UK; Cambridge, MA: Basil Blackwell, 1995).

12. One example is to be found in the collection of various lectures by Ali Shariati, *What Is To Be Done: The Enlightened Thinkers and an Islamic Renaissance,* with commentary by Farhang Rajaee (Houston: IRIS Press, 1986), p. 1. Most of the subjects mentioned will be found here. On Shariati himself, see Ali Rahnema, *An Islamic Utopian: A Political Biography of Ali Shari'ati* (London: Tauris, 1998).

13. Iranian armed groups in the years 1960–1970 consisted mainly of the Peoples' Fedayeen, founded in 1963 (a Marxist-Leninist organization inspired by Che Guevara which took to the bush and had some spectacular encounters with the shah's forces), and the People's Mujahedeen, in which Islamic philosophy was more pronounced. Shariati had no specific links with them, but he had in part inspired the Islamo-Marxist synthesis they had developed. "The Shi'ite martyrs (of Karbala) were exactly like Che Guevara today. They accepted martyrdom as their revolutionary obligation, and considered armed struggle against class oppression as their social duty": quoted in Ervand Abrahamian, *The Iranian Mojahedin* (New Haven: Yale University Press, 1985), p. 92.

14. For an account of these events see Jean-Pierre Digard, Bernard Hourcade, and Yann Richard, *L'Iran au XXe siècle* (Paris: Fayard, 1996).

15. One can get an idea of this doctrinal and moral dimension through the French translation of certain of these pre-1970 texts in *Principes, politiques, philosophiques sociaux et religieux de l'ayatollah Khomeini* (Paris: Editions Libres-Hallier, 1979). The choice of extracts gives a particularly dogmatic and retrograde image of their author (suppressed by his Western admirers at the time), but it cannot explain the social and political phenomenon that the Islamic Revolution represented. It at least illustrates its cultural ambivalence.

16. For an interpretation of the transformation of Khomeini's thought with the 1970 lectures, I follow Ervand Abrahamian, *Khomeinism: Essays on the Islamic Republic* (Berkeley: University of California Press, 1993), esp. pp. 17–38.

2. Islam in the Late 1960s

1. On the end of the caliphate and the various aspects of pan-Islamic feeling that emerged at this time, see Bernard Lewis, *The Emergence of Modern Turkey* (Oxford: Oxford University Press, 1961); Jacob Landau, *The Politics of Pan-Islam,* 2nd ed. (Oxford: Oxford University Press, 1994); Martin Kramer, *Islam Assembled: The Advent of the Muslim Congresses* (New York: Columbia University Press, 1986).

2. On the creation of the Great Mosque in Paris, see Gilles Kepel, *Les banlieues de l'islam* (Paris: Seuil, 1987).

3. The Tablighi Jamaat was very little studied until the 1990s. Elements of it are

mentioned in Kepel, *Les banlieues;* in Mumtaz Ahmad, "Islamic Fundamentalism in South Asia: The Jamaati-Islami and the Tablighi Jamaat of South Asia," in *Fundamentalisms Observed,* ed. Martin E. Marty and R. Scott Appleby (Chicago: University of Chicago Press, 1991), pp. 457–530; in Muhammad Khalid Massud, Barbara D. Metcalf, and William Roff, eds., *Travellers in Faith Studies of the Tablighi Jama'at as an International Movement* (Leiden: Brill, 2000).

4. On these questions with respect to Egypt, see K. T. Barbar and G. Kepel, *Les waqfs dans l'Egypte contemporaine* (Cairo: Cedej, 1981).

5. Although Turkish secularism separates religion from the state, the latter still exercises control over the former. The government authority for religious affairs publishes works giving a version of Islam acceptable to those in power, it directs how religion is taught in schools, it decides what officiating clerics should be paid, and so on.

6. See the pioneering work of Olivier Carré, *La Légitimation islamique des socialismes arabes* (Paris: Presses de la FNSP, 1979). On the subject of the Islamic book market in Egypt at the time of Nasser, see Yves Gonzalez-Quijano, *Les gens du livre* (Paris: Editions du CNRS, 1998).

7. A collection of essays edited by Alexandre Popovic and Gilles Veinstein, *Les voies d'Allah* (Paris: Fayard, 1997), presents a wide panorama of this form of Islamic religious practice today.

8. The Mourides of Senegal are one of the most remarkable examples of a brotherhood that uses the religious vocabulary of Islam but retains forms of piety and devotion that are deeply rooted in African religion, while also developing into a major economic force whose primary motivating factor is absolute obedience of its members to the orders of the marabout or caliph.

9. See Reinhardt Shultze, *Islamischer Internationalismus im 20. Jahrundert: Untersuchungen zur Geschichte der Islamischen Weltliga* (Leiden: Brill, 1990). In 1969, following a terrorist attack on the Dome of the Rock in Jerusalem (under Israeli occupation since 1967), a meeting of Muslim heads of state created the Organization of Islamic Conferences (OIC), whose aim was to bring unity to the common position held by Islamic states on major international issues (essentially the Palestinian question at that time). The divergent interests of the member states have imposed constraints preventing the OIC from fulfilling the same ideological function as the Muslim World League, but Saudi Arabia plays an important role.

10. These two authors—particularly the first, who lived from 1263 to 1328—were to become the major references for the Sunni Islamist movement from the 1970s onward, no doubt leading to the widespread diffusion of their works into mosques worldwide as a result of Saudi Islamic propagation.

11. See Ayman Al-Yassini, *Religion and State in the Kingdom of Saudi Arabia* (Boulder: Westview Press, 1985), esp. pp. 67ff. This balance was put to the test after 1970.

12. On the reform of Al Azhar and the question of the ulemas in contemporary Egypt in general, see Malika Zeghal's *Gardiens de l'islam: Les oulémas d'Al Azhar dans l'Egypte contemporaine* (Paris: Presses de Sciences Po), 1996.

13. On the relationship between the throne and the ulemas in Morocco, see Tozy, *Monarchie et islam politique.*

14. See Ali Merad, *Le réformisme musulman en Algérie de 1925 à 1940* (Paris-La Haye: Mouton, 1967).
15. The daily paper of the FLN, the only political party until 1989, is called *El Moudjahid*, referring, in the vocabulary of the jihad, to the war of liberation (by which the ruling party claims legitimacy).
16. On the expansion of training schools for preachers, see Ilter Turan, "Religion and Political Culture in Turkey," in *Islam in Modern Turkey*, ed. Richard Tapper (London: I. B. Tauris, 1991).
17. The Nahdatul ulema has been the subject of detailed study by Andrée Feillard in *Armée et islam en Indonésie* (Paris: L'Harmattan, 1996). On Sukarno's interest in the reforms of Ataturk, see François Raillon, "Islam et ordre nouveau ou l'imbroglio de la foi et de la politique," *Archipel* 30 *(L'Islam et l'Indonésie)* (1985): 229–262.
18. See Clifford Geertz, *The Religion of Java* (Chicago: University of Chicago Press, 1960).
19. The years 1950–1960 saw Islamic insurrection breaking out in three places in Indonesia. In addition to Darul Islam Java, one movement took up arms at Aceh (Sumatra), the region of the archipelago where Islam had been established longest and in its most "puritan" form, and another at Celebes. See Manning Nash, "Islamic Resurgence in Malaysia and Indonesia," in Marty and Appleby, *Fundamentalisms*, pp. 691–739.
20. The Deobandi school (and other revivalist religious movements which involved Islam on the subcontinent at the end of the nineteenth century) is described in Barbara D. Metcalf, *Islamic Revivalism in British India: Deoband, 1860–1900* (Berkeley: University of California Press, 1982).
21. Personal observations, Islamabad and Karachi, April 1998.
22. An analysis of the struggles that took place during Pakistan's formative years, the result of many years of field work, is found in Leonard Binder, *Religion and Politics in Pakistan* (Berkeley: University of California Press, 1961).

3. Building Petro-Islam on the Ruins of Arab Nationalism

1. Head of the Department of Philosophy at the University of Damas, Sadeq Jalal al-Azm is one of the leading contemporary Arab thinkers and a defender of secularism. His book on the 1967 war, published in Beirut, has prompted a wide variety of reactions.
2. Ahmed Abdallah, *The Student Movement and National Politics in Egypt* (London: Al Saqi Books, 1985).
3. See Olivier Carré, *Septembre noir: Refus arabe de la résistance palestinienne* (Brussels: Complexe, 1980).
4. Demographic information concerning the Islamic world must be treated with some care since it comes from states where statistics are often little to be trusted, either because they are difficult to obtain or because their figures are subject to manipulation. In this light, the United Nations' publication *World Population Resource* (New York, 1994) to which I make reference itself depends on information

supplied by those states. Between 1955—when a number of Muslim countries acquired or were about to acquire independence—and 1970, the increase in population for some of the most important Muslim countries was as follows: Algeria, +41.2%; Bangladesh, +46.6%; Egypt, +42.9%; Indonesia, +39%; Iran, +49.4%; Morocco, +51.5%; Pakistan, +48.6%; Saudi Arabia, +58.3%; Turkey, +48.3%.

5. The term *achwaiyyat* literally denotes "improvised [dwellings]"; *gecekondu* translates as "built overnight," since many of these illegal homes were constructed during the hours of darkness, to avoid police obstruction.

6. Formed by the Arabic word *hit* ("wall") and the French suffix *"iste"* ("ist"), this humorous Algerian term refers to unemployed youths who pass their days leaning against a convenient wall. By implying that these youths prop up the walls to stop them from falling over, it gives them a kind of imaginary job, pointing up the irony of the full employment that was promised to the entire population by Algerian socialism.

7. It is generally considered that U.S. political support for conservative Islam dates back to the meeting between President Roosevelt and King Ibn Saud on board the cruiser *USS Quincy*, at the mouth of the Red Sea on February 14, 1945, just after the Yalta Conference. The meeting resulted in long-term American support of the Saudi regime, in return for exclusive rights for Aramco to exploit the petroleum at Hasa. An interesting American discussion of U.S. foreign policy toward Islam can be found in Scott W. Hibbard and David Little, eds., *Islamic Activism and U.S. Foreign Policy* (United States Institute of Peace, 1997).

8. The support of the Tudeh Iranian Communist Party in the Islamic Revolution of 1978–79, as well as the generally favorable reception afforded it by the communist movement throughout the world, was largely due to its anti-American bias. Thus, events in Iran were interpreted as a religious manifestation of Third World revolutions that had evolved toward socialism over preceding decades, following the example of Nasser in Egypt.

9. In the case of Saudi Arabia, the average supplying cost of the operating petroleum companies rose from $2.01 per barrel on October 1, 1973, to $10.24 on January 1, 1975, a five-fold increase within 15 months. During the second petroleum crisis, caused by the Iranian revolution, official prices rose from 120 to 165%, according to the quality of the oil, between December 1978 and May 1980. The spot market price, which varied according to the level of speculation in a deregulated market, rose to $40 per barrel in May 1979. Revenue from petroleum products among the principal Islamic oil-exporting countries is shown below, in millions of dollars per annum, before (1973) and after (1974) the October war, after the Iranian revolution (1980), and during the market turnaround in 1986:

	Saudi Arabia	Kuwait	Indonesia	Algeria	UAE
1973	4.3	1.7	0.7	1.0	0.9
1974	22.6	6.5	1.4	3.3	5.5
1980	102.2	17.9	12.9	12.5	19.5
1986	21.2	6.2	5.5	3.8	5.9

Source: Ian Skeet, *OPEC: Twenty-Five Years of Prices and Politics* (Cambridge: University Press, 1988).

Iran and Iraq, both large producers, underwent fluctuations in respective revenues, first linked to the chance events of the Islamic Revolution and subsequently to the war between the two countries from 1980 to 1988; the resources at the disposal of Saudi Arabia during this period were immeasurably greater than those available to the other oil-producing countries.

10. The four Sunni Islamic law schools *(madhhab)* refer respectively to the Imams Abu Hanifa *(ob.* 767), Malik *(ob.* 795), Al Chafii *(ob.* 820), and Ibn Hanbal *(ob.* 855).

11. See Kepel, *Les banlieues de l'islam*, ch. 4.

12. See Jonathan S. Addleton, "The Impact of the Gulf War on Migration and Remittances in Asia and the Middle East," *International Migration* 4 (1991): 522–524, and *Undermining the Centre: The Gulf Migration and Pakistan* (Karachi: Oxford University Press, 1992), p. 192.

13. This sociological phenomenon, frequently observed, is also the object of humorous comment in a novel by the Egyptian writer Sonallah Ibrahim, *The Years of Zeth.*

14. In Cairo's Medinet Nasr district, residential areas have been created to house members of the devoutly Islamic business class who have returned from the Gulf. The Al Salam Shopping Centers Li-l Mouhaggabat have specialized in providing shopping facilities for veiled women.

15. See the data provided by Ignace Leverrier in "L'Arabie Saoudite, le pèlerinage et Iran," *Cemoti* 22 (1996): 137.

16. Kepel, *Les banlieues de l'islam*, pp. 211ff.

17. This expression was coined by Z. Laïdi. See Z. Laïdi, ed., *Géopolitique du sens* (Paris: Desclée de Brouwer, 1998).

18. Noor Ahmad Baba, "The Organization of the Islamic Conference: Conceptual Framework and Institutional Structure," *Iranian Journal of International Affairs* 9, no. 3 (Autumn 1997): 341–370.

19. See Hassan Moinuddin, *The Charter of the Islamic Conference and the Legal Framework Economic Cooperation among Its Member States* (Oxford: Clarendon Press, 1987), pp. 113ff.

20. See Leverrier, "L'Arabie Saoudite, le pèlerinage et Iran."

21. Martin Kramer, "Tragedy in Mecca," in *Orbis*, Spring 1988, pp. 231ff.

22. On the calculation of zakat at the time, see G. Causse and D. Saci, "La comptabilité en pays d'islam," in Pierre Traimond, *Finance et développement en pays d'islam* (Vannes: Edicef, 1995), pp. 62–68.

23. "There are 99 types of usury. The least reprehensible can be likened to fornication between a man and his mother." From the *Collection of Hadith* (Sayings of the Prophet) by Moshim, one of the two "authentic" collectors.

24. On the debate surrounding the legal aspects of insurance from the point of view of the sharia, see the clear summary in Ernest Klingmüller, "Islam et assurances," in *Les capitaux de l'islam*, ed. Gilbert Beaugé (Paris: Presses du CNRS, 1990), pp. 153ff.

25. This "trick" of allowing a tax to be levied on interest while pretending that it does not in fact exist is especially striking in the case of the Iranian economy, which has been completely "Islamized" by decree in the Islamic Republic. Investments there are in effect paid for by a "tax on guaranteed profit," which corresponds to a tax on interest and is viewed as such by those who lend money on the black market.

26. On the question of whether interest-earning loans are permissible or not according to modern and contemporary Egyptian ulemas, see Michel Galloux, *Finance islamique et pouvoir politique: le cas de l'Egypte* (Paris: Presses Universitaires de France, 1997), in particular pp. 40–45. The present (2001) sheik of Al Azhar, who at the time was mufti of the republic, declared a fatwa in 1989 that permitted a conventional banking system of interest-bearing loans. This followed a decade in which Islamic investment companies attracted huge numbers of savers away from conventional Egyptian banks.

27. The development of Islamic finance has created a new and remunerative occupation for well-known Muslim theologians, that is, those capable of sitting on a "sharia board" and giving a bank or an investment company serious religious credibility. The Egyptian Sheik Yusuf al-Qaradawi, a fellow-traveler of the Muslim Brotherhood based in Qatar, is much in demand by Islamic banks because he favors allowing market forces to operate freely.

28. See Chibli Mallat, "Muhammad Baqer as-Sadr," in *Pioneers of Islamic Revival*, ed. Ali Rahnema (London: Zed Books, 1994), pp. 263–267.

29. Fuad al-Omar and Mohammed Abdel-Haq, *Islamic Banking: Theory, Practice and Challenges* (London: Zed Books, 1996), pp. 1–19.

30. See Galloux, *Finance islamique*, pp. 23–25.

31. For the correlation between the explosion in oil prices and the rise of Islamic banking, see Abdelkader Sid Ahmed, "Pétrole et économie islamique," in *Les capitaux de l'islam*, ed. Beaugé, pp. 73ff.

32. With a share capital of $2 billion, mainly supplied by Saudi Arabia, Kuwait, and Libya, the IDB tried to create an Islamic economic and financial trading arena. However, less than 10% of exchanges made by Muslim countries were in fact transacted between themselves, the rest being mainly with Western countries. The IDB financed infrastructure projects but also had to contribute aid to poor countries for the importation of Western goods, which went against its initial aims.

33. See Clement Henry Moore, "Islamic Banks and Competitive Politics in the Arab World and Turkey," *Middle East Journal* 44, no. 2 (Spring 1990): 243–249.

34. See Samir Abid Shaik, "Islamic Banks and Financial Institutions: A Survey," *Journal of Muslim Minority Affairs* 27, no. 1 (1997): 118–119. The author, secretary general of the International Association of Islamic Banks, based in Jeddah and directed by Prince Mohammed al-Faisal Al-Saud, lists 187 banks and institutions in total, but only takes into account the 144 on which he was able to obtain precise information.

4. Islamism in Egypt, Malaysia, and Pakistan

1. This chapter puts into perspective and updates the information presented in Gilles Kepel, *The Prophet and Pharaoh: Muslim Extremism in Egypt* (London: Al Saqi; Berkeley: University of California Press, 1985).

2. For an examination of the rise of Islam in Malaysia during the 1970s, consult the comprehensive study by Judith Nagata, *The Reflowering of Malaysian Islam: Modern Religious Radicals and Their Roots* (Vancouver: University of British Columbia Press, 1984). In addition, an analysis by a closely involved witness can be found in Chandra Muzaffar, *Islamic Resurgence in Malaysia* (Penerbit Fajar: Petaling Jaya, 1987). Many aspects are discussed in N. John Funston, "The Politics of Islamic Reassertion: The Case of Malaysia," in *Readings on Islam in Southeast Asia*, ed. A. Ibrahim, S. Siddique, and Y. Hussain (Singapore: Institute of Southeast Asian Studies), and in Nash, "Islamic Resurgence in Malaysia and Indonesia."

3. This calls to mind the social and intergenerational difficulties over the use of French or classical Arabic by the ruling class in North Africa at the same period.

4. Its name (The Home of Arqam) derives from a friend of the Prophet, who had offered him hospitality.

5. For the growth of Islam between the years 1980–1990, see Chandra Muzaffar, "Two Approaches to Islam: Revisiting Islamic Resurgence in Malaysia," unpublished, May 1995; David Camroux, "State Responses to Islamic Resurgence in Malaysia: Accommodation, Co-option, and Confrontation," *Asian Survey,* September 1996, pp. 852ff. Much factual information translated from the local press is to be found in Laurent Metzger, *Stratégie islamique en Malaisie (1975–1995)* (Paris: L'Harmattan, 1996).

6. Born in Mecca in 1936 and rector of the International Islamic University since 1988, Dr. Abdulhamid Abu Sulayman is a stalwart of the international Islamist establishment. He was secretary-general of the World Assembly of Muslim Youth (WAMY), part of the Muslim World League, from 1973 to 1979, and is author of several works, notably *Towards an Islamic Theory of International Relations* (Herndon: International Institute of Islamic Thought, 1993).

7. The events of autumn 1998 are examined by an eyewitness, Raphael Pouyé, in *Mahathir Mohamad: L'Islam et l'invention d'un "universalisme alternatif,"* a memoir (Paris: Institut d'Études Politiques de Paris, November 1998).

8. Dispatch dated January 28, 1999 (my thanks to David Camroux for calling my attention to this).

9. In fact, an attaché from the Thai embassy was pursued by the religious police (armed with bar-code scanners) who had discovered him in a hotel room with his wife; he was unable to prove the legality of his marriage. Anwar Ibrahim's elder brother fell victim to the same type of religious zealotry; the young woman with whom he was discovered was none other than his second wife (polygamy being perfectly legal in the eyes of the sharia). Following the orders of the regime, the press, which had been quick to make ironic comments about the family's libido,

found it had wasted its time, since it could only give way, faced as it was with polygamy sanctioned by Islamic edicts that were treated with the greatest respect in
all circumstances.

10. Munawwar A. Anees, "Jefferson vs. Mahathir: How the West Came to This Mus-
    lim's Rescue," *Los Angeles Times*, September 13, 1999.
11. See the interview with Anwar Ibrahim, then minister of finance, during a session
    of the World Bank in Washington by Joyce M. Davis, *Between Jihad and Salaam:
    Profiles in Islam* (London: Macmillan, 1997), pp. 297ff.
12. For the debates within the Islamic sphere of influence on the subject of democrati-
    zation, faced with "Asiatic values" and the Islamic legitimacy of Mahathir's power,
    see S. Ahmad Hussein, "Muslim Politics and the Discourse on Democracy in Ma-
    laysia," in *Democracy in Malaysia: Discourses and Practices*, ed. Loh Kok Wah and
    Khoo Boo Teik (London: Curzon, 2000).
13. On-the-spot analysis can be found in Mohammed Ayoob, "Two Faces of Political
    Islam: Iran and Pakistan Compared," in *Asian Survey* 29, no. 6 (June 1979): 535–
    536.
14. Mumtaz Ahmad, "The Crescent and the Sword: Islam, the Military and Political
    Legitimacy in Pakistan, 1977–85," *Middle East Journal* 50, no. 3 (Summer 1996):
    372–386. Markus Daechsel, "Military Islamization of Pakistan and the Spectre of
    Colonial Perceptions," *Contemporary South Asia* 6, no. 2 (1997): 141–160, puts the
    accent on the use of Islam by the military hierarchy, without the latter being af-
    fected by any ideological conviction.
15. Between 1971 and 1988 the transfers of Pakistani emigrants to the Middle East cre-
    ated the primary source of currency and was a very important factor contribut-
    ing to the emergence of autonomous social groups that did not depend on the
    state for their social advancement—the opposite of what went on under state-
    controlled nationalism. On such matters, see Addleton, *Undermining the Centre*,
    pp. 200ff. On the strengthening of ties with the Middle East after the 1971 defeat,
    see ibid., pp. 45–48.
16. See the 1990 calendar of the International Islamic University.
17. See S. J. Burki, *Pakistan under Bhutto* (New York: St. Martin's Press, 1982).
18. On Ali Bhutto's last months in government, see in particular William L. Richter,
    "The Political Dynamics of Islamic Resurgence in Pakistan," *Asian Survey* 6, no. 29
    (June 1979): 551–552, and John Adams, "Pakistan's Economic Performance in the
    1980s: Implications for Political Balance," in *Zia's Pakistan*, ed. Craig Baxter (Boul-
    der: Westview Press, 1985), pp. 51–52.
19. See S. V. R. Nasr, "Islamic Opposition to the Islamic State: The Jama'at-I Islami
    1977–1988," *International Journal of Middle East Studies* 25, no. 2 (May 1993):
    267.
20. Baxter, *Zia's Pakistan*, describes the support that the regime enjoyed among the
    different social groups.
21. See Anita M. Weiss, ed., *Islamic Reassertion in Pakistan: The Application of Islamic
    Laws in a Modern State* (New York: Syracuse University Press, 1986), esp. pp. 11–
    17.

22. See Grace Clark, "*Zakat* and *'ashr* as a Welfare System," in ibid., pp. 79–95, esp. p. 93.
23. Jamal Malik, *Colonialization of Islam: Dissolution of Traditional Institutions in Pakistan* (New Delhi: Vanguard Books, 1996), esp. pp. 179ff, "Mushroom-Growth."
24. See, among others, Human Rights Commission of Pakistan, *HCPR Newsletter* 7, no. 2 (April 1996): 32, which reports the case of madrassa students in chains.
25. Malik, *Colonialization of Islam*, p. 196, notes that the number of madrassas controlled by the Deobandis grew by 500% between 1979 and 1984. He counts 1,097 establishments for the Deobandis at that date; see his tables on pp. 198–199.
26. The internal crisis suffered by the Jamaat-e-Islami over what attitude to take toward Zia is presented in great detail by Nasr, "Islamic Opposition to the Islamic State," and returned to in Nasr, *The Vanguard of the Islamic Revolution*, pp. 188–205.
27. Zia died when the military aircraft he was in exploded. With him were the American ambassador to Islamabad and General Akhtar, the mastermind of the Afghan jihad.

5. Khomeini's Revolution and Its Legacy

1. For Saïd Amir Arjomand, author of the influential book *The Turban for the Crown: The Islamic Revolution in Iran* (Oxford: Oxford University Press, 1988), the revolution was an antimodernist movement, which (unlike the French Revolution) brought traditional groups like the clergy and the bazaar merchants into power. Nikki Keddie, *Roots of Revolution: An Interpretative History of Modern Iran* (New Haven: Yale University Press, 1981), accords a central role to the ulemas and their capacity to give meaning to a reactionary social movement opposing a destructuring modernity. Ahmad Ashraf and Ali Banuazizi, "The State, Classes and Modes of Mobilization in the Iranian Revolution," *State, Culture and Society*, Spring 1985, pp. 3–40, identifies the role of three groups, the ulemas, the intellectuals, and the bazaris, and makes one of the first attempts to classify the progress of the revolution, which in turn is detailed with great precision in Mohsen Milani, *The Making of Iran's Islamic Revolution: From Monarchy to Islamic Republic* (London: Westview Press, 1988), chs. 7–10. Finally, the works of Farhad Khosrokhavar, in particular *Le discours populaire de la révolution Iranienne* (with Paul Vieille) (Paris: Contemporanéité, 1990); *L'utopie sacrifiée: Sociologie de la révolution Iranienne* (Paris: Presses de la FNSP, 1993); and *L'islamisme et la mort: Le martyre révolutionnaire en Iran* (Paris: L'Harmattan, 1995), stress the part played by the working class in the revolutionary movement.
2. Information on the secular middle class in Iran is found in Azadeh Kian-Thiébaut, *Secularization of Iran: A Doomed Failure? The New Middle Class and the Making of Modern Iran*, Travaux et mémoires de l'Institut d'études Iraniennes, vol. 3 (Paris, 1998).
3. The reference work on the People's Mujahedeen is E. Abrahamian, *The Iranian Mujahidin*.

4. Information on the working class and immigrants from rural districts is to be found in Farhad Kazemi's *Poverty and Revolution in Iran* (New York: New York University Press, 1980), and Khosrokhavar, *L'utopie sacrifiée,* p. 98, which points out that, on the eve of revolution, almost half of the population of Tehran had been born elsewhere.

5. This expression, used by Khosrokhavar, shows the continuance and inability to adjust of rural people, faced with the new situation of being urban immigrants.

6. Assef Bayat, *Street Politics: People's Movements in Iran* (New York: Columbia University Press, 1997), recounts from the author's own experience the position of a young peasant migrant who became assimilated into society through the Islamic educational network that existed in the popular district in which he lived; see pp. xiii–xv.

7. In September 1977 Khomeini wrote to the ulemas at a time when repression was eased, encouraging them to demonstrate against the shah and not leave the monopoly of opposition to the intellectuals. See Milani, *The Making of Iran's Islamic Revolution,* p. 187.

8. The anniversary of the 40th day after death *(dhikrat al arbain)* is celebrated in the Middle East.

9. *Tekkiye* are places where the martyrdom of Shiite imams is celebrated, and they have been used for all kinds of ceremonial gatherings, as well as revolutionary assemblies. The *heyat* are local religious associations, an essential part of the social fabric through which commands are issued and rallies are organized. The *Hosseiniye* are in principle used in commemorating the martyrdom of the Imam Hussein, killed at Karbala.

10. For the use of these terms by Khomeini at various times, see Abrahamian, *Khomeinism,* pp. 27–31, which observes that after the revolution, Khomeini extended the meaning of the term *mustadafeen* to include the traditional middle class, who supported the new social order.

11. Khomeini's refusal to find fault with Shariati (noted by Rahnema in *An Islamic Utopian,* p. 275) contrasts strongly with his continued opposition to the People's Mujahedeen.

12. Although numerous writers estimate that the lower strata of society played only a minor role in the revolution, I use here the analyses by Vieille and Khosrokhavar, who concluded that studies based on these writings underestimate the political part played by social groups without access to literacy.

13. On these actions, see the data given by Bayat in *Street Politics,* chs. 2, 3.

14. See the interview that appeared in the Lebanese paper *Al Safir* on January 19, 1979, quoted by David Menashri in "Khomeini's Vision: Nationalism or World Order?" in *The Iranian Revolution and the Muslim World,* ed. D. Menashri (Boulder: Westview Press, 1990), p. 51.

15. On these events, see Al-Yassini, *Religion and State in the Kingdom of Saudi Arabia,* pp. 124ff.

16. On November 28, which was the date of the celebration of the Achoura festival commemorating the martyrdom of the Imam Hussein, there was a demonstration

involving thousands of Shiites for the first time in the history of the Saudi kingdom. The Shiites confronted the police in a protest against the discrimination to which they were subjected, chanting pro-Khomeini slogans. At the beginning of February 1980, on the first anniversary of the Ayatollah's return to Tehran, further incidents took place in the town of Qatif, where more Shiites demonstrated, brandishing pictures of Khomeini and setting fire to several buildings.

17. In July 1979 Saddam Hussein, until then vice-president under General Hassan al-Bakr, took power in Baghdad. This act was accompanied by the execution of officials for "conspiracy."

18. Mohammad Baqir as-Sadr (1935–1980), one of the founders of the Shiite Iraqi Islamist party Dawa (Call to Islam) in 1958, is revered to this day in the Islamist movement, Sunni as well as Shiite, as the founder of the Muslim economy, through his 1961 book *Iqtisaduna* (Our Economy). Sadr was at the forefront of the power struggle between the Baathist and Marxist parties in Baghdad and played an important role in the politicization of the religious faction of Nadjaf, where Khomeini lived between 1964 and 1978. See Amazia Baram, "The Radical Shi'ite Movement in Irak," in *The Iranian Revolution and the Muslim World*, ed. Menashri, pp. 133ff, and Hanna Batatu, "Shi'ite Organizations in Irak," in, *Shi-ism and Social Protest*, ed. J. Cole and N. Keddie (New Haven: Yale University Press, 1986), pp. 139ff. Also Pierre Martin (pseud.), "Le clergé chi'ite en Irak hier et aujourd'hui," in *Maghreb-Machrek* 115, January 1987.

19. With the onset of war, the Baathist doctrine was toned down in Iraq, since it was proving an embarrassment to Saddam Hussein's regime in its competition for Muslim supremacy. The phenomenon expanded during the 1991 Gulf War, when Iraq would oppose the Arab states, disputing their Islamic legitimacy, in particular that of Saudi Arabia.

20. Some of the leaders, among them Yasir Arafat, had associated with the Muslim Brothers in their youth but had become more moderate in their political maturity in pursuit of Arab nationalism.

21. See Dalal Bizri, "L'islamisme libanais et palestinien: rupture dans la continuité," *Peuples méditerranéens* 64–65, July–December 1993, pp. 265ff, and Michel Seurat, "Le quartier de Bab Tebbané à Tripoli (Liban)," in *L'État de Barbarie* (Paris: Seuil, 1989), pp. 110ff.

22. On Christian denominations in the Near East, see J.-P. Valognes, *Vie et mort des chrétiens d'Orient* (Paris: Fayard, 1994), a book that is unabashedly engaged but which contains a great deal of clearly presented information.

23. The fullest description of the Palestinian presence in Lebanon appears in Yezid Sayigh, *Armed Struggle and the Search for the State: The Palestinian National Movement, 1949–1993* (Oxford: Clarendon Press, 1997), esp. part 3: "The State in Exile, 1973–1982," pp. 319–544.

24. On the prudence of the Palestinian Muslim Brothers, see Ziad Abu-Amr, *Islamic Fundamentalism in the West Bank and Gaza: Muslim Brotherhood and Islamic Jihad* (Bloomington: Indiana University Press, 1994), esp. ch. 2.

25. See Mohga Machhour and Alain Roussillon, *La Revolution Iranienne dans la presse*

égyptienne (Cairo: CEDEJ, 1982), pp. 45–54, for extracts from this work. Published under the pseudonym of Fathi Abdel Aziz, this book, the first to appear in Arabic on the victory of the Islamic Revolution in Iran, sold out its first print run of 10,000 copies and earned the author a brief spell of detention by the Egyptian police. See Rifat Sid Ahmed, ed., *Al amal al kamila li-l shahid al douktour fathi al-shqaqi* [Complete Works of the Martyr Doctor Fathi Shqaqi] (Cairo: Yafa, 1997), vol. 1, pp. 53, 459–534.

26. On the Palestinian Islamic Jihad movement, in addition to Abu-Amr, *Islamic Fundamentalism in the West Bank and Gaza*, ch. 4, see Elie Rekhess, "The Iranian Impact on the Islamic Movement in the Gaza Strip," in *The Iranian Revolution and the Muslim World*, ed. Menashri, pp. 189–206; and Jean-François Legrain, *Les voix du soulèvement palestinien* (Cairo: CEDEJ, Cairo, 1991), pp. 14–15.

27. On the organizational elements of this movement, see J.-F. Legrain, "Autonomie palestinienne: la politique des néo-notables," *REMMM* 81–82 (March–April 1996): 153–206.

28. On the sociology of the Lebanese Shiite community and its transformations in the 1970s, see A. R. Norton, *Amal and the Shi'a: Struggle for the Soul of Lebanon* (Austin: University of Texas Press, 1987), esp. pp. 13–38.

29. See Fouad Ajami, *The Vanished Imam: Musa al Sadr and the Shia of Lebanon* (New York: Cornell University Press, 1986).

30. Until the mid-1970s, the Lebanese leftist movements, in particular the Lebanese Organization for Communist Action, known by its Arabic name *Al-Mounazzamé* (The Organization), recruited many educated young Shiites who were first-generation city-dwellers. Musa Sadr's movement also tried to attract this group.

31. This is the belief to which Ajami's title, *The Vanished Imam*, refers. According to tradition, the Imam Mahdi, Mohammad al-Muntazar, made himself disappear in 874.

32. On the Lebanese Hezbollah and its links with Iran, see M. Kramer, "The Pan-Islamic Premise of Hizballah," in *The Iranian Revolution and the Muslim World*, ed. Menashri, pp. 105ff. On the the part the Lebanese Islamic party played in the geopolitics of the time as one of Iran's allies against the West, see Magnus Ranstorp, *Hizb'Allah in Lebanon: The Politics of the Western Hostage Crisis* (New York: St. Martin's Press, 1997).

33. Financial aid given by the Islamic Republic to the Lebanese Hezbollah between 1982 and 1989 is reckoned at half a million dollars by J. R. Norton in "Lebanon: The Internal Conflict and the Iranian Connection," in J. Esposito, ed., *The Iranian Revolution: Its Global Impact* (Miami: Florida International University Press, 1990), p. 126.

34. In this event, 241 U.S. marines and 56 French legionnaires were killed. In Tyre, the attack resulted in 29 dead, of whom six were Lebanese.

35. For a chronology and detailed interpretation of the kidnapping and hostage-taking, see Ranstorp, *Hizb'Allah in Lebanon*, pp. 86ff.

36. These actions, carried out in response to the financial support of Kuwait in the Iraqi war against Iran, implicated activists from the Iraqi Dawa party as well as Lebanese militants, united by family connections among their leaders.

37. The pressure brought to bear on France also revealed itself in a series of attacks in Paris and the provinces during 1985 and 1986.
38. See the reports by Martin Kramer, "Intra-Regional and Muslim Affairs," in *Middle East Contemporary Survey (MECS)* 6:290, 7:240, 8:168.
39. *Wal Fadjri* 1 (January 13, 1984), p. 2. Editorial signed by the founder, Sidy Lamine Nyass.
40. *Wal Fadjri* 2:14. Egypt was suspended from the OIC after the signing of the Israeli-Egyptian peace accords in March 1979 and was then reinstated at the Casablanca conference in 1984.
41. Moriba Magassouba, *L'islam au Sénégal: Demain les mollahs?* (Paris: Karthala, 1985).
42. The Iranian embassy in Dakar was closed in the spring of 1984, giving rise to protests in *Wal Fadjri* 3:8–9.
43. Interview with Sidy Lamine Nyass, Dakar, February 1998.
44. See Fred von der Mehden, "Malaysian and Indonesian Islamic Movements and the Iranian Connection," in Esposito, *The Iranian Revolution*, p. 248. A director of the ICMI, founded in December 1990, who went to Iran in 1979, also told me of his enthusiasm for the events in Iran. Yet he did not wish matters in Indonesia to take precisely the same course, preferring to see the revolution as an inspiration rather than as a pattern to be followed. Interview, Jakarta, August 1997. See examples given by Esposito, ed., *The Iranian Revolution*, for an overview. In December 1982 five people close to Alija Izetbegovic, coming from an organization of Young Muslims in Bosnia-Herzegovina, attended the Friday meeting of the imams in Tehran. This was used against them in August 1983, when they were among twelve "Muslim fundamentalists" sentenced to long terms in prison in Yugoslavia.
45. In addition to grants to various Muslim associations and invitations to congresses held in Tehran (such as the one in May 1984 mentioned above), the Islamic Republic published journals of propaganda in several languages praising its achievements and the regime's objectives.
46. For a detailed analysis of this phenomenon, see Kepel, *Les banlieues de l'islam*, pp. 313–352.
47. This information on the movement by Kalim Siddiqi is collected in Gilles Kepel, *Allah in the West* (London: Polity Press; Stanford: Stanford University Press, 1994).
48. The Baqi cemetery was said to have been the last resting place of four of the imams and of the Prophet's daughter, Fatima, wife of Ali (from whose line the Shiites claim descent). It was ransacked by the *Ikhwan* of Ibn Saud when they seized Medina.
49. The Iranians made up the largest contingent of pilgrims, with almost 18% of the total.
50. The degree of Iranian pressure was linked to the progress of the war against Iraq, which had turned to Tehran's advantage in 1984, and to Iranian attempts to separate Saudi Arabia from Saddam Hussein.
51. For the development of pilgrimages to Mecca, the reader is referred to the reports of Martin Kramer in *MECS* 8–12. For the 1987 pilgrimage, see Kramer, "Tragedy in Mecca," *Orbis*.

6. Jihad in Afghanistan and Intifada in Palestine

1. Mark Adkin and Mohammad Yousaf, *The Bear Trap* (rpt. Havertown, PA: Casemate, 2001). It is now known that from the summer of 1979 onward the American CIA was supplying the Afghan anti-communist resistance with arms and money, and this eventually prompted the intervention of Moscow.

2. To three million refugees in Pakistan were added some two million in Iran, mostly minority Shiites from a population concentrated in western Afghanistan.

3. Directorate of Interservices Intelligence, the army secret service.

4. The term "jihadists" will be used in the pages that follow to mean foreign partisans of the jihad. During the 1990s, radical militants of this kind referred to themselves as "salafist-jihadists" *(salafiyyun jihadiyyun)*.

5. Barnett R. Rubin, in a key reference work on the present-day Afghan situation, *The Fragmentation of Afghanistan: State Formation and Collapse in the International System* (New Haven: Yale University Press, 1995), ch. 4, pp. 85–105, develops the parallel between the social origins and the cultural trajectory of communists and Muslims.

6. Babrak Karmal's Parcham faction was eliminated in July 1978. Nour Mohammed Taraki, historic leader of the khalq, was strangled by order of his second-in-command, Hafizullah Amine, who took power on September 15, 1979.

7. Egypt had signed a peace treaty with Israel and for this reason was suspended from the OIC, a suspension that was to last until 1984.

8. See the text of the declaration of the OIC's third summit and the resolutions and recommendations in *MECS* 5 (1980–81): 137–145.

9. Islamic jurisprudence makes a distinction between defensive jihad and offensive jihad. The former is proclaimed when a territory of the Umma is attacked by infidels and the continuity and existence of Islam is under threat. This explains why the ulemas consider that the declaration of a fatwa, a legal judgment made with reference to the sacred texts, obliges all Muslims to take part in the jihad, by fighting or contributing to the cause financially or through charity and prayer. On the other hand, when jihad is declared to attack "the lands of the impious" (dar el-kufr), to conquer them and submit their inhabitants to the law of Islam, there is only a collective duty, or fard kifaya, with responsibility resting on the army chief and his men, without the entirety of Muslims being obliged to take part. On this theme, there are no very recent works available, but Alfred Morabia, in *Le gihad dans l'islam médiéval: Le combat sacré des origines au douzième siècle* (Paris: Albin Michel, 1993), covers the classic texts. For the modern era there is a collection of articles by Rudolf Peters, *Islam and Colonialism: The Doctrine of Jihad in Modern History* (The Hague: Mouton, 1979). Ramadan al-Bouti, *Le jihad en islam: Comment le comprendre? Comment le pratiquer?* (Damascus: Dar el-Fikr, 1996), explains the jihad from the point of view of a leading Syrian ulema, along with the debates raised by these questions.

10. The genesis of the Afghani Islamic movement is described with precision in the key work by Olivier Roy, *Islam and Resistance in Afghanistan,* 2nd ed. (Cambridge: Cambridge University Press, 1990), from which most of the data here are taken.

11. This "putschist" faction in the Islamist movement appeared at about the same time in Egypt, where an aborted uprising took place at the military academy in Heliopolis in April 1974, influenced by the power-seizing strategy of the Party for Islamic Liberation, founded in Palestine in 1948 by Taqi al-din al-Nabahani. He advocated taking control of the state by force, as a reaction to what he considered to be the failure of the implantation strategies of the Muslim Brothers championed by Hassan al-Banna. For further reading on this party see Soha Taji-Faruqi, *A Fundamental Quest: Hizb-al Tahrir and the Search for the Islamic Caliphate* (London: Grey Seal Books, 1996).

12. See Rubin, *The Fragmentation of Afghanistan*, pp. 26ff.

13. The secularized urban middle class, not numerous in Afghanistan, was one of the main targets of communist repression.

14. Interview with the deputy amir of the Jamiat-e-Islami, Mansourah (Lahore), in April 1998. According to this official, the Arabs of the peninsula, not knowing the difference between the Afghan parties, relied on the JI, who, in turn, financed the parties known to them—privileging the Hezb.

15. In 1984, he received King Faisal's international prize awarded for distinguished services to Islam—which each year singles out a figure admired by the Saudi king and rewards him with a prize of 350,000 Saudi rials.

16. This policy is made explicit and defended by one of its leading advocates, Brigadier (retired) Mohammad Yousaf, author of *Silent Soldier: The Man Behind the Afghan Jehad* (Lahore: Jang Publishers, 1991). Yousaf was also a coauthor of *The Bear Trap*.

17. See Rubin, *The Fragmentation of Afghanistan*, pp. 196–225, esp. tables on pp. 208–209.

18. Ibid., p. 215.

19. The Arabic term *qawm* denotes the traditional primary "solidarity group" through which Afghans are linked to their environment (the state, other individuals, and so on).

20. Before 1947 the Deobandi movement was linked with various radical movements whose aim was to shake off British administration—such as the Khilafat movement, which mobilized Muslims from the Indian subcontinent until Ataturk's abolition of the Ottoman caliphate in 1924.

21. American involvement in support of Afghanistan lifted most of the prejudice against Pakistan's nuclear development program, at least until 1987. In 1982 Pakistan became the fourth largest beneficiary of American military aid, after Israel, Egypt, and Turkey. On these points, see Leo E. Rose and Kamal Matinuddin, eds., *Beyond Afghanistan: The Emerging U.S.-Pakistan Relations* (Berkeley: University of California Press, 1989).

22. The precise figures as well as a description of the mechanics of the aid process are given in Rubin, *The Fragmentation of Afghanistan*. Total aid from the CIA is estimated at $3 billion. According to Milton Bearden, former CIA chief in charge of the Afghan department, "The Saudi dollar-for-dollar match with the US taxpayer was fundamental to the success [of the ten-year engagement in Afghanistan]." http://www.pbs.org/wgbh/pages/frontline/shows/binladen/interviews/bearden/html.

23. Pakistan's border regions with Afghanistan, classified as "tribal zones," benefited from internal autonomous government, which allowed them to import tax-free merchandise, a pretext for large-scale smuggling. Opium poppies were cultivated without much interference, and arms of all kinds were openly sold. Their prices were very low because so many had been diverted from supplies to the Afghani war (personal experience, April 1998).

24. In 1988, the Muslim World League, through its branch in Peshawar, claimed to have opened 150 Koran study centers and 85 Islamic schools for Afghans, in addition to Saudi humanitarian aid valued at 445 million Saudi rials. Prince Salman has claimed that his support committee spent 539 million Pakistani rupees on humanitarian aid (see *MECS* 1986, p. 133, and 1988, p. 197).

25. A biography (in effect a hagiography) of Abdallah Azzam is featured on the Azzam Brigades website, http://www.azzam.com. I especially thank M. Ibrahim al-Gharaibeh in Amman for having worked out Abdallah Azzam's itinerary with me.

26. For details of the International Islamic University of Islamabad, see p. 95.

27. On this phenomenon and its development in Sudan, see J. Bellion-Jourdan, "L'humanitaire et l'islamisme soudanais: les organizations *Dawa Islamiyya* et *Islamic African Relief Agency*," *Politique africaine* 66 (1997): 61ff.

28. The brochure published under the title of *Ilhaq bi-l qafila* (Join the [Jihad] Caravan) ends with practical help to foreign jihadists arriving at Peshawar: how to obtain a passport and visa, which telephone number to call, instructions about the vehicle that will pick them up at the airport and take them to the relevant offices, and so on. Abdallah Azzam, *Ilhaq bi-l qafila* (rpt. Beirut: Dar Ibn Hazm, 1992). The Azzam Brigades website (which sells this text by mailorder) describes it as "a source of inspiration for Muslims from all quarters, on their way to fight in Afghanistan and Bosnia."

29. The Azzam Brigades website, http://www.azzam.com, which originated in London, was started after Abdallah Azzam's death; in the past it has specialized in information about the jihads of the 1990s, mainly in Bosnia and Chechnya.

30. Abdallah Azzam, *Al difa': 'an aradi al muslimin ahamm furud al a'yan,* 2nd ed. (Peshawar: Jamiat al dawa wa-l jihad, 1405–6 Hegiran [1984–85]). An English translation, entitled *Defense of Muslim Lands,* "made by members of the Brotherhood who were fighting in Bosnia in 1995" and available by correspondence on the same website (see preceding note), is introduced as follows: "This book is centered on the famous fatwa of Ibn Taïmiyya (d. 1328 A.D.): the first obligation after the Faith is to repel the enemy aggressors who attack religion and the world." The same fatwa was to be used, after Azzam's death and extrapolating its interpretation, to justify the "jihad against the Americans occupying the land of the Holy Places" which was called by Osama bin Laden. The text of this "Declaration of Jihad" refers to Azzam.

31. Abdallah Azzam, *Jihad sha'b muslim* (The Jihad of a Muslim People) (Beirut: Dar Ibn Hazm, 1992), p. 24.

32. Azzam, *Ilhaq bi-l qafila,* p. 44, among other references.

33. Azzam, *Bacha'ir al-nasr* (The Omens of Victory), same edition, p. 28. Text of the

sermon preached at Peshawar during the prayer of Eid al-Kebir (Id al-Adha, or Feast of Sacrifice) in 1988.

34. Not to take part in the jihad once it became an "individual obligation" was a sin comparable to not saying daily prayers or not fasting during Ramadan, according to the consensus of most clerics (with the exception of some Hanbalites who considered that prayers had priority), explains Azzam in *Jihad sha'b muslim,* p. 25, among others.

35. Ibid.

36. Ibid., pp. 26, 59.

37. Assem Akram, *Histoire de la guerre d'Afghanistan* (Paris, 1996), p. 268n1, for the first estimate; Xavier Raufer, *VSD* (September 3, 1998): 20, quoting British sources of information, for the second. According to Milton Bearden, the former CIA chief in Afghanistan, there were never more than 2,000 Arabs actually in Afghan territory at one time, and their participation in the fighting was minimal.

38. On the visits made by Sheik Omar Abdel Rahman to Peshawar, see the records collected by Mary Anne Weaver, *A Portrait of Egypt* (New York: Farrar, Straus & Giroux, 1999), pp. 169ff.

39. Osama bin Laden was an exception, according to his admirers. He apparently personally led his troops into murderous engagements against the Soviets, showing great physical courage. This earned him a reverence that riches alone could never have compelled.

40. Secretly negotiated in Oslo, the "Oslo Accords," as they were known, were signed in Washington on September 13, 1993, by Itzhak Rabin, prime minister of Israel, and Yasir Arafat, president of the PLO, in the presence of U.S. President Bill Clinton.

41. Salah Khalaf, quoted in *MECS* 1988, p. 237.

42. The best-documented account of the beginnings of the intifada remains that of Z. Schiff and E. Ya'ari, *Intifada: The Palestinian Uprising, Israel's Third Front* (New York: Simon & Schuster, 1990).

43. In 1991, the birthrate in the West Bank and Gaza was 46.5/100 and 56.10/100 respectively; and the reproduction rate was 8.1 and 9.8 children, respectively, for each woman. See P. Fargues, "Démographie de guerre, démographie de paix," in G. Salamé, ed., *Proche-Orient, les exigences de la paix* (Brussels: Complexe, 1994), p. 26.

44. See Sayigh, *Armed Struggle,* pp. 608, 628.

45. In 1987 almost one half of the land of the territories occupied by Israel in 1967 had passed under control of the Jewish state, and more than 60,000 Israeli settlers were installed in the West Bank and Gaza. For information on Gaza's economy under the occupation, see Sara Roy, *The Gaza Strip: The Political Economy of De-Development* (Washington, D.C.: Institute for Palestine Studies, 1995).

46. See Adil Yahya, "The Role of the Refugee Camps," in *Intifada: Palestine at the Crossroads,* ed. Jamal R. Nassar and Roger Heacock (New York: Praeger, 1990), p. 95.

47. For the degree of participation of various social groups in the first year of the intifada, see these contrasting analyses: H. J. Bargouti, "The Villages in the Intifada"; J. R. Hiltermann, "The Role of the Working Class in the Uprising"; and S. Tamari,

"Urban Merchants in the Palestinian Uprising"—all in *Intifada: Palestine at the Crossroads,* ed. Nassar and Heacock, pp. 107–125, 143–175. For a balanced survey of the part played by the shebab for the duration of the intifada, see Laetitia Bucaille, *Gaza: La violence de la paix* (Paris: Presses de Sciences Po, 1998), pp. 29–51.

48. The date of the beginning of the intifada has been the subject of debate between Islamic Jihad (who fixed it as October 6, the same date as a military operation led by its militants) and the PLO and Hamas, who remember it as December 9.

49. "To criticize the Palestinian central authority was to be perceived as comforting the enemy: whence the difficulty encountered throughout the 1980s by Palestinian Islamists in their struggle for political, ideological and social legitimacy," observed Jean-François Legrain in "La Palestine: de la terre perdue à la reconquête du territoire," *Cultures et Conflits,* 21–22 (Spring 1996), p. 202.

50. See J.-F. Legrain, *Les voix du soulèvement palestinien, 1987–1988* (Cairo: Cedej, 1991), p. 15. Original text of the official statement p. II/12.

51. See J.-F. Legrain, "L'intifada dans sa troisième année," *Esprit,* July–August 1990, pp. 16–17.

52. Articles 15 and 13, quoted from Legrain's translation in *Les voix du soulèvement palestinien,* pp. 155–156. The charter is a grab-bag of common themes in Islamist groups, its content being rhetorical rather than operational. Article 24 picks up all the clichés of twentieth-century anti-Semitism, which recur regularly in the writings of the Muslim Brotherhood. For more on this, see Kepel, *The Prophet and Pharaoh,* pp. 118–124. Sayigh, *Armed Struggle,* pp. 631–632, attributes its mediocrity of ideas and style to its having been edited by young activists from Gaza. There is a detailed analysis of the document by Legrain in "La Palestine: de la terre perdue à la reconquête du territoire," pp. 204–210.

53. "In the first three years of the uprising, the GNP per head dropped by 41% in the Gaza Strip—from $1,700 to $1,000 U.S., which was below the threshold of poverty for a couple with a family of four living in Israel in 1989," S. Roy, *The Gaza Strip,* p. 295.

54. See *MECS* 14 (1990): 252.

55. See J.-F. Legrain, "A Defining Moment: Palestinian Islamic Fundamentalism," in *Islamic Fundamentalism and the Gulf Crisis,* ed. James Piscatori (Chicago: The American Academy of Arts and Sciences, 1991), p. 79.

56. See *MECS* 14 (1990): 252.

7. Islamization in Algeria and the Sudan

1. Information from the International Monetary Fund, *Algeria: Stabilization and Transition to the Market* (Washington D.C.: IMF, 1998), p. 4.

2. The term *trabendo* derives from the colloquial Spanish word *estraperlo* ("contraband, black market").

3. The Algerian "delay" is attributable in part to the late independence of the country (1962, compared with Nasser's seizure of power in Cairo in 1952). It was only at

the beginning of the 1980s that the first generation grew up who had not lived under colonial rule.

4. Séverine Labat, *Les islamistes algériens: Entre les urnes et le maquis* (Paris: Seuil, 1995), pp. 90–94.

5. For a more detailed account of the events of November 1982, see Kepel, *Allah in the West*. Many of the individuals who belonged to the nonviolent Islamist movement of the time were to play an important part after 1988.

6. The traditional training centers for Maghreb ulemas were Qarawayyin University in Fez, Morocco, and Zitouna University in Tunis. The nationalization and subsequent dismantling of the Zaouias and the closing of the Franco-Arab madrassas founded during the colonial era deprived religious Algerians of institutions in which to train for the priesthood. For the development of mosques during the 1980s and the foundation of the Islamic University of Constantine, see Ahmed Rouadjia, *Les Frères et la mosquée* (Paris: Karthala, 1990).

7. Sheik Mohammed al-Ghazali, who died in 1996, began as a member of the Muslim Brotherhood and later distanced himself from them. He remained in contact with the Egyptian regime and with the various governments on the Arabian peninsula. Yusuf al-Qaradawi, an Egyptian naturalized citizen of Qatar, also with origins in the Muslim Brotherhood, became a key figure among Sunni Muslims at the end of the 1990s. A head of the sharia faculty at the University of Qatar and a member of the sharia boards of the principal Muslim banks, he also presented a religious program on the satellite channel Al-Jazeera, "Al charia wa-l hayat" (The Sharia and Life). He had his own website, "The Yusif al-Qaradhawi homepage." See the critique of his television show on the situation in Algeria by Mohammed El-Oifi, "La guerre en Algérie vue du monde arabe: La chaîne satellitaire *Al Jazeera*," *Pouvoirs* 86 (September 1998).

8. Rémy Leveau, *Le sabre et le turban: L'avenir du Maghreb* (Paris: Bourin, 1993), pp. 130ff.

9. The party's name refers to a verse in the Koran, *surat* III, 103: "You were on the brink of a precipice of fire: He saved you."

10. Born in 1938, Mahfoud Nahnah early became involved with the Islamist movement; arrested in 1976 for sabotage, he was reprieved in 1981. He had contact with Bouyali but refused to break all relations with the government, which made many militants regard him with suspicion. He was the link with the International Association of the Muslim Brotherhood in Algeria and was contemptuous of Islamists who were too preoccupied with local activities, referring to them as djazaristes. Refusing to join the founders of the Islamic Salvation Front (FIS), among whom his rival Abassi Madani quickly won the favor of the majority, Mahfoud Nahnah founded the Hamas party in 1990—using the same acronym as the Palestinian Islamist Movement but with a different significance (*Harakat al Moujtama' al islami*: Movement for Muslim Society). This party succeeded in splitting the Islamist vote in the 1991 legislative elections. Later, in 1996, Hamas became the acronym for a different party name: *Harakat Moujtama' al Silm*: Movement for a Society of Peace, after the ban on political parties bearing denominational names.

11. Abdallah Jaballah represented the November 1982 movement in the Constantine region of Algeria, and like Nahnah he refused to surrender his reserve of militants to the group led by Madani. Instead, he started the Al Nahda (Rebirth) movement, which deepened the split in the Islamist vote in 1991. Originating in western Algeria, the djazarist movement derived its name from a nickname coined by Nahnah (*al djazara*, "Algerianists"). It was largely made up of high-level French- or Anglo-American-trained academics, who were excluded from positions of responsibility by the *nomenklatura* originating in the east of the country. These embodied the "technocratic" faction within the Algerian Islamist movement, but they had little broad-based popular support. Their adversaries within the movement likened the djazarists to a sort of Islamic freemasonry, structured around networks designed for seizing political power.

12. On the personality of Benhadj, see Labat, *Les islamistes algériens*, pp. 53ff.

13. Luis Martinez, *La guerre civile en Algérie* (Paris: Karthala, 1998), p. 51.

14. Ibid., pp. 53–81.

15. Interview with Slimane Zeghidour, *Politique internationale*, Autumn 1990, p. 156.

16. L. Addi, *L'Algérie et la démocratie: Pouvoir et crise du politique dans l'Algérie contemporaine* (Paris: La Découverte, 1994).

17. For example, *Al Munqidh* 18, pp. 1, 7.

18. The FIS obtained 4,331,472 votes (54.25% of those who voted) in June 1990, and 3,260,222 votes (47.27%) in December 1991, according to official figures, which cannot be guaranteed (the FIS has contested them). J. Fontaine, "Les élections législatives algériennes," *Maghreb-Machrek* 135 (March 1992): 155ff.

19. For information on the beginnings of the movement, see Hassan Mekki, *Harakat al Ikhwan al muslimin fi-l sudan, 1944–1969* (The Muslim Brothers Movement in the Sudan), 4th ed. (Khartoum, Ed. Dar al balad li-l tiba'a wa-l nachr, 1998). In English, see Abdelwahab al-Effendi, *Turabi's Revolution: Islam and Power in the Sudan* (London: Grey Seal Books, 1991).

20. J.-L. Triaud, "Introduction," in *Islam et islamismes au sud du Sahara*, ed. Ousmane Kane and J.-L. Triaud (Paris: Karthala, 1998), pp. 16–20.

21. For information about the Ansars at this period, see Gérard Prunier, "Le mouvement des Ansars au Soudan depuis la fin de l'état mahdiste (1898–1987)," in *Islam et islamismes*, ed. Kane and Triaud, pp. 41ff.

22. Of the 33 million inhabitants of the Sudan in 1998, 70% were Sunni Muslim; the remaining 30% were either Christian (5%) or Animist (25%)—the latter lived chiefly in the south, but thanks to forced migrations during war in the region, they have been moving into new areas on the outskirts of Khartoum. In ethnic terms, 52% of the population is described as "black" and 39% "Arabic." See *Facts on Sudan*, http://www.sudan.net (May 1999).

23. Sudan has two electoral colleges, one for the "masses" and one for "graduates," giving each a measure of representation according to his or her sociocultural group.

24. Mekki, *Harakat al Ikhwan al muslimin fi-l sudan*, pp. 72–73.

25. Sudanese emigration within the Arabian peninsula after 1973 involved more than a million workers, of whom a certain number occupied positions of responsibility,

notably in the armed forces. The transfer of the currency they earned was usually effected by parallel arrangements, their confidence in the state banks being weak. The militant Islamists on both sides of the Red Sea were quick to take advantage of this economic opportunity, thanks to networks of reliable money-changers, who paid the workers' families back home the equivalent in Sudanese pounds, minus commission, of the money paid to them by the workers. This was one of the sources of prosperity for businessmen from Turabi's party in exile, which gave them a place in the Islamic financial system.

26. Information on the Faisal Bank in the Sudan can be found in a book by a journalist close to Prince Faisal, Moussa Yaqoub, *Muhammad Faysal Al Saoud: malamih min tajriba al iqtissadiyya al islamiyya* (Aspects of Experience in the Islamic Economy) (Jeddah: Saudi Publishing and Distributing House, 1998), esp. pp. 54–55, 60.

27. It concerns Abd el-Rahim Hamdi, who became finance minister and then director of the Khartoum Stock Exchange under the Islamic regime.

28. For information on the Islamic African Centre, see Nicole Grandin, "Al-Merkaz al-islami al-ifriqi bi'l-Khartoum: La République du Soudan et la propagation de l'islam en Afrique noire (1977–1991)," in *Le radicalisme islamique au sud du Sahara: Dawa, arabisation et critique de l'Occident,* ed. R. Otayek (Paris: Karthala, 1993), pp. 97ff. The financing of the centre was badly affected when the Sudan under General Bashir sided with Saddam Hussein, and it became the International University of Africa, which continues to welcome foreign students, though with a smaller budget and less of a tendency to proselytize in its approach to teaching (interview with Hassan Mekki, IUA, Khartoum, May 1999).

29. Mahmoud Mohammed Taha advocated a "second Islamic mission" based on the oldest verses in the Koran that were revealed to the Prophet in Mecca. He considered them to be "a call to responsibility and freedom" in opposition to more recent verses revealed at Medina and bound up with the constraints of the time, at the moment when the Prophet was founding a state. Such an interpretation was held to be heresy by the traditional ulemas, who accused him of apostasy. An English translation of his work was published by his disciple Abdullah al-Naim as *The Second Mission of Islam* (New York: Syracuse University Press, 1987).

30. Anne M. Lesch, "The Destruction of Civil Society in the Sudan," in *Civil Society in the Middle East,* vol. 2, ed. A. R. Norton (Leiden: Brill, 1996), p. 163.

31. The putsch was led by 300 soldiers, with support from the head of the Faisal Islamic Bank, observed A. Chouet, who pointed out that the new regime was immediately recognized by Saudi Arabia. See A. Chouet, "L'islam confisqué: Stratégies dynamiques pour un ordre statique," in *Moyen-Orient: migrations, démocratisation, médiations,* ed. R. Bocco and M.-R. Djalili (Paris: PUF, 1994), p. 381.

32. See Haydar Ibrahim Ali, "Islamism in Practice: The Case of Sudan," in *The Islamist Dilemma,* ed. Laura Guazzome (London: Ithaca Press, 1955), p. 202.

33. Among Islamic leaders, one is struck by the number of *halaba* (the generic name for people of Levantine origin living in the Sudan and distinguished by their pale skin) excluded from the brotherhood networks who saw the Islamist party as a way of achieving access to political office that was otherwise denied them.

34. Originally from northern Nigeria and Chad, the Fallata traditionally crossed the Sudan on their pilgrimages to Mecca. Employed as day laborers in the cottonfields, they constituted a despised agricultural proletariat to whom the Islamist party was able to offer both social revenge and religious integration (in a country where they were marginalized by the Chufii brotherhoods for belonging to the Maleki school). In the 1986 elections, the parliamentary seats won by the NIF, except in constituencies reserved for those with appropriate qualifications, were obtained thanks to the Fallata vote.

35. Interview with Habib Mokni from MTI, Paris, 1993, in addition to numerous statements along the same lines by Rashidd al-Gannushi, head of the movement. For Hamas, see *MECS* 1991, p. 184.

36. On the setbacks to the Sudanese economy since 1989 and the enrichment of businessmen associated with the NIF, see H. I. Ali, pp. 204–207.

37. The participants and the progress of the three Khartoum conferences are described in *MECS* 1991, pp. 182–183; 1993, pp. 143–146; and 1995, pp. 107–109. A personal account of the progress by one of the participants, F. Burgat, is in *Maghreb-Machrek* 148 (April–June 1995): 89ff.

38. The Sudanese leader is well disposed toward the large Western media corporations, who have presented him as the "acceptable face of Islamic fundamentalism," capable of arousing anxiety in their readers, yet speaking to them in a language they understand.

8. The Fatwa and the Veil in Europe

1. The interpretation of the Rushdie affair given here is based on researches carried out for Kepel, *Allah in the West*, in which can be found bibliographic references to works up to 1994.

2. The difference between the fatwa sentencing Rushdie to death and its apostate modification comes from the declaration that the latter, should the author show penitence, permits him to escape the death penalty. In the first case it is a sentence without leave of appeal, in the second an arraignment allowing (in principle) the presentation of a contradictory argument.

3. Quoted in Reinhardt Schulze, "The Forgotten Honor of Islam," *MECS* 1989, p. 175.

4. For the history of the initial progress of Islam in France, see Kepel, *Les banlieues de l'islam*, whose outlines are given again here and placed in a European and genealogical perspective in the light of events subsequent to the book's publication (1987).

5. Quoted in Schulze, "The Forgotten Honor of Islam," p. 178.

9. From the Gulf War to the Taliban Jihad

1. In spite of the dramatic situation in the Muslim world during the first days of August 1990, the foreign ministers of the OIC devoted their energy to adopting the Cairo Declaration on the Rights of Man in Islam (August 5). It acceded

to Wahhabite conceptions on the matter, making it clear, in Article 24: "All the rights and liberties stipulated in this declaration are subject to the authority of the sharia," thus standing against the universal Declaration of the Rights of Man.

2. For more on the different conferences organized by Saudi Arabia and Iraq to gather support for the Islamic religious authorities, see Martin Kramer, "The Invasion of Islam," *MECS* 1990, pp. 177–207, and "Islam in the New World Order," *MECS* 1991, pp. 172–205. For the Islamic dimension of the war in general terms, and how it was perceived in the Muslim world, see Piscatori, ed., *Islamic Fundamentalisms and the Gulf Crisis,* notably the chapter "Religion and Realpolitik: Islamic Responses to the Gulf War," pp. 1–27.

3. A fourth session was planned for 1998, but the opponents of Turabi in Sudanese power circles moved to cancel it, judging it to be inopportune at a time when they were trying to rejoin the community of nations by refuting all accusations of "supporting terrorism" (interview with Baha el Din Hanafi, Khartoum, May 1999).

4. Mamoun Fandy, *Saudi Arabia and the Politics of Dissent* (London: Macmillan, 1999).

5. See J. Teitelbaum, "Saudi Arabia," *MECS* 1992, p. 677.

6. There is a division within traditional Saudi Bedouin society between the tribes of "noble" lineage descended from camel-breeding nomads and the lower classes *(khediri)* limited to domestic work; marriage contracts are not made between the two—a prohibition that is still in force in spite of the egalitarianism that Islam claims to practice. The fact that Masari belonged to the second group was seized upon by his critics, who also made much of the fact that he had an Ethiopian woman among his ancestors. As a result, he had dark skin, plus an Egyptian mother, and an American wife, whom he married during long years spent studying in the West. These were all factors that would discredit him in the eyes of Saudi mainstream opinion. See Fandy, *Saudi Arabia and the Politics of Dissent,* pp. 121ff. For tribal differences, see Al-Yassini, *Religion and State in the Kingdom of Saudi Arabia,* esp. p. 53.

7. For reactions to the Gulf War in Pakistan, see Mumtaz Ahmad, "The Politics of War: Islamic Fundamentalisms in Pakistan," in *Islamic Fundamentalisms,* ed. Piscatori, pp. 155–185.

8. For information on salafist-jihadism, see Kepel, "Le GIA à travers ses publications," *Pouvoirs,* Autumn 1998. This term, used by the Imam Abu Hamza, one of the representatives of this movement, in the course of an interview (London, April 1998), reappears regularly in his pamphlets and audio-visual releases.

9. On Sayyid Jamal al-Din al-Afghani (1838–1897), Muhammad Abduh (1849–1905), and Rashid Rida (1865–1935) and their relationships with contemporary Islamist movements, see Nikki Keddie, "Sayyid Jamal al-Din al-Afghani," in *Pioneers of Islamic Revival,* ed. Rahnema, pp. 27–29.

10. Criticizing Sayyid Qutb, Abu Hamza (Talmi al-Ansar lil-sayf al-battar [The Companions Burnish the Cutting Sword], London, April 1997) rebukes him for having read the Koran only from his own modern standpoint, and not being an official exegete.

11. Boujema Bounouar, known as Abdallah Anas, one of the members of the salafist movement, took part in the jihad in Afghanistan and married one of Abdallah Azzam's daughters. The attack on the Algerian frontier-station of Guemmar on November 28, 1991, which is held to be the symbolic departure point of the jihad, took place two years and four days after the assassination of Abdallah Azzam in Peshawar.

12. The working of the Pakistani ulema parties brings to mind those of the "ultra-orthodox" *(haredim)* parties in Israel, a state that was founded one year after Pakistan. In both cases the religious parties, who wanted strict observance of Judaism or Islam to take precedence over the simple belonging which was at the root of Israeli or Pakistani nationalism, began to take part in the political system in order to benefit from the state subsidies to their schools; later, in both countries they participated in coalition governments. See Gilles Kepel, *The Revenge of God* (London: Polity Press; Pittsburgh: Penn State Press, 1992), ch. 4, on Israel.

13. For more on these questions, see studies by Mariam Abou Zahab, especially "The Regional Dimension of Sectarian Conflicts in Pakistan" (Paris: Ceri conference, December 7, 1998, in press).

14. The Sahaba, or Companions of the Prophet, are especially revered by the pious Sunnis, who consider their testimony on the origins of Islam as authoritative. The caliph successors to Mohammed were born into their milieu, the Omayyad dynasty in particular. But the Shiites detest them and blame them for the defeat of Ali in 657 as well as the massacre of Hussein and his companions at Karbala in 680. In a Pakistani context, reference to the Companions is directly seen as anti-Shia.

15. The expression refers to Haq Nawaz Jhangvi, a figure who stood midway between banditry and fanatical devotion to Islam. His nickname, Haq Nawaz Pistol, alludes to that of Hassan Karate, famed throughout the "Islamic Republic of Embaba" in Cairo, or that of the amir of the GIA, "Seif Allah Djafar" (Djafar, Sword of God) in Algiers. In the history of Islam, the term *Ansar* refers to the "partisans" whom the Prophet found at Medina when he sought refuge there in 622, after fleeing from Mecca with his first disciples, the *mouhajiroun* ("migrants").

16. Just like the name of the SSP, that of the SMP (of which it is virtually a copy) has controversial associations that are immediately obvious: for the militant Shia, defending the Prophet includes defending his family, stripped of power by the Sahaba to whom the Sunnis claim alliance.

17. See Mariam Abou Zahab, "Islamisation de la société ou conflit de classes? Le *Sipah-e Sahaba Pakistan (SSP)* dans le Penjab," *Cemoti,* Spring 2000.

18. See Ahmad, "Islamic Fundamentalisms," p. 166.

19. See Ahmed Rashid, "Pakistan and the Taliban," in *Fundamentalism Reborn? Afghanistan and the Taliban,* ed. William Maley (London: Hurst & Co., 1998), pp. 72–89. Also, by the same author, *Talibans* (London: Tauris, 2000).

20. See Richard Mackenzie, "The United States and the Taliban," in *Fundamentalism Reborn?* ed. Maley, pp. 90ff.

21. See Andreas Rieck, "Afghanistan, Taliban: An Islamic Revolution of the Pashtun,"

Orient, January 1997, pp. 135ff, and Mariam Abou Zahab, "Les liens des Taleban avec l'histoire afghane," *Les Nouvelles d'Afghanistan* 85 (3rd quarter, 1999).

22. These impressions of Kabul under Taliban domination come from my stay there during April 1998.

23. The institution of the *moutawia* goes back to Ibn Abd al-Wahhab, the imam who gave his name to Wahhabism and who, as soon as he had gained spiritual power over the first Saudi state (1745–1811), set up this "religious police," whose brief was to oversee the public's behavior, seek out and punish every infringement, and ensure that believers took part in all the prayers.

24. See Rashid, "Pakistan and the Taliban," p. 76.

25. See Mumtaz Ahmad, "Revivalism, Islamization, Sectarianism and Violence in Pakistan," *Pakistan 1997*, ed. Craig Baxter and Charles Kennedy (Boulder: Westview, 1998).

26. On this question, see especially "Le Tadjikistan existe-t-il?" *Cemoti* 18 (1995); and M.-R. Djalili and F. Grare, *Le Tadjikistan à l'épreuve de l'indépendance* (Geneva: IUHEI, 1995).

27. Ibn al-Khattab, who probably came from the Arabian peninsula, seems to have decided to leave Afghanistan for Chechnya in 1995 with eight companions, after he had established the nature of the jihad being carried out in that country against the Russians. On April 16, 1996, he seems to have led a force of 50 fighting men in an attack on a retreating Russian military convoy, causing many fatalities; this prompted Shamil Bassayev, the Islamist leader of the local resistance, to make him a Chechnyan general. He also took part in uprisings in villages in Daghestan in August 1999, which triggered the new Russian offensive in Chechnya in the second half of that year. For information on the part played by the jihadists from Afghanistan in this war, see the interview with Ibn al-Khattab in *Al Hayat*, September 30, 1999, as well as the website of the Azzam Brigades (http://www.azzam.com), which contains lengthy descriptions of the part they played in Chechnya. See in particular the hagiography of the Egyptian "martyr" Abu Bakr Aqeedah, killed on December 23, 1997, whose militant career began in Upper Egypt, included Sheik Abdul Rahman, and continued in Afghanistan and then in Chechnya.

10. The Failure to Graft Jihad onto Bosnia's Civil War

1. The Ottoman empire conquered Bosnia in 1463 and Herzegovina in 1482. For information on Islam in the Balkans in general, see the reference work by Alexandre Popovic, *L'islam balkanique* (Wiesbaden: Otto Hassarowitz, 1986).

2. At the time of the 1991 census, the Republic of Bosnia, which was still a part of Yugoslavia, had 4,364,574 inhabitants, of whom 43.7% declared themselves to be Muslim, 31.4% Serb, 17.3% Croat, 5.5% Yugoslav, and 2.1% "other." Source: Xavier Bougarel, *Bosnie, anatomie d'un conflit* (Paris: La Découverte, 1996), p. 141. Independence was declared on March 3, following a referendum in which it was approved by a virtually unanimous 63.4% of the registered electorate who took

part in the vote (the Serbs, who made up one third of the electorate, boycotted it). The date on which the war in Bosnia began is conventionally given as April 6, 1992—the same day that Serb forces began their siege of Sarajevo and the European Community recognized the independence of Bosnia-Herzegovina, declared one month earlier. The following day a Serb Republic of Bosnia-Herzegovina was declared in Pale, a small town on the outskirts of Sarajevo.

3. The term "ethnic cleansing" passed into the language during the war in former Yugoslavia. It denotes the forced expulsion, from any given territory, of people considered non-indigenous by those controlling it. This phenomenon acquired a particular significance where populations claiming to belong to different communities had lived as neighbors for centuries.

4. For more of the realities and the spread of ethnic cleansing and genocide as well as the use of these terms, see remarks by Bougarel, *Bosnie, anatomie d'un conflit*, pp. 11–14.

5. See Xavier Bougarel, "Islam et politique en Bosnie-Herzégovine: Le parti de l'Action démocratique" (Ph.D. thesis, Institut d'Études Politiques de Paris, 1999), p. 342. Subsequent interpretations in this chapter are largely based on the pioneer work of Bougarel, the breadth and depth of whose knowledge are only touched on in this study.

6. For reactions within the Arab world to the start of the war in Bosnia, see Tarek Mitri, "La Bosnie-Herzégovine et la solidarité du monde arabe et islamique," *Maghreb-Machrek*, January 1993, pp. 123–136, and reports in *MECS* 1992, pp. 218–220; 1993, pp. 109–111; 1994, p. 127; and 1995, pp. 98–100.

7. In the overall result for all nationalities in Bosnia, the SDA obtained 30.4%, the SDS Serb party 25.2%, and the Croat HDZ 15.5%—which assured the success of the nationalist parties, in opposition to which the "citizen" parties only got 28.9% of votes cast.

8. Surveys carried out in 1990 indicated that the number of Muslims practicing their religion was one of the lowest of all Yugoslav nationalities: only 34–36% declared themselves to be "religious," and 61% of young people said they never went to a mosque. See Xavier Bougarel, "Discours d'un Ramadan de guerre civile," *L'Autre Europe* 26–27 (1993).

9. See Xavier Bougarel, "Un courant panislamiste en Bosnie-Herzégovine," in *Exils et royaumes*, ed. Kepel, pp. 275–299.

10. Amine al-Husseini, mufti of Jerusalem—opposed to the setting up of a Jewish center in Palestine and hostile to Great Britain, who had made it possible in the wake of the Balfour Declaration of 1917—threw in his lot with Hitler and became director of the Islamic Institute in Berlin. His task was to change hostility to Zionism in the Arab and Muslim world into support for the Nazi regime.

11. Bearing the inscription: "Our goal: The Islamization of Muslims. Our motto: Have faith and fight," the Islamic Proclamation, "A synthesis of ideas that are beginning to be heard more and more often everywhere, and which have the same value in all parts of the Muslim world," calling for "action organized with a view to realization."

12. Croat independence was declared in June 1991, while Serb regions of Bosnia declared autonomy that autumn.

13. Resolution of the Security Council dated September 25, 1991.

14. See Shereen T. Hunter, "The Embargo That Wasn't: Iran, Arms Shipments into Bosnia," *Jane, Intelligence Review* 12 (1997).

15. The Republican opposition feared that, through the expedient of arms deliveries, Iran would be able to build a power base and important relay points in the heart of Europe. See Ali Reza Bagherzadeh, *Une interprétation paradigmatique de l'ingérence iranienne en Bosnie-Herzégovine* (Paris: post-graduate study, IEP, 1999), presentation and analysis of arguments, pp. 11–14.

16. American pressure in the wake of the Dayton Accords made it a condition of the implementation of the aid program, "Train and Equip," that the vice minister of defense in Bosnia, Hassan Cengic, believed to be close to Tehran, resign. *Time*, September 30, 1996, quoted with commentary by A. R. Bagherzadeh, p. 38.

17. See Iman Farag, "Ces musulmans d'ailleurs: La Bosnie vue d'Égypte," *Maghreb-Machrek*, January 1996, pp. 41–50.

18. See Bellion-Jourdan, "L'humanitaire et l'islamisme soudanais," and M. Kramer, "The Global Village of Islam," *MECS* 1992, p. 220.

19. Biographical details and the intentions of Commandant "Barbaros" are taken from an interview he gave in August 1994 to the magazine *Al Sirat al-Mustaqim* (The Right Path), no. 33. English translation available on the website of the Muslim Students Association of North America: http://msanews.mynet.net// MSANEWS/199605/19960509.0.html.

20. It concerned Nasir al-din al-Albani (who advised caution, in view of the disproportionate size of the forces), and the two salafist sheiks close to power in Saudi Arabia, Abd al-Aziz Ben Baz, who later became mufti of the kingdom, and Mohammed Ben Otheimin.

21. The Azzam Brigades website contains ten hagiographies of "martyrs" who died in Bosnia, as well as an account that gives some information about other combatants.

22. There are photographs such as this on the MSANEWS website, http://msanews. mynet.net//MSANEWS/199605/19960509.0.html.

23. See Bougarel, "Islam et politique en Bosnie-Herzégovine," pp. 357–359, for the translation of some ironic writings on Islam viewed by the "Arab Brothers" and their clumsy attempts to implement it in Bosnia.

24. The departure of the jihadists was difficult to accomplish, due to their terror that they would be eliminated while leaving Bosnian territory to reach the airport at Zagreb. In March 1996 more than 300 of them left Sarajevo for Istanbul, where, after a warm welcome from the Turkish Islamist party Refah, they were examined by the MIT (the Turkish intelligence service): 100 of them were sent to a training camp in Northern Cyprus (under Turkish control), while 200 were returned to Jalalabad, to a camp under the command of Hekmatyar, there to await transfer to Chechnya. Others left for Albania, another potential jihad front that was to fail. See MSANEWS website (note 22).

25. Enes Karic, "Islam in Contemporary Bosnia," *Islamic Studies* 36, nos. 2, 3 (1997): 480.

11. The Logic of Massacre in the Second Algerian War

1. Along with others, this opinion was formulated by an analyst from the Rand Corporation, Graham Fuller, in a study entitled *Algeria: The Next Islamist State?* (Santa Monica, CA: Rand Corporation, 1995).
2. See the interview with an "Afghan" leader on the origin of the GIA, in *Al-Ansar* (organ of the "Jihad Partisans in Algeria and Throughout the World" and overseas voice of the GIA, founded in July 1993), November 5, 1993, p. 17, quoted by Camille al-Tawil in *Al haraka al islamiyya al mussallaha fi-l jazaïr: man "al inqadh" ila "al jama'a"* (The armed Islamic Movement in Algeria: From the FIS to the GIA) (Beirut: Dar al Nahar, 1998), pp. 84–85.
3. "Al Afghani" is an alias frequently adopted by those who took part in the jihad in Afghanistan (without implying any family relations among all those who bear that name).
4. The appellation of "Qutbist" was given by its enemies to a group of "Afghani" elders led by Ahmed el-Wad, who adhered to theories in the work of Qutb, such as the jahiliyya and the hakimiyya on understanding the modern world. See Al-Tawil, *Al haraka al islamiyya al mussallaha fi-l jazaïr*, p. 65, and an analysis of those who idolize Sayyid Qutb in Abu Hamza al-Misri, *Talmi al Ansar li-l seif al battar* (The Companions Burnish the Cutting Sword) (London, March 1997), pp. 20–21. The takfirist movement, which derives its name from the Al Takfir wa-l Hijra (Excommunication and Hegira) group, first appeared in Egypt in the 1970s, and, under the leadership of Shukri Mustafa, included in particular those who had fought in Afghanistan centered around Ahmed Bou Amara, known as "The Pakistani." In excommunicating all except his own personal followers, he reduced the number of those potentially available for recruitment to the jihad. He was violently opposed by the salafist-jihadists for that reason, and the accusation of takfirism (excommunication from the community) was frequently cited during the liquidations and purges of the GIA from 1995 onward. The last statement from Amir Antar Zouabri, printed on September 26, 1997, in *Al-Ansar*, justified the massacres of that month under the name of *kufr al mujtama* (excommunication of society), showing how, near its end, the GIA had swung toward takfirism, as we shall see later. See Al-Tawil, *Al haraka al islamiyya al mussallaha' fi-l jazaïr*, pp. 280–283. The figurehead of the djazarists was Lounès Belkacem, known as Mohammed Said, who joined the GIA in May 1994 and was eliminated in November 1995.
5. Published in Stockholm by Algerian Islamists close to the GIA, *Al-Shahada* first appeared in November 1992.
6. Layada names four Algerian Islamist thinkers: Sheiks Misbah, Abdellatif Soltani, and Al-Arbaoui (former members of the Algerian ulemas who stood in opposition to the regime after 1962), and the reformist thinker Malek Bennabi (1905–1973).

7. Layada wishes to make it clear that the GIA came from "the union of the Mansouri Meliani group, of Abu Ahmed (Ahmed el-Wad), and of Moh Leveilley." The Arabic expression used by Layada refers to salafism in its strictest sense *(ittiba' minhaj ahl al sunna wa-l jamaa' wa fahm al salaf al salih)*.

8. Koran, V (The Laid Table), 51: "You who have faith, do not establish alliances with Jews or Christians. Let them make alliances among themselves! Whosoever among you shall make such relations, he will as a consequence become one of them."

9. The expression "join the *Jihad* caravan" brings to mind the title of one of Abdallah Azzam's books on the same theme, *Ilhaq bi-l qafila!* ("Join the caravan!").

10. Between the fall of Kabul at the hands of the mujahedeen in April 1992 and its conquest by the Taliban in September 1996, Afghanistan was in a state of anarchy, which did harm to the "victory" claimed by adherents of the jihad. Key passages from the "interview" are reproduced in Al-Tawil, *Al haraka al islamiyya al mussallaha fi-l jazaïr*, pp. 79–84. See also pp. 74–78 for extracts from the GIA, second statement, as well as the transcription of an audiocassette of Layada.

11. The 466 Assemblées Populaires Communales taken over by the FIS in June 1990 were dissolved in April 1992 and put under the administration of officials nominated by the state, which were targeted with a vengeance by the armed groups.

12. Martinez, *La guerre civile en Algérie.*

13. See Labat, *Les islamistes algériens*, pp. 236–237.

14. The word "Ansar" refers to the first followers of the Prophet Mohammed when he arrived in Medina after Hegira in the year 622. Presenting itself as "the voice of the Jihad in Algeria and throughout the world," the 16-page newsletter, written and produced on a computer, was distributed on Fridays outside various mosques and spread widely through the use of photocopiers and electronic mail. In contrast to the clarity and "modern" style of writers such as Sayyid Qutb, whose writing addressed the intelligence of his readers in a straightforward fashion, the jargon of the salafist-jihadists was deliberately obscure, designed to excite a fanatical and unquestioning following. It was certainly beyond the understanding of the average GIA militant drawn from the young urban poor.

15. On August 21, 1993, the date when Djafar al-Afghani became head of the GIA, Kasdi Merbah, the former prime minister of President Chadli until the summer of 1989 and long-time head of the security services, was assassinated. Condemned by agents of the FIS in Europe as a murder carried out by the Algerian intelligence service itself (which disliked the contacts that the victim had with certain Islamists abroad), the responsibility for the assassination was claimed by the GIA. It was the first far-reaching operation in which the question of manipulation of the GIA was posed within certain FIS circles.

16. On October 26 three employees from the French Consulate in Algiers were kidnapped and then released, carrying a letter from the GIA demanding the departure from Algeria of all foreigners.

17. *Al Wasat*, published in London, printed on January 21, 1994, an interview from Peshawar through an intermediary, with a leader of the GIA who was later identi-

fied as Cherif Gousmi, which led people to assume that he had spent time in the Afghan-Pakistani region.

18. Al-Tawil, *Al haraka al islamiyya al mussallaha fi-l jazaïr*, pp. 144–154, gives a detailed description of the meeting, from the transcription of a video cassette shown in Islamist circles and in which the various participants aired their views. There is a French translation of the "Communiqué de l'unité" by F. Burgat, "Algérie: L'AIS et le GIA, itinéraires de constitution et relations," *Maghreb-Machrek* 149 (July–September 1995): 111.

19. A. Redjem made use of his title as head of the executive branch of the FIS, and S. Mekhloufi signed his own name as well as that of A. Chebouti, who was absent and seriously ill.

20. A. Haddam, head of the Parliamentary Delegation of the FIS overseas, resident in the United States, and Ahmed Zaoui, a Belgian resident, were excluded from the IEFE. On July 8 the former issued a communiqué blessing the union of May 13.

21. Al-Tawil, *Al haraka al islamiyya al mussallaha fi-l jazaïr*, pp. 184–189, puts forward various accounts of the circumstances surrounding the discarding of Mahfoud Tajine.

22. "Algérie: Un colonel dissident accuse," *Le Monde*, November 27, 1999, pp. 14–15.

23. During the hijacking, a statement from the GIA demanded the liberation not only of Islamist leaders held in Algeria (notably Layada, Madani, and Benhadj) and in Saudi Arabia (sheiks al-Auda and al-Hawali) but also of those held in the United States (the Egyptian Sheik Omar Abdel Rahman, at the time of the attack on the World Trade Center in New York), thus re-emphasizing the group's membership in the International salafist-jihadists.

24. The Rome meeting was set up by the Sant' Egidio community, close to certain circles within the Vatican, although this initiative did not meet with unqualified approval in the Roman Curia.

25. Called in Arabic *Hidaya rabb al-'Alamin* (literally, "The Guidance of the Lord of the Worlds [Allah]"), this short work, which is filled with sacred quotations from great writers in the salafist tradition (in the front rank of which is Ibn Taymiyya), appears to be the work of a scholar of profound Islamic learning, which it is difficult to associate with Zitouni.

26. The text of the Hidaya considers that the Muslim Brotherhood and the djazarists "are carriers of impiety [*kufr*] and associationism [*shirk*: to associate Allah with other divinities] in their doctrine," the former for referring to democracy and the latter for having declared that "the *Jihad* is an uncivilized system."

27. Together with A. Chebouti and S. Mekhloufi.

28. The "trial" of Lamara and Tajine took place on January 4, 1996, according to Al-Tawil, *Al haraka al islamiyya al mussallaha fi-l jazaïr*, pp. 240ff, who transcribes part of the cassette's content. The "confessions" of the two men and their sentences were to be the object of much discussion in a later study, *Al seif al battar*, originating in the amirate of Zouabri.

29. The monks had remained in this high-risk mountainous territory near the Islamist

stronghold of Medea, thanks to safe conduct from the local GIA amirs. For more on this, see Mireille Duteil, *Les martyrs de Tibhirine* (Paris: Brépols, 1996).

30. Al-Tawil, *Al haraka al islamiyya al mussallaha fi-l jazaïr*, pp. 230–239. Zitouni saw himself reproached chiefly for not having offered "sharia proofs" to justify the elimination of M. Said and A. Redjem and other elders of Afghanistan. He was also accused of "exaggeration" *(ghoulou)*, a term used in connection with followers of the Kharijites.

31. Written at the request of Abu Hamza by the head of the Religious Affairs Committee of the GIA, Abu Moundher, and with a preface by Zouabri, the 60-page text bears, like other publications of this nature, a title written in assonant prose *(saj')*, which translates as "The Cutting Sword, in answer to those who have stabbed the devout Mujahedeens in the back and are living among the ungodly" (see also Abu Qatada and Abu Musab, who criticized Zitouni's GIA from London in June 1996). The work is essentially a justification of the purges that took place under Zitouni's amirate, on which subject it offers a good deal of evidence, as well as a critique of Algerian society.

32. *Al seif al battar*, pp. 39–40 (ch. 8: "Pertinent Observations Concerning the Classification of the People of This Country by the GIA"). At the beginning of the chapter, the author points out that the GIA has never accused Algerian society as a whole of impiety (unlike the takfiris), for "Islam is its foundation." But the book urges penalties for those who drag their feet in this matter or who are afraid to join the jihad.

33. Statement no. 51 of Zouabri, as published in *Al-Ansar* 165 (September 17, 1997), along with Abu Hamza's explanation, are reproduced in Al-Tawil, *Al haraka al islamiyya al mussallaha fi-l jazaïr*, pp. 280ff.

34. On June 6, Madani Merzag, "national amir" of the AIS, announced "a definitive end to the armed struggle," to which Abassi Madani added his support on the 11th, in a letter to "His Excellency, President Abdelaziz Bouteflika," to whom he was more specific: "If you continue along this much-approved route which coincides with the wishes of our brave people, then by the grace of God you will find me at your side" (*Le Monde*, June 13–14, 1999).

35. In Algerian humor, the French expression *"import-import"* denotes the upward spiral of enrichment of officials in the regime, who held monopolies of import.

12. The Threat of Terrorism in Egypt

1. See Amani Qandil, "L'évaluation du rôle des islamistes dans les syndicats professionels égyptiens," in *Le phénomène de la violence politique: Perspectives comparatives et paradigme égyptien*, ed. B. Dupret (Cairo: Cedej, 1994), pp. 282, 288–289. See also Nabil Abdel Fattah, *Veiled Violence: Islamic Fundamentalism in Egyptian Politics in 1990s* [sic] (Cairo: Sechat, 1993), pp. 36–45, 74–81.

2. Below the Islamic programs were political programs (11,000 hours) and entertainment (8,000 hours), while "immoral" shows (such as dancing) or those held to be

"incompatible with Islamic values" were censored. *Al Ahram,* May 21 and 25, 1985, quoted in Ami Ayalon, "Egypt," *MECS* 1984–1985, p. 351.

3. Between 1981 and 1984 the imprisonment of several hundred radical militants in the same detention centers gave rise to much lengthy debate among the detainees and led to the publication of numerous theoretical pamphlets clarifying the distinction between Al Jihad on the one hand and the Gamaa Islamiya on the other. After 1984, the former refused to recognize Omar Abdel Rahman as "amir" because of his blindness, while the latter decided that a prisoner, A. al-Zomor, could not fulfill the requirements of the amirate of an armed faction. For more on these debates, see *Taqrir al hala al diniyya fi misr 1995 (Report on the Religious Situation in Egypt in 1995;* hereafter called *Taqrir 95),* ed. Nabil Abdel Fattah (Cairo: Al Ahram Center for Political and Strategic Studies, 1996), pp. 185–187.

4. Ayman al-Zawahiri, who played a prominent part in the international radical Islamist networks in the second half of the 1990s, was born in 1951 to a well-known Cairo family of doctors and diplomats, and he qualified as a surgeon himself in 1978. One of his ancestors was an ambassador and another sheik of Al Azhar. In his youth he was a militant member of the clandestine Islamist movement during the Nasser era and joined Sadat's assassins through Abboud al-Zomor. Arrested in 1981 and freed in 1984, he spent the last part of the decade in Afghanistan, while also traveling in Europe from a base in Bulgaria. For more on this, see *Taqrir 95,* p. 280.

5. In the 1970s, Gamaat Islamiya (Arabic uses the plural) denoted the student Islamist movements, with all their different factions. In the 1980s, the term (now used in the singular and sometimes qualified by the epithet *radikaliya* ["radical"]) designated only the clandestine movement engaged in acts of violence under the spiritual leadership of Sheik Omar Abdel Rahman.

6. Born in 1938, a diabetic and blind from the age of ten months, Omar Abdel Rahman was to pursue religious studies (a frequent practice among the blind, whose disability does not prevent them from learning the sacred texts—as in the case of Sheik Kishk, a famous Islamist preacher in the 1970s). Graduating from Al Azhar in 1965, Omar Abdel Rahman received his first prison sentence—of 18 months—in October 1970, when he put out a fatwa forbidding the faithful to pray for Nasser (who had just died), since he had been "impious." After being awarded a doctorate in 1977, he went to teach in Saudi Arabia until 1980, when he became the mufti of the group of Sadat's assassins—for whom he preached a fatwa authorizing them to attack the Copts (see Kepel, *The Prophet and Pharaoh,* p. 226). Arrested in 1981 and found not guilty at his trial, he was freed in 1984. See, among other sources, *Taqrir 95,* p. 280. His life has received much media attention since his arrival in the United States.

7. For more on these incidents, and for a global overview of the role of the Islamist movement in the second half of the 1980s, see Alain Roussillon, "Entre Al-Jihad et Al-Rayyan: Phénoménologie de l'islamisme égyptien," *Maghreb-Machrek* 127 (January–March 1990): 5–50.

8. In January 1990, Zaki Badr, who had just escaped an assassination attempt the previous month and who represented the "hard line," was replaced by Abdel Halim Moussa, who in turn was dismissed in April 1993 after having given encouragement to a mediation committee composed of men of religion, in a period of rapidly growing violence. He was succeeded by General al-Alfi, who remained in the post until the killings at Luxor in November 1997. All three had been governors of Asyut before becoming ministers and were "specialists" in radical Islamism.

9. On the situation of the Egyptian Coptic community, see Dina El Khawaga, "Le renouveau copte: La communauté comme acteur politique" (Ph.D. diss., Institut d'Études Politiques de Paris, 1993). For more on interdenominational strife in the valley, see Claude Guyomarch, "Assiout: Epicentre de la 'sédition confessionnelle' en Égypte," in Kepel, ed., *Exils et royaumes*, pp. 165–188.

10. Alain Roussillon, "Changer la société par le jihad: 'Sédition confessionnelle' et attentats contre le tourisme: rhétoriques de la violence qualifiée d'islamique en Égypte," in *Le phénomène de la violence politique*, ed. Dupret, pp. 299ff; and Guyomarch, "Assiout," pp. 171–172.

11. For more on this, see B. Dupret, "A propos de l'affaire Abu Zayd," *Maghreb-Machrek* 151 (January–March 1996): 18ff; "Un arrêt devenu une 'affaire,'" *Égypte/ Monde Arabe* 29 (1st quarter 1997): 155ff; and "L'affaire Abu Zayd devant les tribunaux" (French translation of extracts from the trial), *Égypte/Monde Arabe* 34 (2nd quarter, 1998): 169–201. See also Nasr Abu Zeid, dossier, published by *Inter-Peuples* 44 (March 1996).

12. Tourism, the prime source of income alongside funds sent back by emigrants, had brought in more than $3 billion in 1991–1992. President Mubarak estimated in December 1993 that the country had lost $2 billion of income from tourists that year (*Akhbar el Yom*, December 11, 1993).

13. The events at Embaba have been the subject of much discussion in the press, of sociological investigations, and of books. Much of this may be found in Hicham Mubarak, *Al Islamiyyoun Qadimoun* (The Islamists Arrive) (Cairo: Mahroussa, 1995). Also see Nimet Guenena and Saad Eddin Ibrahim, *The Changing Face of Egypt: Islamic Activism* (U.S. Institute of Peace, September 1997). Finally, I owe much first-hand information to Patrick Haenni, who shared his extensive knowledge of the Embaba territory with me, for which I am extremely grateful.

14. For an account of life in the suburbs of Algiers, see M. Vergès, "Chroniques de survie dans un quartier en sursis," in Kepel, ed., *Exils et royaumes*, pp. 69ff; and Martinez, *La guerre civile*. The Black Muslims in the United States and some suburban districts of France are discussed in Kepel, *Allah in the West*, parts 3 and 4. The radical anti-Shiite Sunnite Party in Pakistan, Lashkar-e Jhangvi was led by a man who went by the name of Haq Nawaz Pistol, while one of the figures of the Gamaa in Embaba was called Hassan Karate.

15. The principal anti-Christian incidents took place in autumn 1991, their organizers taking advantage of police reluctance to put themselves at risk in a district whose problems were well known.

16. The phenomenon is analyzed by Sameh Eid and Patrick Haenni, "Cousins, voisins, citoyens, Imbaba: Naissance paradoxale d'un espace politique," in Marc Lavergne, ed., *Le pouvoir local au Proche-Orient* (Paris, 2000).
17. Abdel Fattah, *Veiled Violence*, p. 45.
18. For a discussion of the controversies over the law between Islamists and positivists, see B. Dupret, "Représentations des répertoires juridiques en Égypte: Limites d'un consensus," *Maghreb-Machrek* 151 (January–March 1996): 32ff.
19. The ups and downs of the conflict concerning control of the professional unions are discussed by E. Longuenesse in "Le 'syndicalisme professionnel' en Égypte entre identités socio-professionnelles et corporatisme," *Égypte/Monde Arabe* 24 (4th quarter, 1995): 167–168.
20. See Bellion-Jourdan, "Au nom de la solidarité islamique."
21. See Kepel, *The Prophet and Pharaoh*, pp. 185–205.
22. For more on the Mediation Committee, see Roussillon, "Changer la société," pp. 315–318.
23. In 1995, in fact, 93% of recorded acts of violence (which resulted in 366 deaths) took place in Upper Egypt. See *Taqrir 1995*, p. 190.
24. For details of the "de-escalation" in 1996, see the data in *Taqrir 1995*, pp. 235ff.
25. See below for the consequences of the 1993 attack on the New York World Trade Center. See *Taqrir 1995*, pp. 211–212.
26. On April 18, the same day as the attack on the Europa Hotel in Cairo, Israeli artillery bombarded the UNIFIL (United Nations Forces in Lebanon) Center, where 350 civil Lebanese refugees had taken shelter in the wake of the Grapes of Wrath military operation carried out in retaliation against the Hezbollah attacks. The bombardment left 112 dead and 130 wounded, most of them women, children, and old people.
27. The priority of the struggle against "the enemy within" is discussed in a book by Abdessalam Faraj, the ideologist in the group of Sadat's assassins (see Kepel, *The Prophet and Pharaoh*, ch. 7). Through the voice of Ayman al-Zawahiri, the Al Jihad group condemned any idea of a truce, reiterating that the enemy within (apostate, *murtadd*) is worse than any distant enemy (the impious, *kafir asli*). See *Taqrir 1995*, p. 272.
28. Details of these elections are given in Sandrine Gamblin, ed., *Contours et détours du politique en Égypte: Les élections législatives de 1995* (Paris: L'Harmattan-Cedej, 1997), esp. A. Roussillon, "Pourquoi les Frères musulmans ne pouvaient pas gagner les élections," pp. 101ff.
29. In the Koranic perception, the term *wasat* echoes the much-quoted verse II, 143. Details of the Al Wasat Party are in *Taqrir 1995*, pp. 217–230.
30. The number of deaths fell from 366 in 1995 to 181 in 1996.
31. The bulletin referring to the slaughter at Luxor as an "error" was attributed to Ossama Rouchdi, a refugee in Holland and successor to Tala Fuad Qassem; the other one, which had rejected the idea of any cessation of attacks in Egypt, was attributed to Rifai Ahmed Taha, another leader of the group, at that time living in Afghanistan.

32. All this is neatly written up by Patrick Haenni in "De quelques islamisations non islamistes," *Revue des mondes musulmans et de la Méditerranée* 85–86 (1999).

13. Osama bin Laden and the War against the West

1. During the trial in which the Afghan "Egyptians" appeared, at the beginning of 1996, their lawyer, Montasser al-Zayyat, himself a Gamaa militant, pleaded that the state, which had supported his clients at first in the Afghan jihad in the 1980s, could not now make them criminals for this reason without contradicting itself.

2. By means of his construction companies spread throughout the world, Osama bin Laden was to play an important role in moving many jihadists between countries and providing them with various safe houses.

3. See Peter Waldman, "How Sheik Omar Rose to Lead Islamic War While Eluding the Law," *Wall Street Journal*, September 1, 1993, p. A1. This article includes a detailed and balanced biography of Omar Abdel Rahman. See also M. A. Weaver, *A Portrait of Egypt*, a more subjective but well-researched biography of the sheik, based on several interviews with him and his entourage during his time in America.

4. The conditions of interrogation and detention in Egyptian prisons were continually denounced by human rights groups, who asserted that torture was frequently used to extract information and confessions.

5. The official American version, given after the attack on the World Trade Center in February 1993, attributed the issuing of a visa to a "mistake." This, depending on the version, was blamed on a Sudanese employee at the United States consulate or else on a computer error. The idea is scarcely credible, given the sheik's notoriety, the periods between his different journeys, and his rapid acquisition of full resident status (via a "green card") so soon after his arrival in the United States. See also D. Jehl, "Flaws in Computer Check Helped Sheik Enter US," *New York Times*, July 3, 1993, p. 22.

6. Clashes over the financial administration of the center and the use of funds had led to the assassination of Shalabi in March 1991.

7. L. Duke, "Trail of Tumult on US Soil," *Washington Post*, July 11, 1993, p. A1.

8. In the last statement that he was able to make at his trial, the sheik asked why he had not been arrested upon entering the United States in July 1990, if he were indeed at the head of a terrorist conspiracy as charged. U.S. District Court, Southern District of New York, *United States of America v. Omar Ahmad Ali Abdel Rahman [et al.], Defendants*, S5 93 Cr. 181 (MBM), p. 185.

9. During his detention in Egypt at the beginning of the 1980s, the sheik had married the 18-year-old sister of one of his fellow prisoners—his second wife. He had been permitted to consummate the marriage in prison. His American lawyers later stated that he had renounced one of his two wives.

10. To incriminate the sheik for having played a part in the attack himself, in the absence of material evidence, the prosecution linked several events: The assassination of the Jewish extremist leader Meir Kahane on November 5, 1990, killed by a mili-

tant Egyptian Islamist who frequented one of the mosques where Omar Abdel Rahman officiated as sheik, the plot to kill President Mubarak of Egypt, the attack on the World Trade Center, and numerous other plots for attacks and assassinations in New York. Based on the interpretation of passages from his sermons and on recordings of conversations with a police informer, as well as on material facts in the two successful cases, the act of indictment referred to a concept that is rarely used in American law—which led to criticism by the defendants of its having been "fabricated." See U.S. District Court, Southern District of New York, *Indictment S3 Cr. 181 (MBM)*, August 25, 1993 (27 pages).

11. For details of the role of the Egyptian informer to the FBI, Emad Salem, a former army graduate in his native country, see P. Thomas and E. Randolph, "Informer at Center of Case: Hero or Huckster, Salem Shaped Charges," *Washington Post*, August 26, 1993, p. A1.

12. Arriving on September 2, 1992, in New York, on a flight originating in Karachi and carrying an Iraqi passport, Ramzi Yusef entered American territory by requesting political asylum. See "The Bombing: Retracing the Steps," *New York Times*, May 26, 1993, p. B1.

13. From the perspective of the run-down district of "Little Egypt" in Jersey City, the twin towers of the Manhattan skyline appeared like a pagan monument bent on crushing the poor immigrants who prayed in the cramped quarters of the Al Salam mosque where Sheik Abdel Rahman officiated.

14. In actual fact, the Al Jihad group's Internet newsletter was run from London under the supervision of two senior members of the movement, while others were leading the International Committee for the Defense of the Oppressed, which was actively promoting human rights. See *Taqrir 1995*, p. 279.

15. This group was nicknamed Talai al-Fax (Vanguard Faxers) by their opponents, referring to their lack of social foundations and the plethora of faxes they generated. It was run from London by Yasir Tawfiq al-Sirri and also published an Internet newsletter, *Al Mirsad al-I'lami* (The Muslim Information Observatory), which circulated various communiqués and pieces of sectarian information on the international Islamist movement (Chechnya and so on).

16. For more on the reconciliation between the leaders of the Gamaa Islamiya and the Al Jihad group in London in 1996, see *Taqrir 1995*, p. 283.

17. Based in London, the "International Spokesman of the Muslim Brotherhood in the West," M. Kamal al-Halbaoui, of Syrian nationality, is the first non-Egyptian to have responsibilities of this kind. In 1999, Gannushi was to play an intermediary role between President Abdelaziz Bouteflika of Algeria and some of the Islamist leaders to prepare the "national agreement" approved by referendum in September. On the Islamic Foundation, see Kepel, *Allah in the West*, pp. 178–182.

18. With his radical program Bakri brought together enough young Indo-Pakistanis to pack the stadium, thereby transgressing the implicit gentlemen's agreement that controlled relations between the radical Islamists and the British authorities and, according to which, such proselytizing was only allowed if directed overseas. In

1996 he founded the Al Muhajirun. His next meeting, in which the International Spokesman of the Muslim Brotherhood was to participate, was not allowed to take place in August 1996.

19. On the FAF and *Le Critère*, see Kepel, *Allah in the West*, ch. 3.

20. *Le Monde*, November 17, 1993.

21. This policy was implemented in the United Kingdom to the great satisfaction of the local Islamist movement. The many conferences on Islam in Europe organized in the 1990s on its initiative never ceased to hold up the British model as an example and to hold up France to public obloquy.

22. The UOIF congress at Le Bourget, which then used to take place at Christmas, never addressed the Algerian question but rather such topics as democracy, the Republic, secularism, and so on, designed to show the French authorities the movement's commitment to the kind of political debate prevailing at the time. After the assassination of two French surveyors in Western Algeria in October 1993, claimed by the GIA, a massive operation by the French police rounded up more than 110 people supposedly linked to the armed Algerian Islamist movement.

23. The majority of those deported later reappeared among FIS leaders in exile—and condemned the action of the GIA; see statements by D. el Houari, former president of the FAF, in P. Denaud, *Le FIS*, pp. 272–273n49. But since 1994 the djazarists, led by Mohammed Said, paid allegiance to the GIA "amir" Cherif Gousmi, and the FAF became to all intents and purposes djazarist. The video of the "Communiqué d'Unité," which shows the allegiance ceremony as it happened, circulated around Islamist groups in Europe that summer.

24. Extracts from the trial proceedings, which took place in December 1996, are in *Le procès d'un réseau islamiste*, text assembled by C. Erhel and R. de La Baume, as well as in Kepel, "Réislamisation et passage au terrorisme: Quelques hypothèses de réflexion," in *Islam(s) en Europe: Approches d'un nouveau pluralisme culturel européen*, ed. Rémy Leveau (Berlin: Les Travaux du Centre Marc-Bloch, no. 13, 1998), pp. 107–119.

25. Those who favor the theory of manipulation of the GIA note that his assassination was virtually announced in the Algerian daily *La Tribune* some days before the event.

26. Supported by some of the defense counsels in the June 1999 trial, this theory throws suspicion on the leader and the coordinator of the terrorist network, Ali Touchent, known as Tarek (killed in Algiers on May 27, 1997, by the police), of having been an agent of Algerian military security.

27. See the statements by Boualem Bensaid on June 3, 1999, in which he claimed membership of the GIA and denied any links with military security, *Le Monde*, June 5, 1999. A summary of the charges in *Le Monde*, June 1, 1999, and of the official minutes of the hearings of June 3 and 4. The accused swung between refusing the legitimacy of the "crusaders" court, referring to the "justice of Allah," making "insolent remarks" to the judges, and, in some cases, denying membership in the GIA.

28. Three years before the attacks, the German sociologist Dietmar Loch had a long interview with K. Kelkal, by chance, in the course of a survey of immigrant youth in the suburbs of Lyon. It was printed *in extenso* in *Le Monde* on October 7, 1995.
29. See Kepel, *Allah in the West*, pp. 55–56.
30. See Farhad Khosrokhavar, *L'islam des jeunes* (Paris: Flammarion, 1997).
31. For more on these movements, see Kepel, *Allah in the West*; also Jocelyne Cesari, *Musulmans et républicains* (Brussels: Complexe, 1997), in which some of the young militants in these organizations were allowed to speak for themselves.
32. These aspects of the interview with K. Kelkal are examined in Kepel, "Réislamisation et passage," pp. 108–109.
33. See *Libération*, June 8, 1999.
34. On this point, see the work of Michèle Tribalat, based on demographic data, in *Faire France* (Paris: La Découverte, 1996).
35. See the websites of the UOIF and of its sister youth organization, the JMF, who had been put in charge of the organization of the Christmas event at Le Bourget. This site has not been updated since the end of 1999.
36. There were some dissenting voices. According to Milton Bearden, a retired high-ranking CIA officer who was responsible for the agency, aide to the Afghan jihad and later CIA chief in the Sudan, the United States's legal and media handling of bin Laden was simplistic: "To draw a link between him and all known acts of terrorism throughout the decade is an insult to the [intelligence] of most Americans. And it surely doesn't encourage our allies to take us seriously in this respect." See http://www.pbs.org/wgbh/pages/frontline/shows/binladen/interviews/bearden/html.
37. As an example, "Osama bin Laden: An Interview with the World's Most Dangerous Terrorist," *Esquire*, February 1999.
38. In 1979 one of bin Laden's brothers, Mahrous, was under scrutiny after the attack on the Great Mosque in Mecca by conspirators centered around Juhayman al-Utaybi. As a matter of fact his trucks entered and left without being searched, and the attackers had used them to gain access to the holy precinct. But the forces of law and order (and their French advisers) also needed the construction group's help to retake the area, since the bin Ladens possessed the only detailed plans. See "About the Bin Laden Family," http://www.pbs.org/wgbh/pages/frontline/shows/binladen/who/family/html.
39. The Egyptian branch of the group, led by one of Osama's brothers, Abdel Aziz, must have employed more than 40,000 people, which made it the largest private foreign company in the country. See ibid., "About the Bin Laden Family."
40. According to several people I spoke to, Azzam, on the same wavelength as his Saudi bedfellows, wanted to confine the jihadists to Afghanistan, while bin Laden was in favor of internationalizing the jihad. Others maintain that Azzam wanted to focus the jihad on Palestine after Afghanistan.
41. The Iraqi Baathist regime, based on a secular pan-Arab ideology, was condemned as "impious" and "apostate" in Islamist circles. During the Iraq-Iran war of 1980–1988, the conservative states in the Arabian peninsula had played down these at-

tacks, while Khomeini's Iran played them up to the full. After the invasion of Kuwait and the arrival of the forces of the "crusading" international coalition on Saudi soil, the salafist-jihadists and the Iraqi government were united in their opposition to Saudi power.

42. In 1992 and 1993, veterans from Afghanistan, Yemen, and further abroad played a part in destabilizing the Socialist Party that still held power in the southern part of the country (reunified in 1990). Their leader, Tariq al-Fadli, imprisoned in Aden, was accused of being in regular contact with bin Laden, who was based in Khartoum. More information on Yemeni Islamism than it is possible to discuss in this present work can be found in J.-M. Grosgurin, "La contestation islamiste au Yémen," in *Exils et royaumes*, ed. Kepel, pp. 235–250; Paul Monet, *Réislamisation et conflit religieux à Aden* (Paris: a DEA memoir, IEP de Paris, 1995); P. Dresch and B. Haykel, "Stereotypes and Political Styles: Islamists and Tribesfolk in Yemen," *International Journal of Middle Eastern Studies* 27, no. 4 (1995); F. Mermier, "L'islam politique au Yémen ou la Tradition contre les traditions?" *Maghreb-Machrek*, 1997; as well as L. Stiftl, "The Yemeni Islamists in the Process of Democratization," in *Le Yémen contemporain*, ed. R. Leveau, F. Mermier, and U. Steinbach (Paris: Karthala, 1999), pp. 247ff. In the latter work, the activities of T. al-Fadli and his relationship with bin Laden are described by B. Rougier in "Yémen 1990–94: La logique du pacte politique mise en échec," pp. 112–114.

43. See the interview with Baha el Din Hanafi, one of the theorists of Saudi international policy, in Mark Huband, *Warriors of the Prophet* (Boulder: Westview Press, 1998), p. 37.

44. See ibid., p. 40. Also, *Indictment*, U.S. Government, November 4, 1998, at http://www.pbs/wgbh/pages/frontline/shows/alqaeda.html, and "Declaration of jihad," August 23, 1996 (see below).

45. In particular, he was largely responsible for the construction of the motorway known as the "Challenge" *(at-tahaddi)* linking the capital to Port Sudan, 800 km long. He lost more than $150 million in the process, and the Sudanese government never repaid him.

46. This slogan is to be seen, in Arabic and in a "modified" form, on the majority of documents, posters, and so on that extol bin Laden. It means "Expel the Jews and the Christians from the Arabian Peninsula" *(Akhrijou al yahoud wa-l nassara min jazirat al arab)*. It makes reference to a word uttered by the Prophet on his deathbed. Distributed by fax, the declaration includes two English translations (somewhat different in tone): a militant one on the Azzam Brigade's website (http://www.azzam.com/html/body5Fdeclaration.html); the other, made by the CDLR and declared to be "absolutely precise" and entitled "The Ladenese Epistle," on the MSANEWS website (http://msanews.mynet.net.MSANEWS/199610/19961012.3.html).

47. Although one would have expected bin Laden to condemn the practice of lending money at interest, his declaration admitted that the government owed the population "more than 340 million rials, not counting the interest that accumulates daily."

48. "You have suffered the disgrace of Allah and you have retreated."

49. Dated February 23, 1998, published in Arabic in the London Arabic newspaper *Al-Quds al-Arabi,* the text has been translated into English under the title "World Islamic Front Statement Urging Jihad against Jews and Crusaders" on the following website: http://www.fas.org/irp/world/para/docs/980223-fatwa.htm. See Bernard Lewis's interpretation of this—as well as a translation of some passages—in his article "Licence to Kill: Usama bin Ladin's Declaration of Jihad," *Foreign Affairs* 77, no. 6 (November–December 1998), pp. 14–19.

50. The destruction of the Al Shifa factory in the suburbs of Khartoum would appear to have been an attempt to put pressure on the Sudanese government, the substance of the allegations that it was producing dangerous chemicals destined for bin Laden never having been established. The bombarded Afghan camps did not shelter bin Laden but did contain Pakistani militant Islamists who were in training for the war in Indian Kashmir. The American retaliatory measures were condemned in many Muslim countries and coolly welcomed by several traditional allies of the United States. A fervent bin Laden cult grew up in Pakistan as a result of this, with his portrait appearing everywhere in demonstrations organized by the radical Sunni Islamist movements.

51. "Our task consists of instigating, by the grace of Allah; we have done it, and certain people have responded to the instigation" (statement in *Time,* December 23, 1998). In an interview on ABC News the same day, bin Laden denied any involvement in the attacks but ventured his opinion concerning some suspects.

52. At the time of writing, and among so many "instant books" on bin Laden, the best and most reliable work to date is Peter Bergen, *Holy War, Inc.: Inside the Secret World of Osama bin Laden* (New York: The Free Press, 2001).

14. Hamas, Israel, Arafat, and Jordan

1. According to Israeli sources quoted by Elie Rekhess in *MECS* 1993, p. 216, the "funds for firmness" *(amwal al-sumud)* deposited by the PLO in the territories fell from $350 million per year during the intifada to $120 million after the invasion of Kuwait in 1990 and $40 million in 1993. Reports by Meir Litvak and Elie Rekhess that appeared in *MECS* and deal with the years under discussion here provide a useful perspective and have been of great help to me.

2. For an analysis of this point of view, see J.-F. Legrain, "Palestine: Les bantoustans d'Allah," in *Palestine, Palestiniens,* ed. R. Bocco, B. Destremau, and J. Hannoyer (Beirut: Cermoc, 1997), pp. 85–101.

3. Hamas had been banned and its militants hunted down in December 1990. Membership in the movement was punishable by imprisonment.

4. Both the PFLP and the DFLP had Marxist leanings.

5. As in Egypt, the vocational elections, reputedly free, served in Palestine as a test of Islamist influence, especially among the middle class; the same went for the student elections, a good indicator of the strength of the movement on campus.

6. On the foundation and the precise identity of the Brigades, the website of the

Hamas movement gives two conflicting versions. See http://www.palestine-info.org.

7. See Resolution 799, December 1992.

8. On the relations between business and political power in Palestine, see Cédric Balas, "Les hommes d'affaires palestiniens dans un contexte politique en mutation," *Maghreb-Machrek* 161 (July–September 1998): 51–59.

9. The Islamist party translated the function of the Palestine security forces as follows: "Authority, which is upheld by 30,000 armed men forming a police force which goes by various names, must put into practice the obligations required by the accords. The first of these is to oppose and crush the resistance movements." See http://www.palestine-info.org.

10. The difficulties of putting the accords into practice, as well as Israeli and Palestinian mutual accusations, are in the documents compiled by Agnès Levallois, "Points de vue israéliens et palestiniens sur les violations des accords d'Oslo," *Maghreb-Machrek* 156 (April–June 1997): 93ff.

11. See L. Bucaille, also J. Grange, "Les forces de sécurité palestiniennes: Contraintes d'Oslo et quête de légitimité nationale," *Maghreb-Machrek* 161 (July–September 1998): 18–28.

12. Assassinated in Malta on October 26 on his return from Libya, Fathi Shqaqi was opposed from within the movement. His successor, an academic from Florida, did not succeed in preserving the movement as a significant component of Palestinian Islamism. See Rifat Sid Ahmed, *Rihlat al dam*, for details on the life and work of Shqaqi.

13. The sealing-off of territories after the suicide bombings of 1996 put 45% of the active population of the Gaza Strip out of work, along with 30% of workers on the West Bank. The loss of earnings was estimated at $1–2 million per day for the Palestinians. See Anat Kurtz (with the collaboration of Nahman Tal), *Hamas: Radical Islam in a National Struggle*, JCSS, University of Tel-Aviv, Memo, no. 48, July 1997 (http://www.tau.ac.il/jccs/memo48.html, ch. 3, p. 9).

14. Operation Grapes of Wrath against the Lebanese Hezbollah, between April 15 and 27, 1996, which was distinguished by the massacre of civilian Lebanese at Cana due to an Israeli bombardment, also contributed to the defeat of Shimon Peres.

15. In revenge, Israeli agents tried to assassinate the chief of Hamas's political office, Khaled Mishal, in Amman on September 25. They were arrested by Jordanian security forces and released in exchange for the freeing of the religious guide of the Islamist party, Sheik Ahmad Yassin.

16. See the analysis and detailed interpretation of the January 1996 elections by J.-F. Legrain, *Les Palestines du quotidien* (Beirut: Cermoc, 1999).

17. See "Hamas' Position towards the Self-Rule Authority," in http://www.palestine-info.org.

18. See P.-W. Glasman, "Le mouvement des Frères musulmans," the most detailed monograph to date in a Western language, in *Le royaume hachémite de Jordanie, 1946–1996*, ed. R. Bocco (Paris: Karthala, 2000). There is also a well-researched and accurate work in Arabic: *Jama'at al ikhwan al muslimin fi-l urdun 1946–1996* (The

Association of Muslim brothers in Jordan) (Amman: Dar Sindbad, 1997), by Ibrahim al-Gharaibeh (himself a Brother and journalist), and which is completed by an edited work (much of it based upon the former) available in English, *Islamic Movements in Jordan,* ed. Hani Hourani (Amman: Dar Sindbad, 1997). There is also a good overview of the subject recently published by Shmuel Bar, *The Muslim Brotherhood in Jordan,* The Moshe Dayan Center, coll. Data and Analysis, Tel Aviv University, 1998. The Jordanian Muslim Brothers have been looked on in a favorable light in works by British and American academics, who saw in them the possibility of a solution to the equation [Islamists (moderate) = democrats], and campaigned to allow these moderates to participate in power in other parts of the Muslim world. See Glenn E. Robinson, "Can Islamists be Democrats? The Case of Jordan," *Middle East Journal* 51, no. 3 (Summer 1997): 373–387, and Lawrence Tal, "Dealing with Radical Islam: The Case of Jordan," *Survival* 37, no. 3 (Autumn 1995): 139–156, esp. 152.

19. The Brothers participated in the parliamentary elections and gained some seats. Opposed to those in power when they seemed too dependent on the alliance with Britain and later America, and sometimes gently reprimanded for this, they were an important aid against Nasser's opposition and that of the left, receiving favors as a result. There is a detailed analysis on the West Bank during this period in Amnon Cohen, *Political Parties in the West Bank under the Jordanian Regime, 1946–1967* (London: Ithaca Press, 1982).

20. On the participation of families of leading citizens in the governing bodies of the Jordanian Brothers, see Philippe Droz-Vincent, "Les notables urbains au Levant: Cas de la Syrie et de la Jordanie" (Ph.D. diss., Institut d'Etudes Politiques de Paris, 1999), pp. 39–59.

21. On the period of Abdallah Azzam's life between 1967 and 1970 see, in addition to his biography (http://azzam.com), Gharaibeh, *Jama'at al ikhwan al muslimin fi-l urdun 1946–1996,* pp. 77–79 (and interview with the author, Amman, October 1998).

22. See Bar, *The Muslim Brotherhood in Jordan,* pp. 36–39.

23. The first-hand accounts collected by Glasman, in "Le mouvement des Frères musulmans," show that the palace and the Brothers had agreed in advance on the extent of the latter's victory, thanks to the ad hoc electoral arrangements. When the next elections took place, in 1993, a belated change to the voting system allowed a reduction in the number of seats they obtained.

24. On these matters see W. Hammad, "Islamists and Charitable Work," and H. Dabbas, "Islamic Organisations and Societies in Jordan," in Hourani, ed., *Islamic Movements in Jordan,* pp. 169–263.

25. See I. Al-Gharaibeh, "Mu'adalat fi-l haraka al islamiyya al urduniyya" (The Balance of Power in the Jordanian Islamist Movement), *Al Hayat,* July 5, 1997.

26. Beverley Milton-Edwards, "A Temporary Alliance with the Crown: The Islamic Response in Jordan," in Piscatori, ed., *Islamic Fundamentalisms,* pp. 88–108.

27. With the exception of the Party of Islamic Liberation *(Hizb al Tahrir al Islami),* founded in 1948 by Sheik Nabahani, which supported obtaining power by in-

filtration of the elites followed by violent action, and was dismantled in Jordan in the 1950s. On this movement, see Taji-Faruqi, *A Fundamental Quest.*

28. On Mohammed's Army, see B. Milton-Edwards, "Climate of Change in Jordan's Islamist Movement," in *Islamic Fundamentalism in Perspective,* ed. A. Ehteshami and A. S. Sidahmed (Boulder: Westview Press, 1996), pp. 127–130. P.-W. Glasman mentions the arrests of other "Afghans" in 1994 and 1996, charged with terrorist attacks or other attempted attacks. The media exposure of these real or supposed atrocities helped the regime to warn the Brothers that limits exist which could not be exceeded.

29. The Jordanian Islamic Action Front had some similarities with the Centre party (Hizb al Wasat) planned by members of the younger generation of Egyptian Brothers in 1995.

30. The opening of a Hamas office in Tehran, and the regular visits made by exiled leaders of the movement to the Iranian capital since 1994, have been the object of strong criticism by the Palestinian Authority. In particular, among those imprisoned were Khaled Mishal (who had been the victim of an assassination attempt by Mossad in September 1997) and the spokesman Ibrahim Ghawshé. On the other hand, Mussa Abu Marzouq (holder of a Yemeni passport), who had been imprisoned in the United States and freed thanks to the intervention of King Hussein, was expelled to Damascus. On November 20, despite their Jordanian nationality, Mishal and Ghawshé were "removed" to Qatar.

31. On November 22, 1999, four imprisoned leaders who had Jordanian nationality were "removed" to Qatar, as a prelude to a policy of "Jordanization" of Palestinian refugees in the Hashemite kingdom, which was to reduce the possibility of their return to western Jordan.

15. The Forced Secularization of Turkish Islamists

1. Born in 1926 at Sinope on the Black Sea coast, and son of a high-ranking civil servant, Erbakan was educated in German at the German high school for boys in Istanbul and continued his studies at the technical university there. He then qualified as an engineer in Germany, specializing in mechanical engineering and becoming a university professor in 1953, before returning to his own country. One of his friends at the university in Istanbul was Suleyman Demirel, a leading figure of right-wing politics in Turkey and leader of the Justice Party (Adalet Partisi, AP), of which Erbakan was a member until 1969. Demirel was elected president of the Turkish Republic in 1993.

2. The works of the most knowledgeable expert on Islam in contemporary Turkey, the journalist Rusen Cakir, are available at present only in the Turkish language: *Ayet ve Slogan* (Verse and Slogan) (Istanbul: Mètis, 1990), and *Ne seriat ne demokrasi: Refah Partisini Anlamak* (Neither Sharia nor Democracy: Understanding the Prosperity Party) (Istanbul: Mètis, 1990). I owe much to numerous conversations with Mr. Cakir, as well as with Professor Nilüfer Göle, author of pioneering research into the social dimension of this question (although the three of us do not

always agree in our analysis of the Islamist phenomenon as a whole). See R. Cakir, "The City: Trap or Springboard for Turkish Islamists?" *Cemoti* 19 (1995): 83ff, and "The Mobilization of Islam in Turkey," *Esprit*, August–September 1992, pp. 130ff. Analyses of the integration of the Islamist movement into the global sociopolitical context of the country are to be found in a reference work on contemporary Turkey by Eric Zürcher, *Turkey, A Modern History*, 3rd ed. (London: I. B. Tauris, 1997), as well as in Hugh Poulton, *Top Hat, Grey Wolf and Crescent: Turkish Nationalism and the Turkish Republic* (London: Hurst & Co., 1997). A recent synthesis has been published by Nilüfer Narli, "The Rise of the Islamist Movement in Turkey," *MERIA Journal* 3, no. 3 (September 1999).

3. Erbakan was a disciple of Sheik Zahid Kotku of the Naksibendi order. See Serif Mardin, "The Naksibendi Order in Turkish History," in *Islam in Modern Turkey*, ed. Tapper, pp. 121–142, and Thierry Zarcone, "Les Naksibendi et la République turque: De la persécution au repositionnement théologique, politique et social," *Turcica* 24 (1992): 99–107, and also "La Turquie républicaine," in *Les Voies d'Allah: Les ordres mystiques dans le monde musulman des origines à aujourd'hui*, ed. A. Popovic and G. Veinstein (Paris: Fayard, 1996), pp. 372–379.

4. This same "trinity" can also be found a few years later in the pages of the journal of the Egyptian Muslim Brothers, *Al Dawa;* see Kepel, *Prophet and Pharaoh*, pp. 118ff.

5. Binnaz Toprak, "Politicisation of Islam in a Secular State: The National Salvation Party in Turkey," in *From Nationalism to Revolutionary Islam*, ed. Said Amir Arjomand (New York: SUNY Press, 1984), pp. 119–133.

6. See Serif Mardin, "La religion dans la Turquie moderne," *Revue internationale des sciences sociales* 29, no. 2 (1977): 317.

7. This political uncertainty could perhaps be seen as the reason behind the decline in votes for the party in the legislative elections of June 1977, when it gained only 8.6% of the votes cast, as opposed to 11.8% four years previously.

8. The pupils at these "high schools for preachers" were mainly drawn from provincial families rebellious toward the secularization being encouraged by the state—a social group within which the MSP was well established. These schools generally had lower standards than other high schools and recruited from a less privileged sector of society.

9. As well as the Akincilar ("avant-gardists"), a group of young paramilitaries linked to the disbanded Islamist party, there are a multitude of other small groups claiming links to the Iranian or Lebanese Hezbollah (with publications like *Sehadet* and *Tevhid* full of photographs glorifying the Iranian revolution), or to the Palestino-Jordanian Party of Islamic Liberation. Others, like the Ibda (Revelation) movement, look back nostalgically to the Ottoman empire from a radical religious standpoint. See Ely Karmon, "Islamist Terrorist Activities in Turkey in the 1990s," *Terrorism and Political Violence* 10, no. 4 (Winter 1998): 101–121.

10. The elections of November 6, 1983, which took place under strict military surveillance, were intended to mark a return to civil life following the period when the Council of National Security, set up after the coup d'état, had taken over the running of the country and "re-established public order." On November 7, 1982, a new

constitution had been approved by referendum, and General Evren, leader of the CNS, was elected president of the republic for the next seven years. Parties permitted to participate in the legislative elections had to be approved by those in power, who were keen to prevent the re-emergence of old political factions under new names. Of the three authorized parties, the ANAP appeared to be the most independent of the army, although Korkut Ozal had assumed governmental responsibilities in the days following the coup d'état. He won 45.12% of the vote and 211 seats out of 400.

11. Ozal was known for his membership in the Naksibendi order.

12. Poulton, *Top Hat, Grey Wolf and Crescent,* pp. 182–183.

13. Hundreds of members of Islamic brotherhoods and groups were arrested during 1982 when caught attending secret meetings or giving unauthorized religious teaching.

14. The identical phenomenon can be found among the emigrant Turkish population in Western Europe, where Erbakan's closest allies had founded the AMGT (Avrupa Milli Gorus Teskilati, Organization for National Vision in Europe) and were protected from any intervention by the Turkish state. They were also able to guarantee militants who remained in Turkey regular financial aid, boosted by their leader's fund-raising tours.

15. At the origin of this "Turkish-Islamic synthesis" was an influential group founded in May 1970, the Hearth of Intellectuals (Aydinlar Ocagi, AO), which included academics, journalists, men of religion, and right-wing businessmen. Their role is underlined in Poulton, *Top Hat, Grey Wolf and Crescent,* and in B. Toprak, "Religion as State Ideology in a Secular Setting: The Turkish-Islamic Synthesis," in *Aspects of Religion in Secular Turkey,* ed. M. Wagstaff (University of Durham, Centre for Middle Eastern Studies, Occ. Paper no. 40, 1990), pp. 10–15.

16. In 1996 Turkey had 16 national, 15 regional, and 300 local television channels; see Jenny B. White, "Amplifying Trust: Community and Communication in Turkey," in *New Media in the Muslim World,* ed. D. F. Eickelman and J. W. Anderson (Bloomington: Indiana University Press, 1999), p. 169.

17. For an overview of this phenomenon, refer to the works of Nilüfer Göle: "Ingénieurs musulmans et étudiantes voilées en Turquie: Entre le totalitarisme et l'individualisme," in *Intellectuels et militants de l'islam contemporain,* ed. G. Kepel and Y. Richard (Paris: Seuil, 1990), pp. 167–192; *The Forbidden Modern* (University of Michigan Press, 1996); and "Secularism and Islamism in Turkey: The Making of Elites and Counter-Elites," *Middle East Journal* 51, no. 1 (Winter 1997): 46–58.

18. During the local elections of March 1984, the first that the party was able to contest, it obtained only 4.4% of the votes; in the legislative elections of 1987 it won 7.16%. In 1989 it gained 9.8% in the municipal elections, and in 1991, allied to the extreme right-wing nationalists, 16.2% (with one third going to the latter). This maneuver, although it did not greatly increase the Refah party's share of the vote as compared with 1989, allowed it to construct a parliamentary party with an apparatus that was to help in subsequent campaigns, in particular those for the municipal elections of 1994, in which it nearly doubled its votes.

19. The Refah party got 21.4%, the ANAP 19.7%, the Right Path party (DYP), which claimed the support of Demirel (Ozal's successor as president of the republic), gained 19.2%, and Ecevit's Social-Democratic Party, 14.6%.

20. The FIS got more than 54% of the votes in 1990, more than 47% in 1991.

21. Quoted by A. Mango in *MECS* 1989, p. 659.

22. Several authors have noted the paradoxical convergence between the insistence on the veil and feminist demands, or indeed those of transvestites, for whom Islamic moral and ethical thinking had, in principle, little sympathy. See Jean-Pierre Thieck, *Passion d'Orient* (Paris: Karthala, 1990), p. 70.

23. This phenomenon is a part of the general movement toward the expansion of Islamic finance and the emergence of a religious middle class throughout the Muslim world, linked to Saudi interest. The quoted article by Clement Henry Moore, "Islamic Banks and Competitive Politics," contains elements of analysis relevant to the Turkish situation.

24. The acronym Müsiad stands for Müstakil Sanayiciler ve Isadamlari Dernegi (Independent Association of Industrialists and Businessmen), modeled on the Tüsiad (same meaning but with "Tü," the first letters of "Turkish"). It is a grouping of major business leaders, mainly based in Istanbul. The "Mü," which officially stands for "independent," is understood by all as meaning, in reality, "Muslim."

25. Ayse Oncu, in "Packaging Islam: Cultural Politics on the Landscape of Turkish Commercial Television," *Public Culture* 8, no. 1 (Autumn 1995): 51–71, based on the Refah campaign of 1991, shows how Refah's messages avoided the usual quotations from the Koran and deliberately included images of women not wearing the veil saying that they would vote for the party.

26. On the use of the telephone by Refah activists to encourage voters—on the American model—see White, "Amplifying Trust," p. 172.

27. See the analysis of the Refah electorate conducted in 1994 by Ferhat Kentel, "L'Islam carrefour des identités sociales et culturelles," in *Cemoti* 19, pp. 211ff.

28. On the negotiations between Erbakan and Ciller to finalize the coalition between the Refah party and the Right Path party (DYP) as well as the events that took place during Erbakan's period of government, see Aryeh Shmuelevitz, *Turkey's Experiment in Islamist Government* (Tel Aviv: The Moshe Dayan Center for Data & Analysis, May 1999).

29. The Right Path party (DYP) controlled the ministries of Foreign Affairs (which was given to Ciller) and Defense, but also, in particular, Interior and Education (which had been assigned to the MSP in the 1970s, allowing the recruitment of many militant Islamists into the police force and the teaching profession) and Industry. The Refah obtained Finance, Public Works, Employment, Justice, the Arts, Environment, and a Ministry of State, headed by Abdullah Gül, who acted as unofficial foreign affairs minister.

30. I am grateful to R. Cakir, who gave me permission to consult his unpublished article, "Foreign Policy of the Welfare Party," which provides a well-documented analysis of this matter. The first military agreement was signed in 1996 and was denounced by Gül, who promised to retract it when his party controlled power. The

second agreement, which was for the renovation of 60 Turkish Phantom fighter aircraft in Israel, was ratified in August by Erbakan.

31. Details of the accusations and the measures recommended are given in Shmuelevitz, *Turkey's Experiment in Islamist Government*, pp. 24–27.

32. A woman had been elected as member of Parliament on the Fazilet list in April 1999, but the fact that she had decided to sit in the chamber wearing the veil provoked controversy. The daughter of an imam, a doctor, she had studied in Texas (because she could not attend a Turkish university wearing a veil) and there had married an American Muslim of Arabic extraction and become a U.S. citizen. In principle, the Turkish state did not allow citizens of other states to sit in Parliament (this prohibition is seldom applied). Refusing to remove her veil in the chamber, she was expelled and subsequently divested of her Turkish citizenship.

33. The nationalist Social-Democratic Party (DSP) of Ecevit topped the results with 21.6%, the extreme right-wing nationalist party (MHP) obtained 18.4%, the Fazilet 14.9%, and the two parties of the center-right (ANAP and DYP) a little over 13%. Several observers attributed the gains made by the two front-running parties, who were opposed in the political arena but both "chauvinist," to two things in particular. First, the capture of the PKK leader Abdullah Ocalan (which would have benefited Ecevit, the prime minister) after a campaign of intimidation against Syria, where he was being given asylum. Second, the postponement by the European Union of Turkey's application to join the EEC during the European Luxembourg summit in the autumn of 1998.

Conclusion

1. On the coup d'état by which General Bashir removed Turabi from power, see "What Does Bashir's Second Coup Mean for Sudan?" *Mideast Mirror*, December 14, 1999, which gives a very accurate analysis, including many commentaries from the London Arabic press as well as local analyses. A good factual presentation is to be found in "Sudanese Leader Moves against Rival: Bashir Dissolves Parliament, Dismisses Former Mentor Who Challenged Him," *Washington Post*, December 14, 1999.

2. Abdel Wahhab al Effendi, "Al tajriba al sudaniyya wa azmat al haraka al islamiyya al haditha: durus wa dalalat," *Al-Quds al-arabi*, December 29, 1999.

3. In 1994, Arab Islamists and nationalists had been brought together by a conference in Beirut. As a result they overcame their antagonisms in order to fight together against the peace process set in motion by the Oslo Agreements—which they saw as a capitulation to imperialism and Zionism. On this movement, with the Tunisian Islamist Rashid al-Gannushi, a refugee in London, as one of its most eloquent spokesmen, see the edited work published by the Beirut Center for Arab Unity, a nationalist think tank, *Al hurriyyat al 'amma fi-l daoula al-islamiyya* (Public Liberties in the Islamic State) (Beirut, 1993), which indicated approval.

4. In his article M. Effendi incriminates not the "secularists" as such but the "extreme secularists" (al harakat al 'almaniyya al mutattarifa).

5. Thanks to their access to Malaysian wealth, oil and gas extraction, and taxes im-

posed on ethnic Chinese businesses, the Islamists in the footsteps of Anwar contributed to numerous appropriate "causes" all over the world and have since cultivated, especially in American academic circles, a "moderate, business-friendly"
image that is compatible with capitalism.

6. An initial, detailed appraisal of the crisis in the Islamic Republic figures in the
book edited by Saeed Rahnema and Sohrab Behdad, *Iran after the Revolution: Crisis of an Islamic State* (London: I. B. Tauris, 1995). See particularly S. Behdad, "The
Post-Revolutionary Economic Crisis," pp. 97–129, in which the author identifies
the social groups that achieved a dominant position.

7. The fate of those young volunteers who left for the front and ended up seeking
martyrdom, giving up their lives together with the failure of the revolution, has
been the subject of a study by Farhad Khosrokhavar, "Le chi'isme mortifère."

8. For details of the demographic transition in the Muslim world at the end of the
1990s, see J.-C. Chasteland and J.-C. Chesnais, *La population du monde, enjeux et
problèmes* (Paris: PUF-Ined, 1997).

9. For the consequences of the election of Khatami, see part of the *Cahiers de l'Orient*
49 (1st quarter, 1998), entitled "Le printemps Iranien?" ed. Azadeh Kian, in addition to Farhad Khosrokhavar and Olivier Roy, *Iran: Comment sortir d'une
révolution religieuse* (Paris: Seuil, 1999).

10. On this American debate, where scientific and intellectual argument is closely
bound up with political and economic interests, comprehensive documentation
has been available since the mid-1990s. See especially Maria do Céu Pinto, *Political
Islam and the United States: A Study of US Policy towards Islamist Movements in the
Middle East* (London: Ithaca Press, 1999), which summarizes the different policies
applied by successive governments and pressure groups that have promoted them.
See also Fawaz A. Gerges, *America and Political Islam: Clash of Cultures or Clash of
Interests?* (Cambridge: Cambridge University Press, 1999), as well as older compos-
ite works edited by Hibbard and Quandt, *Islamic Activism and US Policy,* and
Kramer, *The Islamism Debate.*

11. Among other examples, *Islam 21,* in an editorial entitled "Politicizing Hijab (the
Veil) and the Denial of a Basic Right," returns to the affair of the Turkish M. P.
Merve Kavakci, elected on the Fazilet Party slate in 1999, then expelled from Parliament and deprived of her citizenship for taking her oath of allegiance wearing
the hijab. Blaming Turkish "secularists," the article points out that the latter made
wearing the veil a sign of female oppression in Islam. To counter these arguments,
the author writes, "This sort of thing must be seen from the point of view of *a
woman's right to choose,* and not from a traditional or political standpoint." It
should be understood that the above phrase (my italics) is exactly that used by the
pro-abortion lobby—and which in English is used as a mark of adherence to the
cause of "civil liberties." *Islam 21,* no. 17, June 1999.

12. http://islam21.org.

13. *Islam 21,* no. 15, February 1999.

14. *Islam 21,* no. 16, April 1999.

15. Tariq Ramadan, *Aux sources du renouveau musulman: D'al-Afghani à Hassan al*

Banna, un siècle de réformisme islamique (Paris: Bayard, 1998), with a preface by Alain Gresh, editor-in-chief of *Le Monde diplomatique*. Other works by this author have appeared on the list of an Islamist publisher, the Lyon bookshop Al Tawhid, close to the Union des Jeunes Musulmans in that city, over which M. Ramadan exerts a spiritual authority. For a discussion of this work, see Frank Frégosi, "Tariq Ramadan ou les habits neuf d'une vieille rhétorique," 2000.

16. Some of the defendants in the trials brought against the support networks of the GIA in Europe had been associating on a regular basis with Islamist groups, notably in the Rhône-Alpes region of France.

17. On the changes in Hezbollah, see H. Jaber, *Hezbollah: Born with a Vengeance* (London: Fourth Estate, 1997).

Glossary

achoura: celebration of the tenth day of the Hegira month of Moharram, when Shiites commemorate the martyrdom of Imam Hussein at Kerbala on October 10, 680.

ahd (dar al-): land of contractual peace in Islamic doctrine; zone where Muslims can live in peace in a non-Muslim state. See also **harb (dar al-)** and **islam (dar-al)**.

amal: hope; acronym of the militia of the Lebanese Movement of the Disinherited.

amir (also emir): lord, endowed with power in the classical Muslim world; chief of a political or military group, especially of an Islamist group.

ayatollah: title in the hierarchy of the Shiite clergy.

baraka: blessing given by God or by a holy man.

Barelwi: Muslim school of mystics, originating on the Indian subcontinent.

dawa: propagation of the faith; call to Islam.

Deobandi: school of **ulemas** on the Indian subcontinent, founded in 1867 as a reaction to British domination.

dzajarist: member of the Islamist movement in Algeria, opposed to **Salafists;** usually well-educated, with technology background.

faqih: jurist specializing in Muslim law.

fatwa: legal opinion based on the holy texts of Islam, in answer to a question about a precise case.

fedayeen (plural of fedai): combatants ready to sacrifice themselves for a sacred cause.

fellah: peasant.

fiqh: Muslim law.

fitna: disorder; sedition; breaking ranks with the Community of the Faithful.

gamaa islamiya (plural, gamaat islamiya): Islamic association; name given to several Egyptian Islamist movements in the 1970s and 1980s.

hajj: pilgrimage to Mecca; one of the Five Pillars of Islam; takes place during a specific Hegira calendar month according to a strictly codified ritual.

halal: authorized by the fiqh (antonym: *haram,* unauthorized; illicit).

Hanbalite: one of the four juridical schools of Sunni Islam, prominent in Saudi Arabia; characterized by extreme rigor and a literal interpretation of the holy texts; has had a strong influence on the Islamist movement.

Hanefite (Hanafi): one of the four juridical schools of Sunni Islam, prominent in Turkey and India.

harb (dar al-): war; in Islamic doctrine, land of infidels (**kufr**) where it is legal to wage jihad.

Hezb: party.

Hezbollah: Party of God, prominent in Iran and Lebanon.

hijab: woman's veil.

Hegira (Hijra): flight of the Prophet from Mecca to Medina in September 622, signifying the founding of Islam and establishing the point of departure of the Muslim (Hegirian) calendar.

hittiste: from *hit* (wall), a young unemployed man leaning against a wall (Algeria).

hudud: legal penalties and punishments prescribed by Islamic religious law in its strictest interpretation (specifically, the stoning of adulterous women, amputation of thieves' hands, and so on).

iltizam: practice of religion, piety.

imam: guide, director of prayer of the community; for Shiites, a descendant of Ali whose person is sacred and whose vocation is to exercise supreme authority.

intifada: uprising, specifically the Palestinian uprisings which began in December 1987 and 2000.

islam (dar al-): land of Islam, where the **sharia** is assumed to be applied.

jahiliyya: pagan or barbaric period prior to the revelation of Islam in Arabia; barbarity.

jamaa (plural, jamaat): association; group; company.

jihad: holy war; effort to propagate Islam within society or in the world by any means; lawful war or holy war, prescribed by the **sharia** against infidels.

kafir: impious, ungodly. See **kufr.**

khalwa: proximity (disapproved of) between two unmarried people.

Kharijite: polemical name applied to a member of certain extremist Islamist groups that condemn all other Muslims as sinners.

kufr (dar al-): land of impiety; opposite of **dar al-islam,** made up of **dar al-ahd** and **dar al-harb.**

madrassa: school where Islamic religion and law are taught.

Mahdi: Messiah who will come to restore religion and justice: twelfth imam expected by the Shiites (Muhammad al-Mahdi, who disappeared in 874).

Malekite: one of the four juridical schools of Sunni Islam, prominent in North and West Africa.

marabout: in North and West Africa, head of a brotherhood; figure venerated by popular religion; sanctuary.

mujahedeen (plural of mujahed): combatants in a **jihad;** name of various militant groups, especially in Iran and Afghanistan, and of armed Islamic formations.

mullah: title of a religious cleric, mostly used in Islamic Asia.

mustadafeen: the "disinherited."

pasdaran: guardians of the Islamic Revolution (Iran).

qawm: tribe (Afghanistan).

salafist: follower of the pious ancestors *(salaf)* or of original Islam, characterized by extreme rigor.

Shafeite: one of the four juridical schools of Sunni Islam, prominent in Southeast Asia and East Africa.

sharia: law distilled from the holy texts of Islam and traditional jurisprudence.

shebab: youth.

sheik: title of respect given to a religious dignitary or to any prominent personality or elderly man.

Shiism: from *shia Ali,* the party of Ali, the doctrine and movement claiming descent from the family of the Prophet, through the line of imams beginning with Ali, the Prophet's son-in-law; includes about 15% of the world's Muslims, chiefly in Iran and Iraq (where they are the majority), and in India, Pakistan, Lebanon, and Bahrain.

shoura: the practice of consultation recommended to sovereigns by the Koran.

Sufi: Muslim mystic.

Sunnism: doctrine of the majority of the world's Muslims (about 85%), which follows the example of the Prophet and legal tradition of the majority of the community (as opposed to the Shiites).

Tabligh: propagation of the faith; abridged name for an Islamic movement which started in India in 1927.

takfir: imputation of impiety; excommunication.

Taliban (Persian, plural of *taleb*): student of a religious school; especially Afghan students from Deobandi madrassas.

ulema (plural. of *alim*): doctor of Islamic law.

Umma: Community of the Faithful.

Wahhabism: doctrine of the disciples of ibn Abd al-Wahhab (1703–1792), puritan preacher whose influence still dominates Saudi Islam.

zakat: legal almsgiving (one of the Five Pillars of Islam).

Zaouia: building containing a marabout, a sacred figure, or a mystical Sufi brotherhood.

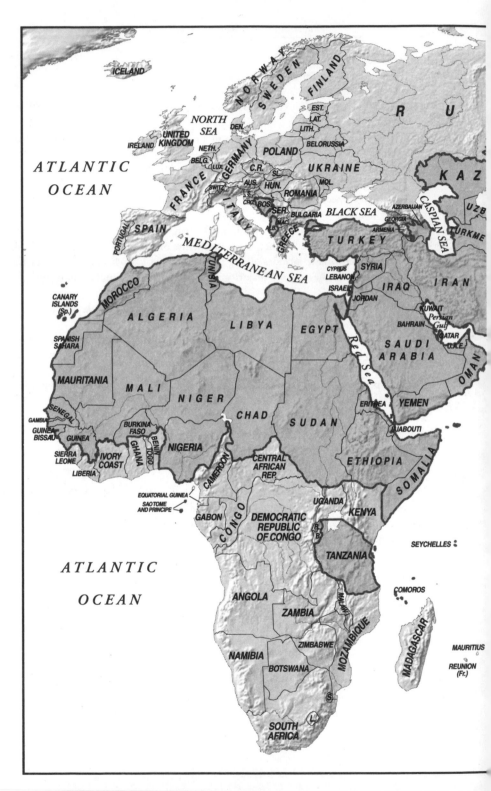

Countries in which the population is predominantly Muslim

RUSSIA

KAZAKSTAN

UZBEKISTAN

TURKMENISTAN

KIRGIZSTAN

TAJIKISTAN

AFGHANISTAN

MONGOLIA

CHINA

N. KOREA

S. KOREA

SEA OF
JAPAN

JAPAN

PAKISTAN

NEPAL

BHUTAN

BANGLA-
DESH

INDIA

MYANMAR
(BURMA)

LAOS

VIETNAM

TAIWAN

PACIFIC
OCEAN

ARABIAN
SEA

BAY OF
BENGAL

THAILAND

CAMBODIA

SOUTH
CHINA
SEA

PHILIPPINES

SRI
LANKA

MALDIVES

BRUNEI

MALAYSIA

SINGAPORE

INDONESIA

INDIAN OCEAN

E. TIMOR

AUSTRALIA

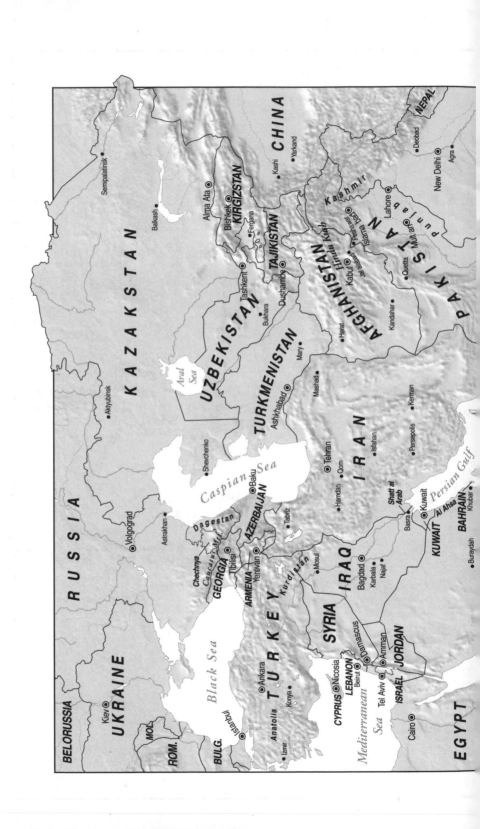

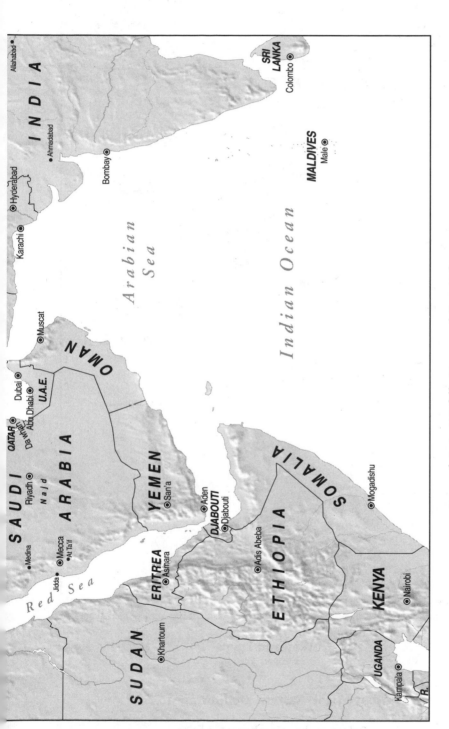

Central Asia, Middle East, and East Africa

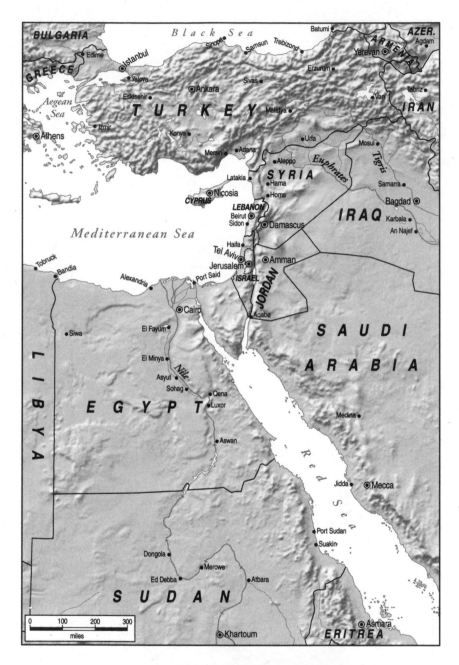

Turkey and Egypt

Above right: Eastern Mediterranean

Below right: Northwest Africa

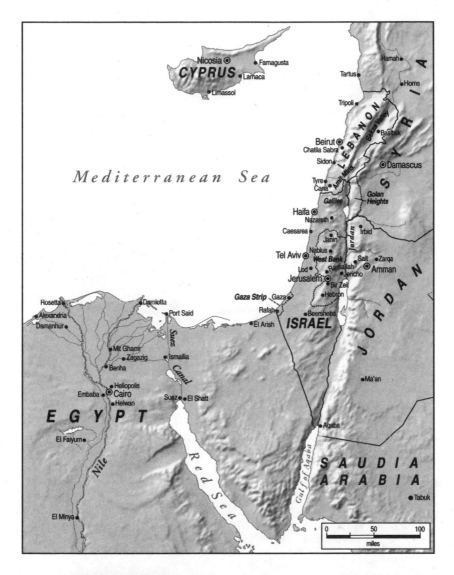

Mediterranean Sea

CYPRUS
Nicosia ◎
Famagusta
Larnaca
Limassol

SYRIA
Hamah
Homs
Tartus
Tripoli
LEBANON
Baalbek
Beirut ◎
Chatila Sabra
Sidon
Damascus ◎
Tyre
Cana
Litany River
Galilee
Golan Heights
Haifa ◎
Nazareth
Caesarea
Irbid
Jahin
Nablus
Jordan
Tel Aviv ◎
West Bank
Salt
Zarqa
Lod
Ramallah
Jericho
Amman
Jerusalem ◎
Bir Zeit
Gaza Strip
Gaza
Hebron
Rafah
Beersheba
JORDAN
El Arish
ISRAEL

Rosetta
Damiotta
Alexandria
Port Said
Damanhur
Mit Ghamr
Zagazig
Ismailia
Suez Canal
Benha
Ma'an
Heliopolis
Embaba
Cairo ◎
Helwan
Suez
El Shatt
EGYPT
Aqaba
El Faiyum
Nile
Red Sea
Gulf of Aqaba
SAUDIA ARABIA
El Minya
Tabuk

0   50   100
miles

PORTUGAL   SPAIN   Mediterranean Sea   Annaba   Bizerte
Seville   Granada   Algiers ◎   Souk Ahras   Tunis ◎
Cádiz   Tipaza   Boufarik   Constantine   TUNISIA
Tangier   Blida   Tebessa   Sousse
Atlantic Ocean   Oran   Medéa   Mitidja   Guemmar   Sfax
Sidi bel Abbès   Batna
Oujda   Tlemcen   Biskra   Gabes
Rabat ◎   Gafsa
Casablanca ◎   Meknès   Fez   Sabaran Atlas Mtns   Laghouat   Touggourt
MOROCCO   ALGERIA   LIBYA
Marrakesh   Atlas Mtns.
El Goléa
Sahara

0   100   200   300
miles

Bosnia and Albania

Malaysia and Indonesia

Abbreviations

ABIM (Muslim Youth Movement of Malaysia)
AIS Armée Islamique du Salut
AMGT Avrupa Milli Görüs Teskilati (Organization for National Vision in Europe)
ANAP Anavatan Partisi (Motherland party)
AO Aydinlar Ocagi (Hearth of Intellectuals)
AP Adalet Partisi (Justice party)
CDLR Committee for the Defense of Legitimate Rights
CIA Central Intelligence Agency
DFLP Democratic Front for the Liberation of Palestine
DMI Dar al Mal al Islami (the House of Islamic Finance)
DSP Social-Democratic party
FAF Fraternité Algérienne en France
FIDA Front Islamique du Djihad Armé
FIS Front Islamique du Salut
FLN Front de Libération Nationale
GIA Groupe Islamique Armé
HDZ Hrvastska Demokratska Zajednica (Croatian Democratic Community, Croatian nationalist party in Bosnia)
HMS Harakat al-Muqawama al-Islamiyya (Hamas)
IAF Islamic Action Front
ICF Islamic Charter Front
IEFE Instance Exécutive du FIS à l'Etranger (FIS Foreign Executive)
IJT Association of Islamic Students
IKIM (Institute for Islamic Understanding)
ISI Inter-Service Intelligence
IUA International University of Africa
IZ Islamska Zajednica (Islamic Community)
JI Jamaat-e-Islami
JMF Jeunesse Musulmane de France
JMO Jugoslavenska Muslimanska Organizacija (Yugoslav Muslim Organization)
JUI Jamiat-e-Ulema-e-Islam (Association of Ulemas of Islam)
JUP Jamiat-e-Ulema-e-Pakistan (Association of Pakistani Ulemas)

KHAD	the Afghan equivalent of the KGB
MECS	*Middle East Contemporary Survey*
MEI	Mouvement de l'Etat Islamique
MHP	Milliyetçi Haeket Partisi (Nationalist Movement party, Turkey)
MIA	Mouvement Islamique Armé
MIT	(Turkish intelligence service)
MNP	Milli Nizam Partisi (Party of National Order)
MSP	Milli Selamet Partisi (Party of National Salvation)
MTI	Mouvement de la Tendance Islamique
NGO	Nongovernmental organization
NIF	National Islamic Front
OIC	Organization of the Islamic Conference
PA	Palestinian Authority
PAS	(Malaysian Islamic party)
PFLP	Popular Front for the Liberation of Palestine
PIC	Popular Islamic Conference
PIR	Party of the Islamic Revolution
PKK	(Kurdistan Workers' party)
PLO	Palestine Liberation Organization
PNA	Pakistani National Alliance
PPP	Pakistan People's party
RCD	Rassemblement pour la Culture et la Democratie
SDA	Stranka Demokratske Akcije (Party for Democratic Action)
SDS	Srpska Demokratska Stanka (Serbian Democratic party, Serbian nationalist party in Bosnia)
SMP	Sipah-e-Mohammed Pakistan (Soldiers of the Prophet Mohammed in Pakistan)
SSP	Sipah-e Sahaba Pakistan (Deobandi paramilitary group)
TIS	Turk Islam Sentesi (Turkish-Islamic Synthesis)
UJM	Union des Jeunes Musulmans
UMNO	United Malay National Organization
UNIFIL	United Nations Forces in Lebanon
UNLU	Unified National Leadership of Uprising
UOIF	Union des Organisations Islamiques de France
WAMY	World Assembly of Muslim Youth

Index